M000166963

THE ROUTLEDGE HISTORY OF
THE HOLOCAUST

'It serves as a comprehensive introduction to the history of the Holocaust but also adds depth to current debate, both geographically and topically, by covering issues that have previously been under-investigated.'

Simon Brown, *The Historical Association*

The genocide of Jewish and non-Jewish civilians perpetrated by the German regime during World War II continues to confront scholars with elusive questions even after nearly seventy years and hundreds of studies. This multi-contributory work is a landmark publication that sees experts renowned in their field addressing these questions in light of current research.

A comprehensive introduction to the history of the Holocaust, this volume has 42 chapters which add important depth to the academic study of the Holocaust, both geographically and topically. The chapters address such diverse issues as:

- continuities in German and European history with respect to genocide prior to 1939
- the eugenic roots of Nazi anti-Semitism
- the response of Europe's Jewish communities to persecution and destruction
- the Final Solution as the German occupation instituted it across Europe
- rescue and rescuer motivations; the problem of prosecuting war crimes
- gender and Holocaust experience
- the persecution of non-Jewish victims
- the Holocaust in post-war cultural venues.

This important collection will be essential reading for all those interested in the history of the Holocaust.

Dr Jonathan C. Friedman is Professor of History and Director of Holocaust and Genocide Studies at West Chester University, USA, and has worked as a historian at both the United States Holocaust Memorial Museum and the Survivors of the Shoah Foundation. He is the author of six books, including *The Lion and the Star: Gentile–Jewish Relations in Three Hessian Communities* (1998) and *Rainbow Jews: Gay and Jewish Identity in the Performing Arts* (2007).

THE ROUTLEDGE HISTORIES

The Routledge Histories is a series of landmark books surveying some of the most important topics and themes in history today. Edited and written by an international team of world-renowned experts, they are the works against which all future books on their subjects will be judged.

THE ROUTLEDGE HISTORY OF WOMEN IN EUROPE SINCE 1700
Edited by Deborah Simonton

THE ROUTLEDGE HISTORY OF SLAVERY
Edited by Gad Heuman and Trevor Burnard

THE ROUTLEDGE HISTORY OF SEX AND THE BODY
Edited by Kate Fisher and Sarah Toulalan

THE ROUTLEDGE HISTORY OF EAST CENTRAL EUROPE
Edited by Irina Livezeanu and Arpad von Klimo

THE ROUTLEDGE HISTORY OF THE HOLOCAUST

Edited by
Jonathan C. Friedman

LONDON AND NEW YORK

First published 2011
by Routledge

First published in paperback 2012
by Routledge
2 Park Square, Milton Park, Abingdon, Oxon, OX14 4RN

Simultaneously published in the USA and Canada
by Routledge
711 Third Avenue, New York, NY 10017

Routledge is an imprint of the Taylor & Francis Group, an informa business

© 2011, 2012 Jonathan C. Friedman for selection and editorial matter; individual chapters, the contributors

The right of Jonathan C. Friedman, and the contributors to be identified as authors of this work has been asserted by them in accordance with sections 77 and 78 of the Copyright, Designs and Patents Act 1988.

All rights reserved. No part of this book may be reprinted or reproduced or utilised in any form or by any electronic, mechanical, or other means, now known or hereafter invented, including photocopying and recording, or in any information storage or retrieval system, without permission in writing from the publishers.

Trademark notice: Product or corporate names may be trademarks or registered trademarks, and are used only for identification and explanation without intent to infringe.

British Library Cataloguing in Publication Data
A catalogue record for this book is available from the British Library

Library of Congress Cataloging in Publication Data
The Routledge history of the Holocaust / edited by Jonathan C. Friedman.
    p. cm. – (The Routledge histories)
    Includes index.
    1. Holocaust, Jewish (1939-1945) 2. Jews–Germany–History–1933-1945. 3. Germany–Ethnic relations. I. Friedman, Jonathan C., 1966-
    D804.3.R76 2010
    940.53'18–dc22
            2010021664

ISBN: 978-0-415-77956-2 (hbk)
ISBN: 978-0-415-52087-4 (pbk)
ISBN: 978-0-203-83744-3 (ebk)

Typeset in Sabon
by Taylor & Francis Books

TO STEPHEN FEINSTEIN

IN HONOR AND MEMORY OF HIS LIFE'S WORK
IN HOLOCAUST AND GENOCIDE STUDIES AND
FOR HIS EFFORTS IN BRINGING THIS PROJECT
TO FRUITION

TO DAVID BANKIER, SYBIL MILTON, HENRY
FRIEDLANDER, AND SAUL FRIEDMAN

FOR THEIR SCHOLARSHIP AND INSPIRATION

AND TO MY WIFE LESLIE, DAUGHTERS TESS
AND MAYA, AND MY MOTHER NANCY

FOR HOPE

TABLE OF CONTENTS

TABLE OF CONTENTS

LIST OF TABLES

ACKNOWLEDGMENTS

The editor would like to thank Syracuse University Press for permission to reprint the following:

Stephen C. Feinstein, ed., *Absence/Presence: Critical Essays on the Artistic Memory of the Holocaust* (Syracuse University Press, 2005), 229–34, 241–50, 256–58.

LIST OF CONTRIBUTORS

Kirk C. Allison directs the Program in Human Rights and Health at the University of Minnesota School of Public Health.

Michael J. Bazyler is professor of law and the "1939" Club Law Scholar in Holocaust and Human Rights Studies at Chapman University. He is also the author of the book *Holocaust Justice: The Battle for Restitution in America's Courts* (New York University Press, 2003), contributor of chapters to various books on genocide and the law, and co-editor with Roger Alford of *Holocaust Restitution: Perspectives on the Litigation and its Legacy* (New York University Press, 2006).

Michael Berenbaum received his doctorate from Florida State University in 1975 and is also an ordained rabbi. He has served as deputy director of the President's Commission on the Holocaust, project director of the US Holocaust Memorial Museum, and director of the museum's Research Institute. From 1997 to 1999, Professor Berenbaum was the president and CEO of Steven Spielberg's Survivors of the Shoah Visual History Foundation. He has taught at a number of universities, including Yale University, Georgetown University, and the University of Maryland, and is currently director of the Sigi Ziering Center for the Study of the Holocaust and Ethics at American Jewish University, where he is also a professor of Jewish Studies. His vast publication record includes 18 books, among them *The World Must Know* (Johns Hopkins University Press, 2005), *Anatomy of the Auschwitz Death Camp* (Indiana University Press, 1998), and *The Yad Vashem Encyclopedia of the Ghettos during the Holocaust* (Yad Vashem, 2010).

Christopher Browning is the Frank Porter Graham Professor of History at the University of North Carolina at Chapel Hill. Among his books on the Holocaust are: *Ordinary Men: Reserve Police Battalion 101 and the Final Solution in Poland* (HarperCollins, 1993), *The Origins of the Final Solution: The Evolution of Nazi Jewish Policy, September 1939–March 1942* (University of Nebraska Press, 2004), and, most recently, *Remembering Survival: Inside a Nazi Slave Labor Camp* (W.W. Norton, 2010).

Bjarte Bruland is the chief curator at the Jewish Museum in Oslo. His research involves the persecution and murder of Norwegian Jewry during the Holocaust.

William Brustein is vice provost for global strategies and international affairs at Ohio State University. He came to Ohio State from the University of Illinois at Urbana-Champaign, where he was associate provost for international affairs and director of international programs and studies. The author of numerous articles and four books, including *Roots of Hate: Antisemitism in Europe Before the Holocaust* (Cambridge University Press, 2003), Professor Brustein received his PhD in sociology from the University of Washington.

Boaz Cohen is head of the Holocaust Studies Program of the Western Galilee College in Akko, Israel. He received his PhD from the Department of Jewish History at Bar Ilan University, writing his dissertation on "Holocaust research in Israel 1945–80: Characteristics, trends, developments." His work focuses on Jewish post-Holocaust society and the development of Holocaust memory and historiography in its social and cultural context. Dr Cohen's current research is on early children's Holocaust testimonies in their historical, social, and cultural context. He has published articles in both *Yad Vashem Studies* and *Holocaust and Genocide Studies*.

John M. Cox is an assistant professor of history at Florida Gulf Coast University, where he directs the Center for Judaic, Holocaust, and Human Rights Studies. His first book, *Circles of Resistance: Jewish, Leftist, and Youth Dissidence in Nazi Germany*, was published in 2009 (Peter Lang), and he is currently writing a book on genocide in the modern world for Pearson Prentice Hall. Dr Cox, who serves on the editorial board of the *Journal of Jewish Identities*, completed his PhD at the University of North Carolina in 2005.

Lynne Fallwell is assistant professor of German History at Texas Tech University, where she teaches, among others, courses on the Third Reich and the Holocaust. Her broader research interests include questions of national identity formation and construction of social frameworks. She is currently completing a manuscript tracing German-American relations within post-World War II mass tourism. Fallwell has an article looking at Nazi propaganda feature films in the forthcoming book *Cinema Inferno*.

Helen Fein is a historical sociologist who is author and editor of 12 books and monographs on genocide and human rights. She serves as Chair of the Board of the Institute for the Study of Genocide in New York, and was a founder and first President of the International Association of Genocide Scholars.

Stephen C. Feinstein was director of the Center for Holocaust and Genocide Studies and adjunct professor at the University of Minnesota from 1999 to 2008. He received his PhD from New York University in 1971, and from 1969 to 1999 he was a professor in the department of history at the University of Wisconsin at River Falls. A prolific scholar, with publications on art and the Holocaust such as *Absence/Presence: Critical Essays on the Artistic Memory of the Holocaust* (Syracuse University Press, 2005), Dr Feinstein was also a beloved teacher and community leader.

Ronit Fischer is the Dean of Students Yzreel Valley College. She has also served as a research colleague at the Struchlitz Holocaust Research and Study Institute at the Haifa University, from where she received her PhD in 2005. Her dissertation dealt with the fate of Bessarabian and Bukovinian Jewry during the Holocaust.

Jonathan C. Friedman is currently the director of Holocaust and Genocide Studies and professor of history at West Chester University in West Chester, Pennsylvania. He is the author of five books, including *Rainbow Jews: Gay and Jewish Identity in the Performing Arts* (Rowman & Littlefield, 2007) and *The Lion and the Star: Gentile–Jewish Relations in Three Hessian Communities* (University Press of Kentucky, 1998). His PhD is in history from the University of Maryland.

Saul S. Friedman retired from Youngstown State University in 2006 after 37 years' service. He received his PhD from Ohio State University in 1969, and went on to publish 13 books on Middle East and Jewish History and to receive six Distinguished Professorship awards from YSU, along with six Regional Emmy Awards. Dr Friedman also received a lifetime achievement award from the Ohio Humanities Council in 1998.

Kinga Frojimovics has been the director of the Hungarian Section in Yad Vashem Archives in Jerusalem since 2007. She holds a PhD from Bar-Ilan University, and has published a number of works on the history of the Jews of Hungary, including *Stranger in a Strange Land: The Hungarian State and Jewish Refugees in Hungary, 1933–1945* (The International Institute for Holocaust Research at Yad Vashem, 2007).

James Frusetta received his PhD in history from the University of Maryland in 2006. He is currently teaching at Hampden-Sydney college, where he specializes in the history of modern southeastern Europe. Among his publications are "Divided Heroes, Common Claims: IMRO between Macedonia and Bulgaria," in John Lampe and Mark Mazower, eds, *Ideologies and National Identities* (Central European University Press, 2004).

Stephen Howard Garrin is a practicing attorney at law in New York City, an adjunct associate professor of history at Herbert H. Lehman College of the City University of New York, and an adjunct associate professor of comparative literature at Bernard Baruch College of the City University of New York. He was the recipient of a Post Doctoral Fulbright Scholarship at the University of Bonn and a DAAD Grant at the University of Berlin.

David Gaunt is professor of history at Södertörn University, Stockholm, Sweden. His publications on genocide include *Collaboration and Resistance during the Holocaust. Belarus, Estonia, Latvia, Lithuania* (Peter Lang, 2004), *Massacres, Resistance, Protectors: Muslim–Christian Relations in Eastern Anatolia during World War I* (Gorgias, 2006), and *Anti-Jewish Violence. Rethinking the Pogrom in East European History* (Indiana University Press, 2010).

Shirli Gilbert is Karten Lecturer in Jewish/non-Jewish relations at the University of Southampton. She obtained her Master's in Musicology and DPhil in Modern History from the University of Oxford. Her research is currently focused on two principal areas: music in the aftermath of the Holocaust, and Holocaust memory in apartheid and post-apartheid South Africa. She has published widely on the subject of music, oppression, and resistance, and her book *Music in the Holocaust: Confronting Life in the Nazi Ghettos and Camps* (Oxford University Press, 2005) was a finalist for the 2005 National Jewish Book Award.

Geoffrey J. Giles is associate professor of history at the University of Florida. He received his PhD from Cambridge University in 1975. A member of many prestigious editorial boards for journals in German history as well as a member of the board of directors of the Friends of the German Historical Institute in Washington, DC, Professor Giles has an illustrious publication record. Among his books are *Students and National Socialism in Germany* (Princeton University Press, 1985) and *Homosexuality and the Nazis* (forthcoming).

Myrna Goldenberg was professor of English at Montgomery College from 1971 to 2003, and has held leadership positions in a number of academic organizations, including the Modern Language Association. She was the director and founder of the Humanities Institute: A College/Smithsonian Partnership, and since 2005, she has been an academic consultant on the Holocaust. Among her many publications are *Tensions, Testimony, and Tikkun: Teaching the Holocaust in Colleges and Universities* (with co-editor Rochelle L. Millen, University of Washington Press, 2007) and *Experience & Expression: Women, the Nazis, and the Holocaust* (with co-editor Elizabeth R. Baer, Wayne State University Press, 2003).

Wolf Gruner received his PhD in history in 1994 from the Technical University in Berlin. Currently, he holds the Shapell–Guerin Chair in Jewish Studies and is Professor of History at the University of Southern California. He is author of seven books on the Holocaust, including *Jewish Forced Labor under the Nazis: Economic Needs and Nazi Racial Aims* (Cambridge University Press, 2006).

Ian Hancock is a professor of English and the director of the Program of Romani Studies at the University of Texas at Austin. He is author of *We are the Romani People* (University of Hertfordshire Press, 2002).

Patricia Heberer has served as a historian with the Center for Advanced Holocaust Studies at the United States Holocaust Memorial Museum in Washington since 1994. There she functions as the Museum's in-house specialist on medical crimes and eugenics policies in Nazi Germany. She is currently producing a volume, *Children and the Holocaust*, for the Center source edition series *Documenting Life and Destruction*. A further publication, *Atrocities on Trial: The Politics of Prosecuting War Crimes in Historical Perspective*, co-edited with Jürgen Matthäus, was published in 2008 by the University of Nebraska Press.

Rita Horváth received her PhD from Bar-Ilan University in 2003. She has been a post-doctoral fellow at both Indiana University and the Hebrew University of Jerusalem. She currently teaches English at Bar-Ilan University, and is working on a manuscript entitled *Escaping Traumatic Circularity: Testimonies and the Novel of Formation*.

Margery Grace Hunt is currently a student in the Master of Arts program in Holocaust and Genocide Studies at West Chester University.

Lee H. Igel is an assistant professor at New York University. He received his PhD in industrial and organizational psychology.

Marion Kaplan is the Skirball Professor of Modern Jewish History at New York University. She received her PhD from Columbia University and is the author of a number of articles and books, including most recently, *Jewish Daily Life in Germany, 1618–1945* (Oxford University Press, 2005) and *Between Dignity and Despair: Jewish Life in Nazi Germany* (Oxford University Press, 1998).

Hans-Lukas Kieser is a *Privatdozent* (adjunct professor) at the University of Zürich and in 2010 a Kratter Professor at Stanford University (Kratter professorship). He is the author of *Nearest East* (Temple University Press, 2010) and *Der verpasste Friede* (Chronos, 2000), the editor of *Turkey beyond Nationalism* (I.B. Tauris, 2006), and a co-editor (with Dominik J. Schaller) of *The Armenian Genocide and the Shoah* (Chronos, 2002).

Alexander Korb is lecturer in modern European history and deputy director of the Stanley Burton Centre for Holocaust Studies at the University of Leicester. He received his PhD at Humboldt-University of Berlin in 2010, writing a dissertation on Ustaša mass violence in Croatia during World War II.

Dieter Kuntz received his PhD in history from the University of Kansas, and he has worked as a historian at the United States Holocaust Memorial Museum since 1999. His publications include the co-edited reader *Inside Hitler's Germany* (Wadsworth, 1991) and the co-edited exhibition catalogue *Deadly Medicine: Creating the Master Race* (University of North Carolina Press, 2004).

Paul A. Levine is a senior lecturer in Holocaust history at Uppsala University in Uppsala, Sweden. He has served as a historical advisor on museum exhibitions related to the Holocaust, and has authored and edited several works, including *Raoul Wallenberg in Budapest: Myth, History, and Holocaust* (Vallentine Mitchell, 2010), (with professor David Cesarini) *"Bystanders" to the Holocaust: A Re-Evaluation* (Frank Cass, 2002), and *From Indifference to Activism: Swedish Diplomacy and the Holocaust, 1938–1944* (Acta Universitatis Upsaliensis, Studia Historica Upsaliensia, 1996).

James Irvin Lichti received his PhD in history from the University of California, Los Angeles, where he also taught for 5 years. In addition, he has worked as archivist for the Los Angeles Museum of the Holocaust, and as a historian with the Shoah Foundation. He is author of the book *Houses on the Sand? Pacifist Denominations in Nazi Germany* (Peter Lang, 2008). Currently, Dr Lichti teaches history at the Milken Community High School in Los Angeles.

Franklin Hamlin Littell was a Methodist minister and pioneering scholar before his death at age 92 in 2009. Author of over 30 books, he taught the first American seminar on the Holocaust at Emory University in 1959, and established the first doctoral program in Holocaust studies in 1976 at Temple University. In 1998, together with his wife, Marcia Littell, established the first master's degree program in Holocaust Studies at Richard Stockton College of New Jersey. He co-founded the Annual Scholars' Conference on the Holocaust and the Churches in 1970.

Marcia Sachs Littell is Professor of Holocaust and Genocide Studies at the Richard Stockton College. Editor of 24 books, including *Confronting the Holocaust: A Mandate for the 21st Century* (University Press of America, 1997), *Women in the Holocaust: Responses, Insights and Perspectives* (Merion Westfield Press, 2001), and *The Genocidal Mind* (Paragon House, 2005).

Joanna B. Michlic is Director of the Hadassah–Brandeis Institute Project on Families, Children, and the Holocaust at Brandeis University. Her major publications include (with Antony Polonsky) *Neighbors Respond: The Controversy about Jedwabne* (Princeton University Press, 2003) and *Poland's Threatening Other: The Image of the Jew from 1880 to the Present* (University of Nebraska Press, 2008).

Bradley Nichols is a PhD candidate at the University of Tennessee in Knoxville. His areas of emphasis include the Holocaust, Nazi anti-Slavic policy, and Germany's relationship with eastern Europe. He is currently working on his dissertation, a study of the SS Germanization program in occupied western Poland during World War II, under the advisorship of Dr Vejas Gabriel Liulevicius.

Devin Pendas is associate professor of history at Boston College. He received his PhD from the University of Chicago in 2000, and has published extensively on war crimes trials. His book *The Frankfurt Auschwitz Trial, 1963–1965: History, Genocide and the Limits of the Law* was published by Cambridge University Press in 2006.

Wolfgang Seibel is a Full Professor of Politics and Public Administration at the University of Konstanz and an Adjunct Professor of Public Administration at the Hertie School of Governance in Berlin. He received his PhD from the University of Kassel in 1982. He has been a visiting professor at the University of California at Berkeley, as well as a temporary member of the Institute for Advanced Study at Princeton. His publication record is vast, and he has edited (with Gerald Feldman) *Networks of Nazi Persecution* (Berghahn, 2005). Professor Seibel serves as member of the editorial boards of *Public Administration Review, Public Administration, Voluntas/International Journal of Voluntary and Nonprofit Organizations*, and the *Journal of Civil Society*. He was recently elected a member of the Heidelberg Academy of Science.

Helene Sinnreich is the Director of Judaic and Holocaust Studies and Assistant Professor of History at Youngstown State University. She received her PhD from Brandeis University in 2004, writing a dissertation on "The supply and distribution of food to the Lodz Ghetto: A case study in Nazi Jewish policy, 1939–45."

Sybille Steinbacher is a Full Professor in Contemporary History at the University of Vienna. She is author of *Auschwitz: Geschichte und Nachgeschichte* (C.H. Beck, 2004), published in German, English, Italian, Dutch, and Finnish. She has written monographs on the Nazi concentration camps of Auschwitz and Dachau and is contributor to *Bertelsmann im Dritten Reich* (Bertelsmann, 2002), edited by Saul Friedländer *et al.* In 2004/05 she was the Alexander von Humboldt Foundation Visiting Fellow at Harvard University.

Guillaume de Syon teaches history at Albright College in Reading, Pennsylvania, including related courses for the Holocaust Studies Program. He is the author of *Zeppelin! Germany and the Airship, 1900–1939* (Johns Hopkins University Press, 2002).

Robert Jan van Pelt is a professor of architectural history at the University of Waterloo in Ontario. He is a leading expert on the Auschwitz concentration camp and has written numerous articles and books, including *The Case for Auschwitz* (Indiana University Press, 2002), *The Holocaust: A History* (W.W. Norton, 2003, with Deborah

Dwork), and *Flight from the Reich: Refugee Jews, 1933–1946* (W.W. Norton, 2009, with Deborah Dwork).

Robert G. Weiner is associate Humanities Librarian at Texas Tech University and librarian for Film Studies and Art/Sequential Art. He is the author of *Marvel Graphic Novels: An Annotated Guide 1965–2005* (Mcfarland, 2007) and editor of *Captain America and the Struggle of the Superhero* (Mcfarland, 2009). He has been published in numerous journals, including the *International Journal of Comic Art* and *East Texas Historical Journal*. Weiner has also written various book chapters on film and other sequential art topics. He is co-editor of a forthcoming book looking at transgressive cinema: *Cinema Inferno* (Scarecrow Press, 2010).

Eric D. Weitz is Distinguished McKnight University Professor of History at the University of Minnesota, where he also holds the Arsham and Charlotte Ohanessian Chair in the College of Liberal Arts. He is a historian of Germany and modern Europe. In recent years his work has extended to the history and politics of genocides, crimes against humanity, and international human rights. Professor Weitz's major publications include *Weimar Germany: Promise and Tragedy* (2007), *A Century of Genocide: Utopias of Race and Nation* (2003), and *Creating German Communism, 1890–1990* (1997), all with Princeton University Press.

INTRODUCTION

Jonathan C. Friedman

Elie Wiesel, the Nobel Prize-winning novelist and poet, once wrote that "Auschwitz defies imagination and perception ... Between the dead and the rest of us there exists an abyss that no talent can comprehend."[1] While Wiesel directed his thoughts at representations of the Holocaust in art, his words have relevance to the broader issue of genocide. The organization Genocide Watch estimates that 100 million civilians around the globe have lost their lives as a result of genocide in only the past 60 years. Political scientist Rudolph J. Rummel has argued for a number closer to 150 million over the period from 1900 to 1987, 85 percent of which one can attribute to totalitarian and authoritarian regimes, specifically the Soviet Union, China, Khmer Rouge Cambodia, Vietnam, Yugoslavia, and Nazi Germany and its fascist allies.[2] World War II, history's deadliest military conflict, accounted for 72 million of these deaths, 47 million civilians in total, 12 million of whom were murdered in the Holocaust, the genocidal wartime policy of the German state. To put it another way, it is estimated there were over 550 million people in Europe (including the Soviet Union) on the eve of World War II. By war's end, one out of every eight European citizens who had been alive in 1939 was dead—two out of every three European Jews including one-and-a half million Jewish children. In terms of aggregate numbers, the 72 million well exceeded the entire population of Germany as of 1933.

The United States Holocaust Memorial Museum in Washington, DC defines the Holocaust as the systematic, bureaucratic, state-sponsored persecution and murder of approximately six million Jews by the Nazi regime and its allies during World War II. Never before had so many Jews suffered wrongful death in Christian Europe. Indeed, nearly one out of every eight civilian deaths during World War II was a Jew. Never before had a European or world government adopted the policy that all Jews, every last Jewish man, woman, and child, would be exterminated. At the same time, while Jews were the primary victims, slated for total physical annihilation, six million non-Jewish victims also suffered grievous oppression and destruction, including several hundred thousand Roma-Sinti, two million Polish civilians, three million Soviet prisoners of war, several thousand gay men and Jehovah's Witnesses, tens of thousands of political prisoners, and 200,000 persons with disabilities. Never before had a government and its operating ideology grouped these disparate European outcasts together as part of a program of persecution. In fact, I would argue that what is illustrative of Nazism is the conflation of these out-groups. Hitler's variant of fascism had no room for any group that stood in the way of his desire to re-engineer European society based on principles of race and heredity.

This compilation of essays attempts to make a contribution to the discussion of what historians Yehuda Bauer and Saul Friedländer argue are the existential problems which the Holocaust poses to humanity.[3] Here again, historians are well advised to heed Wiesel's warning of "the impossibility one stumbles upon in trying to tell the tale."[4] There is a dual significance to this statement for me as editor. This project was originally the undertaking of Stephen Feinstein, the eminent historian of the Holocaust who taught at the University of Minnesota before his sudden death in 2008. When Routledge offered me the opportunity to continue his work, I did so with the idea that the book would be dedicated in his honor, a lasting reminder of his tireless commitment to Holocaust and genocide studies. During the editing of the book, we lost another major historian in the field, David Bankier, who passed away on 24 February 2010. Although I never had the opportunity to meet either scholar, their work was foundational for me as a graduate student. I am indebted to two other academicians for their mentoring when I worked at the United States Holocaust Memorial Museum in the 1990s. They are Sybil Milton, who passed away in 2000, and Henry Friedlander. Without their support, I would not have had the opportunity to research and publish in the field. Most importantly, though, I owe my calling to Holocaust and Jewish studies to my father, Saul Friedman, who taught these subjects among many others in his 40 years at Youngstown State University. Therefore, in addition to dedicating this book to my wife, Leslie, daughters Tess and Maya, and to my mother, Nancy, for the hope they represent to future generations, I dedicate it as well to Stephen, David, Sybil, Henry, and my father for their numerous important contributions to scholarship over the course of their lives.

There are other scholars whom I must recognize for their guidance, including my doctoral advisors James Harris and Marsha Rozenblit from the University of Maryland, and Michael Berenbaum, for whom I worked at the Survivors of the Shoah Visual History Foundation. As editor of this text, I am guided by the need to proceed with humility and awe at the body of work that has gone before and to attempt to add a voice to the conversation. It is my hope that by bringing together over 40 scholars from across the globe, this volume will achieve this goal and complement existing edited works, such as François Furet's *Unanswered Questions: Nazi Germany and the Genocide of the Jews* (1989), Michael Berenbaum's *The Holocaust and History: The Known, The Unknown, The Disputed, and the Re-Examined* (2002), and Dan Michman's *Holocaust Historiography: A Jewish Perspective: Conceptualizations, Terminology, Approaches, and Fundamental Issues* (2003).

The manuscript presented here is both broad and deep in its approach, aiming at comprehensiveness that reaches as wide an audience as possible. I have adopted a framework that is chronological and then thematic, assessing the Final Solution as the German occupation instituted it across Europe, and covering issues that merit further investigation, such as the diverse responses of the Jewish communities, the problem of prosecuting war crimes, gender and Holocaust experience, the persecution of non-Jewish victims, and the issue of representations of the Holocaust in postwar cultural venues (music, film, and museums). The ensuing chapters are organized in such a way that they address a question or questions about the Holocaust, convey its historical narrative given the limitations of language, and perhaps revise, refine, or reshape that narrative.

I have divided the volume into five sections. The first section addresses the issue of continuity in an evaluation of European Jewry and German history. To that end, there are essays on the varied Jewish communities in Europe on the eve of World War II; the links between antisemitism and Nazi ideology; the role of Germany in the Armenian genocide; the collapse of the Weimar Republic; the program of persecution implemented by the Nazis in the German Reich from 1933 to 1939; and the responses to this persecution by Germany's Jews. The second section focuses on the wars launched by Germany against Poland in 1939 and the Soviet Union in 1941. Questions to be addressed in this section include: (i) How was the war that began in 1939 different from the war that came in 1941? Put another way, how did the murderous policies implemented by the German government evolve between 1939 and 1941? (ii) When was the decision made to implement the Final Solution? Authors in the third section describe Germany's implementation across occupied Europe of its state-sanctioned policy of murder from 1942 to 1945. The fourth section explores the responses of Jewish and non-Jewish victims and non-Jewish bystanders to the Nazi murder program. Additional issues here include the role of gender in impacting victim experiences and the extent to which displacement at the end of the war perpetuated trauma for Holocaust survivors. Finally, the fifth section confronts the legacy of the Holocaust in law and culture. The connection between these realms is best expressed through the question: How can there be justice or representation in the wake of such a human cataclysm as the Holocaust?

For some academicians, the Holocaust is one of many heuristic pursuits, one that should be handled as neutrally as possible, lest it be tarnished by emotions and identity politics. For some theologians and philosophers, the Holocaust is a transcendental mystery; for others still, it was not the end but the beginning of a new chapter in Jewish history. I do not share these views. While as a professional historian I aim for detachment, I cannot help but be overwhelmed by the moral ramifications of an event such as the Holocaust. I tend to agree with Zygmunt Bauman, who sees the Holocaust as a blistering commentary on modernity, unprecedented in terms of the theory and technology of murder, specifically the taxonomic classification of victims, the desire for "efficient" killing methods, the use of poison gas in gas chambers, and the assembly-line process of the killing centers.[5] My lifetime has been shaped by events, civic discourse, and government policies that have been equally as shattering—from the near nuclear destruction and/or ecological devastation of the planet, to the fear of terrorism and the Orwellian exploitation of that fear. The sheer scope of killing and suffering from the genocides that continue to occur has a weight that is inescapable, and it has almost come to define who we are as a human civilization. For me, the bracing and sobering words of Primo Levi are never far from my thoughts.[6] We may be alone in a universe in which only we have the capacity and the moral duty to cherish and safeguard the lives of all individuals.

Notes

1 Elie Weisel, "Does the Holocaust Lie Beyond the Reach of Art?" *New York Times*, 17 April 1983; Michael Marrus, *The Holocaust in History* (New York: Meridian, 1987), 3.
2 www.hawaii.edu/powerkills/DBG.CHAP1.HTM#8#8;
3 Yehuda Bauer, *Rethinking the Holocaust* (New Haven, Connecticut: Yale University Press, 2001), 7, 276; Saul Friedländer, *Nazi Germany and the Jews* (New York: HarperCollins, 1997); Saul Friedländer, "The 'Final Solution': On the Unease in Historical Interpretation," in *Lessons and Legacies*, ed. Peter Hayes (Evanston, Illinois: Northwestern University Press, 1991), 23–35.
4 Elie Wiesel, "Trivializing the Holocaust: Semi-Fact and Semi-Fiction," *New York Times*, 16 April 1978; and Marrus, *The Holocaust in History,* 4.

5 See Zygmunt Bauman, *Modernity and the Holocaust* (Ithaca, New York: Cornell University Press, 2001).

6 In *The Drowned and the Saved*, Levi describes the one and only time he contemplated prayer: "This happened in October of 1944, in the one moment in which I lucidly perceived the imminence of death. Naked and compressed among my naked companions with my personal index card in hand, I was waiting to file past the 'commission' that with one glance would decide whether I should immediately go into the gas chamber or was instead strong enough to go on working. For one instant I felt the need to ask for help and asylum; then despite my anguish, equanimity prevailed: you do not change the rules of the game at the end of the match, nor when you are losing. A prayer under these conditions would have been not only absurd (what rights could I claim? and from whom?) but blasphemous, obscene, laden with the greatest impiety of which a non-believer is capable. I rejected the temptation: I knew that otherwise, were I to survive, I would have to be ashamed of it." Levi, *The Drowned and the Saved* (London: Abacus, 1991), 118.

Part I
THE NAZI TAKEOVER AND PERSECUTION IN HITLER'S REICH TO 1939

1

THE JEWISH COMMUNITIES OF EUROPE ON THE EVE OF WORLD WAR II

Jonathan C. Friedman

In 1913, the Czech-Jewish writer Jeri Langer set out on a spiritual journey that took him away from his acculturated roots in Prague and brought him to the Hasidic world of Belz, Poland. Many years later, a 19-year-old Isaac Deutscher moved in the opposite direction. Raised in an ultra-orthodox Hasidic home in Cracow, Deutscher joined the Polish Communist Party and began stretching the boundaries of Jewish identity with the belief that even heretical Jews remain Jews. Langer and Deutscher represented two shades of the rich complexion of Jewishness in Europe before the Holocaust, a spectrum of identity that ran the gamut from students of the Talmud to followers of Karl Marx. European Jewry numbered some nine million by 1933, approximately 60 percent of the world Jewish population, but less than two percent of Europe's total population; in a few short years, six million Jews would die as a direct consequence of the murderous policies of the German government and its non-German allies. This chapter explores the shape and scope of the Jewish communities in Europe before the outbreak of World War II in 1939 in order to appreciate fully the diverse Jewish civilization which the Nazis destroyed.

For centuries, Europe had provided the physical space for Jews to live, but the extent to which this space was ever "home" for the Jews remained a contested issue into the twentieth century, and the events of World War II made further discussion moot. Jewish communities had existed in Greece since before the time of Alexander the Great; the earliest Jews in Rome date from 161 BC; and there were Jews in Germany (specifically Cologne) as early as the fourth century AD. Yet for the bulk of their time in Europe, Jews experienced a fragile dynamic—not an inevitably doomed one, but one that was tenuous and plagued by periods of physical assault which threatened annihilation. Segregated from and subjugated by the Christian world in which they lived, Jews constituted a second-class "corporation" utterly dependent on the whims of Christian authorities. By the beginning of the twentieth century, European Jewry still had not put to rest the central question: Would Europe's Christian population, its leaders and ordinary citizens, ever accept Jews as equals? In the first three decades of what would be humanity's most violent century, this question framed the existence of all Jews despite significant geographical variations and degrees of intensity.

Geography represented perhaps the most obvious marker of the diversity of the Jews, and there were quantitative and qualitative differences between the Jewish and non-Jewish worlds of western, central, and eastern Europe. As table 1.1 demonstrates, on the eve of World War II, over six million of the eight million Jews in Europe lived in eastern

Table 1.1 Jewish Population in Europe by 1939 and Jewish Fatalities in the Holocaust

Country	Jewish Population Number	Approximate Number of Jews Murdered
Poland	3,300,000	2,900,000
Soviet Union	ca. 2,500,000	1,200,000
Romania	756,000	280,000
Germany	525,000	130,000
Hungary	445,000	200–500,000*
Czechoslovakia	357,000	260,000
Great Britain	ca. 300,000	**
France	ca. 250,000	90,000
Austria	191,000	50,000
Netherlands	156,000	106,000
Lithuania	155,000	130,000
Latvia	95,000	70,000
Greece	73,000	65,000
Yugoslavia	68,000	60,000
Belgium	60,000	25,000
Bulgaria	48,500	11,000
Italy	48,000	7,500
Sweden	6,700	NA
Denmark	5,700	60
Estonia	4,560	1,500
Spain	4,000	NA
Finland	1,800	7
Norway	1,400	870
Portugal	1,200	NA
Albania	200	***

* This number varies in part because of the inclusion of tens of thousands of Romanian Jews from Transylvania, who came under Hungarian control in 1940.
** The Germans were able to seize and deport to concentration camps a handful of Jews during their wartime occupation of the British Channel Islands.
*** The *Holocaust Chronicle* estimates that between ten and twelve Albanian Jews were deported to Bergen-Belsen.

Sources: http://www.ushmm.org/wlc/article.php?ModuleId=10005161; http://www.holocaustchronicle.org/holocaustappendices.html; Raul Hilberg, *The Destruction of the European Jews*, 3rd Ed. (New Haven, Connecticut: Yale University Press, 2003), 3: 1321.

Europe—three million in Poland, 2.5 million in the Soviet Union, 756,000 in Romania, 155,000 in Lithuania, 95,000 in Latvia, and 4,500 in Estonia. Germany had the largest Jewish population in central Europe (at 525,000), followed by Hungary (with 445,000 Jews), Czechoslovakia (357,000), and Austria (191,000). In western and southern Europe, the Jewish communities were noticeably smaller, in terms of both percentages and actual numbers (with Britain's Jewish population of 300,000 and France's 250,000 Jews as the notable exceptions).

By the 1920s, Jews had become an urban, if not metropolitan group with urban-oriented occupations. External factors more than anything else, specifically longstanding restrictions on Jewish landowning and guild membership that persisted in western and central Europe into the nineteenth century, helped to shape this unique socio-economic structure. In Germany in the 1920s, for example, over 60 percent of Jews engaged in commercial pursuits, with an additional 12.5 percent in public service or the free professions, as compared with 18 and eight percent, respectively, of the general population.[1] The trend towards metropolitanization increased during the 1920s so that by the beginning of the next decade, 85 percent of the Jews in Germany were large city-dwellers, 80 percent in Hungary, and 70 percent in Romania. Almost all of Denmark's Jews lived in Copenhagen, 92 percent of Austria's Jews in Vienna, and some 65 percent of French

Jews in Paris.[2] In Greece, the principal center of Jewry was the northern port city of Thessaloniki or Salonika, controlled by the Turks until 1912. There, Jews had found refuge after their expulsion from Spain in 1492, and at 80,000 strong in the early 1900s, they accounted for half the city's population and nearly three-quarters of its business owners. After 1912, and into the interwar period, when the city reverted to Greek control, a policy of increasing the ethnic Greek population, as well as a spike in antisemitism, resulted in a decline in the actual and relative numbers of Salonika's Jews.[3] In Russia–Poland, the majority of Jews lived in large towns, and some half million (almost one-tenth of the total Jewish population) lived in three cities—Warsaw, Odessa, and Łódź.[4] As of 1931, over 40 percent of Polish Jews made their living in industry, while some 37 percent were engaged in commerce and retail trade.[5]

Poland's particular place in European Jewish history began at the time of the first Crusade, at the beginning of the twelfth century, when King Boleslav III (1103–39) welcomed Jewish refugees from western Europe. For centuries to come, Poland served as a haven for Jews fleeing persecution, and one of the hallmark features of Jewish demography in the so-called "premodern" or "early modern" period in Europe was forced movement of Jews from the west to Poland in the east. By the eighteenth century, this scenario reversed itself, as the west cultivated a more tolerant space for Jews, and Poland became more unwelcoming. From Britain to the German-speaking regions of central Europe, Jews became one of the beneficiaries of a nascent market economy and an intellectual culture that sought to reorganize society away from superstition and irrationality towards reason and progress. Jews received civic and political rights in return for adopting the national citizenship of their Gentile countries. Jews were to become Germans, Frenchmen, British, and so on, drop their separate national identity and language (Yiddish), and transform themselves into productive citizens. On the surface, the change in rhetoric and legal status of Jews portended a brighter future for Jews, yet antisemitism did not disappear in any realm. Even many of the proponents of emancipating or bestowing rights upon Jews embraced language that belied the notion of Jewish equality, casting Jews as debased and in need of improvement. The often unspoken (often overt) assumption on the part of a good many Gentile leaders was that Jewish identity would ultimately disappear with the acquisition of a non-Jewish national, civic identification.[6]

For Jews, however, the new reality was not to be a process of group effacement, but rather a process of acculturation and limited structural integration, a process by which Jews could enter the social realm with non-Jews without converting to Christianity and abandoning any sense of their ethnic heritage. The results were new incarnations of Judaism and Jewish identity which imbued Jews with a sense of themselves as both citizens of their respective countries, and members of a faith that emphasized universal values of education and humanitarianism.[7]

In eastern Europe, with the dismantling of Poland altogether at the end of the eighteenth century, many Jews found themselves under the control of one of the most hostile regimes they had ever encountered, Tsarist Russia. The policies of the tsars confined Jews to a physical space (the so-called Pale of Settlement, which stretched from Lithuania through Poland and into Ukraine), and subjected them to forced conscription, Russification, and physical assault. Economically more backward than western Europe, and generally devoid of a discourse and policy of emancipation, eastern Europe molded a distinct transformation on the part of its Jews. The bulk of eastern European Jews remained more traditional in terms of religious observance, maintained Yiddish as their primary language, and preserved a greater sense of themselves as a separate Jewish nation. Yet change did occur. Hasidism challenged existing rabbinical authority with an emphasis on one's own connection to God through ecstasy rather than Talmudic learning, and in the nineteenth century, Russian Jews engaged in political activism with a rhetoric of "autoemancipation," which envisioned Jews, and not the Gentile state, as the agency of civil rights. Within this new framework came Zionism (which advocated a Jewish homeland in Palestine), Jewish folkism (which sought territorial autonomy for Jews in Europe), and Jewish socialism or Bundism (which looked to solve the dual problems of antisemitism and oppression of the working class).[8]

The shape of Jewish acculturation and the pace of social change among Jews in both eastern and western Europe changed dramatically in the wake of World War I. Testing the very premise of emancipation, Jews demonstrated their loyalty to their respective countries by fighting and dying alongside their non-Jewish countrymen. In Germany, 85,000 to 100,000 Jews mobilized for the war effort, and 12,000 died; 46,000 Jews fought in the French army, of whom 6,500 died; 41,500 British Jews served in the war, with 2,000 casualties; and even in Russia, an estimated 600,000 Jews risked their lives for the hated tsar.[9] One revealing matrix into the level of acceptance of Jews in the postwar period was the rise in intermarriages, especially in western Europe. In places such as Berlin, Hamburg, and Frankfurt, nearly one-third of all marriages involving a Jewish partner in the 1920s were mixed couplings.[10]

Jewish participation in cultural forums of all manifestations was vibrant throughout Europe in the first decades of the twentieth century, and it intensified in many ways after the war. The Jewish Enlightenment or *Haskalah* had paved the way for the development of the modern Hebrew language and an accompanying Hebrew and Yiddish literary culture,[11] and scholars such as Simon Dubow, Martin Buber, Gershom Scholem, and Franz Rosenzweig put their considerable talents to developing new theories of Jewish history and theology.[12] In terms of the world outside Judaism, Jews over the course of the nineteenth and into the twentieth century made unparalleled contributions to world civilization. Consider as examples Albert Einstein, Sigmund Freud, Emile Durkheim, Marc Chagall, Arthur Schnitzler, Marcel Proust, Franz Kafka, Franz Werfel, Jakob Wassermann, Else Lasker-Schüler, Arnold Schönberg, Kurt Weill, Max Reinhardt, and Fritz Lang. While for most of these individuals, their craft, not their Jewishness, came first, many did engage their Jewish identity in a number of overt ways, from Chagall's cubist depictions of shtetl life to Wassermann's reflections on his own life as a German and a Jew.[13]

Despite the richness of this Jewish cultural contribution and the clear commitment shown by Jews to their countries, antisemitic sentiment never lagged far behind. During the war, military officials in Germany charged that Jews were shirking their duties, and they conducted a "Jew census" as a result, which ironically showed that the proportion of Jewish combat soldiers was roughly similar to (if not greater than) that of their German Christian counterparts.[14] Russian authorities, for their part, regarded the Jews as German spies, and in April 1915 the Russian military ordered the expulsion of Jews from much of Lithuania.[15] After the war, tens of thousands of Jews in Polish and Ukrainian territories were victims of pogroms in the context of the warfare with Russia. Scholars estimate that between 1918 and 1921, more than 2,000 anti-Jewish pogroms took place, with the majority in Ukraine, resulting in the deaths of over 100,000 Jews and the displacement of 500,000 more.[16] The demographic consequences of this violence were clear. Although the European Jewish population increased between 1900 and 1925, it did so extremely slightly and at an increased rate that lagged behind that of non-Jews.[17] There was an upsurge in immigration as well; Jews, who had already been leaving Europe by the hundreds of thousands (an estimated 1.6 million between 1901 and 1914), continued their exit over the course of the 1920s.

Additional developments during the war had uneven effects upon the Jewish communities of Europe. The issuing of the Balfour Declaration and the Bolshevik Revolution in November 1917 (coming literally within five days of each other) radically altered the political landscape for Jews, as did the emergence after the war of numerous countries carved out of the defeated Austria–Hungary. As to the first development, British support for a Jewish national home in Palestine gave Zionists a dose of diplomatic legitimacy, and in the interwar period, Zionists continued to grow as a political force due to the persistence of antisemitism. In Russia, the revolution of February/March 1917 toppled the tsar and brought the emancipation of the Jews. The Bolshevik government that came to power in the fall of 1917 adopted rhetoric against antisemitism as counter-revolutionary, but Jews became targets for persecution once again, not because of the content of their religion, but because of communism's overarching hostility towards all religions. Jews were a decidedly "bourgeois" group as well: the 2.7 million Jews in the Soviet Union represented two percent of the total population, but eight percent of its urban residents, 20 percent of its businessmen, and 40 percent of its craftsmen.[18] A Jewish section of the Communist Party (the *Yevsektsiya*) was established in 1918 to speed up the communization of the Jews, and while communist officials permitted the use of Yiddish in this process, they did so only insofar as it was used to disseminate party propaganda and proletarianize the Jews. Moreover, despite the lip service paid by Soviet officials to stamping out antisemitism, the visible edifices of Jewish life, such as schools and synagogues, were either abolished or neglected, and antisemitism surged during Stalin's regime, as a number of Jews, including prominent Jewish party members, lost their lives in his intra-party purges.[19]

In the newly created states of Poland, Austria, Hungary, and elsewhere in east central Europe, Jews experienced animosity for a host of reasons. Hungary lost territory and non-Hungarian minorities (except for Jews) as a result of the treaties ending World War I. Although smaller in number than they had been in 1910, down from 900,000 to 445,000, Jews were perhaps the most visible minority in Hungary in the interwar period. They also bore the stigma of the failed communist regime of Béla Kun, whose father had Jewish ancestry. In the aftermath of the Kun regime, which lasted from March to August 1919, conservative forces under Miklós Horthy turned on communists, liberals, Jews, and other perceived opponents. Thus, although Jews in Budapest had a relatively favorable existence in the 1920s, entering areas such as medicine, law, and the arts as never before, and Horthy himself held contradictory opinions towards Jews, some favorable, some not, a palpable hostility lingered towards Jews as revolutionary and possibly disloyal. As an example of this, in 1920, the Horthy regime instituted a *numerus clausus* to restrict the percentage of Jewish students at universities to five percent. The *numerus clausus* signalled a change in rhetoric towards Jews in Hungary as well, casting them in racial rather than in religious terms.[20] In Poland, there was a growing backlash against the Minorities Treaty of June 1919, which Polish officials had to sign as a precondition for membership in the League of Nations. The broader provisions of this treaty had specific ramifications for Jews. Jewish schools became eligible for public funding, and

Jews could be exempted from working on the Sabbath. Both possibilities engendered resentment on the part of a Polish population that was already well-steeped in religious and economic antisemitism.[21]

The creation of micro-countries in east central Europe also unsettled what it meant to be a Jew. In the regions of the former Austria–Hungary, where, prior to 1918, multiple identities had been possible for Jews, and where the contours of postwar identities had not yet taken shape, the Jews found themselves addressing once again who they were, and to whom they owed their loyalties. In Hungary, nearly half of all Jews lived in Budapest, the other half in small towns in the countryside. Jews in the capital were of a western type in that they spoke Hungarian, identified as Hungarian citizens, and were more liberal in religious matters, while those in the countryside tended to be more traditional. As Ezra Mendelsohn points out, the distinctions in Hungarian Jewry in the interwar period were less about language and more about religion, because the Yiddish-speaking Jews in Transylvania, Slovakia, and Subcarpathian Rus lived in areas that had been handed over to other countries as a consequence of the postwar peace arrangement.[22] In Czechoslovakia, one could speak of three separate Jewish groups—one in the Czech regions of Bohemia and Moravia, a more western European type, with Prague at its center; one in Subcarpathian Rus, an eastern European type of Jewry both in terms of religious and national identification as well as socio-economic structure; and one in Slovakia, which was somewhere in between the two other groups. In Slovakia and Subcarpathian Rus, Jews generally perceived their national identity as Jewish, while in Bohemia, Jews spoke German and had German cultural identification, with an increasing plurality identifying themselves as Czech by nationality.[23] In Austria prior to 1918, as Marsha Rozenblit maintains, Jews developed a "tripartite" identity through which they could identify as culturally German and ethnically Jewish, with a civic allegiance to the Habsburg monarchy. With the demise of the Habsburgs after World War I, Jews found it difficult to navigate the new cultural terrain with its more chauvinistic, pan-German rhetoric.[24]

There was just as much complexity in eastern Europe, with its comparative lack of acculturation among Jews. Eastern European Jews became more like their non-Jewish neighbors during the interwar period, but they retained a strong sense of themselves as a distinct national group. The Jews of Lithuania were perhaps the paradigmatic eastern European Jewish community—non-acculturated, lower middle class, with a longstanding tradition of Jewish education, as well as a newer trend of Jewish nationalist political activity. In Poland, there were three distinct Jewish groups: one in the central region (known as "Congress" Poland, which held five percent of the country's three million Jews); Jews of the so-called *kresy* or Lithuania-Belorussia; and Jews in Galicia (located in southern Poland). Jews in Galicia differed from Jews in the other two regions because they had lived under Austrian rule in the nineteenth century, and had been emancipated and Germanized. As a result, even though the overwhelming majority of Polish Jews identified themselves as Jewish by nationality, and a majority of Jews considered Yiddish to be their mother tongue, these sentiments were weaker in Galicia. Eighty percent of Warsaw's Jews self-identified as nationally Jewish, and 89 percent claimed Yiddish as their mother tongue, compared with 50 and 63 percent, respectively, in Galician Cracow.[25] According to Celia Heller, Poland's Jews also broke into three groups relative to acculturation, with 10 percent comprising the most assimilated, Polonized Jews; another 33 percent as the most traditionally religious and least acculturated into Polish society; and the rest with one foot in tradition and the other in modernity.[26]

Romania presented yet another multilayered environment for Jews, with its shifting allegiances and governments, gains and losses of territories in the interwar period, and contradictory policies towards its Jewish population (which included stonewalling on granting rights of citizenship). Romania benefited after World War I because it sided with the Entente Powers, acquiring Transylvania from Hungary, as well as parts of Bessarabia (which had been part of Russia), Bukovina (part of Austria), and the Banat (which had been Hungarian). By 1940, Romania had lost 30 percent of its territory after Germany's victory over France, Romania's chief unofficial ally in the 1920s and 1930s. The Jews of Romania included those of the Wallachia, with its center in Bucharest, a relatively small, acculturated Jewish community (that did not adopt Romanian national identity or a Reform religious movement); Moldavia, where Jews were primarily Yiddish-speaking and many were Hasidic; Bessarabia and Bukovina, where Jews were also more of the eastern Europe type; and Transylvania, where rural Jews could be Yiddish-speaking and traditional, and urban Jews could be both German- and Magyar-speaking.

By contrast, in western Europe and Germany, Jews who had become citizens held the national identity of their respective countries and a religious or ethnic identity as Jews, but they were no less diverse. The majority of Jews in western Europe lived in cities— Paris, Antwerp, Oslo, Copenhagen, and Amsterdam—but these were by no means monolithic communities, with liberal and orthodox incarnations, Sephardic (Spanish) and Ashkenazic (central European) synagogues, and émigré Jews from eastern Europe. In fact, of the 350,000 Jews in France in the interwar period, approximately half were not French citizens, and only six percent of Belgium's Jews held citizenship as of 1939.[27] Both countries were appealing alternate destinations for eastern European (and later German) Jewish immigrants unable to leave for the United States due to restrictive immigration policies. By the late 1920s, hundreds of small immigrant synagogues came to dot the Parisian landscape, and in 1926, an umbrella organization known as the *Fédération des Sociétés Juives de France* brought under its aegis nearly 100 different Jewish immigrant associations with a total membership of 20,000 people.[28] As an indication of the diversity of the Jews in western Europe at an even more microcosmic level, in Antwerp alone, with over 50,000 Jews (only about 10 percent of whom were Belgian nationals), there were some 22 Jewish organizations, ranging from left-wing Zionists to the orthodox *Agudath Israel*, and even a veterans' group of Polish Jews.[29]

In Germany, defeat in World War I resulted in the establishment of the Weimar Republic, which, despite advancing rights for Jews, ultimately linked them to its unpopularity. The country's 560,000 Jews (less than one percent of the total population) were placed on an entirely equal footing with non-Jews after 1919, when the country's constitution (penned with the help of a politician of Jewish heritage, Hugo Preuss) officially proclaimed the separation of church and state. In addition to constitutional changes, there were tangible signs that German society was growing more accepting of Jews. Over the course of the 1920s, Berlin and Frankfurt became unrivaled centers of Jewish culture, intermarriage rates rose, and more Jews held public office than ever before. Unfortunately, these contributions served only to link Jews with a democratic order that fell into disfavor because of its association with the Versailles Treaty, political instability, cultural decadence, and economic chaos. The Nazis and other groups hostile to Weimar frequently referred to it as the *Judenrepublik*—the "Jewish Republic." Right-wing propaganda also drew attention to the nearly 100,000 Jewish immigrants from eastern Europe (*Ostjuden*), whose more traditional way of life, socio-economic status, and lower degree of acculturation into

German society provided convenient openings for attack. Mainstream politicians in the political center reacted just as hatefully towards these immigrants. The Prussian Ministry of the Interior issued an order on 1 June 1920 to oversee the deportation of refugees who failed to demonstrate a useful occupation, and one year later, the state set up what it called concentration camps for eastern deportees in Cottbus and Stargard. The Bavarian government ordered a mass expulsion of eastern European Jews in 1923, and in that same year, *Ostjuden* were victims of an anti-Jewish riot in the *Scheuneviertel* district of Berlin. Jewish life in Weimar was therefore both vital and fragile, and an increasing number of groups emerged within local Jewish communities, mainly orthodox and Zionist, to challenge the liberal premise of mainstream Judaism in Germany with its triad of progressive theology, humanism, and acculturation.[30]

The political leanings and activities of the Jews of Europe were further markers of their complex thought and behavior patterns. Although the Jewish national camp (Zionism and Bundism) was stronger in eastern Europe than in the west, there was still a good deal of variety in the politics of interwar Jewry, regardless of geography. Even within Polish Zionism, for instance, there was a general camp, a religious faction (*Mizrahi*), and no fewer than six Zionist socialist groups.[31] Galician Zionists also differed in their overall approach to politics from Zionists in central Poland as they favored compromise over confrontation, a tactic that resulted from Galicia's situation in the nineteenth century under Austrian (as opposed to Russian) rule.[32]

In the 1919 elections that produced Poland's first parliament (the *Sejm*), only 13 out of 444 seats were held by Jews, despite the fact that Jews constituted 10 percent of the Polish population. With six seats, the General Zionists, led by Yitzhak Gruenbaum, comprised the largest Jewish bloc. Gruenbaum sought to carve out a strong position for the non-Polish minority faction in the *Sejm*, and his efforts helped to increase its representation after the 1922 elections to 81 delegates, of whom 35 were Jewish. Polish socialists and minorities helped to elect a liberal as President, but his assassination led the Jewish bloc to retreat from working with other minority parties. For his part, Gruenbaum resigned from the *Sejm* in 1923, and 10 years later he left for Paris (and then Palestine), finding Poland to be an irredeemably chauvinistic state. After a coup by Marshal Josef Pilsudski in 1926 did away with much of the power of the parliament, the number of Jewish delegates was reduced from 13 to six. Pilsudski, however, remained popular among Jews as a figure of national liberation, and although he had the support of forces on the Right, which tended to be antisemitic, he did not enact legislation restricting Jews.[33]

One of the needs in recasting the diversity of Jewish politics is to revise the notion that Jews in the interwar period were squarely aligned with the radical Left. It is true that five of the 21 members of the Central Committee of the Bolshevik Party were Jews, and Jews were present in the secret police (*Cheka*) well beyond their percentage of the general population.[34] Prominent party members who had Jewish ancestry included Trotsky, Zinoviev, Kamenev, Sverdlov, Ioffe, Radek, and Riazanov, and yet this is precisely the point: Jewishness was a thing of their family history and not a cultural or a political identity, and certainly not a religious identity. According to Leonard Schapiro, statistics published in 1928 suggest that the number of [revolutionary] Jews was not disproportionate to the total number of Jews in Russia.[35] Increased party membership over the course of the 1920s and 1930s also lowered the percentage of specifically Jewish members to around four percent, and, as has already been mentioned, Soviet officials under Stalin engaged in a conscious policy of reducing (via purges) the percentage of Jews in leadership positions during the 1930s.[36]

In Germany, Rosa Luxemburg, co-founder of the German Communist Party (*Kommunistische Partei Deutschlands*, KPD), fit into the same category as Trotsky, an individual whose only connection to Jewishness was via genealogy. (By the middle of the decade, following the takeover of the KPD by Stalin protégé Ernst Thälmann, the Jewish presence on its central committee dwindled.) There were other Jewish members of the socialist Left in Germany, such as Hugo Haase, of the independent socialists or USPD, Rudolf Hilferding, the social democratic (*Sozialdemokratische Partei Deutschlands*, SPD) finance minister in 1923 and 1929, and Toni Sender, also of the SPD and one of the few prominent Jewish women in German politics. Sender went on to work for the United Nations after World War II. Of the 63 Jews who served intermittently in the German parliament (Reichstag) from 1919 to 1928, 35 belonged to the mainstream SPD.[37] But Jews could also be found among the ranks of the small, centrist German Democratic Party (*Deutsche Demokratische Partei*, DDP) in the 1920s, including the mayor of Frankfurt am Main, Ludwig Landmann. In terms of voting, most German Jews voted for the DDP until the depression, when that party lurched to the Right and led many Jews to begin splitting their votes between the SPD and the Catholic Center Party. Even the German-Jewish intelligentsia was fragmented; there were leftists, to be sure, like Gustav Landauer, Kurt Tucholsky, Walter Benjamin, and Leon Feuchtwanger, but also liberals like Jakob Wassermann and centrists like Hermann Cohen and Leo Baeck. On the Right, perhaps the most famous Jewish figure was Walter Rathenau, member of the German National People's Party (*Deutschnationale Volkspartei*, DNVP) and foreign minister, who was assassinated in 1922. At one point during the Weimar period, three percent of the approximately 600 delegates to the Reichstag were Jewish, but the trend pointed downward over the course of the 1920s to the point where, in 1932, only one Jewish member remained in parliament.[38]

Jewish participation in German state and society changed radically and quickly with the appointment of Hitler as chancellor on 30 January 1933. Within a few short months, all of the progress towards integration of Jews into the fabric of German life was not only gone, but reversed in such a negative way as to shock even some of the most ardent Jewish skeptics of the supposed German-Jewish symbiosis. By the end of 1933, new laws had begun the process of expelling Jews from the civil service, reducing their percentage in schools and universities in Germany, restricting their ability to become doctors and lawyers, and removing them from cultural and social organizations. Two years later, the Nuremberg Laws prohibited marriage and sexual relations between Jews and non-Jews, and defined the federal legal status of the Jews (denying them an elevated status of citizenship that conferred what few political rights there were left in the dictatorship and not, as is commonly believed, stripping Jews of their German citizenship). Then, in 1938, Jews were subjected to the nationwide pogrom of *Reichskristallnacht*, which crossed into a new territory of violence, forced emigration, and ethnic cleansing. The fact that this was happening in Germany was difficult to comprehend for many Jews, who would have regarded the more antisemitic east as the likely place for such persecution. However, restrictions that mirrored Nazi legislation surfaced there as well. In May 1938, Hungarian officials passed the so-called First Jewish Law, which limited Jewish participation in chambers of industry and commerce and in the legal, medical, and engineering professions. In Poland, following the death of Pilsudski in 1935, antisemitic sentiment increased, Jewish businesses were boycotted, Jewish university students were menaced, and talk surfaced in government circles about deporting Jews to Madagascar, although Polish officials did not actually enact anti-Jewish legislation, in contrast to Hungary and Romania. In the west, fascist officials in Italy proclaimed a law in 1938 that was analogous to the Nuremberg Laws, and they did so despite the fact that Jew-hatred was not a core element of Italian fascism. Indeed, a census in August 1938 revealed that 590 Jewish members of the National Fascist Party were longstanding "old fighters," holding membership from before 1922.[39]

The story of the Jews in the interwar period has an air of inevitability built into it by virtue of bookending the narrative between two catastrophic world wars. This kind of discursive framework is fundamentally ahistorical, and neither Hitler nor the Holocaust was inevitable. There were indices of Jewish integration and cross-ethnic relations that suggested an alternative future for much of European Jewry, in both the west and the east. Still, in some regions, antisemitism remained indisputably strong. In Poland and Romania, old hatreds lingered sometimes overtly, while in Soviet Russia, new rhetoric masked their persistence. In Germany, where Jewish integration continued apace across a broad spectrum of social indicators, the process was too closely linked to the existing (and increasingly unpopular) political order, and was in some respects "overheating," leaving Jews visible and exposed to attacks by virtue of the speed and depth of their social progress. Any sketch of Jewish life during the interwar period must allow for the possibility of a different conclusion, while acknowledging the overt and hidden challenges which Jews confronted across Europe and which, with the rise of Hitler, they were never given the opportunity to overcome.

Notes

1 See Monika Richarz, *Jüdisches Leben in Deutschland: Selbstzeugnisse zur Sozialgeschichte, 1918–1945* (New York: Leo Baeck Institute, 1982); Jonathan Friedman, *The Lion and the Star: Gentile–Jewish Relations in Three Hessian Communities, 1919–1945* (Lexington, Kentucky: The University Press of Kentucky, 1998), 39; Donald Niewyk, *The Jews in Weimar Germany* (Baton Rouge, Louisiana: Louisiana State University Press, 1980).

2 Hayim Ben Sasson, *A History of the Jewish People* (Cambridge, Massachusetts: Harvard University Press, 1976), 946.

3 Mark Mazower, *Salonica: City of Ghosts—Christians, Muslims, and Jews, 1450–1950* (New York: Vintage Books, 2006).

4 Joshua Rothenberg, "Demythologizing the Shtetl," *Midstream* (March 1981): 25–31.

5 Lloyd Gartner, *History of the Jews in Modern Times* (Oxford: Oxford University Press, 2001), 296. See similar statistics in Ezra Mendelsohn, *The Jews of East Central Europe Between the World Wars* (Bloomington, Indiana: Indiana University Press, 1987), 26.

6 See Jacob Katz, *Out of the Ghetto: The Social Background of Jewish Emancipation* (New York: Schocken, 1973), and more recently Shulamit Volkov, *Germans, Jews, and Antisemites: Trials in Emancipation* (Cambridge: Cambridge University Press, 2006).

7 See Jonathan Frankel, "Assimilation and the Jews in Nineteenth-Century Europe: Towards a New Historiography?" in *Assimilation and Community: The Jews in Nineteenth Century Europe,* ed. Jonathan Frankel and Stephen Zipperstein (Cambridge: Cambridge University Press, 1992), 20–30; Paula Hyman, "Recent Trends in European Jewish Historiography," *Journal of Modern History,* vol. 77 (June 2005): 345–56.

8 See Eli Lederhendler, *The Road to Modern Jewish Politics: Political Tradition and Political Reconstruction in the Jewish Community of Tsarist Russia* (New York: Oxford University Press, 1989).

9 Gartner, *History of the Jews,* 268.

10 Friedman, *The Lion and the Star,* 92.

11 Mendelsohn, *The Jews of East Central Europe,* 63.

12 See Michael Brenner, *The Renaissance of Jewish Culture in Weimar Germany* (New Haven, Connecticut: Yale University Press, 1996); Amos Elon, *The Pity of it All: A Portrait of the German-Jewish Epoch* (New York: Picador, 2002); Hugo Munsterberg, *Unspoken Bequest: The Contribution of German Jews to German Culture* (New York: Raymond Saroff, 1995).

13 Ben Sasson, *History of the Jewish People,* 935, 936, 963.
14 Gartner, *History of the Jews,* 269.
15 Gartner, *History of the Jews,* 270.
16 Zvi Gitelman, *A Century of Ambivalence: The Jews of Russia and the Soviet Union* (New York: YIVO Institute, 1988), 116; Benjamin Nathans, *Beyond the Pale: The Jewish Encounter with Late Imperial Russia* (Berkeley, California: University of California Press, 2002).
17 Gartner, *History of the Jews,* 287; Ben Sasson, *History of the Jewish People,* 946.
18 Heiko Haumann, *A History of East European Jews* (Budapest: Central European University Press, 2003), 209, 210.
19 Yitzhak Arad, *The Holocaust in the Soviet Union* (Jerusalem: Yad Vashem, 2009), 19–25.
20 Mendelsohn, *The Jews of East Central Europe,* 104, 105.
21 See Howard Sachar, *Dreamland: Europeans and Jews in the Aftermath of the Great War* (New York: Vintage Books, 2002), 20–42.
22 Mendelsohn, *The Jews of East Central Europe,* 100.
23 Mendelsohn, *The Jews of East Central Europe,* 146.
24 Marsha Rozenblit, *Reconstructing a National Identity: The Jews of Habsburg Austria During World War I* (Oxford: Oxford University Press, 2004).
25 Mendelsohn, *The Jews of East Central Europe,* 30, 31.
26 See Celia Heller, *On the Edge of Destruction: The Jews of Poland Between the Two World Wars* (Detroit, Michigan: Wayne State University Press, 1993), 5, 6.
27 Dan Michman, "Problematic National Identity, Outsiders and Persecution: Impact of the Gentile Population's Attitude in Belgium on the Fate of the Jews in 1940–44," in *Nazi Europe and the Final Solution,* ed. David Bankier and Israel Gutman (Jerusalem: Yad Vashem, 2009), 457.
28 Esther Benbassa, *The Jews of France* (Princeton, New Jersey: Princeton University Press, 1999), 152. See also Paula Hyman, *The Jews of Modern France* (Berkeley, California: University of California Press, 1998).
29 www.bh.org.il/database-article.aspx?48207
30 See Niewyk, *The Jews in Weimar Germany*; Friedman, *The Lion and the Star,* 69.
31 Mendelsohn, *The Jews of East Central Europe,* 59.
32 Mendelsohn, *The Jews of East Central Europe,* 55.
33 See Sachar, *Dreamland,* 20–42.
34 A list of 407 NKVD officials published in 1937 revealed 42 Jewish names. Leonard Schapiro, "The Role of the Jews in the Russian Revolutionary Movement," in *Essential Papers on Jews and the Left,* ed. Ezra Mendelsohn (New York: New York University Press, 1997), 318.
35 Schapiro, "The Role of the Jews," 303, and his citation of N.I. Sidorov, "Statistischesktye svediniya o propagandistakh 70-kh godov v obrabotke III otdeleniya," in *Katagora I Sssylka,* vol. 38 (1928): 27–56.
36 See Salo Baron, *The Russian Jew under Tsars and Soviets* (New York: Macmillan, 1976), 202–4, 285; Benjamin Pinkus, *Russian and Soviet Jews: Annals of a National Minority* (in Hebrew, English Title) (Sdeh Boker: Ben Gurion University Press, 1986), 182–86, 313–15; Leonard Schapiro, *The Communist Party of the Soviet Union* (New York: Random House, 1960), 171, 474; Gartner, *History of the Jews,* 293.
37 Sachar, *Dreamland,* 245.
38 Sachar, *Dreamland,* 245. See also Niewyk, *The Jews in Weimar Germany*; Peter Pulzer, *The Jews and the German State: The Political History of a Minority, 1848–1933* (Detroit, Michigan: Wayne State University Press, 2003).
39 Cristina Bettin, "Jews in Italy Between Integration and Assimilation, 1861–1938," *The European Legacy,* vol. 12, no. 3 (2007): 343.

2

EUROPEAN ANTISEMITISM BEFORE THE HOLOCAUST AND THE ROOTS OF NAZISM

William Brustein

The rise of the Nazi Party in Germany during the interwar period would not have occurred without a hospitable environment for popular antisemitism. Antisemitism in the west between 1870 and 1945 consisted of four principal strains—religious, racial, economic, and political—and each strain contained within itself a distinct antisemitic narrative. Each of these narratives entailed its own set of themes depicting Jewish malfeasance. The catalysts for ignition of the four strains were the deterioration in a nation's economic well being, the impact of increased Jewish immigration, the growth of popular support for the political Left, and the extent to which leadership of the political Left was identified with Jews.

Religious antisemitism in Germany

Of the four roots of antisemitism, religious antisemitism has the longest history in western Christian societies. Religious antisemitism encompasses hostility derived from the Jewish people's refusal to abandon their religious beliefs and practices and, specifically within Christian societies, from the accusation of Jewish collective responsibility for the death of Jesus Christ. By the eighteenth century, the religious root would expand to include the Enlightenment critique that Judaism was responsible for the anti-progressive and exclusionist character of its followers.

The German-speaking populations of central Europe were hardly immune to the mythology of Christian antisemitism during and after the Protestant Reformation. Popular images of the Jews as deniers of Christ, a pariah and demonic people, perpetrators of ritual murder, and agents of the Antichrist were firmly rooted among Germans as among other European Christians. During the Protestant Reformation, Martin Luther turned against the Jews and preached a vision of Jewry as irredeemably corrupt.[1]

German Catholic antipathy toward Judaism had an additional source in the late nineteenth century. In particular, some in the German Catholic church saw the hand of the Jews in Bismarck's anti-Catholic policies of the *Kulturkampf*. Legislators in the Catholic Center Party and writers for Catholic newspapers, citing the presence of prominent Jews in the National Liberal party, used antisemitism to mobilize support against Bismarck's alleged anti-Catholic campaign. At times, popular Catholic antisemitism in

Germany boiled over. Two notable cases surrounded popular religious accusations of Jewish ritual murder. Unsolved local murders led to the Jewish ritual murder allegations in the predominantly Catholic Rhineland town of Xanten in 1891 and the largely Catholic West Prussian town of Konitz in 1900.[2]

German Protestant theologizing did not refrain from occasional assaults on Judaism. Luther had undoubtedly supplied German Protestant churches with ample explosives. John Conway states that attacks on Jewish materialism and intellectualism became commonplace in Protestant sermons during the Weimar era and that the Protestant press frequently caricatured the Jews as corrupt and degenerate, accusing them of seeking to destroy traditional Christian morality within Germany.[3] The darkest chapter in the contemporary history of both German Churches vis à vis antisemitism is the relative silence on the part of the Protestant and Catholic leadership towards the Nazi treatment of German Jews.

With the advent of the Enlightenment, religious antisemitism took on a new leitmotif, emanating interestingly from the attacks leveled on the Jewish religion by such eminent secularists as Voltaire, Diderot, Montesquieu, von Dohm, and d'Holbach. As secularists, these philosophers, in opposing Judaism, did not resort to the ancient religious charges of Jews as Christ-killers or Christ-rejecters. Rather, in their critique of the roots of Christianity, they condemned Judaism for remaining a fossilized religion, persisting in a self-image of its special "election," and upholding anti-progressive beliefs. In this way, the Enlightenment may have contributed to modernizing and secularizing antisemitism.[4] During the nineteenth century, many secularists felt betrayed by Jews who, in their eyes, failed to abandon their distinctive beliefs and practices after having been emancipated and granted civil rights. Whereas traditional religious antisemitism appealed largely to a less-educated public, the secularist critique attracted a more highly educated following.

Within the German-speaking zones of Europe, the secularist interpretation of Jewish particularism found favor among many intellectuals. Some German thinkers, such as Lessing and von Humboldt, embraced a contractual view of the Enlightenment, believing that if granted equality, Jews would abandon their particularistic behavior and attitudes.[5] Other German writers took a more pessimistic view towards Jewish assimilation. For them, a systematic understanding of Jewish religious texts provided the keys to Jewish particularism.[6]

During the second half of the nineteenth century, several prominent German intellectuals questioned the commitment of German Jews to forsaking their historical particularism and to immersing themselves into the German national community. Within this group of German intellectuals, Heinrich von Treitschke, the celebrated German historian, stands out. In a series of articles between 1879 and 1880 in the prestigious *Preussische Jahrbücher*, Treitschke questioned the willingness of Jews to abandon their parochial allegiances and their desire to assimilate fully into German society. He, along with Richard Wagner and Paul de Lagarde, urged German Jews to accelerate the pace of their assimilation.[7] Even German liberals like Theodor Mommsen, Rudolf Virchow, and Johann Gustav Droysen, who by no means shared the overall politically conservative viewpoints of Wagner, de Lagarde, and von Trietischke, pointed to the persistence of Jewish particularism as a barrier to full assimilation.[8]

German socialists embraced the Enlightenment attacks on the Jewish Old Testament and the Jewish origins of Christianity. Bruno Bauer and other "Young Hegelians," heavily influenced by the Voltairian rebuke of Jewish particularism, condemned Judaism as both a fossilized and an antiprogressive belief system. They argued that Jews must be denied emancipation unless they abandoned their exclusionist and particularist essence. Karl Marx equally embraced the Voltairian critique of his fellow "Young Hegelians." His chief statement on the Jewish religion appeared in an 1844 essay, *Zur Judenfrage*. Though this treatise dealt largely with the economic role of Jews as moneymakers, Marx chastised Judaism as a reactionary religion that promoted an antisocial behavior of parasitism and clannishness.[9]

Racial antisemitism in Germany

France had Édouard Drumont, but Germany had Wilhelm Marr. Marr, a journalist, likely did more than anyone else in the last quarter of the nineteenth century to popularize racial hatred of Jews in Germany. Generally recognized as the inventor of the term "antisemitism," Marr published his manuscript *Der Sieg des Judentums über das Germanentum* (*The Victory of Jewry over Germandom*) in 1879. By Marr's account, over the course of 1,800 years, Jews had gained control over German commerce, the arts and media, and had corrupted German civilization. Although Marr cautioned against both hating individual Jews and seeing the Jewish problem as a religious one, he advanced the view that Jews were a racially determined group, unable to alter their ways and properly assimilate into German society. Marr also changed the perception of Jews in German society from a weak group to one holding substantial power. His book proposed that only by a separation of races could Germany solve the "Jewish Problem."[10]

Building on the theme of race war, in 1900 Houston Chamberlain published his landmark work on race, *The Foundations of the Nineteenth Century*. Chamberlain's widely popular book, written in a relatively accessible style, found a favorable reception among intellectuals as well as political and literary elites.[11] In many respects this work interwove religious, economic, political, and racial themes. Chamberlain employed the concept of race to explain the rise and fall of civilizations. In his view, the Germanic races embodied the greatest degree of vitality and creativity by virtue of the interbreeding among the different Aryan branches, the Teutons, Celts, and Slavs. Among the contributions to civilization emerging from the creative nature of the Aryan race were (allegedly) the sciences of botany, physics, chemistry, and mathematics.[12] Chamberlain pitted the creative Teutonic race against the uncreative Jewish race in a war of competing cultures and principles.[13] Pursuing a similar line to Drumont and Marr, Chamberlain argued that the Jews, although inferior in intelligence and numbers and in spite of their persecution, had successfully asserted their domination over the Teutons, Celts, and Slavs and that they, the Jews, threatened to destroy western culture and civilization.[14] Chamberlain's monumental study would become one of the potent molders of racial antisemitism both inside and outside of Germany during the first third of the twentieth century.

In the context of the popularization of Marr and Chamberlain's racial antisemitic arguments and the increasing flood of eastern European Jewish immigration, it was only a matter of time for Darwinian biological and eugenic reasoning to be applied to the "Jewish Question." Indeed, German race scientists such as Eugen Fischer and Fritz Lenz eventually appropriated genetic thinking and applied it to the Jews even before the rise of national socialism in Germany. Fischer linked particular alleged Jewish racial features, such as a large or hooked nose, to recessive genes. Lenz, co-editor of the major

German journal for racial hygiene and a firm proponent of a policy of procreation of "hereditarily worthy" people, claimed that by virtue of their genetic makeup, Jews could never become Germans even if they authored books on Goethe.[15]

Political movements and parties in Germany picked up the racial antisemitic theme beginning in the last quarter of the nineteenth century. Between 1879 and 1898, several antisemitic movements and parties emerged in Germany, and a number of them succeeded in getting candidates elected to the German parliament (the Reichstag). The 1893 Reichstag elections marked a significant victory for Germany's antisemitic parties. With 16 representatives, the antisemites formed their own independent parliamentary group.[16] Among those racial antisemites elected to the Reichstag in 1893 was Hermann Ahlwardt. Ahlwardt, in his attacks on Germany's Jews, invoked racial reasoning, and on a number of public occasions called for the extermination of Jews. In a major speech before the Reichstag on 6 March 1895, Ahlwardt cited the irreconcilable differences between the racial traits of the Jews and the Teutons, and claimed that studies demonstrated that the innate racial characteristics of the Jews acquired over thousands of years had made it impossible for Jews to change their nature. In one of the more memorable passages from his speech, Ahlwardt posited that just as a horse born in a cowshed is still no cow, a Jew born in Germany is still a Jew.[17]

After World War I, Germany witnessed the spawning of new racist antisemitic political parties and movements. Adolf Hitler's German National Socialist Workers' Party (*Nationalsozialistische Deutsche Arbeiterpartei*, NSDAP) is certainly the best known of these.[18] In February 1920, the party issued its official 25-point program. Four of the 25 points applied directly to Jews. Point four read that only those individuals of German blood were considered *Volksgenossen* (or members of the German national community), and only *Volksgenossen* could be German citizens. Point seven addressed the right to deport members of foreign nations; the NSDAP considered German Jews to be foreigners.[19]

Once in power, Nazi leaders drafted a set of policies based on the racial antisemitic ideology of the party. They quickly began to disenfranchise the country's Jewish population. The Civil Service Law of 7 April 1933, coming less than 3 months after Hitler's appointment as chancellor, called for the removal of Jewish civil servants and state employees who had not served at the front in World War I. This law included the "Aryan clause" that approved the forced retirement of Jewish judges, teachers, and other Jewish professionals. On 15 September 1935, at the Nazi Party's annual gathering, Hitler announced the infamous Nuremberg Laws. These laws included the "Law for the Protection of German Blood and Honor" and the "Reich Citizenship Law." Among other things, these laws provided a legal definition of a Jew and a set of policies restricting social relations between Jews and "Aryans," for instance, sexual contact between Jews and non-Jews, and Jewish hiring of non-Jews for domestic help. In November 1935, the Nazi regime followed up on its Nuremberg Laws with a law specifying in more detail the Nazi definition of a Jew.

In the world of German politics in the 1920s, the Nazis did not have any ideological monopoly on antisemitism and xenophobia. Antisemitic utterances found a home among other Weimar political parties other than the NSDAP. While it should come as no surprise that the more conservative parties, the German National People's Party (DNVP) and the German People's Party (DVP), frequently employed racial antisemitic rhetoric, the German Left could also be counted on to tap opportunistically into antisemitism.

Economic antisemitism in Germany

Before the nineteenth century, popular economic antisemitism in Europe typically embodied accusations about alleged unethical business practices in second-hand trade, petty commerce, and money lending conducted by Jews. As the nineteenth century unfolded, economic antisemites added the charge that Jews inordinately controlled the major means of production and, by virtue of this power, successfully manipulated both the domestic and foreign policies of states. The allegation of Jewish economic dominance tended to wax large during periods of economic or financial crises, which occurred periodically during the last quarter of the nineteenth century. Though a number of Jewish families in Europe had acquired sizable fortunes before the 1800s, principally as court agents of aristocratic families, the myth of Jewish economic dominance truly gained widespread currency as a result of several key factors, including Jewish emancipation and European industrialization.

By the end of the nineteenth century, Jewish prominence in German banking, industry, and commerce was staggering. According to Robert Wistrich, while Jews comprised only one percent of the total German population, they accounted for nearly 18 percent of bank owners and directors in the German Reich, and 33 percent in Berlin.[20] Jewish influence was felt equally in commerce and industry, where Jews held positions of prominence in roughly one-third of Germany's largest companies between 1900 and 1910.[21] Jews were well represented among Germany's greatest fortunes. Of the 29 German families in 1908 with aggregate fortunes in excess of 50 million marks, nine were Jewish. Jewish wealth within Germany's largest state, Prussia, in 1908 was even greater. Of the 200 Prussian millionaires in 1908, 55 came from Jewish origins, and 33 of these had made their fortunes in finance and banking.[22]

German Jews were also overrepresented within the German middle classes. Arthur Ruppin observed that, within the German state of Prussia, the percentage of Jews working in commerce was 56.6 percent in 1882 and 49.3 percent in 1925.[23] Among non-Jews, the percentages were 2.0 percent in 1882 and 10.3 percent in 1925. Jews made up roughly 22 percent of all employees in the Prussian banking and stock exchange in 1882. However, these numbers changed significantly by the 1920s. During the Weimar period, Jews directed less than one percent of Germany's more numerous and important credit banks.[24] Perceptions nevertheless trumped truth. More problematic were statistics that showed that by 1925, German Jews comprised 18 percent of all doctors, 15 percent of all dentists, and 25 percent of all lawyers in the German state of Prussia. By 1933, Jews made up slightly more than 16 percent of Germany's lawyers and nearly 11 percent of the country's physicians. We need to keep in mind that Jews comprised a little more than one percent of the total German population in 1933.[25]

During the last quarter of the nineteenth century, economic antipathy towards Jews benefited from the perception of a growing flood of foreign or eastern European Jews entering the new Reich. The outbreak of antisemitic pogroms in Russia in the 1880s turned the stream of eastern European immigration into a flood. Eastern Jews settling in Germany engaged primarily in peddling. Jack Wertheimer observes that the occupational structure of the Jewish immigrants in Germany differed significantly from that in other western destinations. Whereas nearly 70 percent of the Jewish immigrants in the United States and Great Britain participated in industrial labor, roughly half of the Jewish immigrants settling in Germany pursued careers in commerce.[26] Competition from immigrant peddlers constituted one source of friction, but competition for places in Germany's technical schools and universities became an additional arena of antagonism, out of which restrictionist campaigns aimed at immigrant Jewish students emerged. Some German states during the early 1900s instituted quotas or a *numerus clausus* on all foreigners attempting to enter German faculties, but others singled out Russian Jews.[27]

Germany's sudden military collapse in November 1918 ushered in a period of economic insecurity that lasted into the 1930s. The striking magnitude of the German economic decline during the interwar years bears repeating. The value of the German gold mark in relation to the US dollar, which stood at 4.2 in 1914, fell to 4.2 trillion in November 1923. Between 1921 and 1938, the average annual unemployment rate in Germany was 15.5 percent compared with 7.0 percent in France and 13.7 percent in Great Britain.[28] The economic misery hit German agriculture particularly hard. Agriculture and forestry accounted for 30.5 percent of Germany's employed population in 1925. Between 1925 and 1933, the cycle of crop failures, credit shortages, low prices for agricultural products, low tariffs, rising taxes, bankruptcies, and falling net profits increasingly ravaged Germany's farming community.[29]

After 1924, the fate of independent artisans and shopkeepers mirrored that of German farmers. Falling prices, shrinking markets, and expensive credit forced an increasing number of artisans and shopkeepers into heavy debt. Between 1925 and 1933, the average yearly income of the self-employed fell from 3,540 to 2,500 marks, while the income of people who were not self-employed dropped from 1,710 to 1,520 marks. Almost 50,000 business firms went bankrupt between 1930 and 1932.[30]

The deleterious effects of the interwar economic crises on Germany's working class are well known. By December 1923, more than half of Germany's labor force was either unemployed or underemployed. For those who had jobs, the high inflation eroded their income, so that real wages fell to nearly half their 1921 level. With the revival of the German economy in 1924, due in large part to the influx of foreign capital, conditions improved dramatically for many of Germany's blue-collar workers. However, the halcyon days were short-lived. Beginning in 1930, unemployment among blue-collar workers skyrocketed, while wages declined precipitously. In September 1929, 17 percent of organized metalworkers were either unemployed or working part-time. One year later, that figure jumped to nearly 45 percent. Unemployment continued to climb. By the summer of 1932, more than 40 percent of Germany's unionized workers were either unemployed or forced to work part-time.[31]

The Weimar years (1919–33) hardly disabused the harboring of economic antisemitic resentment. During the Weimar period, many of the same charges leveled against the Jews before and during World War I retained their potency. In fact, antisemitic rhetoric grew in intensity as more and more Jews entered into the ranks of Germany's economic, political, and cultural elite. Beside the traditional charge of Jewish economic power, there were the allegations of unfair economic competition from eastern European Jewish immigrants, and Jewish involvement in financial and political scandals. These accusations were hardly new, but they occurred in a context of severe economic trauma and in a climate of renewed eastern European immigration into Germany.

Economic antisemitic rhetoric had established a base throughout Weimar's political culture. Between 1925 and 1933, at a time when the Nazi Party sought to build its membership base and attract a sizable electoral following, the party opportunistically employed economic antisemitism where and when it concluded that such propaganda would attract support. From early in the party's history, Hitler targeted what he referred to as the particular brand of Jewish capitalism. He stressed that point 17 of the Nazi Party's official 1920 platform, calling for the "unremunerative expropriation of land for the common weal," applied to only land wrongfully acquired (obtained illegitimately or administered without regard for the good of the people) and primarily owned by "Jewish property speculation companies" (jüdische Grundspekulationsgesellschaften).[32] Hitler distinguished between productive and unproductive capitalism. The party, Hitler argued, favored productive capitalism (bodenständigen Kapitalismus), which embodied profit from one's own labor; but it disapproved of unproductive capitalism or loan capitalism, which derived profit from speculation. The Nazis incessantly associated the Jews with unproductive or loan capitalism. By distinguishing between good capitalists and bad capitalists, the Nazis staked out their own space between the Left, which was critical of all forms of capitalism, and the Right which was a staunch proponent of big business.[33]

Economic motives appear to have played a major role in the acquiescence of so many non-Jewish Germans to the implementation of Nazi antisemitic measures between 1933 and 1939. David Bankier has argued convincingly that self-interest led many Germans to welcome the expulsion of Jews from employment in the universities, public service, and professions.[34] In a time of relatively high unemployment, the sacking of Jews opened up numerous career opportunities for non-Jews. Also, the "aryanization" of the economy, which resulted in the closing of many Jewish businesses and the forced sale of Jewish property, appealed to the self-interest of many non-Jewish Germans.

In a context marked by the disastrous effects of the hyperinflation of the early 1920s, the agricultural slump of the mid-1920s, and the Great Depression, it is not surprising that a groundswell of economic resentment against Germany's Jews arose. Jews became targets of economic resentment for many reasons, including the general perception that Jews dominated many of Germany's financial and industrial institutions and the widely held view of Jewish overrepresentation in certain professions. The reality was, though, that the Great Depression did not discriminate; Jews were just as likely to be impoverished by the economic collapse as non-Jews.

Political antisemitism in Germany

At various times throughout the modern period, the myth of a "Jewish world conspiracy" has attracted adherents. Jews have been accused of plotting to take over the world by undermining the existing social and political order. In more recent times, Jews were assumed to be the backers or originators of radical and subversive movements whose chief aim was allegedly to bring down the reigning national political order. According to this line of thought, the Jewish predisposition towards radical and subversive movements derived from a combination of the intense internationalism of the Jews, which was a product of the Jewish dispersion throughout the world, and from a Jewish messianism.[35]

Political antisemitism, defined as hostility towards Jews based on the belief that Jews sought to control national and/or world power, experienced a momentous upsurge after 1879 in Europe. We can attribute the dramatic rise in political antisemitism between 1879 and 1945 largely to the emergence and rapid development of an international socialist movement and, concomitantly, to the popularization of the notorious Protocols of the Elders of Zion in the aftermath of the Bolshevik Revolution.

The advent of revolutionary socialism and labor activism during the second half of the nineteenth century triggered an outburst of German political antisemitism lasting until the Holocaust. Two of the principal founders of nineteenth-century socialism, Karl Marx and Ferdinand Lassalle, were German and had Jewish backgrounds. After the deaths of Marx (in 1883) and Lassalle (in 1864), prominent Jews continued to serve in important positions within the German Social Democratic Party (*Sozialdemokratische Partei Deutschlands*, SPD).[36] In addition to the fact that many Jews were Social Democrats, what likely made the perception of the link between Jews and revolutionary socialism more menacing to many Germans was the growing electoral popularity of the SPD. The party's share of the popular vote climbed from 27.2 percent in 1898 to 34.8 percent in 1912. Between 1881 and 1914, 43 of the 417 Social Democratic party deputies elected to the German Reichstag were Jews, representing a rate ten times the Jewish proportion of the German population. Anxiety about socialist popularity and the Jewish presence within the socialist movement became especially apparent in the wake of the stunning SPD victory in the 1912 Reichstag elections. In these elections, the number of SPD deputies rose from 43 to 110, giving the party the largest share of seats in the Reichstag. The SPD's electoral landslide, and the fact that 20 of the 25 Jews elected to the Reichstag belonged to the SPD, caused considerable consternation among Germany's antisemitic and conservative camps. The antisemitic and right-wing press attacked the supposed subversive activities of "international Jewry" and dubbed the 1912 elections the "Jewish elections" (*Judenwahlen*).[37]

The association of immigrant Jews from eastern and central Europe with subversive revolutionary movements further enhanced German political antisemitism. If German antisemites sought to reinforce the picture of immigrant Jews as adherents of revolutionary socialism, they only had to point to the central role that eminent east European Jews played in the German revolutionary socialist movement. Moreover, within the SPD, the Russian and Polish immigrant Jews tended to gravitate toward the party's extreme leftwing. No single individual personified the purported Jewish affinity for extreme revolutionary socialism better than the renowned Polish-Jewish immigrant Rosa Luxemburg. Thus it comes as little surprise that, in the aftermath of the Bolshevik Revolution, the perception that Polish and Russian Jews fleeing the violence of antisemitic pogroms carried with them the "Bolshevik virus" attained epidemic proportions.[38]

As we have seen above, political antisemitism made a quantum leap after the successful Bolshevik Revolution. The disproportionate representation of Jews in the newly emerging Communist movement and the spreading popularity of the *Protocols* gave an impetus to the charge of a Jewish plot to sow disorder as a means to the Jewish conquest of world power. In Germany, in the immediate aftermath of Germany's surrender in November 1919, German antisemites quickly highlighted the disproportionate presence of Jews within the new Reich government, the revolutionary Spartacist movement, and the newly founded German Communist Party. With the ensuing establishment of the Weimar Republic, notable Jews from the ranks of both the Social Democrats and German Democrats found themselves in important governmental positions.

Eastern European Jews played pivotal roles in the revolutionary unrest of 1918 and 1919 in Germany. Kurt Eisner, to whom the German Right and antisemites referred as a "Galician Jew," became the first prime minister and minister for foreign affairs of the new Bavarian Socialist Republic. In Berlin, seven Jews were among the founding party members of the Spartacists and the German Communist Party. The notable Jewish presence in the revolutionary turmoil of 1918 and 1919, and in the establishment of the Weimar Republic, became a godsend for the German antisemitic crusade. It would be wrong to assume the perception in Germany of a Jewish affinity for the revolutionary Left resided solely with ardent German antisemites and zealous nationalists. The notions that Jews performed a leadership role in the revolutionary Left, and that many of these Jewish socialist revolutionaries (such as Kurt Eisner) harbored anti-nationalist sentiments, had spread to the general population.[39]

Political antisemitism in Germany picked up steam after 1930 with the onset of the Great Depression, the resurgence of Germany's Communist party, and the growing popularity of the antisemitic Nazi Party. The German Communist Party had seen its share of the national vote rise from 10.6 percent in the 1928 national elections to 16.9 percent in November 1932. During the crisis years of 1930 through 1932, with skyrocketing unemployment, collapsing governmental coalitions, and incessant street battles between rightist and leftist paramilitary groups, many Germans feared a communist takeover. And in the minds of many, the link between revolutionary socialism and Jews seemed real. Hitler's Nazi party opportunistically capitalized on the rising fear of revolutionary socialism. Nazi speeches and writings were frequently peppered with references to the threat of communism. The *"Gefahr des Bolschewismus in Deutschland"* was dramatized in conjunction with the growth of support of the German Communist Party. The Nazi Party relentlessly hammered home an association between Jews and Marxist socialism, and even after forcing the socialist and communist parties to go underground after March 1933, it continued to highlight this alleged association until the final days of the Third Reich.[40]

Conclusion

Indifference to the fate of German Jewry on the eve of the Holocaust resulted largely from a culture of antipathy towards Jews derived from ingrained religious, racial, economic, and political antisemitic narratives. These narratives were ignited on the eve of the Holocaust by the increase in east European Jewish immigration, the economic depression, and the identification of Jews with revolutionary socialism. Europe's antisemitic environment produced fertile ground for the rise of German Nazism and the destruction of Europe's Jews.

Notes

1 John Weiss, *Ideology of Death: Why the Holocaust Happened in Germany* (Chicago: Ivan R. Dee, 1996), 22–25; Pierre Birnbaum, *Anti-Semitism in France: A Political History from Léon Blum to the Present*, trans. M. Kochan (Oxford: Blackwell, 1992), 12.

2 Albert S. Lindemann, *Esau's Tears: Modern Anti-Semitism and the Rise of the Jews* (Cambridge and New York: Cambridge University Press, 1997), 122; David Blackbourn, "Roman Catholics, the Centre Party and Anti-Semitism in Imperial Germany," in *Nationalist and Racialist Movements in Britain and Germany before 1914*, eds Paul Kennedy and Anthony Nicholls (London and Basingstoke: St Antony's College Press, 1981), 114; Gavin I. Langmuir, *History, Religion, and Anti-Semitism* (Berkeley, California: University of California Press, 1987), 326; Robert F. Byrnes, *Antisemitism in Modern France* (New Brunswick, New Jersey: Rutgers University Press, 1950), 1: 81.

3 J. S. Conway, "National Socialism and the Christian Churches during the Weimar Republic," in *The Nazi Machtergreifung*, ed. P.D. Stachura (London: Unwin Hyman, 1983), 140–41.

4 Arthur Hertzberg, *The French Enlightenment and the Jews* (New York: Columbia University Press, 1968); John M. Efron, *Defenders of the Race: Science in Fin-de-Siècle Europe* (New Haven and London: Yale University Press, 1994); Peter Pulzer, *Jews and the German State: The Political History of a Minority, 1848–1933* (Oxford: Oxford University Press, 1992); Jacob Katz, *From Prejudice to Destruction: Anti-Semitism, 1700–1933* (Cambridge, Massachusetts: Harvard University Press, 1980); Bruce F. Pauley, *From Prejudice to Persecution: A History of Austrian Anti-Semitism* (Chapel Hill, North Carolina: University of North Carolina Press, 1992); Robert S. Wistrich, *Antisemitism: The Longest Hatred* (New York: Schocken, 1991); Lionel B. Steiman, *Paths to Genocide: Antisemitism in Western History* (New York: St Martin's Press, 1998); George L. Mosse, *Germans and Jews: The Right, The Left, And The Search For a "Third Force" in Pre-Nazi Germany* (New York: Grosset and Dunlap, 1970); Rosemary R. Ruether, "The Theological Roots of Anti-Semitism," in *The Persisting Question: Sociological Perspectives and Social Contexts of Modern Antisemitism*, ed. Helen Fein (Berlin and New York: Walter De Gruyter, 1987); Michel Winock, *Nationalism, Anti-Semitism, and Fascism in France*, trans. J.M. Todd (Stanford, California: Stanford University Press, 1998).

5 Richard S. Levy, *The Downfall of the Antisemitic Political Parties in Imperial Germany* (New Haven, Connecticut: Yale University Press, 1975), 9.

6 George L. Mosse, *Toward the Final Solution: A History of European Racism* (Madison, Wisconsin: University of Wisconsin Press, 1985), 129–40; Lindemann, *Esau's Tears*, 87.

7 Donald L. Niewyk, "Solving the 'Jewish Problem': Continuity and Change in German Antisemitism 1871–1945," *Leo Baeck Institute Year Book* 35 (1990): 338; Byrnes, *Antisemitism*, 81; Lindemann, *Esau's Tears*, 131–36.

8 Ibid.

9 Robert S. Wistrich, *Socialism and the Jews: The Dilemmas of Assimilation in Germany and Austria–Hungary* (Rutherford, New Jersey: Farleigh Dickinson University Press, 1982), 19–30; Lindemann, *Esau's Tears*, 161; Paul W. Massing, *Rehearsal for Destruction: A Study of Political Anti-Semitism in Imperial Germany* (New York: Harper and Brothers, 1949), 159; Byrnes, *Antisemitism*, 115–17; Niall Ferguson, *The World's Banker: The History of the House of Rothschild* (London: Weidenfeld and Nicolson, 1998), 464.

10 Weiss, *Ideology of Death*, 97; Steiman, *Paths to Genocide*, 152; Lindemann, *Esau's Tears*, 128–30; Pauley, *From Prejudice to Persecution*, 28–29; Paul E. Grosser and Edwin G. Halperin, *Anti-Semitism, Causes and Effects: An Analysis and Chronology of 1,900 Years of Antisemitic Attitudes and Practices* (New York: Philosophical Library Inc., 1978), 219–20; Roger Eatwell, *Fascism: A History* (New York: Allen Lane, 1996), 28.

11 Lindemann, *Esau's Tears*, 351–53.

12 Steiman, *Paths to Genocide*, 165; Lindemann, *Esau's Tears*, 351–52; Martin Woodroffe, "Racial Theories of History and Politics: The Example of Houston Stewart Chamberlain," in *Nationalist and Racialist Movements*, 145; Mosse, *Toward the Final Solution*, 107.

13 Woodroffe, "Racial Theories of History and Politics," 152.

14 Steiman, *Paths to Genocide*, 165; Lindemann, *Esau's Tears*, 351–52; Woodroffe, "Racial Theories of History and Politics," 145; Leon Poliakov, *The Aryan Myth: A History of Racist and Nationalist Ideas in Europe*, trans. E. Howard (New York: Basic Books, 1971), 516–19.

15 Efron, *Defenders of the Race*, 19; Richard Lerner, *Final Solutions: Biology, Prejudice, and Genocide* (University Park, Pennsylvania: Penn State University Press, 1992), 31.

16 Massing, *Rehearsal for Destruction*, 71; Hajo Holborn, *A History of Modern Germany 1840–1945* (Princeton, New Jersey: Princeton University Press, 1982), 321.

17 Massing, *Rehearsal for Destruction*, 300–305; Weiss, *Ideology of Death*, 104.

18 Weiss, *Ideology of Death*, 223–24.

19 Eric Johnson, *Nazi Terror: The Gestapo, Jews, and Ordinary Germans* (New York: Basic Books, 1999), 87; H.L. Lebovics, *Social Conservatism and the Middle Classes in Germany, 1914–33* (Princeton, New Jersey: Princeton University Press, 1969), 206.

20 Wistrich, *Socialism and the Jews*, 61.

21 In his *Die Juden und das Wirtschaftsleben,* Werner Sombart, the noted German sociologist, pointed out that Jews constituted nearly one quarter of the members of the boards of directors within the ten largest branches of German industry (Wistrich, *Socialism and the Jews*, 61).

22 Jonathan Steinberg, *All or Nothing: The Axis and the Holocaust 1941–1943* (London and New York: Routledge, 1990), 235–36; W.D. Rubinstein, *A History of the Jews in the English-Speaking World: Great Britain* (New York: St Martin's Press, 1996), 124; Roberto Finzi, *Anti-Semitism: From Its European Roots to the Holocaust* (New York: Interlink Publishing Group, 1999), 57.

23 Arthur Ruppin, *Jews in the Modern World* (London: Macmillan, 1934), 209.

24 Donald Niewyk, *The Jews in Weimar Germany* (Baton Rouge, Louisiana: Louisiana State University Press, 1980), 14.

25 Wistrich, *Socialism and the Jews*, 56–57; Ruppin, *Jews*, 219.

26 Jack Wertheimer, *Unwelcome Strangers: East European Jews in Imperial Germany* (New York and Oxford: Oxford University Press, 1987), 92.

27 Wertheimer, *Unwelcome Strangers*, 34, 70.

28 Peter Temin, *Lessons from the Great Depression: The Lionel Robbins Lectures for 1989* (Cambridge, Massachusetts: Harvard University Press, 1989), 3; Angus Maddison, *Dynamic Forces in Capitalist Development: A Long-Run Comparative View* (Oxford and New York: Oxford University Press, 1991), 87–89; Rondo Cameron, *A Concise Economic History of the World: From Paleolithic Times to Present* (New York and Oxford: Oxford University Press, 1989), 351–521; Charles Kindleberger, *A Financial History of Western Europe* (London: Allen & Unwin, 1984), 306, 366.

29 G.D. Feldman, *The Great Disorder: Politics, Economics, and Society in the German Inflation, 1914–1924* (New York: Oxford University Press, 1993), 840; D. Petzina, "Germany and the Great Depression," *Journal of Contemporary History*, vol. 4 (1969): 59; Michael Kater, *The Nazi Party* (Cambridge, Massachusetts: Harvard University Press, 1983), 58; Detlev Peukert, *The Weimar Republic: The Crisis of Classical Modernity*, trans. R. Deveson (New York: Hill Wang, 1989), 65; M. Sering, *Deutsche Agrarpolitik: Auf geschichtlicher und landeskundlicher Grundlage* (Leipzig: H. Buske, 1934), 115; Harold James, *The German Slump: Politics and Economics 1924–1936* (Oxford: Oxford University Press, 1986), 258–59; David Abraham, *The Collapse of the Weimar Republic*, 2nd edn (New York: Holmes and Meier, 1986), 55, 59; William Brustein, *The Logic of Evil: The Social Origins of the Nazi Party, 1925–1933* (New Haven and London: Yale University Press, 1996), 64–66, 68–69.

30 Jürgen W. Falter, "Economic Debts and Political Gains: Electoral Support for the Nazi Party in Agrarian Commercial Sectors, 1928–33" (paper presented at the 85th annual meeting of the American Political Science Association, Atlanta, Georgia, 1989), 5; Brustein, *The Logic of Evil*, 73.

31 Thomas Childers, *The Nazi Voter: The Social Foundations of Fascism in Germany, 1919–1933* (Chapel Hill, North Carolina: University of North Carolina Press, 1983), 102–3, 244; Abraham, *The Collapse of the Weimar Republic*, 117; Feldman, *The Great Disorder*; *Wirtschaft und Statistik*, vol. 12 (1932): 147–48, 471–73.

32 H. A. Winkler, *Mittelstand, Demokratie und Nationalsozialismus* (Cologne: Kiepenheuer and Witsch, 1972), 100; H. Gies, "The NSDAP Agrarian Organization in the Final Phase of the Weimar Republic," in *Nazism and the Third Reich*, ed. H.A. Turner (New York: Quadrangle Books, 1972), 46; W.T. Angress, "The Political Role of the Peasantry in the Weimar Republic," *Review of Politics*, vol. 21 (1959): 546; D. Gessner, "The Dilemma of German Agriculture during the Weimar Republic," in *Social Change and Political Development in Weimar Germany*, eds R. Bessel and E.J. Feuchtwanger (London: Croom Helm, 1981), 150; J.H. Grill, "The Nazi Party's Rural Propaganda Before 1928," *Central European History*, vol. 15 (1982): 164.

33 Brustein, *The Logic of Evil*, 91; M. Kele, *Nazis and Workers: National Socialist Appeals to German Labor, 1919–1933* (Chapel Hill, North Carolina: University of North Carolina Press, 1972), 43; Thomas Childers, "The Social Language of Politics in Germany: The Sociology of Political Discourse in the Weimar Republic," *American Historical Review*, vol. 95 (1990); Sarah Gordon, *Hitler, Germans and the "Jewish Question"* (Princeton: Princeton University Press, 1984), 67.

34 David Bankier, *The Germans and the Final Solution: Public Opinion under Nazism* (Oxford: Oxford University Press, 1992), 69.

35 Jaff Schatz, *The Generation: The Rise and Fall of the Jewish Communists of Poland* (Berkeley, California: University of California Press, 1991), 38–43.

36 Lindemann, *Esau's Tears*, 172; Wistrich, *Socialism and the Jews*, 81–82.

37 Jonathan Sperber, *The Kaiser's Voters: Electors and Elections in Imperial Germany* (Cambridge: Cambridge University Press, 1997), 258; Wistrich, *Socialism and the Jews*, 75–76, 80–81; Anthony Kauders, *German Politics and the Jews: Düsseldorf and Nuremberg 1910–1933* (Oxford: Oxford University Press, 1996), 31, 35; Steiman, *Paths to Genocide*, 161; Saul Friedländer, *Nazi Germany and the Jews: The Years of Persecution, 1933–1939* (New York: Harper Perennial, 1997), 75.
38 Wistrich, *Socialism and the Jews*, 82–83; Wertheimer, *Unwelcome*, 24–25, 39–40, 103–4; David Blackbourn, "Roman Catholics," 119–20.
39 Kauders, *German Politics and the Jews*, 56–58, 67, 77.
40 Brustein, *The Logic of Evil*, 57; Gordon, *Hitler, Germans and the "Jewish Question,"* 67.

3

GERMANY AND THE ARMENIAN GENOCIDE OF 1915–17

Hans-Lukas Kieser

Was the Armenian genocide a genuine project of the reigning Young Turks, or was there driving German agency and doctrine, *ta'lim-i Alman*, as many said on the ground? Was Turkey's ally in World War I instrumental in, and co-responsible for, the Armenian catastrophe? Was there a road, a German road, from the Armenian death camps in the Ottoman Syrian desert in 1915–17 to the eastern European extermination camps in 1942–45? Did the Old World's seminal catastrophes after July 1914, its *descente à l'enfer*, follow the compelling logics of good and evil forces, with the German state being a main actor of evil?

United States Ambassador Henry Morgenthau and the Entente powers, like some later historians, "overplayed the influence of Germany in Istanbul," British historian Donald Bloxham recently stated, while Vahakn Dadrian, a pioneer of Armenian genocide studies, insisted on "German complicity, namely, the willingness of a number of German officials, civilian and military, to aid and abet the Turks in their drive to liquidate the Armenians." Others have argued similarly.[1] The German debate is as old as the famous question of guilt for the beginning of the "Great War." Whereas the general *Schuldfrage*, after heated discussions during and shortly after the First World War, came largely back into academic debate a few decades later—remember the Fischer debate—German involvement in the Armenian genocide began to be discussed only again at the end of the twentieth century.

It was not historians employed at universities, but a retired journalist, Wolfgang Gust, who recently edited the German state documents with regard to the Armenians in the 1910s. This is a highly important documentation of the Armenian genocide that, at the same time, sheds a great deal of light on our main issues—Germany's involvement in the Armenian genocide and the extent to which the experience of this genocide influenced German political thinking up to World War II.[2] Is there a historical record of concrete German–Ottoman interaction leading to the deportation, forced starvation, and massacre of the Ottoman Armenians of Anatolia and European Turkey? How did official Germany react when faced with the destruction of Anatolia's (not only Armenian) Christians? What was the impact of the experience of the Armenian genocide for Germany and Germans after World War I? And finally, was there a road from Der ez-Zor to Auschwitz?

Ally of a dictatorial and "revolutionary" regime

First, let us understand the background for the German–Ottoman war partnership concluded in 1914, which proved a decisive setting. Sporadic German–Ottoman interactions intensified after the Congress of Berlin, which Chancellor Bismarck convened in June 1878. The young Sultan Abdulhamid II sought alternatives to British support for the late Ottoman status quo, after the British won a foothold in Cyprus at the Congress and then, in 1882, invaded Egypt. The Germans sent a military mission to the Ottoman Empire in 1883 in order to reorganize the Ottoman army, which had collapsed in the Russian–Ottoman war in 1878. Colmar von der Goltz was a leader of that mission; his seminal book *Das Volk in Waffen* (The People in Arms) was translated into Ottoman.[3] Both German military doctrine and German arms began to permeate the Ottoman army. Even more importantly, a huge politico-economic project began to crystallize at the end of the 1880s.

The famous *Bagdadbahn* (Baghdad railway), financed by the Deutsche Bank, a project of economic and industrial penetration, was for its promoters an alternative to the colonialism–imperialism as practiced by Germany's senior rivals, Great Britain and France. Rightly or wrongly, the Wilhelminian elite, the elite of the *Kaiserreich* of Emperor Wilhelm II, felt it was deliberately excluded from enjoying its own portion of *Weltgeltung* and *Weltmacht*, the global power that it claimed to deserve according to its economical and military weight. The Entente Cordiale of 1904 between France and Britain, including Russia in 1907, was felt as an alliance among established powers that proved again unwilling to integrate newcomers. Not only German right-wing and liberal nationalists, but also socialists, contributed at that time to both anti-Russian and anti-British feelings and to the conviction that Germany deserved a brilliant, world-shaping future, a fatal *Grossmannssucht* according to Marion Dönhoff.[4]

The *fin de siècle* cooperation with the Ottoman Empire germinated as an answer to German ambition and frustration. Bismarck himself had been skeptical about German involvement in the "Orient" because he judged the Oriental Question to be a bottomless pit and Article 61 of the Berlin Treaty, intended to protect the Armenians, as purely "cosmetic."[5] The largely agrarian Ottoman Empire suffered an existential crisis that had begun in the late eighteenth century, and dramatically worsened during the 1870s and the Russian–Ottoman war of 1877–78. Marked by the loss of territory in the Balkans and eastern Asia Minor, the young sultan Abdulahmid II was determined to save the state by means of reform, a more authoritarian rule, and state-sponsored Islamism. The politics of Muslim unity concerned an imperial interior that, since the Berlin Treaty, had been demographically much more Muslim and geographically more Asiatic. In diplomacy, the sultan exploited the growing inter-European concurrence and German ambitions.

Abdulhamid risked diplomatic isolation when the press in the West depicted him as the *sultan rouge*, the ruler responsible for large-scale anti-Armenian massacres in 1894–96. The main massacres in Anatolia in autumn 1895 began precisely after the sultan had signed, under international pressure, a reform plan for the Ottoman eastern provinces of Asia Minor, according to Article 61 of the Berlin Treaty. They cost the lives of about 100,000 Armenians, mostly men and boys, who were killed in a wave in pogrom-like violence perpetrated by individuals who had organized in mosques and whom the local authorities tolerated or encouraged.[6] The Armenian massacres of the *fin de siècle* were to remain in western cultural memory, up to World War II, *the* pivotal reference for mass violence against civilians.[7]

Sultan Abdulhamid was particularly content in October 1898 to receive the German Kaiser Wilhelm II. By then, British-led diplomacy had failed in orchestrating a strong response to the mass violence that had deeply shocked the West.[8] British diplomacy and transnational humanitarians argued that the reforms agreed upon in Article 61, guaranteeing safety for the Armenians in the Ottoman eastern provinces, their main region of settlement, needed urgently to be implemented. Among the humanitarians, one of the most articulate, a vociforous critic of European diplomacy, was the German pastor Johannes Lepsius.[9]

The reform plan of 1894–95 was not implemented despite or, fatally, because of the massacres. Germany was in the forefront of those powers that ostentatiously put their interests above an international consensus on reforms for a safe Ottoman, including Armenian, future. During his visit in Istanbul in 1898, Wilhelm II was given the provisional concession for the continuation of the railway project, which had started 10 years before, extending as far as Baghdad. Although the Young Turks in opposition criticized German support for Abdulhamid, the Young Turk Revolution of 1908 did not put into question the Ottoman–German friendship. The American railway project (the Chester Project) for the eastern provinces failed because the Ottoman government wanted to prevent trouble with the Germans.[10]

The German economic politics of the *Bagdadbahn* reached their peak in the beginning of 1914. On 8 February 1914, the Ottoman government signed a new reform plan for the eastern provinces drafted by the jurist André Mandelstam, chief dragoman at the Russian Embassy, and thoroughly revised with German participation, after Germany had abandoned in 1913 its hitherto anti-Armenian stance. The "Armenian Reforms," as the plan was shortly called, in its final version divided the eastern provinces into a northern and a southern part; put them under the control of two powerful European inspectors, to be selected from neutral countries; prescribed to publish the laws and official pronouncements in the local languages; provided for a fair proportion of Muslims and Christians in the councils and the police; and demobilized the *Hamidiye*, an irregular Kurdish cavalry that, since its creation in 1891, had threatened non-Sunni groups of the eastern provinces. The close Russian–German collaboration had been the key to this great moment of *Belle Époque* diplomacy that promised to solve the so-called Armenian question, a crucial part of the so-called Eastern question. Lepsius himself had contributed to the negotiations; he now stood side-by-side with a German "Orient" policy he hoped would incorporate both economic penetration and the evangelical aims of his Deutsche Orient-Mission. In a similar vein, Paul Rohrbach, a member of the executive board of the Deutsche Orient-Mission, propagated German "ethical imperialism." In those months, two German–Ottoman friendship associations were founded, the Deutsch–Türkische Vereinigung by Ernst Jaeckh, and the Deutsch–Armenische Gesellschaft by Lepsius, both sponsored by the German Foreign Office.[11]

The Ottoman government, a dictatorial regime controlled by the Young Turk Committee of Union and Progress (CUP) since 1913, signed the Armenian Reforms under pressure. It felt these to be a blow against its goal of "national sovereignty." In spring 1914, it began to implement a diametrically opposed, Turkist, agenda of demographic engineering in Anatolia. The men of its newly founded Special Organization terrorized and expelled some 150,000 *Rûm* (Greek- or Turkish-speaking Ottoman Christians) from the Aegean littoral. When, on 6 July, the Ottoman Parliament discussed the expulsions, Talat, minister of the interior and member of the CUP's central committee, using evasive language, emphasized the need to settle the Muslim refugees of the Balkans in those emptied villages. If he had sent them to the vast deserts of Syria and Iraq (as he did a year later with the Armenians), they would all have died, he added.[12]

The international crisis of July 1914, after the assassination of Archduke Franz Ferdinand of Austria in Sarajevo, saved the regime from a diplomatic backlash against the expulsion and gave it the opportunity to win a formal ally. Even though a German military mission led by Liman von Sanders had already been in Istanbul since 1913, German diplomats did not seriously consider an official alliance with Turkey until right up to the outbreak of World War I, and even as late as mid-July 1914, Germany rejected an Austrian proposal for such an alliance. This changed, however, at the end of July, after war minister Enver Pasha made a proposal to Wangenheim. Fears had arisen of an Ottoman alignment with the Entente, and Emperor Wilhelm stressed reasons of opportunity.[13]

The secret alliance was concluded on 2 August 1914. Under its shield, the Young Turk regime began to implement its own interior agenda and, despite being the junior allied partner, improved its bargaining position vis-à-vis a senior partner eagerly anticipating Ottoman action against Russia. At the same time, the Young Turks were proud of their alliance with a great power which they admired.[14] They felt pressed to show themselves to be a valuable military ally and to obey the compelling geodynamics as seen from Istanbul–Berlin.

Germany and the implementation of the Armenian genocide in 1915

What was the impact of war exigencies upon the CUP's interior agenda and the implementation of this agenda? For General Joseph Pomiankowski, the Austrian military attaché in Istanbul, a frequent companion of Enver Pasha, the regime's intention to eliminate the Armenian question and the Armenians themselves had "an important influence" upon the regime's decision for war on the side of the Triple Alliance, and was a matter of internal politics into which the CUP rejected any immixture.[15] The Germans who had been involved in the reform negotiations did not anticipate, let alone actively prevent, this worst case. On 6 August, Wangenheim accepted six proposals, among them the abolition of the capitulations and "a small correction of her [Turkey's] eastern border which shall place Turkey into direct contact with the Moslems of Russia."[16] Strong panturkist and panislamist propaganda, soon to be coupled by jihadist propaganda made in Germany, began to appear in the Ottoman press in early August. This discourse, together with the suspension of the reform plan and the recall of both inspectors mid-August, alienated and intimidated the Ottoman non-Muslims. In contrast to Germany, Russia insisted on the continuation of the Armenian Reforms in the case of an alliance, after Enver had started deceitful talks with Russian representatives on an alliance with the Entente on 5 August.[17]

Bahaeddin Şakir, a senior CUP member and chief of the Special Organization, invited the leaders of the Armenian Revolutionary Federation (ARF), who had been meeting in Erzurum since late July, to lead an anti-Russian guerilla war in the Caucasus, aimed at preparing the Ottoman conquest. The ARF stated, however, that all Armenians had to remain loyal to the country in which they lived. Despite the ARF's refusal, attempts at revolutionizing the Caucasus began in early August. In September, the regime announced the abrogation of the capitulations, closed down numerous foreign post offices in the Empire, and succeeded in obtaining large sums of money from Germany in order to prepare for attack. Though the Empire officially entered the war only in November 1914, the Ottoman army began in early August to mobilize and requisition to a degree it had never done before. The requisitions hit, in particular, the non-Muslims in the eastern provinces.[18]

On 2 October, Enver stated to his confidant Hans Humann, the navy attaché of the German Embassy, that the great mobilization "had to advance the people's *völkisch* [ethnonationalist Turkist] education," part of which was a paramilitary education of the youth that had already begun in early 1914. On 11 November, when the Ottoman Empire officially entered the war, a CUP circular declared that the Muslims had to be liberated from the infidels and that the national ideal was driving the Turks to destroy the Muscovite enemy in order to obtain a natural frontier that would include all branches of the Turkish race. The ruling single-party of a huge empire used both Islamist and radical *völkisch* language, a striking foretaste of something more extreme than Wilhelminian Germany. Orientalists in the service of the German Foreign Office contributed to the ideological polarization by fabricating holy war propaganda. Max von Oppenheim, the author of a seminal memorandum entitled *Revolutionizing the Islamic Possessions of our Enemies*, dated October 1914, used highly derogatory language when speaking of the Armenians and other Oriental Christians, as if German diplomacy had not reassessed its attitude toward the Armenians in 1913–14 and exactly criticized such language.[19]

While units of the Special Organization began in September to terrorize Armenian villages on the side of and beyond the eastern frontier of Russia, German-led naval attacks against installations on the Black Sea initiated open anti-Russian aggression at the end of October. In reaction, Russia declared war and its Caucasus army crossed the frontier at Erzurum, but stopped before Turkish defenses. Unsatisfied by his generals' defensive attitude and accompanied by his German chief of staff Bronsart von Schellendorf, but against the advice of Sanders, Enver Pasha himself took the command for an offensive towards the Caucasus. At the end of 1914, however, his campaign failed catastrophically in the mountains of Sarıkamış. Tens of thousands of soldiers perished, and epidemics began to spread.[20]

In January and February 1915, the campaigns by Rauf Bey and Enver's brother-in-law Jevdet, with irregular forces in Northern Persia, failed in similar fashion. As a consequence, the panturkist dream, which had galvanized the mobilization in August 1914, had turned to trauma in spring 1915; the long eastern front was brutalized as irregulars and regulars, militias and forces of self-defense spread violence; most Christians had lost any trust in the government; and the catastrophic, frustrating situation at the long eastern front infuriated CUP leaders. Armed Christian forces relied, where possible, on Russian help in those zones. Best known is the Russian relief of the Armenians in Van, who, since 20 April, had resisted Jevdet's efforts of repression.[21]

In contrast to the east, the Ottoman army in the west commanded by the German General Sanders won its first decisive victory against the Entente offensive at the Dardanelles on 18 March. In this double strategic and psychological setting in spring 1915, the regime decided on a policy of complete Armenian removal that was implemented by extermination. Exploiting a distorted version of the Van events and the situation on the eastern front, propaganda was spread throughout Anatolia of a general Armenian uprising and of scorpion- and serpent-like Armenian neighbors. The Ministry of the Interior under Talat coordinated the removal in three main steps:[22] first, there was the arrest of Armenian political, religious and intellectual leaders, beginning with those in Istanbul on 24 April; second, from late spring to autumn, the Armenian population of Anatolia and European Turkey was transferred to camps in the Syrian desert east of Aleppo, excluding Armenian men in eastern Anatolia who were systematically massacred

34

on the spot; third and finally, there was the forced starvation to death of those in the camps and the final massacre of those who still survived. A last death march followed to and beyond Der ez-Zor, excluding a large group of Armenians whom Jemal Pasha, governor of Syria, had converted pro forma to Islam and resettled in Syria and Palestine. Among the points that distinguish the murder of the Armenians from that of the Jews in World War II is this exception, as well as the assimilatory absorption of an unknown, but considerable, number of Armenian children and women into the "perpetrator nation."[23]

German reactions to "removal" and mass crime

From a German perspective, the war on the Ottoman eastern front, though the offensive had failed, absorbed growing Russian forces and made the distressed regime even more dependent on German assistance. Anti-Russian and anti-British propaganda projected a German-led Europe extending its dominance up to Baghdad and beyond. A few so-called democratic, liberal, socialist or "ethical" imperialists between Berlin and Istanbul, such as Jaeckh, Oppenheim, Erwin Nossig, Friedrich Naumann, Helphand Parvus, and Rohrbach, were the leading ideologues in this matter. Whereas Rohrbach, though hesitantly, understood in summer 1915 that, once and for all, the extermination of the Armenians "broke the moral neck of the alliance with Turkey," the others continued to do their business as if, in terms of political culture, Germany did not risk losing the war and "its soul" precisely because of this moral atrocity. The iron logics of geostrategy and georevolution left no consideration for victims and collateral damage, the propagandists argued, the German *Endsieg* needed the alliance at all costs, and with it the anti-British incitement of the Muslim world and Russia's defeat.[24]

Although large-scale anti-Armenian massacres had taken place in peacetime in the 1890s, the centralist policy of 1915 and its extremist ideology would have been inconceivable without a general war that paralyzed internal discussion and international diplomacy. Removal-cum-extermination in the shadow of war and of a war alliance was possible only with a senior ally that did not set, right from the start, critical political and ethical limits to its alliance. For the German officers and leading diplomats, Armenian removal in the war zones, that is, the eastern provinces, was justified by military reasons. In this sense, German officers on the spot and representatives in the capital communicated approvingly with the CUP officials. There was a similar logic of thinking with regard to the *Rûm* on the Aegean coast. Greece's geographical proximity and intended neutrality in the war, however, demanded a more careful policy of removal. It led henceforth not to Greece or to desert, but to the interior of Anatolia. Again, Muslims were resettled in the evacuated *Rûm* villages. In the case of the *Rûm*, Germany pressured its ally several times.[25]

The provisional law of 31 May, often called the Law of Deportation, officially sanctioned removal and served as a legal cover for beginning destruction of the Armenians. Although it did not limit removal to clearly defined zones and the Entente had publicly warned of crimes against humanity, the German officials still did not anticipate or counter the risk of massive abuse. After, in May, they had approved of limited removal for military reasons, they began to back, on the contrary, the public Ottoman denial[26] and made efforts in order to appease friends of the Armenians and experts of the region. In the Foreign Office in Berlin, Lepsius was shown a telegram of 31 May by Wangenheim, who asked for their understanding with regard to removal. Lepsius, however, was alarmed and decided to travel to Turkey.[27] The uncritical approval of removal in the eastern provinces was a decisive breakthrough for a regime which, a few months previously, had found itself strictly bound to implement, jointly backed by Germany, a monitored coexistence of Christians and Muslims, Armenians, Syriacs, Kurds, and Turks in eastern Asia Minor. The breakthrough was all the more poignant as, in a few instances, German officers on the ground signed or approved removals. The best documented case is Lieutenant Colonel Böttrich, head of the railway department of the Ottoman general staff. Against the will of the civil direction of the *Bagdadbahn*, he signed an order of deportation for Armenian employees of the *Bagdadbahn*, though he knew well in October 1915 that this would involve the death of most or all of them.[28]

As early as mid-June 1915, Humann qualified the extermination as "hard, but useful."[29] Ottoman officials succeeded in the provinces to create the impression that the removal was German doctrine, and its horrors the consequence of German agency. The lack of human and Christian solidarity struck many Ottomans; Europe's long-proclaimed ethics and protection of minority Christians appeared to have been sacrificed. "I often notice how embarrassed silence or a desperate attempt to change the subject took hold of their [the German officers'] circles," wrote the former teacher in Aleppo Martin Niepage, "when a German with deep feelings and an independent judgment came to speak of the dreadful misery of the Armenians."[30] Officer Wolffskeel contributed to crush the desperate Armenian resistance in Urfa—like Van and the Musa Dagh an exceptional case—describing this on the ground in cool and smug words to his fiancée.[31] Only a few officers, such as Sanders in Izmir and Erwin von Scheubner Richter in Erzerum, locally prevented, or tried to prevent, the anti-Armenian policy.[32]

Ambassador Wangenheim began to understand in mid-June 1915 that the so-called removal from the war zones was part of a fully fledged program of removal-cum-extinction throughout Asia Minor. "It has come to light that the banishment of the Armenians is not only motivated by military considerations," he wrote on 17 June to Bethmann-Holweg. "The Minister of the Interior, Talaat Bey, recently spoke about this without reservation to Dr. Mordtmann, who is currently employed by the Imperial Embassy. He said 'that the Porte is intent on taking advantage of the World War in order to make a clean sweep of internal enemies—the indigenous Christians—without being hindered in doing so by diplomatic intervention from other countries.'"[33]

Wangenheim felt abused and tricked, and began to send clear-cut reports to Berlin; first and foremost in his mind, however, was Germany's prestige. "The expulsion and relocation of the Armenian people was limited until 14 days ago to the provinces nearest to the eastern theatre of war," he wrote to Bethmann-Holweg on 7 July, "since then the Porte has resolved to extend these measures also to the provinces [...] even though these parts of the country are not threatened by any enemy invasion for the time being. This situation and the way in which the relocation is being carried out shows that the government is indeed pursuing its purpose of eradicating the Armenian race from the Turkish Empire.[...] I have considered it my duty to point out to the Porte that we can only approve of the deportation of the Armenian people if it is carried out as a result of military considerations and serves as a security against revolts, but that in carrying out these measures one should provide protection for the deportees against plundering and butchery."[34] The last sentences were wishful thinking.

Later on, during talks with Ambassador Wolff-Metternich, the successor of Wangenheim who had died in autumn 1915, the regime argued that military reasons had justified the comprehensive removal.[35] Wolff-Metternich intervened more energetically than his predecessor and wanted public condemnation of the horrors, but was not backed by Berlin. The governmental attitude condensed in Chancellor Bethmann-Hollweg's fatal note of 17 December, saying that "The proposed public reprimand of an ally in the course of a war would be an act which is unprecedented in history. Our only aim is to keep Turkey on our side until the end of the war, no matter whether as a result Armenians do perish or not. If the war continues much longer, we will need the Turks even more. I cannot understand how Metternich can make such a suggestion [...]."[36]

In Germany, a few public voices, in particular Lepsius and the socialist deputy Karl Liebknecht, spoke for loyalty to truth and humanitarian action. In lectures and in his report on the situation of the Armenians in Turkey, a brilliant piece of investigative journalism, which exploited sources collected during his travel to Istanbul in July–August 1915, Lepsius gave the German intelligentsia the means to understand what was happening.[37] When Lepsius, in a lecture to German journalists in Berlin in October 1915, complained that the extermination of the Armenians was having a disastrous impact upon Turkey's economy, the rejoinder from Julius Kaliski, a right-wing socialist, was that the Ottoman Armenians would easily be replaced by Jews. Another socialist proclaimed in his freshly launched journal in favor of the German war effort in the late summer 1915: "We do not want to be influenced in our judgment by considerations for friends or comrades, not even by the pity for poor and persecuted people." German power, in his perspective, had alone to bring about Russia's defeat and a socialist world revolution. A collaborator of the Foreign Office published a panegyric of the main CUP leaders after having interviewed them during the high noon of the extermination in late summer 1915 in the Ottoman capital. Another collaborator of the Foreign Office wrote from Istanbul that "this extermination of a rebellious Turcophobe and Anglophile human race, which had been stirred up by foreign money, could be the first step towards the amelioration of the economic situation" in Turkey – that is towards a "national economy," *millî iktisad*, which suppressed the "compradore bourgeoisie."[38]

Could Germany have prevented the genocide? General Pomiankowksi answered no, because of the constraints of the alliance, including the CUP's strict separation between internal politics and military matters. He argued that only a timely declaration of war by the United States, which possessed important missionary institutions throughout Anatolia, could have prevented the extinction of the Anatolian Armenian community. Closer to the reality and the possibilities of early 1915 would have been an Entente strategy that seriously considered a landing at the poorly defended coast of Adana or Iskenderun, instead of stubbornly trying and failing to break through at the Dardanelles. An invasion from that coast would have prevented at least the final phase, the death camps in Syria. The political and military authorities of Germany could indeed have prevented the Armenian catastrophe right from the start, if they had possessed in time the audacity to radically reassess their political self-understanding, overstretched war policy, and ill-conceived alliance with the CUP regime.

It is improbable that any European power would have decided, in times of total war, on steps in favor of universal ethics and political self-denial; this hard fact lies at the core of Europe's unending catastrophe after 1914. However, one could argue that the German authorities could have bargained much better in the summer of 1915 in order to exclude certain groups and regions from removal. Since Germany did not possess the means to control the whole interior, the CUP regime would, in the long run, have found ways to implement its policy of de-Armenization. Arguably, Germany's last best chance to prevent the Armenian genocide would have been in late March and early April 1915, when, after the first victory at the Dardanelles, the Turkish elite's depression turned to chauvinist exuberance and when, combined with events in Zeytun and Dörtyol, the anti-Armenian atmosphere began to condense. German diplomacy was informed in time. "After my return [from Zeytun], Jelal Bey, the Vali of Aleppo, let me know," the German consul in Aleppo Walter Roessler wrote to both Wangenheim and the Chancellor on 12 April, "that apparently in the Turkish government a current is gaining the upper hand which is inclined to consider all Armenians as suspicious or even hostile. He thinks of this development as a misfortune for his fatherland and begged me to persuade His Excellency the Imperial Ambassador to counteract this trend."[39] Emphasizing leading German agency for the first Ottoman victory at the Dardanelles and for the further defense of the Ottoman capital, German diplomacy could then have made clear, once and for all, that it remained committed to the Armenian reforms of 1914, vetoed henceforth any anti-Armenian steps, and did not fear a break in the alliance.

Yet once it understood the extermination, German diplomacy remained egocentric. It worked only to limit damage to prestige, to refuse accusations of guilt and, in the same perspective, to facilitate some humanitarian assistance. In early June 1915, an outraged Roessler asked Wangenheim to intervene for the first deportees arriving in Aleppo, informing him that Jelal was being sacked and that a special CUP envoy had taken power in Aleppo. Jelal had been one of those few high officials who had courageously defended a sense of honor and humanity.[40] Beside some early aid by local agents, German diplomacy began late, in autumn 1915, to facilitate humanitarian help. The Swiss teacher Beatrice Rohner, a member of a German missionary organization, was called to the Ottoman capital for secret talks in November. Helped by local Armenians and backed by German and American diplomacy, in early 1916 she set up legal orphanages in Aleppo and began to communicate illegally with the deportees in the camps. This work was sponsored mainly by American and Swiss sources. The money collected by Lepsius went to his collaborators in Urfa, whose humanitarian work, also for Kurdish deportees, was co-sponsored by the American Near East Relief. This had begun in autumn 1915; it remained backed by American and German diplomacy even after the United States entered the war.[41]

The impact of the Armenian genocide on interwar Germany

The Armenian genocide could have been a tremendous lesson, but to point at the main Turkish culprit, as did Lepsius, did not suffice. At issue was to grasp the lack of German resistance against and response to unexpected, but expectable mass crime next door, whose victims were humans for whom European diplomacy in 1878 and again in 1913–14, this time with central German involvement, had guaranteed security and future. Liebknecht, Lepsius, Rohrbach, and others had felt in 1915 that something had gone wrong in German political and ethical culture, that Germany missed the poignant challenge the Armenians had addressed. Evil, in the sense of a hushed up genocide, entered Germany's political realm through a backdoor. One could consider this a consequence of an ill-begun war and an ill-conceived war alliance, thus part of the war guilt question. After 1918, most political and intellectual actors, including Lepsius, blended together the questions of war guilt (or co-guilt) and of co-responsibility for the murder of the

38

Armenians and answered them in the negative. In a Weimar Republic that broadly cultivated the myth of German innocence, the decisive damage of 1914 and 1915 could not be repaired. Even worse, several actors began to rationalize and endorse extermination, referring implicitly or explicitly to the Armenians. In this sense, the underdiscussed, and wrongly discussed, German experience of the Armenian genocide contributed to the acceptance and adoption of exterminatory schemes in the interwar period.

In February 1918 already, Emperor Wilhelm had endorsed paramilitary action against the "Jew-Bolsheviks" in the Baltic referring to "analogy Turks in Armenia." He again assimilated, as was done so often in the Wilhelmine era, Armenians and Jews, and saw in 1918 the "Russian people at the mercy of the revenge of the Jews."[42] Max von Scheubner-Richter, German officer and vice-Consul in Erzerum, had tried to help the victims and to intervene in their favor through German diplomacy in May and June 1915. However, within a few years this seemingly upright man became a fanatic, obsessed by fear of internal enemies that would annihilate Germany. What haunted him was not the Armenian qua Levantine Jew, but the Armenian victim experience. In the general context of German defeat, the Versailles Treaty and inflation, and of a personal trauma as a refugee from Riga, his native town having been occupied by the Red Army, Scheubner-Richter's ethical references completely broke down. "All illusions on the solidarity of the international proletariat, all illusions that it suffices to be in one's self peace-loving in order to lead the neighbor to peace, all illusions that a nation is justly dealt with if itself it is righteous, all illusions that foreign nations will not permit the destruction of the German nation […] all these stupid dreams and illusions must die."[43] Introduced to Hitler by Alfred Rosenberg, himself a native of the Baltics, Scheubner-Richter was one of the first National Socialists in Munich. In Munich, they internalized together the fear of "becoming like the Armenians" and the conclusive idea of preventive annihilation. Their fear and hate of Bolshevik Russia echoed the panturkist resentments against Tsarist Russia before and during World War I.

"A solution of the Jewish question has to be found," Hitler said at the end of 1922 to a Munich newspaper, probably echoing talks with Scheubner-Richter. "If no solution is achieved, there will be two possibilities, either the German people will be a people like the Armenians or the Levantines, or a bloody clash will follow."[44] For Scheubner-Richter in early 1923, the "rise of Germany and the German nation from today's shame and defenselessness" could only take place "if first of all we remove ruthlessly and completely from Germany and the German lines all those that carry guilt for the destruction of the German national body and for the failure of resistance of the German nation." Like radical Turkists and pan-Turkists after the Balkan wars, Scheubner-Richter now pleaded for "ruthless cleansing from Germany of all elements that are intentionally hostile and that work against the *völkisch* union of all German tribes."[45] A German officer who had moved among Pan-Turkist officers and perpetrators in Erzurum in 1915, next to the Russian front, knew what these words meant.

The military engineer and interwar author Karl Klinghardt had been in the service of Jemal Pasha. Like many other Germans, a witness to death caravans, massacres, and starvation camps, he suffered from a memory filled with traumatic images. "But I have not spoken about these experiences. Nothing to help. With the brutality of natural events a stroke of human history produced itself. […] These experiences should forever be silenced." In a text for *Der Orient*, he nevertheless wanted to prove that he knew what the "true misery of the Armenians" had been. Arguing against a "propaganda of consternation," Klinghardt revealed a fascination with cold-blooded, rational, functional mass killings. "The mass killing was executed almost every time in a quick and functional manner, without any inhibition of blood [*Blutscheu*], but also without any particular cruelty." Turkey would have been "damned to a *völkisch* and national death," had it not annihilated the Armenians, Klinghardt concluded in 1928.[46]

"If we abstract from the human aspect," Dagobert von Mikusch, an early successful biographer of Mustafa Kemal in 1929, wrote with similar logic and a sweeping comparison, "the exclusion of the Armenians from the body of their state was no less a constraining necessity than [...] was the extermination of the Indians for the new state of the white people in America."[47] Many German patriots of those years admired the Turkish nationalists, their successful revision of the Paris-Sèvres Treaty in Lausanne in 1923 and their rapid construction of a nation-state based on Turkism. Dazzled by this success, they went on to accept the whole creation of the state in Asia Minor, including preparatory demographic engineering and extermination. In an article of 1929, the renowned orientalist Richard Hartmann saw the killing of the Armenians as part of a racial war, and described Turkey "after the racial wars" as a nation free from "notable *völkisch* minorities."[48] A healthy homogeneous nation-state, many came to believe, was incompatible with egalitarian plurality. Though they admired the Turkish success and tried to rationalize what had happened to the Armenians, most of them, however, still did so with hesitation, marking distance by referring to "true Asiatic ruthlessness."[49] They were both confused and fascinated by the eliminatory logics—the silent approval of mass killing and the refusal to acknowledge anything criminal in it. "In the Armenian question they [the Kemalists] have covered up for the Young Turks and not explicitly, but tacitly, approved their policy of extermination," Mikusch stated.[50]

The Berlin trial against Salomon Teilirian, the killer of Talat Pasha in Berlin in 1921, polarized between right-wing patriots and voices such as the circle of Lepsius, the left-wing newspaper *Vorwärts*, and students of law such as Robert M. W. Kempner. These welcomed the trial and Teilirian's acquittal as a step towards international justice for unpunished mass crimes. The context of this trial in Germany and the release "of all Turkish war criminals" in 1922 made another student of law, Raphael Lemkin, aware of the need for a new concept in international law—whence he finally coined the term "genocide." Rosenberg, in contrast, praised Talat and condemned the "Jewish press of all colors" who had welcomed the outcome of the trial.[51] When Rosenberg's party was in power, it burned Franz Werfel's 1933 *The Forty Days of Musa Dagh*, the story of a successful Armenian resistance in 1915. As a symbol of hope, Werfel's novel was widely read among eastern European Jews; it formed an important link from the Armenian to the Jewish experience of genocide.[52]

Conclusion

A few differences, analogies and links between the Armenian genocide and the Shoah have been touched upon in this chapter, though comparison is not its main topic. In both cases, young imperial elites and would-be saviors of empire had traumatically witnessed the loss of power, prestige, territory, and homes. In an unstable political situation and fearing imperial and personal ruin, they succeeded in establishing a single-party regime that allowed them to implement policies of expulsion and extermination based on crazy, but calculated social Darwinist engineering. The extermination of the Armenians as part of a comprehensive demographic engineering, which considered Anatolian Christians to be non-assimilable, turned out to be a brutal but successful model for eliminating the issue of minorities, due to its ethno-nationalistic rationale condoned by Western diplomacy at the Near East Conference of Lausanne in 1922–23. The revisionist Treaty of Lausanne tacitly endorsed comprehensive policies of expulsion and extermination of hetero-ethnic and hetero-religious groups, with fatal attraction for German revisionists and many other nationalists. The reception of this paradigm is the bridge from a Wilhelminian Germany on the whole deeply embarrassed by the genocide of its junior partner, to a Nazi Germany that approved of and adopted it.

For a long time, the international setting in both politics and academia did not allow for calmly exploring possible German paths from the Armenian to the Jewish Genocide. The heated *Historikerstreit* of the 1980s had its important points, but certainly did not excel in contextualizing and historicizing Nazi Germany's exterminatory policies. Among other reasons, this deficit had to do then with the striking lack of research into the experiences of the Ottoman Armenians. Contemporary observers, however, had linked both experiences. Lemkin, in particular, pioneer of the Genocide Convention, thought of the death camps in the Syrian desert, the final phase of the Armenian genocide, when he evoked the "heat of the ovens of Auschwitz and Dachau" and the "murderous heat in the desert of Aleppo which burnt to death the bodies of thousands of Christian Armenian victims of genocide in 1915." For him, a road, crooked though it may be, led from Der ez-Zor to Auschwitz, and in turn from both to the Genocide Convention.[53]

Notes

1 Donald Bloxham, *Genocide, the World Wars and the Unweaving of Europe* (London: Vallentine Mitchell, 2008), 87; Vahakn N. Dadrian, *German Responsibility in the Armenian Genocide: A Review of the Historical Evidence of German Complicity* (Watertown, Massachusetts: Blue Crane Books, 1996), 186; Christoph Dinkel, "German Officers and the Armenian Genocide," *The Armenian Review*, vol. 44 (1991): 77–130; *Der Völkermord an den Armeniern 1915/16: Dokumente aus dem Politischen Archiv des deutschen Auswärtigen Amts*, ed. Wolfgang Gust (Springe: Zu Klampen, 2005), 76–108; Eberhard Graf Wolffskeel Von Reichenberg, *Zeitoun, Mousa Dagh, Ourfa: Letters on the Armenian Genocide*, ed. Hilmar Kaiser (Princeton, New Jersey: Gomidas Institute Books, 2001), x–xvi.
2 Internet edition on www.armenocide.de, of which a selection is printed and introduced in Gust (ed.), *Der Völkermord an den Armeniern*. All PA-AA documents quoted in this chapter have been accessed on this site in December 2009.
3 Colmar von der Goltz, *Millet-i müsellaha: asrımızın usul ve ahvali askeriyyesi* (Istanbul: Matbaa-ı Abüzziya, 1305).
4 Marion Dönhoff, *Preussen, Mass und Masslosigkeit* (München: Goldmann, 1991).
5 Norbert Saupp, *Das Deutsche Reich und die armenische Frage* (Köln: n.p., 1990), 30.
6 Jelle Verheij, "Die armenischen Massaker von 1894–96. Anatomie und Hintergründe einer Krise," in *Die armenische Frage und die Schweiz (1896–1923)*, ed. Hans-Lukas Kieser (Zürich: Chronos, 1999), 69–129.
7 Describing persecutions of the Jews, René de Weck, Swiss legate in Bucarest during World War II, referred to the Armenian massacres of the *fin de siècle*, which were more present to his mind than the genocide of 1915; letter of 28 November 1941, quoted by Gaston Haas, "*Wenn man gewusst hätte, was sich drüben im Reich abspielte ...*": *1941–1943: was man in der Schweiz von der Judenvernichtung wusste* (Basel: Helbing und Lichtenhahn, 1994), 82.
8 Hans-Lukas Kieser, *Nearest East. American Millennialism and Mission to the Middle East* (Philadelphia: Temple University Press, 2010), 60–61.

9 Johannes Lepsius, *Armenien und Europa: Eine Anklageschrift wider die christlichen Grossmächte und ein Aufruf an das christliche Deutschland* (Berlin: W. Faber, 1896).

10 Under attack from aggressive young states like Italy and those in the Balkans in 1911–13, and realizing that European assurances of the status quo proved futile in the event of war, Ottoman diplomacy did not focus exclusively on Germany when seeking a formal alliance with a European power. Britain, the diplomatically ideal partner, was rejected, however, since it remained doubtful whether the CUP would have taken Britain's side in the rivalry with Germany over the *Bagdadbahn*. John A. Denovo, *American Interests and Policies in the Middle East: 1900–1939* (Minneapolis, Minnesota: University of Minnesota Press, 1963), 58–87; Joseph Heller, *British Policy towards the Ottoman Empire: 1908–1914* (London: Frank Cass, 1983), 62–64.

11 Roderic H. Davison, *Essays in Ottoman and Turkish History, 1774–1923: The Impact of the West* (Austin, Texas: University of Texas Press, 1990), 180–205; *Deutschland, Armenien und die Türkei 1895–1925. Thematisches Lexikon*, eds Hermann Goltz and Axel Meissner (München: Saur, 2004), 35–36, 122–23, 246. According to Joseph Pomiankowski, the German commitment to reform was insincere since the leading representative, Ambassador Hans von Wangenheim, did not believe in the pluralistic, egalitarian order being aimed for. Joseph Pomiankowski, *Der Zusammenbruch des Ottomanischen Reiches: Erinnerungen an die Türkei aus der Zeit des Weltkrieges* (Zürich: Amalthea-Verlag, 1928), 163; for the German documentation on the reforms see PA-AA/R14077–84.

12 Fuat Dündar, *Modern Türkiye'nin şifresi. İttihat ve Terakki'nin etnisite mühendisliği (1913–1918)* (Istanbul: Iletisim, 2008), 223, 257.

13 For the alliance with Germany and its implementation, see Mustafa Aksakal, *The Ottoman Road to War in 1914: The Ottoman Empire and the First World War* (Cambridge: Cambridge University Press, 2008), 93–118; Ulrich Trumpener, *Germany and the Ottoman Empire 1914–1918* (Princeton: Princeton University Press, 1968), 21–61.

14 Djemal, *Erinnerungen eines türkischen Staatsmannes* (München: Drei Masken Verlag, 1922), 119.

15 Pomiankowski, *Der Zusammenbruch des Ottomanischen Reiches*, 162–63.

16 Trumpener, *Germany and the Ottoman Empire*, 28.

17 Aksakal, *The Ottoman Road to War*, 107–8, 127–30.

18 Dikran M. Kaligian, *Armenian Organization and Ideology under Ottoman Rule: 1908–1914* (New Brunswick, New Jersey: Transaction Publishers, 2009), 219–22; Ramond Kévorkian, *Le génocide des Arméniens* (Paris: Odile Jacob, 2006), 221, 275; Wolfdieter Bihl, *Die Kaukasus-Politik der Mittelmächte* (Wien: Böhlau Verlag, 1975), 1: 230–45; Taner Akçam, *A Shameful Act: The Armenian Genocide and the Question of Turkish Responsibility* (New York: Metropolitan Books, 2006), 136–38; Hans-Lukas Kieser, *Der verpasste Friede. Mission, Ethnie und Staat in den Ostprovinzen der Türkei 1839–1938* (Zürich: Chronos, 2000), 331, 335–36, 445.

19 Aksakal, *The Ottoman Road to War*, 169; Handan N. Akmeşe, *The Birth of Modern Turkey: The Ottoman Military and the March to World War I* (London: I. B. Tauris, 2005), 163–76; Erol Köroğlu, *Ottoman Propaganda and Turkish Identity. Literature in Turkey during World War I* (London: I. B. Tauris, 2007); CUP circular quoted in Tekin Alp, *Türkismus und Pantürkismus* (Weimar: Kiepenheuer, 1915), 53; Gottfried Hagen, "German heralds of holy war: Orientalists and applied oriental studies," *Comparative Studies of South Asia, Africa and the Middle East*, vol. 24, no. 2 (2004): 149–50. See also the report of Wangenheim to Chancellor Bethmann-Hollweg of 24 February 1913, PA-AA/R14078.

20 Maurice Larcher, *La Guerre Turque dans la Guerre Mondiale* (Paris: Chiron & Berger-Levrault, 1926), 367–436; Pomiankowski, *Der Zusammenbruch des Ottomanischen Reiches*, 98–105.

21 Once relieved, they themselves acted revengefully against Muslim civilians. Kieser, *Der verpasste Friede*, 448–53; Bihl, *Die Kaukasus-Politik der Mittelmächte*, 233.

22 The most systematic, detailed and up to date account based on primary sources is Kévorkian, *Le génocide des Arméniens*. For a review of recent literature, see Hans-Lukas Kieser, "Der Völkermord an den Armeniern 1915/16: neueste Publikationen (Rezension)," *sehepunkte*, vol. 7, no. 3 (March 2007), www.sehepunkte.de/2007/03/10400.html, accessed 11 December 2009.

23 For recent comparative and contextualizing approaches, see *The Armenian Genocide and the Shoah*, eds Hans-Lukas Kieser and Dominik J. Schaller (Zurich: Chronos, 2002); Bloxham, *Genocide, the World Wars and the Unweaving of Europe*.

24 Hans-Walter Schmuhl, "Friedrich Naumann und die 'armenische Frage,'" in *The Armenian Genocide and the Shoah* (eds Kieser and Schaller), 503–16; Ernst Jäckh, *Das grössere Mitteleuropa: ein Werkbund-Vortrag* (Weimar: Kiepenheuer, 1916); Rohrbach's quotation in Ernst Jäckh papers, Yale University Library, reel 1366.

25 Dündar, *Modern Türkiye'nin şifresi*, 230–36.

26 Trumpener, *Germany and the Ottoman Empire*, 209–10.

27 Johannes Lepsius, *Der Todesgang des armenischen Volkes: Bericht über das Schicksal des armenischen Volkes in der Türkei während des Weltkrieges* (Potsdam: Tempelverlag, 1919), v–vii.

28 PA-AA/BoKon/171, 18 November 1915.

29 Humann quoted by Hilmar Kaiser, "Die deutsche Diplomatie und der armenische Völkermord," in *Osmanismus, Nationalismus und der Kaukasus. Muslime und Christen, Türken und Armenier im 19. und 20. Jahrhundert*, eds Fikret Adanır and Bernd Bonwetsch (Wiesbaden: Reichert, 2005), 213–14.

30 PA-AA/R14093, report to the Chancellor of 10 September 1916.

31 Von Reichenberg, *Zeitoun, Mousa Dagh, Ourfa*.

32 Gust (ed.), *Der Völkermord an den Armeniern*, 87–91.

33 PA-AA/R14086, 17 June 1915, English translation on the site.

34 PA-AA/R14086.

35 "Die Türkische Regierung vertritt den Standpunkt, daß die Umsiedelungsmassnahme nicht nur, wie wir zugegeben haben, in den Ostprovinzen, sondern im ganzen Reichsgebiet durch militärische Gründe gerechtfertigt war." Ambassador Wolff-Metternich to Bethmann-Hollweg, 3 April 1916, PA-AA/R14091.

36 Note on an Embassy report of 7 December 1915, PA-AA/R1408.

37 Johannes Lepsius, *Bericht über die Lage des Armenischen Volkes in der Türkei* (Potsdam: Tempelverlag, 1916). Published only in July 1916 and soon (not strictly) confiscated, parts of the *Bericht* circulated since autumn 1915. Cf. Goltz and Meissner (eds), *Thematisches Lexikon*, 72–74.

38 Ernst Jäckh papers, Yale University Library, 461-2-52; Christian Gerlach, "Nationsbildung im Krieg: Wirtschaftliche Faktoren bei der Vernichtung der Armenier und beim Mord an den ungarischen Juden," in *The Armenian Genocide and the Shoah* (eds Kieser and Schaller), 382–83; Alfred Nossig, *Die neue Türkei und ihre Führer* (Halle, Saale: Otto Hendel, 1916); Parvus, *Die Glocke* no. 1, 1 September 1915, 2.

39 Roessler to Bethmann-Hollweg, 12 April 1915, DE/PA-AA/R14085, translation on the site.

40 PA-AA/BoKon/169; see also Roessler's reports of 3 and 6 June 1915.

41 Hilmar Kaiser, *At the Crossroads of Der Zor. Death, Survival, and Humanitarian Resistance* (Princeton, New Jersey: Taderon, 2001), 33–38; Hans-Lukas Kieser, "La missionnaire Beatrice Rohner face au génocide des Arméniens," in *La résistance aux génocides. De la diversité des actes de sauvetage*, ed. Jacques Sémelin (Paris: Presses de Sciences Po, 2008), 383–98; Kieser *Der verpasste Friede*, 348–55, 482–87.

42 Quoted by Donald Bloxham, *The Final Solution: A Genocide* (New York: Oxford University Press, 2009), 80–81.

43 Scheubner-Richter, quoted by Paul Leverkühn, *Posten auf ewiger Wache. Aus dem abenteuerreichen Leben des Max von Scheubner-Richter* (Essen: Essener Verlagsanstalt, 1938), 192. Translations by the author, if not otherwise remarked.

44 Adolf Hitler, *Sämtliche Aufzeichnungen: 1905–1924*, eds Eberhard Jäckel and Axel Kuhn (Stuttgart: Deutsche Verlags-Anstalt, 1980), 775; English translation in Mike Joseph, "Max Erwin von Scheubner-Richter: The personal link from genocide to Hitler," in *The Armenian Genocide, Turkey and Europe*, eds Hans-Lukas Kieser and Elmar Plozza (Zurich: Chronos, 2006), 165.

45 Leverkühn, *Posten auf ewiger Wache*, 190.

46 Karl Klinghardt, "Als Augenzeuge der armenischen Katastrophe," *Der Orient*, 1928–5 (finally suppressed proof), 160–65, copy of the University Library Basel.

47 Dagobert von Mikusch, *Gasi Mustafa Kemal zwischen Europa und Asien. Eine Lebensgeschichte* (Leipzig: Paul List, 1929), 83.

48 Richard Hartmann, "Die neue Türkei," *Der vordere Orient*, vol. 4 (1929): 105, quoted by Dominik J. Schaller, "Die Rezeption des Völkermords an den Armeniern in Deutschland, 1915–45," in *The Armenian Genocide and the Shoah* (eds Kieser and Schaller), 539–40.

49 For example, Klinghardt, "Als Augenzeuge der armenischen Katastrophe," 159.

50 Mikusch, *Gasi Mustafa Kemal zwischen Europa und Asien*, 83.

51 Kempner and Rosenberg, quoted by Schaller, "Rezeption des Völkermords an den Armeniern," 537–38; Raphael Lemkin, "Totally Unofficial Man," in *Pioneers of Genocide Studies*, eds Samuel Totten and Steven L. Jacobs (New Brunswick, New Jersey: Transaction Publishers, 2002), 371.

52 Yair Auron, *Banality of Indifference: Zionism and the Armenian Genocide* (New York: Transaction Publishers), 293–311.

53 Letter of July 1950 quoted in *The Encyclopedia of Genocide* (Santa Barbara, California: ABC-Clio, 1999), 79; "Dr. Lemkin, Father of Genocide Convention, reviews work relating to Turkish massacres," *The Hairenik Weekly*, 1 January 1959, 1.

4

EUGENICS, RACE HYGIENE, AND THE HOLOCAUST

Antecedents and consolidations[1]

Kirk C. Allison

"'Do you then breed from all indiscriminately, or are you careful to breed from the best? ...
And if they are not thus bred, you expect, do you not, that your birds and hounds will greatly
degenerate? ... ' I said, 'that the best men must cohabit with the best women in as many cases
as possible ... ' 'The offspring of the good, I suppose, they will take to the pen or crèche, to
certain nurses who live apart in a quarter of the city, but the offspring of the inferior, and any
of those of the other sort who are born defective, they will properly dispose of in secret ...
That is the condition,' he said, 'of preserving the purity of the guardians' breed.'"

Plato[2]

"Eugenics is the science which deals with all influences that improve the inborn qualities of a
race; also with them that develop them to the utmost advantage ... It must be introduced into
the national consciousness like a new religion ... What nature does blindly, slowly, and
ruthlessly, man may do providently, quickly, and kindly. As it lies in his power, so it becomes
his duty to work in that direction ... Then let its principles work into the heart of the nation,
which will gradually give effect to them in ways that we may not wholly foresee."

Francis Galton[3]

"The subjugation of 350,000 Helots by 6,000 Spartans was possible only because of the racial
superiority of the Spartans. This, however, was the result of systematic racial preservation, so
we see in the Spartan state the first racialist state. The abandonment of sick, frail, deformed
children—in other words, their destruction—demonstrated greater human dignity and was in
reality a thousand times more humane than the pathetic insanity of our time, which attempts
to preserve the lives of the sickest subjects—at any price—while taking the lives of a hundred
thousand healthy children through a decrease in the birth rate or through abortifacient agents,
subsequently breeding a race of degenerates burdened with illness."

Adolf Hitler[4]

The relationship between race hygiene, eugenics, and National Socialism emerged selectively,
but not illogically, within an international movement for human betterment spanning
the mid-nineteenth and twentieth centuries. Proponents understood themselves to be scientific, socially progressive, advancing public health[5] and a hereditarily fitter future. They
engaged broader scientific debates on evolution, heredity, and anthropology, regarding

population or race as the depository of biological and social value.[6] In Germany, as internationally, hope for a biologically controllable human future drew adherents across the spectrum: Right (Ernst Haeckel), center (Hermann Muckermann), and Left (Alfred Grotjan;[7] Helene Stöcker[8]). Such sought to ameliorate impacts of perceived hereditary deficits: physical, mental, and social maladies; race deficiency; biological degeneration; population decline.[9] Rational breeding of desirable stock and elimination of the undesirable comprised positive and negative eugenics. Means ranged from persuasion to coercion, non-lethal to lethal. For some of the committed, an emergent political movement advancing its principles as "applied biology" was welcomed.[10] It is tempting today to dismiss *Eugenik* and *Rassenhygiene* as "pseudoscience," and yet proponents were often highly regarded scientists practicing within, even leading, elite institutions.

Gobineau, Darwin, Social Darwinism, and Galton

Shortly before Darwin's *On the Origin of Species* (1859), Alsatian Count Joseph Arthur Gobineau (1816–82) published *Essai sur l'inégalité des races humaines*, claiming the superiority of the "Aryan race," with racial psychology and interbreeding determining the fates of peoples.[11] Gobineau's ideas attracted composer Richard Wagner, whose son-in-law Houston Stewart Chamberlain subsequently fused race-hygienic, Social Darwinist and antisemitic concepts, inspiring future Nazi theoretician Alfred Rosenberg.[12]

Darwin's *On the Origin of Species by Means of Natural Selection or the Preservation of Favoured Races in the Struggle for Life* (1859) advanced the framework of "natural selection," where race indicated variety. Darwin's *Descent of Man and Selection in Relation to Sex* (1871) argued monogenetic human origin over polygenism. Previously, physician John Atkins' (1685–1757) polygenism had informed Voltaire (*Traité de métaphysique*, 1734), who declared whites "superior to these negroes as the negroes are to the apes and the apes are to the oysters."[13] Also in 1871, Jewish sociologist and Social Darwinist Ludwig Gumplowicz published *Rassenkampf* (Race Struggle), promoting *Rassenkunde*, raceology.

Darwin's chapter "Natural Selection as Affecting Civilized Nations" relied on W.R. Greg, Alfred Russel Wallace (1823–1913), and Darwin's cousin Francis Galton (1822–1911): "With savages the weak in body or mind are soon eliminated" while the civilized "do our utmost to check the process of elimination." Vaccination propagated the weak. "No one who has attended to the breeding of domestic animals will doubt that this must be highly injurious to the race of man" as "reckless, degraded, and often vicious members of society, tend to increase at a faster rate. ... "[14] Yet Darwin was no Social Darwinist, stating "but if we were intentionally to neglect the weak and helpless, it could only be for a contingent benefit, with a certain and great present evil."[15]

Social Darwinism, associated with Herbert Spencer (1820–1903), while multiform, held that biological laws apply to social existence descriptively and normatively.[16] Natural selection brought social hygiene (public health) conceptually into question.[17] Infant mortality was often considered to serve population purification.[18] Berlin's infant mortality rate in 1871 was 41 percent.[19] London's 1901 rates, stated David Heron, "show the infantile mortality of the fertile classes does not compensate for their predominant fertility."[20]

In 1883, Francis Galton took the Greek phrase for "good birth" and coined the term "*eugenics*," a construct for the "cultivation of race" for "men, brutes and plants."[21] Having considered expressions of race, breeding, beauty, class, and roots,[22] the original

[handwritten margin note: modern science helped the weak survive]

46

Greek concept spanned nobility of birth and mind, pure breeding, bodily excellence, and elevation; its negation indicated low birth, meanness, or things sordid or unproductive.[23] Galton's eugenics, "the study of agencies under social control that may improve or impair the inborn [or racial[24]] qualities of future generations, either physically or mentally,"[25] comprised three stages nationally: an academic question; a subject of practical importance; and ultimately its introduction "into national conscience like a new religion."

Galton warned against "holding out expectations of a near golden age, which will certainly be falsified and cause the science to be discredited."[26] Galton, Karl Pearson, and R.A. Fischer developed and applied ground-breaking statistical techniques to this study. Galton also established the Eugenics Education Society (1907), succeeded by Leonard Darwin, who attempted to reconcile eugenics with religion,[27] an impulse also manifest in the United States.[28]

Social Darwinism and eugenics overlap, but are not mutually implied. German Social Darwinism paradoxically exhibited pacifist strains domestically, while accommodating exterminationist racism toward non-Europeans.[29] Pacifist Georg Friedrich Nicolai's *Biology of War* (1919) lamented: "war protects the blind, the deaf and dumb ... the epileptics, the dwarfs, the freaks ... all of this residue and dross of the human race ... ."[30]

1891 brought Germany's first eugenic tract, authored by physician Wilhelm Schallmayer[31] (1857–1919), *Concerning the Threatening Physical Degeneration of Cultured Humanity and the Nationalization of the Medical Profession*, emphasizing "prophylactic" medicine.[32] A Krupp-sponsored competition in 1900 queried "What can we learn from the principles of evolution for the development and laws of states?"[33] Schallmayer's winning entry, *Heredity and Selection in the Life Course of Peoples*, was "a state-scientific study on the basis of the newer biology"[34] directed at "race-hygienists, demographers, physicians, anthropologists, sociologists, educators, criminal experts, higher civil servants, and politically educated members of all estates." His lesson: "complete submission of the individual interest to that of the species."[35] *Better the group and not the individual*

Social improvement: early lethal proposals

In the 1894 *Westminster Review*, W.J. Corbet, Irish lawmaker and mental health administrator, offered "a drastic remedy might apply with greater reason to certain classes of lunatics ... than a decennial holocaust of criminals."[36] In America, W. Duncan McKim noted an "inspiring new idea" in *Heredity and Human Progress* (1899): "Poverty, disease and crime are traceable to one fundamental cause, *depraved heredity*."[37] Learning "nature's method" is "an expression of enlightened pity." "The surest, the simplest, the kindest, and most humane means for preventing reproduction among those whom we deem unworthy of this high privilege, is a gentle, painless death ... In carbonic acid gas, we have an agent which would instantaneously fulfill the need."[38] German psychiatrist Alfred Hoche and lawyer Karl Binding published *The Release for Destruction of Life Unworthy of Life* in 1920,[39] replacing a sanctity-of-life ethos with a "sacrificial ethic" open to untreatable psychiatric patients.[40] Against Hoche and Binding, asylum head Ewald Meltzer argued for patients, but considered emergency "sacrifices."[41] He surveyed parents. Seventy-three percent countenanced having their impaired child killed. "Sacrifice" had already transpired between 1914 and 1919, when 70,000 institutionalized people died of infection or starvation, including up to half of psychiatric patients.[42] Karl Bonhoeffer (1868–1948) stated in 1920: "in the years of hunger during the war we had to come to terms with watching as our institutionalized sick died en masse of malnutrition, and nearly to sanction this in the thought that this sacrifice may have saved the lives of the healthy."[43]

Alfred Ploetz, acolyte of race hygiene

Physician Alfred Ploetz published *Basics of a Race Hygiene* (1895), *Part I, The Efficiency of our Race and the Protection of the Weak*.[44] He identified (Plutarch's) Spartan despot Lycurgus,[45] who decreed infanticide to be a very self-conscious race hygienist.[46] In Lycurgus's stead, Ploetz suggested that physicians' panels grant either citizenship or a "soft death."[47] Twenty-five years prior, Monist League founder Ernst Haeckel (1834–1919) also lionized Sparta,[48] and became the first German academic to advocate for infanticide,[49] and later for lethality for disabled adults. To Haeckel, humanity's timber comprised four genera and 12 species (Indogermanic superior; Hamo-Semitic inferior).[50] For Ploetz, race was "a totality of people living through generations in view of their physical and mental characteristics."[51] Humanity at its best coincided with its Aryan fraction;[52] its hygiene also excepting notable smaller races including the Jewish race which "highly probably in its majority is Aryan."[53] Ploetz's *Nordic Ring* society, established in 1907, cultivated this supremacist ethos.[54]

Ploetz framed "the needs of a physician" to see infirmity through hereditary, social, and economic conditions while "viewing with worry the dangers with which the growing protection of the weak threatens the efficiency of our race."[55] A new discipline investigating and mastering variation, *Rassenhygiene*, would vitalize multi-generational organisms whose perishing cells are people.[56] While social hygiene is synchronous, *Rassenhygiene* is transgenerational, selectional, and thus superior.[57] Eugenics was possible without race hygiene, but *Rassenhygiene* essentially required eugenics.

In 1904, Ploetz launched the Archive for Race and Social Biology including Race and Social Hygiene, targeting "the essence of race and society and of their mutual relationship," "fundamental problems of the theory of evolution," controversies, and reviews. With race the continuing, self-preserving, developing unit of life, *Rassenhygiene* was therapy against degeneration.[58] After 1921, Germany's leading medical publisher, Munich's J.F. Lehmanns Verlag, published Ploetz's *Archiv*, *Volk und Rasse* (*People and Race*) as well as the German translation of Madison Grant's *The Passing of the Great Race* (1916/1925), Hitler's "Bible."[59]

Max Weber (1864–1920) criticized Ploetz's research as lacking empirical foundations.[60] Spurned by sociology, Ploetz and Swiss psychiatrist Ernst Rüdin (1874–1952) founded their own Society for Race Hygiene, and despite Weber's skeptical reception, the movement caught on like wildfire within the life sciences. The German Association for Public Health Care became *Rassenhygiene*'s haven and it was welcomed by the prestigious Society of German Natural Scientists and Physicians Medical Section in 1913.[61] Before 1933, over a dozen eugenic/race-hygienic periodicals appeared, plus "Life Reform Movement" publications.[62] *Kraft und Schönheit (Power and Beauty)* was the "Journal for Reasonable Love-breeding." Richard Ungewitter promoted nudism philosophically and practically as selective against degeneration.[63] Haeckel student Willibald Hentschel's *Mittgart: A Path to Renewal of the German Race* (1904),[64] promoted Aryan supremacy through serial polygamy. His utopian, antisemitic Artamanen League (1923) drew Heinrich Himmler, R. Walther Darré, and future Auschwitz Kommandant Rudolf

Hoess.[65] In 1914, Heinrich Wilhelm Poll (1877–1939), a twins researcher, gene eugenicist of Jewish extraction and Lutheran confession,[66] advocated "[j]u organism ruthlessly sacrifices degenerate cells," higher organic entities ought from intervening on liberty to prevent spreading diseased heredity.[67] Pathologist Ludwig Aschoff (1866–1942) considered war "the loftiest expression of the struggle for existence among nations,"[68] seizing an unprecedented opportunity during World War I to establish anthropometric baselines and variances, collecting over 70,000 autopsy reports for Berlin.[69] (In 1933 he described pathology as "overrun with Jews" with "cleansing" "absolutely necessary,"[70] "eradication" from "our *Volkskörper.*"[71])

Establishing the race-hygienic state

In January 1919, railway locksmith Anton Drexler founded the German Workers Party (DAP), renamed National Socialist German Workers Party (NSDAP) in 1920. Its 55th member, Adolf Hitler, became *Parteiführer* on 29 July 1921[72] and established the SA (*Sturmabteilung*, August 1921) and SS (*Schutzstaffel*, January 1923). In Landsberg prison, over 8 months after his failed Munich *Putsch* (November 1923), Hitler read *Principles of Human Heredity and Race Hygiene* by Bauer, Fischer and Lenz, and wrote *Mein Kampf.*[73] Chapters from the latter on "Nation and Race" and "The State" linked positive and negative racial eugenics with folkish state, placing race and health at life's center: the healthy child as national treasure; *not* begetting honorable if infirm, but shameful if healthy.[74] Opposite nature, Hitler utterly dismissed ethical conceptions as "only pure expressions of feeling" compared to "exact scientific truth" and "cold logic."[75] Reviewing *Mein Kampf*, Fritz Lenz approvingly called National Socialism "applied biology": "Hitler is the first politician of really great influence, who has recognized racial hygiene as a central task of all politics and wants to engage himself forcefully in action for this."[76] While depictions of Jews were "one-sided and exaggerated," Lenz affirmed much of the program.

In August 1929, Gerhard Wagner founded the National Socialist German Physicians League. It is estimated that one in six Germans physicians were Jewish, and only six percent of physicians supported the NSDAP; however, that number grew to 27 percent months after Hitler's appointment as chancellor in January 1933.[77] By the summer of that year, the Nazis began implementing eugenic legislation. On 14 July 1933, non-Nazi parties were banned and the Law for the Prevention of Congenitally Ill Offspring (drawing on US model legislation by Harry Laughlin)[78] was passed for "purifying the *Volkskörper* and gradually eradicating diseased heredity,"[79] a significant step toward a biology-driven society.[80] A 1935 amendment included eugenic abortion. The Law against Dangerous and Habitual Criminals (November 1933) extended sterilization. Ultimately, ca 400,000 people were sterilized (1934–45), including 40,000 in occupation, eight times US totals (1907–45) and 30 times higher by rate.[81] After the September 1935 Law for the Protection of German Blood and German Honor, Himmler established *Lebensborn e.V.* (Fount of Life) for non-marital progeny, particularly of the SS.[82]

The October 1935 Law for the Protection of the Hereditary Health of the German People targeted Jews, Roma and Sinti (Gypsies) as "alien races." Gypsies were doubly stigmatized as aliens with a hereditary compulsion to wander.[83] Heading Himmler's Reich Central Office for the Fight against the Gypsy Nuisance (1936), psychiatrist Robert Ritter began their classification. "Relocation" of Gypsies came in September 1939. In 1940, Ritter reported 90 percent of "native Gypsies" had mixed blood, recommending concentration camp incarceration for 21,498 of 30,000.[84] After deportation to Auschwitz in February 1943, 20,078 of some 23,000 perished at Birkenau BIIe.[85]

Himmler's Reich Central Office for Combating Abortion and Homosexuality (1936) was established to ensure population growth. Under expanded Paragraph 175 some 50,000 (mostly male) homosexuals were arrested with 10,000–15,000 sent to concentration camps. Many perished or remained incarcerated, unrecognized as Nazi victims by the German states until long after the war.[86] Himmler's December 1937 crime-prevention decree targeted "asocials," sweeping vagrants into concentration camps.[87] The Interior Ministry classified asocials as community aliens "by virtue of a hereditarily determined and therefore irremediable attitude of mind" (July 1940).[88]

Kaiser Wilhelm Institute for Anthropology, Human Heredity, and Eugenics (1927–45)

Physician–agronomist Erwin Baur (1875–1933), Berlin Society for Race Hygiene chairman,[89] advocated from 1921 a national genetics and eugenics institute within the prestigious Kaiser Wilhelm Society.[90] Supporters included Social Democratic and Catholic Center Party elements. SDP physician and research subject protection advocate[91] Julius Moses (1868–1942) who would die in Theresienstadt, became persuaded that the institute could be politically disinterested. With Eugen Fischer (1874–1967) directing, the Kaiser Wilhelm Institute for Anthropology, Human Heredity and Eugenics (KWI-A) opened in Berlin-Dahlem, timed with the 1927 Fifth International Conference on Hereditary Research, where biologist Raymond Pearl blisteringly critiqued eugenics, and the socialist eugenicist Herman Joseph Muller announced X-ray-induced mutations.

Fischer had a noted career as a researcher in social biology. In 1913, Fischer published *The Rehoboth Bastards and the Problem of Miscegenation in Man*. This study illustrated Mendelian heredity using mixed-race children from his research in German southwestern Africa[92] as genocide against the Herero and Nama tribes (1904–08) ended, adding to his ossuary, and mixed marriages were annulled. Fischer framed the KWI-A as a "purely theoretical institute for the study of the nature of man," nationally crucial for sociology, national economics, anthropology, and eugenics.[93] In 1926, Fischer stated "the very question of the Jewish population that lives among non-Jews is a problem that must be seriously addressed by anthropology, free of any tendential attitudes."[94] At the opening, he emphasized generating race knowledge, not prejudice.[95] In 1930, Ostermann, Fischer, Lenz, and Rüdin launched *Eugenik, Erblehre, Erbpflege* (*Eugenics, Heredity, Hereditary Care*). Their editorial adopted an aggressive stance: "An oppressive and continually growing ballast of useless humans unworthy of life is entertained and cared for in institutions—at the expense of the healthy."[96] Early on in Hitler's reign, Fischer naively sought to refine state racial discourse and was summoned to clarify himself.[97] After his appointment as University of Berlin rector in May 1933, he did not condemn antisemitism, dismissal of Jewish colleagues, nor the 10 May book burning.

Nazi doctor Arthur Gütt visited the KWI-A on 5 July, stressing the political expectation that it "systematically place itself at the service of the Reich with regard to race hygiene research," shifting it toward the National Socialist-driven program.[98] On 3 November, Fischer wrote Minister of Science, Education and National Culture Bernhard Rust, "I place myself unconditionally at your service."[99] KWI-A's new constitution §2 pledged "support of the government in the realization of race-hygienic efforts."[100]

Bridging Weimar and Third Reich, the KWI-A seeded the polity with applied *Eugenik/ Rassenhygiene*: public health officer courses (1930–31, 1933); physician and civil service courses (1932); Conti, Fischer, Gütt, Lenz, and Verschuer trained officers of 220 Hereditary Health Courts (1933); and a 9-month Race Policy Office SS doctors' course (1934–35).[101] Graduates conducted camp experiments (Helmut Poppendick) and turned Hartheim's gas valve (Georg Renno).[102] Altogether, KWI-A educated some 1,100 physicians.[103] Co-instructor Leonardo Conti was appointed Reich Physician's *Führer*, Reich Health *Führer*, National Health Office head and State Secretary for Health Care (replacing Gütt) in 1939.

Otmar von Verschuer (1896–1969)[104] headed the KWI-A's Department of Human Heredity, bringing expertise in neurologic disease, twin[105] and blood group research, psychiatry, and eugenics. He succeeded Fischer as director (October 1942) following a 3-month interim by Lenz. Verschuer launched *Der Erbarzt* (The Genetic Physician, 1934) and *Advances in the Field of Genetic Pathology, Race Hygiene and Boundary Areas* (1937). Although he rejected SA brutality and prized technical rigor, he subordinated the individual to the collective[106] and described voluntary sterilization as Christian charity.[107] The Race Policy Office considered Verschuer neutral and useful, awarding him a race hygiene professorship in Frankfurt. In 1938, Verschuer and Fischer's expertise were called upon against 385 French-colonial/German children, "Rhineland Bastards,"[108] resulting in their extra-legal sterilization.[109]

Popular media: eugenics, dehumanization, and elimination

Turning popular and bureaucratic sentiment against biopolitically rejected humans was an essential state project. Adolf Dorner's *Mathematics in the Service of National-Political Education* (1935) offered children *Question 95*: "The construction of an insane asylum costs 6 million RM. How many houses @ 15,000 RM could be built for that amount?"[110] Between 1935 and 1936, the Nazi Race Policy Office produced insider films, *Was du ererbst* (*What You Inherit*) and *Erbkrank* (*Hereditarily Ill*), dehumanizing institutionalized patients.[111] For public consumption, *Das Erbe* (*The Inheritance*), a nature-film-within-the-film, maintained birds kill weak offspring "by pure instinct." Before dehumanizing asylum shots, the attractive laboratory assistant pipes up, "so some animals pursue a correct racial policy!"

The *Reichsausschuß für Volksgesundheitsdienst* and Dresden German Hygiene Museum coordinated propaganda as well. Konrad Dürre's drama *Erbstrom* (*Hereditary Stream*, 1933) played to 200,000 in Berlin and Thüringen. *Nürnberger Gesetze*, Table 387 (Nuremberg Laws, 1935) explained Jewish–Aryan *Mischling* levels and prohibitions.[112] Posters in *Volk und Rasse* (August 1936) instructed on low urban birth rates, interbreeding, and "degenerates" swamping healthy stock with illustrations such as "*Hier trägst du mit*" ("This *is* your burden"), depicting a youth carrying the hereditarily ill. *Opfer der Vergangenheit* (*Victims of the Past*, 1937), which Hitler had screened in theaters, proclaimed that "Humans have terribly sinned against this law of nature ... We have not only preserved worthless lives; we have also guaranteed their multiplication."[113] Two October 1939 films, *Geisteskrank* (*Mentally Ill*) and *Dasein ohne Leben* (*Existence without Life*) assuaged accessories to murder. Scripted by "euthanasia" *Aktion T-4* psychiatrists, *Dasein*'s fictitious professor argues that every *reasonable* person would prefer death to that existence. Finally, the feature film *Ich klage an* (*I Accuse*, 1941), also a T-4 assessor's novel, conflated voluntary and involuntary euthanasia.

The road to Aktion T-4 and beyond

The path to the murder of persons deemed racially and hereditarily unfit by the Nazis was abetted by an industry of race classification. Vectors from the 16 June 1933 Prussian census data were converted to IBM Hollerith punch cards. Sorting *religion* by *Polish speaker* would identify *Ostjuden* for deportation. In November 1934, the Reich Health Office ordered asylums and care homes to prepare an index "of family clans affected by hereditary disease." After July 1934, Reich Statistical Offices converted health/insurance forms to punch card (eugenic) profiles.[114] The Reich Interior Ministry's January 1936 "anthropological–hereditary" survey on institutionalized mental patients followed.[115] National Agency for Genealogy punch cards also added Jewish baptisms before 1939.[116] This technology would identify 25,000 Romanian Roma (April 1941), code camps and fates (Buchenwald, Matthausen, and Auschwitz: 2, 7, 1; general execution, suicide, and "special handling": 4, 5, 6).[117]

The catalyst for killing impaired persons, however, was parental request: for the good of child, family, society, and polity. Baby Gerhard Herbert K., near Leipzig, had multiple impairments.[118] After Professor Werner Catel denied treatment, his parents requested the Reich Chancellery to "put him to sleep," hoping for a healthy replacement child. Gerhard was killed on 25 July 1939.

In August 1939, a front organization known as the Reich Commission for the Scientific Registration of Hereditary and Constitutionally Severe Disorders ordered midwives and physicians to report specified impairments through age four. This three-man body, made up of pediatricians Catel and Ernst Wentzler and psychiatry Professor Hans Heinze, deliberated whether infants or children would be killed.[119] *Aktion T-4* (headquarters: *Tiergartenstraße 4*, Berlin) institutionalized killing adults. Nine psychiatry professors and 39 physicians marked 70,723 reports of about 283,000 for permanent "disinfection" (carbon monoxide); 23,000 more were killed by starvation or lethal *pharmaka*.[120] Fischer's colleagues Julius Hallervorden and Hugo Spatz (KWG Institute of Brain Research) received 700 brains from branch Brandenburg-Görden killing center. In 1942, Heinze had 100 more children and youth murdered, their brains sent to Hallervorden.[121] Beginning in April 1941, T-4 physicians under *Aktion 14f13* selected so-called ballast existences, prisoners to be gassed at Hartheim and Sonnenstein, a crucial transition toward the generalized killing of Jews under German occupation. In 1942, 92 T-4 personnel joined *Aktion Reinhardt* in Poland, engaging in the systematic gassing of Jews in the killing centers of Belżec, Sobibor, and Treblinka.[122] Their culpability: 1,700,000 deaths.[123] Alfred Ploetz' *ersatz* Sparta had finally been realized.

Dr Dr med. Mengele and the KWI-A

Josef Mengele (1911–79) received his PhD in anthropology at the University of Munich in 1935 for comparing the anterior mandible across racial groups. He obtained his physician's approbation in 1937, and a second doctorate *cum laude* in 1938 at Verschuer's institute, tracing families of children with cleft lip, jaw or palate. Absent war or its failure, Mengele's trajectory was toward a professorial chair.[124] He joined the NSDAP in 1937 and SS in 1938, volunteering in 1940 as *Waffen-SS* (Medical Corps Inspection Office) assigned to the Race and Settlement Main Office (RuSHA) in November. Transferred to the eastern front in late 1941, Mengele was wounded, decorated (Iron Cross 1st and 2nd class), then ordered to Berlin's "Reich Physician and SS" office (concentration camp and experimentation oversight), but was delayed by Stalingrad. By the end of January 1943, Mengele was with Verschuer in Berlin before transferring in May to SS Group DIII (Main Administrative Economic Office), which meant service in the group Medical Care and Camp Hygiene for Concentration Camps, Section BIIe Auschwitz-Birkenau. Mengele served as First Camp Physician and then Executive Camp Physician in the "Gypsy Camp."[125]

Hans Münch, Auschwitz Hygiene Institute Director (1943–45), stated Mengele was drawn by research possibilities, ideal working conditions,[126] of which it would be a "sin and a crime" *not* to take advantage.[127] Indeed, Mengele built functional research capacity, exploited prisoner expertise, acquired "material" by ramp *Selektion*, established twin and family camps allowing experiment and comparative autopsy—unconstrained either morally or legally.[128]

Mengele visited Berlin-Dahlem around July 1943, joining Verschuer's "Experimental Research on the Determination of the Heredity of Specific Proteins as the Foundation of Genetic and Race Research." During 1943–44, he provided over 200 Auschwitz blood samples toward a seriological determination of race,[129] "a new total solution to the Jewish problem" (as quoted in Verscheur's 1944 *Manual of Race Hygiene*).[130] Mengele also supplied heterochromous Sinti eyes to KWI-A's Karin Magnussen, enthusiastic Nazi and *Race and Population Policy Armamentarium* author.[131] Magnussen photographed twins and the family Mechau before Auschwitz (1943), receiving their eyes postmortem.[132] Her 1944 iris studies were published in 1949.[133] Mengele's iris color-change experiments were informed by his KWI-A research relationship. Miklós Nyiszli, Hungarian Jew and self-described Auschwitz forensic doctor, reported sending "countless" anatomical specimens to Berlin-Dahlem.[134] Other Auschwitz twins researchers had KWI-A connections: Siegfried Liebau (advanced training) and SS physician Erwin von Helmersen (with Mengele in 1942).[135] Affiliate Gerhard Wagner surveyed Gypsy twins in 100 locations for his 1943 dissertation, continuing research into March/April 1945 as they were progressively annihilated. Verschuer denied knowing source details.

Race hygiene, the Great Racial War, and genocide

Hermann Göring declared with customary bluntness, "This is not the Second World War, this is the Great Racial War."[136] Goebbels expounded in 1943, "Our policy may here or there lead to difficult decisions but they are trifling by comparison with the menace. For this war is a racial war."[137] Diversions to genocide disadvantaged military objectives. The arc from *Lebensraum* through *Mein Kampf* to the Holocaust was constructed from the beginning through the rhetoric of race hygiene.[138]

In 1939–40, Eugen Fischer launched anthropological studies in the Łódź ghetto.[139] There, Goebbels and Hippler completed scenes for *Der ewige Jude* (*The Eternal Jew*) in October 1939. The film ends with Hitler's *Reichstag* speech of 30 January 1939, in which he proclaims "the annihilation of the Jewish race in Europe" in case of war. Narration concludes: "The eternal law of nature, to keep one's race pure ... ."[140] Goebbels announced in *Das Reich* (on 16 November 1941) that "the Führer's prophecy of 30 January 1939 ... is now coming true," calling the yellow star "a hygienic and prophylactic measure."[141]

Before retiring in 1942, Fischer knew elements of the race-hygienic policies in German-occupied Europe; he knew of deportations and plans for ethnic "cleansing," and facilitated training and collaboration.[142] KWI-A theoretical work materially contributed to eugenic sterilization, euthanasia selection, *Lebensraum* planning, racial classification, and annihilation, while receiving unparalleled access to "material"[143] over pathways constructed from race-hygienic concepts. Toward war's end, KWI-A was vacated, becoming a reserve hospital, and subsequently never reopened.

In the decade after the war, notable racial hygienists and eugenicists (i.e. Lenz, Verschuer, Heberer, Just, Lehmann, Grebe, Loeffler, Schade, Stumpfl, Gieseler, and Pansa) were reappointed to academic positions in human genetics, anthropology, hereditary, social biology, human genetics, and psychiatry.[144] Careers continued without significant reckoning.

Coda

One writes with the historical end in mind, while choices, claims to knowledge, social-political values and policies co-emerge.[145] *Historia docet*. Variations on race hygiene and eugenics continue. Differences between totalitarian and non-totalitarian settings are indeed significant, yet not completely distinguishing. While North Korea's racialist regime eliminates impaired and mixed-race people,[146] closer to home, the documentary *Liebe Perla* on the Auschwitz-surviving Ovitz family ("Mengele dwarves") interrogates postwar rhetoric of equality, given socio-medical pressure toward elimination of their kind.[147] Elements of population control,[148] trait-selection,[149] and infanticide[150] have emerged in new enculturations. Should these give one pause? The antecedent history of eugenics and race hygiene in relation to specific consolidations in National Socialism, its eugenic purge, racial war, and Holocaust admonish that lethal endpoints often have long pedigrees, marshalling claims of greater good, scientific prestige, and social opportunity.

Notes

1 Dedicated gratefully in memory of Stephen Feinstein and in honor of Susan Feinstein.
2 Plato, *Republic* in *Plato in Twelve Volumes*, vols 5–6, trans. Paul Shorey (Cambridge, Massachusetts: Harvard University Press, 1969), 5.458e–5.460c. wwwperseus.tufts.edu
3 Francis Galton, "Eugenics: Its Definition, Scope and Aims," *American Journal of Sociology*, vol. 10 (1904): 1, 5.
4 Adolf Hitler, *Hitler's Second Book*, ed. Gerhard L. Weinburg, trans. Krista Smith (New York: Enigma Books, 1995), 21.
5 Thurman B. Rice, *Racial Hygiene: A Practical Discussion of Eugenics and Race Culture* (New York: Macmillan, 1929).
6 Peter Weingart, Jürgen Kroll and Kurt Bayertz, *Rasse, Blut und Gene: Geschichte der Eugenik und Rassenhygiene in Deutschland* (Frankfurt am Main: Suhrkamp Verlag, 1988), 18.
7 Michael Schwartz, *Sozialistische Eugenik: Eugenische Sozialtechnologien in Debatten und Politik der deutschen Sozialdemokratie 1890–1933* (Bonn: Verlag J.H.W. Dietz Nachfolger, 1995).
8 Helene Stöcker, "Rassenhygiene und Mutterschutz," *Die neue Generation*, vol. 13 (1917): 138–42.
9 Otto Helmut, *Volk in Gefahr* (München: J.F. Lehmann Verlag, 1933).
10 Stefan Kühl, *The Nazi Connection* (Oxford: Oxford University Press, 1994), 36, 121n39.
11 Paul Weindling, *Health, Race and National Politics between National Unification and Nazism, 1870–1945* (Cambridge: Cambridge University Press, 1989), 48–49.
12 Michael Burleigh and Wolfgang Wippermann, *The Racial State: Germany 1933–1945* (Cambridge: Cambridge University Press, 1991), 36.
13 Voltaire, *Traité de métaphysique, œuvres complètes* (Paris: Éditions Moland, s.d.), V. XII, 210, in Bernhard-Henri Lévy, ed., *L'idéologie française* (Paris: Bernard Grasset, 1981), 100, 314n9.
14 Charles Darwin, *The Descent of Man and Selection in Relation to Sex. In Two Volumes with Illustrations* (London: John Murray, 1871), 168–69, 174.

15 Darwin, *The Descent of Man*, 169.
16 Mike Hawkins, *Social Darwinism in European and American Thought, 1860–1945* (Cambridge: Cambridge University Press, 1997), 3–38.
17 Alfred Grotjahn, "Soziale Hygiene und Entartungsproblem," in *Handbuch der Hygiene*, ed. Th. Weyl, 4th suppl. vol. (Jena: Gustav Fischer, 1904), 727–89.
18 Weindling, *Health, Race and National Politics*, 111.
19 Sigrid Stöckel, *Säuglingsfürsorge zwischen sozialer Hygiene und Eugenik* (Berlin: Walter de Gruyter, 1996), 7–8.
20 Karl Pearson, *The Scope and Importance to the State of the Science of National Eugenics*, 2nd edn (London: Dulau and Co, 1909), 36.
21 Francis Galton, *Inquiries into Human Faculty and Its Development* (London: Macmillan, 1883), 24–25, 24n1.
22 Galton Papers, University College London, 138/1. s.d.
23 Henry George Liddell and Robert Scott, *A Greek–English Lexicon with a Supplement* (Oxford: Clarendon Press, 1968), 708.
24 Francis Galton, "Eugenics," *Westminster Gazette*, 26 June 1908. http://galton.org
25 Karl Pearson, *Life, Letters and Labors of Francis Galton* (Cambridge: Cambridge University Press, 1930), 3a: 223.
26 Francis Galton, "Eugenics: Its Definition, Scope and Aims," *American Journal of Sociology*, vol. 10, no. 1 (1904): 1–6.
27 Leonard Darwin, *The Need for Eugenic Reform* (New York: D. Appleton and Company, 1926), 505–23.
28 Christine Rosen, *Preaching Eugenics* (Oxford: Oxford University Press, 2004).
29 Richard Weickart, "Progress through Racial Extermination: Social Darwinism, Eugenics, and Pacifism in Germany, 1860–1918," *German Studies Review*, vol. 26 (2003): 273–94.
30 Hans-Walter Schmuhl, *The Kaiser Wilhelm Institute for Anthropology, Human Heredity, and Eugenics, 1927–1945* (Dordrecht: Springer, 2008), 9.
31 Shiela Faith Weiss, *Race Hygiene and National Efficiency: The Eugenics of Wilhelm Schallmayer* (Berkeley, California: University of California Press, 1987).
32 Weingart, Kroll and Bayertz, *Rasse, Blut und Gene*, 37–40.
33 Weindling, *Health, Race and National Politics*, 116.
34 Wilhelm Schallmayer, *Vererbung und Auslese im Lebenslauf der Volker. Eine staatswissenschaftliche Studie auf Grund der neueren Biologie* (Jena: G. Fischer, 1903).
35 Peter Weingart, "The Rationalization of Sexual Behavior: The Institutionalization of Eugenic Thought in Germany," *Journal of the History of Biology*, vol. 20 (1987): 169.
36 W.J. Corbet, "How Insanity is Propagated," *Westminster Review*, vol. 142 (1984): 162–63.
37 W. Duncan McKim, *Heredity and Human Progress* (New York: W.W. Putnam and Sons, 1899), 185.
38 McKim, *Heredity and Human Progress*, 188. See also Jay Joseph, "The 1942 'Euthanasia' Debate in the American Journal of Psychiatry," *History of Psychiatry*, vol. 16, no. 2 (2005): 171–179.
39 Karl Binding and Alfred E. Hoche, *Die Freigabe zur Vernichting lebensunwerten Lebens. Ihr Maß und ihre Form* (Leipzig: Felix Meiner Verlag, 1920).
40 Michael Burleigh, *Ethics and Extermination: Reflections on Nazi Genocide* (Cambridge: Cambridge University Press, 1997), 115.
41 Ewald Meltzer, *Das Problem der Abkürzung 'lebensunwerten Lebens'* (Halle a.S.: C. Marhold, 1925).
42 Schmuhl, *The Kaiser Wilhelm Institute*, 9.
43 Schmuhl, *The Kaiser Wilhelm Institute*, 10.
44 A. Ploetz, *Grundlinien einer Rassen-Hygiene. Theil 1. Die Tüchtigkeit unserer Rasse und der Schutz der Schwachen. Ein Versuch über Rassenhygiene und ihr Verhältnis zu humanen Idealen, insbesonders dem Sozialismus* (Berlin: S. Fischer, 1895).
45 Robert Garland, *The Eye of the Beholder: Deformity & Disability in the Graeco-Roman World* (Ithaca, New York: Cornell University Press, 1995), 13–18.
46 Ploetz, *Grundlinien einer Rassen-Hygiene*, 5–8.
47 Ploetz, *Grundlinien einer Rassen-Hygiene*, 144.

48 Burleigh and Wippermann, *The Racial State*, 30.
49 Ernst Haeckel, *Natürliche Schopfungsgeschichte*, 5th edn (Berlin: Georg Reimer, 1874), 152–56.
50 Ernst Haeckel, *Natürliche Schopfungsgeschichte*, 11th edn (Berlin: Georg Reimer, 1911), 754–56.
51 Ploetz, *Grundlinien einer Rassen-Hygiene*, 2.
52 Ploetz, *Grundlinien einer Rassen-Hygiene*, 11.
53 Ploetz, *Grundlinien einer Rassen-Hygiene*, 6.
54 Weickart, "Progress through Racial Extermination," 284.
55 Ploetz, *Grundlinien einer Rassen-Hygiene*, V.
56 Ploetz, *Grundlinien einer Rassen-Hygiene*, 1, 11, 48–49.
57 Ploetz, *Grundlinien einer Rassen-Hygiene*, V–VI, 13.
58 Alfred Ploetz, "Die Begriffe Rasse und Gesellschaft und die davon abgeleiteten Disziplinen," *Archiv für Rassen-und Gesellschafts-Biologie*, vol. 1 (1904): 2–26.
59 Jonathan Peter Spiro, *Defending the Master Race: Conservation, Eugenics and the Legacy of Madison Grant* (Lebanon, New Hampshire: University Press of New England), 357.
60 Paul Weindling, *Darwinism and Social Darwinism in Imperial Germany: The Contribution of the Cell Biologist, Oscar Hertwig, 1849–1922* (Stuttgart: Akademie der Wissenschaften und der Literatur, 1991), 286.
61 Schmuhl, *The Kaiser Wilhelm Institute*, 12.
62 Robert Proctor, *Racial Hygiene: Medicine under the Nazis* (Cambridge, Massachusetts: Harvard University Press, 1988), 39.
63 Peter Cohen, *Homo Sapiens 1900* (Arte Factum, 1998; First Run Features DVD, 1999).
64 Willibald Hentschel, *Mittgart. Ein Weg zur Erneuerung der germanischen Rasse* (Leipzig: Mittgartbund, 1904).
65 Burleigh and Wippermann, *The Racial State*, 35.
66 James Braund and Douglas G. Sutton, "The Case of Heinrich Wilhelm Poll (1877–1939): A German-Jewish Geneticist, Eugenicist, Twin Researcher, and Victim of the Nazis," *Journal of the History of Biology*, vol. 41 (2008): 1–35.
67 Heinrich Poll, "Über Vererbung beim Menschen," *Die Grenzboten*, vol. 73 (1914): 308, in Braund and Sutton, "The Case of Heinrich Wilhelm Poll," 9.
68 Ludwig Aschoff, "Über die Bedeutung der Kreigspathologie," *Deutsche Militärärztliche Zeitschrift*, vol. 47(1918): 81–87, 86, in Cay-Rüdiger Prüll, "Holism and German Pathology (1914–33)," in *Greater Than The Parts: Holism in Biomedicine, 1920–1950*, eds Christopher Lawrence and George Weisz (Oxford: Oxford University Press, 1998), 49, 61n28.
69 Prüll, "Holism and German Pathology," 46–67.
70 Aschoff to Ernst Rüdin, Freiburg, 18 August 1933, in Prüll, "Holism and German Pathology," 57, 66n92–93.
71 Aschoff to Fischer, Freiburg, 18 August 1933, in Prüll, "Holism and German Pathology," 57, 66n92,95.
72 Michael H. Kater, *The Nazi Party: A Social Profile of Members and Leaders 1919–1945* (Cambridge, Massachusetts: Harvard University Press, 1983), 20–22.
73 Benno Müller-Hill, *Murderous Science: Elimination by Scientific Selection of Jews, Gypsies and others in Germany, 1933–1945* (Oxford: Oxford University Press, 1988), 8.
74 Adolf Hitler, *Mein Kampf*, trans. Ralph Mannheim (Boston: Houghton Mifflin, 1971), 403–4.
75 Hitler, 277–78.
76 F. Lenz, "Die Stellung des NS zur Rassenhygiene," *Archiv für Rassen- und Gesellschafts-biologie*, vol. 25 (1931): 300–308.
77 Proctor, *Racial Hygiene*, 65, 155; Kater, *The Nazi Party*, 112, figure 6.
78 *Gesetz zur Verhütung erbkranken Nachwuchses. Vom 14. Juli 1933, Reichsgesetzblatt, Theil I*, 86, July 15, 1933, 529–30.
79 Arthur Gütt, Ernst Rüdin and Falk Ruttke, *Gesetz zur Verhütung erbkranken Nachwuchses (erläutert)* (München: Ernst Lehman Verlag, 1934), 52.
80 Roland Staudinger, *Rassenrecht und Rassenstaat* (Hall in Tirol: Berenkamp, 1999), 310–11.
81 Schmuhl, *The Kaiser Wilhelm Institute*, 215.
82 Weindling, *Health, Race and National Politics*, 500.
83 Schmuhl, *The Kaiser Wilhelm Institute*, 357–58.
84 Müller-Hill, *Murderous Science*, 13–14.

85 Burleigh and Wippermann, *The Racial State*, 126.
86 Burleigh and Wippermann, *The Racial State*, 182–97.
87 Burliegh, *Ethics and Extermination*, 162.
88 Burliegh and Wippermann, *The Racial State*, 181–82.
89 Schmuhl, *The Kaiser Wilhelm Institute*, 19–20.
90 Weindling, *Health, Race and National Politics*, 430.
91 Wolfgang U. Eckart, "First Principles: Julius Moses and Medical Experimentation in the Late Weimar Republic," in *Man, Medicine and the State*, ed. W. Eckart (Stuttgart: Franz Steiner Verlag, 2006), 44–46; Schmuhl, *The Kaiser Wilhelm Institute*, 175, 414.
92 Weingart, Kroll and Bayertz, *Rasse, Blut und Gene*, 100–102.
93 Schmuhl, *The Kaiser Wilhelm Institute*, 28–29.
94 Eugen Fischer, "Aufgaben der Anthropologie, menschlichen Erblehre und Eugenik," *Die Naturwissenschaften*, vol. 14 (1926):749–55, in Schmuhl, *The Kaiser Wilhelm Institute*, 27–28.
95 Schmuhl, *The Kaiser Wilhelm Institute*, 38.
96 *Eugenik. Erblehre. Erbpflege*, vol. 1 (1930): 1, in Weingart, Kroll and Bayertz, *Rasse, Blut und Gene*, 252–53.
97 Schmuhl, *The Kaiser Wilhelm Institute*, 134–39.
98 Schmuhl, *The Kaiser Wilhelm Institute*, 133, 118.
99 Schmuhl, *The Kaiser Wilhelm Institute*, 135.
100 Weingart, "The Rationalization of Sexual Behavior," 190–91.
101 Schmuhl, *The Kaiser Wilhelm Institute*, 167.
102 Schmuhl, *The Kaiser Wilhelm Institute*, 205–6.
103 Schmuhl, *The Kaiser Wilhelm Institute*, 93–94, 203, 409.
104 Kühl, *The Nazi Connection*, 20.
105 Schmuhl, *The Kaiser Wilhelm Institute*, 61–66.
106 Schmuhl, *The Kaiser Wilhelm Institute*, 156–156.
107 Schmuhl, *The Kaiser Wilhelm Institute*, 97–98.
108 Schmuhl, *The Kaiser Wilhelm Institute*, 224–30.
109 Müller-Hill, *Murderous Science*, 30.
110 Adolf Dorner, *Die Mathematik im Dienste der nationalpolitischen Erziehung* (Frankfurt: Verlag Moritz Diesterweg, 1935) in Proctor, *Racial Hygiene*, 184.
111 John Michalczyk, "Euthanasia in Nazi Propaganda Films: Selling Murder," in *Medicine, Ethics, and the Third Reich: Historical and Contemporary Issues*, ed. Michalczyk (Kansas City, Missouri: Sheed and Ward, 1994), 64–70.
112 Willi Hackenburger, *Die Nürnberger Gesetze*, Tafel 387 (Berlin: Reichsausschuß für Volksgesundheitsdienst, 1935), http://commons.wikimedia.org/wiki/File:Nurembergracechart.jpg
113 Stewart Lansley, Joanna Mack and Michael Burleigh, *Selling Murder: The Killing Films of Third Reich* (London: Domino Films, 1991), VHS.
114 Edwin Black, *IBM and the Holocaust* (New York: Crown Publishers, 2001), 52–57, 92–95.
115 Volker Roelcke, "Funding the Scientific Foundations of Race Policies: Ernst Rüdin and the Impact of Career Resources on Psychiatric Genetics, ca. 1910–1945," in Eckart, *Man, Medicine and the State*, 81.
116 Edwin Black, *War Against the Weak: Eugenics and America's Campaign to Create a Master Race* (New York: Four Walls Eight Windows, 2003), 290.
117 Black, *IBM and the Holocaust*, 370, 22.
118 Ulf Schmidt, "Reassessing the Beginning of the 'Euthanasia' Program," *German History*, vol. 17 (1999): 543–50.
119 Müller-Hill, *Murderous Science*, xvi–xvii, 40–41.
120 Burleigh and Wippermann, *The Racial State*, 153.
121 Schmuhl, *The Kaiser Wilhelm Institute*, 179n260.
122 Nizan Avarim, *Healing by Killing* (New York: New Yorker Films, 1998), VHS.
123 Burleigh and Wippermann, *The Racial State*, 166.
124 Schmuhl, *The Kaiser Wilhelm Institute*, 362–64.
125 Schmuhl, *The Kaiser Wilhelm Institute*, 366.
126 Alexander Smoltczyk, "Der Doktor und sein Opfer," *Der Spiegel*, vol. 42, no. 14 (5 April 1999): 116–21; cf. 117.

127 Schmuhl, *The Kaiser Wilhelm Institute*, 414.
128 Schmuhl, *The Kaiser Wilhelm Institute*, 367–68.
129 Schmuhl, *The Kaiser Wilhelm Institute*, 387–89.
130 Schmuhl, *The Kaiser Wilhelm Institute*, 239–41.
131 Schmühl, *The Kaiser Wilhelm Institute*, 369.
132 Schmühl, *The Kaiser Wilhelm Institute*, 382–84.
133 Karin Magnussen, "Über die Beziehung zwischen Irisfarbe, hisotlogischer Pigmentverteilung und Pigmentierung des Bulbus beim menschlichen Auge," *Zeitschrift für Morphologie und Anthropologie*, vol. 41 (1949): 295–312.
134 Miklós Nyiszli, *Im Jenseits der Menschlichkeit. Ein Gerichtsmediziner in Auschwitz* (Berlin: Dietz Verlag, 1992), 42, in Schmuhl, *The Kaiser Wilhelm Institute*, 369.
135 Schmuhl, *The Kaiser Wilhelm Institute*, 385, 370.
136 Sarah Gordon, *Hitler, Germans and the "Jewish Question"* (Princeton, New Jersey: Princeton University Press, 1984), 100–101.
137 Sarah Gordon, *Hitler, Germans and the "Jewish Question,"* 100–101; Müller-Hill, *Murderous Science*, 182–83 n86.
138 Japanese Biological Research Units (1932–45), most extremely Unit 731 in Harbin, performed lethal experiments, vivisection and research brutalities exceeding even the Nazis on those judged to be racially inferior (including Chinese and prisoners of war). Till Bärnighausen, "Barbaric Research—Japanese Human Experiments in Occupied China: Relevance, Alternatives, Ethics," in *Man, Medicine and the State*, Eckart, ed., 167–96.
139 Schmuhl, *The Kaiser Wilhelm Institute*, 269.
140 Stig Hornshøj-Møller and David Culbert, "'Der ewige Jude' (1940): Joseph Goebbels' unequaled monument to antisemitism," *Historical Journal of Radio, Film and Television*, vol. 12 (1992): 41, 67.
141 Joseph Goebbels, "Die Juden sind schuld!" *Das eherne Herz* (Munich: Zentralverlag der NSDAP, 1943), 85–91.
142 Schmuhl, *The Kaiser Wilhelm Institute*, 371.
143 Schmuhl, *The Kaiser Wilhelm Institute*, 3, 360–61, 369, 382–84.
144 Weindling, *Health, Race and National Politics*, 567.
145 Weingart, Kroll and Bayertz, *Rasse, Blut und Gene*, 22.
146 B.R. Myers, *The Cleanest Race* (Brooklyn: Melville, 2010); Michael Sheridan, "Nation under a Nuclear Cloud. 'Racially Impure' Children Killed," *TimesOnline*, 15 October 2006.
147 Shahar Rosen, *Liebe Perla* (Tel Aviv: Eden Productions, 1999), DVD.
148 Stefan Kühl, *Die Internationale der Rassisten* (Frankfurt am Main: Campus Verlag, 1997), 233–38.
149 Jürgen Habermas, *The Future of Human Nature*, trans. Hella Beister and William Rehg (Cambridge: Polity Press, 2003); contrastingly: Nicholas Agar, *Liberal Eugenics: In Defense of Human Enhancement* (Malden: Blackwell Publishing, 2004).
150 Eduard Verhagen and Pieter J.J. Sauer, "The Groningen Protocol—Euthanasia in Severely Ill Newborns," *New England Journal of Medicine*, vol. 352 (2005): 959–62.

5

WEIMAR GERMANY AND THE DILEMMAS OF LIBERTY

Eric D. Weitz

Nazism was a product of Weimar Germany (1918–33). This is true not only in the simple matter of chronology, that the Nazi party was founded and flourished in this period, and that the naming of Adolf Hitler to the chancellorship on 30 January 1933 marked the definitive destruction of the Republic. It is also that the many travails of the Weimar Republic and the deep-seated conflicts of German society in the 1920s and early 1930s nourished the Nazi Party. "The System," one of the more polite pejorative terms the Nazis and others on the Right used for the Weimar Republic, was a hobbled entity, weighted down by the burdens of Germany's defeat in World War I, civil strife, and economic depression. The widespread discontent that these trends engendered ultimately redounded to the benefit of the Nazis, helping to create their mass base.

But to focus only on Weimar's difficulties is terribly one-sided; even worse, to see Weimar as primarily the prelude to the Third Reich, as a system whose collapse was virtually inevitable, misreads the history of one year of revolution (1918–19) and 14 years of the Republic (1919–33). It was Weimar's many *achievements* that the Nazis could not abide. In the Revolution, workers won major improvements in working conditions and forms of direct representation in the factories and mines. The Weimar Constitution established a republic with extensive civil and political rights. New social welfare programs dotted the landscape. The modern arts flourished. Whether people had more and better sex is impossible to determine; certainly, they talked more openly about it, and women had greater choices in their lives than ever before.

In short, it was precisely the accomplishments of the era in so many areas, the emancipatory developments that revolution and republic nourished, which characterized Weimar Germany. To be sure, all of these achievements were highly contested, and many, like modernism in the arts and the new openness about sex, proved utterly disorienting to many Germans. The hostility to Weimar's achievements provided the Nazis and the radical Right generally with great possibilities for political mobilization. But the victory of the anti-emancipatory parties on the Right was by no means pre-ordained.[1]

For decades after Germany's defeat in 1945, the scholarship on both sides of the Atlantic focused on the end of the Republic and the rise to power of the Nazis. Weimar's history was significant only as a failed experiment that paved the way for the Nazi takeover. *Germany Tried Democracy, The Dissolution of the Weimar Republic, The Path to Dictatorship*—these and other book titles all suggested the utter failure of the Republic.[2] Internally, the system could generate neither the will nor the sustenance to survive. "Collapse" or "fall" were other terms commonly applied, and suggested that Weimar was a house of cards that, unsurprisingly, fell in on itself.[3] The movement from Republic to Reich was seen as virtually seamless, at the very least inevitable, given the grave, life-long weaknesses of the Republic.

To be sure, there is a large element of truth in these accounts. Weimar Germany was battered by more crises than any democracy, especially a fledgling one, can legitimately be expected to endure. But the Republic did not just collapse. It was systematically attacked, virtually from the day of its founding. It was the victim of an assault, and the ultimate success of the attackers came when the old-guard conservative Right gave up its caution about the radicals and allied with the Nazi Party. The alliance would be fraught with difficulties throughout the history of the Third Reich, but it essentially held until the German surrender on 8 May 1945.

The narrative of failure, collapse, prelude proved so powerful because it was lodged in three critical centers. First, it was the émigrés' story, their retrospective account of their own biographies, of the dreariness of crisis leading into the Nazi years. But it was not how they experienced Weimar. As they lived the 1920s, they felt a sense of possibility, of professional advancement and personal liberation. But from exile, the atrocities of the Nazi period, coupled with their own difficult and often tragic experiences of exile, colored their view of the 1920s and early 1930s. Decay, depravity, and disaster, Weimar as prelude to the Third Reich, came to be their prevailing view. From the émigrés, that understanding entered into the historical literature.

It was also the narrative of the two Germanies after 1945. In the Federal Republic, "Bonn ist nicht Weimar," as the saying went, was repeated over and over and over. Institutionally, the story went (and this part certainly was true), Bonn was a more stable entity, characterized by its integration into the West, limited proportional representation, unification of the labor unions, social welfare economy, and conservative family values. Although most of the Republic's founders were Weimar veterans, they distanced themselves from the more radical accomplishments of the 1920s, especially in the realm of bodies and sex.

The German Democratic Republic had its own variant of Weimar as prelude to the Third Reich. Both were forms of capitalism, according to the official GDR account, the Third Reich only more open and virulent. Weimar had failed because Communists had not been able to seize power and transform state and society. "Never again Weimar democracy!" was the death-bed proclamation of one Communist resistor executed by the Nazis.[4] In the East, also, the system's founders were Weimar veterans, and they too distanced and disparaged the past as a way of creating something new, in this case, a communist state and society.[5]

These three narratives diminished and disparaged Weimar's very significant achievements. Inadvertently or not, they focused on the Right's virulent reaction to Weimar's successes. Three areas in particular define Weimar's successes, however contested and temporary they were: workers' power, modern art, and bodies and sex.

Weimar was born in conflict, and much of it was over the nature of relations in the workplace. More specifically, the fight was over the extent of workers' power in the factories and mines and, by extension, the larger society.[6] In Leipzig, Berlin, Essen, and many other places, beginning in 1916, workers went on strike and at first demanded higher wages and better food provisions. But by their very nature, the wartime strikes posed the issue of power because workers challenged the claims of the military state to all-encompassing authority.[7] By 1917, workers were demanding an end to the war and, soon, the abdication of Kaiser Wilhelm II, making still more explicit the political nature of their actions. While such actions never included a majority of the working population in Germany, those workers who were willing to engage in such actions defined the political agenda for Germany.

The oft-belittled German Revolution of 1918/19 was, indeed, a revolution. It is certainly true that democratic transformations were already underway, but the actions of sailors in the port cities, women in the marketplace, crowds in the streets, and workers in the mines and factories sent the Kaiser into exile, quickened and radicalized the democratization process, and, not least important, gave people a sense of power, an understanding that they could transform their own circumstances.

Mass actions and workers' councils constituted the institutional form of revolution. Sailors invented councils when they mutinied at the end of October 1918, sparking the Revolution. Alongside the sailors' councils, there would also be soldiers' councils, workers' councils, workers' and soldiers' councils, peasants' councils, even artists' councils. Their activities were often confused and chaotic, their politics inchoate. But they were, everywhere, a grassroots form of democracy that allowed a wider range of political participation, addressed a broader range of issues, than had ever existed before in Germany. Councils were elected at mass meetings of workers on strike, of soldiers defying orders, of artists planning the future of a gallery or a theater. The delegates would then go off to negotiate with the forces of order, be they bosses, foremen, city officials, theater managers, or army officers, and come back and report. They might be unceremoniously deposed by those who, hours or days before, had elected them. They might return to rousing cheers. Chaotic, loud, unruly, usually masculine, the mass meeting and the council served as very basic and important forms of democratic expression. Once institutionalized over the course of 1918–19, the councils were usually content merely to supervise the work of regular civil servants or factory managers. But they also inspired great hopes and dreaded fears. To their mainly working-class supporters, the councils, especially in the most heated revolutionary movements, like the winter of 1918–19 or the spring of 1920, were the vehicles for bringing, at long last, democracy and socialism to Germany. To their opponents, including moderate Social Democrats, the councils were the very embodiment of "Bolshevik conditions," which, to them, meant political terror, insecurity, chaos, and economic disaster.

The wave of council organization, strikes, and mass demonstrations in the Revolution resulted in a wide-ranging program of reform. Workers won the 8-hour day (7½ hours in the mines), union recognition, and higher wages.[8] In highly limited fashion, the councils became incorporated into the landscape of labor relations through a corporatist form of workers' representation at the point of production. Taken as a whole, there was nothing remotely comparable in the German past to these achievements.

They did not last. Galloping inflation that began in 1922 undermined wage gains. More important, business owners took advantage of the multidimensional crisis of 1923—the occupation of the Ruhr by France and Belgium, the German policy of passive resistance, hyperinflation, and attempted revolutions by Nazis and by Communists—to roll back the gains workers had won in the Revolution. The 12-hour day was reimposed in industry, 8½ hours in the mines. Worker councils became largely ineffective. The stabilization of the currency, while carried out largely at the expense of the middle class, also had a deleterious impact on workers. Perhaps most important, structural unemployment, connected both to insufficient demand and to the deliberate strategy of slashing labor costs via rationalization, severely affected workers, and some young people never experienced a stable working life.

Yet within a few short years, by the late 1920s, the Labor Ministry, generally in the hands of Catholics or Social Democrats, managed again to force a decrease in the working day and higher wages. An unspoken alliance emerged between the Labor Ministry and the labor movement in an effort to improve workers' lives. The demands were certainly not as far-reaching as in the first few years after World War I. "Workers' power" would be too strong a term to characterize the situation. But there certainly existed labor influence in the state, and even more so at the local and regional levels in particular areas. The great expansion of public housing would hardly have been possible without the political influence and cash reserves of the labor unions. In this sense, Weimar very much remained a system dominated by the Weimar Coalition, that is, by Social Democrats and reform-minded Catholics and liberals. That was something the Right, both traditional and radical, could not abide. The onset of the world economic crisis in late 1929 would afford it the opportunity finally to destroy labor power and influence.

It was not only workers who were inspired by revolution. So were writers and artists, and the feeling was heady indeed. Years later, remembering the Revolution, Arnold Zweig wrote, "with what hopes had we come back from the war!"[9] He threw himself into politics, then into his writing, like a demon. "I have big works, wild works, great well-formed, monumental works in my head!" he wrote to his friend Helene Weyl in April 1919: "I want to write! Everything that I have done up until now is just a preamble."[10] And it was not to be "normal" writing. The times were of galloping stallions and wide-open furrows, and talent was everywhere. War and revolution had drawn people out of the confining security of bourgeois life. "The times have once again placed adventure in the center of daily life, making possible once again the great novel and the great story."[11]

The panoply of modernist movements and ideas, Expressionism, Dada, Bauhaus, and more, the plays, paintings, photographs, photomontages, films, textiles, and buildings that resulted, continue to dazzle us into the twenty-first century. But it was not only that artists and writers produced innovative and challenging works. Weimar art was a serious thing. It was not about decoration, and making pretty this or that corner or canvas, though artists and writers did also produce works of great beauty. Weimar art was about the totality of being, and was infused with powerful visions of transforming society—and humanity—once and for all. As the artist Hermann Finsterlin wrote in 1920, "If you don't long for the impossible, how can you achieve the possible?"[12]

The architect Erich Mendelsohn stands as a fine example of the Weimar spirit. He is little known today. Many of his most striking buildings have not survived; they were destroyed by some combination of Nazi misuse, Allied bombings, and the perverse urban planning drives of both East and West Germany in the post-World War II years. Moreover, Mendelsohn has long been overshadowed by his great rival, Walter Gropius, the founder of the Bauhaus.[13]

But Weimar modernism was so much more than Gropius and the Bauhaus, and Mendelsohn's riveting buildings were perhaps even more expressive of the Weimar era than those of his rival. By the late 1920s, Mendelsohn had become one of Germany's most prominent and successful architects. He presided over a firm with 40 employees and was designing some of the most distinctive commercial and private architecture in the world.[14] He had admirers all across Europe, from London to Moscow. They came to Germany to study his fanciful Einstein Tower, sleek Schocken department stores, and cube-like private homes. These buildings revealed an architect with a deep streak of humanity, a man strongly attentive to human interaction with the built and natural environments.

Mendelsohn had daydreamed about establishing his own practice during the three long years he had languished in the trenches of World War I. With the armistice he quickly returned to Berlin. He was eager to get on with things; nothing would stop him from launching his career or impinge on his enormous self-confidence and determination. But he was hardly oblivious to the dramatic events unfolding around him. Revolution was his stimulus: it opened up great possibilities, in culture as well as politics. It inspired creative thoughts and utopian hopes. Despite a life so deeply etched by the waste of war, Mendelsohn, like so many of Weimar Germany's leading cultural and intellectual figures, joyously celebrated modern times and the prospects of building a freer, more creative, more stimulating, and, yes, organic world—"organic," the word beloved by Germans of all political persuasions.

"A revolution is not only in politics," Mendelsohn told a small group of well-placed listeners, gathered in the Berlin salon of Molly Philippson, in the winter of 1918–19. Revolution is dramatic, chaotic, and forceful, moving and exciting, and also wonderfully embracing.[15] Mendelsohn was no socialist, and he cultivated very close relations with businessmen. But he always spoke in these terms of revolution, of new beginnings, of great possibilities, in Germany and beyond. He never abandoned the modernist hubris that the new art had to be a total art and would transform human relations.[16]

Mendelsohn's soaring ambition for architecture and society, along with his brimming self-confidence, enabled him to design some of the most beautiful buildings of the Weimar era. To businessmen, fellow architects, and an educated public he trumpeted the excitement of the present, its new construction techniques and materials, mass consumption, automobiles, and advertising. "It is unthinkable," he wrote in 1929, "that we can turn back time ... unthinkable that we leave unused the greatly broadened possibilities of technology. That we see the machine as the enemy of humanity, instead of as our powerful tool that we need to master."[17] His love for the organic beauty of a Bach fugue and a Gothic cathedral did not prevent him from seeing the same possibilities in the "hard clang" of a machine's movements, the "metallic sheen" of its material, and the "precision of its rotations."[18]

Like so many other brilliant Weimar figures, Mendelsohn sought to resolve the tensions of modern life by grasping, not rejecting, modernity. But modern times also create a distinct nervousness and unease among men, Mendelsohn wrote. Architecture, the most unified of all the arts, was the medium best suited to stimulate as well as to calm, to establish the balance. A great building has a dynamic sense of movement that creates the sense of harmony needed to calm the nervousness of the modern age.[19]

Mendelsohn's first great building (and his very first commission), the Einstein Tower, with its smooth, soaring exterior and lack of ornamentation, was (and is, since it is still standing) a striking expression of Weimar modernism. The tower reflected the architect's determination to construct something utterly new and daring, a building that would challenge and soothe at the same time. Constructed out of reinforced concrete, it joyously celebrated modern, industrial society. Built in circular and spiral fashion out of a variety of materials, the Einstein Tower arises seamlessly out of its low-slung base. The horizontal base situates the building in the surrounding field, the vertical tower mimics the upward thrust of the trees that envelop the site. The building is firmly connected to its setting, the wooded park and other nearby research institutes, and thrusts upward to the heavens.[20] As an observatory and laboratory, the building expressed the questing, scientific spirit exemplified by Albert Einstein and admired by Mendelsohn.

In his great buildings in the decade that ensued—the department stores for the Schocken family in Nuremberg, Stuttgart, and Chemnitz; the Universum movie palace on Kurfürstendamm in Berlin; his Columbus House on Potsdamer Platz in Berlin; a number of private homes—Mendelsohn tamed the Expressionism so vividly conveyed in the cement and plaster of the Einstein Tower. In these constructions, Mendelsohn deployed the curvatures, absence of ornamentation, smooth exteriors, and attentiveness to lighting that were evident in his first building. Mendelsohn transformed the playfulness of the Einstein Tower into the pleasure of shopping in Chemnitz. But both buildings were designed to elicit joy as well as wonder, and to evoke the cry of "organic!" that Einstein discovered in his tower.[21]

The modernism that Mendelsohn so powerfully represented evoked fierce responses. Potsdam officials had initially rejected Mendelsohn's design for the Einstein Tower as unsuitable to the site, and the sharp-witted art critic Paul Westheim described it as the work of a dilettante, an advertisement for the architect rather than a celebration of the building's namesake.[22] To more traditionallyminded Germans, the placement of the Schocken department store and the Columbus House among far more traditional German buildings, some dating back to the sixteenth century and even earlier, seemed like a deliberate affront. Mendelsohn's contemporary, Bruno Taut, built in Berlin some of the best public housing of the twentieth century, yet the flat roofs that he designed were criticized as distinctly un-German, modernism in general as sterile, mechanical, and "Jewish."[23]

As in the modern arts, as in the claims for workers' power, the advocates of a full and pleasurable sex life for all people had a broad, encompassing vision. A humane, democratic society was one in which women and men enjoyed sex, had the leisure to indulge in the pleasures of the body, and could do so in various ways, in and out of marriage, in heterosexual or homosexual relations. The Revolution and the Republic had, in their understanding, not only destroyed the authoritarian political elements of Imperial Germany and established a new democratic political order. They had also opened the possibility for moving Germans beyond the cramped, repressed sexual lives that most had endured to a new, sunny world of pleasure that also enabled women to limit reproduction. Joyful sex was an intimate element of the new democratic order.

Many Germans, apparently, suffered from a widespread disease: sexual misery (*sexuelle Not*). Legions of sex reformers, mostly physicians, many Social Democrats or Communists, provided the diagnosis and the cure. With explicit descriptions of sexual techniques and friendly counseling, they showed Germans how to lead pleasurable and healthy sex lives. And that, in turn, would create a sound, flourishing, productive, and fertile society, they believed.

Ideal Marriage, written by the Dutch physician Theodor Hendrik van der Velde, was one of the many, very popular sex manuals published in Weimar Germany. The book articulated a deeply humanistic sensibility, a concern for the difficulties people faced in the most intimate aspects of their lives. They did not have to suffer in silence, Velde counseled. Science tempered by paternalistic solicitude would show them that their marriages, "often a hell of torment," could become a state of bliss.[24] The key to "enduring happiness" in marriage lay in mutual, ongoing sexual pleasure.[25]

Men have to be the guides, according to Velde, that is their natural role in life. But he was scathing about the way most men made love. They were fast and sometimes even brutal, concerned only with their own orgasms.[26] Men have to learn that "strictly within the bounds of *normality*," all sorts of variations are possible that "can banish the mechanical monotony of the too well-known from the marriage-bed."[27] The husband has to learn that his wife's sexual rhythms are different, and that "the true lover achieves ecstasy by giving the joy of love." If he is not an "erotic genius" (and Velde clearly thought that few men were), then he needs "explicit knowledge." He must learn how to make love, and science will be the instructor.[28]

Other reformers went further. Magnus Hirschfeld accepted homosexuality and campaigned against homophobic legislation and prejudices. Wilhelm Reich drew on Bronsilaw Malinowski's idyllic portrait of the sex lives of Trobriand Islanders in the Pacific to show the dismal results of repressive bourgeois life. As Reich quotes Malinowski, Trobriand Islanders ridiculed white men's sexual performance because they reached orgasm too quickly, while the natives engaged in long love-making that was pleasurable to both partners.[29] Another reformer, Max Hodann, found an alternative model in "the Orient" and the gentle art of lovemaking, so he said, that Indians, Japanese, and Muslims all practiced.[30] In this view, the task of a democratic Germany was somehow to join the sex practices of traditional, non-western societies with the fast-paced character of modern life.

The sex reformers counseled, wrote, and lectured in a highly politicized, highly activist environment. They found critical support especially at the municipal level, where Social Democrats or at least the Weimar Coalition parties dominated many city councils and governments. A huge expansion of family- and sex-counseling clinics resulted, even in small towns. Most were led by physicians, women activists, and officials of various sex-reform leagues—often one and the same person performing multiple roles.[31] The sex-reform leagues had over 150,000 members, and an influence far beyond their numbers through their publications, lectures, clinics, and sales of condoms and other birth-control devices. The leagues included lay people, healthcare professionals, social workers, activists in the socialist and communist parties, and government officials.[32] Many of them were involved in the vibrant public campaign against paragraph 218, the legal provision that criminalized abortion.

The "new woman" was perhaps the most renowned symbol of the sexual revolution of the 1920s. She had short hair, the famed *Bubikopf*, was slender, athletic, erotic, and amaternal. She smoked, and sometimes wore men's clothes. She went out alone, had sex as she pleased. She worked, typically in an office or in the arts. She lived for today and for herself, as Elsa Herrmann wrote in *So ist die neue Frau* (This Is the New Woman), yet another of the Weimar books devoted to the topic. The woman of yesterday lived for her husband and her children and sacrificed for the family. The new woman believed in equal rights and "refuses to be regarded as a physically weak being in need of assistance" and strove to be self-reliant in economic terms.[33] The "new woman" was in large part a class-bound image, of middle- and upper-class women who had the independence and the means to pursue their interests and desires. For the vast majority of women, the sheen and glimmer of the good life lay very distant. But it was a compelling image, nonetheless, and it did trickle down to the lower classes.

The image of liberated sex and, especially, of the new woman, inspired visceral and vitriolic responses. The issues of sex and the family, and of women—what they did, how they looked—struck at the heart of what Germans did in their intimate and spiritual lives. All sorts of commentators railed against what they perceived as unbridled licentiousness of new women, who limited their fertility or refused to have children altogether, thereby threatening religion, family, and society by the selfish pursuit of their own pleasures. The Protestant and Catholic churches thundered their opposition to all the sex talk and the public display of lightly clad bodies. All of this was a sign of the spiritual crisis of the age, one fostered by the Republic. An unbridgeable chasm lay between those who believed that the sober, sexually modest Christian family would undergird a moral society, and the advocates of erotic fulfillment as part and parcel of the new, democratic Germany.

The Left could never win a majority for its program. Internally, it was deeply divided. The Social Democrat–Communist split, perhaps more virulent in Germany than anywhere else, was only one divide. Workers in both parties may have been supportive of greater access to birth control; it is not at all clear that they supported sexual liberation and the emancipated woman. Similarly, the more abstract and experimental forms of modern art hardly accorded with the artistic predilections of the labor parties, which tended to venerate classical German culture in the form of Goethe, Schiller, and Beethoven. Nonetheless, alliances between left-wing artists and writers and the Social Democrats and Communists did exist, and they sometimes could prove immensely productive, as when Social Democratic communal leaders supported the Bauhaus or promoted sex-counseling clinics, or when Communists helped launch the large, public campaign against Germany's highly restrictive abortion law. Though difficult to sustain over the long haul, these tacit alliances did much to support Weimar's innovations in all the various realms of society.

But the Right literally hated Weimar's accomplishments. Workers' power made class rather than nation the defining pole of politics and identity, and suggested horizontal loyalties across national boundaries, the identification with workers in other countries and, most threatening, with Soviet Russia. Modern buildings were a powerful, visual statement about the need to break with tradition, to forge a new, creative, joyous, dynamic, and humane future. Free and pleasurable sex and the emancipated woman inspired the deepest sexual and existential anxieties of more conservative-minded Germans. Ultimately, the alliance between the traditional and the radical Right was founded on their visceral opposition to Weimar's emancipatory promise. Together, they brought Hitler to power and destroyed the Republic.

Notes

1 See Eric D. Weitz, *Weimar Germany: Promise and Tragedy* (Princeton, New Jersey: Princeton University Press, 2007).

2 For example, S. William Halperin, *Germany Tried Democracy: A Political History of the Reich from 1918 to 1933* (1946; New York: Norton, 1965); Karl Dietrich Bracher, *Die Auflösung der Weimarer Republik: Eine Studie zum Problem des Machtverfalls in der Demokratie*, 5th edn (1955; Düsseldorf: Droste, 1984); *Der Weg in die Diktatur* (Munich: Piper, 1982), published in English as *The Path to Dictatorship, 1918–1933: Ten Essays by German Scholars*, trans. John Conway (1962; New York: Anchor, 1966).

3 Martin Broszat, *Hitler and the Collapse of Weimar Germany*, trans. V. R. Berghahn (1984; Leamington Spa: Berg, 1987) (although the German original is different since the title uses *Zerstörung* or "Destruction"); A. J. Nichols, *Weimar and the Rise of Hitler* (1968; New York: St Martin's, 1991); Alex de Jonge, *The Weimar Chronicle: Prelude to Hitler* (New York: New

American Library, 1978); Michael N. Dobkowski and Isidor Wallimann, eds, *Radical Perspectives on the Rise of Fascism in Germany, 1919–1945* (New York: Monthly Review, 1989). David Abraham, *The Collapse of the Weimar Republic: Political Economy and Crisis*, 2nd edn (New York: Holmes and Meier, 1986), also uses the "collapse" terminology, but the analysis is more about destruction led by the elites.

4 Anton Saefkow, member of the KPD's "operative leadership" and leader of the Saefkow–Jacob–Bäustlein resistance group, in his political testament written shortly before his execution by the Nazis in 1944. Quoted by Siegfried Suckut, *Die Betriebsrätebewegung in der Sowjetischen Besetzten Zone Deutschlands (1945–1948)* (Frankfurt am Main: Haag und Herchen, 1982), 172.

5 See Eric D. Weitz, *Creating German Communism, 1890–1990: From Popular Protest to Socialist State* (Princeton, New Jersey: Princeton University Press, 1997).

6 Recent histories of the Weimar period have been excessively one-sided in their focus on the cultural realm. They have ignored critical issues of political economy. See, for example, Moritz Föllmer and Rüdiger Graf, eds, *Die "Krise" der Weimarer Republik: Zur Kritik eines Deutungsmusters* (Frankfurt am Main: Campus, 2005); Rüdiger Graf, *Die Zukunft der Weimarer Republik: Krisen und Zukunftsaneignungen in Deutschland 1918–1933* (Munich: Oldenbourg, 2008).

7 See Jürgen Kocka's classic, *Klassengesellschaft im Krieg: Deutsche Sozialgeschichte 1914–1918* (Göttingen: Vandenhoeck und Ruprecht, 1973).

8 See the articles by Gerald D. Feldman, "German Business between War and Revolution: On the Origins of the Stinnes-Legien Agreement," in *Entstehung und Wandel der modernen Gesellschaft: Festschrift für Hans Rosenberg zum 65. Geburtstag*, ed. Gerhard A. Ritter (Berlin: Walter de Gruyter, 1970), 312–41; Gerald D. Feldman and Irmgard Steinisch, "Die Weimarer Republik zwischen Sozial- und Wirtschaftsstaat: Die Entscheidung gegen den Achtstundentag," *Archiv für Sozialgeschichte*, vol. 18 (1978): 353–439.

9 Arnold Zweig, "Freundschaft mit Freud: Ein Bericht" (1947/48) in *Arnold Zweig, 1887–1968: Werk und Leben in Dokumenten und Bildern*, ed. Georg Wenzel (Berlin: Aufbau, 1978), 103–4, quotation 103.

10 Arnold Zweig to Helene Weyl, 4 April 1919, in Arnold Zweig, Beatrice Zweig and Helene Weyl, *Komm her, Wir lieben dich: Briefe einer ungewöhnlichen Freundschaft zu dritt*, ed. Ilse Lange (Berlin: Aufbau, 1996), 149–51, quotation 150.

11 Arnold Zweig, "Theater, Drama, Politik," 10 January 1921, in Wenzel (ed.), *Arnold Zweig*, 115–18, quotation 117.

12 Hermann Finsterlin, 3 February 1920, in *The Crystal Chain Letters: Architectural Fantasies by Bruno Taut and His Circle*, ed. and trans. Iain Boyd Whyte (Cambridge, Massachusetts: MIT Press, 1985), 53.

13 MoMA mounted a major Bauhaus exhibit in 2009–10, the first since its fabled exhibit in 1938 that did so much to promote Gropius's career.

14 Ita Heinze-Greenberg and Regina Stephan, eds, *Luise und Erich Mendelsohn: Eine Partnerschaft für die Kunst* (Ostfildern-Ruit: Hatje Cantz Verlag, 2004), 109.

15 First lecture in Philippson salon, in Ita Heinze-Greenberg and Regina Stephan, eds, *Erich Mendelsohn: Gedankenwelten* (Ostfildern-Ruit: Hatje Cantz, 2000), 14–20, here 14.

16 Eighth lecture in Philippson salon, 1919, in *Erich Mendelsohn* (Heinze-Greenberg and Stephan, eds), 38–44, here 44.

17 Mendelsohn, "Das neuzeitliche Geschäftshaus" (1929), in *Erich Mendelsohn* (Heinze-Greenberg and Stephan, eds), 96–103, here 103.

18 Erich Mendelsohn, "Die internationale Übereinstimmung des neuen Baugedankens oder Dynamik und Funktion" (1923), *Erich Mendelsohn* (Heinze-Greenberg and Stephan, eds), 48–53, here 48–49.

19 Mendelsohn, "Die internationale Übereinstimmung des neuen Baugedankens oder Dynamik und Funktion" (1923), in *Erich Mendelsohn* (Heinze-Greenberg and Stephan, eds), 50–51.

20 A point rightly emphasized by Norbert Huse, "Facetten eines Baudenkmals," in Huse, ed., *Mendelsohn: Der Einsteinturm. Die Geschichte einer Instandsetzung* (Stuttgart: Karl Krämer, 2000), 14–27, here 21–23.

21 Or so Mendelsohn claimed, in Erich Mendelsohn, "My Own Contribution to the Development of Contemporary Architecture," lecture at UCLA, 17 March 1948, in *Erich Mendelsohn: Letters of an Architect*, ed. Oskar Beyer, trans. Geoffrey Strachan (London: Abelard Schuman, 1967), 161–74, here 166.

22 Paul Westheim, quoted in Huse, "Facetten eines Baudenkmals," 24–25.
23 See Barbara Miller Lane, *Architecture and Politics in Germany, 1918–1945* (Cambridge, Massachusetts: Harvard University Press, 1968), 125–47, especially 136–37, 138, and 139.
24 Th. H. van de Velde, *Ideal Marriage: Its Physiology and Technique*, rev. edn, trans. Stella Browne (German original 1926; New York: Random House, 1939), 1.
25 van de Velde, *Ideal Marriage*, 2.
26 van de Velde, *Ideal Marriage*, 7–8.
27 van de Velde, *Ideal Marriage*.
28 van de Velde, *Ideal Marriage*, 9.
29 Wilhelm Reich, "The Imposition of Sexual Morality" (1932), in Wilhelm Reich, *Sex-Pol: Essays 1929–1934*, ed. Lee Baxandall, trans. Anna Bostock et al. (New York: Random House, 1966), 123–24.
30 Max Hodann, *Sex Life in Europe: A Biological and Sociological Survey*, trans. J. Gibbs (German original 1929; New York: Gargoyle Press, 1932), 17–18.
31 See Atina Grossmann, *Reforming Sex: The German Movement for Birth Control and Abortion Reform, 1920–1950* (New York: Oxford University Press, 1995).
32 Figure from Grossmann, *Reforming Sex*, 14.
33 Elsa Herrmann, "This is the New Woman," in *The Weimar Republic Sourcebook*, eds Anton Kaes, Martin Jay and Edward Dimendberg (Berkeley, California: University of California Press, 1994), 206–8, quote 207.

6

HITLER AND THE FUNCTIONING OF THE THIRD REICH

Dieter Kuntz

On the evening of 30 January 1933, Joseph Goebbels exhilaratingly recorded in his diary: "It seems like a dream ... the *Wilhelmstrasse*[1] is ours ... the *Führer* is appointed Chancellor ... Germany is at a turning-point in her history ... like a fairy tale ... Germany has awakened!"[2] Over the course of approximately the next year-and-a-half, an astonishingly rapid transformation engulfed Germany. Beginning on this momentous eve—marked by a mesmerizing torchlight parade and iconic pageantry that symbolized both the Nazi movement's revolutionary vigor as well as regime change—and followed shortly by measures calculated to consolidate and extend Hitler's authority and the influence of the NSDAP (German National Socialist Workers' Party, *Nationalsozialistische Deutsche Arbeiterpartei*), sweeping changes were set in motion that established the dictatorship. Hitler, as leader of a political "movement" rather than a political "party," projected himself as a messianic visionary pursuing a vital mission, and had written in *Mein Kampf*[3] that only he and his movement possessed the necessary ideological convictions, and were "alone capable not only of halting the decline of the German people, but of creating the granite foundation upon which some day a state will rest which represents, not an alien mechanism of economic concerns and interests, but a national organism: A Germanic State of the German Nation."

Hitler had no reservations about his goal to restructure the German state under his personal leadership, and in 1933, he began to implement the plan that he long envisioned, beginning with his manipulation and utter rejection of the republic's constitutional limitations. In 1923, he had already proclaimed that "the *völkisch* state must free all leadership and especially the highest—that is, the political leadership—entirely from the parliamentary principle of majority rule—in other words, mass rule—and instead absolutely guarantee the right of the personality." Now, with political power in hand, he embarked on a path that jettisoned the constraints of democratic parliamentary government and created instead a system defined by his own increased personal authority and by a struggle for influence and power among those close to him. This ultimately would have far-reaching consequences in the implementation of Nazi policies that were so deeply rooted in racial ideology.

Immediately following his appointment, Hitler convinced President Paul von Hindenburg to dissolve the Reichstag and call for new elections for 5 March 1933, expecting to receive a majority of seats in the new parliament. For the next 7 weeks, the nation was governed via emergency decrees. On his second day in office, Hitler delivered a radio address to the German people wherein he vowed to raise the nation from what he characterized as 14 years of "decay" and "ruin" under the Weimar government, a system he castigated as being

69

strongly influenced by Marxism. Foreshadowing the campaign against leftist parties that followed in the coming weeks, he warned of the continued threat of Bolshevism, promising to "declare a merciless war" against what he defined as "political nihilism." He promised that his government would rebuild the Reich, and asked the German people to "give us four years' time and then put us on trial and judge us."[4] A swift and pronounced repression of political opponents soon followed, and although the Nazis claimed that they had effected a legal, bloodless revolution, in fact, considerable violence accompanied the Nazi takeover of power. From spring to summer of 1933, about 27,000 political prisoners were interned in concentration camps and subjected to inhumane treatment and physical abuse, so that by the fall of that year some 600 had perished.[5]

A number of pseudo-legal acts facilitated the Nazis' grasp of control at the national and state levels. In early February, a decree was issued that curtailed freedom of the press and the right to assemble. Aimed at the communists, this measure enabled the arrests of KPD (German Communist Party, *Kommunistische Partei Deutschlands*) leaders and members and severely hindered party activities. The decree, however, did not affect the activities of the NSDAP, which instead stepped up its campaign of physical intimidation of opponents. In Prussia, the largest state, Hermann Goering, the new Prussian Minister of the Interior, tightened Nazi control by directing a purge of the police force of those perceived to be non-supporters or opponents of the Nazis. He followed this up on 22 February by appointing members of the party's paramilitary wing (the SA, *Sturmabteilung*) and "praetorian guard" (the SS, *Schutzstaffel*) to positions of special police auxiliaries, ostensibly to help "restore order" to what was alleged to be a surge in violent acts by leftist radicals. When, on the evening of 27 February, the Reichstag building was set on fire, the regime portrayed it as the start of the expected communist revolution, announcing on the next day a state of emergency and suspending civil liberties by issuing the "Decree for the Protection of People and State." This, the so-called "Reichstag Fire Decree," established the basis for the creation of a police state by enabling the Nazis to suspend those sections of the constitution that guaranteed civil liberties and individual rights. The decree authorized the government to use any methods necessary, including house searches and arrests, to guard against "Communist acts of violence endangering the state." The regime rounded up communists and Social Democrats, as well as other opponents. On the basis of this decree, Reich police commissioners were dispatched to various states not only to assume control of the police, but also to pressure resignations from legally constituted state governments and engineer the formation of Nazi governments to take their place. This established the basis for the peculiar organizational structure of the Nazi state, which came to be, in effect, a "dual state," characterized by a governing system whereby the NSDAP's party structure and state-government administrative bodies functioned side-by-side. The regime, on 23 March, put an end to parliamentary democracy after intimidating and coercing the *Reichstag* to vote for the Enabling Act. Officially named the "Law for the Removal of the Distress of People and Reich," this act suspended parliament and allowed the government to rule via decree for the subsequent four years. In 1937, the law was renewed, and by 1943 was simply declared to be perpetual. Hitler was able to enact laws through his cabinet without actually obtaining consent of the *Reichstag*, although by 1938 cabinet government, too, lapsed entirely. After 1933, the *Reichstag* met only when Hitler called it into session to vote on laws such as the 1935 Nuremberg Laws. Representative democracy was replaced by a series of referenda, such as the plebiscites that approved withdrawal from the League of Nations, and the 1938 incorporation of Austria into the

Reich.[6] Consequently, the Enabling Act not only altered the Weimar Constitution, but legalized the Nazi revolution, and provided the foundation for the establishment of the totalitarian regime.

With a firm grip on the Reich government, Hitler, at the end of March 1933, moved to bring state governments and their bureaucratic structures fully under his control with a law that dissolved and reorganized the state governments. This was followed by a further law that allowed Hitler to appoint Reich governors—many of whom were the NSDAP's regional leaders (*Gauleiter*)—to head these new state governments. Nominally subordinate to the Ministry of the Interior, these new state officials also continued to hold the top party posts in each state, and were thereby simultaneously also directly answerable to Hitler, personifying the new order's slogan of "unity of party and state." Soon after, the Nazis continued their incursions into the hitherto relatively independent realm of the state bureaucracies with the first civil service decree, the 7 April "Law for the Restoration of the Professional Civil Service," which legalized a wide range of arbitrary and violent acts, and made it possible summarily to dismiss employees on the basis of their "Aryan" suitability or political allegiances. The civil service legislation not only achieved an intimidation and political leveling of the state bureaucracy, but also enabled the Nazis to incorporate their antisemitism into law for the first time. Whereas state governments quickly lost all autonomy, control over the administrations of local government was a longer, ongoing process, and some towns and cities even continued to be governed by mayors who were not Nazi Party members.[7]

The incursions of the NSDAP into the bureaucracy of the judicial arena were particularly acute, and were based on the passage of the "Law on Admission to the Practice of Law," and the aforementioned "Civil Service Law," which removed lawyers and judges from their posts based on political and racial lines. This was followed by the coordination (*Gleichschaltung*) of lawyers through the creation of the Nazi-controlled German Law Front, whose head was also appointed Reich Commissar for the Coordination of Justice in the States. Pressure was brought to bear on judges to join the NSDAP, and the entire judicial system was systematically purged and molded into a compliant and loyal body that sought to interpret laws according to National Socialist principles.[8] In the place of an independent judiciary, the regime sought not only compliant, but "activist" judges, who were committed to National Socialist values and who administered justice as the "agents of the national community (*Volksgemeinschaft*)." In the later years of the Third Reich, rather than representing the will of the people, judges increasingly came to be direct instruments of the *Führer's* authority.[9]

Consequently, the duality of party and state was most pronounced in the field of law, and led to a legally justified dictatorial system of terror that created a number of new special courts, and meted out thousands of jail terms and death sentences to "traitors and saboteurs" as defined by the party. In March 1933, special courts were created to prosecute "treason" cases, from which there were no appeals, and which dispensed draconian justice, imposing some 11,000 death sentences. Hearing cases of "high treason" was the People's Court (*Volksgerichtshof*), established in 1934, and which alone imposed some 5,200 death sentences during the war years.[10] Over 200 special "Hereditary Health Courts" (*Erbgerichte*) were created to preside over compulsory sterilization cases of individuals judged "genetically diseased" and therefore unsuitable for reproduction. More than 400,000 individuals were forcibly sterilized in the Third Reich. Victims of this "second track" of justice had no recourse to the normal legal process, and no appeal from special measures such as "protective custody," since the police agencies of the party and the SS stood outside all judicial control. The testimony of a district court judge, deposed at the military tribunal in Nuremberg in 1945, described this process:

> The strongest interference with the administration of Justice developed increasingly after 1933 "outside of" [*neben*] the administration of justice. The police, under the command of the *Reichsführer* SS, arrested persons who were persona non grata for political or even for other reasons without judicial procedure (and, indeed, without any procedure at all) and detained them in prisons and concentration camps. In political cases, it was the rule rather than the exception that accused persons who had been acquitted by the court were taken immediately after trial into "protective custody" by the police and thus disappeared into concentration camps.[11]

Within days of the seizure of power, improvised detention sites were created for political opponents, as the SS and SA simply translated political orders into the terrorist justice of the Nazi camp system. These early detention sites consisted of protective custody camps, torture sites, and concentration camps, many of which were established in structures ranging in size from wings of already existing prisons, to sections of castles, workhouses, and large factory buildings that had been forced to close due to the dire economic circumstances.[12]

Simultaneously with the move to control the police and judicial system, and in order to prevent possible united opposition to their consolidation of power, the Nazis broadened their efforts to control and coordinate all aspects of state and society through the policy of *Gleichschaltung*. In an attempt to neutralize potential opposition from the labor movement, trade unions were crushed and replaced with the German Labor Front. Professional organizations in the fields of medicine, education, and culture saw doctors, teachers, artists, writers, and editors forced to align themselves with newly created Nazi organizations that now represented these fields and oversaw their ideological and institutional coordination. Yet by early 1934, one full year after the takeover of power, two important sources of potential opposition continued to remain outside Hitler's direct control—the army and the SA.

The radicalism of the SA and the talk of a "second revolution" in a more socialist direction, which Ernst Roehm and others in the leadership of the organization were clamoring for, grew increasingly problematic for Hitler, who by June 1934 determined to put an end to it. With his proposal to create a new "people's army" by combining the SA and the *Reichswehr* (army) under his command, Roehm had also alienated the army, whose support Hitler regarded as crucial for his future expansionist plans. During the night of 30 June 1934, Hitler not only unleashed the SS in an assassination campaign against the rebellious SA leadership, but also used the opportunity to settle old scores against hundreds of other perceived enemies and potential threats. Gaining control of the army was a more gradual process, but was crucial to the consolidation of power. When President Hindenburg died in early August, the title of Reich President was abolished, and the president's powers were transferred to Hitler, whose new official title became *Führer* and Chancellor—underscoring the duality of the structure of power in the new Third Reich. On one level, Hitler was still chancellor and head of the supposed parliamentary government, yet by illegally adding the powers of the presidential office, he trampled on what remained of Weimar's constitutional limitations on authority, demonstrating thereby that the institutions of the democratic state could be abolished simply through his will. By designating himself *Führer*, Hitler laid claim to an even more important source of power that allowed him to go beyond the restrictions of his constitutional office. His position as *Führer* transcended the formally defined authority of the chancellor, and his powers as *Führer* emanated not so much from the machinery of government as from his role as leader of the National Socialist movement, which uniquely empowered him to undertake his historical mission to reshape the destiny of the German people. Hitler's new dual title was also representative of the fluidity of the party–state relationships which characterized the *Führer* state in the years prior to the war.

Since opposition parties had voluntarily dissolved themselves or had been eliminated, the "Law against the Founding of New Parties," promulgated in July 1933, consolidated the NSDAP's monopoly. The December 1933 "Law to Secure the Unity of Party and State" affirmed that " ... the National Socialist German Workers' Party has become the upholder of German state thinking and is indissolubly linked to the state." This law not only legalized the supreme position of the NSDAP within the state, but also established the Party as the official purveyor of political ideology. In theory, the machinery of the state served to implement the will of the party, and the regime aimed for the integration of structure and personnel of state mechanism and party apparatus. Hitler as both *Führer* and chancellor personified the unity of party and state, and served as the model for the intended merging of the two entities at all administrative levels. Yet the actual "unity of party and state" varied in practice, did not function smoothly, and certainly did not mean that the two were equal entities. The state apparatus was subordinate to the party, as stipulated by the Civil Service Code's assertion that "the *Volk*, not the state, is the decisive element." The party represented the *Volk* (the people), and the state was merely the mechanism through which the future goal of the desired *Volksge-meinschaft* could be attained. Rather than a system of two opposing forces, the "dual state" can more aptly be defined as an *intertwining* of party and state. This intertwining or enmeshing can, however, best be characterized as a tangle of parallel bureaucracies. In the analysis of some legal scholars, this dual organizational structure was sanctioned by Hitler as it served to strengthen his own position of power.[13]

Gleichschaltung eliminated all sources of potential opposition and those members of the civil service who held democratic convictions, still many civil-service administrative bodies that had long-established traditions and a strong sense of cohesiveness continued to function, coexisting with the various new National Socialist organizations and personnel. For instance, within the Berlin ministerial bureaucracy, the National Socialist leadership was largely unable to effect the desired degree of "political accountability" that could be relied upon to obediently carry out the will of the Party. An administrative apparatus that was run exclusively by militant party members and loyalists could not be realized, because many party functionaries simply lacked the necessary administrative experience, or were simply too inept. Accordingly, the relationship between the civil service administration and the Nazi political leadership was defined by both collaboration and antagonism, as well as by continued, traditional, established jurisdictions and the new extra-legislative powers of the *Führer*.[14]

Old and new administrative authorities simultaneously attempting to exercise jurisdiction became a feature of all levels of government in the Third Reich, from the local to the district, and to the state or regional level—as different ruling bodies claimed primacy within their perceived sphere of authority. Inevitably, an overlapping and entangling jurisdictional system resulted, evidenced by hostile rivalries between state administrative bodies and party offices. Rather than simplifying administration, the Third Reich's expansion of the one-man and one-party rule actually served to complicate jurisdictional relations, leading to an often-chaotic system defined by inefficiency, waste, duplication, friction, and sometimes even contradictory policies.

This is exemplified in a memorandum written at the end of 1935 by a high-level state government official in the Rhineland, who lamented that lower-level party offices were "still staffed by thoroughly unqualified individuals." Cooperation between the party and state officials continued to be "unsatisfactory" in the eyes of the NSDAP, which claimed that government officials "do not toe the line sufficiently." The state official pointed to grievances of the party that were seemingly contrived "in order to have reasons for interfering in state business, so that state officials will feel that they are under Party supervision." Mayors and council members, he lamented, felt that they were

> more under the command of the Party than of higher administrative offices. Not only has this created dissatisfaction among a large segment of the public, but it has led to frequent criticism of and opposition to city government offices, which in the end is detrimental to the National Socialist movement.

He confirmed the primacy of party over the state apparatus, citing "continued meddling in [state] affairs by Party officials." The civil service grudgingly accepted these conditions, he surmised, and "put up with this in order to avoid serious conflict."[15]

The conflicting relationship between party and state was also central to Hitler's maintenance of personal power. Rather than fusing party and state, Hitler allowed the two entities to remain separate, with both depending on his personal intervention to settle the competency squabbles that invariably arose. The *Führer* could act as supreme arbiter and had the decisive voice on all critical issues, and through the police and SS (unified by 1936 under Himmler, who derived his authority directly from Hitler), also commanded the extralegal instruments of coercion and terror in the state. Within only a few months after taking the reins of power in the state, the Nazis had transformed a parliamentary democracy into a personal dictatorship in which the *Führer* had unlimited power. Hitler sat atop a hierarchical organizational structure that was rooted in the ideological concept of the "*Führer* (leadership) principle." Established early in the development of the National Socialist movement, the *Führer* principle was the structural principle of party organization prior to the seizure of power, emphasizing discipline and a chain of command, and culminating in the charismatic position of the *Führer*. Hitler expounded on this concept in *Mein Kampf*, and felt that it was the best organizational structure for the state as well as the party, because it

> raises the best minds in the national community to leading position and leading influence ... but, the able men cannot be appointed from above, but must struggle through for themselves ... From the smallest community cell to the highest leadership of the entire Reich, the state must have the personality principle anchored in its organization.[16]

After the seizure of power, the *Führer* principle indeed became state doctrine, and the regime aimed to apply the concept to the organizational structure and functioning of the Third Reich. Guidelines in *The Organization Book of the NSDAP*[17] defined how the system was intended to function in theory:

> The *Führer* principle requires a pyramidal organization structure ... The *Führer* is at the top. He nominates the necessary leaders for the various spheres of work of the Reich's direction, the Party apparatus and the State administration ...
>
> The Party was created by the *Führer* out of the realization that if our people were to live and advance towards an era of prosperity they had to be led according to an ideology suitable for our race. They must have as supporters men above average, that means, men who surpass others in self-control, discipline, efficiency, and greater judgment. The Party will therefore always constitute a minority, the order of the National Socialist ideology which comprises the leading elements of our people. Therefore the party comprises only fighters, at all times prepared to assume and to give everything for the furtherance of the National Socialist ideology. Men and women whose primary and most sacred duty is to serve the people. The NSDAP as the leading element of the German people control the entire public life, from an organizational point of view, as well as from that of affiliates, the organizations of the State administration, and so forth ... Furthermore, the Party shall create the prerequisites for a systematic selection of potential *Führers* ...

The *Führer* principle, however, was only a vague concept that was not codified into law, had no legal or traditional basis, and was based largely on the mythical, messianic-like notion that Hitler had a "divine calling." Yet it affirmed his position of absolute supremacy, and commanded obedience to his authority—so that even his *will* came to be regarded as binding.

Analyzing the Third Reich in 1944, Franz Neumann, a contemporary observer, noted in his now classic work *Behemoth: The Structure and Practice of National Socialism, 1933–1944*, "Adolf Hitler is top leader. He combines the functions of supreme legislator, supreme administrator, and supreme judge; he is the leader of the party, the army, and the people. This person is leader for life." His powers, Neumann concluded, derived from a charismatic leadership principle that "rests on the assertion that the Leader is endowed with qualities lacking in ordinary mortals. Superhuman qualities emanate from him and pervade the state, party, and people."[18]

The *Führer's* authority could not be defined constitutionally. He was independent of all other governmental institutions, did not swear the constitutional oath to parliament as required under the Weimar constitution, and could not be deposed by a popular initiative. "His power is legally and constitutionally unlimited," lamented Neumann.[19] Moreover, his leadership role was something abstract that could only be grasped "intuitively." It was anchored in an "unwritten constitution" and in the "Germanic values" of the *Volksgemeinschaft* (national community) that called for higher virtues such as "readiness for sacrifice" and "purity of the blood," and which rejected the legal definitions and moral standards of the previous liberal system. The judicial community accepted the *Führer's* authority, set aside the principle of separation of powers, and nullified all constitutional norms and the traditional concept of law. Law became simply the "expression of the will of the *Führer*."[20]

The governmental system of the Third Reich, based on Hitler's seemingly omnipotent position, stood in stark contrast to the parliamentary democracy of the Weimar Republic. Hitler perceived parliamentary government and its need for majority decisions to be the source of democracy's weakness and as inevitably deleterious to the unity of the nation. Alan Bullock emphasizes, in his masterful biography of Hitler, that

> as soon as Hitler began to think and talk about the organization of the State, the metaphor which dominated his mind was that of an army. He saw the State as an instrument of power, in which the qualities to be valued were discipline, unity and sacrifice. It was from the Army that he took the *Führerprinzip*, the leadership principle, upon which first the Nazi Party, and later the National Socialist State, were built.[21]

The *Führer* principle, Bullock asserts, placed all power in Hitler's hands, but his authority did not derive from a bureaucratic hierarchy, but came instead from "his exceptional, charismatic gifts as a person, recognized and accepted by all members of the party."[22] The foremost legal theoretician of the Third Reich, Carl Schmitt, professor of law (expert on constitutional law) at the University of Berlin from 1933 to 1945, in reflecting on the constitutional aspects of authority and the delegation of power in the Hitler state, concluded that the *Führer* had indeed created a "personal regime."[23]

> Because of the concentration of power in Hitler's hands, which was carried to an extreme, access to him became one of the most important problems of internal politics in the Third Reich. Such a concentration of total power in a single human being—who insisted on ruling a modern industrial state of 70 million people, even down to the smallest detail, and on conducting a modern total war personally, down to issuing detailed individual orders—exceeds all known examples of a "personal regime" ... Correspondingly, the significance of being quite close to the leader was greater than in any previous regime ... The higher Hitler rose, and with him all those who had access to him or were in personal contact with him, the lower sank the Reich ministers who did not belong to this privileged group ... The Reich cabinet did not meet after 1937.
>
> Hitler's personal position of power implied a colossal claim to omnipotence ... Therefore the first practical question was who would feed the omnipotent *Führer* the information on which he could formulate his decisions and his decrees, and who would select from the incoming mass [of letters and petitions] what was or was not to be submitted to him. The second question dealt with who should pass on orders and decisions to those carrying them out, a question that is of special importance because there were no clearly defined forms for the so-called *Führer* directives, and the orders were frequently very brief and abrupt ...

Yet, despite his seeming omnipotence, the *Führer* did not concern himself with the everyday affairs of running the government, and was content to leave these tasks to subordinates. Moreover, despite the hierarchical intent of the *Führer* principle, there were, in fact, no clearly delineated lines of authority below Hitler that defined administrative responsibilities—within either the party or the state structure—and his directives were often extremely vague and open to interpretation. Neumann labeled this governing system a "task state," wherein assignments were doled out to trusted plenipotentiaries who frequently competed with other authorities, creating what Peter Hayes has called an "institutional Darwinism."[24]

Hitler's aloofness to the daily business of running a government certainly reflected his utter disdain for mundane bureaucratic tasks, but, as the historian Ian Kershaw has maintained, it was also the "product of the deification of the leadership position" and the awareness of a "need to sustain prestige to match the created image."[25] The idealized image of the *Führer* cultivated by Nazi propaganda portrayed Hitler as a strong leader, firmly in command atop the pyramidal hierarchy, and in control of a centralized authority and unified nation. This concept was imprinted on the minds of the German people by the slogan *"Ein Volk, Ein Reich, Ein Führer."*[26] Some, however, have argued that his leadership style, and the overlapping and conflicting institutional structure of the Third Reich, belied the image of a powerful or "strong dictator," and that Hitler was actually "weak" and ineffectual, and that the Third Reich was not a centralized state, but was instead a polycratic regime.

Otto Dietrich, Press Chief of the Third Reich from 1933 to 1945, experienced first-hand how the *Führer* state functioned. His observations describe a system of personal and institutional conflict that created administrative confusion and chaos.

> In theory Hitler had built up an ideal Leader State. But in practice he created utter chaos in the leadership of the state ... In the twelve years of his rule Hitler created in the political leadership of Germany the greatest confusion that has ever existed in a civilized state ... He destroyed all clarity in the administration of government and established an utterly opaque network of overlapping authorities. It was almost a rule with Hitler to establish dual appointments and conflicting agencies ...
>
> For example, by making Goering head of the Four-Year Plan authority he gave him control of the entire German planned economy. But then at the same time he kept in office a rival minister of the economy (Schacht-Funk) whose functions were practically the same. Later on he added to these a minister for war production (Todt-Speer) who, just by the by, was engaged in a permanent feud with the OKW over problems of armament ... In the sphere of culture Goebbels and Rosenberg quarreled incessantly; in art Goering and Goebbels, Rosenberg and Buhler tilted against one another ... in the Party organization Ley and Borman had the same radius of activities; in Party education Rosenberg and Ley were in competition. In the armed forces the interests of the army, Waffen-SS (Armed-SS) and air force field divisions were inextricably confused and incompatible. Hitler had arbitrarily set up these organizations side by side ... In the sphere of justice he had a Minister of Justice and a Head of the German Legal Front (Gürtner and Frank) who feuded with one another ...

Dietrich claimed that there was purpose and intent to the administrative tangle, arguing that Hitler, through "systematic disorganization," sought to enhance his position of authority by playing his subordinates against each other.

> Everywhere in the Reich and in the occupied territories Hitler established the same conditions: dual appointments, special commissioners, a horde of officials

with overlapping jurisdictions ... [but] there was method in the madness. In this way Hitler had at his disposal two or three "chiefs" in every field, each with an extensive apparatus. He could ensure the execution of his plans by playing one man off against the other or showing preference to one rather than another. His method systematically disorganized the objective authority of the higher departments of government—so that he could push the authority of his own will to the point of despotic tyranny.[27]

Historical analysis of Hitler's role, the structure of the state, and the functioning of the Third Reich is also linked to the debate surrounding the origins of the Nazis' "Final Solution." Some historians have taken what is referred to as the "intentionalist" position, arguing that what is paramount in assessing Hitler's role was his determination to achieve his ideological goals. Norman Rich, for instance, maintains that the "systematic extermination of the Jews, the ruthless implementation of racial policies in Germany and the German-occupied territories, and the massive population transfers to alter the racial configuration of Europe ... cannot be dismissed as the policies of a political opportunist ... [but] can only be explained as the policies of a fanatical ideologue."[28] Rich, too, sees the Third Reich as "an administrative maze" and a "crisscross of competencies and overlapping of powers and responsibilities." However, he also posits that despite the "vicious conflicts for authority among the officials of the Third Reich, there was never any question of challenging the authority of Hitler himself," because Hitler had simply "imposed his personal authority on the German people and state." He argues that it cannot be stressed too strongly that "Hitler was master in the Third Reich."[29] The analysis of Karl Dietrich Bracher also emphasizes the omnipotence and pivotal role of Hitler's ideologically-driven actions within what he terms the "totalitarian dictatorship."[30] Similarly focusing on the centrality of Hitler's position and the motivational impetus of his *Weltanschauung* (his world view or ideological fixation), the intentionalist interpretation of Eberhard Jäckel describes the Nazi regime as *Alleinherrschaft* or "sole rule," in which "the essential political decisions were taken by a single individual."[31] Klaus Hildebrand also argues the Hitler-centric, "strong" dictator, monocratic position—especially in the development of Nazi racial policy—and simply equates Nazism with Hitlerism: that Hilters's role was decisive and unique.[32]

By contrast, a number of other scholars offer a differing interpretation of the power structure of the regime. Rejecting what they regard as an overemphasis on the centrality of Hitler's role, and stressing instead the chaotic nature of the organizational hierarchy within the regime—and the structural limitations this imposed—they depict Hitler as a "weak" dictator. Termed either structuralist or functionalist (or sometimes revisionist), this approach downplays Hitler's role as absolute ruler, and rejects the view that he purposely abetted administrative rivalries within his government in order to enhance his own powers. Instead, it underscores the competitive and polycratic structural nature of the Third Reich, as well as the spontaneous and opportunistic—or "functional"—rather than "intentional" process of policy-making. Historians such as Martin Broszat and Hans Mommsen concentrate on what they see as Hitler's "inability" to create a monocratic, centralized structure, and argue that the Third Reich's power structure was not monolithic but multidimensional, where, in addition to the *Führer*'s authority, party offices (especially regional *Gauleiter*), various economic planning agencies, and the SS also exerted considerable power and competed for influence.

Broszat attributes the administrative chaos not so much to a consciously planned scheme on Hitler's part to "divide and rule," but rather regards it as a system that haphazardly developed from his administrative ineptitude.[33] Rather than seeing all policy emanating directly from Hitler, Broszat describes his role as authorizing the initiatives undertaken by subordinates competing to interpret the will of the *Führer*. Mommsen goes even further in arguing that Hitler's primary role was as propagandist for what were only vaguely defined ideological goals, and sees him as incapable of articulating clear and rational policies. Nazi racial policy and even the implementation of the "Final Solution," Mommsen maintains, should not be seen as merely carrying out Hitler's intent, but as an evolutionary process of the regime's ever-increasing radicalization.[34] Moreover, he does not even acknowledge that Hitler derived power from his role as arbiter of quarrels among subordinates, contending that the *Führer* "instead of functioning as a balancing element in the government" actually "disrupted the conduct of affairs by continually acting on sudden impulses ... and by delaying decisions on current matters."[35]

A more synthetic approach has been developed by Ian Kershaw, who also rejects the notion of Hitler's planned "administrative anarchy" but regards the Third Reich's organizational structure as "systemless."[36] This, says Kershaw, was a reflection of Hitler's personality and leadership style, because his "instinctive Darwinism made him unwilling and unable to take sides in a dispute till the winner emerged. But the need to protect his infallible image also made him largely incapable of doing so." Yet this structural disorder was accompanied by a tremendous increase of his authority that already by early 1938 (with the neutralization of the army's independence through the Blomberg–Fritsch affair) was practically unrestrained. According to Kershaw, Hitler's position as charismatic and quasi-deified leader served to unify quarrelling factions, and stimulated the activism and initiative of various agencies looking to realize the *Führer*'s aims. Even more importantly, he argues that Hitler's authority was an enabling factor because it legitimized and sanctioned the actions of anyone—no matter how extreme their measures—as long as they were furthering the overall aims of the *Führer* and the movement. Simply by working toward the creation of the *Volksgemeinschaft* and the goal of a racially pure and expanded Reich, anyone exercising initiative toward these goals had free rein and could count on official approval from the highest level.[37]

With all constraints removed, the regime was able to undertake ever more radical actions that became totally unchecked under the cover of war. Yet Hitler personally needed to do little to initiate the implementation of murderous measures, since he could rely on his lieutenants in the occupied eastern territories to enact his will. Kershaw cites the statement of a party functionary as exemplary of this notion: "Anyone who really works towards the *Führer* along his lines and towards his goals ... will have the finest reward in the form of the sudden legal confirmation of his work." This spirit of "working towards the *Führer*" reflects the power of Hitler's charismatic authority to stimulate action from his followers—even in the absence of specific orders.[38] Being aware of what the *Führer* wanted gave rise to, and validated, local initiative and often spontaneous actions by Nazi ideological zealots as well as by those seeking to advance careers. This notion was clearly at work, for instance, when, in the absence of a formal "euthanasia" law, only the *Führer*'s signed "authorization" was required to sanction the Nazi medical community's murder of more than 200,000 physically and mentally disabled patients. This was underscored by the medical killings through starvation and medication at the hands of directors of mental institutions and asylums that continued even after Hitler, who—in yielding to public criticism—halted the gassing phase of the "euthanasia" program in 1941. To that point, specially established killing centers had already claimed some 70,000 lives deemed expendable by the regime. Yet the murders continued through the war years (and even beyond), claiming more than 130,000 additional victims solely on the basis of individual enterprise motivated to fulfill the *Führer*'s wishes by working for the greater good of the *Volksgemeinschaft*. Similarly, the SS, in carrying out the *Führer*'s will, had free rein to initiate barbarous measures in meting out "special treatment" to Jews, and in working towards Hitler's desired "Final Solution" to the "Jewish Question."

The mission of National Socialism in establishing the *Volksgemeinschaft* was to bring to full consciousness the awareness of race, blood, and soil among all Germans. This entailed the creation of a "new man" and "new woman" with the strength of character and the dedication to the *Führer* necessary for the creation of this *Volk* community. The *Führer*'s "divine calling" and his sense of "mission" in leading Germany towards the chimerical goal of a racially pure national community defined the purpose and justified the actions of the Third Reich. Hitler's *Weltanschauung*, grounded in the principle of the supposed inequality of races, and in the belief that racial struggle—or competition between races—was the driving force in human biological evolution, in social development, and in cultural achievement. Hitler prided himself on being able to see more clearly than others that this was what had defined the course of history, and that it was therefore necessary for him to undertake the mission to ensure Germany's future survival in the immense struggle that lay ahead in the coming millennia. This, then, was the logic that justified mass murder and became the central policy of the Nazi regime. This ideological policy, based on the racial restructuring of Germany and ultimately of Europe, identified a multitude of perceived racial enemies, and led to the systematic persecution and murder of millions of people. The Nazis regarded themselves as coming to power via a revolution in 1933, and the regime subsequently did not discard the dynamic principle of revolution. In order to legitimize their measures and their use of unrestricted power in working toward their goal, the Nazis continued to employ the concept of an unfinished mission, or a "permanent revolution." In this view, as long as there were Germans who were still recalcitrant, as long as "total unity" of the people had not been achieved, as long as the all-important racial goals, both domestically and in the occupied East, had not been attained, the Hitler state needed to continue its perpetual activity toward the ultimate goal—as defined by Hitler—and which became ever more destructive.

Notes

1 Refers to the Wilhelmstrasse, the street in Berlin where the chancellery was located. The name was synonymous with the German government.
2 Joseph Goebbels, *My Part in Germany's Fight* (London: Hurst and Blackett, 1935), 234–37.
3 Adolf Hitler, *Mein Kampf*, trans. Ralph Manheim (Boston: Houghton Mifflin, 1943, 1971), 329.
4 *Völkischer Beobachter*, 2 February 1933.
5 Wolfgang Benz, *A Concise History of the Third Reich*, trans. Thomas Dunlap (Berkeley and Los Angeles: University of California Press, 2006), 118–20.
6 Michael Burleigh, *The Third Reich. A New History* (New York: Hill and Wang, 2000), 155.
7 Benjamin Sax and Dieter Kuntz, *Inside Hitler's Germany: A Documentary History of Life in the Third Reich* (Lexington, Massachusetts: D. C. Heath and Company, 1992), 146.

8 Office of the US Chief Counsel for the Prosecution of Axis Criminality, Nazi Conspiracy and Aggression (Washington, DC: US Government Printing Office, 1946), vol. 5, doc. no. 1964-PS, 673–76.

9 Diemut Majer, *Non-Germans under the Third Reich*, trans. Peter Thomas Hill, Edward Vance Humphrey and Brian Levin (Baltimore and London: Johns Hopkins University Press, 2003), 22.

10 Benz, *A Concise History of the Third Reich*, 115–16.

11 Office of the US Chief Counsel for the Prosecution of Axis Criminality, Nazi Conspiracy and Aggression (Washington, DC: US Government Printing Office, 1946), vol. 5, doc. no. 1964-PS, 673–76.

12 Geoffrey P. Megargee, *Encyclopedia of Camps and Ghettos* (Bloomington and Indianapolis: Indiana University Press, 2009), 1:15.

13 Majer, *Non-Germans under the Third Reich*, 25–27.

14 Majer, *Non-Germans under the Third Reich*, 4–7.

15 Sax and Kuntz, *Inside Hitler's Germany*, 170–71.

16 Hitler, *Mein Kampf*, 449–50.

17 Office of the United States Chief Counsel for the Prosecution of Axis Criminality, Nazi Conspiracy and Aggression (Washington, DC: US Government Printing Office, 1946), vol. 4, doc. no. 1809-PS, 411–14.

18 Franz Neumann, *The Structure and Practice of National Socialism, 1933–1944* (Chicago: Ivan R. Dee: 2009, orig. 1944), 84–85.

19 Neumann, *The Structure and Practice of National Socialism*, 84.

20 Majer, *Non-Germans under the Third Reich*, 12–16.

21 Alan Bullock, *Hitler. A Study in Tyranny* (New York: Harper Perennial, 1971), 227.

22 Alan Bullock, *Hitler and Stalin. Parallel Lives* (New York: Alfred A. Knopf, 1991), 430.

23 Carl Schmitt, *Verfassungsrechtliche Aufsätze aus den Jahren 1924–54* (1958), in Sax and Kuntz, *Inside Hitler's Germany*, Dieter Kuntz, trans., 161–62.

24 Neumann, *The Structure and Practice of National Socialism*, x.

25 Ian Kershaw, *Hitler, the Germans, and the Final Solution* (New Haven and London: Yale University Press, 2008), 38.

26 Joseph W. Bendersky, *A Concise History of Nazi Germany* (Lanham and Plymouth: Rowman and Littlefield, 2007), 105.

27 Otto Dietrich, *Hitler*, trans. Richard and Clara Winston (Chicago: Regnery Gateway, 1955), 112–19.

28 Norman Rich, *Hitler's War Aims: Ideology, the Nazi State, and the Course of Expansion* (New York and London: W. W. Norton and Co., 1973), xiii.

29 Rich, *Hitler's War Aims*, 11–13.

30 Karl Dietrich Bracher, *The German Dictatorship. The Origins, Structure, and Effects of National Socialism* (New York: Holt, Rinehart and Winston, 1970).

31 Eberhard Jäckel, *Hitler in History* (Hanover, New Hampshire: University Press of New England, 1984), 28–30.

32 Klaus Hildebrand, "Nationalsozialismus oder Hitlerismus?" in *Persönlichkeit und Struktur in der Geschichte*, ed. Michael Bosch (Düsseldorf: Europäische Verlagsanstalt, 1977), 56–57.

33 Martin Broszat, *The Hitler State* (London: Longman, 1981). K. Hildebrand, *The Third Reich* (London: George Aller & Unwin, 1984), 112.

34 See Ian Kershaw's analysis of Mommsen's position in his *The Nazi Dictatorship. Problems and Perspectives of Interpretation* (London: Edward Arnold, 1985), 66.

35 Hans Mommsen, "National Socialism. Continuity and Change," in *Fascism, A Readers Guide*, ed. Walter Laqueur (Berkeley: University of California Press, 1976), 196.

36 Kershaw, *Hitler, the Germans, and the Final Solution*, 38.

37 Kershaw, *Hitler, the Germans, and the Final Solution*, 40

38 Kershaw, *Hitler, the Germans, and the Final Solution*, 41–42.

7

THE THOUSAND YEAR REICH'S OVER ONE THOUSAND ANTI-JEWISH LAWS

Michael J. Bazyler

The German authorities knew that some Jews, desperate for survival, were attempting to escape deportation and death by posing as Christians. To put a stop to this practice, squads of SS troopers converged on churches throughout that sick nation. One such group entered a Berlin Evangelical Church while the services were in progress. "I want to make an announcement to your congregation," said the squad leader. The minister could only shrug helplessly. "Fellow Germans," began the Nazi, "I am here in the interests of racial purity. We have tolerated the inferior race for far too long, and now the time has come when we must spew them out from our midst." The Nazi glared at the congregation. "All those whose mothers and fathers were both Jews are ordered to line up outside this church—at once!" A pitiful few rose from their seats and were hustled outside. "And now, all those whose fathers were Jews are to get outside!" A few more white-faced people rose and left. "Finally, all those whose mothers were Jewish, get out!" The minister took a figurine of Jesus Christ from its niche near the pulpit. "Allow me the honor, dear Lord, of escorting you to the door!"[1]

One of the most important and least considered aspects of the Holocaust is law. The Nazis were fastidious about following legal requirements, and for this reason the law played an important role in the measures taken which led to the death of the six million Jews of Europe.

Long before Adolf Hitler came to power in January 1933, Germany had a widely admired legal system. The two major documents creating modern civil law, and which thereafter became leading influences for legal systems worldwide, were the 1804 French Napoleonic Civil Code and the 1898 German *Bürgerliches Gesetzbuch* (BgB) Civil Code, which came into being on 1 January 1900. The BgB has been widely emulated by legal drafters in other countries, and its structure serves as a template for all modern legislation. German legal philosophy likewise was well known, respected, and emulated worldwide for many years before the Nazi era; the innumerable and still-ongoing debates to define the term "law" have their roots in ideas first formulated by German legal philosophers in the nineteenth century. Many American legal theorists looked to German jurisprudence as a source of inspiration for their writings. In pre-Nazi Germany, lawyers played an important role, judges were independent, and a law-based state existed that was not too dissimilar to the United States. A significant percentage of German lawyers, judges, and law professors were also Jews.

The jurisprudential doctrine in favor in the west during the first part of the twentieth century was legal positivism, the theory that legal rules are valid only because they are enacted by an existing political authority and then accepted as binding by the citizenry. Morality and natural law are not proper sources of law-making in a positivist-based state. The German society's allegiance to the necessity of written laws was recognized by the Nazis when they came to power, and the recognition that policies had to appear to be law-based persisted throughout the peacetime years of Nazi rule. In 1938, when the number-two Nazi Hermann Göring suggested in the course of a discussion that German travelers could always kick Jewish passengers out of a crowded compartment on a train, the Propaganda Minister Josef Goebbels replied: "I would not say that. I do not believe in this. There has to be a law."[2]

The anti-Jewish legislation enacted by the Nazis defined Jews by genealogy rather than religion, using the bogus concept of a Jewish "race." In Nazi Germany, a person did not have to practice Judaism in order to be a Jew; lifelong Christians could be Jews, be forced to wear the yellow star, and be transported to the "East." Of course, practitioners of Judaism were the primary victims, but due to race-based classification, the number of persons cast as Jews increased exponentially and included those who were not classified as Jews before or after the Third Reich. The number of those victims is unclear. It is estimated that in 1933, the Jewish population of Germany was about 600,000, or 1 percent. This included both those who practiced Judaism and those whose parents were half-Jewish. The racial classifications enacted by the Nazis expanded that number by several hundred thousand (by some Nazi estimates to several million).

Among the Nazis' first targets were the 5,000 Jews working for the government, 0.5 percent of the total government personnel. The first major anti-Jewish law, pre-dating the infamous Nuremberg Laws that came 2 years later, was the "Law for the Re-establishment of the Professional Civil Service," enacted on 7 April 1933. Like much antisemitic legislation, this law carried an innocuous title; by its force, however, it intended to expel from government service Jewish civil servants and those individuals "whose previous political activities afford no assurance that they [would] at all times give their fullest support to the national State," that is, communists and socialists.[3] In a gesture to the aged president of Germany, World War I hero Field Marshal Paul von Hindenburg, the law exempted Jewish World War I veterans from expulsion. This exemption did not last long, as the Jewish veterans were also soon banished from their government jobs.

Between the civil service law of April 1933 and the September 1935 Nuremberg Laws, the Nazis passed all sorts of anti-Jewish legislation, some major and some minor, but all meant to make life extremely difficult for Jews living in Nazi Germany. These included: a 19 April 1933 decree entered by the State of Baden, prohibiting the use of the Jewish language (Yiddish) in cattle markets; a 13 May 1933 decree issued by the State of Prussia decreeing that Jews may only change their names to other Jewish names; a 27 November 1933 decree issued by the Reich Interior Ministry forbidding the listing of Jewish holidays on office calendars; and a 5 May 1934 decree issued by the Reich Propaganda Ministry forbidding the appearance on stage of Jewish actors.

From 11 to 15 September 1935, the Nazis held their annual party congress at Nuremberg. It is believed that the Nuremberg Laws were drafted on the last two days of the congress, even though much preliminary work had been accomplished before that.[4] The 15 September 1935 "Reich Citizenship Law" reduced the status of (but did not deprive) German Jews of citizenship. Instead, it created a new, superordinate category of Reich citizenship for persons of German or "kindred" blood. As a result, those whom the Nazis considered to be non-German were now deprived of the few remaining (if any) civil rights possessed by citizens.

Jews were now subjects of the German state, with limited rights, and subject to an often bewildering barrage of national, state, and local laws, executive orders, decrees, and ordinances directed at them. The "Law for the Protection of German Blood and German Honor" prohibited marriage and extramarital sexual relations between Jews and citizens of German or "kindred" blood. Jews were also forbidden to employ in their households German women younger than 45 years of age, and were forbidden to fly the national flag.

Since the Nazis classified Jews on the basis of race, not religion, they were forced to develop an entire set of legal rules to determine who would be classified as a person of "Jewish blood" and a person of "German blood." The practical problem was the hundreds of thousands of Germans who had some Jewish heritage, but who were baptized as either Catholic or Protestant, or who did not consider themselves to be Jews by religion and did not belong to any Jewish community or congregation. These individuals were labeled *Mischlinge*, a German word for half-breed or mixed-cast. Not all persons labeled as *Mischlinge* fell under the scrutiny of the anti-Jewish legislation. *Mischlinge* who could keep themselves out of the Jewish category, under the laws' definition, were able to retain all the rights and privileges of Reich citizenship. Considering the broad scope of the definition, however, many who never considered themselves Jewish were faced with the repercussions of the lethal label.[5]

Since specific definitions were now required, supplementary decrees were published. The first supplementary decree to the Reich Citizenship Law, published on 14 November 1935, defined as Jewish (1) all persons who had at least three full Jewish grandparents, or (2) who had two Jewish grandparents and were married to a Jewish spouse, or (3) who belonged to the Jewish religion at the time of the Law's publication, or who entered into such commitments at a later date. From 14 November on, therefore, the civil rights of these legally defined Jews were cancelled, their voting rights abolished, and Jewish civil servants who had kept their position owing to their veteran status were now forced into retirement.

A 26 November 1935 supplementary decree to the Law for the Protection of German Blood specified the various categories of forbidden marriages, but in so many ways added an absurd degree of legal complexity to the issue, confounding a number of local officials charged with preparing marriage licenses. Marriage was now forbidden between a Jew and *Mischling* with one Jewish grandparent (*Mischling* of the second degree); between a *Mischling* and another, each with one Jewish grandparent; and between a *Mischling* with two Jewish grandparents and a German, the last one subject to waiver by special exception from the Interior Minister. *Mischlinge* of the first degree (two Jewish grandparents), therefore, could marry Jews, and thereby become Jews, or marry one another. *Mischlinge* of the second degree (one Jewish grandparent) had even more severe legal restrictions: they could not marry a Jew, and could not marry each other.

A 21 December 1935 supplemental decree ordered the dismissal of Jewish professors, teachers, physicians, lawyers, and notaries who were state employees and earlier had been granted exemption. What this meant was that one's religion did not matter, nor the religion of one's parents. The critical fact determining who was to be considered a Jew was the religion of one's grandparents.

The Nazis, either for personal gain or convenience, would make exceptions to these legal categories. The most notorious case was that of Gerhard Milch, the State Secretary of the Aviation Ministry. A *Mischling* of the second degree, he was turned into a person of German blood by the Nazis. When a Bavarian priest, Father Wolpert, stated to his children in religion class that General Milch was of Jewish origin, charges were brought against him. Another exception was made for cancer researcher and Nobel laureate Otto Warburg. He was a *Mischling* of the first degree, but was transformed into a *Mischling* of the second degree on Hermann Göring's orders. Many non-Jewish Germans also succeeded in hiding their partial Jewish background; those not so lucky had the full force of the anti-Jewish legislation thrust upon them.[6]

The 14 November 1935 supplementary decree also forbade sexual relations between Germans and persons of "alien blood." Days after the issuance of this decree, a circular from the Reich Ministry of the Interior clarified the ambiguity: alien blood referred to "Gypsies, Negroes, and their bastards."[7] As Saul Friedländer, in volume one of his landmark study, *Nazi Germany and the Jews*, explains:

> Proof that one was not of Jewish origin or did not belong to any "less valuable" group became essential for normal existence in the Third Reich. And the requirements were especially stringent for anyone aspiring to join or to remain in a State or Party agency. Even the higher strata of the civil service, the party, and the army could not escape racial investigation. The personal file of General Alfred Jodl [who would later become one of the defendants at the Nuremberg trial of major war criminals] contains a detailed family tree in Jodl's handwriting, which, in 1936, proved his impeccable Aryan descent as flit back as the mid-18th century.[8]

A major legal hurdle encountered by experts attempting to interpret the Nuremberg Laws was the definition of "intercourse." Litigation on this question even came before the Supreme Court of Germany. In a December 1935 decision, the Supreme Court held:

> The term "sexual intercourse" as meant by the Law for the Protection of German Blood does not include every obscene act, but it is also not limited to "coitus." It includes all forms of natural and unnatural sexual intercourse, that is, coitus as well as those sexual activities of those persons of the opposite sex which are designed, in the matter in which they are performed, to serve in place of coitus to satisfy the sex drive of at least one of the partners.[9]

On 13 March 1942, the Special Court for the District of the Court of Appeals in Nuremberg issued a decision in a criminal case brought against defendants Katzenberger and Seiler. Leo Katzenberger was an elderly Jewish widower who had befriended Irene Seiler, a German woman 37 years his junior, who lived in Katzenberger's apartment building. The three-judge court handed down a death sentence for Katzenberger (he was beheaded), and a sentence of 2 years of hard labor and an additional 2 years of loss of civil liberties for Seiler. Seiler's offense was committing perjury while being questioned by the police in the course of their investigation into whether Katzenberger had committed "race defilement" or *Rassenschande*.[10]

This is how the Court justified the classification of their contact as "sexual intercourse," even though the two defendants maintained that their acts amounted to no more than a case of fatherly friendliness towards a younger neighbor:

> In view of the behavior of the defendants towards each other, as repeatedly described, the court has become convinced that the relations between Seiler and

Katzenberger which extended over a period of years, were of purely sexual nature. This is the only possible explanation of the intimacy of their acquaintance. As there were a large number of circumstances favoring seduction, no doubt is possible that the defendant Katzenberger maintained continuous sexual intercourse with Seiler. The Court considers as untrue Katzenberger's statement to the contrary that Seiler did not interest him sexually, and that the statements made by the defendant Seiler in support of Katzenberger's defense the Court considers incompatible with all practical experience. They were obviously made with the purpose of saving Katzenberger from his punishment.

The Court explained its rationale for imposing the death sentence upon the 70-year-old Katzenberger:

The political form of life of the German people under National Socialism is based upon the community. One fundamental factor of the life of the National Community is the racial problem. If a Jew commits racial pollution with a German woman, this amounts to polluting the German race and, by polluting a German woman, to a grave attack on the purity of German blood. The need for protection is particularly strong. Katzenberger practiced pollution for years. He was well acquainted with the point of view taken by patriotic German men and women as regards racial problems, and he knew that by his conduct the patriotic feelings of the German people were slapped in the face. Neither the National Socialist Revolution of 1933, nor the passing of the Law for the Protection of German Blood in 1935, neither the action against the Jews in 1938 [referring to *Kristallnacht*, the Jewish pogrom in November of that year], nor the outbreak of war in 1939 made him abandon this activity of his.[11]

The opinion issued by the Court mirrors the structure of opinions regularly issued by judges in western liberal democracies: a detailed recitation of facts, the statement of applicable law, and then a dutiful application of the law to the facts, with statutory analysis to fill in any gaps. The German judges appear to be doing what judges presiding over criminal cases in the United States and other modern democracies do every day. Yet the laws that the judges were applying and interpreting were obscene. This did not stop them, however, from doing their job. Only the last portion of the Katzenberger opinion quoted above reveals that the three judges were ardent believers in such laws.

David Fraser, in his study, *Law after Auschwitz: Towards a Jurisprudence of the Holocaust*, correctly describes the Holocaust as "the culmination of the acts of ordinary people in the ordinary course of events within ordinary governmental and legal structures ... Throughout the Nazi period, German lawyers continued to act as lawyers ... judges judged, even while Auschwitz spewed its smoke and ash ... Law continued while six million died."[12] Bernhard Lössner, the expert on Jewish affairs in the German Interior Ministry, saw himself as a good lawyer who conscientiously both drafted and applied laws having to do with his job of legally persecuting Jews.

German historian Ingo Müller, in his landmark study *Hitler's Justice: The Courts of the Third Reich*,[13] explains in detail how German jurists eagerly began, using his phrase, to "coordinate" themselves into the new reality created by the Nazis, and even to profit from it. The scope of the new reality took place not only inside the courtroom. In the academy, young up-and-coming non-tenured law professors at German law schools eagerly took up the spots of their senior mentors who had been expelled from their posts because of their Jewish origins. These younger professors were quickly granted tenure to replace the shortage created by the expulsion. Ironically, these professors reached their scholarly heights after the war, and so became the most influential post-war German law teachers and scholars, teaching the new generations of German youth into the 1970s.

In the aftermath of the March 1938 incorporation of Austria into the German Reich, the anti-Jewish legislation became applicable to the former Austrian Republic, and with conquest of other countries, Jews living in those portions annexed into the Reich were likewise subject to anti-Jewish legislation. In conquered territories not annexed to the Reich, German officials enacted numerous decrees applicable to the *fremdvölkvische* (literally "foreign people"), legal and pseudo-legal measures with specific characteristics based on the classification of each person as being a Jew, Gypsy, Slav, or belonging to another group considered to be non-German and therefore racially inferior.[14]

Resistance from the bench and bar did occur to some degree. Hubert Schorn, a retired judge, wrote a book after the war listing accounts of resistance by judges. Schorn asserted that "the overwhelming majority" of judges had opposed the Nazi system, and that a judge had "no alternative but to apply the unjust laws, and risked his own life if he objected."[15] That the Nazis created their own party court, the *Volksgerichtshof* (or People's Court) in 1934 to prosecute political offenses, circumventing existing constitutional law, also suggests that portions of the legal establishment were not necessarily as ideological as the Nazis wanted.

Fritz Hartunger, a justice of the Supreme Court in West Germany, who had worked for the courts during the Nazi era, also claimed in a study that if the judges had made any other decisions, they would have risked their lives. Müller, in his study, doubts the accuracy of these statements, but does point out that two prominent judges were executed by the Nazis. Both were murdered by the Nazis in early 1945 for their participation in a plot against Hitler; therefore these individuals were persecuted not for their conduct on the bench, but rather for their political activities. In the waning years of the war, as the tide turned against Nazi Germany, these two judges joined the underground German resistance movement, even secretly assisting the few remaining Jews in Germany.

There is only one documented case of resistance by a judge in the course of carrying out his professional duties. Dr Lothar Kreyssig, a family law judge in Brandenburg, appointed in 1928, began complaining about the Nazis in 1934. Kreyssig began receiving complaints from his superiors, beginning in 1936, yet he continued to express his displeasure with the acts being committed by the Nazis. An inquiry with the aim of removing him from the bench began in 1937, when he referred to Nazi policies as "injustice – masquerading in the form of law." A criminal investigation was also opened against him in 1938 for some of the statements he made during church services.

Kreyssig was not fired or imprisoned, however, only reassigned to another court, where he continued to issue rulings to ameliorate the harshness of Nazi legal decrees. In one such move, Judge Kreyssig issued injunctions to several hospitals in his capacity as a judge of the Court of Guardianship, prohibiting the hospitals from transferring mental patients to authorities of the Nazi T4 program, in which tens of thousands of physically and mentally persons with disabilities were murdered between 1940 and 1941. When Judge Kreyssig learned that Phillipp Bouhler, head of Hitler's private chancellery, was responsible for the euthanasia program, he filed criminal charges before the public prosecutor in Potsdam against Bouhler. The tenacious judge was then summoned before the Minister of Justice, Franz Gürtner, who tried to persuade him that the program was lawful because it had come from an "order of the Führer." Gürtner also indicated that if Judge Kreyssig "did not recognize the will of the Führer as the [force] of law," then he could no longer serve as a judge.[16] Soon thereafter, Judge Kreyssig wrote to Gürtner requesting early retirement, since his conscience would not allow him to withdraw the objections against the hospital. He was allowed to retire at the end of 1940, and was given full pension rights. In April 1942, a month after his early retirement was finally confirmed, the criminal investigation against him was dropped. "[F]rom then on[,] the Third Reich left the courageous judge in peace."[17]

Such cases of judicial resistance were few and far between, as the heralded German judiciary "became a smoothly functioning part of the National Socialist's system of intimidation; today they prefer to say they became 'enmeshed' or 'entangled' … "[18] Martin Hirsch, a retired judge of the post-war West German Federal Constitutional Court, has estimated that the courts during the Nazi era handed down between 40,000 and 50,000 death sentences, not counting the multitude of verdicts in the summary proceedings of the military and the police tribunals that took place in both Nazi Germany and its conquered territories. As put by Müller: "The jurists of the Third Reich had no peers anywhere in the world."[19] The Thousand Year Reich may have lasted only 12 years, but its over 1,000 anti-Jewish laws, and the legal actors drafting and enforcing those laws, were instrumental in the death and destruction of the Jews of Europe.

Notes

1 William Novak and Moshe Waldoks, *The Big Book of Jewish Humor* (New York: HarperCollins, 1981), 193.
2 Raul Hilberg, *Perpetrators, Victims, Bystanders: The Jewish Catastrophe 1933–1945* (New York: HarperCollins, 1992), 71.
3 www1.yadvashem.org/about_holocaust/documents/part1/doc10.html.
4 Saul Friedländer, *Nazi Germany and the Jews: Volume One, The Years of Persecution, 1933–1939* (New York: HarperCollins, 1997).
5 For an autobiography of a German woman who had been a member of the Hitler Youth but then classified as a *Mischling* and stripped of her civil rights because she had one Jewish grandparent, see Ilse Koehn, *Mischling, Second Degree: My Childhood in Nazi Germany* (New York: Greenwillow Books, 1977).
6 For a discussion of German soldiers serving in the Nazi military, see the two books by Bryan Mark Rigg: *Hitler's Jewish Soldiers: The Untold Story of Nazi Racial Laws and Men of Jewish Descent in the German Military* (Lawrence, Kansas: University Press of Kansas, 2002); *Lives of Hitler's Jewish Soldiers: Untold Tales of Men of Jewish Descent Who Fought for the Third Reich* (Lawrence, Kansas: University Press of Kansas, 2009). Rigg estimates that several thousand Jews and over 100,000 others of Jewish descent fought for the Nazi regime between 1939 and 1945, many of them hiding their partial Jewish ancestry.
7 Friedländer, *Nazi Germany and the Jews*, 1: 153.
8 Friedländer, *Nazi Germany and the Jews*, 1: 153.
9 Quoted by Ingo Müller, *Hitler's Justice: The Courts of the Third Reich*, trans. Deborah Lucas Schneider (Cambridge, Massachusetts: Harvard University Press, 1991), 99–102. For other books on law in Germany during the Nazi era, see Michael Stolleis, *Law under the Swastika: Studies in Legal History in Nazi Germany* (Chicago: University of Chicago Press, 1998); H.W. Koch, *In the Name of the Volk: Political Justice in Hitler's Germany* (London: I.B. Tauris, 1997); Richard Lawrence Miller, *Nazi Justiz: Law of the Holocaust* (New York: Praeger, 1995).

10 For the full story of the Katzenberger and Seiler saga and the postwar trials by the German judges who presided over the original proceedings, see Christiane Kohl, *The Maiden and the Jew: The Story of a Fatal Friendship in Nazi Germany*, trans. John Barrett (Hanover, New Hampshire: Steerforth Press, 2004).

11 The Katzenberger case opinion is translated and reproduced in Volume III of the *Trials of War Criminals Before Nuremberg Military Tribunals Under Control Council Law No. 10*, conducted by the United States and other Allies after the trials of the International Military Tribunal (IMT) at Nuremberg. Oswald Rothaug, presiding over Katzenberger's criminal trial, was himself a defendant in so-called Justice Trial, the third of the 12 post-IMT trials held at Nuremberg by the Americans under Law No. 10. Rothaug was sentenced to life imprisonment in 1947 but released 9 years later. His trial at Nuremberg later formed the basis of a subplot in the 1961 film *Judgment at Nuremberg*, with Judy Garland playing the Seiler character.

12 David Fraser, *Law after Auschwitz: Towards a Jurisprudence of the Holocaust* (Durham, North Carolina: Carolina Academic Press, 2005), 36.

13 Müller, *Hitler's Justice*.

14 The best study on law in Nazi-occupied Europe is Diemut Majer, *"Non-Germans" Under the Third Reich: The Nazi Judicial and Administrative System in Germany and Occupied Eastern Europe, with Special Regard to Occupied Poland, 1939–1945*, trans. Peter Hill, Edward Humphrey and Brian Levin (Baltimore, Maryland: Johns Hopkins University Press, 2003). For an excellent study of French law's complicity in the Holocaust, see Richard H. Weisberg, *Vichy Law and the Holocaust in France* (New York: Routledge, 1998).

15 Müller, *Hitler's Justice*, 21.

16 Müller, *Hitler's Justice*, 195.

17 Müller, *Hitler's Justice*, 195. For a German-language biography of Kreyssig, see Konrad Weiss, *Lothar Kreyssig: Prophet der Versöhnung [Lothar Kreyssig: Prophet of Reconciliation]* (Gerlingen, Germany: Bleicher Verlag, 1998). After the war, Kreyssig, who lived in East Germany and became President of the German Evangelical Church's National Synod, founded *Aktion Suehnezeichen* (Action through Reconciliation), dedicated to reconciliation and atonement by sending young Germans to work in Israel, the Soviet Union, and Poland with surviving victims of Nazism. See "Israel: The Penance Corps," *Time*, 23 November 1962. He died in 1986, aged 87.

18 Müller, *Hitler's Justice*, 196. See also Michael Burleigh, *The Third Reich: A New History* (New York: Hill and Wang, 2001), 398–99, for a further discussion of Judge Kreyssig's resistance from the bench.

19 Müller, *Hitler's Justice*, 196.

8

PERSECUTION AND GENDER

German-Jewish responses to Nazism, 1933–39

Marion Kaplan

Germany's Jews had enjoyed over 60 years of emancipation by the time the Nazis came to power in January 1933. They had achieved educational, economic, cultural, and political successes, even if antisemitism still limited their careers in the army, civil service, and professoriate until 1918. Socially, too, they experienced a level of integration in community, organizational, and public life never before imagined. Although the multiple economic and political crises of the Weimar era raised anxieties about an increase in political and economic instability with a concomitant rise in antisemitism, most Jews felt part of German society.

Starting in 1933, however, Germany's Jewish community, of about 525,000 Jews (by faith), or under one percent of the total population, faced frightening, bewildering, and unprecedented state harassment, discrimination, and violence. In addition, the Nazis persecuted another 35,000 "mixed" marriages (by "race") and as many as 300,000 *Mischlinge* ("mixed breeds") or offspring of these marriages.[1] This chapter touches on the Nazi regime's persecution of Jews, as well as how most Germans transformed their "neighbors into Jews."[2] But it focuses on Jewish reactions and, in particular, on the gendered nature of these reactions. Memoirs, diaries, and letters help us reconstruct the grassroots experiences of Jews from the perspective of daily life, underlining the confusion and the gradual nature of changes that appear clear and catastrophic only from hindsight.

German Jews, mostly urban, middle class business people, confronted a growing menace bewilderingly embedded in life as they had known it. As government polemics reached crescendos of antisemitism, those Jews whose business or career could be maintained, albeit at reduced levels of activity, felt less urgency to leave their homeland than those (usually young people) whose education and career prospects looked bleak. Until the violent pogrom of November 1938, German Jews suffered the agonizing double-bind of preserving the sanity and normality of their lives while assessing the mounting danger around them, helpless to stop it. Their dilemma was magnified by their ties to Germany—their friends, culture, and identity—and by Nazi policy, which vacillated enough to keep its victims off guard.[3] Indeed, contradictory government pronouncements, the economic depression, regional variations, lack of coordination, and the attempt to appear moderate to other nations gave most contemporaries profoundly mixed signals.

But the Nazis clarified one point even before 1933: they conflated Jewish men with "Jews." The vast majority of antisemitic caricatures as well as propaganda attacked

Jewish men.[4] Nazi newspapers and newsreels depicted "the Jew" as a male with hideous facial features and a distorted body, as a rapacious capitalist or communist, a rapist of pure Aryan women, and a dangerous "race defiler." Occasionally Nazi propaganda highlighted an obese Jewish woman bedecked in jewelry and her grotesque children. But (until the beginning of deportations in late 1941) the Nazis focused on males, attacking Jewish men both physically and economically, demolishing their careers and businesses, and leaving women to maintain their households and communities. Still, the Nazis ultimately saw Jewish women as procreators, hence enemies in their "race war," and Jewish children as the racial enemies of the future. Thus racism and sexism were intertwined in the minds of the torturers.

Legal and economic attacks on Jews and Jewish organizational responses

In April 1933, the "Law for the Restoration of the Professional Civil Service" excluded opponents of the regime and "non-Aryans." The decree's "Aryan Paragraph" defined the latter as people who had one "non-Aryan" grandparent. This included people who had been raised as Christians. This, and further exclusionary decrees that month, affected Jewish men in great numbers, but hurt Jewish women disproportionately because the two exemptions, having held their job before August 1914 and having served in World War I, applied to very few women. Most universities had allowed women entry only in 1908, so they could hardly be employed by 1914, and they had not fought in the war. The April laws forced the dismissal of about half of Jewish judges and prosecutors and almost a third of Jewish lawyers. A significant proportion of Jewish doctors lost their German National Health Insurance affiliation (severely limiting or ruining their practices). Since the civil service in Germany encompassed a vast number of jobs, the April laws meant that teachers, professors, postal officials, and clerks, and even train or Reichsbank employees, had to be "Aryans." Further decrees put quotas on Jews in schools and universities. These discriminatory acts affected over 850,000 people: Jews, political opponents, and other "non-Aryan" Christian Germans (such as Sinti, Roma, Jewish, and Afro-Germans who were baptized Christians).[5] Joseph Goebbels' takeover of the Chamber of Culture in September 1933 further excluded Jews from German cultural life, film, theater, music, fine arts, literature, and journalism—areas in which Jews had been disproportionately active.

Boycotts of Jewish businesses and professionals led to further economic decline. On 1 April 1933, the government declared a national boycott, attempting to expose German Jews to public opprobrium and to destroy Jewish businesses. The boycott met with mixed reception and the regime canceled it after one day, but it frightened Jews, and continued unofficially and sporadically throughout the 1930s until the Nazis completely "aryanized," or confiscated, Jewish businesses. Simultaneously, many private businesses and state licensing boards demanded that their employees be "Aryans." Unemployment began to plague the Jewish community. Already by spring 1933, nearly one-third of Jewish clerks sought jobs.[6] Also, about three-quarters of Jewish women in business and trade were affected by the discriminatory laws and the early anti-Jewish boycotts.[7] About one-third of Jews in Germany received some form of public assistance by 1935, and by 1938 over 60 percent of all Jewish businesses no longer existed.

Jewish organizations responded to these attacks. The Central Organization of German Jews (*Reichsvertretung der deutschen Juden*), founded in 1933 and encompassing most major Jewish organizations and communities, supported Jewish schools, helped needy Jews, and prepared people for emigration. The Jewish Cultural Association (*Jüdischer Kulturbund*), also organized in 1933, hired over 1,300 men and 700 women artists, musicians, and actors fired from German institutions, and grew to about 70,000 members.[8] It provided cultural events throughout Germany until 1941. The League of Jewish Women (*Jüdischer Frauenbund*), founded in 1904, expanded its aid to housewives, established day-care centers, participated in the Jewish Winter Relief collections (once the Nazis refused to provide needy Jews with German Winter Relief), and attended to the physical and emotional needs of women.[9] Still, Jewish organizations' enormous efforts could not withstand new governmental onslaughts and increasing social ostracism.

In September 1935, the Nuremberg Laws deprived Jews of their rights as citizens and established racial segregation. Most infamously, the laws created a pseudoscientific classification system that labeled people according to the amount of their "Jewish blood," creating categories of "full Jew" and "first-degree" and "second-degree *Mischlinge*." The laws forbade intermarriages as well as sexual intercourse between "Aryans" and "non-Aryans," with "race defilement" viewed as seriously as high treason.[10] In effect, the Nazis created two categories, "*Mischlinge*" and Jews, with the former spared the expropriation, ghettoization, and destruction later reserved only for Jews. This decree also had a chilling effect on any relationship between males and females of opposite "races." These relationships, as well as general friendships and neighborly exchanges, had already suffered increasingly since 1933.

Social ostracism, social death, and mixed signals

One of the first signs of a "new era" had been the disassociation of former friends. Memoirs are replete with personal disappointments.[11] One woman reported that she had stopped attending a monthly café circle in the city of Dortmund, not wanting to embarrass her non-Jewish friends. One day she met one of the women, who assured her they would all welcome her. However, when she arrived at the café, she found no-one. But, "I couldn't blame them. Why should they have risked the loss of their jobs only to prove to me that Jews could still have friends in Germany?" Moreover, she understood the processes at work: "With each day of the Nazi regime, the abyss between us and our fellow citizens grew larger. Friends whom we had loved for years did not know us anymore."[12] Organizations, too, swiftly expelled Jewish members and friends even before they were forced to do so. Philosopher Hannah Arendt concluded: "Our friends nazified themselves!"[13] As Germans increasingly treated *each other* with reserve and suspicion, many broke emphatically with Jews.[14]

Neighbors turned away most abruptly in small towns and villages, where about 17 percent of the Jewish population lived. In one town, a Jewish woman and her non-Jewish neighbor had spent the previous 20 years gardening in their adjoining plots, chatting as they worked. As a result of Germany's new mood, they no longer spoke. Classmates, too, broke with Jewish children or refused to sit next to them. Strangers also made life miserable for Jews. On trams, in stores and restaurants, and on the street they tested their knowledge of who "smelled" or "looked" Jewish and mortified their victims by pronouncing their suspicions loudly.[15] Since Jews were not as dark nor

"Aryans" as blond as the stereotypes portrayed, some Germans were quickly disabused of their arrogant certainty, as the "Jew" they had identified turned out to be another "Aryan."[16]

Mixed marriages suffered similar disapproval from neighbors, employers, and the state. Members of these families lost jobs, financial status, previous homes, and friends. But unlike Jewish couples, mixed marriages were intimately connected to "Aryans." Some faced cold rejection by "Aryan" relatives who had previously either welcomed or, at least, tolerated the Jewish partner, or by relatives who had always opposed the Jewish partner and now, arguing that the individuals had brought bad times "upon themselves," ostracized them. In contrast, some "Aryan" relatives proved loyal and courageous, helping their Jewish relatives, including saving their lives.

Social ostracism could and did lead to what Orlando Patterson has called "social death," a state of domination, excommunication from the "legitimate social or moral community," and a perpetual condition of dishonor.[17] In tracing the daily interactions of Jews with other Germans, we note the increasing numbers of "Jews not Wanted" signs, the gradual segregation of Jewish children from their classmates, and the growing power that Germans, from Nazi officials to strangers on a tram, had over Jews. Over 6 years, as more and more Germans brutally banished Jews from their ethnic community, the majority became inured to the suffering of the minority. Their racial war at home led many to stand by as the government and party transformed social death into actual murder.[18]

Importantly, not all Germans abandoned their Jewish friends. Acts of simple neighborly decency, as little as a "good morning" greeting, came as a great relief. They meant that there were still "good Germans." One woman wrote that every Jewish person "knew a decent German" and recalled that many Jews thought "the radical Nazi laws would never be carried out because they did not match the moderate character of the German people."[19] And it was often precisely an experience of loyalty, such as a former classmate who shook hands with a Jewish woman in a crowded store, that gave Jews mixed messages, letting some deceive themselves into staying on. In addition, random kindnesses, the most obvious "mixed signals," gave some Jews cause for hope. Moreover, the mixed messages affected individual lives unevenly: in 1933, a 10-year-old observed Nazis marching with placards reading "Germans, don't buy from Jews. World Jewry wants to destroy Germany ... "; but in 1935, Berlin's Chief of Police gave her father a medal for his World War I service. Finally, it is worth recalling that, like most other Germans, Jews did not understand that Hitler was an entirely new leader. Most Germans "saw in him ... a caricature of something old and known; they adjusted him to their own limited imagination."[20] This was certainly the case for German Jews. At worst, they expected a return to some form of earlier, pre-emancipation status. They did not (and could not) predict their end.

Gendered responses to persecution

Jewish women shared the predicament of Jewish men: economic decline, political disenfranchisement, concern for their children's futures, and increasing social ostracism. Jewish women also shared the reactions of Jewish men: disbelief, outrage, and fear. Still, their experiences and responses were gendered, based on their socialization and their economic and familial roles. The desire to emigrate presents a striking example. Wives usually saw the danger signals first and urged husbands to leave Germany. One woman's memoir noted that, in a discussion among friends about a doctor who had just fled in the spring of 1936, most of the men in the room condemned him:

"It takes more courage to leave," the ladies protested vigorously. "What good is it to stay and to wait for the slowly coming ruin? Is it not far better to go and to build up a new existence somewhere else in the world, before our strength is crippled by the everlasting strain on our nerves, on our souls? ... " Unanimously we women felt that way ... while the men, with more or less vehemence, [spoke] against him.[21]

The different attitudes of men and women seem to reflect a gender-specific reaction remarked upon by sociologists and psychologists: in dangerous situations, men tend to "stand their ground," whereas women avoid conflict, preferring flight as a strategy. A more important reason why men hesitated came from their role as breadwinners. Those still employed, or whose business limped along, could not imagine how they would support their family abroad, without the language, capital, or skills needed in countries of emigration. In addition, men's connection to their work and women's lack of ties to the public world of job or business made it easier for women to take their leave. Although their decision to flee was as fraught with practical consequences as their husband's, since they, too, would face uncertainty and poverty, women did not have to tear themselves away from their life work, whether a business or practice, whether patients, clients, or colleagues. In short, in light of men's primary identity with their work, they often felt trapped into staying. Women, whose identity was more family-oriented, struggled to preserve what was central to them by fleeing with it.

Men and women also interpreted daily events differently. Although less integrated than men into the economy and culture, women were more integrated into their community. They were accustomed to neighborly exchanges and courtesies, occasional visits to the school, attendance at concerts or local lectures, and participation in local women's organizations. Raised to be sensitive to interpersonal behavior and social situations, they registered the increasing hostility of their immediate surroundings and their children's schools, unmitigated by a promising business prospect, a deep feeling for German culture (as experienced by their more educated husbands), or the patriotism of husbands who had fought in World War I. In contrast, men mediated their experiences through newspapers and broadcasts. Carol Gilligan's psychological theories may apply here: men tended to view their situation in terms of abstract rights, women in terms of actual affiliations and relationships.[22]

Like Jewish couples, those in mixed marriages had to make the decision to stay or to go. This was an excruciating decision for couples in which both partners were Jewish. One can only imagine how much more difficult it was for mixed couples, who might have thought that the "Aryan" spouse, or their Christian faith, or their *Mischling* children would somehow serve to ameliorate Nazi wrath.[23] Moreover, unlike Jewish couples who saw relatives flee, mixed couples saw Jewish relatives flee while Christian relatives stayed.[24] But here, too, anecdotal evidence suggests that wives took notice first. For example, Verena Hellwig, an "Aryan," pressed her Jewish husband to leave and eventually preceded him with their children.[25] Summing up, Peter Wyden recalled these family debates:

It was not a bit unusual in these go-or-no-go family dilemmas for the women to display more energy and enterprise than the men. ... Almost no women had a business, a law office, or a medical practice to lose. They were less status-conscious, less money-oriented than the men. They seemed to be less rigid, less cautious, more confident of their ability to flourish on new turf ... [26]

Role reversals among Jewish women and men

Gender differences in perceiving danger do not mean that gender roles remained static. On the contrary, in what Raul Hilberg has described as communities of "men without power and women without support,"[27] we find, for the most part, anxious but highly energetic women who, early on, greatly *expanded* their traditional roles. As the family became more central to the practical and emotional needs of Jews, women took on the increased burdens of daily survival, from living in tighter quarters, to preparing *ersatz* foods, to providing sociability and diversion. Housewives and mothers strove to preserve a sense of "normalcy" in the midst of desperation, while learning to cope with less and to expect even worse. But they also accepted new responsibilities as partner, breadwinner, family protector, and defender of the business or practice, duties often strange to them, and which they recorded in memoirs with the apprehension they felt at the time.

Many Jewish women, who had never worked outside the home before, now searched for employment. Some did not have to look far. They worked for husbands who had to let paid help go. Jewish newspapers found "relatively few families in which the wife does not work in some way to earn a living," and noted that women were also sole supporters in many a family.[28] Statistics indicate that women eagerly trained for new careers and retrained where old careers no longer provided employment. Social workers saw women as "more versatile and adaptable," with "fewer inhibitions" than men. Women seemed willing to change their lives, entering retraining programs at older ages than men.[29] In Berlin, for example, Jewish employment services were more successful in placing women than in placing men.

Increasingly women found themselves representing or defending their men with the authorities, behaviors rarely before attempted by any middle-class German women. Some saved a male family member from the arbitrary demands of the state or from the Gestapo. In these cases, it was always assumed that the Nazis would not break gender norms: they might arrest or torture Jewish men, but would not harm women. Thus traditional gender norms afforded women greater freedom at first, and they regularly mediated between state and family. In one small town, a Jewish family sent two of its women to the city hall in order to ask that part of their house not be used as a meeting place for the Nazi party.[30] Other women interceded for family members with German emigration or finance officials. In some cases, they broke not only gender barriers but also normal standards of legality, reporting that Nazi officials had to be bribed.[31]

Some women took responsibility for the entire family's safety. Eva Wysbar, the Jewish wife of an "Aryan" film producer, traveled to six countries until she found a safe haven for her family.[32] Another woman went to England to negotiate her family's emigration with British officials and medical colleagues. Her daughter noted: "It was thanks to her pertinacity and determination that we were able to leave Germany as soon as we did, and it was always to be a great source of pride to her that it was she who obtained the permit allowing us to come to England."[33] Women also found themselves in threatening situations, in which their bravery benefitted from luck. Ruth Abraham regularly accompanied her father to the Gestapo for his weekly interrogation. When her uncle was arrested, she hurried from jail to jail until she found his location and appealed for his release.[34] Women's new roles may have increased familial stress in some cases, but in general both women and men appreciated the importance of women's new behavior.

Yet, even if women picked up and reacted to warning signals differently from men, and even if women expanded their former gender roles dramatically, we should be very clear that neither women nor men had actual control over the situation. First, the signals of Nazi intentions occurred in stages, and women, too, could be confused by policies and events. The writing was not clearly on the wall. That conclusion emerges largely with the advantages of hindsight. Alice Nauen and her friends "saw it was getting worse. But until 1939 nobody in our circles believed it would lead to an end" for German Jewry.[35] Then, women could not magically create safe havens for their families. We need to remember that *perceptions* of women or men were not the main factors effecting emigration. Even if all Jews had tried to escape in good time, the major obstacle to mass Jewish emigration lay in foreign governments bolting their doors against refugees.[36]

The November Pogrom

The Nazis increased their persecution of Jews in 1938 with the German annexation of Austria and the brutal public humiliation of Austrian Jews. Thereafter, German Jews had to report the value of all of their property and had to register and identify all "Jewish" commercial establishments (thus forced to make themselves targets for future vandalism). That summer, the Nazis destroyed three synagogues. In fall, after having won a major international victory, the Munich Agreement, in which Britain and France acquiesced in Germany's annexation of part of Czechoslovakia, the Nazis deported 17,000 Polish Jews to Poland, which refused them entry. As the deportees languished in the cold borderland, young Herschel Grynszpan, whose family was among them, was driven to despair. In Paris, he killed a German diplomat. The Nazis used this as an excuse to launch a brutal, nationwide attack on all of Germany's Jews.

Although the November Pogrom represented the intensification of the political disenfranchisement, economic strangulation, and social segregation that had begun in 1933, no-one expected the widespread violence—a pogrom of the sort Germans connected only with Czarist Russia. The public manifestations of Jewish life in Germany— synagogues, Jewish stores, institutions, and homes—stood covered with broken glass. The marauders, often easily recognized neighbors, also destroyed private homes, interior spaces. Thirty-two thousand Jewish men, arrested *en masse* for the first time as Jews, suffered torture in concentration camps. Jewish women faced the onerous job of freeing their men, repairing their homes, and helping their families flee for their lives.

One of the lasting images of the November Pogrom, or "Crystal Night," is that of "crystal," the broken glass scattered on the streets. A more mundane image, mentioned often in Jewish women's memoirs, is that of flying feathers—feathers covering the internal space of the home, hallway, front yard, or courtyard. Similarly to pogroms in Russia at the turn of the century, the marauders tore up feather blankets and pillows, shaking them into the rooms, out the windows, down the stairways. Broken glass in public and strewn feathers in private spelled the end of Jewish security in Germany.

The image of feathers flying is one of a domestic scene gravely disturbed. This was women's primary experience of the pogrom. The marauders beat and arrested men.[37] With some exceptions, most women were forced to stand by and watch. Then they turned to rescue. Prisoners' families learned that their men would be released only if they could present emigration papers. Women summoned the courage to overcome gender stereotypes of passivity, and to face unhelpful to hostile non-Jews in order to find any means to have their men freed. Charlotte Stein-Pick wrote of the November Pogrom:

> I ran to Christian acquaintances, friends, or colleagues, but everywhere people shrugged their shoulders, shook their heads and said 'no.' And everyone was glad when I left. I was treated like a leper, even by people who were positively inclined towards us.[38]

After the pogrom, Mally Dienemann raced to the Gestapo to prove that she and her 63-year-old husband, a rabbi who languished in Buchenwald, were ready to emigrate. Next, she rushed to the passport office to get their passports back.

> After I had been sent from one office to another the entire morning ... I had to go to ... the Emigration Office in Frankfurt, the Gestapo, the Police, the Finance Office, [send] a petition to Buchenwald, a petition to the Secret State Police in Darmstadt, and still it took until Tuesday of the third week, before my husband came ... Next came running around for the many papers ... for emigration. And while the Gestapo was in a rush, the Finance Office had so much time and so many requests, and without certification from the Finance and Tax offices one did not receive the so-called certificate of harmlessness, and without [that] one did not get a passport, and without a passport a tariff official could not inspect the baggage.[39]

Finally arriving in Palestine in March 1939, Rabbi Dienemann died from his ordeal.

Women who saw to their husbands' releases and papers also often sold the couple's businesses and property, and decided on emigration destinations. Accompanying her husband home after his ordeal in a camp, one wife explained that she had just sold their house and bought tickets to Shanghai for the family. Her husband reflected: "That was all right with me, just as long as we didn't have to stay any longer in a country where we were fair game for everyone."[40]

Once the Nazis began releasing some men, women organized emergency assistance near the concentration camps.[41] But not all Jewish men were that lucky: "On a daily basis one heard that the ashes of a dead person had been delivered to this or that family. These urns were sent C.O.D. (for which the post office took the sum of 3.75 marks)."[42] And those women and men faced remaining behind faced increasing brutality after the November Pogrom, when the Nazis began treating both sexes with shocking savagery, crowding them into "Jew houses," requiring forced labor from both sexes, restricting their food and heating fuel, forcing them to wear a yellow Star of David on their outerwear, tearing them away from their family, and, as of October 1941, loading them onto trains bound for destruction.

Who stayed behind

A gender analysis of the *desire* to emigrate highlights women's different expectations, priorities, and perceptions. It does not follow, however, that more women than men actually left. In fact, the opposite seems to be the case. Why was this so? There were still compelling reasons to stay, although life became increasingly difficult. First, women, especially young women, could still find jobs more easily than men in the Jewish sector of the German economy, especially in social welfare institutions.

While the employment situation of Jewish women helped keep them in Germany, that of men helped get them out, as some had business connections abroad facilitating their immediate flight. Other men emigrated alone in order to establish themselves and then send for their families. In addition, before the war, men faced more immediate, physical danger than women and fled promptly. In a strange twist of fortune, the men arrested during the November Pogrom were released from concentration camps only upon showing proof of their ability to depart from Germany immediately. Thus women sent men ahead, hoping to join them later.

Further, as sons left, daughters remained the sole caretakers of elderly parents. One female commentator noted that she knew of "a whole slew of young women who can't think of emigration because they don't know who might care for their elderly mother in the interim, before they could start sending her money. In the same families, the sons went their way ... ." As early as 1936, the League of Jewish Women expressed serious concern regarding the "special problem of the emigration of women which is often partly overlooked. ... ."[43] In January 1938, the Hilfsverein, one of the main emigration organizations, announced that "up to now, Jewish emigration ... indicates a severe surplus of men" and promised that women's emigration would become a priority.[44]

And fewer women went to Palestine. Between 1933 and 1936, more German Jews went to Palestine than anywhere else. Some men had the wherewithal to purchase a £1,000 "capitalist visa" needed to enter Palestine; and the main youth emigration organization, Youth Aliyah, preferred men to women, accepting about 60 percent males and 40 percent females.[45] Moreover, young women hesitated to go to Palestine, and faced gender role discrimination when they arrived there. Articles appearing on Palestine, often written by committed Zionists, must have given pause. In one piece, the (male) author described a situation in which eight girls took care of 55 young men. Besides cooking, they washed "mountains" of laundry, darned hundreds of socks, sewed ripped clothing, and worked long days. Additionally, numerous news items about Arab–Jewish discord left most young women looking elsewhere. One survey of graduating classes from several Jewish schools in late 1935 showed that 47 percent of the boys and only 30 percent of the girls considered Palestine a possible destination.[46]

The growing disproportion of Jewish women in the German-Jewish population also resulted from the fact that, even in 1933, there were more Jewish women than men in Germany. In order for the numbers to stay even, a greater absolute number of women would have had to emigrate. The slow rate of female emigration meant that the female proportion of the Jewish population rose from 52.3 percent in 1933 to 57.5 percent by 1939. Looking around in 1939, one woman wrote: "Mostly we were women who had been left to ourselves. In part, our husbands had died from shock [or] ... in a concentration camp and partly some wives who, aware of the greater danger to their husbands, had prevailed upon them to leave at once and alone. They were ready to ... follow their husbands ... but ... it became impossible ... and quite a few ... became martyrs of Hitler."[47] The combination of gender and age was lethal. In 1941, two-thirds of the Jewish population was past middle age. Thus women, and elderly women in particular, unwilling to become a burden on their children abroad or unable to maneuver through the Nazi bureaucracy, sent their young out first and were trapped. About 61,000 elderly people, including a disproportionate number of widows, remained in Nazi hands. When Elisabeth Freund, who took the last train out of Germany in 1941, went to the Gestapo for her emigration papers, she observed: "All old people, old women" waiting on line.[48]

Conclusion

Some historians have explained the behavior of the German population in the face of the persecution and genocide of the Jews as the result of a combination of authoritarian mentality and moral apathy, not so much an antisemitic bias. They have blamed the growing distance between Jews and non-Jews after 1933, both physically and socially, on German "ignorance and indifference" toward Jews.[49] On the other side is the argument that, generations before the Nazis, Germans, uniquely, adopted an "eliminationist anti-semitism" which craved the annihilation of Jews. The Nazis mobilized this violent hatred, permitting "ordinary Germans" to take pleasure in tormenting and, ultimately, exterminating Jews.[50]

Research on Jewish daily life challenges both sides. Through Jewish eyes, it shows that (with poignant exceptions, particularly those people who hid Jews), many Germans took an active, not passive, role in persecuting Jews, and that, throughout the Nazi era, German racism was widespread and deep. Still, "ordinary Germans" were *not* bent on killing Jews as much as ostracizing them. Their racism led them to hope that the Jews would simply "disappear,"[51] first economically and politically, then socially, and later, to avert their eyes when this process escalated hideously. This wish among Germans that Jews "disappear" was not the same as wishing for or condoning genocide. Nevertheless, it is valuable to examine the meaning of "disappearance" wishes for people on both sides of the racial or ethnic divide.[52] It is also crucial to analyze how endemic prejudice becomes epidemic, how bigotry turns into massacre.

Simply because so many Germans wished for the Jews to disappear does not mean that we can leap to the conclusion that genocide was inevitable in the 1930s. Unless one reads history backwards, the 1930s were ambiguous. They were frightening, even ominous, but gave no clear indication of the genocide to come. What the 1930s do show us is how intensely menacing racism is, how it demeaned the perpetrators as it devastated the victims, and how social death can lead to physical death.

Nazi persecution also shows us how its victims responded in gendered ways. Women's roles in the family and society affected both their approach to events in the 1930s and their options during the war. They reacted to the Nazi threat earlier than men, pushing for emigration. When the Nazis blocked Jewish men's economic survival, Jewish women took on employment. Jewish women also strained to rescue loved ones from the clutches of the Gestapo. They preserved shrinking family and friendship circles, which drew sustenance from each other. They also volunteered to aid the Jewish community. During and after the November Pogrom, Jewish women displayed extraordinary determination, facilitating the exodus of thousands. Yet, when emigration turned into a rout, more Jewish women were trapped. Some were too aged to leave; others had sent husbands ahead; still others hesitated to leave their parents or did not have the wealth or vocations required by countries of refuge.

Examining women's experiences raises the question, why, until recently, have historians looked primarily at men in studying the Holocaust? Today's research makes it clear that "[t]he end—namely, annihilation or death—does not describe or explain the process," that "along the stations toward extinction ... each gender lived its own journey."[53] I have emphasized the importance of gender not only because it helps us to tell a fuller and more nuanced story, but to give Jewish women a voice long denied them and to offer a perspective long denied us. Studying the differing ways in which women and men were treated and the frequently distinctive manner in which they reacted demonstrates how gender mattered, especially in extreme situations.

Notes

1 Interfaith marriages became legal in 1871.

2 Hazel Rosenstrauch, *Aus Nachbarn wurden Juden: Ausgrenzung und Selbstbehauptung, 1933–1942* (Berlin: Transit, 1988).

3 See Karl Schleunes, *The Twisted Road to Auschwitz: Nazi Policy toward German Jews, 1933–1939* (Illinois: University of Illinois Press, 1970); Herbert Strauss, "Jewish Autonomy within the Limits of National Socialist Policy: The Communities and the Reichsvertretung," in *The Jews in Nazi Germany*, ed. Arnold Paucker (Tübingen: J.C.B. Mohr, 1986), 126.

4 See Nazi papers such as *Der Stürmer* and *Der Völkische Beobachter*.

5 These figures are from June 1933, when some people had already fled. Günter Plum, "Wirtschaft und Erwerbsleben," in *Die Juden in Deutschland, 1933–1945*, ed. Wolfgang Benz (Munich: C.H. Beck, 1988), 282; Herbert Strauss, "Jewish Emigration from Germany, Part I," *Leo Baeck Institute Year Book*, vol. 25 (1980): 326. See also Avraham Barkai, "Der wirtschaftliche Existenzkampf der Juden im Dritten Reich, 1933–38," in *The Jews in Nazi Germany* (ed. Paucker), 155.

6 Erich Rosenthal, "Trends of the Jewish Population in Germany, 1910–39," *Jewish Social Studies*, vol. 6 (1944): 262; Wolf Gruner, "Die Reichshauptstadt und die Verfolgung der Berliner Juden 1933–45," in *Jüdische Geschichte in Berlin: Essays und Studien*, ed. Reinhard Rürup (Berlin: Hentrich, 1995), 232; Clemens Vollnhals, "Jüdische Selbsthilfe bis 1938," in *Die Juden in Deutschland* (ed. Benz), 377.

7 Women's jobs in *Blätter des jüdischen Frauenbundes (BJFB)*, Berlin, January 1934, 7; March 1935, 2; *Israelitisches Familienblatt (IF)*, 23 February 1933, 9; *Jüdische Wohlfahrtspflege und Sozial Politik (JWS)*, 1931, Heft 2, 77–78.

8 Ingrid Schmidt and Helmut Ruppel, "Eine Schwere Prüfung ist über Euch: Aspekte zur Geschichte des Jüdischen Kulturbunds," in *Geschlossene Vorstellung: Der Jüdische Kulturbund in Deutschland 1933–1941*, ed. Akademie der Künste (Berlin: Hentrich, 1992), 39.

9 Marion Kaplan, *The Jewish Feminist Movement in Germany: The Campaigns of the Jüdischer Frauenbund, 1904–1938* (Greenwood, Connecticut: Greenwood Press, 1979).

10 For a chart widely circulated to explain the marriage laws, see www.historyplace.com/worldwar2/timeline/nurem-laws.htm

11 Memoirs are among my most important sources. I used archives at the Leo Baeck Institute, NY (LBI); the Houghton Library, Harvard University (Harvard); and Yad Vashem in Israel. I also used interviews from the Research Foundation for Jewish Immigration, NY (Research Foundation).

12 Marta Appel, in *Jewish Life in Germany*, ed. Monika Richarz (Bloomington, Indiana: University of Indiana Press, 1991), 352–53.

13 Hannah Arendt, in Eike Geisel, *Die Banalität der Guten: Deutsche Seelenwanderungen* (Berlin: Edition Tiamat, 1992), 137.

14 Germans referred to "der deutsche Blick" (the German glance), looking over one's shoulder to see who was listening before commenting on the regime.

15 Marion Kaplan, *Between Dignity and Despair: Jewish Life in Nazi Germany* (New York: Oxford University Press, 1998), 34–35.

16 Kaplan, *Between Dignity and Despair*, 35–36.

17 Orlando Patterson, *Slavery and Social Death* (Cambridge, Massachusetts: Harvard University Press, 1982). He used social death to describe the slave condition. The condition of Jews in Nazi Germany illustrates many similarities (with important differences).

18 "Racial War at Home," chapter 10 in Claudia Koonz, *The Nazi Conscience* (Cambridge, Massachusetts: Harvard University Press, 2003).

19 Charlotte Hamburger, LBI, 41, 46.

20 Fritz Stern, "Germany 1933: Fifty Years Later," in *Dreams and Delusions: The Drama of German History*, ed. Fritz Stern (New York: Random House, 1987), 125.

21 Appel in *Jewish Life in Germany* (ed. Richarz), 356.

22 Carol Gilligan, *In a Different Voice: Psychological Theory and Women's Development* (Cambridge, Massachusetts: Harvard University Press, 1982).

23 In a typically racist and sexist decision, couples with an "Aryan" husband and Jewish wife held "privileged" status over those with a Jewish husband and "Aryan" wife. See Kaplan, *Between Dignity and Despair*, 148–49.

24 Kaplan, *Between Dignity and Despair*, 83–87.

25 Verena Hellwig, Harvard, 25–26.

26 Peter Wyden, *Stella: One Woman's True Tale of Evil, Betrayal, and Survival in Hitler's Germany* (New York: Simon and Schuster, 1992), 47.

27 Raul Hilberg, *Perpetrators, Victims and Bystanders* (New York: HarperCollins, 1992), 127.

28 *IF*, 13 January 1938, 13–14.

29 *JWS*, 1937, 80.

30 Margaret Moses, Harvard, 44–45.

31 Kaplan, *Between Dignity and Despair*, 131–35.

32 Eva Wysbar, in *Germans no More: Accounts of Jewish Everyday Life 1933–1938*, eds Margarete Limberg and Hubert Rübsaat (New York: Berghahn Books, 2006), 87–94.

33 Ann Lewis, LBI, 264

34 Ruth Abraham, LBI, 2.

35 Alice Nauen, Research Foundation, 8.

36 Debórah Dwork and Robert J. van Pelt, *Flight from the Reich: Refugee Jews, 1933–1946* (New York: Norton, 2009).

37 For attacks on women, see Rita Thalmann and Emmanuel Feinermann, *Crystal Night* (New York: Holocaust Library, 1974), 70, 81; and my long endnote in *Between Dignity and Despair*, 253, n15.

38 Charlotte Stein-Pick, LBI, 41.

39 Mally Dienemann, Harvard, 35.

40 Siegfried Neumann, in *Germans no More* (eds Limberg and Rübsaat), 167.

41 *Deutschland-Berichte der Sozialdemokratischen Partei Deutschlands, 1939* (Frankfurt, 1980), 924.

42 Margot Littauer, Harvard, 33.

43 *BJFB*, April 1937, 10; *BJFB*, December 1936, 1.

44 *Central Verein Zeitung*, 20 January 1938, 5.

45 Youth Aliyah assumed boys would contribute more to the kibbutz. See Brian Amkraut, *Between Home and Homeland: Youth Aliyah from Nazi Germany* (Tuscaloosa, Alabama: University of Alabama Press, 2006); M. Mossek, *Palestine Immigration Policy under Sir Herbert Samuel, British, Zionist and Arab Attitudes* (London: F. Cass, 1978), 1–35. The Mandatory Immigration Department in Palestine allocated labor certificates according to a ratio of approximately 70 males to 30 females. Thus most women arrived under category D, "dependent." Aviva Halamish, "Against Many Odds: Immigration of Jewish Women to Palestine between the World Wars" (paper presented at the Seventh European Social Science History Conference, Lisbon, Portugal, 2008). Thank you to Dr Halamish of the Open University of Israel for sharing her work.

46 Kaplan, *Between Dignity and Despair*, 142.

47 Elizabeth Bamberger in *Women of Exile: German-Jewish Autobiographies since 1933*, ed. Andreas Lixl-Purcell (Greenwood, Connecticut: Greenwood Press, 1988), 92.

48 Elizabeth Freund, LBI, 146.

49 Hans Mommsen, "The Reaction of the German Population to Anti-Jewish Persecution and the Holocaust" in *Lessons and Legacies: The Meaning of the Holocaust in a Changing World*, ed. Peter Hayes (Evanston, Illinois: Northwestern University Press, 1991), 153.

50 Daniel J. Goldhagen, *Hitler's Willing Executioners: Ordinary Germans and the Holocaust* (New York: Knopf, 1996).

51 Kaplan, *Between Dignity and Despair*, 234–35.

52 For minority responses to a majority's "disappearance" wish, see Hugo Brettauer, *Stadt ohne Juden* (Vienna: Gloriette Verlag, 1922) for a Jewish response; Jeanne Wakatsuki Houston, *Farewell to Manzanar* (Boston: Houghton Mifflin, 1973) for a Japanese-American response; William Melvin Kelley, *A Different Drummer* (New York: Doubleday, 1962), Douglas Turner Ward, *A Day of Absence* (New York: Okpaku, 1966), Derrick Bell's "Space Traders," in his *Faces at the Bottom of the Well* (New York: Basic Books, 1992), Sidney Willhelm, *Who Needs the Negro?* (Cambridge: Schenkman, 1970) for African-American responses.

53 "The end," in Joan Ringelheim, "Reflections on Gender," paper presented at the Women and the Holocaust Conference, Hebrew University, Jerusalem, June 1995; "Stations" in Mary Felstiner, *To Paint Her Life: Charlotte Salomon in the Nazi Era* (New York: HarperCollins, 1994), 204–7.

9

THE FATE OF THE JEWS IN AUSTRIA, 1933–39

Lee H. Igel

It is well accepted that the variety of books published at a certain place and time reveals a great deal about a society. Even more so, books can reveal the importance and freedom of a particular community. This is certainly the case of Jewish communities throughout history, including the one in Vienna, which developed a European center of publishing after the monarchy permitted a Jewish printing press to be operated in the early 1780s. Within one half-century, printing presses in Vienna published a number of religious items, including Bibles, prayer books, multiple editions of the Talmud, and *Haggadot*. Of the *Haggadot*, each of which contains the Exodus narrative to be recited at the *seder* on the first two nights of the Jewish Passover, among the most acclaimed is an 1823 printing with superb engravings of biblical scenes that were originally drawn by a Christian. Neither the Viennese Jew of 1823 nor of 1923 is likely to have seen much irony in the illustrations. Ten years later, however, the conditions in Vienna and other parts of the country tell a different story altogether—one that is highly important to an understanding of the fate of the Jews in Austria throughout most of the 1930s.

Several significant social, economic, and political transformations came to a head in the handful of years prior to the onset of World War II. Much of the change was centered in Vienna, which had long been a political, craft, and trading center that, by the middle of the nineteenth century, became an industrial city. Fifty years later it was an intellectual and artistic center, having flourished despite the defeat of Austria in the Austro-Prussian War of 1866.

As the capital of a defeated country, Vienna should have been spiritless. But the city was organized along the same lines as Baron Haussmann's vision for Paris, and became flush with economy, society, and technology that vitalized the professional middle class—the bourgeoisie—and released their energy.[1] In turn, Vienna experienced a population explosion.

From 1860 to 1900, the population of Vienna increased several-fold to nearly 1,700,000 people—and fewer than every one in two people living in Vienna had been born there.[2,3] Among these swelling numbers was an influx of Jews. Where, in the middle part of the nineteenth century, they represented two percent of the Viennese population, not 50 years later Jews represented more than eight percent of the city's inhabitants; they multiplied in number from about 6,000 to nearly 200,000.[4,5] A good reason for this rise in numbers was the easing of policies that restricted Jews from the rights of citizenship in the Austro-Hungarian Empire.

The inflow of Jewish immigrants to Vienna included the range from wealthy Bohemians to poor Galicians. Richer Jews became more integrated into the mainstream Austro-Hungarian society than poorer ones, although Jews in general tended to be better received in Vienna than in other parts of Austria-Hungary. Across the territory, if they were not hated in one part for being of German heritage, they were hated in another part for their loyalty to the Habsburg crown or for being Jewish.[6] But over time, and certainly by the first two decades of the twentieth century, Jews in Austria identified themselves with *Kultur* and further allegiance to the monarchy.[7] That is, they perceived themselves as Austrians. And, more specifically, with almost 93 percent of the Jews in Austria living in Vienna by 1930,[8] most perceived themselves as Viennese.

That the Jews inhabited a major city such as Vienna and the outlying urban areas was mostly a result of well-ingrained state policies across western and central Europe that restricted Jews from landownership and guild membership. Because of these restrictions, there were few Jews who did not take up work in commerce and trade. The result was a bourgeois society in which Jews merged with Gentiles. Together, they were socially and politically discouraged and discriminated against by the upper classes. This trend was encouraged by the Imperial government and upper classes because they perceived a healthy bourgeoisie as a potential threat. Yet, at the same time, the ruling classes were aware that the middle class was vital to the development of capitalist society.

By the late nineteenth century, the development of the bourgeoisie in the city brought upward mobility. In the embodiment of *Stadtluft Macht Frei* ("city air frees"), the German proverb that dates to the Middle Ages, the bourgeoisie filled and defined the business, engineering, artistic, and intellectual, academic, and medical occupations. The city provided a means not only of acquiring knowledge, but also of establishing a network. Much of it was defined by the Viennese Jewish stock, who became prominent contributors to the professions and the arts of the period: the psychoanalyst Sigmund Freud; the economist Ludwig von Mises; the sociologist and political economist Otto Neurath; the philosopher Martin Buber; most of the philosophers of the Vienna Circle; the anatomist Emil Zuckerkandl and salon hostess Bertha Zuckerkandl-Szeps; the Jung Wien writers such as Arthur Schnitzler and Stefan Zweig; and the classical composer Gustav Mahler, to name a few. And the Austrian branch of the Rothschild banking dynasty functioned on an entirely different rung out of its palatial estate on the Theresianumgasse. Yet, despite the position and influence of these and other Jews, Austria and most surrounding countries continued to deal with the "Jewish Question."

The Jewish Question—what to do about the status, rights, and toleration of Jews— was an ages-old matter across Europe. It was even a matter of discussion at the Congress of Vienna in 1814 and 1815, though considerably rehashed around 1843 with the diffusion of opposing commentaries by German thinkers Bruno Bauer in *Die Judenfrage* (*The Jewish Question*) and Karl Marx in *Zur Judenfrage* (*On the Jewish Question*). But an attempt to reconcile the Jewish Question in a new and different way came with the Viennese journalist Theodor Herzl's authorship of *Der Judenstaat* (*The Jewish State*) around 1895. Using an increase in antisemitism as part of his basis, the justification for the creation of a Jewish homeland outside of Europe, which, unbeknownst to Herzl, followed Leon Pinsker's 1882 writing of *Selbstemanzipation* (*Auto-Emancipation*), provided an alternative to the long-running strategy that encouraged Jews to assimilate themselves into the community in which they lived.

The integration of Jews into Viennese society had been well under way when Herzl completed his manuscript. Popular accounts have it that when Herzl invited the chief rabbi of Vienna into his home to discuss the text, the visit was hosted within sight of the family Christmas tree.[9] That the home of the journalist and future father of modern Zionism was as likely to contain a Christmas tree as a Passover *seder* plate would not likely have surprised the rabbi, for such decoration in the home of secular, upper-middle-class Viennese professionals was common and near-requisite.

The presence of a Christmas tree in a Jewish home is emblematic of the merger of Jews and Gentiles in the upper middle class. This class developed as Vienna became a center of the *Haskalah*, or the Jewish Enlightenment movement, and through the inclusive business and social relationships that were a response to common discrimination by the upper class. As these relationships and the class itself prospered, the Jews, who had traditionally insulated themselves as a means of protection, became progressively less defensive against changes to the orthodoxies of their religion. But as Jews gained increased equality within the class, at the same time they experienced a decline in the numbers of people who identified themselves as Jewish.

The 200,000-member-strong community of Jews in Vienna comprised 20 percent of the bourgeoisie and, together with "Non-Aryans," accounted for about 75 percent of the entire class.[10] The acceptance of the Jewish community was due in part to the socially free practice of marrying outside the religion, which was by then common in Vienna as in other German-speaking areas of Europe. But Jews were excluded from holding state-paid positions as officers in the military, as judges in the courts, or as full professors in universities, which prevented them from achieving a full sense of citizenship.[11] This is why a large number of Jews who sought and gained high-ranking positions in public service frequently—and freely—converted to Christianity.

By the turn of the twentieth century, Jews were beginning to attain positions in the higher ranks of the civil service. Yet being a Jew remained a disadvantage, and the top positions in the prominent ministries were still reserved for, and filled by, Christians. Thus, upon nearing promotion to such a post in a respective ministry, a good many Jewish high civil servants underwent baptism by the Emperor's chaplains or an esteemed pastor, albeit usually with little publicity and near-full discretion.[12] But the policy that led to this practice was not a form of hostility against them based on physical characteristics or ethnicity. It was, rather, discrimination of religious belief.

By contrast, Jews were entering medical and scientific professions as never before; upwards of 60 percent of the physicians in Vienna were Jewish.[13] Like plenty of Jewish civil servants and professionals across the German-speaking parts of Europe, however, many underwent conversion and baptism, and chose specific attire and comportment as means of assimilation. To claim Christianity as one's religion was anyway better than to claim no religion at all, as Albert Einstein learned when his prospective appointment to the faculty at the University of Prague was run through the Imperial education ministry in Vienna in 1911. The German-born physicist, despite being a non-believing Jew, was initially passed over in favor of a candidate whose advantages were being Austrian and not Jewish. When Einstein later received the appointment, it was due in part to his agreement to claim on official forms that he was of the "Mosaic" faith.[14]

The example of Einstein may reveal more about the individual than the status of Jews in the Austro-Hungarian Empire and their relationship with it. But to achieve as much, Jews found it necessary to at least reconcile, often overcome, and sometimes renounce any hint of their Jewishness. For example, Sigmund Freud was among those of the professional set who wrestled painfully with being Jewish by birth. But while the full explanation for his personal and professional conflict with Judaism is beyond the scope of this analysis, it is largely explained by his self-identification as a German nationalist, which was in lockstep with most other Austrians of his generation. It is not for nothing that in his final book, *Moses and Monotheism*, Freud cast the biblical hero Moses not as a Jew but as an Egyptian nobleman, and the Jewish religion as an Egyptian conception that was spread to Palestine.

While Freud and others of his class sought to transcend religious barriers in the movement to merge all German people, the Jewish community had become accepted in Viennese society. There alone, while antisemitism was strong among shopkeepers and craftsmen, prejudice against Jews was considered to be in bad taste by those in the Imperial court and in intellectual and professional circles.[15] Outside Vienna, in Austrian Poland, for example, Jews were the only people in the region who, on the whole, spoke German. Yet whatever amount of acceptance Jews had achieved by the turn of the twentieth century began to decrease with the defeat of the Austro-Hungarian Empire in World War I.

The first result of the defeat was the fragmentation of the "Dual Monarchy"; the empire that stretched from the Alps to the Russian border and ruled more than 50 million subjects was reduced to an amalgam of national and religious republics. Terms of the Treaty of Saint-Germain-en-Laye, the war accord signed in 1919 by the victorious Allied Powers and defeated Austrian representatives, established a republic of 6.5 million people from the German-speaking regions of the dissolved Habsburg Empire. What emerged beyond the signal-end of Habsburg rule over Austria, which dated to the reign of Rudolf I in the late 1200s, was the Republic of German-Austria, declared by Austrians to be a part of the democratic Weimar Republic of Germany. But the treaty forbade any political or economic union with Germany, and the violation of terms forced Austrian officials to establish alternatively an independent Republic of Austria.

The treaty also imposed harsh economic terms. In almost no time, there emerged a depressed economic and social spirit that loaded down the rump Austrian state with hyperinflation and rising unemployment. A response by the socialist government to balance the budget could not, however, overcome political bickering and maneuvering.[16] Nor did anyone seriously entertain the proposal by Joseph Schumpeter to counteract the turbulence through a policy grounded in a free economy.[17] Schumpeter, who at the time briefly held the post of finance minister, proposed that a free economy required profit-making, which could be achieved through the practice of innovation that was unique to businessmen—the bankers, merchants, manufacturers, industrialists, and other such professionals.

Yet, as Schumpeter observed, Austro-Hungarian politics of the period was not interested in businessmen. Businessmen were members of the bourgeoisie; they reflected an inherently peaceful society in an Austria dominated by a military aristocracy created by war and subsistent on new war.[18] It therefore came as no surprise to Schumpeter when the Austrian government chose to deal with inflation and sizable war reparation payments by taking on huge loans from the League of Nations. The first of these came in 1922, during a time when there was a growing policy rift between the two most influential political parties: the Social Democrats and the Christian Socialists. The tensions resulted in the growth of several paramilitary organizations bent on supporting one ideology or the other through daily mass demonstrations.

Things turned increasingly turbulent into the 1930s, by which time a new government had resolved to take on another loan from the League of Nations, but to no avail.[19] In 1933, Chancellor Engelbert Dollfuss, a Christian Socialist, attempted to right the deteriorating conditions in Austria by abolishing all political parties and the legislature, and reforming the constitution along fascist lines.[20] These moves were heavily criticized by Social Democrats, Pan-German nationalists, and Austrian Nazis, and served to intensify their latest round of calls for the annexation of Austria by the German republic.

The fall of the monarchy after World War I cleaved the "old world" and gave rise to the socialist governments and the bourgeoisie. With the emergence of the bourgeoisie as the power class, the mix of Jews and Gentiles were attracted to, and filled, an increased number of available jobs in white-collar trade, industrial, professional, and artistic occupations. This shift would have been profound in its own right. Yet the shift and its implications became even more so when this class failed amidst the turbulence of the 1920s and into the 1930s. And this dimension became altogether perilous as the masses grew increasingly desperate.

In early 1934, about one year after Dollfuss abolished constitutional law, a brief civil war broke out following Social Democratic resistance to actions by the right-wing, state-supported paramilitary. The Social Democrats were defeated and Dollfuss maintained power until the summer, when he was assassinated in a failed *coup d'état* by Austrian Nazis. The seat Dollfuss held at the head of the chancellery was assumed by Kurt Schuschnigg, a fellow ultra-conservative. But like his predecessor, Schuschnigg could neither appease Nazi Germany nor obtain support from Britain and France against the growing pressure of intervention by the Hitler regime. By 1936, despite the Nazi Party having been banned in Austria, the feeling of urgency to reach some accord with Germany caused Schuschnigg to release some imprisoned Nazis and to permit some Nazi Party members into the government. The government then became reorganized during the next year-plus through an increasing number of influential Nazis and via political agreements that favored Germany. At the same time, Germany continued its mobilization of German troops near the Austrian border. This created a *fait accompli* that was realized on 13 March 1938, when, after German troops crossed the border and occupied Austria the day before, Austria was declared to be a province of Germany. The *Anschluss*—annexation and reunification of the Austrian region with the German fatherland—had been accomplished.

The German republic, like its Austrian neighbor, was among the defeated in World War I. It experienced its own rough going in the interim, and had come under Nazi control with the appointment of Adolf Hitler to the chancellorship in 1933. Hitler was not German by birth; he was born in Braunau am Inn, Austria, a city in the north-western portion of the country near the border with Germany, and raised in the northerly city of Linz. In 1908, at the age of 16, he left school and his middle-class upbringing for Vienna. But not long after arriving, he was rejected from art school and took to something of a vagrant existence in the capital city.

Writing in his manifesto *Mein Kampf*, Hitler recalled the "five years of hardship and misery" he spent in Vienna as the "saddest period of my life."[21] But also during this period, Hitler witnessed and became fascinated with the mass protests organized by workers. He began to study the politics of their party, the Social Democrats, as well as the activities of the Pan-German nationalists and the Christian Social Party. He equally studied the demagoguery of Karl Lueger, an antisemite who was the mayor of Vienna from 1897 to 1910. In turn, Hitler gained perspective on their antisemitic slants, despite noting that he initially considered the "tone" of the antisemitic literature to be "unworthy of the cultural tradition of a great nation."[22] Yet he is said to have experienced in Vienna an incontrovertibly defining moment, one in which he "encountered an apparition in a black caftan and black hair locks"; that is, a Jewish man whose particular physical appearance was qualitatively different from the Germanic look of the Jews that Hitler had known in Linz.[23] Henceforth, Hitler distinguished Jews "from the rest of humanity" and became an avowed antisemite.[24]

Whether the presence of one orthodox Jew so suddenly transfixed and truly transformed Hitler cannot be known with absolute certainty. What is known, however, is that to whatever extent that Jewish man existed, he would have been one among a diverse and accepted Jewish community of nearly 200,000 within a Viennese citizenry that numbered 2,000,000. Further, by appearance and place, the man likely would have been one of the many Jewish peddlers who inhabited in sufficient numbers the run-down districts to the north of the city center. These sectors historically contained the Jewish ghettos, which provided community to both rich and poor traders, most of whom subscribed to the appeals of Marxism and Zionism.[25,26] And it is from this Vienna that Hitler left for Munich, age 24, to avoid mandatory service in the military of the Empire he had come to loathe.

The next time Hitler came to Austria, he had achieved the *Anschluss* and was met by cheering crowds as he rode in an open-topped Mercedes on a route that took him from his birthplace to Vienna. The attractiveness of totalitarianism under the Nazi banner was immediately apparent when Hitler arrived in Vienna on 14 March 1938. It was still at a fever pitch there not two weeks later, when Field Marshal Hermann Goering delivered a speech in which he outlined the German program for Austria. Two points professed in that speech were that Nazism would tolerate the church so long as it did not interfere with political matters; and that Jews should not live among Austrians, particularly the Viennese.

Immediately following the *Anschluss*, Vienna remained a center of activity, especially for Jewish emigration from Austria. An emigration process was organized out of the beginnings of the *Zentralstelle für jüdische Auswanderung*, the Central Office for Jewish Emigration, and developed chiefly by Adolf Eichmann, a quickly rising member of the Nazi *Schutzstaffel* (SS), who was dispatched there as specific mastermind.[27,28,29] Eichmann worked closely with the Inspector of Security Police and the Security Service, Walter Stahlecker, who a few years later would find himself commanding one of the SS *Einsatzgruppen*, which executed Soviet and Jewish civilians during the German military onslaught against the Soviet Union. Together and with others, Eichmann and Stahlecker managed a process that included forcing Jews into long lines outside municipal buildings in order to receive emigrant documentation, to pay high taxes and fees, and to have much of their property—both immoveable and moveable—confiscated by officials.[30]

The Nazi form of revolution under the *Anschluss* seized every concept of society, as evidenced by the German takeover of Austria's professional football association and the outlawing of Jewish sports clubs. When, on 3 April 1938, the middling German national football team came to Vienna's Prater Stadium to play a match against the premier Austrian team in a celebration of Germanic unity, Jewish players and officials were in the process of being, or had already been, banned. The German control and spirit of things very likely influenced the decisions of the world-renowned Austrian team captain, Matthias Sindelar, who refused requests by Nazi officials for him to join the newly organized German national team.[31,32] In addition, he not only ran up the score in the game, which had been orchestrated by the Nazis to end in a draw, but almost immediately thereafter quit playing football and purchased a small café. The café had been owned by a Jewish acquaintance, and became available when "Aryanization" dispossessed Jews of their businesses. But though Sindelar bought the business for a song, he apparently paid its former owner more money than was offered by the government *apparatchiks*, and maintained its clientele enough that the Nazi Gestapo labeled him a "social democrat and a Jews' friend."[33] That the 35-year-old football star ended up being found dead in his Vienna flat some months later was due to accident, according to government-sponsored media. Several months later, during *Kristallnacht*, on 9 and 10 November, Nazis and civilians took to the streets in Vienna, torching synagogues, vandalizing Jewish-owned businesses, and physically assaulting Jews. In the days following the pogrom, Nazi officials placed blame for the events on the Jews and began to institute more and more antisemitic policies, including the expedited forced emigration of Jews and "Aryanization" of their property.[34]

By the summer of 1939, Nazi policy resulted in the emigration of about 110,000 Austrian Jews; of the numbers who remained, they were fewer in Vienna than in other parts of the country.[35,36,37] Yet to what extent is the rapid increase in antisemitic activity, specifically in the years from the rise of Hitler in Germany to the outbreak of World War II, explained by purely antisemitic motives? One popular explanation is that Austria, like Germany, contained strains of antisemitism as far back as anyone could remember. The Austrian strain was perceived to be a particularly threatening form, due largely to its being oriented in a manner that was especially appealing to workers and oppressed ethnic groups.[38] Another is that non-Jews were economically envious, which explains the support for policies that deprived Jews of their property and positions. But while valid, both are too simple and convenient to explain the sharp increase in antisemitic activities.

The common thinking that the Jews were blamed for the depressed conditions in the Austro-Hungarian Empire and Germany because of pure antisemitism is misleading to a certain extent. In *The End of Economic Man*, a late-1930s treatise on the growing threat of totalitarianism across Europe, Peter F. Drucker propounded that such hostility toward Jews was due not to outright antisemitism, but rather to a particular form of discrimination against the bourgeoisie that had developed in capitalist society. As specified by Drucker, who was born and raised in turn-of-the-century Vienna, it would have been far easier to lay blame for the rotting way of life on the corrupt municipal governments than on a group of non-Aryans that personified the forces of bourgeois capitalism and liberalism. But, unlike the bourgeoisie across western Europe, who were emancipated through revolt against the crown governments, the middle class in Austria was liberated by the upper class. That the rise of the bourgeoisie was top-down meant political and social rule did not transfer from the aristocracy to the middle class. This explains why, as mentioned above, many if not most bourgeois professionals—businessmen, Jews, and Gentiles, individually and collectively—were not recognized as socially equal to those who held positions in the military or the highest ranks of the civil service.

During the years of the First Republic (1918–38), the vast majority of Austria's chancellors were members of the conservative and Catholic Christian Social Party. Only from 1918 to 1920 was Austria led by a Social Democrat. One would have thought, therefore, that the depression would have resulted in stunning losses for a party that had been in power for so long and represented both the old aristocratic order as well as big industry and business, but this was not the case. The Christian Socialists simply moved rightward and transformed into an Austrian variant of fascism in the Fatherland Front (under Dollfuss). The forces of the old order were able to retain their power by diverting attention away from their failings, creating an umbrella of patriotism, and assailing Marxism and socialist politicians, who, Drucker argues, were also part of the problem.

The majority of members of the Nazi Party, as well as the civilians who were enamored of Nazism, probably did not understand such a distinct element of the creed to which they subscribed. This is likely because there is little evidence to indicate that they understood the economic and social conditions well enough to realize the effects of Nazism and its strategy of "Aryanization." For instance, competitors who expected an increase in business activity as a result of the elimination and liquidation of Jewish-owned retail stores, banks, doctors' offices, and law firms often saw business disappear as their industry shrank.[39] Yet, not only did those out of work not blame Nazi policy for these results, they and other workers who joined the Nazi ranks became more convinced that Nazism would protect against the total collapse of capitalist society and deliver better circumstances.

It stands to reason that many Austrian Jews might have joined the Nazi cause had they been welcomed to do so, and had antisemitism not been such a central principle. Here is where Drucker's argument might benefit from nuance; Austrofascism was not Nazism, and in fact what differentiated the two was the primacy of antisemitism in the latter. One cannot ignore, either, the time-and-place-specific events that led to the takeover of Nazism in Austria. German aggression, not indigenous legal or illegal efforts, produced the "union." At the same time, one should not underemphasize the latent dimensions of anti-semitism that persisted in Austrian society before the *Anschluss* in order to give better context to the support for the persecution of Jews after 1938. Very quickly, Austria's Jews were reduced to scrubbing the streets while other citizens either looked on and did nothing, or publicly mocked them. This, along with increasingly harsh regulations imposed on the Jewish community through the Nuremberg Laws, brings to mind the word "demeaning" in its original form, that is, to drive away animals by use of threat. It was not long until the Nazi apparatus sealed the fate of the Jews in cattle car transports to concentration and death camps when the outbreak of World War II ended the policy of legal emigration and permitted their deportation from Nazi-occupied lands.

Notes

1 Peter Drucker, *The Age of Discontinuity* (New York: Harper & Row, 1968), 34.
2 Ian Kershaw, *Hitler, 1889–1936: Hubris* (New York: W.W. Norton, 1998), 31.
3 Kershaw, *Hitler*.
4 Kershaw, *Hitler*.
5 Hannah S. Decker, *Freud, Dora, and Vienna 1900* (New York: Free Press, 1991), 22.
6 Amos Elon, *The Pity of It All* (New York: Picador, 2002), 252.
7 Marsha Rozenblit, *Reconstructing a National Identity: The Jews of Habsburg Austria During World War I* (Oxford: Oxford University Press, 2004).
8 Haim Ben Sasson, ed., *A History of the Jewish People* (Cambridge, Massachusetts: Harvard University Press, 1976), 946.
9 Michael A. Meyer, ed., *German-Jewish History in Modern Times: Volume 3 Integration in Dispute: 1871–1918* (New York: Columbia University Press, 1997), 82.

10 Peter F. Drucker, *The End of Economic Man: The Origins of Totalitarianism* (New York: John Day, 1939), 206.

11 Drucker, *The End of Economic Man*, 200.

12 Peter Drucker, *Adventures of a Bystander* (New York: John Wiley and Sons, 1994), 33.

13 C.A. Macartney, *The Habsburg Empire, 1790–1918* (New York: Macmillan, 1969).

14 Walter Isaacson, *Einstein: His Life and Universe* (New York: Simon & Schuster, 2007), 163–64.

15 Drucker, *Adventures of a Bystander*.

16 C.A. Macartney, *The Social Revolution in Austria* (Cambridge: Cambridge University Press, 1926).

17 Joseph Schumpeter, *Imperialism and Social Classes* (New York: Augustus M. Kelley, 1951).

18 Arno J. Mayer, *The Persistence of the Old Regime: Europe to the Great War* (London: Croom Helm, 1981), 111.

19 David Clay Large, *Between Two Fires: Europe's Path in the 1930s* (New York: W.W. Norton, 1990), 77.

20 Stanley G. Payne, *A History of Fascism, 1914–1945* (Abingdon: Routledge, 1995), 248–49.

21 Adolf Hitler, *Mein Kampf* (New York: Stackpole Sons, 1939).

22 Hitler, *Mein Kampf*.

23 Hitler, *Mein Kampf*.

24 Hitler, *Mein Kampf*.

25 Steven Beller, *Vienna and the Jews, 1867–1938: A Cultural History* (Cambridge: Cambridge University Press, 1989), 17.

26 Ian Kershaw, *Hitler*, 32.

27 David Cesarani, *Becoming Eichmann: Rethinking the Life, Crimes, and Trial of a "Desk Murderer"* (Cambridge, Massachusetts: Da Capo Press, 2006), 66.

28 State of Israel Ministry of Justice, *The Trial of Adolf Eichmann: Record of Proceedings in the District Court of Jerusalem* (Jerusalem: Trust for the Publication of the Proceedings of the Eichmann Trial, in cooperation with the Israel State Archives and Yad Vashem, the Holocaust Martyrs' and Heroes' Remembrance Authority, 1992–95).

29 Hannah Arendt, *Eichmann in Jerusalem: A Report on the Banality of Evil* (New York: Viking Press, 1963).

30 Saul Friedländer, *Nazi Germany and the Jews* (New York: HarperCollins, 1998), 1: chapter 8.

31 Ulrich Hesse-Lichtenberger, *Tor!: The Story of German Football* (London: WSC Books, 2003), 83.

32 Roman Horak and Wolfgang Maderthaner, "A Culture of Urban Cosmopolitanism: Uridil and Sindelar as Viennese Coffee-house Heroes," in *European Heroes: Myth, Identity, Sport*, eds Richard Holt, J.A. Mangan and Pierre Lanfranchi (Abingdon: Routledge, 1996).

33 Hesse-Lichtenberger, *Tor!*, 83.

34 US Presidential Advisory Commission on Holocaust Assets in the United States, *Plunder and Restitution: The U.S. and Holocaust Victims' Assets: Findings and Recommendations of the Presidential Advisory Commission on Holocaust Assets in the United States and Staff Report* (Washington, DC: The Commission, 2000), SR-18.

35 Richard L. Rubenstein and John K. Roth, *Approaches to Auschwitz: The Holocaust and Its Legacy* (Louisville, Kentucky: Westminster John Knox Press, 2003), 398.

36 United States Holocaust Memorial Museum, "Vienna," *Holocaust Encyclopedia*. www.ushmm.org/wlc/article.php?ModuleId=10005452 (accessed 11 November 2009).

37 Austrian State Archives Department: General Administrative Archives, Withdrawal of [status as] legally recognized public corporation from the Jewish Community of Vienna, 1762/1, 12 June 1939. www1.yadvashem.org/about_HOLocaust/documents/part1/doc61.html (accessed 11 November 2009).

38 Elon, *The Pity of It All*, 252.

39 Drucker, *The End of Economic Man*, 201.

Part II

GERMANY'S RACIAL WAR IN POLAND AND THE SOVIET UNION, 1939–41

10

VICTIM AND PERPETRATOR PERSPECTIVES OF WORLD WAR II-ERA GHETTOS

Helene Sinnreich

"To the Jews the ghetto was a way of life; to the Germans it was an administrative measure."[1]

Raul Hilberg

During World War II, Nazi Germany and its allies forcibly interned Jews and Roma in segregated residential districts called ghettos. The size of the ghettos varied greatly. The area could be as small as an individual building or as large as several neighborhoods. Often the border of the area would be marked with signs or delineated with a wall, barbed wire, fence, surrounding trench or other barrier. Although ghettos were prevalent in Nazi-occupied Eastern Europe, there were many ghettos in areas that were not under the direct control of Nazi Germany. Therefore there existed both ghettos controlled by Nazi German authorities and those controlled by non-German authorities. Ghettos under both Nazi and non-German control varied greatly in administration and structure. It is therefore not possible to speak of a typical Holocaust-era ghetto. Rather, ghettos must be characterized to reflect differences brought on by variations in regional government, geographical and population size, and other factors. The diverse ghetto administrations, size, and structure contributed to a variety of experiences of ghettoization by the victims. This chapter first deals with the diversity of ghettos from an administrative perspective, then focuses on the experiences of the inhabitants of the ghettos.

Ghettoization has long been studied as part of the Nazi annihilation program directed against the Jews of Europe during World War II. However, until recently, most studies of ghettos focused on Nazi-controlled ghettos, particularly the large ghettos of Poland such as those in Warsaw and Łódź. Therefore many current perceptions and definitions of ghettos are based on research into these larger Polish ghettos. While there were large numbers of individuals in these larger ghettos, there were over 1,000 ghettos in Nazi-occupied eastern Europe, the former Soviet Union, Romania, and Hungary, which varied in size and structure.[2] As a result of more recent research on these smaller ghettos, and ghettos located outside of Nazi-occupied areas, scholars' conceptions of ghettos and ghetto experiences have been in transition.

Traditionally, the ghettos of Nazi-occupied Europe were seen as part of a deliberate, centralized Nazi plan to kill off the Jewish population; they were, in effect, a laboratory in methods of killing.[3] This thesis was challenged by historians who saw ghettos "as a means by which local authorities first prevented any stabilization of Jewish living conditions and then exploited untenable circumstances to provide them with leverage to press the central government for ever more radical measures."[4] The moderate functionalist Christopher Browning rejects the thesis that the ghettos were centrally planned, and argues that ghettoization was initiated by local authorities, though it was "carried out at different times in different ways for different reasons."[5] Various scholars and those carrying out ghettoization have offered reasons for the creation of ghettos, which include (among others) demographic re-ordering of a city by removing Jews and placing them in crowded conditions and creating space for non-Jews to move in; facilitating expropriation of Jewish valuables, particularly property; public health considerations; concentrating Jews to facilitate deportation; social reasons, such as protecting non-Jews from having to encounter Jews; to decimate the Jewish population; and removing Jews from the general population in preparation for the German invasion of the Soviet Union. More recently, Dan Michman has suggested that ghettos resulted from the circulation of the idea among Nazis that the concentration of Jews into an area of a city was a naturally occurring phenomenon, which gained currency after 1940.[6] Theories about the reasons and motivations for ghettoization will undoubtedly continue to be proposed. Despite these differences, all of the ghettos shared at least three purposes: the concentration of the Jewish population (or, in some cases, the Roma population); at least partial separation of that population from the "Aryan" population; and some form of expropriation of valuables. Ghettos were not necessary for expropriation, but they often facilitated this activity. As a result, expropriation connected to ghettoization was often a central experience of those interned in ghettos.

Ghettos provided abundant opportunity for expropriation. Deportation to a ghetto often involved authorities or neighbors gaining entrance to homes and valuables. Upon entering the ghetto, valuables could be appropriated at check points or through brutal treatment resulting in bribes. Once inside the ghetto, there could be thefts by any number of officials. In Secureni, in Transnistria, police Colonel Manecuta reported on 1 September 1941 that "the Jews complain that they are utterly destitute as they have been looted and whatever they still possessed they were forced to sell for food ... They are patrolled by seven police and 50 pre-military guards ... but the latter are given to thefts and other illegal practices. ... ."[7] In Czernowitz, it was reported by the former mayor that "although the regulations strictly prohibited entry into the Ghetto, no one paid any attention to them. ... the wholesale looting started."[8]

Sometimes the raiding of homes was organized and approved by German and non-German officials. These were often expropriation measures, such as demanding valuables in exchange for food and supplies, or collecting fur coats or valuables such as gems and precious metals. Survivor Malvina Graf described the collection of furs in the Krakow Ghetto in her memoir:

> On December 27, 1941, trucks drove into the ghetto and, through loudspeakers mounted on the trucks, the announcement came that the *Stadthauptmann* (the city captain) had ordered all Jews to give up their furs. These furs were to be brought to a building on Limanowskiego Street. Whoever did not give up their

furs would be put to death immediately ... So on a day that saw the temperature drop well below the freezing point, Jews in painfully thin cloth coats stood in line and handed over the warm furs ... There were, however, a number of people who cut their furs into tiny pieces and buried the pieces in their cellars rather than give them to the Germans.[9]

Those who did not hand over valuables might fall victim to a search by the authorities, or the networks of internal ghetto spies who would identify those with wealth hidden inside and outside the ghetto. Those with hidden wealth would sometimes be summoned by the authorities, beaten until they revealed the hiding places of their wealth, or held for ransom, forcing the family to hand over valuables for their safe return. The authorities would also sometimes hold prominent individuals captive in exchange for a ransom from the community as a whole. Expropriation also took place during deportation from a ghetto through limits on how much could be taken to the deportation site and, in some cases, through body-cavity checks prior to deportation.

Ghettos also sometimes carried out expropriation through the exploitation of available labor. Forced labor was a requirement of many ghetto inmates. Sometimes it was heavy unskilled labor, such as shoveling snow or digging ditches. These difficult work details ended up mainly on the heads of the poor, who could not afford to bribe their way into an easier detail.[10] This work was frequently extremely difficult, and often those with the means to do so would "buy out" of it. There was also skilled labor, which was often highly coveted as it was perceived that this work would provide better conditions, and often could mean extra food rations, or a sense of security that the worker and his or her family would be allowed to remain longer in the ghetto.

Ghettos that proved economically beneficial sometimes found champions among local administrators, who fought to keep the ghettos in existence when plans for extermination became known and began to be carried out. This practical following of personal interest has led some to point out the banality of certain figures such as Hans Biebow, the administrator of the Łódź ghetto, who actively expanded his workforce. By December 1942, 7,000 machines were in operation in the ghetto.[11] By 1943, there were approximately 80,000 employed ghetto inhabitants, and Biebow could boast of 18,000 machines.[12] He pleaded with authorities to continue the existence of the ghetto and provide more sustenance for those employed within.[13] However, the pleading for food for ghetto laborers was not evidence of banality. Rather, ghetto administrators such as Biebow could work diligently to extend the ghetto period and provide its workers with food, while at the same time engaging in rape and beatings of ghetto inmates and brutal ghetto actions. For example, one woman relates her experience with Biebow when the Pabianice Ghetto was being liquidated and the survivors sent to be workers in Łódź:

When the women were being selected, I was taken before Biebow and was asked whether I had a worker's insurance card. I said, 'Yes but I have a child,' Biebow said 'What is a child? That is so much dirt.' He hit me over the shoulder with a whip and tore my three-year-old boy from me and threw him to the ground. The child cried 'Mama' and then Biebow went to it and kicked it with his boots. The child cried once more faintly and did not move any more. Then Biebow hit me again and ordered another man to take me to the other square. I myself saw several small children die on the square as a result of Biebow's brutality.[14]

Extending the existence of the ghetto for economic purposes was not always an indicator of interest in the wellbeing of the population. "Productionists," as Christopher Browning has termed those who sought to exploit ghetto labor forces rather than deport them directly to their deaths, could be just as brutal and deadly as those he termed, "attritionists," who felt providing ghetto-dwellers with sustenance was a waste of resources.[15]

Despite the common purposes of concentration and expropriation, there were different kinds of ghetto, with variations based on geography, population, and other factors. Three basic types of ghetto dominated: "closed," "open," and "temporary" ghettos. The closed ghetto was the archetypical ghetto—a large-scale ghetto based on the models of the largest and second-largest ghettos in Nazi-occupied Europe, the Warsaw and Łódź ghettos, respectively. These ghettos were generally located in urban centers, sealed off, and usually equipped with an autonomous Jewish administration or *Judenrat*. These *Judenräte* often controlled an internal Jewish administration, which maintained order, supplied local social services such as medical care, and was responsible for carrying out Nazi orders such as supplying Jews for labor and appropriating valuables. Although not universal within all ghettos, Jewish ghetto administration was widespread. The Jewish councils were initially established to serve as the liaisons between the authorities and local Jewish communities. With the creation of ghettos, however, these Jewish administrations often became the internal ghetto administration, especially in closed ghettos.[16] *Judenräte* varied from single individuals to multi-member councils. For example, Lvov's Jewish council "was organized in 22 divisions and 6 subdivisions and employed in 1942, some 4,000 persons (4.5 percent of the ghetto inmates)."[17]

The major means of continued existence for these closed ghettos was through trading valuables, and later labor in the form of direct laborers or through manufacturing finished products in exchange for food and supplies from the Nazi administration. The hallmark of the closed ghetto was a wall or barbed-wire fence which surrounded the space and restricted the residents from entering and leaving at will. Basic supplies such as foodstuffs were provided by the German administration, leaving the population vulnerable to amounts set by the Nazi authorities. The result was that these types of ghetto were particularly susceptible to starvation conditions. An example of the type of hunger experienced in the closed ghettos was recorded by an unknown nurse in a hospital in the Warsaw ghetto:

> In the entrance hall lies a boy of five, swollen with hunger. He is in the last stage, his life ending because of hunger. He came to the hospital yesterday. Eyes swollen, hands and feet puffed up like balloons. Every possible analysis is being made; maybe kidneys, perhaps heart. No, neither this nor that. The child still moves his lips, he begs for some bread. I try to feed him something, hoping he could take something down. Alas, [his] throat is swollen shut, nothing passes down, too late. The doctor asks him 'did you get anything to eat at home?' 'No.' 'Would you like to eat now?' 'Yes!' Some few minutes later he utters for the last time 'a piece of bread,' and with this express he sinks into sleep. Dead for a piece of bread.[18]

Although the closed ghetto dominated in Nazi-occupied Poland, they existed in other areas as well, including non-German-controlled areas. For example, the short-lived Czernowitz ghetto was enclosed. Traian Popovici, then mayor of Czernowitz, related the conditions of the Czernowitz ghetto in his "Confessions." He wrote that the section delineated for the ghetto "could hardly have accommodated 10,000 people [but] had to house 50,000 Jews plus the Christian population which lived there ... Many were forced to live in corridors, cellars, garages, under bridges, anywhere to find shelter against snow and rain."[19] Carp writes that "The [Chernovitz] ghetto was so small that people could live there only among the worst conditions. The luckiest settled down in houses, 30–40 per room. Those who arrived later found shelter for themselves in attics, cellars or stables. The last to arrive could not get more than the gutters in the yards and streets."[20]

Congested living conditions were common in most ghettos. The space designated was commonly too small to accommodate the number of inhabitants directed to live there. Relief from these crowded conditions often came immediately after deportations or mass killings. Often, however, this was immediately followed by a reduction in the amount of living space allocated for ghetto inhabitants.

Open ghettos dominated in Nazi Germany's ally, Romania, although they were prevalent in a number of other countries as well. These ghettos usually did not contain a wall, and members of the ghetto population could often leave the ghetto area in a controlled manner. In some cases, inmates of open ghettos were able to go to the market place at designated times to trade for food, or they were able to leave for work outside the ghetto. Dennis Deletant describes one open ghetto, which residents were permitted to enter and leave with a permit between 11 am and 4 pm. They were kept in the ghetto through forced registration and daily roll call for men between 14 and 60.[21] Some, such as the Krakow ghetto, had a wall around them, but at least in the early days functioned as an open ghetto with inmates having the ability to go to the city on a day or overnight pass, or even to visit neighboring villages for a few days. The open ghettos often had less serious food crises due to the inhabitants' ability to barter for food with the surrounding population. There is not a great deal known about open ghettos, and far more research needs to be done on these.

Temporary ghettos were usually quite small, and consisted of a building or a few buildings instead of a section of a city. These temporary ghettos came into existence in the summer of 1941 and afterwards, when the Final Solution was already being undertaken, and where mass executions were the first encounter the Jewish population had with the occupying authorities. While there is some debate about the purpose of the Polish ghettos, most historians agree that ghettoization was meant to be a temporary measure, either in anticipation of a potential emigration plan or with the goal of attrition and concentration before annihilation. The "temporary" ghettos of the occupied USSR were also intended as temporary holding grounds until the ghetto occupants could be massacred.[22]

The Jews of Storojinetz (in Transnistria) were housed in a temporary ghetto consisting of a few buildings, which inhabitants were forbidden to leave.[23] The ghetto was divided into two parts: "women and children [were] locked into the building of the elementary school, men into the orphanages which [were] two kilometers away from the town."[24] These temporary ghettos were usually operated by the *Einsatzgruppen* or Romanian military authorities. The duration of these ghettos was often extremely short-lived. Some existed only a few days, others perhaps a few months. Christian Gerlach writes that on 25 September 1941, the Jews of Moghilev were ordered to move into a ghetto. The liquidation of the ghetto came not long after, and by 19 October 1941, fewer than 1,000 Jews of Moghilev remained. Nearly 6,000 people were killed on three dates between 2 and 19 October 1941.[25] Another example of short-lasting ghettos comes from Jean Ancel, who describes one action in Telenesti on 14 July, during which all the Jews of the town were rounded up and brought to "a large house at Budais, a nearby village ... [creating] ... a virtual ghetto."[26] On 16 July, all the men were killed (about 100 in all). The next day, the women were killed.[27] These types of short-term holding area generally served as precursors to murder.

Whatever the function or layout of the ghetto, there were some similarities in how the ghettos were experienced, which crossed ghetto types and geographical locations. One shared ghetto experience was the breakdown of the family, brought on by a variety of factors: slow death by starvation or disease, deportation of family members, rifts brought on by lower morale or morals, inability to witness the suffering of other family members, feelings of helplessness, or opportunities for improvement of one's individual situation that required abandoning one's family. In the territories occupied by Germany after the summer of 1941, there was often an additional immediate and shocking breakdown of the family due to mass exterminations in the first few days of the invasion, which produced a large numbers of widows and orphans. Similarly, smaller ghettos in Poland experienced this mass murder of large numbers of family members before concentration in the larger ghettos. This is related to another commonality of ghetto experience—that ghetto inhabitants were overwhelmed with a general sense of insecurity about their personal safety. One report of the ghetto in Kishinev disclosed that the members of the Jewish population were "the targets of abuse of soldiers and guards. It is especially the officers who insult them, for whom visiting the ghetto is the funniest thing."[28] Harassing Jews who were forced to remain in the ghettos was not limited to Romanian guards. German officials and others seem to have been able to gain easy access to the ghetto. According to Robert Marshall, in his memoir *In the Sewers of Lvov*, *SS Obersturmführer* Grzymek patrolled the streets of the ghetto himself, "entering the buildings to inspect each home while the inhabitants were at work ... his pathological behavior sent the population into frenzied devotions of washing, sweeping, and polishing whatever they were forced to call home."[29]

This constant fear led to another common experience—widespread bribery to mediate conditions. Bribery seems to have been more widespread in the eastern ghettos than in their more western counterparts in Poland. In her article on the ghettos of Transnistria, Dalia Ofer writes that "Jewish policies in Transnistria reflected the traditional attributes of Romanian administration: slackness, ineffectiveness, corruption, and preoccupation with the economic exploitation of the region. Jewish ghetto and camp inmates took advantage of these conditions which enabled them to create a narrow margin of survival for themselves."[30] Bribery of the administration could range from low-level bribing of individual guards to ignore or assist in food smuggling, letter-carrying or other illegal activities, to higher-level bribing of commanders and even higher officials. Bribery extended to the very highest of levels, as testified by the former mayor of Czernowitz. He wrote that "Oct. 14, the day that Ion Antonescu exempted 20,000 Czernowitz Jews from deportation, saw the budding of a shameless racket: exemptions were sold for 'hard currency' (dollars, British pounds and gold coins)."[31]

Bribery, however, did not save many from one of the most frequent experiences, which was to a greater or lesser degree perpetually present in ghettos throughout Nazi-occupied and Nazi-allied Europe, namely the constant specter of death. The piles of bodies in the streets of the Warsaw ghetto are well documented in contemporary reports and photographs. In Riga, the newly arrived population found "[t]he apartments were in a shambles, and some of the furnishings bore the traces of blood."[32] A survivor, Meyer Sternberg, described arriving at the Bessarabian Merkulesht ghetto:

> From all sides horror, ruin and death stared at us. In the houses, in the cellars, in the attics, in the sheds, in the courtyards, behind fences, in ditches, there lay the bodies of murdered Jews. As we entered the houses the stench was so strong, it was impossible to breathe. The first thing we did was to lift up the dead, and carry them to a nearby synagogue.[33]

He goes on to report that when he opened the chest he was sleeping on top of, he found the dead body of a child. Upon ascending the stairs to the attic, he discovered three more bodies hanging from the beams.[34]

Many Holocaust victims did not have to wait to enter a town to discover that they would be living among those murdered. One survivor relates, "Once within sight of Soroko, a peasant woman approached us, holding her nose. When she came close, she apologized, saying she was holding her nose to shut out the horrible stench from the dead lying about the streets of Soroko."[35] One of the common images described in the ghettos in Romania are of bodies, unburied, and lying on the streets. Both survivors and Romanian officials describe this in their testimonies. St. Dragomirescu, a jeweler who served as an appraiser of valuables to be bought by the Romanian National Bank, reported that when he arrived in Marculesti "all over, [he saw] in cellars, trenches, yards lay corpses of the deportees."[36] Similarly, Dr Mayer Teich wrote of his arrival in Attachi, "Round about lay corpses left by former groups of exiles."[37]

Sometimes the encounters with death related to being forced to desecrate cemeteries and the buried. Aaron Schwartz, along with his brother and cousin, was deported on Passover evening from Debica to Krakow ghetto.[38] Although Aaron identified himself as a tailor, he was put to work breaking up tombstones from the Krakow cemetery into large chunks. Women were then assigned to making gravel out of these pieces of tombstones with hammers. Another group then took away the gravel to make a road over the cemetery.[39] The bodies in the cemetery were dug up and Aaron was put to work extracting gold teeth from their jaws. Sometimes the bones rolled down the hill. Other times, the bodies were not entirely decomposed. The gold was delivered to the Germans.[40]

For those not living among the dead, there was always the specter of death. Deportations and ghetto liquidations were a constant reality for ghetto inmates. Malvina Graf described one deportation from the Krakow ghetto: "On Monday, June 8, the doors [of the holding area] … were unbolted, and the people who had been there for the past two days began a forced march to the railroad station in Prokocim. They passed through Limanowskiego Street and then Wieliczka Street, urged on by the cruel blows of their *Sonderdienst* escort."[41]

Despite the constant reality of death and insecurity, in those ghettos that managed to survive for some length of time, various social entities emerged or managed to remain from the pre-ghetto period. In many ghettos, some sort of secret worship took place; victims of the Łódź ghetto, for instance, record the prevalence of prayers for the dead and prayers said on fast days. Education also continued. In some ghettos it was permitted, while in others it took place in secret schools, held in homes and even inside wardrobes, to avoid the eyes of spies. Larger communal enterprises also continued, such as hospitals, orphanages, charitable organizations, and even social workers' visits to individuals' homes. Cultural life sprang up in many ghettos, with musical and theatrical performances in large halls or in the ghetto streets. One well-known street singer in the Łódź ghetto, Yankele Hershkowitz, would sing about the troubles of the day. In the same ghetto, a House of Culture employed musicians, actors, set designers, and others until deportations and starvation killed off many of its members.

Disease and hunger were perhaps the most common experiences for ghetto-dwellers. Typhus, dysentery, diphtheria, meningitis, and other diseases claimed lives by the thousands, and by 1944, tuberculosis was responsible for close to 40 percent of all deaths in the Łódź ghetto.[42] With respect to hunger, in the Warsaw ghetto, Jews were forced to subsist on approximately 180 calories per day, a quarter of the rations given to Poles, and close to five percent of the rations allotted to Germans.[43] Ghetto inhabitants therefore had to devise numerous coping methods including (among other things) smuggling, theft, and consuming things which were not normally consumed in the prewar period. Potato peels, rotting vegetables, and moldy bread became commonly eaten foods in most ghettos. The most desperate were described by one ghetto writer, Josef Zelkowicz, as the

> hundreds, thousands [who] drag along the ghetto streets now. They are driven from their houses into the streets, into the courtyards where the garbage is piled, and they look, they seek:
> A piece of a broken pot that can still be licked—A rag that once wrapped food and can still be gnawed at—A discarded piece of vegetable—And they live out their last days up to their necks in piles of garbage.[44]

To combat this hunger, ghetto home-makers needed to be extremely creative to stretch the food products they were given. They contrived ways of making soup out of radish and of stretching their meager food allotments. One ghetto cake recipe called for three potatoes, 12–15 spoons of (ersatz) coffee, two spoons of flour, 10 saccharine tablets, one spoon of drinking soda, and a little salt.[45]

In the closed ghettos, some combated hunger through smuggling. Emmanuel Ringelblum wrote of the Warsaw ghetto:

> Smuggling began at the very moment that the Jewish area of residence was established ... [because] If one had wanted really to restrict oneself to the official rations, then the entire population of the ghetto would have had to die of hunger in a very short time. ...
> The German authorities did everything to seal off the ghetto hermetically and not to allow in a single gram of food ... They fixed barbed wire and broken glass to the top of the wall. When that failed to help, the Judenrat was ordered to make the wall higher, at the expense of the Jews, of course. ... [46]

Ringelblum relates that many Jews and non-Jews died trying to smuggle food. Some of the Jewish smugglers were as young as five and six.

> And despite that ... the smuggling never stopped for a moment. When the street was still slippery with the blood that had been spilled, other smugglers already

set out, as soon as the 'candles' had signaled that the way was clear, to carry on with the work. ....[47]

Not everyone experienced extreme hunger. There were those in the ghettos who managed to get enough to eat, and even some with more than enough. Sometimes these were those in open ghettos who had access to help from outside. In closed ghettos, the elite were often smugglers, though sometimes they were ghetto officials or those rewarded for spying on their fellow ghetto-dwellers. For those with the means to pay for it, there were cafés and restaurants where one could obtain hot meals, and even pastry shops at which to buy sweets.

There were varying ghetto experiences, depending both on the type of ghetto one was interned within, and on one's place in the social hierarchy within the ghetto. Nevertheless, there were common traits and experiences which dominated in the ghettos, irrespective of administration, location, or population.

Notes

1 Raul Hilberg, *The Destruction of the European Jews* (New York: Quadrangle, 1961), 153.
2 Dan Michman, *Fear for the 'Ostjuden': The Jewish Ghettos During the Holocaust: Why and How Did They Emerge?* trans. Lenn Schramm (Cambridge: Cambridge University Press, 2009), 11.
3 See, for example, Philip Friedman, "The Jewish Ghettos of the Nazi Era," in *Roads to Extinction: Essays on the Holocaust* (Philadelphia: The Jewish Publication Society of America, 1980); Isaiah Trunk, *Judenrat: The Jewish Councils in Eastern Europe Under Nazi Occupation* (New York: Macmillan, 1972); Lucy Dawidowicz, *The War Against the Jews, 1933–1945* (New York: Holt, Rinehart and Winston, 1975).
4 Christopher Browning, "Before the 'Final Solution': Nazi Ghettoization Policy in Poland (1940–41)," in *Ghettos 1939–1945: New Research and Perspectives on Definition, Daily Life, and Survival, Symposium Presentations* (Washington, DC: Center for Advanced Holocaust Studies, United States Holocaust Memorial Museum, 2005), 3.
5 Christopher Browning, "Nazi Ghettoization Policy in Poland, 1939–41," in *The Path to Genocide: Essays on Launching the Final Solution* (Cambridge: Cambridge University Press, 1992), 30.
6 See Michman, *Fear for the 'Ostjuden.'*
7 Julius Fisher, *Transnistria: The Forgotten Cemetery* (South Brunswick, New Jersey: T. Yoseloff, 1969), 49.
8 Fisher, *Transnistria*, 68.
9 Malvina Graf, *The Kraków Ghetto and the Płaszów Camp Remembered* (Tallahassee, Florida: Florida State University Press, 1989), 42.
10 Shmuel Spector, *The Holocaust of Volhynian Jews, 1941–1944* (Jerusalem: Yad Vashem, 1990), 159.
11 Trunk, *Judenrat*, 150.
12 Browning, *The Path to Genocide*, 43.
13 Browning, *The Path to Genocide*, 56; Primo Levi, *Moments of Reprieve: A Memoir of Auschwitz* (New York: Penguin Classics, 1995), 125.
14 Sworn testimony of Rosa Kamelgarn, United States Holocaust Memorial Museum Archives, Acc. 1998.A.0249.
15 Browning, *The Path to Genocide*.
16 There have been numerous studies of the *Judenräte* and their relationship with the Nazi authorities. This discussion, first raised by Raul Hilberg and perverted by Hannah Arendt, asked what the victims' role—in the form of the Jewish leadership—was in their own destruction. Isaiah Trunk, in his monumental work, *Judenrat*, shifted the debate to focus on the fact that the position of the Jewish Councils as executioners was imposed on them by the Nazi authorities, who, in the end, had final control.
17 Trunk, *Judenrat*, 51.

18 Zoe Vania Waxman, *Writing the Holocaust: Identity, Testimony, Representation* (Oxford: Oxford University Press, 2006), 29. See also Joseph Kermish, *To Live with Honor and Die with Honor!* (Jerusalem: Yad Vashem, 1986), 405.

19 Fisher, *Transnistria*, 68.

20 Matatias Carp, *The Holocaust in Romania: Facts and Documents on the Annihilation of Romania's Jews* (New York: Simon Publications, 2001), 281.

21 Dennis Deletant, "Aspects of the Ghetto Experience in Eastern Transnistria: The Ghettos and Labor Camp in the Town of Golta," in *Ghettos 1939–1945*, 23.

22 Hilberg, *The Destruction of the European Jews*, 231.

23 Fisher, *Transnistria*, 45.

24 Carp, *The Holocaust in Romania*, 268.

25 Christian Gerlach, "Failure of Plans for an SS Extermination Camp in Mogilev, Belorussia," *Holocaust and Genocide Studies*, vol. 11, no. 1 (1997): 62.

26 Jean Ancel, "The Romanian Way of Solving the 'Jewish Problem' in Bessarabia and Bukovina, June–July 1941," *Yad Vashem Studies*, vol. 19 (1988): 218.

27 Ancel, "The Romanian Way of Solving the 'Jewish Problem'," 218–19.

28 Carp, *The Holocaust in Romania*, 270–71.

29 Robert Marshall, *In the Sewers of Lvov: A Heroic Story of Survival from the Holocaust* (New York: Scribner, 1991), 9.

30 Dalia Ofer, "Every Day Life in the Ghettos and Camps in Transnistria," *Yad Vashem Studies*, vol. 25 (1996): 175–208.

31 Fisher, *Transnistria*, 69.

32 Hilberg, *The Destruction of the European Jews*, 233.

33 Jakób Apenszlak, *The Black Book of Polish Jewry* (New York: Roy Publishers, 1943), 168–69.

34 Apenszlak, *The Black Book of Polish Jewry*, 168–69.

35 Apenszlak, *The Black Book of Polish Jewry*, 163.

36 Fisher, *Transnistria*, 52.

37 Fisher, *Transnistria*, 94.

38 Oral Testimony of Aaron Schwartz. United States Holocaust Memorial Museum Archives, RG 50.002*0048.

39 Oral Testimony of Aaron Schwartz.

40 Oral Testimony of Aaron Schwartz.

41 Graf, *The Kraków Ghetto*, 48.

42 www.holocaustresearchproject.org/ghettos/Łódź/Łódźghetto.html.

43 www.deathcamps.org/occupation/warsaw%20ghetto.html.

44 Alan Adelson and Robert Lapides, eds, *Łódź Ghetto: Inside a Community Under Siege* (New York: Viking, 1989), 129.

45 S. Glube, "Meachlim in Łódźer Ghetto" ["Meals in the Ghetto of Łódź,"] in *Fun Letztn Churban: Tzytschrift fur geshichte yidishen laben beten Nazi Rezim* [*From the Last Extermination: Journal for the History of the Jewish People During the Nazi Regime*], no. 9 (Munich: EUCOM Civil Affairs, September 1948), 80.

46 Emmanuel Ringelblum, "Life in the Warsaw Ghetto," in *Documents on the Holocaust*, eds Yitzhak Arad, Israel Gutman and Abraham Margaliot (New York: Pergamon, 1987), 228–29.

47 Ringelblum, "Life in the Warsaw Ghetto," 228–29.

11

FORGING THE "ARYAN UTOPIA"

Nazi racial policy in occupied Poland, 1939–45

Bradley Nichols

While historians have long been researching the experiences of victims of the Nazi genocide, the linkages between separate Nazi policies for Jews, Poles, and ethnic Germans in occupied Poland remain relatively unexamined. What follows is a brief overview of these connections, as well as a study of the similarities between institutional processes and ideological motivations animating racial policy towards different population groups under German occupation. As the setting for some of the most wide-ranging and barbarous initiatives of the National Socialist regime, occupied Poland provides an instructive topic for such an examination. Though within each common pattern lay complex variations and interactive relationships between planning and realization, comparable trends of cumulative radicalization served to unify the seemingly divergent agendas of Nazi Jewish policy, *Polenpolitik*, and the campaign to reclaim "lost" German blood in Poland prior to the 1941 invasion of the Soviet Union. Despite their creation of a racialized hierarchy that distinguished between various groups of undesirables, the Nazis tended to collapse these distinctions into a more general drive of violent racial purification.

The subjugation of Poland

The Polish campaign was a war of racial annihilation from its very inception.[1] The Germans' systematic murder campaign of September 1939 activated and dogmatized prewar anti-Polish and antisemitic attitudes as SS (*Schutzstaffel*) killing squads and army units conducted widespread massacres throughout the region.[2] The murderousness of these operations originated with Hitler's demand for a ruthless racial struggle, beginning with the elimination of the Polish elite. Though specific death lists targeted thousands, the Nazis left the definition of "elite" nebulous so as to encompass a wider range of victims. Therefore, while Polish aristocrats, nationalists, political officials, intelligentsia, and clergy constituted official targets, anyone with the slightest social or cultural prominence could be murdered for anti-German inclinations.[3] Antisemitic atrocities were especially savage by way of comparison, but more spontaneous and uncoordinated.[4] The extension of the euthanasia program into occupied Poland added yet another dimension to this initial phase of ethnic cleansing.[5]

A functional link existed among all of these various manifestations of "cleansing" the eastern territories. The ideological rationale for murder remained relatively consistent—purifying the German race and securing a territorial empire.[6] Nazi anxieties concerning racial pollution and subversive behavior emanated from overlapping perceptions of Jewish and Polish ethnic identity, conditioned by traditional German prejudices and National Socialist race ideology. Jews and Poles were threats by reason of immutable racial traits, a specific danger to national security by virtue of their existence. Within this fusion of racial and security imperatives, radicalization emerged with Hitler's pronouncements and the operational planning of the SS, but assumed its expansive form through the implementation of executions by local commanders. From the outset, key decision-makers in Berlin anticipated, allowed for, and encouraged independent escalation of killings. Taken as a whole, the number of different murder programs in 1939 marked an early microcosm of the processes of cumulative radicalization later developed into extermination policy over the course of the conflict.[7]

The New Order in the East

For Hitler, the consolidation of *Lebensraum* required radical measures beyond selective execution; the Polish territories could not become German until cleared of all alien influences and settled with "persons of Aryan blood." To this effect, in early October 1939, Hitler placed responsibility for resettlement in Poland into the hands of the SS, granting Heinrich Himmler enormous power for the furtherance of racial–ideological goals.[8] Himmler consolidated police authority under Reinhard Heydrich, head of the newly constituted Reich Security Main Office (*Reichssicherheitshauptamt*, RSHA), and established the Staff Office of the Reich Commissioner for the Strengthening of Germandom (*Reichskommissar für die Festigung deutschen Volkstums*, RKFDV) under Ulrich Greifelt to serve as the linchpin agency for the formulation and coordination of resettlement initiatives. The RSHA and the RKFDV each functioned as hubs for directives passed down from Himmler and Heydrich to Higher SS and Police Leaders (*Höhere SS- und Polizeiführer*, HSSPF) at the regional level, and for intelligence on these initiatives transmitted back from the periphery to Berlin.[9] But the SS was not the only source of authority in occupied Poland.

In the Polish territories incorporated to Germany, Himmler contended with regional governors who had plans of their own. While Arthur Greiser in the Warthegau was amenable to Himmler's goals, Josef Wagner in Silesia and Albert Forster in Danzig-West Prussia were resistant and downright hostile. Moreover, the General Government remained an independent administrative entity encompassing most of eastern Poland, under the control of Hans Frank, who put up heavy resistance to SS designs to turn his fiefdom into a dumping ground for racial undesirables. Therefore the administrative security apparatus included competing elements that produced a disorderly situation of adhoc decision-making. However, despite the confused power structure, the officials involved shared similar ideological motivations to forge an Aryan racial utopia in the East.[10]

The onset of civilian administration in October 1939 confirmed these shared propensities by stripping the Poles of all human rights. Provided with substandard food provisions and subject to violence without pretext or provocation, the Polish people experienced policies of decimation and terror that soon became the hallmarks of Nazi rule throughout Eastern Europe.[11] The German occupiers saw the Poles as inferior and dangerous, so they took measures to segregate and remove them, while fixing a draconian legal standard stipulating imprisonment in a concentration camp or execution for any offense. While this doctrine dovetailed with SS and *Wehrmacht* killings, the main technique for Germanizing the land from the fall of 1939 to the spring of 1941 was expulsion, beginning in September with a series of unauthorized "wild" deportations of Poles and Jews.[12]

National Socialist *Polenpolitik*

Himmler's dual task in October conveyed the focal, binary dynamic of Nazi racial policy in Poland—to remove so-called harmful elements and replace them with Germans. After the conclusion of diplomatic arrangements for the repatriation of ethnic Germans from Soviet-held territory, Himmler issued orders on 30 October 1939 for the expulsion of anti-German Poles from the Warthegau, Silesia, and southeast Prussia, all Congress Poles (those having moved to previously German regions after World War I) from West Prussia, and all Jews from the incorporated territories as a whole. In the Warthegau, HSSPF Wilhelm Koppe emphasized on 10 November that security could not be guaranteed until "none of the intellectual elite … [and] criminal or political Polish elements are at all still present."[13] In drafting memoranda for the removal of an estimated 200,000 Poles, subordinates broadened the scope of targets even further to include Catholic clergymen, local business leaders, the "work-shy" and "asocial elements," even a majority of the industrial proletariat.[14] The Nazis linked associations of criminality and anti-German attitudes with those understood to represent Polish national sentiment, yet expanded beyond these definitions, following a classification similar to that which defined killing actions against the Polish elite. As one report indicated, the deportations "included a biological, a political, and a social component."[15] The belief in a hydra-headed threat to Germandom reinforced the conviction that harsh measures were necessary for the indigenous population in general.

However, numerous logistical problems forced Heydrich to intervene in late November to reorganize the operation into several short-range plans working towards a long-term solution. Though the Nazis deported 87,000 people from the annexed territories by early December (usually left to die in deplorable conditions in the General Government), they did not distinguish between Polish and Jewish victims, reflecting the closely interconnected nature of policy towards both groups. Heydrich's intervention changed this stance. The sheer number of Poles slated for deportation meant that the Nazis could not deal with the Jews simultaneously. The plan for the emigration of the Jews entered into a succession of setbacks and postponements as German functionaries first worked to solve their *Polenproblem*.[16] Racial policy toward Poles and Jews began to diverge.

In addition, the stated goal of colonizing ethnic German settlers (*Volksdeutsche*), now pouring into the incorporated territories from the Baltic region, complicated the racial-ideological designs of ethnic purification. The *Volksdeutsche* required housing and employment, and, according to Nazi *Blut und Boden* ("Blood and Soil") ideology, should be settled on farmland. Yet most of the targeted Poles (not to mention a majority of the local Jews, already despoiled in any case) resided in urban areas. Furthermore, alleged criminals and "asocial elements" offered little, in terms of housing or jobs, to dispossess.[17] This tension between ideological initiatives and economic requirements was especially palpable in Upper Silesia and the Warthegau throughout the deportation phase of fall 1939 to spring 1941. In the former territory, deportation proceeded with greater scrutiny due to the employment of Polish skilled labor in vital war industries, while in the latter, more thorough expulsions wreaked havoc on the local economic infrastructure. While alleged security threats continued to take precedence and racial inequality functioned as the fundamental pretext for deportation, practical concerns related to ethnic German settlement forced a compromise with the ideology underlying the removal of the Poles, as economic prerogatives worked their way into the overall scheme of resettlement in late 1939.[18]

If the dogma of racial apartheid could be sidestepped, the inhuman racist perspective could not. As manpower shortages became dire in January and February of 1940, the Nazi leadership responded with a concession that in actuality masked a further radicalization of *Polenpolitik*. In choosing to import Polish slave labor into the Reich, the Nazis violated their own racial security doctrine predicated upon fears of Slavic interbreeding with the German population, a not insignificant ideological compromise in the face of real-life circumstances. However, the reaction to this self-imposed offense against racial purity revealed a *de facto* intensification of brutality. The Nazis worked their pathological hatred into a set of decrees, issued in March 1940, that ordained a regimen of punitive labor for Polish forced laborers designed to exhaust and kill, the vicious treatment subsequently suffered at the hands of their German overseers attesting to an unstated though implicit policy of gradual annihilation through labor. Cruel treatment of Polish laborers ensured their economic productivity would never reach optimum levels.[19] While the economic imperative of labor shortages compelled a deviation from ideological goals, the results of state-sanctioned racism overrode such considerations in practice.

Ideological prerogatives asserted themselves in other ways, while still taking more rational considerations into account. The structural reorganization of the SS racial security apparatus in spring 1940 brought with it not only the task of mass Polish labor recruitment, but the reclamation of "lost" German blood through racial selection and Germanization. The inclination towards this second duty began in fall 1939, with sporadic racial examinations of local inhabitants and the establishment of the *Deutsche Volksliste* (DVL) to register ethnic Germans (*Volksdeutsche*) on Polish soil for preferential treatment.[20] In November 1939, a memorandum issued by the Nazi Party's Racial Political Office stated that, in addition to confirmed ethnic Germans, in the incorporated territories there lived great numbers of *Deutschstämmige*, that is, Polish nationals of German ethnic stock capable of Germanization.[21] The concept of rehabilitating "Polonized Germans" shortly thereafter assumed great importance as a policy measure. During the winter and spring of 1939–40, the Nazis began to emphasize the need for more conclusive determinations of the ethnic identity of deportees in order to prevent the loss of German blood.[22] The creation of the Central Emigration Office (*Umwandererzentralstelle*, UWZ) in April 1940 was an attempt to cull supposed "valuable Aryan bloodlines," prevent the most harmful racial elements from entering Germany, and replace as many undesirable Polish laborers as possible with "reclaimed" Germans. However, while UWZ officials handled labor procurement, property registration, economic deferments, and expulsions, it was the "racial fitness examiners" of the SS Race and Settlement Office (*Rasse- und Siedlungshauptamt-SS*, RuSHA) who determined the ethnic classification and eventual fate of the deportees.[23]

With the inauguration of an official Germanization program in May 1940, known as the *Wiedereindeutschungsfähigenverfähren* (WED), Himmler brought the imperatives of racial selection and Germanization into the open and under the purview of the

RuSHA.[24] The agency's chief, *SS-Brigadeführer* Otto Hofmann, along with his subordinate racial experts, developed a procedure for racial examinations that, while never uniform, adhered to the racist and eugenic principles of Nazi ideology.[25] The RuSHA classification of Polishness in large part conformed to the broad definition of security threats established for executions and deportations during the first six months of the occupation. However, by a bizarre twist of logic, racial ideologues also claimed that the most resistant, anti-German Poles were actually the ones with pure German blood. This novel conception reflected the bifurcated perception of human characteristics underlying the racial selection process. Any personal or social defect, any perceived hereditary or physical malady was an indication of Slavic ethnic character, whereas the assessment of Aryan physiognomy and positive personality traits of all kinds denoted German blood suitable for a type of racial-psychological assimilation.[26] For those entering its embrace, however, the process of Germanization itself conveyed the extent of anti-Polish racism and extreme paranoia within the regime. "Germanizables" faced conditions as appalling as those of the "pure Pole" forced laborers, each the subject of contempt from local party officials, business leaders, and civilians. Greifelt, Hofmann, and others decried this predicament, yet their own suspicions directed at Germanizable Poles paralleled broader concerns about ethnic German resettlers, and colored measures taken towards them. Both were kept in miserable conditions, under constant surveillance by the Gestapo, subjected to ceaseless party meetings, indoctrination, cultural genocide, and physical violence.[27] No matter where they ended up, Poles and "reclaimed" Germans usually faced adverse circumstances.

Polish resettlement in general, and the Germanization program in particular, encompassed the simultaneous striving towards both ideological and economic goals. But as the UWZ–RuSHA procedure continued into 1941, the difficulties of balancing zealous demands for ethnic cleansing of Poles and Jews, the requirements of a wartime economy, and the desire for German settlement became increasingly apparent. By spring 1941, when preparations for the invasion of the Soviet Union and aggrandized labor demands in the Reich terminated the Polish deportations, the Nazis had evicted 923,000 Poles from their homes, the majority expelled into the General Government.[28] Despite regional disparities and an uneasy synthesis of divergent concerns, occupation policy functioned well enough to kill and immiserate a vast quantity of Polish civilians by spring 1941. The chronology of Polish resettlement from 1939 to 1941 reveals the strength of Nazi ideological responses in the face of the practical difficulties. In fact, the setbacks presented by the German invasion of the Soviet Union in June 1941 (Operation Barbarossa) engendered an even greater and more ruthless radicalization of *Polenpolitik*, the common denominator of which was a widely accepted racist perception of the Poles.

Jewish policy in Poland

Though Nazi functionaries devoted much of their time between the fall of 1939 and the spring of 1941 to clearing the incorporated territories of Poles, they did not forget the Jewish question, nor did the Jews lose any semblance of their status as the ultimate ideological enemy. Though the Nazis utilized mass violence from the beginning, the initial goal of Jewish policy in Poland was the same as the aim in Germany—emigration. Heydrich issued instructions on 21 September 1939 for the concentration of Polish Jews into urban areas and the establishment of *Judenräte* (Jewish councils) to facilitate administrative control over the Jewish population. He also distinguished between gradual stages of enactment and a long-term final aim, meaning deportation to the General Government, where, that fall, several Nazis devised plans to create a Jewish reservation in the Lublin district.[29] However, because Himmler's focus was on ethnic German resettlement, the goal of evacuating 700,000 Jews from the incorporated territories subsequently suffered a series of postponements.[30] The Jews could not yet be deported, but their presence was seen as intolerable.

The practice of sealing off Jews in closed ghettos developed from this situation, conceived as a temporary measure in anticipation of future expulsion, and carried out with great reluctance.[31] Though haphazard and inconsistent in its implementation, ghettoization clearly arose within the parameters of racial ideology.[32] In the Warthegau, Greiser claimed the ghetto's purpose was to force Jews to divulge hoarded valuables in exchange for food, whereas in the General Government, the pretexts were more numerous: Jews were claimed to be the source of epidemics, black marketeering, and the partisan threat to German officials.[33] Behind all of these justifications stood the standard requirement of segregation, based on the belief that Jews constituted a collective racial peril. While much of the Nazis' antisemitic legislation served to humiliate Jews, early measures for identification and restriction of movement occurred within the context of national–biological security.

Exploitation of Jewish labor also matured as policy during 1940 and 1941 due to the repeated deferment of wholesale evacuation, a subject of contention between functionaries favoring utilitarian economics and those calling for wholesale murder through neglect. The former (productionists) had little humanitarian sympathy for the Jews, but believed they should be allowed to contribute something of value until they could be expelled. The latter (attritionists) preferred allowing the Jews to perish slowly through starvation and disease, intentionally made endemic in the Łódź and Warsaw ghettos throughout their existence, killing tens of thousands by the end of 1941. Since the predominantly destitute Jews of eastern Poland had far less to offer in terms of property than their more affluent brethren in the annexed territories, labor exploitation became far more widespread in the General Government.[34] From the very beginning, labor camps were in fact death traps. Because Jews were considered racially worthless and expendable, Jewish labor camps cost little to maintain and provided something of an economic incentive for German businesses. But, because death and suffering was so extensive that nothing of worth could be produced, the camps ended up costing more to maintain than the value of Jewish efforts. While no uniform policy ever arose, the irrational organization and brutality of Jewish labor usage shared the purpose of the ghettos, which was to accelerate destruction.[35]

While ghettoization and labor exploitation were not initially intended as preparatory steps for physical extermination, their inherently violent nature spurred radicalization toward that end.[36] Each policy originated as provisional, with killing part of the strategy, yet removal the ultimate goal. In the ghettos, the murderous consequences of deliberate starvation made resident Jews appear to be human examples of Nazi antisemitic stereotypes, confirming their validity to Nazi officials and fueling a self-fulfilling prophesy whereby imposed conditions intensified the sense of a crisis situation, with the pretexts for ghettoization becoming rationalizations for implementing a quicker and more lethal method of removal.[37] Frustration with recurring impasses and failures in the resettlement program as a whole, and with Jewish resettlement in particular, contributed a crucial dynamic of exigency to the escalation of harsh measures.[38] The overarching desire for removal and the deadliness of ghettoization and labor exploitation helped prepare the psychological groundwork for the eventual solution of wholesale annihilation.

The destruction of Polish Jewry

The switch in German military-strategic focus from Britain to the Soviet Union in late 1940, and the abandonment of the proposition to ship the Jews *en masse* to the island of Madagascar, stimulated contemplation of an intentionally murderous solution to the "Jewish Question." From the winter of 1940 to the early summer of 1941, Nazi leaders conceptualized a "Final Solution" through the extermination of Soviet Jewry and the mass deportation of European Jews to labor reservations deep within Russian territory. Accompanying this plan was the conviction that, while the Jews as a whole would gradually die out due to starvation, exhaustion, and the desolate, wasteland conditions of Siberia and the Arctic (to paraphrase Heydrich), a large number of those incapable of work or otherwise undesirable would be executed in, or en route to, the East.[39] The reactions of Nazi functionaries in Poland to this proposal played a crucial role in the process of cumulative radicalization during the period from June to December 1941.

In the zones of Soviet-occupied eastern Poland overrun by the Germans during the first weeks of Operation Barbarossa, SS killing squads immediately exterminated entire Jewish communities. In the General Government, news of steadily enlarged killings in the Soviet Union encouraged local officials to eliminate superfluous Jews under their control by the same method. Galicia, in particular, saw numerous massacres carried out in the context of rationalizing labor projects with planning for complete removal, and throughout Frank's domain, the Security Police and SD consistently attempted to intensify local executions in anticipation of a final evacuation further east.[40] Frank expressed his understanding in September 1941 that expulsion remained the arrangement, while the civilian administration conspired to make conditions in the ghettos as untenable as possible.[41]

Local SS authorities in Upper Silesia were also under the impression that expulsion to Siberia was the intention, and undertook independent killing initiatives in preparation for that eventuality.[42] In short, as the Himmler–Heydrich evacuation plan slowly came into focus, local officials in Poland responded with anticipatory liquidations. While territorial solutions for expulsion to Lublin, Madagascar, and the Soviet Union always implied genocide and eventual extinction, the momentum towards swift, total annihilation was gaining strength.[43]

A similar process took place in the Warthegau, where in July, Rolf-Heinz Höppner, head of the SD office in Poznań, suggested "finishing off" those Jews unable to work "with some quick-acting method" as an alternative to slow death through starvation.[44] When Himmler notified Greiser in September 1941 of the pending influx of German and Czech Jews to the already overcrowded Łódź ghetto, the latter took steps for executions to "make room" for the incoming deportees, irrespective of labor capacity.[45] Preliminary gassings occurred throughout the autumn. In September, several hundred Soviet POWs and Polish prisoners were gassed via Zyklon B in Auschwitz; in November, construction began on the killing center at Bełżec; and the first gassings took place at Chelmno on 8 December. In October, Greiser, through Koppe, concluded an arrangement with Heydrich and Himmler whereby he would accept Reich Jews if the SS agreed to decimate the existing ghetto population.[46] With Hitler's approval of deportations from the Reich in early October, the prescription to eliminate all non-working Jews escalated into designs for the full-scale extermination of Polish Jewry, though lack of coordination continued in the General Government until the "Operation Reinhard" death camps (Bełżec, Sobibor, and Treblinka) became operational in the spring and summer of 1942.[47]

Racial selection, Germanization, and cumulative radicalization

The launch of Operation Barbarossa in June 1941 held ominous implications for the non-Jewish population of Poland as well.[48] The March cessation of deportations and comprehensive RuSHA racial screening of Polish forced laborers marked serious set-backs to resettlement.[49] But the invasion of the Soviet Union also ushered in more direct radicalization of *Polenpolitik*. The RuSHA and UWZ continued to screen and evict Poles through the prism of racial–biological security, following a tripartite model of eviction, Germanization, and mass starvation dubbed "displacement." Between 1941 and 1942, the agency sent some 130,826 Poles to perish slowly in massive reception camps.[50] Poles pressed into labor service endured the same mistreatment and woeful conditions as before, but by 1945 their number had swelled to over two and a half million.[51]

Displaced Poles who escaped from internment frequently joined partisan groups, resulting in expanded German "pacification operations," which wiped hundreds of Polish villages off the map.[52] Nazi authorities in Poland also undertook measures in 1942 to control marriages and encourage abortions as part of an overall genocidal plan to reduce the Polish birthrate.[53] Yet nowhere was the shift in murderous intentionality more obvious than in the formulation of the *Generalplan Ost*. The plan envisioned the expulsion of over 30 million Poles to Siberia for forced labor and gradual extinction, a fate similar to that initially intended for the Jews in the planning of Himmler and Heydrich.

An analysis of the Germanization program in the years of the war after 1941 provides a peculiar and novel insight into this general process of radicalization. The campaign to recover "lost" German blood expanded dramatically in scope during the spring and summer 1941 (and afterwards), as RuSHA personnel began conducting racial examinations on Polish forced laborers and prisoners of war, and Himmler secured jurisdiction for selection and Germanization within the DVL.[54] Yet despite the increasingly vast scale of racial examinations, classification as a potential German remained elusive.[55] While the Nazis convinced themselves that German blood lay dormant in the East, they were never quite able to locate it. They deflected the resulting frustration upon the "Germanizable" themselves, all the while evincing paranoia over potential recidivism and the fear of polluting the German body politic.[56]

In early 1942, concerns about the faults of existing examination techniques compelled the SS to augment the pool of racial–medical experts by allowing public health officials to examine captured Poles and to make determinations of their fitness for Germanization.[57] RuSHA officials proposed a procedure to expel from the program those deemed unfit *ex post facto* and relegate them to "special treatment"—murder—a policy subsequently approved by Greifelt and Himmler, echoing the latter's assertion that all irredeemable German blood must be destroyed.[58] The Germanization program devolved into a grotesque, farcical cycle of abuse, exploitation, and murder. Individuals "accepted" into the WED on a trial basis faced conditions that made life untenable, were then removed under the pretense that their inability to endure was a sign of Polishness, and were replaced by fresh recruits from ever-larger rounds of examinations. In dealing with "Germanizables," SS officials expressed the same anti-Polish racial stereotypes under which Poles had been oppressed and murdered since 1939, and retreated into utopian visions of demographic engineering that became more grandiose with each setback they incurred.

Conclusion

National Socialist occupation policy in Poland wove together a complex relationship of prejudices and motivations to launch a racial war against multiple targets under the auspices of conquest and biological purity. The Nazis believed that different *Reichsfeinde* (enemies of the Reich) simultaneously sought Germany's destruction through a protean, multifaceted conspiracy, at the center of which stood international Jewry. They invested these various "undesirables" with a supposed collective unity of action that stimulated a similarity of approach towards each distinct target group. In Poland, responses to the difficulty of reconciling utopian dreams of imperialism with changing situational dynamics reveal how the Nazis followed similar courses of persecution and mass murder towards Jews, Poles, and "reclaimed" Germans.

Genocidal policies developed not from unilateral decisions or an automatic path towards clear, predetermined political aims, but out of an evolution of initiatives that progressively broadened the scope of action. The reciprocal interaction of high-level planners and regional occupation authorities, with the elite echelons providing the initial framework for their subordinates to pursue ever more brutal measures, meant in each example that utilitarian pretexts became, to a large extent, expressions of ideological dictates.[59] In each case, the basis for action lay in the collective perception of a nexus between racialized, typological characterizations of human behavior on the one hand, and the principles of national–biological security on the other. Jewish policy, *Polenpolitik*, and the Germanization campaign followed comparable patterns of cumulative radicalization. Ideological compromise and perceived setbacks triggered radical goals and enhanced brutality, with seemingly pragmatic concessions masking increasingly grandiose, expansive aims and heinous mistreatment of victims.

Notes

1 Philippe Burrin, *Hitler and the Jews: The Genesis of the Holocaust* (London: Hodder Arnold, 1994).

2 Martin Broszat, *Nationalsozialistische Polenpolitik, 1939–1945* (Stuttgart: Deutsche Verlags-Anstalt, 1961), 218.

3 Alexander B. Rossino, *Hitler Strikes Poland: Blitzkrieg, Ideology, and Atrocity* (Lawrence, Kansas: University Press of Kansas, 2003), 22–23; Tadeusz Piotrowski, *Poland's Holocaust: Ethnic Strife, Collaboration with Occupying Forces and Genocide in the Second Republic, 1918–1947* (Jefferson, North Carolina: McFarland, 1998), 23; Richard C. Lukas and Norman Davies, *The Forgotten Holocaust: The Poles Under German Occupation, 1939–1944* (New York: Hippocrene, 1997), 8.

4 Christopher R. Browning, *The Origins of the Final Solution: The Evolution of Nazi Jewish Policy, September 1939–March 1942* (Lincoln, Nebraska: University of Nebraska Press, 2004), 28–29; Saul S. Friedman, *A History of the Holocaust* (London: Mitchell Vallentine & Co., 2004), 91.

5 Götz Aly, *Final Solution: Nazi Population Policy and the Murder of the European Jews* (London: Arnold, 1999), 70–71.

6 Richard Breitman, *The Architect of Genocide: Himmler and the Final Solution* (New York: Knopf, 1991), 91.

7 Norman Davies, *God's Playground: A History of Poland, Vol. 2: 1795 to the Present* (New York: Columbia University Press, 1982); Doris Bergen, *War and Genocide: A Concise History of the Holocaust* (Washington, DC: Rowman & Littlefield, 2009), 3, 161; Rossino, *Hitler Strikes Poland*, xiv, xv.

8 Hitler's Order for the Strengthening of Germandom, 7 October 1939, United States Holocaust Memorial Museum Archives (USHMMA), RG 15.015m, 1/95/1–2.

9 Helmut Krausnick and Martin Broszat, *Anatomy of the SS State* (New York: Walker & Co., 1968), 278, 283, 286.

10 Robert L. Koehl, *RKFDV: German Resettlement and Population Policy: A History of the Reich Commission for the Strengthening of Germandom* (Cambridge: Harvard University Press, 1957), 49–50, 57; also see Phillip T. Rutherford, *Prelude to the Final Solution: The Nazi Program for Deporting Ethnic Poles, 1939–1941* (Lawrence, Kansas: University Press of Kansas, 2007), 38–39.

11 Dieter Pohl, "War, Occupation, and the Holocaust in Poland," in *The Historiography of the Holocaust*, ed. Dan Stone (New York: Palgrave Macmillan, 2004), 94; also see Bergen, *War and Genocide*, 105.

12 Piotrowski, *Poland's Holocaust*, 28; also see Pohl, "War, Occupation, and the Holocaust in Poland," 96; Rutherford, *Prelude to the Final Solution*, 74–75.

13 The general orders for deportation, as well as the quote, are cited from USHMMA, RG 15.015m/95/8–14 (Koppe's order for the removal of Jews and Poles, 10 November 1939); also see USHMMA, RG 15.015m/1/95/4–7; draft of planning memorandum by Rapp for the deportation of Warthegau Poles, 10 November 1939.

14 Rapp's directive for the removal of Jews and Poles, 12 November 1939, USHMMA, RG 15.015m/95/4–7; Rapp's directive on investigations of those exempted for deportation for economic reasons, 16 November 1939, USHMMA, RG 15.015m/2/144/1–2; Rapp's directive on categories for deportation, 17 November 1939, USHMMA, RG 15.015m/1/96/1–2.

15 Unsigned report on 1 *Nah-plan*, undated, USHMMA, RG 15.015m/2/99/17–22.

16 Browning, *The Origins of the Final Solution*, 49–54.

17 Browning, *The Origins of the Final Solution*, 55; also see Aly, *Final Solution*, 6.

18 Rutherford, *Prelude to the Final Solution*, 82–83; on Silesia, see Sybille Steinbacher, "In the Shadow of Auschwitz: The Murder of the Jews of East Upper Silesia," in *National Socialist Extermination Policies: Contemporary Perspectives and Controversies*, ed. Ulrich Herbert (New York: Berghahn Books, 1999), 276; Debórah Dwork and Robert Jan Van Pelt, *Auschwitz, 1270 to the Present* (New York: W.W. Norton & Co., 1996).

19 Ulrich Herbert, *Hitler's Foreign Workers: Enforced Foreign Labor in Germany under the Third Reich* (New York: Cambridge University Press, 1997), 69, 89; Ulrich Herbert, *A History of Foreign Labor in Germany, 1880–1980: Seasonal Workers, Forced Laborers, Guest Workers* (Ann Arbor, Michigan: University of Michigan Press, 1990), 138; also see Detlev J.K. Peukert, *Inside Nazi Germany: Conformity, Opposition, and Racism in Everyday Life* (New Haven, Connecticut: Yale University Press, 1987), 126–29.

20 "Excerpt of Greifelt's Testimony," in *Trials of War Criminals before the Nuremberg Military Tribunal under Control Council Law No. 10, October 1946–April 1949, Case No. 8, U.S. vs Greifelt (RuSHA Case)* (Washington, DC: US Government Printing Office, 1948–53), 4: 743–45 [LOC/IMT/Vol. IV ("Green Series")]; also see Robert L. Koehl, "The Deutsche Volksliste in Poland, 1939–45," in *Journal of Central European Affairs*, vol. 15 (1956): 354–66.

21 Erhard Wetzel and Gerhard Hecht, "The Question of the Treatment of the Population of the Former Polish Territories According to Racial-Political Points of View," 25 November 1939, National Archives (NARA), T74/9/57/380571ff.

22 Memorandum on the "Establishment of a Central Emigration Office," January 1940, USHMMA, RG 15.007m/8/103/6–13; Rapp's report on Heydrich's conference of 30 January, 1 February 1940, USHMMA, RG 15.015m/2/109/1–2; also see Koppe memorandum, 20 January 1940, USHMMA, RG 15.015m/2/99/24–25.

23 Rutherford, *Prelude to the Final Solution*, 140–42; on the RuSHA, see Isabel Heinemann, *"Rasse, Siedlung, deutsches Blut": Das Rasse- und Siedlungshauptamt der SS und die rassenpolitische Neuordnung Europas* (Göttingen: Wallstein Verlag, 2003); Isabel Heinemann, "'Another Type of Perpetrator': The SS Racial Experts and Forced Population Movements in the Occupied Regions," in *Holocaust and Genocide Studies*, vol. 15, no. 3 (2001): 387–411.

24 Himmler Decree 17/II on Polish nationals capable of Germanization, 9 May 1940, Document No. 514B, LOC/IMT/Vol. IV ("Green Series"), 762–65; RKF Directive concerning Germanization of Polish families, Document No. 84, LOC/IMT/Vol. IV ("Green Series"), 812–13.
25 Hofmann's "Guidelines for the Selection of the Polish Population in the new Eastern Territories," 16 March 1940, USHMMA, RG 15.021m/1/1/15–18.
26 Himmler, "Some Thoughts on the Treatment of the Alien Populations in the East," c. May 1940, NARA, T175/119/2646113ff.
27 Greifelt to HSSPFs in Poland, 3 July 1940, USHMMA, RG 15.015m/4/259/11–13; Greifelt's instructions on treatment of Germanizable Poles, 31 July 1940, USHMMA, RG 15.021m/1/3/3–4; Hofmann to Greifelt, 28 August 1940, USHMMA, RG 15.007m/10/125/8–9; also see Koehl, *RKFDV*, 132.
28 Piotrowski, *Poland's Holocaust*, 22; Browning, *The Origins of the Final Solution*, 109.
29 Instructions by Heydrich on Policy and Operations Concerning Jews in the Occupied Territories, 21 September 1939, in *Documents on the Holocaust: Selected Sources on the Destruction of the Jews of Germany and Austria, Poland, and the Soviet Union*, ed. Yitzhak Arad, Israel Gutman and Abraham Margoliot (London: Yad Vashem, 1999), 173.
30 Browning, *The Origins of the Final Solution*, 38–40, 45, 62.
31 Raul Hilberg, *The Destruction of the European Jews* (New York: Holmes & Meier, 1985), 1: 215.
32 Browning, *The Origins of the Final Solution*, 133.
33 Tim Cole, "Ghettoization," in *The Historiography of the Holocaust*, ed. Dan Stone (New York: Palgrave Macmillan, 2004), 74–78.
34 Browning, *The Origins of the Final Solution*, 117–31; also see Saul Friedländer, *The Years of Extermination: Nazi Germany and the Jews, 1939–1945* (New York: Harper Perennial, 2008), 104; Jacób Apenzlak, Jacob Kenner, Isaac Lewin and Moses Polakiewicz, *The Black Book of Polish Jewry: An Account of the Martyrdom of Polish Jewry Under the Nazi Occupation* (New York: Howard Fertig Books, 1982), 43, 55–56.
35 Christopher Browning, *Nazi Policy, Jewish Workers, German Killers* (London: Cambridge University Press, 2000), 60–64; also see Hilberg, *The Destruction of the European Jews*, 254–66.
36 Yehuda Bauer, *Rethinking the Holocaust* (New Haven, Connecticut: Yale University Press, 2002), 95; Ian Kershaw, *Hitler, the Germans, and the Final Solution* (New Haven, Connecticut: Yale University Press, 2008), 270; also see Cole, "Ghettoization," 74–75.
37 Friedman, *A History of the Holocaust*, 96–97; Hilberg, *The Destruction of the European Jews*, 269.
38 Ulrich Herbert, "Extermination Policy: New Answers and Questions about the History of the 'Holocaust' in German Historiography," in *National Socialist Extermination Policies* (ed. Herbert), 27, 31.
39 Richard Breitman, "Plans for the Final Solution in Early 1941," in *The Holocaust and History: the Known, the Unknown, the Disputed, and the Re-examined*, eds Michael Berenbaum and Abraham J. Peck (Bloomington, Indiana: Indiana University Press, 2002), 191–94; Dwork and Van Pelt, *Auschwitz*, 278–83, 287–93; Browning, *The Origins of the Final Solution*, 213–14.
40 Dieter Pohl, "The Murder of the Jews in the General Government," in *National Socialist Extermination Policies* (ed. Herbert), 94; Thomas Sandkühler, "Anti-Jewish Policy and the Murder of the Jews in the District of Galicia, 1941–42," in *National Socialist Extermination Policies* (ed. Herbert), 123.
41 Herbert, "Extermination Policy," 37–38; Pohl, "The Murder of the Jews in the General Government," 92–95.
42 Dwork and Van Pelt, *Auschwitz*, 287–88, 291–93; Steinbacher, "In the Shadow of Auschwitz," 285–86.
43 Herbert, "Extermination Policy," 33–34; Kershaw, *Hitler, the Germans, and the Final Solution*, 67, 69.
44 Kershaw, *Hitler, the Germans, and the Final Solution*, 66.
45 Friedländer, *The Years of Extermination*, 314.
46 Michael Burleigh, *Ethics and Extermination: Reflections on Nazi Genocide* (New York: Cambridge University Press, 1997), 206; Kershaw, *Hitler, the Germans, and the Final Solution*, 70, 77–78.
47 Browning, *The Origins of the Final Solution*, 374–75; Kershaw, *Hitler, the Germans, and the Final Solution*, 69–70, 98; Yitzhak Arad, *Belzec, Sobibor, Treblinka: The Operation Reinhard*

Death Camps (Bloomington, Indiana: Indiana University Press, 1999), 16, 19, 56; Friedländer, *The Years of Extermination*, 330.

48 Davies, *God's Playground*, 336–38.

49 Rutherford, *Prelude to the Final Solution*, 201–2.

50 UWZ order for displacement, 12 May 1941, USHMMA, RG 15.015m/2/112/1–2, and Report on 3 *Nah-plan*, 20 January 1942, NARA T81/386/VoMi/ 325/2409652ff; also see Aly, *Final Solution*, 153–57, 161.

51 Herbert, *Hitler's Foreign Workers*, 387; Piotrowski, *Poland's Holocaust*, 32.

52 Davies, *God's Playground*, 336–37.

53 Koehl, *RKFDV*, 199.

54 Greifelt to Hofmann, 13 March 1941, USHMMA RG 15.021m/5/36/10–12, and Himmler decree for RuSHA racial examinations in the DVL, 25 April 1941, USHMMA RG-15.021m/6/41/10–11; also see Himmler decree for the examination and sifting of the populations of the incorporated territories, 12 September 1940, USHMMA RG 15.021m/1/3/40–43.

55 Greifelt's report on Germanization, August 1942, USHMMA RG 15.007m/10/125/154–55, and Report on 3 *Nah-plan*, 20 January 1942, NARA T81/386/VoMi/ 325/2409652ff.

56 Dongus to Klinger and Hofmann, 22 January 1941, USHMMA RG 15.021m/1/4/76, and Greifelt to Hofmann, 15 December 1941, USHMMA RG 15.021m/6/41/19–20.

57 Racial examination instructions for Public Health officials, January 1942, USHMMA RG 15.021m/5/37/105.

58 Greifelt to Hofmann, 12 May 1942, USHMMA RG 15.007m/10/125/84–85, and Breitman, *The Architect of Genocide*, 99–100.

59 Herbert, "Extermination Policy," 27–28, 34, 38; Bauer, *Rethinking the Holocaust*, 91; Kershaw, *Hitler, the Germans, and the Final Solution*, 325.

12

THE NAZI "EUTHANASIA" PROGRAM

Patricia Heberer

In 1917, a young woman named Paula Bauer[1] served as a nurse at a military hospital in Belgium. Born in 1892 in Amsterdam, the attractive 25-year-old had worked as a secretary before volunteering with an army medical unit during World War I. Bauer had been healthy as a child and young adult, but now, tending war-wounded near the front lines under intense artillery bombardment, the young nurse experienced the first symptoms of epilepsy. Dispatched to a civilian hospital, Bauer regained her health. In 1920, she married, settling with her husband in the northern German city of Hildesheim, where she bore and raised her only daughter.

In the early 1930s, Paula Bauer's conventional life as housewife and mother began to unravel. She suffered frequent epileptic seizures and found it difficult to function. Recognizing that wartime duties had led to the onset of her illness, German health officials certified her as a war invalid and granted her a pension. As her condition deteriorated, Bauer was admitted to the local mental hospital at Hildesheim. In March 1938, her husband was granted a divorce on grounds that his wife required continual care and showed little sign of improvement. Because Nazi German law mandated compulsory sterilization of individuals suffering from "hereditary" disorders such as epilepsy, a legal suit was lodged that same year to sterilize Bauer on medical grounds. A local sterilization court overturned the petition, not because her epilepsy had manifested itself under extreme wartime conditions and did not appear to be hereditary, but rather because the 47-year-old woman was beyond child-bearing age. In an interview in the 1980s, Bauer's daughter Margot remembered that her institutionalized mother suffered palpably from her illness, yet remained "intelligent, subtle, with a marked sense of justice, and an excellent logic!"[2]

Margot Bauer saw her mother for the last time on the Easter holiday in 1941. At that meeting, Paula confided to her daughter that she feared for her life and begged her to obtain her release. Thus it was with consternation that Margot Bauer received an announcement of her mother's death, posted from the Hadamar state sanatorium just weeks after her last visit. An official death certificate, issued in May 1941, indicated that the 51-year-old patient had died of natural causes. In reality, however, Paula Bauer had been murdered in the gas chamber at the Hadamar facility, a victim of the Nazi "euthanasia" program.

The "euthanasia" campaign,[3] implemented by the National Socialist government beginning in the autumn of 1939, represented one of many radical measures which aimed to restore the "racial integrity" of the German nation. Code-named "Operation T4," the effort aimed to eliminate individuals Nazi authorities deemed "life unworthy of life," that is, people with cognitive or developmental impairment, severe physical disability, or incurable mental illness. Representing the regime's first program of mass murder, T4 targeted for killing mentally and physically disabled patients housed in institutional settings throughout Germany and in German-annexed territories. Considered by many historians as a model and precursor to the "Final Solution," the "euthanasia" program claimed the lives of some 200,000 individuals, including 5,000 children.

This secret murder initiative had its roots in the international eugenics movement, which gained currency in many industrialized nations in the late nineteenth and early twentieth centuries. The term "eugenics" ("good birth") was coined by English naturalist and mathematician Sir Francis Galton in 1883; its German-language counterpart, *Rassenhygiene* (racial hygiene), was first utilized by German economist Alfred Ploetz in 1895. The movement's leading American advocate, Charles B. Davenport, described eugenics as the "science devoted to the improvement of the human race through better breeding."[4] For eugenicists, the ravaging social ills that attended modern society—mental illness, alcoholism, sexually transmitted diseases, tuberculosis, criminality, and even poverty—stemmed from hereditary factors. Proponents of eugenic theory were not prepared to attribute the origins of societal problems to environmental causes, such as the rapid industrialization and urbanization that marked the last half of the nineteenth century in Western Europe and the United States. Advocates noted only that, in a new age of progress, society seemed to languish in a state of degeneration, and mobilized the modern "science" of eugenics to arrest the cycle of decay. Eugenics adherents championed three primary objectives: to discover and enumerate "hereditary" characteristics that contributed to the social ills in their society; to develop biological solutions for these dilemmas; and to campaign actively for public measures that might combat these dangers.

While eugenics was to find its most radical interpretation in Germany, its influence was by no means limited to that nation alone. Throughout the late nineteenth and early twentieth centuries, eugenic societies and research institutions sprang up throughout most of the industrialized world, most notably in Germany, the United States, and Great Britain. Eugenicists lobbied for "positive" eugenic efforts, or, more precisely, public policy which aimed to maintain physically, racially, and hereditarily "healthy" individuals through social welfare for "deserving" families, marriage counseling, and motherhood training. Through these efforts, proponents hoped to encourage "better" families to reproduce. Dovetailing these endeavors to support the "productive," however, came negative eugenic measures or initiatives to exclude and hinder society's "unproductive" elements and to redirect social and economic resources from these "less valuable" to the "worthy." Many members of the eugenics community, in Germany as well as in the United States, promoted strategies that sought to marginalize segments of society with limited mental or social capacity—the "feebleminded," the mentally ill, and persons with disabilities—and to regulate their reproduction through voluntary or compulsory sterilization. Eugenicists targeted the mentally ill and cognitively impaired, arguing a direct link between diminished capacity and depravity, promiscuity, and criminality. They viewed as a menace the racially "inferior" and "shiftless poor" who transmitted their dependency on public funds through the mode of heredity. Tainted through inherited deficiencies, these groups endangered the national hereditary community, eugenicists maintained, and placed a financial burden on the society that sustained them. More often than not, eugenicists' "scientifically" drawn conclusions about disabled individuals or ethnic and racial minorities did little more than incorporate popular prejudice. Yet by employing "research" and "theory" in their efforts, eugenic researchers could assert their own notions of human inferiority and superiority as scientific fact.[5]

German eugenics pursued a terrible and separate course after 1933, but before 1914, the German racial hygiene movement did not differ appreciably from its British and American counterparts.[6] A genuine radicalization of the German eugenics community began, however, shortly after World War I. Here, the unprecedented carnage that accompanied the "Great War" and the economic hardships of the interwar years served in tandem to underscore in popular conception the division between the "useful" Germans who had died on the battlefield and the "unproductive" Germans institutionalized in prisons, hospitals, and welfare facilities on the homefront. While their hereditarily "valuable" countrymen had sacrificed their lives for the fatherland, these "impaired" and "compromised" individuals had remained behind to reproduce and to draw their sustenance from the slender resources of the state. An allegory of the "stab-in-the-back" legend, such argumentation resurfaced consistently in the Weimar and early Nazi eras to justify eugenic sterilization and an abrogation of social services for the disabled and institutionalized. With the radicalization of the discourse, voices in the medical and scientific communities began to call for not only the marginalization of these individuals, but the elimination of society's most "unproductive elements." The focus of this startling discussion pivoted upon the destruction of the so-called "life unworthy of life" ["*lebensunwertes Leben*"].

Until the 1920s, the concept of euthanasia had always remained at the outer margins of the eugenics dialogue. The word, meaning "good death," initially denoted the physician's right to alleviate the suffering of a dying patient, and has come to mean a "deliberate intervention undertaken with the express intention of ending a life [in order] to relieve intractable suffering."[7] In 1920, a publication by jurist Karl Binding and psychiatrist Alfred Hoche, both prominent in right-wing nationalist circles, would frame the euthanasia debate in the German-speaking world. In their *Authorization of the Elimination of Life Unworthy of Life* [*Die Freigabe der Vernichtung lebensunwerten Lebens*], Hoche and Binding argued that there existed human beings who have "so far forfeited the character of something entitled to enjoy the protection of the law that its prolongation represents a perpetual loss of value, both for its bearer and for society as a whole."[8] After careful medical evaluation, Hoche asserted, in his contribution to the monograph, that the state should have the right to intercede for the death of these "ballast existences," even if relatives opposed the measure. The Hoche–Binding treatise had immediate impact and was widely discussed in medical and scientific circles. Although it produced more detractors than defenders, the tract, with its utilitarian arguments of reducing per diem expenditures for "incurables" in order to concentrate more care and resources on the less impaired, was sufficient to make an impression on physicians, psychiatrists, and caregivers already instilled with eugenic arguments.

By 1933, the theories of racial hygiene had embedded themselves into professional and public conception, and influenced the thinking of Adolf Hitler and many of his supporters and followers. Embracing an ideology which blended racial antisemitism with eugenic theory, the Hitler dictatorship provided both the context and latitude for the realization of eugenic measures in their most concrete and radical manifestations. One of the first eugenic efforts undertaken by the Nazi regime closely followed the calls of eugenicists in Germany, as well as the United States and elsewhere, to restrict the reproductive capacity of the "hereditarily compromised" through eugenic sterilization. On 14 July 1933, the Hitler cabinet promulgated the Law for the Prevention of Progeny with Hereditary Diseases [*Gesetz zur Verhütung erbkranken Nachwuchses*], which ordered the compulsory sterilization of German citizens suffering from certain "hereditary" disorders.[9] Five of the diseases specifically designated in the law represented psychiatric or neurological disorders, including schizophrenia, manic-depressive (bipolar) disorder, hereditary epilepsy, Huntington's chorea, and "hereditary feeblemindedness."[10] Physical conditions warranting sterilization under the new legislation were hereditary blindness, hereditary deafness, serious hereditary physical deformity, and chronic alcoholism, which many physicians and scientists felt to have a genetic component. Medical professionals were now legally obligated to report patients who exhibited these illnesses or disabilities to public health authorities. Adjudication of sterilization proceedings came within the jurisdiction of newly constructed hereditary health courts [*Erbgesundheitsgerichte*], a Nazi legal innovation superimposed on the existing German juridical structure. By 1936, there were approximately 230 hereditary health courts throughout Germany; each tribunal was composed of two physicians and one jurist, a fact which ensured that medical professionals held the balance of the decision-making authority in each case. If a particular court ruled for sterilization, the individual in question had 4 weeks in which to appeal the verdict, for it was a legal process. In the absence of an appeal—or if a higher court turned down a standing appeal—the implementing decree for the 1933 law demanded execution of the sterilization procedure within 2 weeks' time at the hospital or clinic designated in the verdict. Paragraph 12 of the legislation sanctioned the use of force on unwilling victims. Those attempting to circumvent the procedure might be escorted by police guard to the facility in question.

The new law took effect in January 1934, and its impact was immediate, with 388,400 proposals for sterilization advanced in the first year alone. The most careful study of available data suggests that from 1 January 1934 until war's end in May 1945, some 400,000 Germans were forcibly sterilized under the terms of the Nazi sterilization law.[11] This figure does not include the thousands of Jews, Roma, Poles, and other victims sterilized outside the law's parameters during the war years. The overwhelming number of candidates for sterilization were individuals suffering from mental illness, especially from diagnoses of schizophrenia and "hereditary feeblemindedness." Particularly these illnesses, whose definition implied a certain elasticity of application, permitted eugenicists to include in their dragnet not only those diagnosed as mentally ill or developmentally disabled, but also those whom National Socialist medical officials deemed "asocial": vagrants, prostitutes, mothers with several illegitimate children, petty criminals, juvenile delinquents, and, in large numbers, German Roma and Sinti, who were viewed at once by Nazi officials as a racial "enemy" and as an ethnic criminal element on German soil.

The compulsory sterilization effort proved the first measure directed against persons with mental, physical, and social disabilities in Nazi Germany, and represented a bridge in policy to the "euthanasia" measure. The immediate impetus for the introduction of the killing program remains unclear.[12] What we do know concretely is that, in the spring and summer months of 1939, a number of planners, led by Philipp Bouhler, director of the Führer Chancellery,[13] and Karl Brandt, Hitler's attending physician, began to organize a secret killing operation targeting disabled children.[14] In the course of time, a planning committee emerged which included Bouhler's trusted subordinates Viktor Brack and Hans Hefelmann, as well as Dr Herbert Linden from the Reich Interior

Ministry's Department IV, which enforced public health policy. Joining their number were four physicians: Hellmuth Unger, Ernst Wentzler, Hans Heinze, and Werner Catel. The latter three men were pediatricians with excellent credentials; Heinze had an established practice at Brandenburg-Görden, a pediatric clinic renowned for its modern facilities and advanced therapies, while Wentzler was the inventor of an incubator for premature infants ubiquitously known as the "Wentzler Warmer." One of the fundamental concerns of this steering committee was to develop a mechanism by which disabled youngsters—who often were not institutionalized until they reached school age—might come to the attention of public health authorities. On the basis of their recommendations, the Reich Ministry of the Interior, on 18 August 1939, circulated a decree, "Requirement to Register Deformed, etc. Newborns," stipulating that all physicians and midwives must report newborn infants and children under the age of three who showed signs of the following:

1 idiocy, as well as Mongoloidism[15] (especially in cases combined with blindness or deafness);
2 microcephaly;
3 hydrocephaly in severe or progressive stages;
4 deformation of every kind, especially the absence of limbs, severe malformation of the head and the spine, etc.;
5 paralysis, including Little's disease [cerebral palsy].[16]

At first only infants and toddlers were incorporated in the effort, but as the scope of the measure widened, juveniles up to 17 years of age were included in the killings. Through the auspices of a fictive "Reich Committee for the Scientific Registration of Severe Hereditary and Congenital Disorders" [*Reichsausschuss zur wissenschaftlichen Erfassung von erb-und anlagebedingten schweren Leiden*], "euthanasia" operatives convinced or cajoled parents to surrender their severely disabled youngsters to one of the Committee's many "special pediatric units"[17] organized throughout the Reich. Conservative estimates suggest that at least 5,000 physically and mentally disabled children were murdered at these specially designated pediatric killing wards through starvation or lethal overdose of medication.[18]

"Euthanasia" planners quickly envisioned extending the killing program to adult disabled patients living in institutional settings. In the autumn of 1939, Adolf Hitler signed a secret authorization in order to protect participating physicians, medical staff, and administrators from prosecution; this authorization was backdated to 1 September 1939, to suggest that the effort was related to wartime measures. Because his *Führer* Chancellery was insular, compact, and separate from state, government, or Nazi Party apparatuses, Hitler chose this organization to serve as the engine for the "euthanasia" campaign. Its functionaries called their secret enterprise "T4." The operation took its code-name from the eventual street address of the program's coordinating office in Berlin: Tiergartenstrasse 4. According to Hitler's directive, Führer Chancellery director Phillip Bouhler and physician Karl Brandt undertook leadership of the killing operation. Under their auspices, T4 operatives established six gassing installations for adults as part of the "euthanasia" action: Brandenburg, on the Havel River near Berlin; Grafeneck in southwestern Germany; Bernburg and Sonnenstein, both in Saxony; Hartheim, near Linz on the Danube in Austria; and Hadamar, in Hessen.[19]

Utilizing a practice developed for the child "euthanasia" program, in the autumn of 1939, T4 planners began to distribute carefully formulated questionnaires to all public health officials, public and private hospitals, mental institutions, and nursing homes for the chronically ill and aged. The limited space and wording on the forms, as well as the instructions in the accompanying cover letter, combined to convey the impression that the survey was intended to gather statistical data. The form's sinister purpose was suggested only by the emphasis the questionnaire placed upon the individual patient's capacity to work, and by the categories of patients which the inquiry required health authorities to identify: those suffering from acute psychiatric or neurological disorders; those not of German or "related" blood; those committed to the facility on criminal grounds; and those who had been confined to the institution in question for more than 5 years. Secretly recruited physicians and psychiatrists—many of significant reputation—worked in teams of three to select patients for the program, often without seeing the individuals in question. On the basis of their decisions, T4 functionaries began in January 1940 to remove designated patients from their home institutions and to transport them by bus or by rail to one of the central gassing installations for killing. Within hours of their arrival at such centers, the victims perished in especially designed gas chambers, disguised as shower facilities, utilizing chemically produced carbon monoxide gas. Thereafter, T4 functionaries burned the bodies in crematoria adjacent to the gassing facilities. Other workers took the ashes of cremated victims from a common pile and placed them in urns to send to the relatives of the victims. The families or guardians of the victims received such an urn, along with a death certificate and other documentation, listing both a fictive cause and date of death.

Despite elaborate efforts to conceal its deadly designs, the "euthanasia" program quickly become an open secret. Fearing public unrest at a critical point in the war effort, Adolf Hitler himself gave orders to halt the T4 operation on 24 August 1941. According to T4's own internal calculations—the so-called Hartheim Statistics—70,273 institutionalized mentally and physically disabled persons perished at the six "euthanasia" facilities between January 1940 and August 1941.[20] Yet Hitler's order for the termination of the action did not mean an actual end to the killing. The child "euthanasia" program continued throughout this pause in "euthanasia" operations. Likewise, the T4 centers at Sonnenstein, Bernburg, and Hartheim continued to support the so-called Operation 14f13,[21] or "Invalid Action," the extension of "euthanasia" killing operations to the concentration camps of Nazi-occupied Europe. In the early 1940s, when many concentration camps on German soil lacked facilities to murder detainees in large numbers, the *Reichsführer* SS Heinrich Himmler decided to tap the "euthanasia" program's extensive killing capabilities and appealed to "euthanasia" plenipotentiary Philipp Bouhler to utilize T4 personnel and gassing installations on a limited basis for the concentration camp system.[22] From the spring of 1941 until the winter months of 1944–45, prisoners too ill or exhausted to work were murdered at T4 killing centers, their selection, deportation, and murder carried out by Tiergartenstrasse 4 planners and functionaries. The program found application at several concentration camps on Reich territory, including Dachau, Sachsenhausen, Buchenwald, Mauthausen, Flossenbürg, Gross-Rosen, Niederhagen, Neuengamme, Ravensbrück, and in a few instances at Auschwitz. After Hitler's order to halt the gassing program in August 1941, only prisoners from these sites were supposed to be gassed at T4 centers. Of those four gassing installations still in operation at the time of the halt, Hartheim, Sonnenstein, and Bernburg accepted these victims for killing. Contemporary documentation concerning the 14f13 action is fragmentary, but the most reliable data for this program suggest that

14f13 claimed the lives of 10,000 to 20,000 concentration camp prisoners between 1941 and 1945.[23]

The halt in "euthanasia" killing actions in August 1941 came at an auspicious time, just as plans for the "Final Solution" began to coalesce. It was at this juncture that T4 administrative director Viktor Brack began negotiations to transfer non-essential T4 staff as camp personnel to newly constructed or envisioned extermination camps in the occupied East. Between December 1941 and late spring of 1942, some 130 "euthanasia" operatives arrived in the Lublin District of German-occupied Poland in order to fill key posts in the construction and operation of the *Aktion* Reinhard [Operation Reinhard] killing centers of Belzec, Sobibor, and Treblinka. Charged with the task of murdering the Jews of the General Government [*Generalgouvernement*], the three "Reinhard camps" claimed the lives of 1.7 million Jews. T4 operatives were essential to the successful functioning of these killing centers. They came to occupied Poland with an integral understanding of the gassing and crematory procedures which had been developed by "euthanasia" technicians, and which were further expanded in order to conform to the demands and conditions of the Reinhard camps. Most men had long-standing ties to the T4 organization and had been drawn or recruited to that program on the bases of personal connections or political reliability. Their dependability had been firmly established throughout the "euthanasia" action, and recommended them for inclusion in the Reinhard campaign. Initiated to the killing process and inured to the very routine of mass murder, they brought their knowledge and experience to Operation Reinhard. In doing so, these functionaries of the T4 organization forged a deadly continuity between Hadamar, Sonnenstein, and Hartheim; and Belzec, Sobibor, and Treblinka.

In the summer of 1942, after a year-long hiatus, T4 operatives reinstated the practice of adult "euthanasia." Because of its perceived lack of coordinated activity, many historians—inaccurately—label this second phase of killing operations as the era of "wild euthanasia." Early scholars seized on this nomenclature, originally utilized by T4 operatives themselves, to denote a more diffuse killing process, in which Tiergartenstrasse officials presumably disengaged from organizational and selection procedures, and in which physicians and administrators "on the ground" seized control of the apparatus of destruction. In fact, the coordination and planning for this period was shared between center and periphery. More decentralized than the initial gassing phase, the renewed "euthanasia" effort was still carefully choreographed in Berlin. The T4 central office continued to select, transport, and process its victims, while local authorities often asserted their own priorities and determined the pace of the killing at each facility.

The "euthanasia" program now resumed at a broad range of custodial institutions throughout the German Reich. The majority of institutions pressed into service by the "euthanasia" program functioned at once as killing centers and as normal sanatoria, hospitals, or clinics, so that in each case the murder process had to fit within the facility's regular regimen. In an attempt to camouflage murders more carefully at "euthanasia" sites, adult killing centers introduced a different method of killing. Drawing from the experience of the child "euthanasia" program, T4 installations now relied principally on lethal overdoses of medication to murder their victims. In most cases, medical staff at these killing centers employed Luminal, Veronal, Trional, or a solution of morphine scopolamine either in liquid, tablet, or intravenous form. Although this represented the most common method of killing, many institutions also employed starvation of adult patients. Studies such as Heinz Faulstich's important work *Hungersterben in der*

Psychiatrie [*Starvation Deaths in Psychiatry*][24] have served to highlight the relatively high rates of mortality due to systematic starvation in "euthanasia" facilities, particularly in the last years of the war.

There was one final, important difference that distinguished this second murder phase from the gassing stage which had proceeded it. While it generally proved the case in the first years of the effort that the gas valve belonged—according to the T4 motto—"in the hand of the physician," it was equally true that in "euthanasia's" second stage, the syringe increasingly belonged in the hands of the nurses. All evidence indicates that at most "euthanasia" sites, the nursing staff, both male and female, did the bulk of the killing between 1942 and 1945. As T4 killings were now carried out on a smaller, but sustained basis, physicians with their head nurses often chose a short list of victims on their daily morning rounds, while the caregivers administered the deadly dosages, often on the evening shift. In this way, every sector of the facility's medical personnel—doctors, nurses, and orderlies—were drawn into the killing process.

Prior to 1942, the "euthanasia" program had targeted the institutionalized mentally and physically disabled for killing because they supposedly compromised Germany's genetic and economic resources. In the final years of the war, however, the web of the killing apparatus spiraled outward to embrace a diverse spectrum of victims. Under the auspices of the so-called Operation Brandt, the synchronization of the "euthanasia" program with local and regional disaster planning, hundreds of geriatric and nursing home patients were dispatched to T4 killing centers such as Hadamar and Kaufbeuren in order to free emergency bed space for military casualties and for the victims of Allied bombings. In several instances, these same transports included German air-raid victims themselves. Injured, disoriented or traumatized, many such persons were temporarily housed in lazarettes, hospitals, or welfare institutions for observation or until relatives could collect them. At intervals, municipal authorities in need of bed space for more "valuable" military or civilian casualties dispatched these individuals—almost invariably female, of advanced age, and without family—to T4 facilities.[25]

"Euthanasia" centers also claimed the lives of members of the armed forces who had defended Germany in the field. During T4's gassing phase—from January 1940 until August 1941—"euthanasia" planners Philipp Bouhler and Karl Brandt had specifically forbidden the killing of all servicemen who had fought on the front lines, including veterans of World War I.[26] Yet there exists no doubt that from 1943 to 1945 a number of active military personnel fell victim to T4 killing operations. Invariably, those German soldiers murdered at the facility had suffered sufficient physical or psychiatric impairment to preclude further military service. In these cases, the individuals' transfer to a "euthanasia" facility succeeded their formal release from the armed forces and inevitably followed the individual's entry into the state welfare network.

Finally, beginning in 1944, the "euthanasia" facilities at Kaufbeuren in Bavaria, Mauer-Öhling in Lower Austria, Hadamar in Hessen-Nassau, and Tiegenhof, near Gnesen in the Warthegau, served as collection points and killing centers for physically and mentally incapacitated civilian forced laborers, principally from Poland and the Soviet Union.[27] Early provisions laid out by Brandt and Bouhler had once restricted non-German patients from the "euthanasia" action, but, beginning in mid-1944, these ailing and exhausted "Eastern workers" [*Ostarbeiter*] now found themselves included in the killing campaign when military exigencies and a rapidly advancing Red Army made it impossible to repatriate them. The Hadamar institution in particular earned an infamous reputation in the postwar period for the murders of 468 Soviet and Polish forced laborers suffering from varying degrees of tuberculosis. It is clear that, in these cases, local German labor offices facilitated the murders of the tubercular workers on their own initiative, with the tacit consent of the T4 office, when they perceived that the laborers' illness generated a public health risk in the Frankfurt area.[28] An unknown number of *Ostarbeiter* were also murdered at the "euthanasia" facilities Meseritz-Obrawalde, Eglfing-Haar, Eichberg, Pfaffenrode, Haina, and Merxhausen. In its final spiral of destruction, Operation T4 consumed not only the institutionalized and "incurable," but increasingly "ordinary" individuals whose physical or mental conditions—often ephemeral or treatable—made them a drain on local or regional economies.

The "euthanasia" program continued until the arrival of Allied forces in Reich territory in the spring of 1945. From October 1939, when child "euthanasia" began, until the end of World War II in Europe, Operation T4 and its corollaries claimed the lives of at least 200,000 persons, the vast majority of them institutionalized German patients. For decades, the significance of the "euthanasia" action within the wider context of the Holocaust remained underestimated and misunderstood. Yet, thanks to the works of Ernst Klee and Henry Friedlander, scholars have come to grasp the vital links that united the two killing programs.[29] Technical planners for the Final Solution borrowed hard-won lessons and strategies from the T4 operation. They learned that gassing in a centralized location was the quickest and most efficient method of murdering large numbers of people. All gassing technology used in the extermination centers in Poland—the stationary gas chamber, the assembly-line killing process, and the elaborate efforts at subterfuge and deception—had been developed by T4 planners and technicians for the murder of the mentally and physically disabled. The "euthanasia" program was also a litmus test for killing as comprehensive state policy. The success of the action proved to Nazi leaders that extensive training and intense ideological indoctrination were not necessary to produce "willing executioners." "Ordinary" Germans could and did serve as killers and accomplices in the murder of innocent and defenseless human beings. The complicity or non-interference of official state and local agencies in the transfer and processing of the victims was vital to the accomplishment of the measure; and the unstinting cooperation of the German bureaucracy gave the "green light" to further killing operations. Finally, the ideological justification conceived by medical perpetrators for the destruction of "life unworthy of life" meshed with justifications to murder other categories of biological enemies, most notably Jews. "Euthanasia" and the Final Solution were both components of a biomedical vision which imagined a racially and genetically pure and productive German society and which embraced unthinkable strategies to eliminate those who did not fit within that perverse vision.

Notes

1 In accordance with German privacy laws, the surname of Paula B. has been altered to protect her identity. The medical history of Paula B. is provided in Gerhard Baader, Johannes Cramer and Bettina Winter, "*Verlegt nach Hadamar*": *Die Geschichte einer NS-"Euthanasie"-Anstalt. Historische Schriftenreihe des Landeswohlfahrtsverbandes Hessen* (Kassel: Eigenverlag des LWV Hessen, 1991), 2: 30.

2 Margot B., quoted in *Verlegt nach Hadamar*, 30.

3 Excellent comprehensive sources on the "euthanasia" program include Götz Aly *et al.*, *Aussonderung und Tod: Die klinische Hinrichtung der Unbrauchbaren: Beiträge zur Nationalsozialistischen*

Gesundheits- und Sozialpolitik, Vol. I (Berlin: Rotbuch Verlag, 1985); Götz Aly, ed., *Aktion T4, 1939–1945: Die "Euthanasie"-Zentrale in der Tiergartenstrasse 4* (Berlin: Edition Hentrich, 1989); Götz Aly, Peter Chroust and Christian Pross, *Cleansing the Fatherland: Nazi Medicine and Racial Hygiene*, trans. Belinda Cooper (Baltimore, Maryland: Johns Hopkins University Press, 1994); Michael Burleigh, *Death and Deliverance: Euthanasia in Germany, 1900–1945* (Cambridge: Cambridge University Press, 1994); Henry Friedlander, *The Origins of Nazi Genocide: From "Euthanasia" to the Final Solution* (Chapel Hill, North Carolina: University of North Carolina Press, 1995); Hans-Walter Schmuhl, *Rassenhygiene, Nationalsozialismus, Euthanasie: Kritische Studien zur Geschichtswissenschaft*, Vol. LXXV (Göttingen: Vandenhoeck and Ruprecht, 1987); Winfried Süss, *Der "Volksko?rper" im Krieg: Gesundheitspolitik, Gesundheitsverhältnisse und Krankenmord im nationalsozialistischen Deutschland, 1939–1945* (Munich: Oldenbourg, 2003).

4 Friedlander, *The Origins of Nazi Genocide*, 4.

5 See Patricia Heberer, "Science as Enabler," in John Roth and Peter Hayes, eds, *The Oxford Handbook of Holocaust Studies* (Oxford: Oxford University Press, 2010).

6 See Sheila Faith Weiss, "Die rassenhygienische Bewegung in Deutschland, 1904–33," in Christian Pross and Götz Aly, *Der Wert des Menschen: Medizin in Deutschland, 1918–1945* (Berlin: Edition Hentrich, 1989), 153–73.

7 See N. M. Harris, "The Euthanasia Debate," *Journal of the Royal Army Medical Corps*, vol. 147, no. 3 (October 2001): 367–70.

8 Karl Binding and Alfred Hoche, *Die Freigabe der Vernichtung lebensunwerten Lebens*, quoted by Michael Burleigh, *Death and Deliverance,* 17–18.

9 See Gisela Bock's excellent *Zwangssterilisation im Nationalsozialismus: Studien zur Rassenpolitik und Frauenpolitik* (Opladen: Westdeutscher Verlag, 1986).

10 The term "feebleminded" was utilized throughout the nineteenth and first half of the twentieth century to describe what physicians might today recognize as a wide number of developmental and cognitive disabilities.

11 Bock, *Zwangssterilisation im Nationalsozialismus*, 230–46.

12 Until recently, it was generally believed that the impetus for the "euthanasia" program stemmed from a personal petition made to Hitler on the part of a certain "Knauer" family, requesting that he sanction the mercy killing of their severely disabled infant. Hitler's attending physician, Karl Brandt, testified at the Nuremberg Medical Trial in 1946 that the *Führer* had tasked him with investigating the matter and granting authorization for euthanasia of the child in his name, if warranted. Brandt further testified that on his return to Berlin, Hitler had instructed him to proceed in the same manner in similar cases, and that this directive had been the basis for a systematic child "euthanasia" program. According to postwar statements, this original instance happened in late 1938 or early 1939. Recent scholarship, however, has shown that the killing of the infant actually transpired in the summer of 1939, when planning for the child "euthanasia" program was already well under way. The timing thus suggests that the "Knauer case" was a "trial balloon" rather than an impetus for child "euthanasia."

13 Hitler's private chancellery, a small office which managed Hitler's private affairs as head of state and responded to correspondence and petitions directed to him personally. See Ulf Schmidt, "Reassessing the Beginning of the 'Euthanasia' Programme," *German History*, vol. 17 (1999): 543–50.

14 Ernst Klee, *"Euthanasie" im NS-Staat: Die "Vernichtung lebensunwerten Lebens,"* 2nd edn (Frankfurt am Main: Fischer Taschenbuch Verlag, 1985), 79.

15 That is, Down's syndrome; the term "Mongol" is considered pejorative today.

16 Bundesarchiv Berlin-Lichterfelde (BAB), R 1501/5586 (Reichsinnenministerium), Circular Decree of the Reich Minister of the Interior, re Obligatory Registration for Deformed etc., Newborns, 18 August 1939.

17 *"Kinderfachabteilung,"* literally "children's ward," but used in this context to denote a secret killing center belonging to the child "euthanasia" program.

18 Michael Burleigh and Wolfgang Wippermann, *The Racial State: Germany, 1933–1945* (Cambridge: Cambridge University Press, 1991), 144.

19 Only four killing centers operated at any given time. In the early winter of 1940, the T4 centers at Brandenburg and Grafeneck were dismantled, and their operational responsibilities taken over by Bernburg and Hadamar, respectively.

20 "Die Zahl der Vergasten, verteilt auf die einzelnen Anstalten für die Monate der Jahre 1940/ 1941" (Hartheim Statistics), reprinted in Ernst Klee, *Dokumente zur "Euthanasie"* (Frankfurt am Main: Fischer Taschenbuch Verlag, 1985), 233.

21 Also called *Sonderbehandlung* [Special Treatment] 14f13, the program's codename stemmed from file numbers regularly utilized by the Inspectorate of Concentration Camps: "14f" marked those dossiers concerning prisoner deaths, while the number "13" denoted transfer to a T4 facility. "*Sonderbehandlung*," or "special treatment," was the term applied to killings by SS and police language regulations.

22 See Walter Grode's still seminal *Die "Sonderbehandlung 14f13" in den Konzentrationslagern des Dritten Reiches: Ein Beitrag zur Dynamik faschistischer Vernichtungspolitik* (Frankfurt/ Main/Bern/New York: Peter Lang, 1987), 82.

23 Grode, *Die "Sonderbehandlung 14f13" in den Konzentrationslagern des Dritten Reiches*, 253; Friedlander, *The Origins of Nazi Genocide*, 150; Ute Hoffmann, *Todesursache: "Angina": Zwangssterilisation und "Euthanasie" in der Landes-Heil-und Pflegeanstalt Bernburg* (Magdeburg: Eigenverlag des Ministeriums des Innern des Landes Sachsen-Anhalt, 1996), 87.

24 Heinz Faulstich, *Hungersterben in der Psychiatrie, 1914–1949: Mit einer Topographie der NS-Psychiatrie* (Freiburg/Breisgau: Lambertus, 1998).

25 See Götz Aly, "Die 'Aktion Brandt': Bombenkrieg, Bettenbedarf und 'Euthanasie'," in Götz Aly, *Aktion T4*, 174–75.

26 BAB, R 96 I//2 (Reichsarbeitsgemeinschaft für Heil-und Pflegeanstalten), Memorandum von Philipp Bouhler and Karl Brandt, betr. Entscheidung der Euthanasie-Beauftragten hinsichtlich der Begutachtung, 10 March 1941. In the same way, war veterans were initially excluded from deportations of German Jews from the Reich to the East.

27 See BAB, R 1501/3763, Runderlass des Reichsministers des Innern, betr. Geisteskranke Ostarbeiter und Polen, 6 September 1944.

28 See Holker Kaufmann and Klaus Schulmeyer, "Die polnischen und sowjetischen Zwangsarbeiter in Hadamar," in *Psychiatrie im Faschismus: Die Anstalt Hadamar, 1933–1945*, eds Dorothee Roer and Dieter Henkel (Bonn: Psychiatrie-Verlag, 1986), 264.

29 See Ernst Klee, "Von der 'T4' zur Judenvernichtung: Die 'Aktion Reinhard' in den Vernichtungslagern Belzec, Sobibor und Treblinka," in Götz Aly, *Aktion T4*, 147–52; Henry Friedlander, *The Origins of Nazi Genocide*, 150.

13

THE *EINSATZGRUPPEN* AND THE ISSUE OF "ORDINARY MEN"

Guillaume de Syon

The *Einsatzgruppen*, or "task forces," were mobile militarized units assigned to maintain security in the rear echelons of the German front by ensuring the collection of political intelligence. Their task quickly evolved into the extermination of persons considered dangerous by the Nazi leadership, including approximately one million Jews and thousands of Gypsies. Organized initially for the Polish campaign, these special task forces operated under the command of the German field army headquarters, but received their orders from the Reich Security Main Office (*Reichssicherheitshauptamt*, RSHA) under Reinhard Heydrich. Their activities are fairly well documented, and became known during and immediately after the war ended.[1] However, significant details, notably the fact that they were assisted by police battalions, the German army, and non-German volunteers, did not become clear until two decades ago.

The *Einsatzgruppen* originated in informal task commandos established by Heydrich in the wake of the German annexation of Austria in 1938. These groups were given the responsibility of securing government buildings and public documents. In the summer of 1938, in advance of Hitler's planned war against Czechoslovakia in October (averted by the Munich conference), Heydrich commissioned *Einsatzgruppen* to engage in similar activities—securing buildings and documents, but this time they were given wide latitude to use lethal force when they saw fit. When the Germans finally invaded Czechoslovakia, the *Einstatzgruppen* secured the offices of the former Czech government. Eventually disbanded, the *Einsatzgruppen* were re-established in the summer of 1939 in preparation for the German invasion of Poland. Five *Einsatzgruppen* were formed in August 1939, numbered I–V, and stationed along the Polish border. They were divided into 12 *Einsatzkommandos*. Later, two more *Einsatzgruppen* (VI and VII) were also formed alongside an extra *Einsatzkommando*.

The German attack on Poland on 1 September 1939 is generally best known as the first successful implementation of the concept of "Blitzkrieg." However, as more recent examinations, such as that of Alexander Rossino,[2] have shown, it was also a striking example of the escalation of violence against civilians and prisoners of war, in contravention of established war practices. The corollary to this escalation involves the ideological justification for murdering specific social groups. By December 1939, for example, the *Einsatzgruppen* may have murdered some 50,000 Polish civilians, including at least 7,000 Jews. These numbers have yet to be fully re-examined in light of the discovery of new materials in eastern European archives. Early historical accounts, notably Helmut

Krausnick's investigation of the *Einsatzgruppen* in Poland, do not include an examination of Polish sources.

Still, the evidence of mass murder confirms several things. First, the "Final Solution" had not been hatched by late 1939, as functionaries still favored the notion of expulsion and resettlement, notably in the stillborn "Madagascar Plan." Furthermore, at the time, the Nazis viewed other groups with as much suspicion as Jews, notably members of the Polish clergy and the Polish intelligentsia. But which victims to target was less of an issue than the strong protests Himmler and his deputy, Heydrich, encountered from the *Wehrmacht*. Army commanders strenuously protested the arbitrary mistreatment and murder of the Polish population, arguing notably that the process of pacification had the reverse effect. In March 1940, Himmler, in an attempt to smooth over difficulties between the army and the SS over the latter's actions, emphasized that nothing was done without the approval of Hitler. In so doing, he offered the basis for the third point, namely that the early SS *Einsatzgruppen* were committed Nazis fully willing to carry out their orders on the basis of ideology. Their selection reflected preparation for a different kind of conflict, but it was the actual operations that would determine the evolution of *Einsatzgruppen* tasks.

On 3 March 1941, Hitler rejected the army's proposed guidelines for the planned invasion of the Soviet Union (Operation Barbarossa), and he issued a directive to the Army High Command demanding that the elimination of the "Jewish-Bolshevik intelligentsia" be given the highest priority in any subsequent blueprint.[3] Ten days later, "Guidelines for Special Fields to Directive No. 21" were approved, removing the actions of German soldiers toward Russian civilians from the jurisdiction of military courts and giving official sanction to collective reprisals against entire villages. More importantly, the draft outlined the official duties of the *Einsatzgruppen*: "In order to prepare the political and administrative organization, the *Reichsführer SS* (Heinrich Himmler) has been given by the Führer certain special tasks within the operations zone of the army; these stem from the necessity finally to settle the conflict between two opposing political systems. Within the framework of these tasks, the *Reichsführer SS* will act independently and on his own responsibility. This is however, without prejudice to the overriding plenary power hereby accorded to the Commander in Chief of the Armed Forces. The *Reichsführer SS* is responsible for seeing that military operations are not affected by any measures necessary to carry out his task."[4] Speaking to over 200 commanding officers and chiefs of staff in the Reich Chancellery on 30 March, Hitler reiterated his belief that Operation Barbarossa constituted an extraordinary war of extermination against communism.[5] In the final agreement between the army and SS in April 1941, the *Einsatzgruppen* were empowered to carry out security and police duties in occupied Soviet territory and to take executive measures against the civilian population. Although Jews were absent from this agreement, they were consciously identified in the "Guidelines for the Conduct of Troops in Russia," issued on 19 May 1941: "The battle demands ruthless and vigorous measures against Bolshevik inciters, guerillas, saboteurs, Jews, and the complete elimination of all active and passive resistance."[6] Two additional orders that approved of "extraordinary" measures against civilians were the "Barbarossa Jurisdictional Order" of 13 May and the "Guidelines for the Treatment of Political Commissars" of 6 June.[7]

The *Einsatzgruppen* were constituted into four groups, with approximately 500–600 individuals in each. *Einsatzgruppe A*, led by Dr Walter Stahlecker, the head of the

Gestapo in Württemberg, functioned in the Baltic region; *Einsatzgruppe B*, led by Artur Nebe, the head of the German Criminal Police (*Kriminalpolizei*, KRIPO), operated in the central front; *Einsatzgruppe C*, led by Dr Otto Rasch, followed Army Group C into central Ukraine; and *Einsatzgruppe D*, led by Dr Otto Ohlendorf, a scholar of economics and the law and head of *SD-Inland* (Domestic Security Service of the Party), moved into southern Ukraine, Romania, and Crimea. These units were, in turn, subdivided into smaller groups known either as *Einsatzkommandos* or *Sonderkommandos*. Considerable discussion took place at the time with the German army, partly in response to the tensions that had affected the relationship with the SS during the Polish campaign. A series of meetings followed, resulting in the latter allowing the SS to accompany the attacking troops and operate independently near the front lines.

Shortly before the start of Operation Barbarossa against the Soviet Union, the *Einsatzgruppen* leaders were assembled at Pretzsch in Saxony and informed of their upcoming mission. There exists doubt, however, as to what exactly they were told. Several members of the *Einsatzgruppen*, notably Otto Ohlendorf (*Einsatzgruppe D*) and Martin Sandberger (*Sonderkommando 1a*), claimed in postwar interrogations that a *Führerbefehl* (Hitler order) had been relayed orally, in particular by their superior, Bruno Streckenbach. The claim was later challenged when Streckenbach, presumed dead, returned from Soviet captivity. In fact, the briefings and lectures given at Pretzsch appear to have contained the essential elements for an ideological war that would involve extermination, but the exact shape lacked specificity.

The *Einsatzgruppen*'s initial targets in the Soviet Union involved communists, as confirmed in Reinhard Heydrich's order of 2 July 1941. In it, Himmler's deputy expanded the description to include "Jews in party and state positions." All Jewish men, especially of military age, were also to be shot, partly because troops had been warned of Stalin's call to the civilian population to resist. The *Wehrmacht* cooperated in the matter, often handing over Jewish civilians to *Einsatzgruppen* units. On 17 July, a further order from Heydrich asked for the execution of all Jews found in German PoW camps. Only toward the end of July, and increasingly through August, did the killers destroy entire communities (men, women, and children), often returning to places where they had already acted. But even this was not a universal or definitive pattern. On 3 July, just days after the German invasion, 322 persons were shot in Georgenburg in Lithuania; five were women. That same day, 316 persons were shot in Augustowo, also in Lithuania; among the victims were 10 women. At the end of the month, Himmler issued a directive to 1st and 2nd SS-Cavalry Regiments at the southern border of Rear Area, Army Group Center, clarifying the position of the Reich government: "All Jews are to be shot. Jewish women to be driven into the swamps."[8] Himmler's actions point to a shift in policy in Berlin which was confirmed orally to various *Einsatzgruppen* leaders. Other postwar interrogation points to a "Führer order" transmitted orally in August 1941. While that point remains under discussion, there is further confirmation of a shift in policy during Himmler's visit to *Einsatzkommando 8* in Minsk on 14–15 August. Then, and in the presence of several high-level persons, the *Reichsführer* reportedly stated that all Jews would now be targeted. However, written documentation to the *Einsatzgruppen* in October 1941 targeting "Jews in general" confirms the definitive policy shift by fall.

Based on these elements, it becomes clear that the *Einsatzgruppen* were part of a multi-staged, but also multi-pronged evolution of the "Final Solution." Ghettoization, which had accompanied the Polish campaign, was a temporary solution pending the end of the war. As Christopher Browning notes, the improvised nature of Nazi wartime racial policy reflects confusion up to 1941, and only becomes certain by late summer, opting for genocide, first through the elite *Einsatzgruppen*, and eventually with the assistance of police battalions and non-German units, notably *Hilfswilligen* (volunteers) from Ukraine and the Baltic states.

The number of those involved in the killings also increased. Though early postwar investigations emphasized *Einsatzgruppen* activities, they either overlooked or under-estimated the fact that the mobile units received substantial assistance from local forces (notably in Ukraine and the Baltic states). Reviving antisemitic feelings in Ukraine, for example, *Einsatzkommandos* were able to accelerate the completion of their mission in certain regions, notably Ponary, where some 24,000 Jews were murdered over several months.

Furthermore, many German police units assisted, too. The collaboration of police and SS was the result of close contact between Himmler and Kurt Daluege, chief of the *Ord-nungspolizei* (Orpo), which gave him control over uniformed police throughout Germany. Though Orpo units and associated Reserve Police Battalions did not receive the same kind of indoctrination as their SS counterparts, they did undergo basic training as paramilitary rather than police units. They also were given special briefings concerning their upcoming mission in support of the *Einsatzgruppen*. That they fulfilled their assignments fairly completely, as shown in the analyses of Christopher Browning and Edward B. Westermann, raises the matter of motivation for carrying out mass murder (see below).[9]

Because of the shifting nature of the *Einsatzgruppen* tasks, from murdering cadres to destroying entire communities, the scale of the massacres increased substantially by late summer 1941. The SS made multiple visits to various regions and towns in response to evolving orders from Berlin. Initial instructions from early July called for killing all Jews in professional and leadership positions, but by August, the killing campaigns began to include Jewish women and children, as reflected in camouflaged and oral instructions. The former do not call for actual execution (such as an order from Himmler on 1 August 1941), but for such actions as driving women into the Pripet marshes. The confirmation that such orders were carried out affirms that civilian massacres took place on an enlarged scale.

Other actions involved "reprisal shootings" for alleged or real partisan attacks. *Einsatzgruppen* activities reflect the incremental nature of the Final Solution. Such was the case of the Babi Yar massacre, a large ravine on the edge of Kiev where 34,000 Jews met their deaths at the hands of members of *Einsatzgruppe C* on 28–29 September 1941. But this method of killing, though applied on a wide scale, was deemed problematic. Several *Einsatzgruppen* reports cite men breaking down despite receiving generous sup-plies of alcohol and cigarettes to carry out their deeds. Requesting more "humane" kill-ing conditions (for the killers), leaders wondered about the possibility of using other methods to carry out mass murder. The use of gas vans was thus introduced.

The gas vans, or S-wagen ("*Sonderwagen*" or "*Spezialwagen*"), is not as well docu-mented as the shooting activities of the *Einsatzgruppen*. It appears that the first use of a truck that had its exhausts redirected into the sealed cargo area dates back to January 1940 and falls in line with operation T4, the forced euthanasia program and the first wave of *Einsatzgruppen* activities. In fall 1939, these murdered about 3,700 patients in mental institutions in Bromberg, Poland. When an SS *Sonderkommando* emptied the Koscian Bernardine monastery, an asylum, near Poznan, it injected patients with a morphine mixture and placed them inside a modified truck painted to simulate a coffee company lorry. The trailer was then driven for some 20 minutes, by which time the victims had been killed. All told, some 1,500 patients were murdered that way. The experiment led to the modification of more trucks, some 30 of which operated in the Minsk region between December 1941 and June 1942. (Others were assigned to the Chelmno death camp and to the region of Semlin in Yugoslavia.) A secret report of 16 May 1942 notes that *Einsatzgruppen* C and D were able to use some of the trucks only in fair weather, while other vehicles were no longer airtight as a result of rough terrain. Still, *Einsatzgruppen* reports, though confirming the deaths of at least 97,000 people by such means, also complain of the difficulty in carrying out the assignment. Victims screamed, shifted the balance of the truck, damaging its suspension, and vomited and defecated as they expired. The end of the "S-Wagen" experiment coincides with the beginning of the death camps of Operation Reinhard.

The question of motivation

In his seminal study of Police Battalion 101, Christopher Browning considered very specifically the killers' backgrounds and rationalization for the killings. His conclusions suggested that antisemitism, while a motivating factor in a few cases, was not central to the majority of men involved. Instead, a combination of peer pressure, conformism, and personal gain was invoked.[10] Browning thus confirmed, at the field level, several of the conclusions of Raul Hilberg. His main sources, trial records, and methodology that included the Stanford prison experiment and the Milgram experiment, sought to reconcile the notion of the banality of evil with the level of violence associated with the *Einsatzgruppen* and their support units. In essence, most killers displayed pragmatism rather than fanaticism in their decision to kill.

Though generally well received, Browning's approach drew criticism from one young scholar in particular, Daniel Jonah Goldhagen, who was completing a dissertation that included an examination of police battalions. While Goldhagen looked at similar sources, he argued in his thesis that eliminationist antisemitism was paramount in explaining the killers' behavior. He maintained that the police battalions were not sufficiently indoctrinated in Nazi ideology and generally not staffed by party members. For officers in these groups to engage willingly in murder, their thought patterns towards Jews had to be shaped by something broader and more systemic in German society. To support his view, Goldhagen tracked down testimonies of Jewish survivors, and complemented these with an emphasis on the power of Nazi propaganda on the individual.

The debate culminated with the release of Goldhagen's book and a public debate between him and Browning in spring 1996 at the United States Holocaust Memorial Museum. The sharp debate that took place there showed the limitations of using victims' testimony to assume perpetrators' motives. Goldhagen maintained that perpetrators' testimony was far too fraught with lies to be considered valuable. The debate shifted beyond methodology to include counterfactual arguments. For example, if German eliminationist antisemitism was indeed the *modus operandi* of SS killers, how did one explain the cooperation in the murder process of countless non-Germans? Eventually, the debate and its aftermath opened up new venues of investigation. On the one hand, it rekindled an interest in victim and bystander testimony; on the other, it encouraged the search for greater precision in the motivations of the killers.[11]

More recently, writer Richard Rhodes, whose work on nuclear weaponry led him to examine other instances of extreme violence, re-examined the history of the *Einsatzgruppen* and applied a different psychological theory. Borrowing from criminologist Lonnie Athens' model of the socialization of violence, Rhodes applies a four-stage process to members of the *Einsatzgruppen*.[12] Though fitting in some cases, the hypothesis excludes the role of ideology and incorporates the notion of provocation, a far more difficult notion to apply when considering the cowering civilian victims most *Einsatzgruppen* members dealt with. More recent studies have sided with Christopher Browning's summary of motivation, yet have given a more measured response to the role of ideology within peer group psychology.

Comparing the atrocities by the *Wehrmacht* in fall 1939 with those of summer 1941, authors Klaus-Michael Mallmann and others have found that, while confrontation between the German army and the SS did occur, as documented in numerous cases, there was a greater tendency toward cooperation because of the notion of a common enemy, this time crystallized into "Jewish Bolshevism."[13] In fact, antisemitism as professed in public propaganda proved less important than convincing killers that they belonged to a vanguard group that alone understood the necessity of extreme action to protect the fatherland. This indoctrination may not have functioned across the board, but was clearly sufficient in offering those participating in the massacres a rationale for their usage. Hilary Earl's look at the background of *Einsatzgruppen* leaders also suggests that antisemitism was not as foundational as we would think.[14]

Still, no complete explanation is available. Patrick Desbois' recent contribution, a cross between oral history and memoir, shows the depravity of the *Einsatzgruppen* in their actions, but muddles the field by allowing collaborators and non-German perpetrators to point the finger at the SS.[15] The task of unearthing explanations is further complicated by the various strategies defendants used at Nuremberg.

The trials

The Nuremberg *Einsatzgruppen* trial was held in 1948, one of 12 additional trials following the International Military Tribunal. The prosecution offered no evidence of *Einsatzgruppen* criminal activity before May 1941 or after July 1943, when most were disbanded (though *Einsatzgruppe A*, notably, remained in operation till 1944), but substantial documentation supported the intervening period. The massacres the *Einsatzgruppen* carried out were well documented, for they reported their activities directly to Heydrich's office in Berlin. Some 195 reports were filed as daily and weekly reports from the *Einsatzkommandos* and *Einsatzgruppen*. Most of these gave direct accounts of executions, extermination, and liquidation, but some used the camouflage words "special treatment," "evacuation," and "resettlement." Many killings were often described as "reprisals" for alleged partisan actions, but the broadness of the charge includes such alleged offenses as refusal to work, or spreading rumors.

Because police battalions were not considered criminal organizations, the prosecutors overlooked their role. Among oral sources, Otto Ohlendorf had already admitted, as a witness before the International Military Tribunal, that *Einsatzgruppe D*, which he commanded, had killed about 90,000 people. Although in this trial he drastically reduced this estimate, neither he nor his co-defendants attempted to deny the fact that their units committed mass murder, but claimed that they acted legally under superior orders; when pressed, some further explained that their actions were motivated not by antisemitism, but by the need to defend Germany against the threat of Bolshevism. Though clearly members of the elite SS, these leaders generally were average men who happened to believe in all or part of Nazi ideology, which allowed them to carry out the massacres. Using the field reports, the prosecution estimated the total number of persons killed by the four *Einsatzgruppen* to approximately one million. Five of the 20 defendants were hanged in 1951, while the others, though found guilty, were all released between 1951 and 1958. That year, a trial of members of the Gestapo and SD opened in Ulm, which further investigated *Einsatzgruppen* activities. Later trials, notably in the Soviet Union, also provided substantial documentation on *Einsatzgruppen* activities, though these have yet to be fully examined by historians.

The *Einsatzgruppen* represent a key stage in the evolution of the Final Solution, one which not only increased the level of violence and the scope of the killing, but also paralleled the murders in death camps. The highly detailed documentation that exists for the period 1941–43, nonetheless, lacks contextual analysis, which is only now coming out in historical investigations. As such, it continues to raise questions pertaining to the chronology of orders, the roles of support troops (including foreign ones), and the motivations of the killers.

Notes

1 Richard Breitman has shown that British intelligence knew of the activities of the *Einsatzgruppen* as early as late summer/early fall 1941. Richard Breitman, *Official Secrets: What the Nazis Planned, What the British and Americans Knew* (New York: Hill and Wang, 1998).
2 Alexander Rossino, *Hitler Strikes Poland: Blitzkrieg, Ideology, and Atrocity* (Lawrence, Kansas: University Press of Kansas, 2003).
3 Jürgen Förster, "The Wehrmacht and the War of Extermination against the Soviet Union," *Yad Vashem Studies,* vol. 14 (1981): 11; Hans-Adolf Jacobsen, ed., *Kriegstagebuch des Oberkommando der Wehrmacht (Wehrmachtführungsstab)* (Frankfurt am Main, 1961), 1: 341.
4 Förster, "The Wehrmacht and the War of Extermination against the Soviet Union," 11–13. For the actual document, see Nuremberg Document PS 447.
5 Förster, "The Wehrmacht and the War of Extermination against the Soviet Union," 13.
6 Förster, "The Wehrmacht and the War of Extermination against the Soviet Union," 15.
7 Helmut Krausnick, "Kommissarbefehl und Gerichtbarkeitserlass 'Barbarossa' in neuer Sicht," in *Vierteljahrheft für Zeitgeschichte,* vol. 25 (1977): 628–738.
8 Operational Situation Report USSR, No. 19, from the Chief of the Security Police and of the SD, Berlin, 11 July 1941, in *The Einsatzgruppen Reports: Selections from the Dispatches of the Nazi Death Squads' Campaign Against the Jews, July 1941–January 1943,* eds Yitzhak Arad, Shmuel Krakowski and Shmuel Spector (New York: Holocaust Library, 1989), 16; Befehl RFSS, 28 July 1941 an das SS-Kav.Regiment 2, cited in J. Büchler, "Kommandostab Reichsführer SS: Himmler's Personal Murder Brigades in 1941," in *Holocaust and Genocide Studies,* vol. 1, no. 1 (1986): 15; Bestätigung dieses Befehls im Einsatzbericht des SS Kav.Rev. 2 vom 12 August 1941, Kriegshistorisches Archiv (KHA), Prague, box 5, folder 30, p. 209, all cited in Hannes Heer, "Killing Fields: The Wehrmacht and the Holocaust in Belorussia, 1941–42," *Holocaust and Genocide Studies,* vol. 7 (Spring 1997): 83, 96.
9 Edward Westermann, *Hitler's Police Battalions: Enforcing Racial War in the East* (Lawrence, Kansas: University Press of Kansas, 2005).
10 Christopher Browning, *Ordinary Men. Reserve Police Battalion 101 and the Final Solution in Poland* (New York: HarperCollins, 1992).
11 *The "Willing Executioners"/ "Ordinary Men" Debate Selections from the Symposium, April 8, 1996* (Washington, DC: United States Holocaust Memorial Museum Research Institute

Occasional Papers, 1996). See also Daniel Goldhagen, *Hitler's Willing Executioners* (New York: Alfred A. Knopf, 1996).

12 Richard Rhodes, *Masters of Death: The SS-Einsatzgruppen and the Invention of the Holocaust* (New York: Alfred A. Knopf, 2002).

13 Klaus-Michael Mallmann, Jochen Böhler and Jürgen Matthäus, *Einsatzgruppen in Polen: Darstellung und Dokumentation* (Darmstadt: Wissenschaftliche Buchgesellschaft, 2008).

14 Hilary Earl, *The Nuremberg Einsatzgruppen Trial, 1945–1958: Atrocity, Law, and History* (New York: Cambridge University Press, 2009).

15 Patrick Desbois, *The Holocaust by Bullets: A Priest's Journey to Uncover the Truth Behind the Murder of 1.5 Million Jews* (New York: Palgrave Macmillan, 2009).

Multiple Final Solutions
1) Forced Emigration

14

THE ORIGINS OF THE FINAL SOLUTION

Christopher Browning

Between 1933 and 1939, various players in the Nazi regime had sought a solution to their self-imposed "Jewish question" within the framework of the expanding boundaries of the Third Reich. The victims were first German, then also Austrian and Czech, Jews; the ultimate goal—as articulated by the SS in 1935—was the creation of a Germany "free of Jews." This was to be achieved by emigration, coerced through an escalating persecution that would convince Jews that they had no future in Germany and thus had to find a way to leave, despite the ever-raising barriers to immigration elsewhere. Waves of anti-Jewish laws achieved the "civic death" of German Jews in 1933 through the end of legal equality; their "social death" in 1935 through the Nuremberg Laws, which criminalized sexual relations between Jews and Germans; and their "economic death" in 1938–39 by completing the expropriation of Jewish property. All of this persecution through legal measures was accompanied by rituals of exclusion, humiliation, and degradation that climaxed with the unfettered violence, wanton destruction, sporadic killing, and mass arrests of *Kristallnacht* in November 1938. By 1939, half the Jews of the Third Reich had left, and virtually all the rest were desperate to follow. But they were trapped, first by lack of immigration opportunities, and then by the outbreak of war. The first solution to the Nazis' Jewish question—forced emigration of all Jews from the Third Reich—was only half-complete when it was completely superseded in September 1939.

Knowing that war was imminent, Hitler signaled a new level of expectations to his followers in his Reichstag speech of 30 January 1939. If international Jewry precipitated another world war, he prophesied, the result would be not "Bolshevization of the earth" and Jewish victory, but rather "the annihilation of the Jewish race in Europe." This speech signaled to all those "working toward the Führer" that, with the outbreak of war, the Jewish question would have to be solved throughout German-dominated Europe, not just within the boundaries of the Third Reich. The vicious circle that had become apparent with the annexation of Austria and the Czech provinces of Bohemia and Moravia, namely that every diplomatic and military success meant a step backwards in solving the Jewish question because additional territory also meant more Jews, was to be broken. But how did Hitler's followers understand the phrase "the annihilation of the Jewish race in Europe"? The subsequent plans, which they concocted and Hitler approved in 1939 and 1940, indicate that they envisaged a solution in terms of mass uprooting and expulsion on a scale that dwarfed the coerced emigration of the 1930s and was accompanied by population decimation, but not yet in terms of systematic and total mass murder.[1]

With victory over Poland and its partition with the Soviet Union according to the terms of the Hitler–Stalin pact assured, Heinrich Himmler submitted proposals to Hitler

Himmler told Hitler about the new Jews they would bring in w/ the new territory

concerning the demographic remaking of German-occupied Poland in late September 1939. The western half of the German share was to be annexed directly to the Third Reich, and the eastern half turned into a German colony called the General Government. The annexed or "incorporated territories" were to be demographically transformed and made fully German by ethnic cleansing and expulsion into the General Government of the seven and one-half million Poles and 500,000 Jews who lived there, and repopulation through the repatriation of ethnic Germans from those territories (the Baltic states, eastern Poland, and Bessarabia) ceded to the Soviet Union in the Hitler–Stalin pact. The Polish Jews expelled from the incorporated territories, to be followed by all the German, Austrian, and Czech Jews still remaining in the Third Reich, were to be sent to the district of Lublin at the most eastern extremity of the German empire. This Lublin Reservation was deemed an especially appropriate reception area because the "severe, marshy nature" would "induce a severe decimation of the Jews."[2]

The growing opposition of Hans Frank, head of the General Government, who wanted his bailiwick to become a model colony rather than the demographic dumping ground of the Third Reich, and of Hermann Göring, who needed Polish workers and farmers to harness the incorporated territories to the war economy, drastically slowed the realization of Himmler's plans for demographic revolution through massive ethnic cleansing—what the Nazi documents euphemistically called "resettlement." By the spring of 1940, the plan for the Lublin reservation had given way to other priorities. But the unexpectedly rapid victory over France rekindled Himmler's hopes and ambitions. On 25 May, with the best units of the French and British armies trapped at Dunkirk, Himmler met with Hitler and offered renewed proposals for the erasure of Poland as a national concept through a combination of ethnic cleansing, cultural genocide, and reduction of the Polish population to a reservoir of forced labor. As for the Jews, he now suggested—in recognition that the French empire would soon be at Germany's disposal—they could be sent overseas to some colony, perhaps in Africa. "However cruel and tragic each individual case may be," Himmler argued, these proposals were "still the mildest and best, if one rejects the Bolshevik method of physical extermination of a people out of inner conviction as un-German and impossible." Hitler deemed the proposals "very good and correct," and authorized Himmler to let the other Nazi leaders know he had "recognized and confirmed" them.[3] This is a rare case in which historians can actually document how Hitler and Himmler interacted in the decision-making process. Himmler, sensing the moment was opportune, made proposals to Hitler privately. Hitler verbally approved, but signed no order. Rather, he authorized Himmler to proceed and also to invoke his name, should others still oppose.

Simultaneously, a minor official who had just been named head of the Jewish desk in the German Foreign Office, Franz Rademacher, proposed that, in the looming peace negotiations, Germany demand the French colony of Madagascar as the site of a reservation to which the Jews of Europe could be expelled. Hitler approved the notion submitted to him by the Foreign Minister, Joachim von Ribbentrop, and through the summer months of 1940 the SS and Foreign Office each concocted its own version of a Madagascar Plan. Despite real enthusiasm for the Madagascar Plan, however, it was quickly stillborn when Germany's failure in the Battle of Britain meant that the necessary opening of the sea lanes and use of British shipping would not be forthcoming.

With the collapse of this second, potentially even more lethal, reservation scheme for the expulsion and decimation of Europe's Jews, Germany's racial planners had to await

[handwritten annotation: Nazi's planning invasion of S.U., had to plan Final solution in Europe]

Hitler's next key strategic decision. When, in December 1940, he ordered preparations for an invasion of the Soviet Union the next spring, they followed suit. They now prepared for "a final solution to the Jewish question within the European territories ruled or controlled by Germany" to take place "at the end of the war" through their deportation to "a territory yet to be determined."[4] Due to the secrecy surrounding preparations for the surprise attack on the Soviet Union, German planning documents could not specify that the third expulsion and decimation plan—following Lublin and Madagascar—now envisaged sending the Jews of Europe to the inhospitable wastelands of Siberia and the Arctic.

In the spring of 1941, as military planning proceeded, Hitler once again signaled to those "working toward the Führer" what he expected, namely that this war would be not just a conventional war, as fought against France, but rather a racial and ideological struggle that called for a "war of destruction." How did his followers interpret this incitement? The military altered the jurisdiction of its own military code of justice to deprive the civilian population of protection of the law and mandated for its troops policies of collective reprisal and killing of captured communist functionaries or "commissars." Furthermore, it made no logistical plans for the care of the vast numbers of Soviet PoWs that its tactical plans for vast encirclements were intended to produce. The economic experts envisaged what historians have subsequently come to call a "hunger plan," whereby not only the invading German army, but the German homeland, would be fed at the expense of the Soviet population. As the protocol of one meeting of high-ranking economic officials noted bluntly: "Umpteen million people will doubtless starve to death, if we extract everything necessary for us from the country."[5] The SS formed four mobile firing squads, totaling 3,000 men, called *Einsatzgruppen*. They would receive their operational orders from the SS concerning the execution of potential enemies but, in accordance with an agreement with the military, would receive logistical support from the latter as well as permission to operate up to the front lines. In speaking to his top officers in a final pre-invasion briefing, Himmler envisaged "a racial struggle of pitiless severity, in the course of which 20 to 30 million Slavs and Jews will perish through military actions and a crisis of food supply."[6] Himmler then authorized his demographic planners to draw up a General Plan for the East (*Generalplan Ost*) to make this macabre prophecy self-fulfilling.

In short, contrary to postwar alibis that the unparalleled savagery of the Eastern Front was imposed on Germany by the ferocity with which the Red Army and Soviet citizenry fought, the "war of destruction" was fully premeditated, and based on the assumption that Germany's victory would be so quick and total that the Nazi occupiers could act with total impunity, and hence without limit or restraint. Only one aspect of the prewar planning remained ambiguous and undocumented, namely the exact fate of the Soviet Jews. In the past, whenever there were food shortages, Jews starved first; wherever there were mass executions, Jews were killed in disproportionate numbers; and wherever mass expulsions were envisaged, no Jews were to remain. Under the circumstances of planning for all of the above on an unprecedented scale, the "war of destruction" against the Soviet Union implied the genocide of Soviet Jewry, even if by an as yet indefinite timetable and an unspecified combination of executions, starvation, and expulsion.

What was implicit concerning the fate of Soviet Jews before the invasion became explicit just weeks after it was launched on 22 June 1941. In the opening weeks, the *Einsatzgruppen* reported numerous executions, but above all other categories of victims were adult male

Jews, whose killings were still justified by various rationales. Then, in the wake of stupendous initial victories and expecting the imminent collapse of the Soviet regime, Hitler met with Himmler on 15 July and other top leaders on 16 July. Hitler opened the second meeting with a monologue that amounted to a victory speech. Germany would never withdraw from these territories it had conquered. It would instead transform them into a "Garden of Eden" through "all necessary measures—shootings, resettlements, etc."[7] Himmler, who rarely failed to understand Hitler's signals, immediately reinforced the meager 3,000 men of the *Einsatzgruppen* by assigning to the Higher SS and Police leaders behind the front two brigades of Waffen-SS and at least 11 battalions of Order Police for a sixfold increase in manpower. Furthermore, he approved the recruitment of native populations into auxiliary police units, whose numbers reached 33,000 by the end of the year. In addition to this massive build-up of manpower, Himmler paid frequent visits to these units. Following his visits, a "re-targeting" occurred, in which the shooting of Jewish women, children, and elderly now eclipsed the shooting of adult male Jews. And word then spread from the initiated units to others. In short, there was no single, comprehensive killing order issued on a single date and disseminated in a single, uniform fashion. However, by the end of the summer, virtually every German killing unit knew it was participating in a "Final Solution to the Jewish Question" on Soviet territory through the systematic mass shootings of Soviet Jews.

In the Baltic, Eberhard Jäger, in command of *Einsatzkommando 3*, kept meticulous statistics concerning his unit's body count. On 15 August 1941, following a Himmler visit to the Baltic, Jäger's numbers jumped sharply and henceforth regularly included large numbers of Jewish women and children.[8] Following a Himmler visit to Ukraine in mid-August, the police units of Higher SS and Police Leader Friedrich Jeckeln perpetrated the first five-figure massacre at Kamenets Podolsky, enabling him to report that for the month of August, units under his command had "shot a total of 44,125 persons, mostly Jews."[9] This was quickly surpassed by *Einsatzkommando 4a* and several Order Police units, which reported killing nearly 34,000 Jews in a single two-day action in the ravine of Babi Yar outside Kiev on 29–30 September 1941. The new mind set of the perpetrators was reflected in their reports. Earlier, the *Einsatzgruppen* reports had provided various rationales for the killing of adult male Jews. In September, Otto Rasch of *Einsatzgruppe* C, in contrast, felt the need to justify why he had not killed all Jews immediately, but temporarily kept some alive for labor. Putting these Jews to work was necessary economically and would "result in a gradual liquidation of the Jews" in any case, he noted.[10]

Hitler's call for a war of destruction in a no-holds-barred, racial and ideological struggle against the Soviet Union had inaugurated the decision-making process that led to the genocide of Soviet Jews, and their fate was sealed when this decision-making process reached closure in July/August 1941. When, then, was the Final Solution—the policy to kill every last Jew in the German grasp—extended from Soviet Jews to the Jews in other parts of German-dominated Europe? The process began on 31 July 1941, when Himmler's deputy, Reinhard Heydrich, visited Göring (in charge of the overall coordination of Jewish policy since *Kristallnacht*) and procured his signature on a simple, three-sentence document that authorized Heydrich to make "all necessary preparations" for a "total solution" to the Jewish question in Europe, to coordinate the participation of those agencies whose jurisdictions were involved, and to report back on the plan for this "final solution" as soon as possible. This document was not an order for the destruction of the European Jews, but rather the authorization for a "feasibility study" as to how the problem they posed to the Nazis might be solved—procured by Heydrich exactly at the moment when systematic mass killing of Jews was being inaugurated on Soviet territory.[11]

In the following month of August, the Nazi military advance ground to a halt, as exhausted units needed refitting and the logistical support bases for a new advance had to be moved up. Simultaneously with the military stall, Hitler rejected the proposals of both Heydrich and Goebbels to begin deporting Jews from the Third Reich. On 19 August, Hitler promised Goebbels that such deportations could begin "immediately after the end of the campaign in the east." Concerning the fulfillment of Hitler's *Reichstag* prophecy, Goebbels noted that "in the east the Jews are paying the price" while in Germany they would have "to pay still more in the future."[12] If Heydrich and Goebbels were frustrated by Hitler's hesitancy at this moment, so were middle-echelon planners. Rolf-Heinz Höppner, in charge of ethnic cleansing from the Warthegau and already the author of a proposal for the mass killing of non-working Jews in the Łódź ghetto through some "quick-acting" means, was eager to expand his operations to all of Europe. He wanted to organize the deportation of unwanted populations into the Soviet Union, but all such planning had to remain "patchwork" because he did not know "the intentions of the Führer." To organize such deportations, "first of all the basic decisions must be made" and "total clarity" had to prevail "about what shall happen" to the deportees. "Is it the goal to ensure them a certain level of life in the long run, or shall they be totally eradicated?"[13] Clearly a Nazi zealot like Höppner did not shy from the prospect of committing mass murder, but even he was unwilling to proceed without clear authorization from above.

The "basic decisions" and "total clarity" that people like Höppner required—in order to confidently "work toward the Führer" in implementing the genocide of European Jews—emerged between mid-September and late October 1941. One key to the change in Hitler's receptivity was the renewed military advance. In the first week of September, the German army successfully cut off Leningrad on the northern front. In mid-September, the German army launched a breakthrough offensive in the south that quickly encircled and then captured Kiev on 26 September. Following meetings with Hitler and others, Himmler wrote on 18 September that the Führer had now decided that the Third Reich was to be freed of Jews as soon as possible. "As a first step," 60,000 Jews would be deported to the ghetto of Łódź, from which they would be sent "yet further to the east next spring."[14] On 23–24 September, Hitler met with top leaders, including Himmler, Heydrich, and Goebbels. Heydrich assured Goebbels that deportation of the Jews could begin "as soon as we arrive at a clarification of the military situation in the east." Following his conversation with Hitler, Goebbels recorded in his diary: "The spell is broken. In the next three to four weeks we must once again expect great victories." Hitler believed serious resistance would be over by 15 October.[15]

On 2 October, the German armies on the central front launched their offensive, which within just a few days resulted in the spectacular double-encirclement victory of Vyazma and Bryansk. As final Soviet resistance seemed to be collapsing, Hitler returned to Berlin to deliver a public address on 4 October, and Goebbels again noted that Hitler was "exuberantly optimistic."[16] It was precisely at this moment, as historian Saul Friedländer has noted, that Hitler's "hitherto low-key rhetorical stance regarding the Jews came to an abrupt end," and that subsequently his "anti-Jewish diatribes became torrential."[17]

On 15 October, the very date that Hitler had estimated for the end of Soviet resistance, the deportation of Jews from the Third Reich to the eastern ghettos of Łódź, Minsk, and Riga began.

Hitler's victory euphoria and the decision to begin deporting Jews from the Third Reich in anticipation of imminent Soviet collapse, rather than waiting until after the war, raise two questions. First, at this point in time, what was the intended fate of the deportees who were to be housed in the ghettos of Łódź, Minsk, and Riga over the winter, but sent "yet further to the east next spring"? Was there clarity yet between Höppner's options of minimal subsistence and total eradication? And, second, to what extent were all European Jews, and not just the deported Jews of the Third Reich, facing this ultimate fate? As historians lack any "smoking gun" document in this regard, they must extrapolate from the conjuncture of fragmentary evidence concerning two key developments. The first concerns the effort to develop sophisticated killing methods that were both more efficient in terms of manpower than the mass shootings on Soviet territory, and more appropriate in terms of secrecy for mass killing of Jews from outside the war zone. Killing in gas chambers with pure carbon monoxide transported from chemical factories in steel canisters had been inflicted on the mentally and physically handicapped since late 1939. Suddenly, in September 1941, a flurry of additional experiments in killing with poison gas took place. In Belarus, scientists from the Berlin laboratory of the criminal police injected the carbon monoxide-laden exhaust gas from internal combustion engines of two motor vehicles into a sealed room of mental patients, with lethal effect. In the Lublin District of the General Government, Christian Wirth, formerly involved in the killing of the mentally and physically handicapped, experimented with engine exhaust gas injected into sealed peasant huts. At Auschwitz, the fumigant Zyklon B, widely used in the concentration camps to control infestation, was successfully used to kill prisoners sealed up in the basement of Block 11. Following consultation with the returning scientists from Belarus, Heydrich authorized the construction and testing of a gas van, after which 30 were ordered. Three of these were dispatched to the camp at Chelmno outside Łódź, where an earlier generation of gas van still using bottled carbon monoxide began gassing Jews on 8 December 1941. The SS and Police Leader in Lublin, Odilo Globocnik, urgently requested a meeting with Himmler. It took place on 13 October, and on 1 November construction of the death camp at Bełżec in the Lublin District, near where Wirth had conducted his experiment, began. Bełżec began the mass killing of Jews in March 1942. In Auschwitz, Zyklon B was used in the fall of 1941 to kill Jews in the morgue of the camp's crematory. By late October, the design for a more advanced crematory–morgue–gas chamber complex had been drawn up. Before four of these complexes were constructed in Birkenau, large-scale gassing of Jews with Zyklon B began in two peasant huts in May 1942.

Moreover, on 23 October 1941, Himmler was in Mogilev, promising Nazi killers there that their burden of killing Jews would soon be made easier by the construction of gas chambers. And, on the same day, Eichmann in Berlin discussed with an official of Rosenberg's Ministry for the Eastern Occupied Territories the possibility of constructing gas vans in Riga. Also on 23 October, Eichmann met with his team of deportation specialists and Jewish experts whom he had summoned back to Berlin. No official record of this meeting has survived, but one man "who works in the east on the settlement of the Jewish question" indiscreetly told a friend that very day that "in the near future many of the Jewish vermin will be exterminated through special measures."[18] In short, in the third week of October 1941, plans were being made for gassing facilities at five sites, three of which—Mogilev near Minsk, Chelmno near Łódź, and Riga—were located at or near the sites from which Jews who were being deported from the Third Reich were to be sent further east the next spring, and Eichmann's cadre of experts (middle-echelon SS activists such as Höppner, who craved "clarity") were being informed of "special measures" to exterminate the Jews.

Did these plans for the deportation of Jews to camps equipped with gassing facilities apply only to eastern Jews, who had to be killed to make room in crowded ghettos for Jews deported from the Third Reich? Did they apply only to the eastern and deported Third Reich Jews? Or did the Nazis already envisage at this point in time a comprehensive killing program for all European Jews? Several key documents suggest the last alternative. In the late summer of 1941, a number of Spanish Jews had been arrested and interned in France. This led the Spanish government to suggest that, in return for their release, it would evacuate all Spanish Jews residing in France (some 2,000) to Spanish Morocco. As the expulsion of Europe's Jews overseas was very much in line with Germany's previous plans, the Foreign Office eagerly and expectantly sought SS approval on 13 October 1941. Four days later, it received a surprising rejection from Heydrich. If these Jews were sent to Spanish Morocco, he explained, they would be "too much out of the direct reach of measures for a basic solution to the Jewish question to be enacted after the war." One day later, on 18 October, Himmler and Heydrich had a lengthy telephone conversation, the conclusion of which was cryptically noted in Himmler's phone log: "No emigration by Jews to overseas." On 23 October, the official circular was sent out, announcing the end to any further Jewish emigration from all territories under German control.[19]

What was to happen to those European Jews, none of whom was now to be allowed to escape the German grasp? At the very moment that Eichmann had summoned his various specialists back to Berlin, where they were informed of "special measures" to exterminate the Jews, Eichmann's right-hand man, Friedrich Suhr, travelled to Belgrade, where he discussed the eventual fate prescribed for the Jewish women and children, after the liquidation of the Jewish men who were in the process of being shot in mass reprisals carried out by the German army. The women and children were to be interned over the winter. "Then as soon as the technical possibility exists within the framework of a total solution to the Jewish question, they will be deported ... to reception camps in the east."[20] In short, as part of the "basic" or "total solution" to the Jewish question, not even Spanish Jews in France nor Jewish women and children in Belgrade were to be spared deportation to "reception camps" in the east, construction of which would be finished by the following spring. I conclude, therefore, that the Nazi regime had crossed a key watershed. The old vision of solving the Jewish question by making Europe judenrein through a combination of expulsion and decimation had been superseded by a new vision of comprehensive mass murder to be achieved through deportation to camps equipped with gassing facilities still to be built.

If the new vision was now in place, the Nazi regime still had many questions to answer and decisions to make. The decision-making process did not come abruptly to an end. Would the prototype death camps under construction provide an adequate techno-logical and logistical solution to the staggering and unprecedented task now facing the Nazis, and what adjustments would have to be made? Could the killing of Reich Jews, a potentially far more sensitive issue politically, be managed in the same way as the killing of foreign Jews, or would it require more numerous exceptions and greater deception? How could the economic exigencies of the wartime economy, especially the growing shortage of labor, be reconciled with the mass destruction of Jewish labor potential? How would the necessary collaboration of allied and satellite regimes, whose Jews were targeted and whose help was needed, be obtained? In what sequence should the Nazi regime implement the Final Solution in the countries under its control or influence? The implementation of the Final Solution never became routine, and the Nazi regime experienced frustrations as well as lethal successes. But the "basic decision" of September/October 1941 and the "clarity" of the ultimate goal as "extirpation," to cite Höppner once again, were never again in doubt.

This interpretation of the origins of the Final Solution is one historian's view. Over the decades, this issue has been hotly debated and contested. While differences have narrowed on some aspects and near consensus has been achieved on others, the debate still remains vigorous on certain points. The first round of this debate, which began in the early 1970s and reached its peak in the 1980s, was characterized as the intentionalist–functionalist controversy. The difference of opinions was stark.[21] Intentionalists believed that the course of events in Nazi Germany was best explained on the basis of Hitler's intentions and decisions, which in turn were logically derived from his ideology.[22] In the "ultra-intentionalist" view, Hitler alone made the key decisions, and he operated from a blueprint or grand design for the Final Solution from the earliest years of his political career.[23] Functionalists believed the course of events in Nazi Germany was best explained by how the government functioned. They viewed the regime as a polycratic system consumed by rival factions and internal power struggles, presided over by a relatively aloof and improvisatory Hitler. He reacted to changing circumstances rather than according to a predetermined blueprint, and was as much concerned with preserving his popularity and the loyalty of his followers as he was with realizing some specific program.[24] In the "ultra-functionalist" view, Hitler never made a decision for the Final Solution. Rather, a series of increasingly murderous local improvisations, in response to local frustrations, only gradually coalesced or crystallized into a Europe-wide program of systematic mass murder by the summer of 1942. In a process of unplanned but highly destructive "cumulative radicalization," conception in effect followed practice.[25]

Following the collapse of communism in Eastern Europe, historians took a new look at the origins of the Final Solution. Empirically grounded in significant new documentation now accessible in East European archives, and many of them from a younger generation free from defending the entrenched and polarized positions of the intentionalist–functionalist controversy, these historians have narrowed the spectrum of interpretational differences on a number of important issues over the past two decades. What are the areas of broad agreement, and what issues are still being contested? First, most historians now agree that there was no "big bang" theory for the origins of the Final Solution, predicated on a single decision made at a single moment. The decision-making process was prolonged and incremental, and the ongoing debate is about emphasis, that is, which stages of the decision-making process were more pivotal or decisive than others.

Second, most historians agree on emphasizing two connections. The history of the evolution of Nazi Jewish policy cannot be separated from the history of the war, and the crucial developments of 1941 and early 1942—where debates over the relative weighting of decisions is still hotly debated—cannot be sharply separated from the wider Nazi plans and visions of demographic engineering that first emerged in 1939. In short, the Final Solution emerged from both the way in which the war developed, and the ultimate Nazi aim for which the war was being fought, namely a fundamental demographic revolution based on Nazi racial axioms.

Third, there is a growing acceptance among historians that the Final Solution was based on a form of consensus politics. Hitler played a key role, both as instigator and legitimizer of the ongoing search for a solution to the Nazis' self-imposed Jewish problem and also as a key decision-maker, but he did not proceed according to the script of some premeditated grand design or blueprint. He signaled his expectations, often through prophecies, and others sought to make these prophecies come true by making suggestions or designing concrete proposals, for which they then sought Hitler's approval. In an interactive process between the center and periphery, between top leaders and lower-ranked activists and functionaries, what united the Nazis in their determination to solve the Jewish problem was more important than the rivalries and power struggles that divided them.

What, then, is still contested? First is the issue of the relative weighting between the initiatives of local and regional authorities on the one hand, and the decisions of central authorities (most importantly Hitler and Himmler) on the other. A large number of important regional studies have been published in the past two decades,[26] and a tendency of many of these local studies is to highlight the local initiatives this research has uncovered, while downplaying the role of the central authorities. In this "center vs periphery" debate, I have argued for greater emphasis on the role of Himmler and his relationship to Hitler. If one wants to know what Hitler was thinking, I have argued, watch what Himmler was doing, for no-one anticipated and understood Hitler's wishes in this period with greater alacrity than Himmler. In 1939–40, Himmler and those under him were devising manic schemes of "population resettlement." In the spring of 1941, he organized the manpower for targeted killing of potential enemies. Then, in the summer of 1941, he traveled extensively behind the front, instigating the comprehensive killing of all Jews. In the fall of 1941, he and those under him began the deportation of Jews from the Third Reich to the east, ended emigration, and began the construction of death camps. These were the parameters within which local and regional authorities could work, as even the most lethally zealous—such as Rolf-Heinz Höppner—realized.

The relative weighting and dating of events in 1941 and early 1942 is also contested. Such weighting and dating is not arcane hair-splitting. The "when" question is important, because the debate over the weighting and dating of key decisions is inseparable from the circumstances in which they were taken, and thus crucial to the "why" question as well. Two historians have maintained the greatest continuity with the old intentionalist position. Richard Breitman has argued that a "basic decision" for the Final Solution was taken during the preparations for Barbarossa in early 1941, a stance which implies the primacy of ideological factors and central decision-making.[27] Philipp Burrin has argued for what he calls "conditional intentionalism," positing a Hitler determination as early as 1935 to destroy the Jews if and when he faced a prolonged war on all fronts. He dates Hitler's realization that this condition had been fulfilled to late summer and early fall 1941, with the failure to achieve quick victory over the Soviet Union.[28]

A number of historians have put great emphasis on Hitler's reaction to the United States in 1941 as a, if not the, decisive factor in his thinking. Tobias Jersak argues that August 1941—with the Blitzkrieg stalled and the US–British announcement of the Atlantic Charter—was the fatal point at which Hitler decided to vent his rage and take his revenge by destroying the Jews.[29] Shlomo Aronson also emphasizes the importance of imminent US entry into the war, but dates this crucial turning point in Hitler's mind to October 1941, when Lend-Lease was extended to the Soviet Union.[30] Hans Safrian, L.J. Hartog, and Christian Gerlach place Hitler's key decision in December 1941. Crucial for them was the US entry into the war after Pearl Harbor, which fulfilled the conditions of Hitler's *Reichstag* prophecy speech (which specified a true "world war" as opposed to a mere continental conflict) and deprived European Jews of any value as hostages for American behavior.[31]

Peter Longerich argues for "stages of escalation" from 1939 to 1942. The first stage, in 1939, already committed Nazi Germany to a "policy of annihilation" of one kind or another. In the final stage of April/May 1942, a cluster of decisions cast Nazi "annihilation policy" in the ultimate form of the Final Solution. In comparison with others, he somewhat downplays the events of the summer and fall of 1941. Longerich, along with Ian Kershaw, remains closest to the old functionalist tradition in portraying Hitler as approving the initiatives of those "working toward the Führer" in a series of incremental decisions culminating without clear and decisive turning points in the Final Solution.[32]

I have argued for two key decision-making processes: one for the mass murder of Soviet Jews that reached closure in July/August 1941; and one that sealed the fate of European Jews in September/October 1941. In contrast to others with similar dating, however, I have not emphasized the context of Hitler's frustrations and rage over the failure to obtain quick victory against the Soviet Union and the looming entry of the USA into the war. Instead, I have emphasized the correlation between the peaks of Hitler's victory euphoria and the radicalization of Jewish policy that, in my opinion, form a persuasive pattern. In September 1939, flush with victory over Poland, Hitler approved Himmler's first large-scale schemes for population resettlement, which also involved sending the Jews under German control to the Lublin Reservation. Flush with victory over France in May/June 1940, Hitler approved Himmler's revived proposals for demographic revolution and the Madagascar Plan. Expecting imminent collapse of the Soviet Union in July 1941, Hitler gave the "green light" for the extermination of Soviet Jewry. And in late September/early October, once again Hitler was "exuberantly optimistic" over the prospects of a decisive victory over the Soviet Union. He was in constant contact with Himmler, who, in this same period, began deporting the Jews of the Third Reich eastward, closed any further Jewish emigration out of Europe, and began building death camps. When just a few weeks later the weather turned and exhausted German troops were stopped at the gates of Moscow, the Soviet Union was saved. The Jews of Europe were not.

Notes

1 For detailed studies of the various Nazi "resettlement" schemes, see Götz Aly, *"Final Solution": Nazi Population Policy and the Murder of the European Jews* (London: Arnold, 1999); Phillip Rutherford, *Prelude to the Final Solution: The Nazi Program for Deporting Ethnic Poles, 1939–1941* (Lawrence, Kansas: University of Kansas Press, 2007); Christopher Browning and Jürgen Matthäus, *The Origins of the Final Solution: The Evolution of Nazi Jewish Policy, September 1939–March 1942* (Lincoln, Nebraska: University of Nebraska Press, 2004), chapter 3.

2 Arthur Seyss-Inquart, report on his trip to Poland, 17–22 November 1939, Nuremberg Document 2278-PS, in *Trial of the Major War Criminals before the International Military Tribunal, Nuremberg, 14 November 1945–1 October 1946* (Nuremberg: Allied Control Council, 1947–49), 30: 95 (*IMT*).

3 Helmut Krausnick, ed., "Denkschrift Himmlers über die Behandlung der fremdvölkischen im Osten," *Vierteljahrshefte für Zeitgeschichte*, vol. 5, no. 2 (1957): 194–98.

4 Theodore Dannecker memorandum, 21 January 1941, printed in Serge Klarsfeld, *Vichy-Auschwitz: Die Zusammenarbeit der deutschen und französischen Behörden bei der "Endlösung der Judenfrage" in Frankreich* (Nördlingen: Delphi Politik, 1989), 361–63.

5 Economic conference of state secretaries, 2 May 1941, Nuremberg Document 2718-PS, *IMT*, 31: 84–85.

6 Bach-Zelewski testimony, in *Justiz und NS-Verbrechen: Sammlung deutscher Strafurteile wegen nationalsozialistischer Tötungsverbrechen, 1945–1966*, Vol. 20, No. 580 (Amsterdam: University Press of Amsterdam, 1968–2008), 413 (JNSV).

7 Conference of 16 July1941, Nuremberg Document 221-L, *IMT*, 38: 86–94.

8 Jäger Report, 1 December 1941,Yad Vashem Archives, O-53/141/30–38.

9 Einsatzgruppen Report No. 94, 24 September 1941, in *The Einsatzgruppen Reports: Selections from the Dispatches of the Nazi Death Squads' Campaign against the Jews in Occupied Territories of the Soviet Union*, eds Yitzhak Arad, Shmuel Krakowski and Shmuel Spector (New York: Holocaust Library, 1989), 158.

10 Report No. 86, 17 September 1941, in *The Einsatzgruppen Reports* (ed. Arad *et al.*), 137.

11 Göring authorization to Heydrich, 31 July 1941, Nuremberg Document 710-PS, *IMT*, 26: 266–67.

12 Goebbels entry of 19 August 1941, in *Die Tagebücher von Joseph Goebbels*, Part II (Munich: K.G. Saur, 1987–2008), 1: 265–69.

13 Höppner to Eichmann, 16 July 1941, in *Documents of Destruction*, ed. Raul Hilberg (Chicago: Quadrangle, 1971), 87–88; Höppner memorandum, 2 September 1941, United States Holocaust Memorial Museum Archives, RG 15.007m, 8/103/45–62.

14 Himmler to Greiser, 18 September 1941, National Archives microfilm, T 175/54/2568695.

15 Goebbels entry of 24 September 1941, *Die Tagebücher von Joseph Goebbels*, Part II, 2: 480–85.

16 Goebbels entry of 14 October 1941, *Die Tagebücher von Joseph Goebbels*, Part II, 2: 49–50.

17 Saul Friedländer, *Nazi Germany and the Jews 1939–1945: The Years of Extermination* (New York: Harper Perennial, 2009), 272.

18 Wurm to Rademacher, 23 October1941, Political Archives of the German Foreign Office, Inland II A/B 59/3.

19 Luther memoranda of 13 and 17 October 1941, Political Archives of the German Foreign Office, Pol. Abt. III 246; Entry of 18 October 1941, *Der Dienstkalendar Heinrich Himmlers 1941/1942*, eds Peter Witte et al. (Hamburg: Christians, 1999), 238. Until this point, the emigration of Jews from the Third Reich had been permitted, though emigration of non-German Jews from German occupied territories had already been forbidden in order to give precedence to making the Third Reich *judenrein* first.

20 Rademacher report, 25 October 1941, *Akten zur deutschen auswärtigen Politik*, Series D, Vol. 13, no. 2 (Baden-Baden: Impr. Nationale, 1950–91), 570–72.

21 For the origin of these terms, see Tim Mason, "Intention and Explanation: A Current Controversy about the Interpretation of National Socialism," *Der Führerstaat: Mythos und Realität* (Stuttgart: DVA, 1981), 21–40. As Ian Kershaw has noted, at the conference at the Cumberland Lodge in 1979, during which Mason applied these terms to current historiography on Nazi Germany, the Holocaust—still a marginalized academic topic at that time—was not discussed. Ian Kershaw, *Hitler, Germans, and the Final Solution* (New Haven, Connecticut: Yale University Press, 2008), 12–13. These terms were first applied to the debate over Nazi Jewish policy and the origins of the Final Solution at a conference in Paris in 1982. Christopher R. Browning, "The Decision Concerning the Final Solution," in *Unanswered Questions: Nazi Germany and the Genocide of the Jews*, ed. François Furet (New York: Schocken, 1989), 96–118.

22 Eberhard Jäckel, *Hitler's Weltanschauung: A Blueprint for Power* (Middletown, Connecticut: Wesleyan University Press, 1972); Andreas Hillgruber, "Die Endlösung und das deutsch Ostimperium als Kernstück des rassenideologischen Programms des Nationalsozialismus," *Vierteljahrshefte fur Zeitgeschichte*, vol. 20, no. 2 (1972): 133–51.

23 Lucy Dawidowicz, *The War Against the Jews 1933–1945* (New York: Holt, Rinehart and Winston, 1975).

24 Karl Schleunes, *The Twisted Road to Auschwitz: Nazi Policy toward German Jews 1933–1939* (Urbana: University of Illinois Press, 1970); Uwe Dietrich Adam, *Judenpolitik im Dritten Reich* (Düsseldorf: Droste, 1972).

25 Martin Broszat, "Hitler and the Genesis of the Final Solution," *Yad Vashem Studies*, vol. 13 (1979): 73–125; Hans Mommsen, "Die Realisierung des Utopischen: Die 'Endlösung der Judenfrage' im 'Dritten Reich,'"*Geschichte und Gesellschaft,* vol. 9 (1983): 381–420.

26 This was particularly the case of the hitherto relatively understudied regions of eastern Europe. For Lublin, see Dieter Pohl and Bogdan Musial; for Eastern Galicia, Dieter Pohl and Thomas Sandkühler; for Silesia, Sybille Steinbacher; for Radom, Robert Seidel and Jacek Andrzej Mlynarczyk; for the Łódź ghetto and the Warthegau, Gordon Horwitz, Michael Albertini, and Peter Klein; for Latvia, Andrew Ezergailis and Andrej Angrick/Peter Klein; for Estonia, Anton Weiss-Wendt; for Belarus, Christian Gerlach; for the Ukraine, Wendy Lower.

27 Richard Breitman, *Architect of Genocide: Himmler and the Final Solution* (New York: Knopf, 1991).

28 Philipp Burrin, *Hitler and the Jews: The Genesis of the Holocaust* (London: Arnold, 1994).

29 Tobias Jersak, "Die Interaktion von Kreigfsverlauf und Judenvernichtung: Ein Blick auf Hitlers Strategie im Spätsommer 1941," *Historische Zeitschrift,* vol. 268 (1999): 311–49, and "Decisions to Murder and to Lie. German War Society and the Holocaust," *Germany and the Second World War, Vol. IX/1: German Wartime Society 1939–1945: Politicization, Disintegration, and the Struggle for Survival* (Oxford: Clarendon Press, 2008), 287–368, esp. 306–25.

30 Shlomo Aronson, "Die dreifache Fälle: Hitlers Judenpolitik, die Allierten und die Juden," *Vierteljahrshefte für Zeitgeschichte*, vol. 32, no. 1 (1984): 28–65. In his more recent book, *Hitler, the Allies, and the Jews* (New York: Cambridge University Press, 2004), Aronson is less explicit about the specific impact of Lend-Lease, but continues to emphasize the impact on Hitler of Allied reactions to his previous provocations in October/November 1941.

31 Hans Safrian, *Die Eichmann Männer* (Vienna: Europaverlag, 1993); L.J. Hartog, *Der Befehl zum Judenmord: Hitler, Amerika, und die Juden* (Bodenheim: Syndikat Buchgesellschaft, 1997); Christian Gerlach, "The Wannsee Conference, the Fate of German Jews, and Hitler's Basic Decision in Principle to Exterminate all European Jews," *Journal of Modern History*, vol. 70 (1998): 759–812. The December dating has now been accepted as the most probable by Saul Friedländer, *Nazi Germany and the Jews, Vol. 2, The Years of Extermination* (New York: HarperCollins, 2007).

32 Peter Longerich, *Politik der Vernichtung: Eine Gesamtdarstellung der nationalsozialistischen Judenverfolgung* (Munich: Piper, 1998); Ian Kershaw, *Hitler 1936–1945: Nemesis* (New York: Norton, 2000), esp. chapter 10.

15

FORCED LABOR IN NAZI ANTI-JEWISH POLICY, 1938–45

Wolf Gruner

In Mauthausen concentration camp, the SS forced prisoners to climb up and down a stone stairway carrying heavy loads until the victims were totally exhausted; this often fatal labor had no economic rationale. Does this example provide the main characteristics of forced labor for Jews during the Third Reich, or does it constitute the exception from the rule? For a long time, research studies have scarcely considered forced labor to be a significant factor in Nazi anti-Jewish policy. Instead, historians have regarded forced labor as an intermediate solution or as a particular step on the way to mass murder.[1] Some authors even equated labor with extermination from the outset.[2] Yet, despite the common assumption that labor was used only to exhaust Jewish lives, forced labor was a key feature of Nazi policy.[3] Whether in Germany, the annexed territories, or the occupied countries, Nazi rule usually ended the Jews' free access to any given job market by placing prohibitions on employment and trade. As a consequence, the majority of the Jews were left without any source of income and thus depended on public assistance. Hence, the National Socialists regularly imposed forced labor as one of the first persecutory measures on the local Jewish population, whether in Poland, the Soviet Union, Norway, Serbia, the Netherlands, France, or even Tunisia.[4] Forced labor assured a minimum income to Jewish families, provided the German state with cheap labor, and at the same time guaranteed strict control over individuals within the Jewish population who were capable of resistance. At its maximum extent, more than one million Jewish men and women toiled for Nazi Germany, thus providing significant manpower for the war economy.[5]

Germany and Austria

Today, Jewish labor in Nazi Germany is still associated primarily with use of Jews in concentration camps. Scholarly interest in their exploitation by the SS and in the concentration camps has continued without interruption until today.[6] It was a little known fact that forced labor served as an integral part of Jewish persecution outside that context. Moreover, the predominant form of forced labor performed by Jews in Europe was neither exploitation in concentration camps, nor in other SS camps, but in the "*Geschlossene Arbeitseinsatz*," that is, segregated labor deployment, developed and organized by the German labor offices (*Arbeitsämter*). This concept referred to involuntary, segregated, and discriminatory employment of workers who had been selected on the basis of racial criteria. The leadership of the labor administration ensured that compulsory labor was set up with an eye to economic interests.[7]

This special labor program started in Germany and Austria after *Kristallnacht* in 1938, with obligatory assignment of Jews to manual labor for municipalities as well as public and private businesses. The fact that compulsory labor for Jews originated in Germany itself and played a significant role in persecution has remained unnoticed for a long time. A different view still held sway during World War II and in the years that followed.[8] This view promptly disappeared when the process of analyzing the historical events began. Indeed, few documents on Jewish forced labor surfaced at first, since Nazi labor officials, conscious of their crimes, had destroyed most files. However, historical studies on the crimes against the Jews provided a rough picture of this matter during the 1960s and 1970s.[9] Later, though, the erroneous view spread among historians that forced labor for German Jews had not been introduced until March 1941.[10] As a consequence, the duration, extent, and historical significance of forced labor were gravely under-estimated.[11] Only from the mid-1990s onwards did new research fundamentally alter this picture.[12]

Although the stereotype of the "lazy Jew" had been widespread in Germany since the nineteenth century, the leading National Socialists did not develop any concept of forced labor during the first years of power, because the expulsion of Jews had priority. However, every measure taken by the Nazis to expel the Jews since 1933 increased unemployment and poverty among Jews and thus obstructed speedy individual emigration.[13] After the March 1938 annexation of Austria, and with 200,000 more Jews living in the German Reich, the inherent contradictions became increasingly pronounced by the radicalized Nazi policy. The brutal nationwide pogrom in November 1938 did not achieve the desired goal—the fast emigration of all Jews. Now, Nazi leadership sought to reorient anti-Jewish policy by forcing emigration by any means available, and by completely separating those Jews unable to emigrate from the rest of society. Under Göring's supervision, persecution was organized centrally and involved division of labor. Since all avenues for Jews to earn a living independently were now blocked, as part of the new program, the forced employment of Jews without income was introduced, which was to be arranged by the Reich labor administration. Forced labor was thus not an interim solution, but rather a key element in a remodelled persecutory process after 1938.[14]

The idea to exploit Jews registered with the labor offices was first launched in Vienna. Radical persecution of Jews after the *Anschluss* had resulted in mass dependence on public welfare and unemployment insurance. In September 1938, the Austrian labor administration reacted with the novel measure of forcing Jews receiving unemployment benefits to perform excavation work in separate columns.[15]

After the November pogrom, the Austrian model became the prototype for segregated labor deployment of Jews in the Reich. Following the 20 December 1938 decree of the Reich Institute for Labor Placement and Unemployment Insurance, labor offices began to deploy Jews, first men supported by government unemployment insurance, and principally for manual work. In many towns, Jews were especially assigned dirty and humiliating work such as street cleaning or garbage removal. While activities such as garbage sorting, construction, and street cleaning dominated the program in the beginning, Jews soon were also used in agriculture and forestry. In summer 1939, 20,000 German Jews worked in segregated labor deployments. The labor offices sent many Jews to newly erected labor camps, where they toiled on road and dam construction for months, sometimes even years.[16]

As in the Reich, Jews in Austria who received unemployment assistance were taken first. However, as soon as the summer of 1939, much earlier than in Germany, the labor offices started to exploit all able-bodied men and women. They were assigned to garbage-dump jobs and brickworks in Vienna, to the Reich Autobahn, and road and power plant projects in other Austrian regions, as well as to dam and dike projects in Germany.[17]

The fact that hundreds of special forced-labor camps were erected for German, Austrian, and later even for Polish Jews inside the Reich, and that they existed entirely independently of the SS-administered concentration camp system, is scarcely known even today. The camps were established and supported by private companies, public builders, even municipalities. For example, as early as spring 1939, the small city of Kelkheim in Hesse established its own "Jews' camp." For a local road construction project, the mayor received upon his request 20 Jewish laborers from the Frankfurt am Main labor office. Most of the Jewish men had never before performed excavation work, and were entirely overtaxed physically by toiling up to 60 hours a week; that was not at all usual in the prewar period. The difficult living circumstances soon led to suicide. After 6 months, in October 1939, the road was built, the men sent back, and the camp closed.[18] Such labor camps were by no means as well shielded from the population as the concentration camps, since town residents often guarded, inspected, or supplied the facilities. But as many of the camps existed only for a limited time, they are forgotten in Germany and Austria today.[19]

From the outset, Jews were subject to unwritten special regulations: in being forced to work based on racial criteria, in being utilized segregated from other workers, and in being allocated to unskilled labor regardless of former qualifications or their suitability. A special feature of segregated labor deployment consisted of the fact that Jews were employed under individual work contracts. But such contracts were by no means an indicator of voluntariness, as "assignment by the labor office" replaced "the employee's declaration of intention."[20] Decrees of the Reich Trustee of Labor and various decisions of German labor courts progressively created a special legislation for Jewish forced labor, which was finally codified by a 3 October 1941 order.[21]

After the rapid takeover of Poland, Hitler dropped the idea raised in spring 1939 of introducing forced labor for all able-bodied German Jews in case of war. Instead, all German, Austrian, and Czech Jews would be relocated to the occupied territories.[22] Yet, in spring 1940, after initial deportation plans failed, the German labor offices responded, in light of the looming campaign against France, to new labor shortages by recruiting all able-bodied Jews. While the deployment for minor construction projects was stopped, forced labor for industry or other activities requiring skills now grew rapidly, especially towards the end of 1940. These transformations in labor policy indicate how specific war needs were able to reshape persecutory measures. In the summer of 1941, the number of Jews toiling in Germany and Austria reached its peak at over 60,000, now more than half of them women, including many elderly and even children. In Berlin alone, Jews worked for over 230 companies. None of the enterprises was obliged to employ Jews; on the contrary, they could release any forced laborer within a day.[23]

In Germany, the labor administration had increasingly organized forced labor to benefit the war economy, especially industry and armaments, without the SS and Gestapo being involved in any way. This situation would change with mass deportations of Jews after fall 1941. Although transport timing compatible with production was to be coordinated with the labor administration and the *Wehrmacht* offices responsible for armaments (*Rüstungskommandos*), power relationships between the different local agencies provided the decisive factor in Germany. In some cases, transport dates were cancelled; in others, companies were spared removal of their Jews for extended periods. By contrast, postponing transports was rare in Vienna because industrial work played almost no role at all. By fall 1942, most Austrian Jews had been deported and the labor camps closed. At the same time, after more than a year of deportations, 20,000 armament workers represented the bulk of Jews still remaining in Germany. Only in February 1943, with the notorious *Fabrikaktion* (factory raid), were laborers pulled from the companies and deported.[24]

In 1943, the labor administration organized further segregated labor deployment, now for Jews in mixed marriages, mostly at manual labor or, less frequently, in industry. Based on a decision by Hitler in 1942, Jewish *Mischlinge* (individuals with a Jewish parent or grandparent) were also taken to perform forced labor, initially in France, and then later in Germany. After Himmler pushed in fall 1944 for accelerated forced deployment to dozens of newly established forced-labor camps, mostly for *Organisation Todt* projects, the labor offices employed around 20,000 *Mischlinge*.[25]

Forced labor thus shaped, decisively and for years, the everyday life of most German victims of Nazi anti-Jewish policies. However, it was very differently perceived by the people affected, given that they were employed in various sectors of the economy. Whereas the father of Karla Wolf collapsed physically and mentally while working as a painter's assistant,[26] the writer Gertrud Kolmar regarded her work in an armaments operation as a challenge.[27] Marga Spiegel remembered, "My husband had to perform forced labor. Jews could be deployed only in columns of about 17 men and had non-Jewish supervisors … They had supervisors who ordered them around like slaves and harassed them when in the mood."[28]

The Protectorate of Bohemia and Moravia

After the occupation of Czech territory by Nazi Germany in March 1939, Hitler granted the newly founded Protectorate a limited autonomy. Thus anti-Jewish policies would be introduced by both the German Reichprotector and the Czech government. The ensuing exclusion of Jews from employment resulted in impoverishment of the Jewish population and dependence on social assistance. As the original plan to deport the Jews to occupied Poland failed, the first compulsory labor measures were introduced at the local level in mid-1940. Several central orders in succession established the segregated labor deployment for Jews in 1941. In early fall, 12,000 Jews, 16–60 years old, toiled in construction and farm work. In some labor office districts, that was almost 100 percent of all Jews physically capable of working; in others more than 50 percent.[29]

Until this point, women were scarcely recruited in the Protectorate, in striking contrast to Germany and Austria. Despite the commencement of mass deportations in October 1941, the labor offices surprisingly were even able to expand forced labor. Now, the labor offices assigned Jews increasingly to industry. Thus the peak of the forced labor program in the former Czech territories was reached a year later than in Germany and Austria. In May 1942, private companies and public agencies exploited more than 15,000 men and 1,000 women. In July, the forced laborers were placed on the same legal footing as those in most of the territories under German rule. The labor administration directed labor for Jews in the Protectorate, but diverging from the rest of the Reich, the Central Office for

Jewish Emigration (*Zentralstelle für jüdische Auswanderung*) of the SS Security Service (*Sicherheitsdienst* or SD) in Prague took partial control in May 1941 of the supervision of outside deployments. The Protectorate thus held a transitional position in relation to the forced-labor program introduced in occupied Poland.[30]

The Polish territories

While many books on persecution in occupied Poland have surfaced, researcher have seldom paid much attention to Jewish forced labor, with the exception of Christopher Browning, who studied developments in the General Government.[31] Limited attention has been paid to the SS labor camps in eastern Poland.[32] Indeed, the focus on the Lublin and the Galicia districts, in which the SS developed special programs, has forged our image of forced labor in occupied Poland,[33] a perspective which must be thoroughly revised.

In occupied Poland, persecution was organized, as in the Reich, with a division of labor. While in Polish regions annexed to Germany, such as the Warthegau or East Upper Silesia, where rapid expulsion was planned in order to Germanize the area, compulsory employment of Jews initially was not organized centrally; instead, local measures predominated. In the General Government, established in October 1939 and earmarked as an area to receive Jews deported from the regions annexed to Germany, one of the first measures introduced forced labor for all Jews. After the conquest, the rapid exclusion of Jews from businesses led to impoverishment. This situation, coupled with labor shortages, was a central motive for the establishment of forced-labor programs in the so-called General Government. While everywhere in the Reich the labor administration directed Jewish forced labor, here the situation would be different: The respective order of 26 October 1939 transferred official responsibility to the Higher SS and Police Leader (*Höherer SS- und Polizeiführer* or HSSPF).[34]

However, only a few months later it was clear that the SS missed paying wages, which left the families of the forced laborers without income, and failed to acknowledge the interests of the labor market. Hence, in summer 1940, the government of the General Government surprisingly took away authority from the SS and handed it over to the labor administration. From now on, the main labor department of the General Government directed Jewish forced labor. Labor offices made sure that Jews were at least paid minimum wages, and placed them according to the needs of the war economy, to modernize the occupied territories' infrastructure through hydraulic, road, and railway construction. Especially after starting to ship non-Jewish Poles as forced laborers to Germany, the entire General Government thus had an interest in the exploitation of Polish Jews. When transport plans failed in 1940 in the annexed Warthegau, the civil authorities began to recruit Jews systematically for forced labor there, too. By the end of 1940, more than 700,000 Jews are believed to have been engaged in occupied Poland's forced-labor program.[35]

However, local and regional ambitions of the SS, the police, the *Wehrmacht*, and the civilian authorities interfered with labor administration operations in Poland. Additionally, the municipal administrations responsible for organization of the newly formed ghettos initiated labor measures, on the one hand to pursue their own economic interests, and on the other to sustain the unemployed ghetto inhabitants. Some established shops in the ghetto, some convinced the Jewish councils to do so, and others, as in Warsaw, even invited private enterprises. At the same time, an increasing number of ghetto inhabitants were sent to newly established camps: Jews from Litzmannstadt (Warthegau) worked in Reich Autobahn construction; Jews from Lublin (General Government) toiled in hydraulic construction. After 1941, the assumption that work might protect against deportation to extermination camps provided the Jewish councils with a strong motivation for cooperation in forced-labor initiatives.[36]

Some of the regional Higher SS and Police Leaders in Poland attempted to set up their own labor systems, which operated side by side with the central program managed by the labor administration. Examples were the SS camps in Lublin district erected after 1940 as well as the SS camps along *Durchgangsstraße* IV in Galicia established after fall 1941; hard labor and malnutrition in those camps resulted in extremely high mortality rates among inmates.[37] In East Upper Silesia, a newly founded SS agency even took over Jewish forced labor in late 1940. The SS Special Commissioner Schmelt developed a forced labor program which, beside the shops in the East Upper Silesian ghettos, encompassed more than 50,000 Jews working in at least 177 camps at the end of 1942.[38]

All those SS forced-labor systems must be viewed as regional phenomena. Yet even when such SS networks surfaced, labor offices remained decisively involved in recruiting, selecting, and placing the forced laborers. Unlike the SS, the labor administration was able to coordinate economic needs with persecutory goals, including isolation and control. Overall, the relationship between the two institutions was characterized retrospectively less by conflict than by agreement and cooperation. Regardless of who was responsible, the work was usually performed by private enterprises. Many operations did not pay wages at all, or diverted them to civilian or municipal administrations that supplied only starvation rations to the Jews or the ghettos from where they came. Construction, equipment, and armaments companies profited the most.[39]

While, in the Warthegau, the labor administration continued to organize Jewish workers, the SS resumed control in the General Government in summer 1942 in the course of the progressing genocide, and economic interests had far more difficulties in prevailing. The SS eliminated the last vestiges of wages and instituted a forced-laborer rental system. Most labor camps were soon transformed into subcamps of SS concentration camps. However, the SS still cooperated closely with the army and armaments companies. During the following months, many laborers were exempted from mass murder because of war needs. As a result, 300,000 Jews, mostly forced laborers, still lived in the General Government at the end of 1942.[40] Despite SS control, labor administration remained involved. By classifying Jews into those capable of working and those incapable of doing so, labor officials often defined the groups determined for murder. The main labor department in the General Governor's office regularly received reports about mass murders.[41]

By contrast, the labor administration at the Posen *Reichsstatthalter*'s office in the annexed Warthegau continued to have the upper hand in organizing forced labor. It placed tens of thousands of Jews with the Wehrmacht and private enterprises. Despite regulations in force in the German Reich to pay forced laborers minimum wages, here the regional labor administration abolished regulations that had been in effect since 1940. A June 1942 order put the labor offices in charge of a forced-labor rental system that strongly resembled the parallel SS rental methods developed in the General Government and in Upper Silesia.[42]

Various camp systems for Jewish forced labor existed in the occupied Polish territories. In the Warthegau, dozens of labor camps were erected for agricultural work or infrastructure improvements. In the General Government, there were three main networks: the Wehrmacht camps; the forced-labor camps established by civilian authorities for hydraulic and road construction; and the SS camps. According to one estimate, the occupied Polish territories held at least 910 camps,[43] but there were probably many more. All the different camp systems intensified the social isolation and physical exploitation of the persecuted, but paradoxically, as a result of economic interests, some of the camps provided better chances of survival for Jews than the ghettos.

Work and/or annihilation?

The results of present research clearly demonstrate that forced labor in the Third Reich can hardly be considered part of the Nazi murder program. The Nazi state introduced forced labor as an element of their persecutory policy years before the decision to commit mass murder. Contrary to previous assumptions,[44] Jewish forced labor represented from the outset a conspicuous economic factor. In the summer of 1941, the labor administration in Greater Germany and the Protectorate of Bohemia and Moravia employed over 70,000 strategically situated Jews, mostly in industry, many in skilled jobs. More than 700,000 Polish Jews were engaged in forced labor in the Polish territories. If the Soviet and western European territories with comparable programs but no precise figures are included, the German war economy had more than one million cheap Jewish workers without any rights at their disposal.[45]

Against this background, one must ask what prompted the order to deport and murder the Jewish population, and with it the forced laborers, a decision that seems quite irrational. This decision is understandable only taking into account the perspective of the Nazi leadership, a perspective shaped by the special situation in Germany in the summer of 1941: while 50,000 Jews performed forced labor, the industry employed more than a million non-Jewish forced laborers from eastern and western Europe inside Germany alone. With that ratio, the removal of the German Jews, without detriment to the national economy, seemed feasible. At the same time, the rapidly advancing conquest of the Soviet Union raised the prospect of a future army of millions of slaves capable of replacing even the hundreds of thousands of Polish Jews.

Of course, this Nazi perspective had its shortcomings. It rapidly became apparent that Jews made up a large proportion of the laborers in certain regions and/or specific war industries; conflicts between political and economic objectives thus arose. The SS and Gestapo, on the one side, and the labor administration and the Wehrmacht offices, on the other, had to cooperate and plan pragmatically according to the interests of production. In Germany, armaments workers received limited-term releases from transports; some companies, such as Siemens, even negotiated collective guarantees preventing temporarily removal of all their hundreds of Jewish forced laborers. Berlin, a center of industrial concentration, clearly illustrates that economic needs led to decisive modifications in the course of deportations: at the end of 1942, 15,000 of all 20,000 Jewish forced laborers and two-thirds of the remaining Jews in Germany lived in the capital—*the* city which Hitler and Goebbels wanted to be "free" of Jews first.[46]

In the former Polish areas, too, the economic importance of forced labor cannot be overestimated. In 1940 and 1941, the labor administration assigned large numbers of Jewish forced laborers to infrastructure measures important for the war, but also to army repair facilities. Because of labor shortages, thousands of Polish Jews from the

Łódź ghetto were even sent to work in Germany against Hitler's outspoken wishes.[47] Moreover, after the SS reassumed control of forced labor in the General Government in 1942, Hitler himself guaranteed the army and industries protection of their Jewish skilled workers—against the demands of SS chief Himmler, who was pushing for total eradication.[48] Jews were especially instrumental in providing the *Wehrmacht* with clothing and other equipment and in building supply roads leading to the Soviet Union. In the East, the SS consequently coordinated its further actions with the German Army, but also with private enterprises and public builders such as the *Organisation Todt*. Forced laborers at important production or construction sites would be exempted from mass murder for months, sometimes years. From the 300,000 Jews still alive in the General Government at the end of 1942, surprisingly, more than half lived in Galicia— the district where mass murders had begun the earliest and the SS control over forced labor was the fiercest.[49] Thus, upon closer examination, the thesis of the total irrationality of the deportation decisions conflicting with the exigencies of war cannot be upheld, either for Greater Germany or for Poland.

The same is essentially true for the thesis of "destruction through work,"[50] which assumes that the prime objective of forced labor was the death of the forced laborer. This is definitely not true for the labor programs of Jews in Germany, Austria, the Protectorate, and Poland between 1939 and 1941. While many historians still view forced labor in Poland only as an integral component of extermination, and usually justify that on the basis of the SS camps,[51] others concede that Jewish forced laborers at least temporarily had better chances of survival than the rest of the population, and therefore the situation after 1942 could be described as a compromise between work and destruction.[52] Christopher Browning's claim that "destruction through work" is not at all accurate, because most of the Jews did not die from labor, but from the horrible living conditions, seems much more plausible, though.[53] Mostly, the exhausted and the sick were murdered and replaced by a new labor force, an effective way to secure the labor tasks. One must not forget: even the SS in occupied Poland used forced labor to achieve concrete goals such as construction of a street or fortification of a border. If murder had been the only objective, the SS would have been able to arrange the task more simply without the detour through labor, which required investment for equipment, maintenance, and supplies. Instead, mismanagement, in combination with the SS belief in its racial superiority, resulted in high mortality rates in many forced-labor camps, as did the colonial-master behavior in civilian agencies and companies responsible for others. In striking contrast to the thesis of "destruction through work," the forced-labor camps were the places where Jews were exempted from extermination the longest. In many camps and some ghettos in occupied Poland, forced laborers escaped genocide until late 1943 and even 1944.[54] Ironically, this was especially true for the regional SS strongholds such as Galicia and Upper Silesia, thus making it clear that the SS itself subordinated the regional murder programs to economic objectives. It is of interest that the latter is a fact also for the occupied Soviet territories, as Jürgen Matthäus, as well as Andrej Angrick and Peter Klein, revealed.[55]

In this light, the notorious "death marches," through which tens of thousands of Jewish and non-Jewish prisoners were evacuated from concentration camps and transferred to the Reich at the end of the war, have to be re-evaluated. Since the marches produced a huge death toll, they are perceived by many as the Nazis' last means to exterminate the Jews.[56] It is true that thousands of evacuees died from starvation, random killing, and illnesses; yet, for the SS guards, it would have been easier to have shot all prisoners on the spot or to have left them behind at the camps. Many prisoners died because the evacuation routes were ill-prepared, without food and shelter in harsh winter times, and the inmates were rejected by their destination camps, which were already overcrowded with arrivals from other camps. But why would the SS transfer camp inmates to the Reich in the first place, in direct contradiction to all former Nazi plans to get rid of Jews in Germany? It was to secure the labor force. That is why the guards desperately tried to bring them by foot, but—and this is mostly overlooked—also by trains, to camps located in Germany.[57]

Conclusion

While millions of Jews perished in the Holocaust, at least a few hundred thousand forced laborers survived due to economic German war interests. After the war, the re-established Republic of Austria as well as West Germany refused to compensate those Jewish victims.[58] Only as the result of mounting international pressure, forced laborers who are still alive recently received a small compensation from a shared fund of the German government and some private enterprises. For countless Jews in Nazi Germany and the occupied countries, forced labor determined the course of their daily lives for up to 6 years. Almost every Jewish family was affected. Hundreds of thousands of men and women had to leave their homes and live for months or years in labor camps. Until recently, historians had not systematically compared the different forms of Jewish forced labor in the different territories of the Third Reich, due to the assumption that forced labor was introduced late, under the control of the SS, and thus organized without an economic rationale.

The notion is still widespread that the SS, at least after 1938 in Germany and later in all occupied countries, determined anti-Jewish policies. Yet forced labor proves otherwise: not the SS, but the labor administrations, planned and managed the obligation for Jews to perform labor in Greater Germany and the Protectorate of Bohemia until the end of the war, and between 1940 and 1942 in the General Government. The SS orchestrated forced labor only as regional exceptions in Upper Silesia or parallel developments in Lublin and Galicia.

As early as late 1938, segregated labor deployment for Jews had been introduced in Germany and annexed Austria as a basic element of anti-Jewish policy. The labor administration responded to increased poverty and unemployment among the Jewish population due to intense persecution as well as growing labor shortages, especially just before and during the war. More than 60,000 men and women would later perform heavy labor in construction, agriculture, and forestry, often in newly erected labor camps, or in industrial enterprises. In 1943, after the deportation of most Jews, forced labor for *Mischlinge* was introduced. Possibly as many as 450 labor camps for Jews, today mostly forgotten and independent of the concentration camp system, existed between 1938 and 1945 in the Old Reich, in Austria, and in the Sudeten regions alone. The forced-labor model developed in Germany was applied in all annexed and occupied territories, often in a more radical manner. While forced labor for Jews was introduced as early as October 1939 in the General Government, it was established in the Protectorate and the annexed Polish territories only in late 1940 or early 1941 after deportation plans had failed.

More than one million Jewish men and women toiled for the Third Reich. The laborers' value lay not only in their numbers, but also in their placement in strategic areas where labor shortages were severe, including infrastructure projects and the armaments industry. The actual beneficiaries of exploiting extremely cheap labor unprotected by any rights were, in all territories, local and regional civil authorities, public builders, and private businesses. Thousands of officials from national, regional, and local administrations, from police, army, and SS, as well as numerous employees of private companies and public enterprises, took part in the development of the forced-labor programs and thus were responsible for their often horrific conditions.

In all territories, the labor administration ran forced labor focusing on consideration of the labor market and war economy interests. For this reason, the German labor administration managed to push through the mass utilization of Jews in skilled industrial jobs in 1940, despite pending planning for deportation; at the same time, the labor administration in occupied Poland took over control of forced labor from the failing SS. While the latter re-obtained control in the General Government after summer 1942, in the shadow of mass murder, it never succeeded to that extent elsewhere. While local persecutory interests of the SS often interfered with the central labor market interests of the labor administration in the General Government during the period prior to 1942, local and regional economic objectives frequently modified central plans for murder afterwards.

These circumstances change previous perceptions of the development of anti-Jewish policy: forced labor of hundreds of thousands of Jews was an important economic factor, which was mainly organized by civil authorities. The fact that even the SS had to coordinate persecution with the needs of the labor market, and therefore many Jews survived, fundamentally refutes the thesis that compulsory work was just another element of the destruction of the Jews.

Notes

1 See Ulrich Herbert, "Arbeit und Vernichtung," in *Europa und der "Reichseinsatz": Ausländische Zivilarbeiter, Kriegsgefangene und KZ-Häftlinge in Deutschland 1938–1945*, ed. Ulrich Herbert (Essen: Klartext, 1991), 90–105.
2 Goldhagen based his claim on the description of three SS camps during times of mass murder: Daniel J. Goldhagen, *Hitler's Willing Executioners. Ordinary Germans and the Holocaust* (New York: Alfred A. Knopf, 1996), 283–326.
3 For a general discussion on the importance of forced labor for Nazi Germany, see Mark Spoerer, *Zwangsarbeit unter dem Hakenkreuz: Ausländische Zivilarbeiter, Kriegsgefangene und Häftlinge im Deutschen Reich und im besetzten Europa 1939–1945* (Stuttgart: Deutsche Verlagsanstalt, 2001).
4 See Martin Gilbert, *Die Endlösung: Die Verfolgung und Vernichtung der europäischen Juden. Ein Atlas* (Reinbek near Hamburg: Rowohlt, 1982).
5 Wolf Gruner, *Jewish Forced Labor under the Nazis. Economic Needs and Racial Aims 1938–1944* (New York: Cambridge University Press, 2006, 2; corrected paperback edition, 2008).
6 Michael Thad Allen, *The Business of Genocide: The SS, Slave Labor, and the Concentration Camps* (Chapel Hill, North Carolina: University of North Carolina Press, 2002); Hermann Kaienburg, *Die Wirtschaft der SS* (Berlin: Metropol, 2003).
7 For this and the following, see Wolf Gruner, *Der geschlossene Arbeitseinsatz deutscher Juden. Zur Zwangsarbeit als Element der Verfolgung 1938–1943* (Berlin: Metropol Verlag, 1997); *Zwangsarbeit und Verfolgung. Österreichische Juden im NS-Staat 1938–1943* (Innsbruck: Studienverlag, 2000); and *Jewish Forced Labor under the Nazis* (op. cit.).

8 Institute of Jewish Affairs, ed., *Hitler's Ten-Year War on the Jews* (New York: Institute of Jewish Affairs of the American Jewish Congress, 1943), 24; *The Black Book. Nazi Crimes against the Jewish People* (New York: The Jewish Black Book Committee, 1946), 170–83.

9 Raul Hilberg outlined the social and historical context of Jewish forced labor in Germany and Poland: Raul Hilberg, *The Destruction of the European Jews* (London: W.H. Allen, 1961), and *Die Vernichtung der europäischen Juden*, new and expanded edition of the translation into German of 1982 edn, Vol. 1 (Frankfurt am Main: S. Fischer, 1990). In 1974, H.G. Adler added new details in his unjustifiably neglected study, H. G. Adler, *Der verwaltete Mensch. Studien zur Deportation der Juden aus Deutschland* (Tübingen: Mohr, 1974), 205–34.

10 See Bruno Blau, *Das Ausnahmerecht für Juden in Deutschland 1933–1945*, reworked 3rd edn (Düsseldorf: Verlag Allgemeine Wochenzeitung der Juden in Deutschland, 1965), 86; Joseph Walk, ed., *Das Sonderrecht für die Juden im NS-Staat. Eine Sammlung der gesetzlichen Maßnahmen – Inhalt und Bedeutung* (Heidelberg and Karlsruhe: Müller, 1981), IV/174, 336; Avraham Barkai, *Vom Boykott zur "Entjudung". Der wirtschaftliche Existenzkampf der Juden im Dritten Reich 1933 –1943* (Frankfurt am Main: S. Fischer, 1988), 195.

11 See, for example, Barkai, Vom Boykott zur *"Entjudung,"* 173–81; Konrad Kwiet, "Nach dem Pogrom. Stufen der Ausgrenzung," in *Die Juden in Deutschland 1933–1945*, ed. Wolfgang Benz (Munich, C.H. Beck, 1988), 574–96. For Austria, see: Herbert Rosenkranz, *Verfolgung und Selbstbehauptung. Die Juden in Österreich 1938 bis 1945* (Vienna and Munich: Herold, 1978), 173–74, 208–10, 234–35, 271–73.

12 Dieter Maier, *Arbeitseinsatz und Deportation. Die Mitwirkung der Arbeitsverwaltung bei der nationalsozialistischen Judenverfolgung in den Jahren 1938–1945* (Berlin: Hentrich, 1994); Gruner, *Der geschlossene Arbeitseinsatz*; Gruner, *Zwangsarbeit und Verfolgung.*

13 For the 1930s, see Saul Friedländer, *Nazi Germany and the Jews, Vol. 1: The Years of Persecution, 1933–1939* (New York: HarperCollins, 1997); Peter Longerich, *Politik der Vernichtung: Eine Gesamtdarstellung der nationalsozialistischen Judenverfolgung* (Munich: Piper, 1998); Wolf Gruner, "Anti-Jewish Policy in Nazi Germany 1933–45. From Exclusion and Expulsion to Segregation and Deportation. New Perspectives on Developments, Actors and Goals," in *The Comprehensive History of the Holocaust: Germany*, ed. Yad Vashem (Lincoln: Nebraska University Press, 2011).

14 See, in general, Gruner, *Der Geschlossene Arbeitseinsatz*; Gruner, *Jewish Forced Labor*, 3–32, 276–95.

15 Gruner, *Zwangsarbeit und Verfolgung*, 47–49.

16 See in extensive detail Gruner, *Der Geschlossene Arbeitseinsatz*, 68–132; Gruner, *Jewish Forced Labor*, 3–8, 32–40.

17 Gruner, *Zwangsarbeit und Verfolgung*, 74–92.

18 For more details see Wolf Gruner, "Terra Inkognita? – The Camps for 'Jewish Labor Conscription' 1938–43 and the German Population," *Yad Vashem Studies*, vol. 24 (1994): 1–41.

19 See Gruner, *Jewish Forced Labor*, 32–83, 105–40.

20 *Jüdisches Nachrichtenblatt*, Viennese edn, 23 January 1942, 1.

21 *Reichsgesetzblatt*, 1941, Vol. I, 675.

22 For more detail on this decision, see Wolf Gruner, "Von der Kollektivausweisung zur Deportation der Juden aus Deutschland. Neue Perspektiven und Dokumente (1938–45)," in *Beiträge zur Geschichte des Nationalsozialismus, Vol. 20: Die Deportation der Juden aus Deutschland. Pläne, Praxis, Reaktionen 1938–1945* (Göttingen, 2004), 21–62.

23 Gruner, *Geschlossener Arbeitseinsatz*, 116–78; Gruner, *Jewish Forced Labor*, 9–19.

24 Gruner, *Geschlossener Arbeitseinsatz*, 204–320; Gruner, *Jewish Forced Labor*, 19–32; Gruner, *Widerstand in der Rosenstraße. Die Fabrik-Aktion und die Verfolgung der "Mischehen" 1943* (Frankfurt am Main: S. Fischer-Verlag, 2005).

25 Gruner, *Jewish Forced Labor*, 83–102. For the general development, see Jeremy Noakes, "The Development of Nazi Policy towards the German-Jewish 'Mischlinge' 1933–45," in *Leo Baeck Institute Yearbook* 34 (1989): 291–354; Beate Meyer, *"Jüdische Mischlinge." Rassenpolitik und Verfolgungserfahrung 1933–1945* (Hamburg: Dölling und Galitz, 1999).

26 Karla Wolf, *Ich blieb zurück* (Heppenheim: Evang. Arbeitskreis Kirche und Israel in Hessen und Nassau, 1990), 26.

27 Gertrud Kolmar, *Briefe an die Schwester Hilde (1938–1943)* (Munich: Kösel, 1970), 158–61, letter of 19 July 1942.

28 Marga Spiegel, *Retter in der Nacht. Wie eine jüdische Familie überlebte,* 2nd edn (Cologne: Röderberg, 1987), 14.

29 For more details, see Gruner, *Jewish Forced Labor,* 141-62.

30 Gruner, *Jewish Forced Labor,* 163-73.

31 Christopher Browning, "Nazi Germany's Initial Attempt to Exploit Jewish Labor in the General Government: The Early Jewish Work Camps 1940-41," in *Die Normalität des Verbrechens: Festschrift für Wolfgang Scheffler zum 65. Geburtstag* (Berlin: Edition Hentrich, 1994), 171-85; "Jewish Workers in Poland. Self-Maintenance, Exploitation, Destruction," in Christopher Browning, *Nazi Policy, Jewish Workers, German Killers* (Cambridge: Cambridge University Press, 2000), 58-88; and *The Origins of the Final Solution: The Evolution of Nazi Jewish Policy, September 1939-March 1942* (Lincoln: Nebraska University Press, 2004), 138-68.

32 Dieter Pohl, "Die großen Zwangsarbeitslager der SS-und Polizeiführer für Juden im Generalgouvernement 1942-45," in *Die nationalsozialistischen Konzentrationslager. Entwicklung und Struktur,* eds Ulrich Herbert, Karin Orth and Christoph Dieckmann (Göttingen: Wallstein, 1998), I: 415-38; Jan Erik Schulte, "Zwangsarbeit für die SS Juden in der Ostindustrie GmbH," in *Ausbeutung, Vernichtung, Öffentlichkeit. Neue Studien zu nationalsozialistischen Lagerpolitik,* ed. Norbert Frei for the Institute for Contemporary History (Munich: Saur, 2000), 43-74.

33 Dieter Pohl, *Von der "Judenpolitik" zum Judenmord. Der Distrikt Lublin des Generalgouvernements 1939-1944* (Frankfurt am Main: Lang, 1993); Bogdan Musial, *Deutsche Zivilverwaltung und Judenverfolgung im Generalgouvernement. Eine Fallstudie zum Distrikt Lublin 1939-1944* (Wiesbaden: Harrasowitz, 1999); Eliyahu Yones, *Die Straße nach Lemberg. Zwangsarbeit und Widerstand in Ostgalizien 1941-1944* (Frankfurt am Main: S. Fischer, 1999); Hermann Kaienburg, "Jüdische Arbeitslager an der 'Straße der SS,'" *Zeitschrift für Sozialgeschichte des 20. und 21. Jahrhunderts,* vol. 11, no. 1 (1996): 13-39; Dieter Pohl, *Nationalsozialistische Judenverfolgung in Ostgalizien. Organisation und Durchführung eines staatlichen Massenverbrechens* (Munich: Oldenbourg, 1996).

34 *Verordnungsblatt des Generalgouverneurs* (1939): 6.

35 Browning, "Nazi Germany's Initial Attempt," 171-85; Browning, "Jewish Workers in Poland," 58-88; Browning, *The Origins of the Final Solution,* 138-52. See the chapters on the GG and the Warthegau: Gruner, *Jewish Forced Labor,* 177-275. For the Warthegau in general, see Michael Alberti, *Die Verfolgung und Vernichtung der Juden im Reichsgau Wartheland 1939-1945* (Wiesbaden: Harrasowitz, 2006).

36 Gruner, *Jewish Forced Labor,* 177-275; Browning, *The Origins of the Final Solution,* 111-68. See also Christoph Dieckmann and Babette Quinkert, eds, *Im Ghetto 1939-1945. Neue Forschungen zu Alltag und Umfeld* (Göttingen: Wallstein, 2009).

37 Pohl, "Die großen Zwangsarbeitslager," 415-38; Gruner, *Jewish Forced Labor,* 244-47; Kaienburg, "Jüdische Arbeitslager," 13-39.

38 See the chapter on Eastern Upper Silesia in Gruner, *Jewish Forced Labor,* 214-29; see also Sybille Steinbacher, *"Musterstadt" Auschwitz. Germanisierungspolitik und Judenmord in Ostoberschlesien* (Munich: Saur, 2000). However, as the comparative analysis of the Polish territories demonstrates, Upper Silesia was not the area of former Poland where forced labor first was used systematically as an instrument of anti-Jewish policy, as Steinbacher claims; *ibid.,* 142.

39 See, in general, Gruner, *Jewish Forced Labor.*

40 Gruner, *Jewish Forced Labor,* 189-95, 257-73.

41 Pohl, *Nationalsozialistische Judenverfolgung in Ostgalizien,* 287-88.

42 Gruner, *Jewish Forced Labor,* 177-95. For more details on the Warthegau, see Alberti, *Die Verfolgung und Vernichtung;* Peter Klein, *Die "Gettoverwaltung Litzmannstadt" 1940-1944. Eine Dienststelle im Spannungsfeld von Kommunalbürokratie und staatlicher Verfolgungspolitik* (Hamburg: Hamburger Edition, 2009).

43 Gudrun Schwarz, *Die nationalsozialistischen Lager* (Frankfurt am Main and New York: Campus, 1990), 75.

44 Herbert speaks of an economic significance for Jewish forced labor only after the turning point in the war at the end of 1941. Herbert, *"Arbeit und Vernichtung,"* 417.

45 Gruner, *Jewish Forced Labor,* 289-93.

46 Gruner, *Widerstand in der Rosenstraße,* 34-55. See also Gruner, *Jewish Forced Labor,* 24-28.

47 For more details, see Gruner, *Jewish Forced Labor,* 196-213.

48 Bundesarchiv Berlin, R 3/1505, fol. 101: Note of Speer's office, 28 September 1942 on meetings with Hitler (20, 21, 22 September 1942), Doc. printed in *Deutschlands Rüstung im Zweiten Weltkrieg. Hitlers Konferenzen mit Albert Speer 1942–1945*, ed. Will Boelcke (Frankfurt am Main, 1969), 189. For more details on this discussion, see Gruner, *Jewish Forced Labor*, 264–65.

49 For the numbers: BA Berlin, NS 19/1570, no fol.: Inspekteur für Statistik beim RFSS, 1 January 1943 (Korherr-report), 14.

50 The phrase was probably never used for Jews. By contrast, Wachsmann is placing "extermination through labor" back in its contemporary context: the transfer of judicial prisoners to concentration camps and their killing in 1942 ordered by the Reich Ministry of Justice. Nikolaus Wachsmann, "'Annihilation through Labor': The Killing of State Prisoners in the Third Reich," *Journal of Modern History*, vol. 71 (September 1999): 624–59.

51 For example, Thomas Sandkühler, "Das Zwangsarbeitslager Lemberg-Janowska 1941–44," in *Die nationalsozialistischen Konzentrationslager* (Herbert *et al.*, eds), Vol. 2, 606; Hermann Kaienburg, "Zwangsarbeit von Juden in Arbeits-und Konzentrationslagern," in *"Arisierung:" Volksgemeinschaft, Raub und Gedächtnis*, eds Irmtrud Wojak and Peter Hayes (Frankfurt am Main and New York: Campus, 2000), 226; Hans Mommsen, *Auschwitz, 17. Juli 1942. Der Weg zur "Endlösung der europäischen Judenfrage"* (Munich: DTV, 2002), 135.

52 Pohl, *Nationalsozialistische Judenverfolgung in Ostgalizien*, 335, and "Die Großen Zwangsarbeitslager der SS," 431–32.

53 Browning, "Jewish Workers in Poland," 87–88.

54 For a detailed account on the suffering and survival of the inmates in one of those camps, see Christopher Browning, *Remembering Survival. Inside a Nazi Slave Labor Camp* (New York: Norton, 2010).

55 See the chapter by Jürgen Matthäus in Browning, *The Origins of the Final Solution*, 244–308; Andrej Angrick and Peter Klein, *Die "Endlösung" in Riga. Ausbeutung und Vernichtung 1941–1944* (Darmstadt: Wissenschaftliche Buchgesellschaft, 2006), esp. 276–360 (in English: Berghahn Books, 2009).

56 See, for example, the chapter in Goldhagen, *Hitler's Willing Executioners*, 327–74. For a critique of his thesis with different arguments from those provided in the following paragraph, see Daniel Blatman, "The Death Marches and the Final Phase of Nazi Genocide," in *Concentration Camps in Nazi Germany: The New Histories*, eds Jane Caplan and Nikolaus Wachsmann (New York: Routledge, 2010), 167–85.

57 For a comparison of several of these evacuations from Silesian camps, see Bella Gutterman, *A Narrow Bridge to Life: Jewish Forced Labor and Survival in the Gross-Rosen Camp System, 1940–1945* (New York/Oxford: Berghahn Books, 2008), 189–218.

58 For the survivors' odyssey and the embarrassing behavior of German companies, see Benjamin Ferencz, *Less than Slaves: Jewish Forced Labor and the Quest for Compensation* (Cambridge: Harvard University Press, 1979; reprinted Indiana University Press, 2002).

16

THE CONCENTRATION AND EXTERMINATION CAMPS OF THE NAZI REGIME

Sybille Steinbacher

A basic characteristic of the Nazi concentration camps—as opposed to the extermination camps—was constant change. In 1933, improvised camps emerged in cellars, factories, barracks, and even in "out-of-service" ships; these had hardly anything in common with the sites of terror that, at the war's end, covered the German Reich in a widely cast net of main and auxiliary camps. Their history was stamped by the dynamic development of the camp system and a permanent functional alteration in various phases of Nazi rule. The number of prisoners confined there for shorter or longer periods can only be estimated, since at the time no statistics were kept in this regard: the total was probably between 2.5 and 3.5 million people.[1] In camps lying within the area of the "Old Reich"—the German Reich in its 1937 borders—around 450,000 prisoners lost their lives, more than a third of them in the war's last phase. At the war's end there were more than 20 main and over 1,000 auxiliary camps; roughly a million people lost their lives within them. The concentration camps differed from the six extermination camps—they were set up only after the war began, in conquered Poland—in that their inmates were not immediately murdered after their arrival. But in the concentration camps they died from bullying, exhaustion, hunger, blows; those who remained alive were subject to wretched conditions.

Concentration camps were not invented by the Nazis. The first of them were already established around the start of the twentieth century to break the resistance of rebels against Spanish colonial rule. Around this time the Americans, as well, set up camps for a similar purpose in the Philippines, and in South Africa the British used them to cope with rebellious Boers. The term did not have to be explained to Germans at the start of the Nazi period: already in the early 1920s, internment camps for undesired foreigners were called "concentration camps." Above all, Jews from Eastern Europe were held in such camps, which were located, for example, in Cottbus-Sielow and Stargard in Pomerania. They were patrolled by the German army and were quickly dismantled.[2]

The development of the camps in the Nazi period

In the Third Reich, the development of the concentration camps was not marked by a plan formulated at an early stage, but rather by a continuous process of alteration, expansion, and radicalization. Camps were put together quickly, furnished sparsely, and hermetically sealed; both individuals and groups considered harmful or dangerous were confined there, in poor conditions, and deprived of any rights. In distinction from the prisons, where people who had been sentenced after trial were incarcerated, concentration camps were used to isolate persons who had not committed crimes in the juridical sense. In other words, the camps were an instrument of terror and despotism. The functional changes they underwent, leading to ever-new tasks and many structural changes,[3] can be separated into five phases.

1   Between the start of Nazi rule in January 1933 and the early summer of 1934, smaller and larger prison-like facilities were set up throughout Germany for confining and maltreating the regime's political opponents. At this time, the main victims of Nazi persecution were Social Democrats and Communists. In the first 6 months alone, the new rulers arrested 26,000 persons, with an orgy of violence accompanying creation of the new camps. There was, however, no unified organization in this early phase, responsibility lying in the hands of various parties: the *Sturmabteilung* (SA) under Ernst Röhm was responsible for many camps; others were under the control of police chiefs in states and cities; and, in sharp competition with the SA, Heinrich Himmler—since 1929 so-called *Reichsführer SS*—himself entered into leadership and administration of the camps.

2   Characteristic of the 1934–36 period was reorganization of the camps. Following Röhm's murder and the elimination of the SA as a political force in the summer of 1934, Himmler quickly succeeded in removing them from the influence of other institutions (the Reich Justice Ministry, the Reich Interior Ministry, and the state governments) and placing them under the SS's control. His goal was to structure all the sites of imprisonment on the model of Dachau: opened in March 1933, this was the first concentration camp managed by the SS, according to an order of punishment and discipline introduced by the camp's commander, Theodor Eicke. In 1934, Himmler appointed Eicke chief of the newly established central Office of Inspection for the camps, henceforth responsible for their administration. The term "concentration camp"—*Konzentrationslager*—now designated all detention sites controlled by this office.

When Himmler was appointed chief of the German police in 1936, and immediately set about bringing the political police and criminal police together under the umbrella of the security police, the reorganization of the camps proceeded swiftly. The number of camp prisoners had by then fallen to its lowest point: in the summer of 1935 it stood at fewer than 4,000. This striking decline shows, on the one hand, that following the isolation and murder of its political opponents, the Nazi regime encountered hardly any public opposition, not to speak of organized resistance. On the other hand, it shows that the camp system was manifestly losing its sense. That it was retained nonetheless lay in Himmler seeking—and soon finding—new functions for it in order for the SS to keep a bastion of power.

3   New concentration camps were now established. Starting after 1936, the third phase in the history of the Nazi terror-centers was characterized by a continuous rise in the number of prisoners and a significant shift in their composition: those confined in the camps were no longer the regime's political opponents alone, but also those "elements" that the Nazis viewed as damaging the "healthy substance" of the German *Volk*. Whoever was considered "criminal" or "asocial," behaved in either a "work-shy" or

sexually loose manner, drank, or indeed was tardy in making alimony payments ran the risk of being sent to a camp. Punishment and discipline were the ingredients of the proper "education" for all those deemed intolerable and fit for social exclusion as *Gemeinschaftsfremde*[4]—persons alien to the German *Volk*-community. The goal was, then, to isolate them from the "healthy" part of the "*Volk* body," in order to increase its "racial" value through selection. In this way, the concentration camps emerged as loci for the new socio-biological shaping of German society. With the widening of the parameters of those considered enemies of both the Nazi regime and German society, the camp system was thus assigned the task of furthering general "racial" prophylaxis. In essence, this meant that the system was now newly invented.

Remove the bad element (handwritten margin note)

The construction of a series of new camps was an organizational outcome of the new orientation. Smaller sites were now closed and several large ones newly built, in particular Sachsenhausen and Buchenwald. In the middle of 1938, Sachsenhausen became the center of the concentration camp system, with Theodor Eicke moving his Office of Inspection there, and the camp also housing the training center for SS guard details.[5]

The expansion and new structuring of the camp system was tied to a change in the significance of prisoners' labor. Where previously forced labor had the character of bullying and punishment, it was now systematized and applied for economic goals.[6] Prisoners at the newly built camps, which included Neuengamme near Hamburg and Mauthausen near Linz, were drawn on for the realization of Hitler's gigantic urban-planning projects. For this reason, the new camps were located mainly near stone quarries; the SS, which already owned various business enterprises of its own, set up a number of brickworks in this context. For the prisoners, use of slave labor in the miserable conditions of quarries and claypits meant torture and often a speedy death.

The organized pogroms in November 1938 did not spark any new functional change in the camps. But the escalation of unrestrained violence against the Reich's Jewish population resulted in a dramatic rise in the number of prisoners. For the first time, the concentration camps were now made use of in "solving the Jewish question." Until then, Jews were not sent to the camps on "racial" grounds, but when they were considered political opponents of the Third Reich. In November 1938, the goal of Nazi anti-Jewish policies was still expulsion; systematic murder began later.[7] It was already clear, however, that the regime had no qualms about using the most violent imaginable measures against Jews. In the course of the pogroms, 25,000 Jewish men were seized across the Reich and transported to the Sachsenhausen, Buchenwald, and Dachau camps—a process quickly leading to their being overfilled. By the year's end, they contained 60,000 persons. Most Jews were kept in the camps for at least 4 weeks; and most tried to leave the German Reich as soon as possible after their release

4 The fourth phase in the history of the Nazi concentration camp system began in the autumn of 1939 and lasted until mid-1941. On the eve of World War II, around 21,000 persons were imprisoned in the camps, roughly a third on political grounds. Following the war's start, the number of prisoners quickly doubled. The SS now divided the camps into three groups or categories, graded according to severity of treatment. Camps in category one were considered a relatively "mild" form of punishment, while in category three, extremely harsh conditions were meant to prevail.

The reason for the new organization was the huge wave of fresh incarcerations, the camps now containing, above all, potential political opponents in the conquered regions. This led to a new preponderance within the camps of various non-German sub-communities of prisoners, including Poles, French, Czechs, Dutch, Yugoslavians, Belgians, and other nationalities; among them were many Jews and so-called Gypsies. From the spring of 1940 until the war's end, German prisoners remained a minority.

Following the war's outbreak, the number of camps in conquered and occupied areas rapidly expanded. Soon they contained more prisoners than those held in the Old Reich. In May 1940, the Auschwitz concentration camp was established on the German Reich's eastern border, in a barren area used in World War I as housing for Polish seasonal laborers, and later as a site for army barracks.[8] The choice of site was tied to Himmler's search for suitable facilities in support of an ambitious project: constructing concentration camps across the Reich's border area, for the sake of securing German rule. Although opting for Auschwitz required several inspections— the barracks were dilapidated and the area was prone to flooding—the responsible SS specialists saw the advantages offered by both the grounds' developed infrastructure and the ease with which they could be sealed off as outweighing such disadvantages. Although more people would be murdered at Auschwitz than any other place in the Nazi domain, at the beginning the camp was by no means a center for mass murder of the Jews. Rather, it was opened in June 1940 as an incarceration center for Polish political prisoners. Its only unusual feature was a capacity to hold 10,000 prisoners— a number reflecting the German calculation of a high number of detained opponents in conquered Poland. In the camp's initial phase, the majority of prisoners were not Jews, but members of the Polish intelligentsia and other groups seen as belonging to the Polish national resistance. Auschwitz took on its function as the center for the extermination of Europe's Jewry only in 1942–43.

Forced labor became increasingly important in the concentration camps after the start of the war. It is the case that prisoners' labor was not exploited for the armaments industry. But the camps were SS sites for producing bricks and other basic building materials. As a result, the number of deaths began to increase exponentially: for example, where in 1938 the Dachau camp registered a death rate of around four percent, in 1942 it was 36 percent; in Mauthausen—a category three camp, meaning especially horrible conditions—the rate increased from 24 percent in 1939 to 76 percent the following year.

With the attack on the Soviet Union in the summer of 1941, the fifth and final phase of the development of the Nazi camp system began. In March 1942, *Amtsgruppe* D of the newly established SS Chief Office of Economic Administration took over administration of the concentration camps.[9] The total number of prisoners in the camps would now rise without stopping: in April 1943, the figure was approximately 200,000; in August 1944, it was more than 520,000; and at the end of the war, it was around 700,000, with non-Germans composing 90 percent of the prisoner population.

This was the phase in which the extermination camps were established, their sole purpose being to immediately murder arriving prisoners. The first such camp, opening at the beginning of December 1941, was Chelmno (Kulmhof) in Warthegau. The SS *Sonderkommando* under Herbert Lange, a police unit that since the war's start had been murdering mentally ill persons in western Poland as part of the Nazi "euthanasia" program, converted an agricultural structure in the middle of the village—the structure was locally referred to as the "castle"—into a death camp. Belzec, Sobibor, and Treblinka, the camps for *Aktion Reinhardt*, did not stand under the economic office but rather under the head of the SS and police in the district of

Lublin, Odilo Globocnik, who was assigned this responsibility by Himmler. The mass of Polish Jews were murdered in these three camps, which were established between November 1941 and June 1942. Death transports from the so-called *Generalgouvernement* (German-occupied but non-annexed Poland) rolled into the camps from March 1942 onward.[10]

The construction of the extermination camps in occupied Poland marked the start of the systematic genocide of the Jews and the mass murder of Poles, Russians, and so-called Gypsies. Following break-up of these murder centers in the war's final phase, only a small portion of the deported Jews, persons who were young and "work-capable" and had survived selection in the extermination camps, were able to enter the concentration camps, where they were used for forced labor under extreme conditions.

In 1941, the Auschwitz camp was the site for the first murder experiments using the cyanide gas Zyklon B. The poison had already been used by the German military in World War I for disinfesting dwellings and clothing; this was also the first use it was put to in Auschwitz. The first mass murders that took place in the main camp (*Stammlager*) were carried out not in the framework of the "final solution to the Jewish question," but as part of a continuation of the "euthanasia" program within the concentration camps; the victims were Soviet war prisoners and other "work-incapable" inmates. Built in September 1942, the Auschwitz–Birkenau camp was located three kilometers from the *Stammlager*. Together with the Majdanek camp near Lublin, which had been set up at the same time, it held a special position in that it was both a concentration camp and extermination camp, thus having a double function. In July 1942, selection according to "work-capable" and "work-incapable" persons became the principle for deciding over life and death at Auschwitz. Following Himmler's second visit to the camp in July 1942 (the first had taken place in March 1941), transports of Jews gradually began to arrive from all over Western Europe, especially from France, Holland, and Belgium; after Mussolini's overthrow in the autumn of 1943, they also came from Italy. In 1943, the construction of enormous crematoria was completed in the camp—in the view of those responsible, they were the "most modern" to be found.[11] At this time, the systematic mass extermination reached a provisional highpoint; a second one came in the spring of 1944 with the murder of ca 400,000 Jews from Hungary over a few weeks.

Himmler evidently intended to be regularly present at the mass murder, since he had an apartment set up in the house of the *Waffen-SS* facing the Auschwitz train station in the summer of 1943, at a time when the camps for *Aktion Reinhardt* were being gradually dismantled and Auschwitz promoted to sole extermination center. In any case, Himmler never used his apartment, presumably because of the fast unfolding of specific events: those following the Warsaw Ghetto revolt in May 1943, and the mass breakouts from Sobibor and Treblinka in August and October of the same year.

According to present knowledge, a total of approximately 1.1 million people were murdered in Auschwitz, a million of them Jews.[12] The trains rolled in with the deported from all corners of Europe. A special railway line into the Birkenau camp was even constructed for the Hungarian Jews; in any case, that something horrible was happening there could not have been hidden from anyone living in the vicinity and wanting to know something, even if details were unavailable. Not only in the immediate area but in the Old Reich as well, the name Auschwitz connoted death and annihilation. In a diary entry of 16 March 1942, the Dresden-based German-Jewish literary scholar Victor

Klemperer noted that "these days I hear of Auschwitz (or something like that) near Königshütte in Upper Silesia. Mine work, death after a few days." Seven months later, in his entry for 17 October 1942, Klemperer revealed a better sense of the place's purpose: "Auschwitz ... which seems to be a fast-working slaughterhouse."[13] It thus appears that already in the Nazi period, the question of knowledge about the death camps was to an extent what it has never really ceased to be since the war's end: a question of wanting to know.

In the last phase of the war, Auschwitz played a central role in the use of forced labor. In the spring of 1942, Albert Speer became the new chief coordinator of the German armaments industry. The SS Chief Office of Economic Administration was now given the task of speedily adapting prisoners' slave labor to the needs of that industry; henceforth exploiting prisoners for war production would be the chief purpose of the concentration camps. For a long time, the productivity involved here was relatively small—around half that resulting from free labor, sometimes only a fifth. The situation changed only with construction of subcamps in the vicinity of private industry.

The prelude to this process was the IG Farben company's construction in 1942 of a gigantic factory in Auschwitz–Monowitz[14] for the intensive production of synthetic benzene and rubber (so-called Buna): one of the most expensive and ambitious investment projects of the Third Reich in World War II. Many firms would now take over the policy of transporting prisoners to their premises and using them for slave labor. In this way, a large number of subcamps sprang up in proximity to the main camps. In the war's last phase, with the development of close—and from the Nazi regime's perspective, successful—cooperation between the SS and private industry, concentration camp prisoners were used to transfer entire factories to underground production sites and to labor there for the war economy. In the tunnels and burrows, their life expectancy dropped to 3 months on average; many did not survive even a few weeks.

The perception of the camps since the war

In the Third Reich, the existence of the concentration camps was no secret. On the contrary, the "opening" of the Dachau camp was announced in the Munich papers on 22 March 1933.[15] The reports in the Nazi-controlled media were, however, drastically sugar-coated—in the *Münchner Illustrierten* of 1936, we find photos of Dachau with flower-decorated prisoners' barracks and card-playing prisoners.

Still, tied to steadily circulating rumors about what was happening in the camps, soon after the Nazis took power a fear-inducing idea of the "camps"—the "*KZ*"—had already taken hold; soon everyone knew the term. In Munich and environs in the mid-1930s, the following saying circulated: "Dear God, please make me dumb, so that I do not to Dachau come" (*Lieber Gott, mach mich stumm, dass ich nicht nach Dachau kumm*). During World War II, this fear-ruled image became stronger, but at the same time a process of habituation set in. One factor contributing to this was certainly the populace's massive experience of violence in the form of Allied bombing. Suspicions, rumors, and concrete knowledge about what transpired in the camps thus lost, so to speak, their uniqueness or were leveled off by the experience of war. After the war, statements and testimony by camp survivors could convey an impression of the horror of what was done to the prisoners, beyond all wartime action. The impression was strengthened by international reporting on the first major trials of camp commanders and guards,[16] and the

186

camps, especially Auschwitz, Buchenwald, and Dachau, became a cipher for all the crimes of the Nazis.

The stylization of the camps into symbols of terror had complex and highly varied effects. One factor that counts here is that, for a long time, the camps were not a focus of historical research in either West Germany or elsewhere: repression, forced labor, and mass murder simply lay far outside what historians considered worth studying. This was closely connected with the process of coming to terms with the Nazi past and the difficulty of confronting complicity in such horrendous crimes.[17] For this reason, for decades the history of the Nazi concentration camps was written not by historians, but by former prisoners.

Accounts by prisoners who had been able to escape already reached the public in the first years of the Nazi regime—for instance, the account by Hans Beimler, a fighter in the Spanish Civil War, who was able to flee Dachau in 1933.[18] For many prisoners, the conviction that the world had to learn what was taking place in the camps already took on great importance. This conviction intensified with the steady expansion of the camps and their population, and the rapid increase in deaths.

The impression of being completely at the mercy of others, of being in a place lacking all law, probity, and safety, and of an omnipresence of death, would lastingly cling to nearly all survivors of the camps. For many, the time spent there would remain the center of their lives—whether in active confrontation with it or decades-long silence over their traumatic memories.[19] The first witness accounts and memoirs in book form came out shortly after the war. Appearing in Munich in 1946, former Buchenwald prisoner Eugen Kogon's *Der SS-Staat. Das System der deutschen Konzentrationslager* (*The SS State: The System of the German Concentration Camps*; republished recently in English as *The Theory and Practice of Hell*) quickly became something of a best-seller in West Germany, and would stamp the public picture of the camps in an authoritative way. At the same time, in the early 1950s, publications by survivors encountered an increasingly negative reception from the general West German public, reflecting the period's widespread silence and will to ignorance regarding Nazi crimes. The groups formed by survivors and their circles of friends found it very difficult to receive any meaningful public support. They often acted in isolation when trying to make former camps into memorials or even to set up plaques. The situation was different in East Germany, where the state's anti-fascist foundational consensus meant that the rapid establishment of memorial sites at former camps served a direct political function for the regime. Instrumentalized in this way, the history of the communist prisoners soon emerged as both a founding myth and historical legitimation for the East German state.

In the west as in the east, the actual number of former camp-prisoners who published reports about their experiences was small. There were many reasons, among them the fact that, above all, persons who succeeded in occupying functional positions in the SS patronage system had chances of survival. These were German-speaking, non-Jewish political prisoners in particular; we presently know a great deal about the conditions they were held in and their experiences in the camps. But their accounts and testimony have offered us only a small excerpt from the camp cosmos, especially since during the war they only formed a minority among mainly non-German prisoners. We know next to nothing about the experiences of so-called criminal and asocial prisoners, together with the Jews, the Soviet war prisoners, and the Sinti and Roma—all groups among whom very few survived.

International historical research turned to the concentration camps in a significant way only in the 1960s, with work in the field above all initiated by Martin Broszat, later director of the *Institut für Zeitgeschichte* in Munich.[20] The Auschwitz trials, held in Frankfurt in 1963, when a few dozen former members of the camps' SS guard details were tried on criminal charges, here served as a starting point, the evaluations prepared by Broszat and other members of the institute for the trial adding up to the first detailed studies of the camp system: the development of these sites of terror, the prisoners' circumstances, the hierarchy and internal structure of the guard details, and the mentality of the SS. The evaluations were published under the title *Anatomie des SS-Staates* (*Anatomy of the SS State*) in 1965—the same year that the verdicts were announced in the Auschwitz trials.[21] Other important work followed soon, including that of Eberhard Kolb on Bergen-Belsen, Hans Günter Adler on Theresienstadt, and Enno Georg on the SS's economic-industrial enterprises.[22]

In 1970, Martin Broszat also published an anthology of studies of various camps.[23] But over the following years, historians' interest in the camps again died down, with empirical research on the camp system and Nazi extermination policies being pushed aside in favor of a discussion that now unfolded of the systemic character of the Nazi regime.[24] It would be the mid-1980s before the approaches Broszat initiated were taken up by a new generation of historians. It soon became apparent that, although the camps played an important role in public and political discussion in West Germany, there was still little concrete knowledge about them. In view of the age of surviving prisoners, it had become clear that a basic task of the historian was to preserve their memories. In the context of the boom of everyday and regional history, a great deal of work was also done on the local ramifications of Nazi rule, with the history of subcamps being explored for the first time. A range of historical projects were now initiated, some of them international.

To the extent that the research intensified, its shortcoming became evident. Even at present, full-length studies of some large and important camps have not appeared, and many former subcamps form a veritable historiographic blind-spot.[25] In view of the missing material, getting a well-founded general study of the camps underway will constitute a great challenge. Although Martin Broszat pointed the way to such a project in the 1960s, the state of research of the time would not have allowed it.[26]

Meanwhile, important studies have appeared suggesting the beginning of a new spate of research. These include Wolfgang Sofsky's sociological analysis of the camps, *Die Ordnung des Terrors* (*The Order of Terror*).[27] Starting with the concept of an "absolute power" based on terror, organization, and extreme murderous violence, Sofsky describes the prisoner-societies that formed by force in the camps. Empirical research on the camp system likewise stands at the center of a new volume of comprehensive, lexically arranged research projects initiated by Barbara Distel and Wolfgang Benz in order to bring together current knowledge about all the camp complexes.[28]

Since the 1990s, historical interest in the history of the Nazi concentration camps has increased impressively,[29] with survivors' testimony now forming an irreplaceable legacy for researchers: a legacy that, to be sure, calls for sensitive evaluation.[30]

Notes

1 Jürgen Zarusky, "Die juristische Aufarbeitung der KZ-Verbrechen," in *Der Ort des Terrors. Geschichte der nationalsozialistischen Konzentrationslager*, eds Wolfgang Benz and Barbara Distel (Munich: Beck, 2005), 1: 345–62.

2 Andrzej J. Kaminski, *Konzentrationslager 1896 bis heute. Geschichte, Funktion, Typologie* (Stuttgart: W. Kohlhammer, 1982).

3 Karin Orth, *Das System der nationalsozialistischen Konzentrationslager. Eine politische Organisationsgeschichte* (Hamburg: Hamburger Edition, 1999); Ulrich Herbert, Karin Orth and Christoph Dieckmann, eds, *Die nationalsozialistischen Konzentrationslager. Entwicklung und Struktur* (Göttingen: Wallstein, 1998).

4 The term stems from Detlev Peukert, *Volksgenossen und Gemeinschaftsfremde. Anpassung, Ausmerze und Aufbegehren unter dem Nationalsozialismus* (Cologne: Bund Verlag, 1982).

5 On the history of the Nazi concentration camps, see the important nine-volume series *Der Ort des Terrors* (Benz and Distel, eds). The Holocaust Memorial Museum in Washington is working on a seven-volume work under the direction of Geoffrey Megaree, *Encyclopedia of Camps and Ghettos, 1933–1945* (Bloomington, Indiana: Indiana University Press, 2009); the first volume, treating the early camps, appeared in 2009; completion of the project is planned for 2018.

6 Ulrich Herbert, ed., *Europa und der "Reichseinsatz". Ausländische Zivilarbeiter, Kriegsgefangene und KZ-Häftlinge in Deutschland 1938–1945* (Essen: Klartext, 1991); Dittmar Dahlmann and Gerhard Hirschfeld, *Lager, Zwangsarbeit, Vertreibung und Deportation. Dimensionen der Massenverbrechen in der Sowjetunion und in Deutschland 1933 bis 1945* (Essen: Klartext, 1999); Wolf Gruner, *Jewish Forced Labor under the Nazis. Economic Needs and Racial Aims (1938–1944)* (New York: Cambridge University Press, 2006).

7 Christopher Browning and Jürgen Matthäus, *The Origins of the Final Solution* (Lincoln, Nebraska: University of Nebraska Press, 2003).

8 Sybille Steinbacher, *Auschwitz: A History* (New York: ECCO, 2005); Sybille Steinbacher, *Germanisierungspolitik und Judenmord in Ostoberschlesien* (Munich: K.G. Saur, 2000); Norbert Frei, Thomas Grotum, Jan Parcer, Sybille Steinbacher and Bernd C. Wagner, eds, *Darstellungen und Quellen zur Geschichte von Auschwitz* (Munich, 2000); Wacław Długoborski and Franciszek Piper, *Auschwitz 1940–1945: Central Issues in the History of the Camps* (Oświęcim: Auschwitz-Birkenau State Museum, 2000).

9 Jan-Erik Schulte, *Zwangsarbeit und Vernichtung. Das Wirtschaftsimperium der SS. Oswald Pohl und das SS-Wirtschaftsverwaltungshauptamt 1933–1945* (Paderborn: F. Schöningh, 2001); Mike T. Allen, *Engineers and Modern Managers in the SS: The Business Administration Main Office (Wirtschaftsverwaltungshauptamt)* (n.p. 1995); Herman Kaienburg, *Die Wirtschaft der SS. Oswald Pohl und das SS-Wirtschafts-Verwaltungshauptamt 1933–1945* (Berlin: Metropol, 2003).

10 Bogdan Musial, ed., *"Aktion Reinhardt." Der Völkermord an den Juden im Generalgouvernement 1941–1944* (Osnabrück: Fibre, 2004).

11 Jean-Claude Pressac, *Die Krematorien von Auschwitz. Die Technik des Massenmordes* (Munich: Piper, 1995).

12 Franciszek Piper, *Die Zahl der Opfer von Auschwitz. Aufgrund der Quellen und der Erträge der Forschung, 1945–1990* (Oświęcim: Auschwitz-Birkenau State Museum, 1993).

13 Victor Klemperer, *Ich will Zeugnis ablegen bis zum letzten: Tagebücher 1933–1945* (Berlin: Aufbau Verlag, 1995), 1: 47, 59.

14 Bernd C. Wagner, *IG Auschwitz. Zwangsarbeit und Vernichtung von Häftlingen des Lagers Monowitz 1941–1945* (Munich: K.G. Saur, 2000).

15 Sybille Steinbacher, *Dachau. Die Stadt und das Konzentrationslager in der NS-Zeit. Die Untersuchung einer Nachbarschaft* (Frankfurt am Main: Peter Lang, 1993). On the complex interweaving between the camps and German society, see Sybille Steinbacher, *"Musterstadt" Auschwitz: Germanisierungspolitik und Judenmord in Ostoberschlesien* (München: K. G. Saur Verlag, 2000); Jens Schley, *Nachbar Buchenwald. Die Stadt Weimar und ihr Konzentrationslager 1937–1945* (Cologne: Böhlau, 1999); *Dachauer Hefte* 17 (2001).

16 Karin Orth, *Die Konzentrationslager-SS. Sozialstrukturelle Analysen und biographische Studien* (Göttingen: Wallstein, 2000); Tom Segev, *Soldiers of Evil: Commanders of Nazi Concentration Camps* (New York: McGraw Hill, 1988).

17 Norbert Frei, *Adenauer's Germany and the Nazi Past. The Politics of Amnesty and Integration* (New York: Columbia University Press, 2002).

18 Hans Beimler, *Four Weeks in the Hands of Hitler's Hell-Hounds. The Nazi Concentration Camp of Dachau* (London: Modern Books, 1933).

19 Dietmar Sedlaczek, " ... *das Lager läuft dir hinterher.*" *Leben mit nationalsozialistischer Verfolgung* (Berlin: Reimer, 1996); Johannes Dieter Steinert and Inge Weber-Newth, *Beyond Camps and Forced Labour. Current International Research on Survivors of Nazi Persecution, Proceedings of the International Conference London, 29–31 January 2003* (Osnabrück, 2005).

20 Norbert Frei, *Martin Broszat, Der "Staat Hitlers" und die Historisierung des Nationalsozialismus* (Göttingen: Wallstein, 2007).

21 Hans Buchheim, Martin Broszat, Hans-Adolf Jacobsen and Helmut Krausnick, *Anatomie des SS-Staates* (Olten: Walter-Verlag, 1965).

22 Eberhard Kolb, *Bergen-Belsen. Geschichte des "Aufenthaltslagers" 1943–1945* (Hannover: Verlag für Literatur und Zeitgeschehen, 1962); Enno Georg, *Die wirtschaftlichen Unternehmungen der SS* (Stuttgart: Deutsche Verlags-Anstalt, 1963).

23 Martin Broszat, *Studien zur Geschichte der Konzentrationslager* (Stuttgart: Deutsche Verlags-Anstalt, 1970).

24 With the exception of the study by Falk Pingel, *Häftlinge unter SS-Herrschaft. Widerstand, Selbstbehauptung und Vernichtung im Konzentrationslager* (Hamburg: Hoffmann u. Campe, 1978).

25 Books have appeared on Mauthausen, Dachau, Ravensbrück, Neuengamme, Groß-Rosen, Mittelbau-Dora, and Bergen-Belsen, but not on large and important camps such as Buchenwald and Sachsenhausen. On Buchenwald and on historical treatment of the SS patronage system after the war, see Lutz Niethammer, ed., *Der "gesäuberte" Antifaschismus. Die SED und die roten Kapos von Buchenwald* (Berlin: Akadamie Verlag, 1995).

26 In 1980, Yad Vashem held a conference on the question of the significance of the concentration camps and death camps in the process of murdering Europe's Jews; the first major scholarly international conference on the history of the Nazi camp system took place only in the autumn of 1995, in Weimar. The two volumes of conference proceedings remain the basis for ongoing research: *Die nationalsozialistischen Konzentrationslager* (Herbert, Orth and Dieckmann, eds).

27 Wolfgang Sofsky, *Die Ordnung des Terrors. Das Konzentrationslager* (Frankfurt am Main: S. Fischer, 1993).

28 *Der Ort des Terrors* (Benz and Distel, eds).

29 Karin Orth, "Die Historiografie der Konzentrationslager und die neuere KZ-Forschung," *Archiv für Sozialgeschichte* 47 (2007): 579–98; Nikolaus Wachsmann, "Looking into the Abyss: Historians and the Nazi Concentrations Camps," *European History Quarterly*, vol. 36, no. 2 (2006): 247–78. Marc Buggeln, *Arbeit und Gewalt. Das Außenlagersystem des KZ Neuengamme* (Göttingen: Wallstein, 2009).

30 Saul Friedländer has powerfully demonstrated the historical eloquence of reports by the persecuted: *Nazi Germany and the Jews. Vol 1: The Years of Persecution, 1933–1939* (New York: Harper Perennial, 1997); *Vol. 2: The Years of Extermination: Nazi Germany and the Jews, 1939–1945* (New York: HarperCollins, 2007).

17

PARADISE/HADES, PURGATORY, HELL/GEHENNA

A political typology of the camps

Robert Jan van Pelt

"I have just seen the most terrible place on the face of the earth," veteran journalist Bill Lawrence wrote in *The New York Times* on 30 August 1944. He had just visited the Majdanek concentration camp, recently liberated by the Red Army. Lawrence reported that he had spoken with captured Germans "who admitted quite frankly that it was a highly systemized place for annihilation, although they, of course, denied any personal participation in the murders."[1]

For the German Jewish refugee Hannah Arendt and her husband Heinrich Blücher, the newspaper report proved another turn in a downward spiral. In 1940, both had spent time in French internment camps. They escaped in the chaos that followed the armistice, and found shelter in Montauban. There they observed how the Germans used the unoccupied south as a dumping ground for Jews, "superfluous" people whom the French immediately locked up in camps. In early 1941, Arendt and Blücher obtained American immigration visas, and traveled via Spain and Portugal to the United States. In safety, Arendt tried to make sense of her experience. In November 1941, she wrote in the German-language, New York-based Jewish weekly *Aufbau* about stateless people as outlaws whose only place was the concentration camp.[2] A year later, Arendt learned that the French and Germans were collaborating in emptying internment camps by sending the inmates—German-Jewish refugees like herself, who had sought refuge in France in the 1930s—to an unknown destination in the east. She felt great solidarity with them: both she and they were people who were put "in concentration camps by their foes and in internment camps by their friends."[3]

In 1943, Arendt and Blücher got a first intimation of what happened to those who had been deported. First they didn't believe it. They obtained proof when they read the report on Majdanek. "It was really as if an abyss had opened. Because we had the idea that amends could somehow be made for everything else, as amends can be made for just about everything at some point in politics. But not for this. *This ought not to have happened.* And I don't mean just the number of victims. I mean the method, the fabrication of corpses and so on—I don't need to go into that. This should not have happened. Something happened there to which we cannot reconcile ourselves. None of us ever can."[4]

In May 1945, Arendt saw in the newsreels original footage from the camps taken by cameramen in Belsen, Buchenwald, and Dachau. Sadly, she did not leave a full description of her experience. In an article published in 1948, she observed, tersely, that she was struck by an "atmosphere of insanity" and shocked that "things which for thousands of years the human imagination had banished to a realm beyond human competence, can be manufactured right here on earth."[5] Peter Weiss has given us a much fuller description of the revelation, and I'll quote it here as I believe that his experience was shared by Jews and non-Jews everywhere. In May 1945, the young German-Jewish refugee Weiss had treated himself to a movie in Stockholm. The newsreels that preceded the feature film carried a report on the liberation of the concentration camps in Germany. "On the dazzlingly bright screen I saw the places for which I had been destined, the figures to whom I should have belonged." He saw an inconceivable and incomprehensible world. "A sobbing could be heard and a voice called out: Never forget this! It was a miserable senseless cry, for there were no longer any words, there was nothing more to be said, there were no declarations, no more admonitions, all values had been destroyed." Weiss observed the mountains of corpses, and between them "shapes of utter humiliation in their striped rags. Their movements were interminably slow, they reeled around, bundles of bones, blind to one another in a world of shadows." Weiss racked his brain for a parallel, for some kind of conceptual framework that would help him understand what he saw. He turned to the traditional iconography of the underworld as told in great works of literature and depicted in great visions of art. Yet he couldn't make the connection. "Everything was reduced to dust and we could never think again of looking for new comparisons, for points of departure in the face of these ultimate pictures. This was no kingdom of the dead. These were human beings whose hearts were still beating. This was a world where human beings lived. This was a world constructed by human beings."[6]

Almost all who witnessed the camps first-hand or watched the newsreels in the cinemas made the association with Hell: most saw it as Hell incarnate, but some, like Weiss, realized the parallel would not go very far. But either through affirmation or through differentiation, Hell provided a useful point of reference to clarify one's thoughts about the camps. Arendt also compared the camps with Hell—but she broke new ground in the way she understood the nature of the analogy. In 1946, she articulated in *Commentary* her evolving understanding of the camps. "The facts are: that six million Jews, six million human beings, were helplessly, and in most cases unsuspectingly, dragged to their deaths." Neglect and deprivation had been followed by starvation and forced labor, to end in the death camps—"and they all died together, the young and the old, the weak and the strong, the sick and the healthy; not as people, not as men and women, children and adults, not as good and bad, beautiful and ugly—but brought down to the lowest common denominator of organic life itself, plunged into the darkest and deepest abyss of primal equality, like cattle, like matter, like things that had neither body nor soul, nor even a physiognomy upon which death could stamp its seal." This was an "equality without fraternity or humanity" in which she saw mirrored "the image of hell." In this equality, all were innocent. "The gas chamber was more than anybody could have possibly deserved, and in the face of it the worst criminal was as innocent as the new-born babe." In this Hell, "saint and sinner were equally degraded to the status of possible corpses."[7] Arendt recognized that a series of events that centered on lack of agency, the equality of inorganic matter, and radical innocence could not be told as a story. "The monstrous equality in innocence that is its *leitmotif* destroys the very basis on which history is produced—which is, namely, our capacity to comprehend an event no matter how distant we are from it."[8]

Yet she tried to find ways to create a narrative that would allow her to think about the camps. In July 1948, Arendt published a first attempt in *The Partisan Review*. The opening sentence was bold and broke conceptually new ground. "There are three possible approaches to the reality of the concentration camp: the inmate's experience of immediate suffering, the recollection of the survivor, and the fearful anticipation of those who dread the concentration camp as a possibility for the future." Arendt observed that the first two approaches, which encompassed the whole literature on the camps that had been created between 1945 and 1948, did not work. Only those who could analyze the camps dispassionately, using the tools of political science, would be able to see beyond the horrors and understand the camps as an essential tool of totalitarianism.[9] Considering the camps from a political point of view, Arendt noted that they were without parallel in history. Comparisons with prisons and penal colonies, exile and slavery led nowhere. These earlier forms of punishment or exploitation had made sense. The killings in the camps did not—giving the whole phenomenon "an air of mad unreality." Yet this very unreality was the key to understanding the camps. "Seen from the outside, they and the things that happen in them can be described only in images drawn from a life after death, that is, a life removed from earthly purposes." Yet Arendt did not simply slap the label "Hell" on the world of the camps. Since 1946, her thinking had evolved. In the same way that Dante needed to articulate afterlife in the threefold hierarchy of Inferno, Purgatory, and Paradise, Arendt introduced her own threefold system, articulating "ideal types" in the sense given to this by the sociologist Max Weber.[10] "Concentration camps can very aptly be divided into three types corresponding to three basic Western conceptions of a life after death: Hades, Purgatory, and Hell." The internment camps designed to getting out of the way bothersome and undesirable elements such as refugees, stateless people, and asocials corresponded to Hades. Purgatory corresponded to the Soviet Union's labor camps, where neglect combined with chaotic forced labor. And the Nazi concentration camps were Hell. There "life was thoroughly and systematically organized with a view to the greatest possible torment." Arendt observed that all three types treated the imprisoned masses "as if they no longer existed, as if what happened to them were no longer of any interest to anybody, as if they were already dead and some evil spirit gone mad were amusing himself by stopping them for a while between life and death before admitting them to eternal peace."[11]

Arendt did not base the threefold typology on an arbitrary division between bad, worse, worst. Her division was based on sound political analysis. In each of the camps, a particular aspect of the human person was killed—ending up with the naked human being who is thrown back to the level of organic life. "The first essential step was to kill the juridical person in man; this was done by placing the concentration camp outside the normal penal system, and by selecting its inmates outside the normal judicial procedure in which a definite crime entails a predictable penalty."[12] In the camps belonging to all three categories, people were interned, but because in camps belonging to Hades—the first circle of Arendt's camp universe—destruction was limited to the annihilation of the juridical person, we may conclude that this was the primary characteristic of those camps. The second step was the murder of the moral person in man. "This is done in the main by making martyrdom, for the first time in history, impossible." In the second circle, death became anonymous, suggesting that neither the life nor the death of the inmate was of relevance to anyone—setting, in short, "a seal on the fact that he had never really existed."[13] The third step in the threefold reduction of human beings to a state of bare life was the erasure of the unique identity of each person. In the third circle, Hell, people were "transformed into specimens of the human beast." This erasure of the uniqueness of each human being "creates a horror that vastly overshadows the outrage of the juridical–political person and the despair of the moral person."[14] Arendt claimed that the Nazis knew what they were doing when they created the death camps that "demonstrated the swiftest possible solution to the problem of superfluous human masses." And she feared that many would be inspired by their example "whenever it seems impossible to alleviate political, or social, or economic misery in a manner worthy of man."[15]

In *The Origins of Totalitarianism* (1951), Arendt preserved the three ideal types of Hades, Purgatory, and Hell. And rightly so: it offered a brilliant scheme to map the perplexing landscape of *l'univers concentrationnaire* on the basis of the political meaning of the camps. Arendt's book offered the first coherent narrative in which the world of the camps was described in the context of the political developments of the twentieth century. It opened magnificent vistas, all held together by the central concept of "super-fluous people." Paradoxically, these also included the men who ran the camp. "The manipulators of this system believe in their own superfluousness as much as in that of all others, and the totalitarian murderers are all the more dangerous because they do not care if they themselves are alive or dead, if they ever lived or never were born." Arendt boldly sketched the continued relevance of the death camps as a political possibility. "The danger of corpse factories and holes of oblivion is that today, with populations and homelessness everywhere on the increase, masses of people are continuously rendered superfluous if we continue to think of our world in utilitarian terms." The camps, therefore, were "as much an attraction as a warning."[16]

Wide-ranging and prophetic, the many important insights in *The Origins of Totalitarianism* overshadowed the discussion on the typology of the camps. In addition, to have understood the typology, one should have been willing to consider the value of distinctions, and as Arendt complained in the 1960s, there was "a silent agreement in most discussions among political and social scientists that we can ignore distinctions and proceed on the assumption that everything can eventually be called anything else, and that distinctions are meaningful only to the extent that each of us has the right 'to define his terms.'"[17] She was right: neither the few sociologists, nor the few political scientists, who wrote about the camps could be bothered by it.

Also, historians did not know what to do with her types. I, for example, held in my own work scrupulously, pedantically, and perhaps also timidly to the bureaucratic distinctions by which the camps were classified in the 1930s and 1940s, knowing well that they often meant little. Since 1990, I always had at hand the reprint of the massive *Catalogue of Camps and Prisons in Germany and German-Occupied Territories September 1939–May 1945*, prepared by the International Tracing Service of the United Nations Rescue and Relief Authority.[18] I knew Arendt's ideal types, but did not take them too seriously—admittedly, I was somewhat put off by the not-so-felicitous labels of Hades, Purgatory, and Hell. As a historian, I found myself constantly engaged in a battle against mythification of the camps, and comparisons with mythical places did not help—and so I always returned to the categories the Germans had used themselves: *Auffangslager* (absorption camps), *Durchgangslager* (transit camps), *Firmenlager* (company camps), *Judenarbeitslager* (labor camps for Jews), *Judenlager* (Jews' camps), *Konzentrationslager* (concentration camps), *Polizeihaftlager* (police detention camps), *Sammellager* (assembly camps), *Zwangarbeitslager* (forced labor camps), and so on.[19]

Part of my resistance was also the result of my irritation with George Steiner's claim that the camps had been created in a deliberate effort to make Hell immanent. "They are the transference of Hell from below the earth to its surface. They are the deliberate enactment of a long, precise imagining," Steiner claimed in 1971. He proposed that modern man felt a loss when he ceased to believe in either Heaven or Hell. "It may be that the mutation of hell into metaphor left a formidable gap in the co-ordinates of location, of psychological recognition in the Western mind. The absence of the familiar damned opened a vortex which the modern totalitarian state filled. To have neither Heaven nor Hell is to be intolerably deprived and alone in a world gone flat. Of the two, Hell proved the easier to recreate."[20] Brilliant, to be sure, and I was quite happy to concede that our fascination with Auschwitz might reflect a need to know the presence of the mystery of horror—but I absolutely refused to accept that the Nazis had built the camps because they missed Hell.

I also admit that my aversion for metaphor had been increased by my love for Imre Kertész's semi-autobiographical novel *Fatelessness*. When his alter ego György Köves returns from the camps, he meets in a Budapest streetcar a journalist who identifies him as someone who had been in "one of the pits of the Nazi hell."[21] In a beautifully written dialogue, Köves refuses to accept the journalist's suggestion that the camps belonged to another world, that they were unnatural. "I told him that in a concentration camp they *were* natural. 'Yes, of course, of course,' he says, 'they were *there*, but ... ,' and he broke off, hesitating slightly, 'but ... I mean, a concentration camp in itself is *unnatural*,' finally hitting on the right word as it were. I didn't even bother saying anything to this, as I was beginning slowly to realize that it seems there are some things you can't argue about with strangers, the ignorant, with those who, in a certain sense, are mere children so to say."[22] When the journalist suggests György might publish his story about "the hell of the camps," György replies that he was not acquainted with hell, and hence could not say anything about it. "He assured me, however, that it was just a manner of speaking. 'Can we imagine a concentration camp as anything but hell?' he asked, and I replied, as I scratched a few circles with my heel in the dust under my feet, that everyone could think what they liked about it, but as far as I was concerned I could only imagine a concentration camp, since I was somewhat acquainted with what that was, but not hell."[23] Of course, György might have been mistaken. He was a somewhat clueless lad after all. But when I read *Fatelessness* for the first time, I felt immediate sympathy for his position, and more suspicious of using myth or metaphor to describe the camps.

And, finally, I concede that the wicked sense of humor of my friend Stephen Feinstein (who took the initiative for this book and who sadly passed away in March 2008) spoilt my taste for the mythical. In 2001 we had a long conversation about Zbigniew Libera's irreverent and provocative Lego Concentration Camp (1996). A conceptual artist from Poland, Libera had been able to convince the Lego company to sponsor a project in which he would use Lego pieces to create an "architecture which could be a factor of transformation of individuals: the architecture which influences those whom it shelters, which provides control, subordinates individuals to cognition and modifies them through discipline."[24] Initially, I had my doubts about the project, considering it sacrilegious, but Feinstein convinced me that it had succeeded in making people think, to keep the debate about the meaning of the camps going. I had to admit that the association of Auschwitz with Lego had made an impact, while the association of the camp with Hell produced only yawns. Once he had convinced me that Libera's interpretation was legitimate, Feinstein also offered to put me in contact with Libera's agent Polina Kolzynska, so that I could obtain a set for my own collection. I declined.

Yet, a few years ago, I changed my mind about Arendt's classification of Hades as the place where inmates were deprived of their juridical person only (a French internment camp like Gurs, where Arendt was imprisoned in 1940); Purgatory as the place where inmates were deprived of their juridical *and* moral person (a German concentration camp like Dachau before 1939); and Hell as the place where they were deprived of their juridical *and* moral person *and* their individuality (a German concentration camp like Auschwitz). This change of mind came in response to the writings of the Italian philosopher Giorgio Agamben. A hero to those concerned about the apparent erosion of civil liberties in Europe and post-9/11 United States, Agamben has brought (with the help of Arendt's *The Origins of Totalitarianism*) important philosophical focus on the so-called "state of exception"—the originally temporary but increasingly permanent suspension of the legal order. In December 1992, Israel expelled 425 Palestinians who got stuck in the no-man's land between Israel and Lebanon; the Lebanese government refused to allow their country to become a "dumping ground." Their desperate situation caused Agamben to read Arendt's 1943 essay on refugees, and he wrote an article in which he quoted Arendt's observations that the stateless and rightless refugees were "the vanguard of their people."[25] Taking Arendt's analysis of the stateless person and the refugee as his point of departure, Agamben defined the refugee as "the central figure of our political history." He then invoked Arendt's typology of the camps, without the mythic labels. "We should not forget that the first camps were built in Europe as spaces for controlling refugees, and that the succession of internment camps–concentration camps–extermination camps represents a perfectly real filiation."[26] But the concentration camp had not only evolved from the internment camp, and the extermination camp from the concentration camp. They were in fact a single phenomenon: once a person had lost their civic rights, which meant that they were fit for internment, they were also doomed to death. Considering the mass of non-citizens living in European countries who do not want to be, and cannot be, either naturalized or repatriated, Agamben urged the nation-states to revisit the whole concept of citizenship "before extermination camps are re-opened in Europe (something that is already starting to happen)." Of course, Agamben meant internment camps, but it appears that his postulate of a necessary continuum between internment and killing allowed him to use the term "extermination camp."[27]

In 1994, Agamben decided to focus on the phenomenon of "the camp" as a general and abstract category. If, a year earlier, he had still acknowledged that the qualifiers "internment," "concentration," and "extermination" might have some residual significance, now he limited his discussion to the concept of "the camp"—singular. He asked "What is a camp? What is its political–juridical structure? How could such events have taken place there?" And in the same way that Arendt had considered the camp as a possibility, so did Agamben: for him "the camp" was not only a phenomenon of the past, but "the hidden matrix and *nomos* [law] of the political space in which we still live."[28] He defined the essence of the camp as "the materialization of the state of exception," and hence discovered this to be everywhere: in a soccer stadium in which the police temporarily herd illegal immigrants, or the holding areas for asylum-seekers in international airports, or certain suburbs of postindustrial cities, or gated communities in North America. In all these places one would find the nation-state, which ordered life and law in the threefold space of nation, state, and territory, in crisis. Therefore the camp was a fourth element, a "dislocating localization" that had been added to, and had broken up, the old trinity of nation, state, and territory, and that formed the hidden

196

matrix of contemporary politics. "We must learn to recognize it in all of its metamorphoses."[29]

While I recognized the importance and brilliance of Agamben's work, I also felt that his erasure of the conceptual distinctions between the various forms of camp was problematic, and I believed that the symbolic nomenclature of Arendt's typology offered a protection against an all-too-easy collapse of the internment camp, the concentration camp, or the extermination camp into the single concept of "camp." In the western tradition, Hades, Purgatory, and Hell are ontologically different, and when one refers to one or all of those imagined regions of the afterlife, one would not be tempted to collapse them all in the singular notion of "Underworld." Rereading Arendt's 1948 essay on the concentration camps and her discussion on the camps in *The Origins of Totalitarianism*, I rediscovered in her analysis of the camps both a subtlety of thought and an existential understanding of the different situations of the inmates in the modern forms of Hades, Purgatory, and Hell, which made Agamben's musings on "the camp" appear to be both crude and somewhat callous.

If Agamben had taught me to appreciate the nomenclature of Arendt's typology of the camps, the first attempt to write a global history of the camps showed me that it might be a useful tool for the historian. In 2000, the French historians Joël Kotek and Pierre Rigoulot published their 800-page-long *Le siècle des camps* (*The Century of Camps*). This book was an attempt to realize Arendt's aborted ambition to write a short (sic!) history of the camps, "from their beginnings in the imperialist countries, passing by their utilization as a temporary measure in wartime, arriving at their institutionalization as a permanent organ of government in regimes of terror. This historical research must be complemented with an analysis of the different juridical aspects of the different types of concentration camps."[30] Kotek and Rigoulot tried to organize the enormous amount of material by applying two kinds of classification. The first was based on the function of the camps, and led them to distinguish between internment camps, concentration camps, and centers for extermination or immediate killing.[31] This classification appeared in the subtitle of the book: *Detention, concentration, extermination: one hundred years of radical evil.*

But they also used a second system of classification, which was based on Arendt's typology of Hades, Purgatory, and Hell. In *Le siècle des camps*, Hades remained reserved for the camps that were designed merely to isolate. These included the so-called areas of concentration created by the Spanish in Cuba during uprising against colonial rule, and the concentration camps built by the British in South Africa during the Boer wars. Kotek and Rigoulot modified Arendt's concept of Purgatory, which they understood as the camps that were designed to profit from forced labor, but where the authorities still assumed that the inmates could be reformed. Purgatory included, as Arendt had suggested, the Soviet camps, but the authors also included the early Nazi concentration camps in this category. The authors applied the category Hell to the Nazi camp system as it evolved from 1939, from a system that held only German nationals to one that was filled with people from the occupied countries. In this second phase, the main purpose of the German concentration camps had become humiliation and elimination. In rearranging the concept of Purgatory and Hell, Kotek and Rigoulot had faithfully followed Arendt's understanding of the three types as places that annihilated the juridical man, the moral man, and the individual. They went beyond Arendt in separating out of the concept of Hell the killing factories, and assigning them to a fourth category: *Gehenna*— the traditional Jewish concept of the part of the afterlife in which, unlike Dante's Hell, the souls are not subjected to eternal tortures, but are quickly destroyed. Gehenna included the Operation Reinhard camps.[32]

In *Le siècle des camps*, the two classifications sit uneasily side by side—it is as if each author had his own favorite, and they couldn't agree which one to use, and therefore used both of them. On reading the book, I found the authors' use of Arendt's (modified) typology very useful in tracing the evolution in the Gulag as it moved from Hades (1917–22) via Purgatory (1923–30) to Hell (1930–53)—a clear example of the slippery slope which made Agamben propose to eliminate all distinctions.[33] Yet I also recognized that Kotek and Rigoulot did not exploit the full potential of the fourfold typology to harness the material: in *Le siècle des camps*, the historical narrative clearly dominates the political (that means typological) understanding of the camps. Yet their book suggested that an analysis of the role of the camps in the Holocaust with the help of Arendt's typology, as modified by Kotek and Rigoulot, might be useful.

Kotek and Rigoulot strengthened Arendt's typology by adding the fourth type of Gehenna to the triad of Hades, Purgatory, and Hell. Yet for this fourfold typology to work, I would like to suggest that the scheme should acknowledge that the corpse factories which they identify as Gehenna mark a clear rupture. Arendt realized this when she first heard about these places, and felt that an unbridgeable abyss had opened for which humankind could not make amends.[34] If their history of the Gulag showed that triad of Hades, Purgatory, and Hell can form a slippery slope, or if Agamben's musings may have convinced some that various forms of camp may be assembled within the single concept of "the camp," I believe that a clear boundary ought to separate the triad of Hades–Purgatory–Hell from Gehenna. Thus the typology is not fourfold, written down as

Hades–Purgatory–Hell–Gehenna

but reveals a structure of "three plus one." On a piece of paper I wrote my scheme down in the following manner:

Hades–Purgatory–Hell
Gehenna

Considering the *Gestalt* of the diagram, I realized that we needed one more addition to this system of classification, adding a fifth type that creates a structure of "one plus three plus one." To justify this addition, I'll invoke a movie that the Nazis intended to shape their image: Leni Riefenstahl's *Triumph of the Will* (1935). Early on, the movie shows a pivotal shift that ends the sequence which began with the magic of flight amidst the clouds, the touch-down of Hitler's plane on the Franconian soil, the jubilant reception of the *Führer* by the crowds, the leader's arrival at hotel Deutscher Hof, and the evening brass band concert in front of the hotel. Separating this overture and the report of the Party Rally is a visual and musical diptych that begins with contemplative shots of the old city of Nuremberg as it awakes to a new day—a romantic evocation of past greatness that dissolves into an aerial view of countless, geometrically arranged tents: The enormous camp outside the city that lodges tens of thousands of storm-troopers, Hitler Youth, Labor Service men, and soldiers who were to be the bit players in the Party Rally and who, as they arise, wash their muscled bodies, obtain breakfast, and play around, providing an effective representation of a vigorous and unified community as it prepares itself for a bright and different future.

Triumph of the Will reminds us of the fact that the Nazis used camps not only to radically change society through the removal of "superfluous" people. To them, camps were also places where they wanted to re-educate young German men in order to change a class-ridden, fragmented society into a unified, strong, and racially pure *Volksgemeinschaft* (national community). As the historian Axel Dossmann, the art-historian Kai Wenzel, and the artist Jan Wenzel have argued, camps were to be key sites in the social revolution that Hitler had promised: located outside the cities, towns, and villages, they offered secluded places of optimization and betterment.[35] Most important of these were the camps of the *Arbeitsdienst* (Labor Service), and they became a symbol of the collective will of the nation to renew itself.

Ideologically, the labor camps were a product of the German youth movement. In the first decade of the twentieth century, many adolescent middle-class Germans felt alienated from bourgeois society, with its stuffy customs and restrictions. In their restlessness, these youngsters were not different from adolescents in other countries.[36] Yet in Germany, the persistence of a century-old romantic tradition helped to shape a unique response. Young people believed that they would be able to create a new national community (*Volksgemeinschaft*) that transcended social divisions. Initially, the central focus of the youth movement were "ramblings" through the countryside. Somehow these journeys were supposed to create the basis for the new society. After the Great War, the focus shifted from communion with nature to the social virtues of comradeship, solicitude, and solidarity—all buttressed by discipline and obedience. Peer-led communities of young people were to be the avant garde of a new and regenerated Germany. Working the land far away from the city, they were to create a "New Man."

The labor camp became the most important tool to realize that aim. Pioneered in Bulgaria in 1920, after 1925 the labor camp became the ideal place to introduce middle-class youngsters to the special virtues of the *Volk*: living the simple life together in a camp allowed young people to experience the essence of national community.[37] Party politics were not allowed inside the camps, and neither were tobacco or alcohol. The central idea was unity, and the erasure of bourgeois individualism. Young people were to work the land as a group, participate in ceremonies as a group; one sported as a group, learned as a group, and sang as a group. "The labor camp is a form of community, a collective, which strongly embraces every person," a youth magazine wrote in 1932. "The labor camp provides a very effective education towards collective thought and action. No-one, not even the greatest individualist, can escape its pull. Here, a new kind of human being is shaped who will be of decisive importance for the future. All the tasks that define the future destiny of the German nation, such as its social unification and settlement, can only be approached and resolved through collective work. The necessary conditions for this are of a human and not of an ideological nature."[38]

Until 1929, the youth movement was largely a middle class phenomenon. When the Depression started, and millions of young people found themselves unemployed, the labor camps also became a tool to fight unemployment. The German government began to support a national *Freiwilliger Arbeitsdienst* (Voluntary Labor Service) in 1931. Now the labor camps of the youth movement broke out of their middle-class isolation, and an ideology that stressed the mixing of social classes became an important element of labor camp life. (Incidentally, Jews did not participate in the German youth movement. They had, however, their own Zionist youth movement, which ran *Hachshara* camps that trained young Jews for a pioneer life in Palestine.)

In 1933, the National Socialist government unified the many youth organizations into the Hitler Youth, and the Voluntary Labor Service (and many other labor services of the youth movement) into a single, national *Nationalsozialistischer Arbeitsdienst* (National Socialist Labor Service). Its official ideology stressed the fact that their camps offered a generation that had not been schooled in war an experience that touched on life in the trenches. Living and working together in the back country, young men were to discover the comradeship that did away with class distinctions and differences. On 1 May 1933, Hitler observed that the German *Volk* was in a state of disintegration and that the Labor Service camps were to be the tool of regeneration. "It remains our firm decision to lead every single German, be he who he may, whether rich or poor, whether the son of scholars or the son of factory workers, to experience manual labor once in his lifetime so that he can come to know it, so that he can here one day more easily take command because he has learned obedience in the past."[39]

In July 1934, the National Socialist Labor Service became compulsory and was renamed *Reicharbeitsdienst* (Reich Labor Service). During the 1934 Party Rally, Hitler told the 52,000 Reich Labor Service men assembled in Nuremberg that "the entire nation will learn the lessons of your lives! A time will come when not a single German can grow into the community of this *Volk* who has not made his way through your community."[40] The ideals and the techniques of the Reich Labor Service spoke to many. The British Ambassador Sir Nevile Henderson believed that the English should imitate the German example. "In my humble opinion, these camps serve none but useful purposes. In them not only are there no class distinctions, but on the contrary an opportunity for better understanding between the classes. Therein one learns the pleasure of hard work and the dignity of labour, as well as the benefits of discipline; moreover they vastly improve the physique of the nation."[41] After the war, the Reich Labor Service was one of the only parts of the Nazi regime which Germans were proud to remember. "A wave of excitement seizes the stands when these 40,000 young people march in singing, with naked, bronzed trunks," Peter Kleist recalled in the 1960s. His eyes filled with tears. "Here is something alive of that youthful devotion to a greater goal, an enthusiasm of pure origin comes into being, and touches the spectators. An American journalist sighs: 'it's a real pity that I can't transmit this. No American paper will let me print this.'"[42] Yes, those were magnificent days ...

The Reich Labor Service camps, and all the other camps in which German men were gathered and trained to carry the weight of Germany's future, provide the political context for our understanding of the German camp system as a tool of societal change. Because the Nazis were willing to subject their own to the rigors of camp life, they were willing to assign those who did not fit to even harder regimes. In their strategy to transform society, the many camps where they were to create the new "German Man" complemented the camps where they were to re-educate those who had been led astray, and the camps where they could dump those who would never fit in. Following the structure of Dante's *Divine Comedy*, we might identify these camps of betterment as Paradise,[43] creating a typology of

Paradise
Hades—Purgatory—Hell
Gehenna

I believe that this modified and expanded version of Arendt's typology will prove to offer a useful tool of analysis. And I might find time to have a crack at writing such a fivefold analysis of the camps. I just might.

Notes

1 William H. Lawrence, "Nazi Mass Killing Laid Bare in Camp," *The New York Times*, 30 August 1944, 1.
2 "Active Patience," Hannah Arendt, *The Jewish Writings*, eds Jerome Kohn and Ron H. Feldman (New York: Schocken, 2007), 138.
3 Hannah Arendt, "We Refugees," *The Menorah Journal*, vol. 31, no. 1 (Winter 1943): 70.
4 "'What Remains? The Language Remains': A Conversation with Günter Gaus," in Hannah Arendt, *Essays in Understanding, 1930–1954*, ed. Jerome Kohn (New York: Harcourt Brace & Co., 1994), 13f.
5 Hannah Arendt, "The Concentration Camps," *Partisan Review*, vol. 15, no. 7 (July 1948): 750f.
6 Peter Weiss, "Vanishing Point," in *Exile*, trans. E.B. Garside, Alastair Hamilton and Christopher Levenson (New York: Delacorte Press, 1968), 194f.
7 Hannah Arendt, "The Image of Hell," in *Commentary*, vol. 2, no. 3 (September 1946): 291f.
8 Arendt, "The Image of Hell," 292.
9 Arendt, "The Concentration Camps," 748.
10 According to Weber, "an ideal type is formed by the one-sided accentuation of one or more points of view and by the synthesis of a great many diffuse, discrete, more or less present and occasionally absent concrete individual phenomena, which are arranged according to those one-sidedly emphasized viewpoints into a unified analytical construct." Max Weber, *The Methodology of the Social Sciences*, eds Edward A. Shils and Henry A. Finch (New York: The Free Press, 1997), 88.
11 Arendt, "The Concentration Camps," 749f.
12 Arendt, "The Concentration Camps," 752.
13 Arendt, "The Concentration Camps," 756.
14 Arendt, "The Concentration Camps," 758.
15 Arendt, "The Concentration Camps," 762.
16 Hannah Arendt, *The Origins of Totalitarianism* (New York: Harcourt, Brace & Company, 1951), 433f.
17 Hannah Arendt, "What is Authority?" in Hannah Arendt, *Between Past and Future*, ed. Jerome Kohn (London: Penguin, 2006), 95.
18 Martin Weinmann, ed., *Das nationalsozialistische Lagersystem* (Frankfurt am Main: Zweitauseneins, 1990).
19 See also Yisrael Gutman and Avital Saf, eds, *The Nazi Concentration Camps: Proceedings of the Fourth Yad Vashem International Historical Conference, Jerusalem, January 1980* (Jerusalem: Yad Vashem, 1984).
20 George Steiner, *In Bluebeard's Castle: Some Notes Towards the Redefinition of Culture* (London: Faber & Faber, 1971), 47f.
21 Imre Kertész, *Fatelessness*, Tim Wilkinson, trans. (New York: Vintage International, 2004), 246f.
22 Imre Kertész, *Fatelessness*, 247f.
23 Imre Kertész, *Fatelessness*, 248.
24 See Stephen C. Feinstein, "Zbigniew Libera's Lego Concentration Camp: Iconoclasm in Conceptual Art About the Shoah," *Other Voices*, vol. 2, no. 1 (February 2000). www.othervoices.org/2.1/feinstein/auschwitz.html
25 Giorgio Agamben, "Beyond Human Rights," in Giorgio Agamben, *Means without End: Notes on Politics*, Vincenzo Binetti and Cesare Casarino, eds (Minneapolis and London: University of Minnesota Press, 2000), 24.
26 Agamben, "Beyond Human Rights," 21.
27 Agamben, "Beyond Human Rights," 23.
28 Giorgio Agamben, "What is a Camp?" in Agamben, *Means without End*, 36.
29 Agamben, "What is a Camp?", 40, 43.
30 Joël Kotek and Pierre Rigoulot, *Le siècle des camps: Détention, concentration, extermination— cent ans de mal radical* (Paris: J.C. Lattès, 2000), 721f.
31 Kotek and Rigoulot, *Le siècle des camps*, 21f.
32 Kotek and Rigoulot, *Le siècle des camps*, 45f.
33 Kotek and Rigoulot, *Le siècle des camps*, 144ff.

34 Arendt, "'What Remains? The Language Remains'," 13f.
35 See Axel Dossmann, Jan Wenzel and Kai Wenzel, "Barackenlager: Zur Nutzung einer Architektur der Moderne," in *Auszug aus dem Lager: Zu Überwindung des modernen Raumparadigmas in der politischen Philosophie,* ed. Ludger Schwarte (Berlin and Bielfeld: Akademie der Künste/Transcript Verlag, 2007), 220ff.
36 See Erik H. Erikson, *Identity: Youth and Crisis* (New York: W.W. Norton, 1968).
37 See Peter D. Stachura, *The German Youth Movement 1900–1945: An Interpretative and Documentary History* (London: Macmillan, 1981), 46ff.; Walter Z. Laqueur, *Young Germany: A History of the German Youth Movement* (London: Routledge & Kegan Paul, 1962), 146f.
38 As quoted in Harry Pross, *Jugend, Eros, Politik: Die Geschichte der deutschen Jugendverbände* (Bern, Munich and Vienna: Scherz, 1964), 314.
39 Adolf Hitler, *Speeches and Proclamations, 1932–1945*, Max Domarus, ed., four vols (Wauconda, Illinois: Bolchazy-Carducci, 1990), 1: 314.
40 Hitler, *Speeches and Proclamations, 1932–1945*, 1: 531.
41 Sir Nevile Henderson, *Failure of a Mission: Berlin 1937–1939* (New York: G.P. Putnam's Sons, 1940), 15.
42 Peter Kleist, *Aufbruch und Sturz des 3. Reich: Auch Du warst dabei* (Göttingen: Schütz, 1968), 150.
43 In fact, Kotek and Rigoulet did include in their book a chapter entitled "Paradise." In it they discussed the dream of a racial elite. Yet they did not connect it to a particular type of camp, therefore they did not include Paradise in their fourfold typology. See Kotek and Rigoulot, *Le siècle des camps*, 459–67.

Part III
THE FINAL SOLUTION IN EUROPE

18

LEVELS OF ACCOUNTING IN *ACCOUNTING FOR GENOCIDE*

A cross-national study of Jewish victimization during the Holocaust

Helen Fein

Accounting for Genocide: National Responses and Jewish Victimization during the Holocaust (hereafter AG) was first published in 1979, attracting widespread attention, mostly very positive, but some critical from reviewers who objected to the use of statistical methodology and victim testimony, and my stress on political and moral responsibility. In this chapter, I discuss both the range of methods in AG, and how I distinguish and relate analytic accounting of the causes and outcomes of social action with moral accounting for the responsibility of human action and inaction.

To begin theoretically, I conceived of the Holocaust as a test-case of national integration and defense by state and society of its citizens, taking account of the fact (often overlooked) that most Jews were citizens of the European states from which they were seized. AG set out first to assess what accounted for the percentage of Jews who became victims (killed and/or incarcerated in German camps) in different states occupied by and allied to Nazi Germany. This ranged from less than one percent to over 99 percent. In eight of the 21 states and regions studied (excluding the USSR for lack of basic information), which were allied with or occupied by Germany during World War II, the majority of Jews were not seized. The second dimension of AG was accounting for the political and moral responsibility of other actors who might be co-perpetrators, collaborators, conformers to authority, or resisters. This included church leaders, the Jewish councils and other sources of Jewish leadership, the Allies, and social defense movements whose mobilization enabled more Jews to survive in some states. The third dimension accounts for the perception and behavior of the victims, viewing them as subjects and actors. Thus the second part complements the macroscopic analysis in the first part, which analyzes Jewish responses principally as objects of others' actions.

The first step in AG began by constructing three hypotheses and finding indicators for the variables they specified. The three alternate hypotheses or theses were based on: 1 solidarity; 2 German control; and 3 value consensus on antisemitism. I shall present these as brief explanation sketches.

1 Jewish victimization might be explained by the disintegration of national solidarity, assuming that Jews were included in the prewar universe of obligation. The less solidarity there was, the greater would be native cooperation with the Germans. Thus

it was expected that the more solidarity in the nation-state before the war, the fewer Jewish victims there would be. An index of solidarity was based upon prewar political experience and partisan cleavage in the 1930s.

2   Jewish victimization might be explained by the directness of German control leading to both lack of cohesion and resistance: anomie and opportunism on the personal level, and state cooperation. German control was conceived of as a scale of relative freedom, based on Weber's conception of the state,[1] which distinguished five categories, eventually classed in three ranks or degrees of freedom from German control: the colonial zone (which included Bulgaria, Croatia, Finland, Romania, France, and Hungary after March 1944); the command zone (German-occupied territory with no self-government, e.g. Denmark as of 1943, Thessaloniki as of 1941, Athens in 1943, Italy in 1943, the Netherlands, and Norway); and the SS zone (of domination and extermination, e.g. Germany, Austria, the Protectorate, Estonia, Latvia, Lithuania, Serbia, and Poland).

3   The value-consensus thesis was based on the extent of agreement within states that Jews were the source of a "problem"; hence eliminating Jews would eliminate the problem. Since the goal of prewar antisemitic movements was to exclude Jews from a common universe of obligation, and the German goal was to exclude and eliminate Jews, one might expect that the more successful such movements were, the more natives would cooperate with German occupiers and the more Jewish victims there would be. Antisemitism was observed by indicators of the success of national antisemitic movements by 1936. The success of the German entrapment strategy depended on how isolated Jews were. The leading cause behind the chain of Jewish isolation and victimization was the success of the national antisemitic movement in the 1930s, which best explained the cooperation of states in segregating the Jews. Two explanations ultimately proved to be complementary—German control and prewar antisemitism.[2]

The moral dimension: the effect of church responses

The above explanation of underlying causes (based on events occurring between 1930 and 1941) does not convey the proximate or intervening causes which invariably depended on human agency at the time. It was not simply the absence of high prewar antisemitism—or even the extent of anti-antisemitism—but the conjunction and coordination of timely social responses which enabled the Jews to survive. Where this was lacking, the majority perished. This was shown in the deviant-case analysis of the Netherlands, a state with low prewar antisemitism.[3]

The response of the dominant (majority or plurality) church was indexed as the church was believed to be a critical institution that was hypothetically related to resistance against discrimination and deportation. How strongly this was related astounded me. "Church protest proved to be the single element present in every instance in which state collaboration was arrested – as in Bulgaria, France, and Romania. Church protest was absent in virtually all cases in which state cooperation was not arrested. Church protest was also the intervening variable most highly related to the immediacy of social defense movements that enabled Jews to successfully evade deportation. The majority of Jews evaded deportation in every state occupied by or allied with Germany in which the head of the dominant church spoke out publicly against deportation before or as soon as it began."[4]

How church protest and resistance worked to deter deportations differed in different zones. Within the colonial zone, Germany could deport Jews only if an agreement was concluded with state authorities, and if native police were mobilized to arrest Jews. Where state and church refused to sanction any anti-Jewish discrimination, as in Denmark prior to the German invasion of September 1943, resistance was highest. In states in which the government began to agree to deport Jews, church threats and protest operated directly to check government readiness to collaborate. The greater the church resistance, the fewer Jews became victims. Resistance ranged from discrete appeals to public exhortation, with the implicit threat of withdrawal of loyalties to the head of state. Perhaps the most dramatic illustration of the latter was in Bulgaria: "Bishop Kiril of Plovdiv (later Patriarch of Bulgaria) also wired the king 'threatening a campaign of civil disobedience, including personally lying down on the railroad tracks before the deportation trains, if the planned operation was carried out.'"[5]

Within the command zone, church protest had no effect on deterring deportation initiated by the Germans, but it could deter collaboration and instigate people to join movements of social defense of the Jews. Such movements systematically helped Jews, finding new homes for children, seeking out routes and guiding adults to safe-havens, and helping them survive in hiding (and passing as Aryans) by organizing shelter, supplies, ration-stamps, and false papers. Among the occupied states, resistance movements' identification and early mobilization on behalf of hunted Jews was strategically more important than church protest. Relying on appeals or official promises alone in the occupied countries could increase the vulnerability of Jews by reducing their apprehension.

We have no evidence of any church protest in the SS zone by dominant churches, and much evidence of their acquiescence and legitimization of anti-Jewish discrimination. Although verbal protests might have provoked German retaliation, we have little evidence of any covert resistance. Where church behavior was consistent regardless of sanctions, it does not seem that it can be explained by the fear of sanctions. For example, in Poland, the Roman Catholic hierarchy did not condemn violence against the Jews either in 1936, 1942, or 1946, failing to speak out under Polish authorities as well as the German occupier.

The lack of church protest in Europe ignited a controversy over the moral responsibility of Pope Pius XII, as head of the Roman Catholic Church, and the leaders of the Protestant churches. The most critical impact of the failure of Pope Pius XII and the Roman Catholic Church to condemn and delegitimize deportations was in the colonial zone, in which state participation in deportations was voluntary. The majority of Roman Catholic churches in Catholic states in the colonial zone did not protest early and publicize the fact that deportations meant death in the period when they might have deterred them. AG compares Jewish victims in the colonial zone in states with dominant Catholic churches and other dominant churches. An average of 72 percent of Jews in the dominant Catholic states were seized—about 856,000 persons—or 2.6 times the 30 percent seized—about 330,000 persons—in the non-Catholic states. Since these averages conceal wide disparities, it is more revealing to examine the individual states.

Among the three non-Catholic states, Finland never agreed to discriminate or deport Jews as a group. Bulgaria and Romania did agree; indeed, anti-Jewish massacres in Romania by Romanians started before deportations, but Romania's leader Antonescu refused to implement negotiated agreements when the time came for the deportation of Jews who were citizens before the war. Church protests were among the pressures causing the head of state to retract cooperation.

In the Roman Catholic states, there was full cooperation of the church, except in France, where state collaboration was arrested. The Vichy government, which sought (and received) Vatican approval for its discriminatory legislation against Jews in 1941, withdrew its cooperation with the deportation of French Jews (whom it planned to denaturalize so that they could be deported) after the protest of the French cardinals and archbishops of the deportation of foreign-born Jews in July 1942. In France, 65–70 percent of the Jews were saved; in Croatia, Hungary, and Slovakia, fewer than 20 percent.

How church leadership went from dissent to resistance (when needed), instigating social defense movements, is illustrated in AG by case studies of Denmark, Belgium, and Bulgaria. Besides illuminating how the Jews were saved, in Holocaust literature most often ascribed to the personal characteristics of helpers viewed as isolated individuals, my study of social defense movements enabled me to confirm a more general theory of how moral action may transform collectivities, enabling the helpers to transcend their everyday selves by helping others.

Three stages were noted.

1 *Recognition*: the victims must be seen or be made visible and viewed as endangered. Further, they must be defined as innocent victims whose plight is due to others' wrongful acts or to chance in order to counteract the common tendency to blame or to suppress sympathy with victims; Lerner attributes this to our need to believe in a "just world."[6] The victims must be defined within a common "universe of obligation."

2 *Acknowledgment*: potential leaders must be shown that their actions can help the group at risk to avoid further victimization. Group acknowledgment of responsibility depends on mobilization by group leaders, who call for support by appealing to pre-existing values and norms held by the group.

3 *Resource mobilization*: the organization of helping behavior depends on the use of pre-existing social networks, group resources, and the norm of helpfulness, which causes helping to snowball once it becomes the norm.

Church protest and resistance was involved in all these stages, but was especially critical in the first stage. The church leaders who spoke up promptly acknowledged Jews within their universe of obligation by affirming either that Jews belonged to a common religious family—"Our Lord was David's Son"—or a common nation or shared a common humanity: "The Jews are men, the Jews are women. All is not permitted against them."[7] Some of those who did not include Jews within their universe of obligation acknowledged this only after most Jews had been killed, or after the war.

A concluding note

Empirical methods may empower us to clarify the awesome task of understanding how social organization produces both good and evil. At the very least, such methods can falsify conventional wisdom: for example, that German Jewry (and other Jewish communities) awaited their fates passively with no attempt at flight. They can also unmask the myths (such as that of the Danish king who put on the yellow star) and provide a fuller explanation, giving all the actors a role. Numbers are valuable first for enabling us to observe what has been overlooked. In the case of AG, what had been overlooked was that in one of three states allied with, or occupied by, Germany during World War II (excluding the USSR), the majority or half the Jews did not become victims. Several methods were used in AG to test competing explanations of the causes of national differences in the victimization of the Jews, enabling scholars both to resolve the issue and to go beyond particularistic explanations, which have inhibited generalization and insight.

Empirical demonstration may also illuminate past controversies about moral evaluation and imputation of responsibility. This was shown in tracing the direct and indirect effects of actions; this reinforces arguments for moral responsibility, which have often been diverted by arguments about the actors' motives and hypothetical defenses; for example, arguing that possible actions not taken by Pius XII would have had no positive effect. Having shown the role of church protest and its effect on saving lives, ethicists can supplement judgments based on an "ethic of ultimate ends" with judgments based on an "ethic of responsibility."[8]

Both historical and statistical methods need to be supplemented by interpretivist methods, which bring the individual—and collectivities—back in as actors. The more we know of them, the more we realize that the victims of the Holocaust were no less rational (and irrational) than we are, enabling us to go beyond both blaming and idealizing the victims.

Lastly, AG sought to develop an explanation, tested by comparing the Armenian genocide and the Holocaust, of the historical preconditions for ideological genocide (not discussed here). This explanation has stimulated similar comparisons (Melson in 1992[9] and many others). The question of the roots of genocide is becoming more pertinent every day as masses of bodies float down rivers and fill ravines in different continents. Scholars concerned with social responsibility must seize the opportunity both to understand genocide and to devise policies to deter it.

Notes

1 Max Weber, "Politics as a Vocation," in Max Weber, *Essays in Sociology*, eds H.H. Gerth and C. Wright Mills (New York: Oxford University Press, 1946), 77, 78.
2 Helen Fein, *Accounting for Genocide: National Responses and Jewish Victimization During the Holocaust* (New York: The Free Press, 1979), 77, 80, 81.
3 Fein, *Accounting for Genocide*, 262–89.
4 Fein, *Accounting for Genocide*, 67.
5 Fein, *Accounting for Genocide*, 162.
6 Ervin Staub, *Positive Social Behavior and Morality* (New York: Academic Press, 1979), 1: 151.
7 Fein, *Accounting for Genocide*, 112, 114–18.
8 Weber, 122.
9 Robert Melson, *Revolution and Genocide: On the Origins of the Armenian Genocide and the Holocaust* (Chicago: University of Chicago Press, 1992).

19

REICHSKOMMISSARIAT OSTLAND

David Gaunt

Germany invaded the Soviet Union on 22 June 1941 and quickly conquered Belarus, Lithuania, and Latvia by the first week of July, and Estonia in the following months. As the German army advanced deeper into Russia, a civilian administration was set up in the Baltic region. The *Reichskommissariat Ostland* (East-land) was a special administrative unit of the Nazi occupation that combined the formerly independent states of Estonia, Latvia, and Lithuania with a newly created territory named *Weißruthenien* (White Ruthenia), made up of former Polish provinces and part of the Minsk region, now in Belarus. Most of this large area had been incorporated into the Soviet Union in 1940 as a consequence of the Hitler–Stalin pact of 1939. Although the Baltic nationalists expected their countries would revive as fully independent countries, as a *Reichskommissariat*, it was instead destined for economic exploitation and inclusion in Greater Germany. The *Ostland* administration existed from September 1941 until the Soviet re-conquest in mid-1944. It controlled a population of 8.5 million with a very large Jewish population particularly in Belarus, Lithuania, and southern Latvia (which had been part of the old Pale of Settlement). A large proportion of the skilled craftsmen, shopkeepers, factory employees, and professionals were Jews who lived in the cities and market towns.

It is difficult to establish the prewar Jewish population of the area because censuses were infrequent and not all were trustworthy. Dramatic changes in the prewar period also affected the size of the Jewish population. The whereabouts of tens of thousands of Polish refugees who had fled from the Nazi invasion of 1939 can only be speculated. About 15,000 Jews had just been caught up in Stalin's mass deportations of June 1941. Most Jews in Belarus, Lithuania, and Latvia found themselves trapped by the German invasion. Only in Estonia did a significant proportion escape by joining the Soviet retreat. Estimates of the Jewish inhabitants are: 4,000 in Estonia (of whom 3,000 managed to flee), 95,000 in Latvia, and 209,000 in Lithuania (including 65,000 in Vilnius). The White Ruthenian province of *Ostland* is very hard to judge since it was newly created out of parts taken from two countries, but it might have contained 250,000 to 300,000 Jews.

On the eve of war

The Hitler–Stalin pact of 23 August 1939 carved out a German and a Soviet sphere. The Baltic countries fell under heavy Soviet influence. The Red Army invaded eastern Poland, and except for Vilnius (given to Lithuania), the occupied territory was divided between the Soviet republics of Belarus and Ukraine. For a time, the three Baltic countries remained independent, but bullying and manipulation resulted in the total absorption of Estonia, Latvia, and Lithuania as Soviet republics in August 1940.

Faced with the prospect of the imminent Soviet takeover, many Jews were desperate to leave. A handful of foreign diplomats began to grant visas to Jews to escape in the short time remaining. In the Lithuanian capital of Kaunas, British Consul Preston provided 1,200 certificates for Jews to settle in Palestine. The Dutch Consul Jan Zwartendijk issued 2,345 visas to the Caribbean colony of Curaçao and arranged transit over the Soviet Union and Japan. The Japanese Consul Chiune Sugihara (acting against his government's orders) matched this and issued transit-visas to Japan. Eventually, over 2,000 Jews made their way to Japan.[1]

Once installed, the new communist regime confiscated private industry, repressed the nationalist political leadership, and set up branches of the *NKVD* (*Narodnyy Komissariat Vnutrennikh Del*, People's Commissariat of State Security). The 1-year experience of brutal Sovietization is a common point of departure for major Baltic Holocaust narratives, because it is believed to have increased popular antisemitism. Nazi propaganda used the brutality of the Soviet reign of terror to recruit collaborators and motivate anti-Jewish violence.[2] The communist ideological perspective targeted established national elites for destruction, and actively enlisted the working class and attracted the hitherto excluded Jewish minority to join the communist party. For the first time ever in the Baltics, Jews attained positions of some authority and held public functions, some rose to high communist party posts, and Jews were prominent in the Soviet security service.[3] A widespread myth in Eastern Europe equated all Jews with support for communism, and vice versa, and the year of Soviet rule did nothing to dispel this belief. In mid-June 1941, just days before the German invasion, Stalin ordered the exile of tens of thousands of the leading Baltic political, intellectual, and economically successful families. Although about 15,000 Jews had also been arrested and many Jewish businesses were confiscated, these arrests and deportations resulted in accusations that the Jews, as pro-Soviet, were collectively responsible. The Nazis expected to be able to benefit from the fresh feelings of antisemitism and believed that the Baltic peoples would spontaneously take revenge on the Jews and communists. When the German army invaded, the local population was still in shock over the deportations; in Kaunas and Riga, some atrocities took place when the German troops arrived, and in a few places pogroms were staged. The degree to which all of these events were spontaneous or initiated by the Nazis is a matter of considerable debate.

The Holocaust in *Ostland* is important for many reasons. First, the mass murder of Jews here signaled the first signs of a Nazi will to total extermination. It is possible to see how the genocidal intent quickly evolved a few weeks after the Nazi invasion. By late 1941, the Jews of the area had been close to being decimated, with nearly 80 percent of the entire Lithuanian Jewish population reported wiped out, and Estonia was declared *Judenrein* (cleared from Jews). Second, the killing here was not hidden away in secret extermination camps, but was carried out in the open through shooting, resulting in mass graves scattered throughout the region. Third, the perpetrators included not just the German soldiers attached to the *SS Einsatzgruppen*, the *Waffen-SS* brigades, the *Wehrmacht*, and reserve police battalions, but also involved tens of thousands of indigenous collaborators in a variety of paramilitary and police organizations. Fourth, from late 1941, untold thousands of European Jews were transported here in order to be murdered or to do slave labor. Fifth, the resistance movement was very significant and included several unique all-Jewish partisan brigades based in the deep, impenetrable forests.

To the disappointment of the Baltic peoples, the defeat of the Soviet regime merely turned into a new occupation, this time by the Nazis. The *Reichskommissariat* was subject to the same confusing decision-making processes that were the mark of Nazi rule. The chain of command in *Ostland* was very complex, with overlapping spheres of responsibility marked by aggressive rivalry between leaders. The civil occupation administration took over when the German army moved further east in the autumn of 1941. Officially, the *Reichskommissariat* was the responsibility of the Ministry for the Occupied Territories in the East, headed by the well-known Nazi publicist Alfred Rosenberg, who was born in Tallinn. Hinrich Lohse, a Gauleiter from Schleswig-Holstein, was appointed *Reichskommissar* for *Ostland*. Thousands of German careerists were placed in administrative offices throughout the area. However, Rosenberg's ministry was never very important as he was excluded from Hitler's inner circle.

Although the Nazi leadership was agreed over targeting Jews, there was disagreement about the tactics and tempo of eradication. The Jewish policy of *Reichskommissar* Lohse was *Vernichtung durch Arbeit*, that is, to keep alive those who could be "useful" to the economy—skilled craftsmen, shoemakers, tailors, seamstresses, and factory workers—in order to do slave labor on short rations. The useful worker-Jews were indeed doomed to die, but they would be placed in supervised camps and worked to death, rather than be shot. Lohse's policy was challenged by Heinrich Himmler, who pressed for quick and total annihilation. A third part in the conflict, the army of the *Wehrmacht*, vacillated. When, in the winter of 1941–42, it needed Jewish-produced supplies, it favored Lohse's line, but as the partisan movement grew stronger in late 1942, the army started perceiving all Jews as security risks and pressed for total extermination.

Himmler was one of Hitler's nearest confidantes. As head of the Reich Security Main Office (*Reichssicherheitshauptamt*, RSHA), the SS, the SS Security Service (*Sicherheitsdienst*, SD), the police, and the agencies dealing with Germans abroad, Himmler became ultimately responsible for concentration camps, ghettos (from the summer of 1943), and methods of extermination of Jews, Roma gypsies and other priority target groups. His nearest functionaries in the *Ostland* were the two Higher SS and Police Leaders (*Höhere SS- und Polizeiführer*, HSSPF), who were in charge of the local police, SS-brigades, and indigenous volunteer *Hilfspolizei* (auxiliary police) and *Schutzmannschaft* (local police). For the Baltic countries, at first this was Hans-Adolf Prützman, but in mid-November 1941, Friedrich Jeckeln replaced him. Jeckeln had developed a unique management system that enabled the killing of 10,000 people per day, the slaughter at Babi Yar being the most notorious of his previous acts. The HSSPF for Belarus was Erich von dem Bach-Zelewski, who was given the extra responsibility of coordinating the war against partisans. The most effective instruments of extermination were the *Einsatzgruppen* task forces that were trained as death-squads.

The first wave of genocide—1941

During the first weeks of the invasion, Himmler himself would visit the SS-brigades and the *Einsatzkommandos*. These visits usually involved oral orders and were followed by changes in the treatment of the Jewish population in the occupied territories. In the last days of July and start of August, Himmler inspected the killing squads in Lithuania and

Belarus. Visiting Riga, he had discussed setting up "police formations of Lithuanians, Latvians, Estonians, Ukrainians, etc. This is possible right away." This build-up of troops, police, and native auxiliaries provided the increased manpower needed for rapid mass murder. Himmler ordered the SS cavalry brigade: "All Jews must be shot. Drive the female Jews into the swamps." The head of *Einsatzgruppe A* urged that conditions required "an almost one hundred percent immediate cleansing of the entire *Ostland*." From this moment, the death-squads changed tactics from small-scale shooting of groups and individuals to large-scale executions with hundreds of victims, with no concern for sex or age. Himmler told the soldiers that they should consider every Jew to be a partisan, and he demanded that they step up the tempo of killing. Perhaps the background was the failure to instigate the Baltic peoples to full-blown anti-Jewish pogroms everywhere, and the realization that the Germans just had to organize it themselves. To perform genocide, the designated German task forces were too small and had to be reinforced by SS units and local collaborators. *Einsatzkommando 3*, together with Lithuanian auxiliaries, killed the first Jewish women and children on 5 August. And at about the same time, *Einsatzkommando 2* did likewise in Latvia. The daily number of victims claimed by the commandos increased greatly as actions grew in size. At Panevesys in Lithuania on 23 August, at a mass execution, 1,609 Jewish children died along with 4,602 women and 1,312 men. This was a sign of a new policy of genocide. Christopher Browning calls it a decision made in the "euphoria of victory."[4]

The German *Wehrmacht* soldiers were given special guidelines just before the invasion. "Bolshevism is the mortal enemy of the National Socialist German people. Germany's fight is against this corrosive world-view and its bearers. This fight requires ruthless and energetic measures against Bolshevik agitators, partisans, saboteurs, Jews and ruthless elimination of active or passive resistance."[5] Other propaganda statements targeted the "Jewish-Bolshevik intelligentsia," the "Jewish-Bolshevik worldview," and the "Jewish-Bolshevik system." However, most of the leading communists had been evacuated at the start of the war, so the full brunt of this hate-speech guideline fell upon the heads of the hundreds of thousands of entrapped Jews.

Behind the German army vanguard followed a few special task forces belonging to the SD. The *Ostland* was the territory of the mobile killing squads of *Einsatzgruppe A*, with 990 men, headed by Franz Walter Stahlecker, which was responsible for the Baltic countries; and *Einsatzgruppe B*, with 655 men, headed by Arthur Nebe, which was active in Belarus and Russia. These task forces were created before the invasion in order to capture and liquidate Soviet functionaries, particularly Jewish communists, but they began to indiscriminately target the entire adult male Jewish population. We know most about *Einsatzgruppe A* from the many *Ereignismeldungen* (Events reports) it submitted to Berlin, which specified, with date and place, the number of Jewish men, women, and children shot. The force was divided into four *Einsatzkommandos* (1a, 1b, 2, and 3), each with between 105 to 170 members. According to the summary report of Karl Jäger, head of *Einsatzkommando 3*, his command performed 112 executions in 71 separate locations in Lithuania, Belarus, and Latvia between 4 July and 1 December 1941. On 17 occasions, the number of victims for one day's shooting exceeded 2,000. The total of victims claimed was 133,346; nearly all of them were Jews, but the number also included communists, POWs, and mental hospital patients. A large part of the killing had been done by a single, small flying squad (*Rollkommando*) headed by Joachim Hamann, which had only eight or 10 Germans, but included many Lithuanian volunteers. In

Jäger's opinion, "the goal of solving the Jewish problem in Lithuania has been reached by EK 3. There are no Jews in Lithuania anymore except the worker-Jews and their families," who totaled 34,500. He complained that the civil administration had stopped him short: "I intended to kill off these work-Jews and their families too, but met with the strongest protest from the civil administration and the *Wehrmacht*, which culminated in the prohibition: These Jews and their families may not be shot dead!"[6] In total, *Einsatzgruppe A* reported that, by the end of 1941, its various units had murdered 249,420 people.

Einsatzgruppe B reported that 45,467 had been executed throughout Belarus. *Einsatzgruppe B* stayed only briefly in *Ostland* and advanced further into Russia, basing itself in Smolensk. It had liquidated only a small proportion of the Belarusian Jews, and as a consequence Himmler diverted various SS brigades, members of *Einsatzgruppe A* and Lithuanian and Latvian paramilitaries, to annihilate Belarusian Jews.[7] By October 1941, there were 4,428 German members of SS death-squads and paramilitary police engaged in the liquidation of *Ostland*'s Jews. But this figure was overshadowed by a total of 31,804 Baltic collaborators enrolled in various auxiliary units, of which the most notorious was the Latvian Arājs commando and the Lithuanian *Tautinio Darbo Apsauga* (National Labor Welfare) battalions.[8]

The Germans sought out or created native groups who would appear to initiate anti-Jewish massacres without the participation of German troops. This was part of a strategy termed *Selbstreinigungsaktionen* ("self-cleansing"), and German photographers would document the events. However, *Einsatzgruppe A* commander Stahlecker reported that initiating spontaneous anti-Jewish pogroms in Lithuania had been "surprisingly" difficult. The only major pogrom he could give details on was that perpetrated by Algirdas Klimaitis's unit in Kaunas on 25 June, which caused the deaths of more than 1,500 Jews. The most publicized event was that of a small gang, possibly prisoners newly released from the Soviet jail, who humiliated, beat, and then slaughtered in broad daylight a group of as many as 50 Jews at the Lietūkis bus garage in Kaunas on 27 June, after the Germans had taken control. German officers looked on and photographers documented the incident.[9] Provoking pogroms proved even more difficult in Latvia, although it was possible to entice the Latvian auxiliary police to kill about 400 Jews and destroy the Riga synagogues on 4 July. In Riga, several hundred Latvians, headed by Viktors Arājs, had already seized the police headquarters, and met with Stahlecker on 1 July 1941. This grew to become the Sonderkommando Arājs that was used as a death-squad not just in Latvia, but in Belarus as well.[10] Although it proved impossible to mobilize the entire Baltic community to anti-Jewish violence, there were enough volunteers who were willing, and they were transported over long distances to perpetrate the atrocities. Historian Alfonsas Eidintas concludes that more than half of Lithuania's murdered Jews died at the hands of Lithuanian executioners, who were nicknamed *žydžaudys* (Jew shooters).[11] In Estonia, the Nazis found that an anti-Soviet partisan organization was already in place—the Forest Brothers, made up of deserters from the Red Army. In early July, the Forest Brothers joined the German campaign, established local authority in municipalities behind the German lines, and built up a large home guard, the *Omakaitse*. Some of the home guard participated in killing Jews and Roma.[12]

In Belarus, the situation was different. Here, the non-Jewish population was Slavic, either Polish or Belarusian, and the Germans did not trust the Polish element. In the Minsk area, which had been Soviet for a generation, little anti-communist opposition existed. The situation was different in the former Polish provinces. But at the most, only auxiliary local police could be recruited, and they might participate in local massacres, but they are not known to have acted far away from their home bases. For instance, in the town of Mir, German soldiers and local police killed about 1,500 Jews on 9 November 1941.[13] In the end, Latvian and Lithuanian executioners were brought in to aid the German killing squads.

In ghettos, the Nazis had ordered the formation of self-administrations to be responsible for the enforcement of German regulations and fill requests for workers, but also to select individuals for extermination. The Germans regulated Jewish life in detail, including wearing of six-pointed stars on clothing, curtailing the possibility to buy food, rationing, and the ability to move about. Most small ghettos lasted for only a short while, but a very few, such as Vilnius, Kaunas, Minsk, and Riga, were kept for several years. In these large ghettos, there would be separate sections, one for the workers and their families, the other for those who were not considered "useful." In the Minsk and Riga ghettos, the eastern Jews were kept separate from the "German" Jewish newcomers.[14] Repeatedly, selections were made from internment camps and groups of Jews were taken for execution. Those who survived were those considered economically useful, often in the hands of the civilian administration, and they were employed in factories and workshops. Slave labor was used on road construction, fortification, loading and unloading supplies, as well as harvesting. Some were even hired out as day laborers. The worker-Jews were an important labor reserve and often were the only skilled craftsmen available for the army's needs.

Up until then, the Nazi leadership had agreed to liquidate the "Russian" Jews, but hesitated to treat the European Jews with the same brutality. In November and December 1941, the killing of eastern Jews increased dramatically, particularly in Latvia, after the appointment of the new, bloodthirsty *Höherer SS und Polizeiführer* Jeckeln. One motive for the intensity of killing was to prepare space in the ghettos for the arrival of Jews from Greater Germany. The arriving German Jews were not to be killed outright, but rather would land in ghettos in Minsk and Riga, where it was expected they would work with German-like efficiency. However, the first five trainloads destined to Riga were diverted to Kaunas. The local SS did not understand the deferential treatment, and these people were killed on arrival at Fort Nine, which was not part of the orders. Alarmed, Himmler sent an urgent telegram on 30 November: "The Jewish transport from Berlin. No liquidation," and the immediate killing of German Jews decreased. However, the decimation of the eastern Jews reached high numbers. In the Minsk ghetto, 12,000 Jews were murdered on 7 November. In Riga, on 29 November and 9 December, a total of 24,000 Jews were marched from the ghetto and shot in the back of the head in open pits.

The second wave of genocide

But the German war machine halted by late 1941 without having defeated the Red Army or having captured Moscow and Leningrad. The Germans needed to rethink as winter approached. Jews deported from Germany had also begun arriving in *Ostland*, and orders came that they were not to be killed. These deportees were settled into separate "German" ghettos and were lured to work hard by promises that after the war they could return home. There is some speculation that there had been a plan to send the

German Jews further east to Mogilev, where an extermination camp was projected.[15] Cremation furnaces intended for it were redirected to Auschwitz–Birkenau. The Germans needed to prepare for a long war, and this meant new supplies, ammunition, uniforms, replacements for lost equipment, and repair shops with skilled mechanics. Extermination of the surviving worker-Jews ceased as they were placed in work groups serving military needs. Instead, the death-squads expanded the spectrum of target priorities to Roma, those defined as "bandits," the mentally ill, criminals, and a catch-all category of *Sonstige Reichsfeinde* (other enemy of the Reich).

In the Baltics, a new group began to be exterminated because it was not "useful." This was the Roma gypsies, 3,800 of whom lived in Latvia, the largest population in the Baltic countries. In the port town of Liepāja, about 100 Roma men, women, and children were arrested and murdered on 5 December 1941. The motive given was that nomadic gypsies spread epidemic disease, were unreliable, and did not do useful work. The civil administration targeted specifically the "non-sedentary" gypsies, who they ordered to be treated "like the Jews." However, it was not easy to distinguish nomadic from sedentary, so most local police arrested all of the gypsies in their district and waited for further orders. Estonian gypsies were incarcerated in the Harku prison, 243 were executed on 27 October 1942, and about 200 women and children were taken from Tallinn Central prison and killed in early February 1943. Throughout 1942, gypsies were killed in *Ostland*; for instance, 301 were murdered by *Einsatzgruppe B* in the last 2 weeks of September.[16] The few still alive in spring 1944 were sent to Auschwitz–Birkenau for destruction.

After the Wannsee conference of January 1942, even more trainloads of European Jews began to arrive from Germany, France, and Czechoslovakia, and they filled the largest *Ostland* ghettos, repopulating even places that had been declared *Judenfrei*. German attitudes to the "civilized" western Jews were quite different from those held for the "savage" eastern Jews. From Minsk, General Commissar Wilhelm Kube complained that he had not minded the killing of Belarusian Jews, but was unwilling to liquidate European Jews. "I am certainly hard and prepared to help with the solution of the Jewish question, but people from our cultural world are something entirely different from the local, degenerate hordes." Selections were made on or just after train-arrival, and persons deemed useless were destroyed outright, while the able-bodied were assigned to workplaces.

With the exception of Belarus, from January 1942 to March 1943 was a period of relative stability in the big Baltic ghettos, particularly for worker-Jews and their families. Even in the countryside, massacres ceased because the very cold weather made digging graves impossible. However, in the Minsk ghetto, there was massive slaughter in March and July 1942. Without any apparent pause, both Russian and European Jews were being killed at the little-known death camp of Maly Trostinetz, just outside Minsk.[17] And in the countryside, killing was much more intense than it had been in 1941. Martin Dean reckons that 60,000–95,000 Jews had been killed in Belarus in 1941, and that number had increased by 125,000–175,000 murders perpetrated in 1942–43.[18]

Mass executions of ghetto prisoners in Lithuania and Latvia resumed in April 1943, and very soon the ghettos would be emptied. It became increasingly clear after defeats at Stalingrad and in North Africa that the Germans would lose the war and the army in Russia was retreating. Partisan sabotage became a serious problem, and whatever support the Nazis had initially received from the non-Jewish population had disintegrated.

Liquidation of the few remaining ghettos stepped up. The SS took over from the civil administration and turned the ghettos into concentration camps. In September, the Jews of the Vilnius ghetto were fired from 72 workplaces, and most were sent to labor camps in Estonia. The ghettos of Belarus were destroyed in August to October 1943. The Kaunas ghetto ceased to exist in autumn 1943. The population of the Riga ghetto was first drastically reduced, and it was then turned into a concentration camp. At this time, a large number of younger Jews managed to escape and join the partisans in the forests. Throughout the region, occupation authorities ordered that corpses from mass graves be recovered and burned.

Many of the Jewish ghetto workers were transferred to a series of small slave-labor camps established by an order of Himmler given on 21 June 1943 to meet acute military needs. At that time, there were about 54,000 Jews left in the Baltic region, and 40,000 were deemed fit to work.[19] The Vaivara concentration camp network was set up in mid-September 1943, and it grew to include 23 subordinate camps throughout Estonia. The main product was artificial oil refined from shale deposits. The Nazis considered shale oil to be the primary strategic resource in the former Baltic states, and it had become even more important as the Germans retreated. Initially, the workers had been Red Army POWs, but 9,207 Jews came to reinforce them.[20] The Jewish prisoners also worked as miners, road-builders, trench-diggers, in fort construction, or as shoemakers and tailors. The slave-laborers in the Vaivara complex were often shifted back and forth between camps as the need for labor varied. Many came from the ghettos of Vilnius, Kaunas, and Kaiserswald (near Riga), but hundreds were newly arrived from central and western Europe. The Vaivara shale works existed up to late August 1944, when the Russian offensive recaptured Estonia. As the Germans retreated, 4,150 Jewish workers were shipped west to the Stutthof concentration camp outside Danzig. Other workers were liquidated, and the corpses at Klooga labor camp were still burning when the Red Army arrived.[21]

By the end of the war, Eidintas estimates that 160,000 (ca 80 percent) of Lithuania's Jews had been murdered, while Ezergailis reckons that about 61,000 (ca 65 percent) of Latvia's Jews were dead. Weiss-Wendt establishes that 963 Estonian Jews were killed, which was about 25 percent. Statistics for Belarus are harder to make. However, Dean, as already noted, believes that the two waves of killing in Weißruthenien resulted in at a minimum 185,000 Jewish deaths of an original prewar population of 250,000.[22] On top of this, the area witnessed the killing of tens of thousands of western and central European Jews.

Jewish resistance

After the first 6 months of universal mass murder and forced deportations, most of the survivors were incarcerated in large or medium-sized ghettos in the cities of *Ostland*. The ghettos were under the authority of the civilian administration until the SS took over through Himmler's order of 21 June 1943. The largest ghettos, Kaunas, Minsk, Riga, Šauliai, and Vilnius, existed up to late summer and fall of 1943, when the able-bodied inmates were dispersed to various labor camps, and the children, elderly, and invalids were exterminated. Conditions in the ghettos were bad, but they were better than in the concentration camps because families could keep together and a multifaceted social and intellectual life emerged. The Nazis decreed that there must be a self-administration council of elders (*Ältestenräte* or *Judenräte*) to implement regulations and keep order in every ghetto. For this purpose there was also a Jewish police force armed with truncheons. Many ghetto Jews worked in the German factories, repair workshops, and even weapon depots, and some could steal guns and ammunition from their workplaces. Unknown to the self-administration, secret resistance movements grew up.

From the start, young people in the ghettos prepared self-defense and stole or bought guns and other weapons. Some ghettos were in terrain that was hard to fence in, or where sewage tunnels ran under the streets. Secret openings could enable some contact with other ghettos and with resistance groups on the outside. Vilnius even received money to buy guns from the Warsaw ghetto. As a rule, members of political associations such as the communists, Bund, the Zionist-revisionist Betar, and the Zionist-socialist *Hashomer Hatzair* and youth clubs formed the hub of activities. Abba Kovner in Vilnius proclaimed the need for armed resistance: "Let us not be led as sheep to the slaughter ... Brethren! Better fall as free fighters than to live at the mercy of murderers. Rise up! Rise up until your last breath."[23]

The character of the resistance differed, however. The Minsk ghetto was dominated by members of communist associations and other Soviet-era groups, but had relatively little presence of Zionists. The Jews in Minsk appear to have had the best contacts with the non-Jewish population and the Red Army partisans. In Vilnius, the ghetto prisoners had a long experience of Polish antisemitism, which prepared them psychologically for self-defense. Here Zionist groups dominated. Successful escape from Minsk and Vilnius was favored by the closeness of the deep forests of Belowiez, Lipszan, Naliboki, Rudninkai, and Nacha. A stream of male and female activists managed to escape and join up with partisan brigades, the rule for acceptance being that each must bring along a gun. The Kaunas ghetto was filled with Lithuanian Jews, and they had a history of passivity, which made them less inclined to resist. Riga's large ghetto had many German Jews who had little possibility of contacting the Latvians and had very far to travel to reach a deep forest; thus activity was lower. But in the small Latvian-Jewish ghetto, guns stolen from the Germans were smuggled in by the Jewish police force. However, preparations ended when the Germans discovered the plans and executed all the policemen.

By the second half of 1942, the general partisan movement in *Ostland* had emerged as a growing danger to the Nazi occupation, and considerable effort was made to stamp it out. In the Vilnius ghetto, the *Fareynigte Partizaner Organizatsie* (United Partisan Organization, FPO) formed on 21 January 1942, and it grew to several hundred members. Its goal was armed defense in case the ghetto was to be liquidated. Members left the ghetto through tunnels and raided weapons from the Germans, and even committed acts of sabotage. The *Yidishe Algemeyne Kamfs Organizatsie* (Jewish General Fighting Organization) was set up in Kaunas ghetto in the summer of 1943, but was less successful than the Vilnius partisans. A total of 1,800 persons managed to flee from the Lithuanian ghettos and at least 4,240 from 16 investigated Belarusian ghettos joined the resistance in the forests.[24]

In the forests along the Lithuanian and Belarusian border zone, the Soviets had organized official but small partisan detachments, built on a core of Red Army soldiers who were stranded behind enemy lines. The first Jews met up with them at the end of 1941. In 1942, the number of Jews among the partisans reached 350. Escapees from the ghettos and camps arrived in such numbers that several official all-Jewish brigades linked to the Red Army were formed in 1943.[25] The usual type of operation was sabotaging bridges and factories, blowing up trains and railroad tracks, destroying communication lines, and ambushing enemy soldiers. The most famous all-Jewish unit was the detachment led by the charismatic Tuvia Bielski in Naliboki forest, which, by the summer of 1944, had grown to 1,200 members. It differed from other partisan groups by accepting any Jew regardless of age or sex and actively seeking out and saving stranded individuals, particularly women. It stood for the largest armed rescue of Jews by Jews in Nazi occupied Europe.[26]

Memory

After World War II, the *Ostland* became part of the Soviet Union's republics of Belarus, Estonia, Latvia, and Lithuania. While the Soviet Union commemorated the heroic sacrifices of what it called the Great Patriotic War, it downplayed the extent of Jewish suffering. There was very little research done on the Holocaust. The well-known writers and journalists Ilya Ehrenburg and Vasily Grossman compiled and edited a massive number of Jewish diaries, witness testimonies, official reports, interrogations, and articles on the fate of the Jews in the Baltic States, Belarus, and Ukraine, in *The Black Book of Russian Jewry*. The book was set and ready for printing in 1946 when it simply disappeared, and the manuscript was not rediscovered until the 1970s, but still could not be issued. An English translation was published in 1980; the Russian had to wait until 1993, after the fall of the Soviet Union.[27]

Symptomatic of the neglect of the Jewish Holocaust, when the Soviet regime placed commemorative plaques at sites of executions or concentration camps, the text would state that the memorial was raised over murdered "Soviet citizens," rather than Jews. After the re-establishment of independence in 1990, the new independent Baltic States set up international historical commissions to investigate war crimes committed during the Nazi occupation, and these focused on the Holocaust and the degree of collaboration. Evidence for collaboration proved strong.

Notes

1 Alfred Erich Senn, *Lithuania 1940. Revolution from Above* (Amsterdam and New York: Rodopi, 2007), 230–31.
2 Andrew Ezergailis, *The Holocaust in Latvia 1941–1944. The Missing Center* (Riga: Historical Institute of Latvia, 1996), 94–106; Alfonsas Eidintas, *Jews, Lithuanians and the Holocaust* (Vilnius: Versus Aureus, 2003; original 2002), 133–57; Estonian International Commission for the Investigation of Crimes Against Humanity, *Estonia 1940–1945. Reports of the Estonian International Commission for the Investigation of Crimes Against Humanity* (Tallinn: Estonian International Commission, 2006), 1–412; Anton Weiss-Wendt, *Murder without Hatred. Estonians and the Holocaust* (Syracuse, New York: Syracuse University Press, 2009), 48–56.
3 Arkadii Zeltser, "Jews in the Upper Ranks of the NKVD, 1934–41," *Jews in Russia and Eastern Europe*, vol. 52 (2004): 64–90.
4 Christopher Browning, *The Origins of the Final Solution. The Evolution of Nazi Jewish Policy, September 1939–March 1942* (London: William Heinemann, 2004), 309–29.
5 Browning, *The Origins of the Final Solution*, 222–23.
6 "The Jäger Report, Kaunas December 1, 1941" Appendix A in Eidintas, *Jews, Lithuanians and the Holocaust*, 488–96.
7 Peter Longerich, *Heinrich Himmler: Biographie* (München: Siedler, 2008), 548–53.
8 Helmut Krausnick and Hans-Heinrich Wilhelm, *Die Truppen des Weltanschaungskrieges: Die Einsatzgruppen der Sicherheitspolizei und des SD, 1938–1942* (Stuttgart: Deutsche Verlags-Anstalt, 1981), 167–70.

9 Eidintas, *Jews, Lithuanians and the Holocaust*, 182–95.

10 Ezergailis, *The Holocaust in Latvia*, 173–202.

11 Eidintas, *Jews, Lithuanians and the Holocaust*, 451.

12 Eugenia Gurin-Loov, *Suur häving. Eesti juutide katastroof* (Tallinn: Estonian Jewish Community, 1994); Meelis Maripuu, "Execution of Estonian Jews in Local Detention Institutions in 1941–42," in Estonian International Commission, *Estonia 1940–1945*, 651–61.

13 Martin Dean, "Microcosm: Collaboration and Resistance during the Holocaust in the Mir Rayon of Belarus, 1941–44," in *Collaboration and Resistance During the Holocaust. Belarus, Estonia, Latvia, Lithuania*, eds David Gaunt, Paul A. Levine and Laura Palosuo (Bern: Peter Lang, 2004), 223–59.

14 Gertrude Schneider, *Journey into Terror: Story of the Riga Ghetto* (Westport, Connecticut: Praeger, 2001).

15 Götz Aly, *Final Solution: Nazi Population Policy and the Murder of the European Jews* (London: Arnold, 1999), 223–24.

16 Michael Zimmermann, *Rassenutopie und Genozid: Die nationalsozialistische "Lösung der Zigeunerfrage"* (Hamburg: Christians, 1996), 267–76; Wolfgang Benz, Konrad Kwiet and Jürgen Matthäus, eds, *Einsatz im "Reichskommissariat Ostland:" Dokumente zum Völkermord im Baltikum und in Weißrußland 1941–1944* (Berlin: Metropol, 1998), 229.

17 *Lager' smerti Trostenets. Dokumenti i materiali* (Minsk: Belarus National Archive, 2003).

18 Martin Dean, *Collaboration in the Holocaust: Crimes of the Local Police in Belorussia and Ukraine, 1941–44* (New York: St Martin's Press, 2000), 170.

19 Weiss-Wendt, *Murder without Hatred*.

20 Ruth Bettina Birn, *Die Sicherheitspolizei in Estland 1941–1944: Eine Studie zur Kollaboration im Osten* (Paderborn: Ferdinand Schöningh, 2006), 171–81.

21 Weiss-Wendt, *Murder without Hatred*, 314–22.

22 Eidintas, *Jews, Lithuanians and the Holocaust*, 16; Ezergailis, *The Holocaust in Latvia*, xix; Dean, *Collaboration in the Holocaust*, 170; Weiss-Wendt, *Murder without Hatred*, 351.

23 Yitzhak Arad, *Ghetto in Flames: The Struggle and Destruction of the Jews in Vilna in the Holocaust* (New York: Holocaust Library, 1982), 232.

24 Shalom Cholawsky, *The Jews of Belorussia during World War II* (Amsterdam: Harwood, 1998), 303.

25 Dov Levin, *Fighting Back: Lithuanian Jewry's Armed Resistance to the Nazis, 1941–1945* (New York: Holmes and Meier, 1985), 109–25.

26 Nechama Tec, *Defiance: The Bielski Partisans* (New York: Oxford University Press, 1993).

27 Ilya Ehrenburg and Vasily Grossman, *The Complete Black Book of Russian Jewry* (New Brunswick, New Jersey: Transaction, 2003; original 1946); Lukasz Hirszowicz, "The Holocaust in the Soviet Mirror," in *The Holocaust in the Soviet Union*, eds Lucjan Dobroszycki and Jeffrey S. Gurock (Armonk, New York: M. E. Sharpe, 1993), 29–59.

20

THE HOLOCAUST IN WESTERN EUROPE

Wolfgang Seibel

When German troops invaded the Netherlands, Belgium, and France in May 1940, some 500,000 Jews were living in these countries. By September 1944, approximately 200,000 Jews had been deported to the death camps in eastern Europe, where almost all of them were murdered in Auschwitz and Sobibor. Following the defeat of their armed forces and the British expeditionary forces in June 1940, the Netherlands, Belgium, and France were under German rule for more than four years, a period stretching from early summer of 1940 until late summer of 1944; parts of Belgium and the Netherlands remained in German hands well into 1945 and even up to the end of the war on 8 May. German officials conceived of this occupation as a supervisory administration (*Aufsichtsverwaltung*) with only a thin layer of German officials at the top and the main body of national, that is, native administration and judiciary remaining entirely intact. Dependence on indigenous human and organizational resources was thus what characterized the situation of the German occupation regime in western Europe, in total contrast to the situation in the east.

This characteristic also impacted the persecution and annihilation of the Jews, which was prepared and carried out by the respective German occupation administration, relying on national agencies. This general pattern, however, varied substantially cross-nationally. The Netherlands, Belgium, and France display significant differences both in the structures of their occupation regimes and the position of the persecutors within those structures, as well as in the respective rates of Jewish victimization, ranging from 25 percent in France to 43 percent in Belgium and 76 percent in the Netherlands.

Legislative and administrative measures of persecution

Persecution and deportation of the Jews by means of modern administration instead of mass murder on the spot was the crucial characteristic of the Holocaust in western Europe. The basic judicial and organizational patterns had been developed and tested in Germany proper, in Austria, and in the "Protectorate of Bohemia-Moravia."[1] It was based on two components. One was a bipolar centralization of the SS and Gestapo apparatus on one side and of the representation of the Jewish community on the other. The second component was a combination of economic and police-repressive persecution, each based on systematic legislation and the human and organizational resources of public administration, and a broad range of subsidiary agencies. Economic measures of persecution, however, were initiated soon after the beginning of the occupation, and were carried out more or less independently from the SS or Gestapo apparatus, while the latter initiated and supervised police-repressive persecution which eventually led to deportation.

The core-group of perpetrators all over German-occupied Europe was formed by the SS and police forces. These were led by a central authority, either a Higher SS and Police Leader (*Höhere SS- und Polizeiführer*, HSSPF), as in the Netherlands, or, starting in 1942, in France; or a Representative of the Head of the Security Police and Security Service (*Beauftragter des Chefs der Sicherheitspolizei und des SD*, BdS).[2] Each of these authorities reported directly to the *Reich* Security Main Office (*Reichssicherheitshauptamt*, RSHA). The RSHA handled the Netherlands, Belgium, and France as a single area, and strove for the highest possible degree of coordination with regard to the execution of the "Final Solution."

The discrimination of Jews, the economic measures taken against them, and the preparations made for their deportation were all conducted according to the same scheme in all three countries, although initiated and monitored by different agencies on the German side. At the command of the German authorities or, in the case of France, the Vichy government of Henri Pétain and Pierre Laval, Jewish representative organizations were created in all three countries to facilitate the command and control of the Jewish communities (the *Joodse Raad* in Amsterdam, the *Association des Juifs de Belgique* and the *Union Générale des Israélites des France*). The members of these "councils" were responsible to the German authorities or their native collaborators for the preparation of the discrimination, expropriation, and deportation measures demanded.

Anti-Jewish legislation and decrees in the Netherlands were published in the *Verordnungsblatt für die besetzten niederländischen Gebiete (VOBl)*. Subsequently, the legislation was implemented through Dutch administrators. Legislation and decrees affecting the Jews were also published in the *Joodsche Weekblad*, which was the only remaining Jewish periodical in the Netherlands. It was edited by the Jewish Council of Amsterdam, which underlined its quasi-official character.

The first decree affecting the Jews not *expressis verbis* but *de facto* was the ban on ritual slaughter published on 31 July 1940, which prohibited "cruelty to animals."[3] On 28 August 1940, German occupation authorities forbade the appointment of Jewish civil servants. A decree of 4 November 1940 permitted mass firing of Jewish civil servants. A decree of 22 October 1940 stipulated that Jewish businesses had to be registered.[4] This was combined with a formal regulation of who was to be defined as Jewish. On 10 January 1941, a decree stipulated that all Jews according to the official definition had to register with the respective Dutch authorities.[5] On this basis, some 160,000 residents with at least one Jewish grandparent were registered, of whom some 140,000 were subsequently declared "full Jews." In April 1941, Dutch authorities issued identity cards (that had not existed before in the Netherlands) in which the capital "J" was stamped if the holder was Jewish. On 12 March 1941, businesses that had been declared "Jewish" were taken over by "Trustees" (*Treuhänder*) on the basis of a decree which also stipulated that the person in charge could sell the property.[6] In early June 1941, Jews were banned from beaches and swim clubs.

A decree of 11 August 1941 on "The treatment of Jewish Assets" stipulated the registration and central administration of any kind of assets owned by Jews.[7] The institution in charge was the bank Lippmann, Rosenthal & Co., Amsterdam, Sarphatistraat, which purposefully was forced to keep the names of its former Jewish owners. The bank, however, was nothing but the main institutional pillar of legalized robbery.[8]

A second decree of 21 May 1942 extended the range of the affected property to artwork, any sort of precious metal, and jewelry.[9] Jewish creditors had to concede their claims to the Lippmann and Rosenthal bank. The same was stipulated for foreign assets owned by Jews, the content of lock boxes, life insurances, etc. With these two decrees, dubbed the "Liro-Decrees" (from Lippmann and Rosenthal), Jews in the Netherlands were entirely stripped of their personal assets. This happened during the weeks immediately preceding the deportations, which began in July 1942. A decree of 27 April 1942 imposed the star of David to be worn by every Jew of 6 years and older, effective 4 June 1942.

Just as in the Netherlands, the ban on ritual slaughtering was the initial step of anti-Jewish legislation in Belgium.[10] It was followed by two decrees explicitly directed against the Jews—the decree of 28 October 1940 stipulating the registration of all Jews living in Belgium with municipal authorities, and a second decree which enabled Belgian authorities to exclude Jews from the civil service.[11] Some 43,000 Jews registered on the basis of the decree of 28 October. On 31 May 1941, a supplementary decree (*Verordnung zur Ergänzung der Judenverordnung vom 28. Oktober 1940*) laid the groundwork for the economic persecution of the Jews.[12] Businesses owned by Jews had to be flagged up as such, Jewish owners had to be excluded from the business, and Jewish assets were subject to seizure. By a decree of 29 August 1941, the cities of Antwerp, Brussels, Liège, and Charleroi were assigned to the Jews as compulsory residential municipalities. The star of David to be worn by every Jew of 6 years of age and older was imposed on 7 June 1942.[13]

What characterized the occupation regime in France and the persecution measures directed against the Jews was the parallel existence of French and German legislation, which, to some extent, turned out to be mutually radicalizing. Immediate jurisdiction of German legislation was restricted to the occupied (northern) zone, while the Germans had to rely on political pressure on French authorities in Vichy for legislation in the southern unoccupied zone. This system was upheld even after the Germans occupied the southern zone in November 1942, because they wanted to avoid violating the terms of the June 1940 armistice with the French.

In July, August, and September 1940, the Vichy government issued a series of decrees which were more or less immediately directed against the Jews. A law of 22 July 1940 stipulated that all naturalizations based on the citizenship law of 10 August 1927 were going to be re-examined.[14] This law affected many immigrants from central and eastern European countries, among them thousands of Jews. A series of decrees issued on 17 July, 14 August, and 10 September 1940 stipulated the dismissal of French citizens whose fathers were not French from the civil service and subsequently from the free professions.[15] This again affected Jewish immigrants and their children to a large extent. By decree of 23 July 1940, French citizens who had taken residence outside French soil (including the territories overseas and the colonies) were stripped of their citizenship.[16] Their property and financial assets were confiscated. Again, those primarily affected were Jews who had fled the country when the Germans invaded France in May 1940.

The first measure taken by the Vichy government that was explicitly directed against the Jews came on 27 August 1940 with the revocation of a law issued in April 1939 banning antisemitic propaganda in the press.[17] This was followed by two decrees of 3 and 4 October 1940, made public on 18 October.[18] These decrees contained a French definition of who was considered to be a "Jew" that went even further than the German version (since it explicitly used the term "Jewish Race" [*race juive*] instead of "Jewish

Denomination" [*religion juive*], the term contained in the first anti-Jewish decree of 27 September 1940 issued by the German military government on 27 September 1940). The French *Statuts des Juifs* of 3 and 4 October 1940 not only stipulated the dismissal of Jews from the civil service, the army, public office, state-owned enterprises, the educational professions, and a series of cultural and journalistic professions, but also empowered the prefects of the departments and the provinces to commit Jews of non-French citizenship to special camps or forced residence areas (*résidence forcée*).

Parallel to these French decrees, the supreme German military authority had issued its own anti-Jewish decrees, the first of which, issued on 27 September 1940, stipulated the compulsory registration of Jews with their respective municipal administration and the marking of businesses owned by Jews. The decree also barred Jews from returning to the occupied zone regardless of their place of residence.[19] The second German decree, issued on 18 October 1940, initiated the economic persecution of the Jews by requiring that businesses owned by Jews could be subjected to provisional administration by non-Jews.[20] In April 1941, this was followed by two additional decrees, which subjected Jewish assets of various sorts to the administration of a special French authority, the *Service du Contrôle des Administrateurs Provisoires* (SCAP).[21] These German decrees were adopted by the Vichy government and thus expanded all over French territory by a series of French laws whose capstone was the law of 22 July 1941, which demanded that Jewish assets—firms, real-estate, securities, life insurances, cash—be registered and transferred to the state-owned *Caisse des Depôts et Consignations*.[22] The deposited assets were administered by the *Commissariat Général aux Question Juives* (CGQJ), the Vichy ministry of Jewish affairs, without whose approval the deposited assets could not be accessed.[23] The Vichy law of 22 July 1941 was the key legislative act in the economic persecution of the Jews in France. It was also used and further institutionalized when German military authorities imposed an arbitrary fine of one billion French francs on the Jews in the occupied zone in December 1941, and plundered the assets deposited in the *Caisse des Depôts et Consignations*.[24]

In early 1942, another wave of anti-Jewish measures was designed to pave the way for the implementation of the "Final Solution" in France as well as in the other German-occupied territories in western Europe. A general curfew was imposed on the Jews in the occupied zone on 7 February 1942.[25] The star of David became compulsory for the Jews in the occupied zone on 1 June 1942.[26] Immediately prior to the large-scale deportations, Jews were excluded from attending public events and establishments. Shopping time for Jews was restricted to 3–4 pm.[27]

From the above scan, it is clear that Jewish legislative and administrative measures were remarkably homogenous in German-occupied western Europe. The implementation of the "Final Solution," the deportation and mass murder of the Jewish population, nonetheless took different trajectories in the Netherlands, Belgium, and France due to differences in terms of occupation regimes and relative strength of the perpetrators.

Occupation regimes and strength of perpetrators

The systematic deportation of Jews to the extermination camps in eastern Europe began in all three countries in 1942 (in France and the Netherlands in July, and in Belgium in August) and continued right up until the arrival of Allied troops in the third quarter of 1944. Of the 320,000 Jews living in France in 1940, 80,000 (25 percent) were eventually deported. The deportation rate for Belgium amounted to 43 percent (25,000 out of 52,000), and for the Netherlands to 76 percent (107,000 out of 140,000).[28] These differences can be explained mostly by the different occupation regimes and the agencies that held power in the German-occupied zones.

In the Netherlands, a *Reichskommissariat* was established under German civilian administration from 1940 to 1944/45. The highest-ranking official was the *Reichskommissar*, Arthur Seyss-Inquart. Under him served four *Generalkommissare* as quasi-ministers. One of these was the *Generalkommissar für das Sicherheitswesen* or "General Commissioner for Security," who simultaneously served as HSSPF, named Hanns Albin Rauter. In addition, there was a BdS, the Commander of the Security Police and Security Service, named Wilhelm Harster. The four General Commissioners reported directly to the *Reich* authorities in Berlin with corresponding areas of jurisdiction. The HSSPF reported to the RSHA and therefore had direct access to all parts of the German and Dutch administration. Beneath the level of the German General Commissioners, the Dutch administration remained intact. Top-ranking Dutch officials were the Secretaries General (*Secretarissen-generaal*) who were running the various departments of the central government.[29]

In Belgium, the territories of Eupen, Malmedy, and Moresnet, which had belonged to Germany prior to 1918, were annexed. From 1940 to 1944, the rest of the country was under a German military administration led by a Military Commander of Belgium and Northern France (*Militärbefehlshaber in Belgien und Nordfrankreich*), General Alexander von Falkenhausen. The transfer to a civilian administration in July 1944 had little effect as most of the country was soon liberated by the Allies. The military commander had a regular command staff and an administrative staff run by a Chief Military Administrator (*Militärverwaltungschef*), Eggert Reeder. The military administration was divided into regional and local units (*Feldkommandaturen* and *Ortskommandaturen*), and was accorded supervising functions according to the German model of supervisory administration (*Aufsichtsverwaltung*). The executive was made up of Belgian General Secretaries as heads of the ministries, as in the Netherlands. From May 1940 onwards, a Belgian government in exile operated in London, although the King and his family did not flee to England. In contrast to the Netherlands and France (since 1942), Belgium lacked an HSSPF, although the RSHA and Himmler both repeatedly tried to implant one.[30] The SS and police apparatus in Belgium was led by a BdS, Constantin Canaris. He was subordinate to the military commander, but he reported directly to the RSHA.[31] The command radius of the military commander covered not only Belgian territory, but also the two northernmost French *départements* (*Nord* and *Pas de Calais*), which is why he was referred to as the commander of "Belgium and Northern France."

In France, the occupation and administration was territorially much more fragmented than that of Belgium and the Netherlands. Moreover, France was the only occupied country with which Germany had signed a formal armistice and continued to maintain formal diplomatic relations throughout the period of occupation. There were no fewer than five occupation regimes on the territory of the French homeland.[32] From June 1940 to November 1942, there was the German-occupied zone, which covered the northern half of France and the Atlantic coast; the unoccupied zone, in which the Vichy government had its capital in the city of that name; the two *départements* in the north which were under the Military Commander in Belgium and Northern France; and the not-yet-formally annexed areas of Alsace and Lorraine, which were under a German civilian administrator (*Chef der*

Table 20.1 Rates of Jewish victimization and organizational attributes of occupation regimes

Country	Victimization rate (%)	Formal status of the occupation regime	Territorial fragmentation	Formal status of Gestapo (HSSPF/BdS)* apparatus
Netherlands	ca 76	Civilian *Reichskommissariat* with German "General Commissioners" according to quasi-ministerial branches supervising Dutch "Secretaries General"	None	HSSPF as "General Commissioner for Security Issues" with BdS
Belgium	ca 43	Military administration supervising indigenous "General Secretaries"	None	BdS as "*Beauftragter des Chefs der Sicherheitspolizei und des SD*" instead of HSSPF
France	ca 25	Military administration supervising indigenous government (Vichy)	High (up to five regimes)	BdS as "*Beauftragter des Chefs der Sicherheitspolizei und des SD*" instead of HSSPF until May 1942; HSSPF and BdS as of May 1942

*HSSPF, *Höherer SS- und Polizeiführer* (Higher SS and Police Leader); BdS, *Befehlshaber der Sicherheitspolizei und des SD* (Commander of the Security Police and Security Service) in France (as of May 1942) and the Netherlands or *Beauftragter des Chefs der Sicherheitspolizei und des SD* (Representative of the Chief of the Security Police and Security Service) in France (June 1940–May 1942) and Belgium.

Zivilverwaltung, CdZ). From June 1940 until November 1942, there was also a strip of territory *ca* 60 km (40 miles) wide in southeastern France under Italian occupation, which was extended to the river Rhône between November 1942 and September 1943 when the fascist regime in Italy eventually collapsed. The Germans also occupied the British Channel Islands.

The varying strength of SS and police in the different occupation regimes had a direct impact on the degree of Jewish victimization during the Holocaust. The less fragmented the overall occupation regime and the more integrated the status of Sipo/SD (Secret Police, *Sicherheitspolizei*/Security Service, *Sicherheitsdienst*) apparatus within the general occupation administration, the higher the degree of victimization among the Jewish minority. This is clearly reflected in the development of the monthly deportation rates 1942–44.

The dynamics of persecution

What shaped the actual dynamics of the persecution was the interplay of hierarchical power and inter-agency rivalry resulting from the various degrees of power differentiation within the respective occupation regimes, and the relative control capacity of the SS and Gestapo apparatus connected to it.

In France, inter-agency rivalry initially spurred rather than impeded the persecution of the Jews. This materialized in two different dimensions. One was the inner-German struggle between the military administration and Sipo/SD, the other was the competition between Vichy authorities and the German military administration for jurisdiction. The Vichy government initially collaborated intensively with the Germans when the large-scale deportation of Jews—the vast majority of them foreigners who had sought refuge on French soil—started, but then reacted with gradually stiffening resistance, leading to the provisional suspension of the deportation scheme in September 1942. Vichy officials left no doubt that the massive protest of the high-ranking clergy of the Catholic church, one of the crucial pillars of the regime, was the main reason why Pétain insisted on having the deportation program suspended, at least temporarily.[33]

Powerful as Sipo/SD seemed to be after the installation of an HSSPF in May 1942, it was not powerful enough to enforce the "Final Solution" in France. In a protracted process, Sipo/SD was negotiating back and forth, since the summer of 1942, to achieve Vichy's approval of the denaturalization of Jews in order to have them deported as well. A Vichy law was drafted that would have stipulated precisely this. Then came 1942/43 and Vichy, even Laval, became more and more reluctant to make such concessions. In August 1943, Pétain finally refused to sign any law that would allow for the denaturalization of Jews. In a note of 24 August 1943, Sipo/SD communicated internally that Pétain's change of mind was probably due to the "current political situation" and the "difficulties" the Reich government was facing.[34] That was a clear allusion to the military situation of Germany, which had worsened dramatically after the defeats of el-Alamein, Stalingrad, Tunis, the allied conquest of Sicily in July 1943, and the imminent threat to the southern flank in the Mediterranean, which in early September 1943 would cause Italy to leave the Axis.

Pétain's refusal saved the lives of tens of thousands of French Jews. In the perception of Sipo/SD, it actually made the "Final Solution" in France impossible, just as his backing of the collaboration had cost, and still would cost, the lives of tens of thousands of foreign Jews living in France. It was the changing terms of trade that transformed French compliance into non-compliance as far as French nationals among the Jews were concerned. The relative value of Vichy autonomy under German occupation shrank in view of the increasing likelihood of a German defeat. At the same time, the costs of compliance began to rise substantially.

Belgium is, in many respects, the deviant case among the three countries under consideration. Throughout the war, Sipo/SD in Belgium remained dependent on *Wehrmacht* benevolence since, despite several attempts by Himmler himself, no HSSPF was installed, and any repressive measure had to be carried out by the *Feldgendarmerie* (military police).[35]

The average percentage of Jewish victims in Belgium (43 percent) conceals the significant differences between the Flemish part and the rest of the country. According to Lieven Saerens,[36] the deportation rate in Brussels was 37 percent, as opposed to 65 percent in Antwerp, figures that have been contested by others, in particular Insa Meinen.[37] What is undisputed, though, is that the persecution of the Jews was much more intense in Antwerp than in Brussels, which made the Belgian capital rather than the Flemish port city the main concentration of the remaining Jews. While native authorities in Antwerp displayed open compliance with the persecution measures enforced by the German military administration, the municipal administration in Brussels was very reluctant to do so.[38] In general, anti-Jewish policy found fertile ground in Antwerp, where a wave of antisemitism had emerged in the 1930s, mainly directed against Jews in the diamond industry. In August 1939, pogrom-like attacks on Jewish businesses and citizens were organized by Flemish nationalists, and under the German occupation regime, the Antwerp municipal administration, including the municipal police, actively collaborated with the German *Feldkommandantur* in the registration of Jews, distributing the star of David and preparing as well as enforcing the deportations throughout most of the first phase of German occupation, until October 1942.[39]

A German decree of 6 October 1942, however, imposed forced labor on male Belgians aged 18–50 and on female Belgians aged 21–35, all of whom could be deported to Germany at the discretion of the German authorities. The decree was issued by the newly installed *Generalbevollmächtiger für den Arbeitseinsatz* (Plenipotentiary for Labor), Fritz Sauckel, without consent of the German military administration. However, when Sauckel requested that Belgian police officers enforce the decree, in the event that Belgian workers refused to sign up for working in Germany, the Antwerp police, which so far had had no qualms about arresting Jews at German request, stopped collaborating.[40] Thereafter, the Germans were not able to carry out large-scale arrests, but instead were dependent on the collaboration of Flemish Nazis and Flemish SS members. Thousands of Jews, almost exclusively non-Belgians, were to survive because of increasing support of individual Belgians and the passive resistance of Belgian authorities, at least outside Antwerp.[41] Indeed, more than 50 percent of the Jews in Belgium who were arrested by German authorities were found either on the streets or in hiding as individuals, as families, or in small groups.[42]

Finally, the impact of the particular structure of the occupation regime in general and the Sipo/SD position within that structure is undeniable as far as the Netherlands is concerned. The persecution apparatus was as fragmented as it was elsewhere and inner-German rivalries were commonplace. Neither was the Dutch side completely powerless. However, the decisive factor was again the bargaining process within which Dutch compliance with the persecution was traded for relative gains in autonomy.

The fundamental difference between the Netherlands on the one hand and Belgium and France on the other was that, at a very early stage, Sipo/SD managed to exclude Dutch central authorities from decision-making while getting control over Dutch police at the local level.[43] From spring 1941 on, Rauter as HSSPF and General Commissioner for Security Affairs insisted vis-à-vis the Dutch Secretaries General on having the Jews treated as non-Dutch "enemies of the Reich" who fell under exclusive German jurisdiction. The Secretaries General, weakened through the brutal repression of a political strike in February 1941, eventually accepted that definition. The struggle against that German imposition kept the central level of Dutch administration busy while, at the local level, the Germans reorganized the Dutch police, which they had put under their direct control by the end of 1941, effectively by-passing the Dutch Secretary General for the Interior and skilfully exploiting the ambitions of local police leaders, especially in Amsterdam. As a result, again at a rather early stage, the Jewish community in the Netherlands found itself completely isolated while facing a powerful police apparatus under direct German control.

The Germans made the Jewish Council of Amsterdam responsible for virtually everything that affected Dutch Jewry. Very similar to the Ghetto administration system imposed in eastern Europe, the Germans created the Council as a sort of state within a state. The Council leadership had a substantial share of power, which was used to alleviate the fate of the Jewish community, but also created tragic illusions about what ultimately could be achieved through an endless chain of concessions, including assistance in preparing the deportations.

Conclusion

Although anti-Jewish legislative and administrative measures were very homogenous in the Netherlands, Belgium, and France, and western Europe as a whole was treated as a single target area by the RSHA, the process and the outcome of anti-Jewish persecution differed significantly in the focal countries. While 25 percent of the Jews living in France in 1940 were eventually deported and mostly murdered, the rate of victimization was considerably higher in Belgium (43 percent) and especially in the Netherlands (76 percent). Two factors essentially account for these differences: the structure of the respective occupation regimes, and the action strategy of the perpetrators and their helpers connected to it.

The civilian occupation regime in the Netherlands, erected in the form of a *Reichskommissariat*, provided for a strong position of the SS and Gestapo or Sipo/SD authorities. Chief SS and Gestapo officials also held ranks in the hierarchy of the *Reichskommissariat* administration, with the HSSPF simultaneously acting as *General-kommissar für das Sicherheitswesen*. Problems of coordination and inter-agency rivalry within the repressive machinery of the occupying power were thus minor. Moreover, the Germans forced the Dutch heads of administration to abandon altogether their jurisdiction over, and responsibility for, the Jews, and to have them represented exclusively by the *Joodse Raad* of Amsterdam. It was basically the administrative isolation and the resulting exclusion from representation by the heads of domestic administration that sealed the fate of the Jews in the Netherlands.

In Belgium, SS and Gestapo authorities were considerably weaker than in the Netherlands, since they remained subordinated to the military commander and lacked an independent HSSPF until July 1944. However, in the process of a protracted power struggle between the *Reichssicherheitshauptamt* and the military administration, a pragmatic compromise was reached in the form of a rather autonomous Gestapo apparatus, which was nonetheless nominally part of the military administration. What shaped the persecution of the Jews most significantly, though, was the divergent action patterns of Belgian municipal administration and the activity of local collaborators in Amsterdam and Brussels. Although exact and undisputed figures are not available, sufficient evidence supports the assumption that initial collaboration of municipal administration and antisemitic climate intensified the persecution of the Jews in Amsterdam, while in Brussels local administration and police, as well as large parts of the population, were rather engaged in passive resistance.

In France, a shifting pattern of collaboration and non-compliance by French authorities characterized the implementation of the Holocaust. In the first phase of the German occupation, stretching from mid-1940 until mid-1942, the Vichy government was eager to defend or even regain administrative jurisdiction, and was ready to extradite to the Germans foreign nationals or "stateless" individuals among the Jews living on French soil. When, in July and August 1942, the deportation of tens of thousands of Jews triggered fierce protest by the Catholic clergy, itself a crucial pillar of the Vichy regime, the Vichy government asked for the temporary suspension of the deportation plan, which Himmler granted in September 1942. The turning tide of the war in 1942/43 only bolstered Vichy reluctance. When Pétain, the head of state, in August 1943 refused to sign a law allowing for mass denaturalization of Jews and their subsequent deportation, the "Final Solution" finally faltered.

Notes

1 Philippe Burrin, *Hitler and the Jews: The Genesis of the Holocaust* (London: Edward Arnold, 1994), 54, 55; Saul Friedländer, *Nazi Germany and the Jews: Vol. 1: The Years of Persecution, 1933–1939* (New York: HarperCollins, 1997), 241–68; Peter Longerich, *Politik der Vernichtung. Eine Gesamtdarstellung der nationalsozialistischen Judenverfolgung* (München und Zürich: Piper, 1998), 187–89. Foundational works on the three countries under consideration here include Jacob Presser, *Ashes in the Wind: The Destruction of Dutch Jewry*, trans. Arnold Pomerans (London: Souvenir, 1968); Michael Marrus and Robert Paxton, *Vichy France and the Jews* (New York: Basic Books, 1981); Werner Warmbrunn, *The German Occupation of Belgium 1940–1944* (New York: Peter Lang, 1993); Dan Michman, ed., *Belgium and the Holocaust* (Jerusalem: Yad Vashem, 1998).

2 Note that the abbreviation *BdS* could stand for *Befehlshaber der Sicherheitspolizei und des SD* or *Beauftragter des Chefs der Sicherheitspolizei und des SD*. *Beauftragter* refers to the weaker position of the two, a representative of the *Chef der Sicherheitspolizei und des SD*, attached to another central administrative unit, usually a military commander, in the occupied territories. *Chef der Sicherheizspolizei und des SD* was a circumscription of the Chief of the RSHA, which was run by Reinhard Heydrich from 1939 to 1942 and by Ernst Kaltenbrunner from 1943 to 1945. A *Befehlshaber der Sicherheitspolizei und des SD*, by contrast, was part of the regular chain of command within the SS and police apparatus.

3 *Verordnungsblatt für die besetzten niederländischen Gebiete* (VOBl). VO 80/1940, VOBl No. 16–1940, 3 August 1940, 247.

4 VO 189/1940, *VOBl* No. 33/1940, 26 October 1940, 546.

5 VO 6/1941, *VOBl* No. 2/1941, 13 January 1941, 19.

6 *VOBl* No. 10/1941, 14 March 1941, 164.

7 VO 148/1941, *VOBl* No. 31/1941, 9 August 1941, 624.

8 Gerald Aalders, *Roof. De ontvremding van joods bezit tijdens de Tweede Wereldoorlog* (Den Haag: Sdu Uitgevers, 1999).

9 VO 58/1942, *VOBl* No. 13/1942, 289.

10 *Verordnungsblatt des Millitärbefehlshabers in Belgien und Nordfrankreich für die besetzten Gebiete Belgiens und Nordfrankreichs* (VOBlBN) No. 8/1940, 25 October 1940, 251.

11 VOBlBN,No. 20/1940, 5 November 1940, 279 and 288.

12 *VOBlBN,* No. 44, 10 June 1941, 607.

13 *VOBlBN,* No.79/1942, 1 June 1942, 943.

14 *Journal Officiel,* 23 July 1940, 4567.

15 *Journal Officiel,* 18 July 1940, 4537, 15 August 1940, 4701, 13 September 1940, 4983.

16 *Journal Officiel,* 24 July 1940, 4569.

17 *Journal Officiel,* 30 August 1940, 4844.

18 *Journal Officiel,* 18 October 1940, 5323.

19 *VOBlBN,* 30 September 1940, 92.

20 *VOBlBN,* 20 October 1940,112.

21 *VOBlBN,* No. 32/1941, May 1943, 255; *VOBlBN,* No. 36/1941, 10 June 1941, 272.

22 *Journal Officiel,* 26 August 1941, 3594.

23 Philippe Verheyde, "Des premières interdictions jusqu'à la spoliation totale," in Caisse des depôts et consignations, La spoliation antisémite sous l'occupation: consignations et restitutions. Rapport définitif (2001): 73–84.

24 Wolfgang Seibel, "The Strength of Perpetrators: The Holocaust in Western Europe, 1940–44," *Governance: An International Journal of Policy, Administration, and Institutions,* vol. 15 (2002): 211–40.

25 *VOBlBN,* No. 53/1942, 11 February 1942, 340.

26 *VOBlBN,* No. 63/1942, 1 June 1942, 383.

27 *VOB/BN*, No. 69/1942, 15 July 1942, 414.
28 See Gerhard Hirschfeld, *Fremdherrschaft und Kollaboration. Die Niederlande unter deutscher Besatzung 1940–1945* (Stuttgart: Deutsche Verlagsanstalt, 1984), and "Niederlande," in *Dimensionen des Völkermordes. Die Zahl der jüdischen Opfer des Nationalsozialismus*, ed. Wolfgang Benz (Munich: Deutscher Taschenbuch Verlag, 1996), 137–66. See also Juliane Wetzel, "Frankreich und Belgien," in *Dimensionen des Völkermordes*, 105–36; Pim Griffioen and Ron Zeller, "La Persécution des Juifs en Belgique et aux Pays-Bas pendant la Seconde Guerre Mondiale. Une analyse comparative," *Cahiers d'Histoire du Temps Présent*, vol. 5 (1999): 73–132.
29 Henk Flap and Will Arts, eds, *De organisatie van de bezetting* (Amsterdam: Amsterdam University Press, 1997).
30 Albert De Jonghe, "La lutte Himmler-Reeder pour la nomination d'un HSSPF à Bruxelles," *Cahiers d'histoire de la Seconde guerre mondiale*, vol. 3 (1974): 103–73, vol. 4 (1976): 6–159, vol. 5 (1978): 5–172, vol. 7 (1982): 95–184, and vol. 8 (1984): 5–234. See also Warmbrunn, *The German Occupation of Belgium*, 96–104; Wolfram Weber, *Die innere Sicherheit im besetzten Belgien und Nordfrankreich 1940–1944. Ein Beitrag zur Geschichte der Besatzungsverwaltungen* (Düsseldorf: Droste Verlag, 1978), 35–43.
31 Weber, *Die innere Sicherheit*, 41.
32 Eberhard Jäckel, *Frankreich in Hitlers Europa. Die deutsche Frankreichpolitik im 2. Weltkrieg* (Stuttgart: Deutsche Verlagsanstalt, 1966), 59–95.
33 Jacques Duquesne, *Les catholiques français sous l'occpuation* (Paris: Grasset, 1966), 244–72.
34 Serge Klarsfeld, "Vichy-Auschwitz. Die Zusammenarbeit der deutschen und französischen Behörden bei der 'Endlösung der Judenfrage'" in *Frankreich* (Nördlingen: Greno Verlag, 1989); Klarsfeld/Centre de Documentation Juive Contemporaine (CDJC), *Receuil de documents des dossiers des autorités allemandes concernant la persécution de la population juive en France (1940–1944)* (New York: Beate Klarsfeld Foundation, n.d.), 9: 2476.
35 Insa Meinen, *Die Shoah in Belgien* (Darmstadt: Wissenschaftliche Buchgesellschaft, 2009); Lieven Saerens, *Étrangers dans la cité. Anvers et ses Juifs (1880–1944)* (Brussels: Étitions labor, 2005); Maxime Steinberg, *Le persécution des Juifs en Belgique (1940–1945)* (Brussels: Éditions complexe, 2004); Rudi Van Voorslaer, Emmanuel Debruyne, Frank Seberechts and Nico Wouters, eds, *La Belgique docile. Les autorités belges et la persécution des Juifs an Belgique durant la Seconde Guerre mondiale* (Brussels: Éditions Luc Pire, 2007).
36 Saerens, *Étrangers dans la cité*, 762–72.
37 Meinen, *Die Shoah in Belgien*.
38 Steinberg, *Le persécution des Juifs en Belgique*, 109–56. See also Nico Wouters, "La chasse aux Juifs, 1942–44," in *La Belgique docile* (Van Voorslaer et al., eds), 547–66.
39 Saerens, *Étrangers dans la cité*, 497–567, 653–740. See also Wouters, "La chasse aux Juifs," 645–56.
40 Wouters, "La chasse aux Juifs," 624–35.
41 Meinen, *Die Shoah in Belgien*, 182–85.
42 Meinen, *Die Shoah in Belgien*, 83–84.
43 Pim Griffoen and Ron Zeller, "Anti-Jewish Policy and Organization of the Deportations in France and the Netherlands, 1940–44: A Comparative Study," *Holocaust and Genocide Studies*, vol. 20, no. 3 (2006): 437–73.

21

NORWAY'S ROLE IN THE HOLOCAUST

The destruction of Norway's Jews

Bjarte Bruland

It was ironic that the registration of Norway's Jews was implemented on 20 January 1942, the same day that Heydrich met with top bureaucrats of the Third Reich at the Wannsee villa in Berlin to discuss "the final solution of the Jewish problem." It was a coincidence that the representative of the Ministry of Foreign Affairs at the conference, the permanent undersecretary Martin Luther, specifically mentioned the Nordic countries in his summary of the problems that might occur in the process of deportation.[1] Luther, a figure of some prominence on the side of the Ministry of Foreign Affairs in negotiations concerning the deportation of Jews from states allied to or otherwise subdued by Germany, was at this point not aware of the latest developments in Norway. Heydrich's implicit goal with the Wannsee conference was to establish the Reich Security Main Office (*Reichssicherheitshauptamt*, RSHA) as the leading operative office in the deportation of Jews to the death camps. In Norway, the representative of the RSHA, the offices of the Chief of the Security Police in Oslo, had already taken the lead by introducing a systematic registration of the Jews, a crucial step towards a subsequent removal of Jews from Norwegian society. And yet, even if the destruction process in Norway included all the intrinsic steps necessary to complete the destruction of the Jews in the country, the perpetrators in Norway would follow their own course when they implemented the registration, the deportation, and the economic liquidation of the Jews.

Occupation—a Norwegian "Sonderweg"?

When Germany's armed forces attacked Norway on 9 April 1940, there were some 2,100 Jews in the country, less than 0.1 percent of the population. Around 1,700 were members of the two organized Jewish communities.[2] The largest of those communities was in Oslo; the other was situated in Trondheim. Besides these communities, Jews lived around the country in more than 60 local municipalities. There had been a Jewish presence in Norway since the 1850s, when the Norwegian parliament finally annulled part of § 2 of the Constitution of 1814 that banned Jews from the country. After 1933, Jewish refugees from Germany and later from Czechoslovakia and Austria started to arrive, despite hard-line Norwegian asylum policies. By 1940, some 350 Jewish refugees had arrived in Norway. Most had temporary visas and were awaiting transfer to the United States or other countries overseas.[3]

In a pre-invasion order for the invasion of Denmark and Norway, the *Wehrmacht* had specified which measures were to be taken and which were not to be taken after the countries were subdued. One of the measures *not* to be taken was the introduction of a German racial regime. The Germans did not want anything to disturb the economic life of Denmark and Norway. The German army had expected little resistance, and hoped that the two countries would accept their presence without too much trouble. In Denmark, the government surrendered almost immediately. In Norway, however, after some initial hesitation and panic, the government decided to fight back. This changed the political situation. Hitler appointed a civilian plenipotentiary in Norway (a *Reichskommissar*), the Gauleiter Josef Terboven. As the war raged in Norway (the battle for Narvik would not end until 8 June 1940), the remnant bureaucracy in Oslo, headed by a County Governor, established an Administrative Council to prepare for the actual administration of the occupied territories. The Administrative Council was established partly to counter the coup d'état by radio by right-wing leader Vidkun Quisling on the day Norway was attacked, 9 April 1940. Quisling, supported by elements within the German Nazi Party (*Nationalsozialistische Deutsche Arbeiterpartei*, NSDAP) and the German navy (*Kriegsmarine*), attempted in this way to seize the political agenda in Norway, and for all practical purposes to render the presence of a German civilian administration unnecessary. *Reichskommissar* Terboven was, at this time, in no way interested in an alliance with Quisling's minuscule party (*Nasjonal Samling*), and also felt that Quisling threatened his power base. Not without a realistic view of the situation, Terboven may very well have felt that an alliance with Quisling would impede his attempt to make the Norwegian bureaucracy cooperate with the German occupation regime. For the initiators of the Administrative Council, practical concerns played along with political motives. Conscious of keeping Quisling and his party from any political influence, their main purpose was twofold: to secure supplies for the civilian population, and to avoid too much direct control of the bureaucracy by Terboven and his staff.

The Norwegian Government did not accept the Administrative Council as anything more than an emergency measure. After their narrow escape from Oslo, the government followed the withdrawal of Norwegian forces in the south of Norway, only to be evacuated to the northern port of Tromsø by the end of April. In June 1940, the king and government, along with some members of parliament and remnants of the civilian and military administration, were evacuated once again, this time to exile in London. From there, they organized the Norwegian resistance and exerted their control over the Norwegian merchant navy, their most important source of income and the most significant Norwegian contribution to the allied war effort. It would take 5 years before they could return to Norwegian soil.

After the surrender of the Norwegian armed forces on Norwegian soil in June 1940, Terboven initiated talks on the permanent administration of Norway with the remnants of the political and administrative establishment.[4] He wanted a new government established, which could sign a legally confirmed peace agreement with Germany much along the lines of the "Danish solution."[5] If this were at all possible from the outset, it was certainly stopped by the instructions given by Hitler to Terboven by the end of July 1940, in which Terboven was instructed to secure power to Vidkun Quisling and his *Nasjonal Samling* party.[6]

By September 1940, all discussions with the remaining Norwegian political establishment had ended. One of the reasons for the Norwegian establishment not to make a deal with the German occupiers was the status of *Nasjonal Samling* and its leader Vidkun

Quisling. The old establishment could, in fact, accept the deposition of the king, but would not allow Quisling's movement a hand on the steering wheel in a new government. This was de facto why a political arrangement between the occupiers and what was left of the political establishment was not possible. On 25 September 1940, a number of new departmental ministers were appointed, responsible to *Reichskommissar* Terboven alone. Terboven announced this in a radio speech the same day. Furthermore, all political parties except *Nasjonal Samling* were declared illegal. Most of the ministers were members of *Nasjonal Samling*, and even if the ministers as such did not constitute a government, they had meetings with Quisling every week. Quisling himself was not a minister. It was not until February 1942 that Quisling was allowed to form his own "national government."[7]

The political arrangements made in Norway were the result of a power struggle between different power structures in Norway and Germany. Quisling had political support in certain quarters in Germany, not least with *Reichsleiter* Rosenberg and the German navy, who intrigued on behalf of Quisling with Hitler and others.[8] According to Norwegian historian Hans Fredrik Dahl, Quisling's goal was an independent Norway and the ending of German occupation through a peace treaty. Afterwards, a new Norway was to be allied with Germany, as an independent member of the anti-Komintern pact and, after the introduction of conscription, to build an army to fight on the side of Germany.[9] *Nasjonal Samling* was, by 1940, a minuscule party with only a few hundred members. It was established in 1933 and fought in general and local elections from that time, but it never managed to gain nationwide support and was only (relatively) strong in a few local municipalities. After the occupation, and particularly after it was declared the only allowed political party, its ranks swelled to more than 40,000 members.[10]

The German occupation regime in Norway thus differed from most other western European countries and became a "hybrid" of different types of occupation regime. On the one hand, Norway was organized as a *Reichskommissariat* with a *Reichskommissar* responsible to Hitler alone, much like in the Netherlands. On the other hand, a national Nazi movement was allowed a much more independent role than in the Netherlands. Norway in February 1942 got its own nationalist and collaborating government, in some ways similar to Vichy, but its government was entirely based on German arms and had very little legitimacy with the populace. For the Germans, relative peace and quiet and the continuation of important industries and fisheries was the most important goal, in much the same way as in occupied France.[11] In the end, the particular and, in some ways, peculiar political structure of occupied Norway would shape the destruction policy prepared by the perpetrators. In a true sense, occupied Norway was organized in the "chaotic" and often irrrational way explained in the literature.[12] Hitler never abandoned *Reichskommissar* Josef Terboven as the chief implementer of his will in Norway, but he still allowed other players in the game for power, most notably Quisling and his movement. In the end, *Nasjonal Samling* and Quisling would play a prominent role in the destruction of Norway's Jews. In this sense, Norway took a *Sonderweg* or "special path" compared with other occupied territories in western Europe.

The destruction process

As mentioned, the anti-Jewish policy in Norway would take its own course, in some ways different from most other western European countries, and yet with the same basic and necessary elements. In the introduction of the different steps of the alienation and final extermination of the Jewish minority, Norway was a latecomer compared with the Netherlands, Belgium or France, occupied or non-occupied zone. The Jews would not be systematically singled out through a series of decrees and a gradual process of "Aryanization" and separation from society as a whole. It is important to note that this was gradually developed into a deliberate decision, at least on the part of the German Security Police and other parts of the German occupation regime in Norway. And yet, when the final blows fell, the policy was just as destructive and had exactly the same purpose as in these other countries. As will be shown later, the result would be statistically more deadly in Norway than in France or even Belgium.

The destruction process in Norway can be said to have three different phases:

1   An early "indecisive" phase from April 1940 to January 1942, dominated by single actions (*Einzelaktionen*) and initiatives not necessarily part of a systematic anti-Jewish policy.
2   A short middle phase from January 1942 to October 1942, when necessary steps were taken and when signs of a far more destructive intent are visible.
3   The destruction phase from October 1942 to February 1943, when the steps came in quick succession, when the Jews were deported, and systematic economic measures were taken against them.

The early indecisive phase

Even if the *Wehrmacht* had not planned for any racial measures to be introduced in Norway after the invasion, such measures were actually taken very early. On 10 May 1940, radios belonging to Jews were confiscated by order of the German Security Police to the Norwegian police in occupied territories. The German Security Police was originally organized as *Einsatzkommandos* in Norway. Led by *SS-Oberführer* Franz Walter Stahlecker, a 200-man-strong *Einsatzgruppe* was ordered to Norway by the leader of the RSHA, Reinhard Heydrich, on 20 April 1940.[13] They established *Einsatzkommandos* in Oslo, Bergen, Stavanger, Kristiansand, and Trondheim.

The actual seizure of the radios was carried out by the Norwegian police in a country where fighting was still going on between Germany and Norway and its allies. This was a systematic measure, but it was not publicized, and it was not based on a definition of the term "Jew."[14] Rather, the Jewish communities were coerced to collaborate to see to it that all Jews, not only members of the two Jewish communities, gave up their radios.[15] The Administration Council discussed the seizure of radios belonging to Jews in their meetings on 16 and 17 May. The chief of the police in Oslo, Kristian Welhaven, was called to the meeting for an explanation. He told the council that the Norwegian police could not oppose a direct order from the Germans. A member of Terboven's staff would later explain to a council representative that the seizure of radios belonging to Jews was founded in a *Führer*-directive.[16]

At the same time, impatient German officials saw to it that Jewish shops and offices were specially marked in a few cities. This was a far more public measure, and most signs were soon removed due to the fear among German officials and Norwegian right-wing factions that it would arouse sympathy for the Jews.[17]

Local branches of the German Security Police also showed signs of impatience, resulting in the closing of Jewish shops here and there and the occasional arrest of Jews around the country. In Trondheim and other towns in mid-Norway, this local "Aryani-zation process" gradually encompassed most Jewish businesses. In Trondheim, many shops continued to operate under a special office set up by the leader of the German Security Police, Gerhard Flesch.[18]

Nasjonal Samling had been antisemitic in its outlook since its beginnings in 1933. From 1935/36, as party membership went down, it became even more antisemitic. After the German invasion, antisemitic propaganda was widespread in all Norwegian news-papers, but even more so in the party press. In 1941, *Nasjonal Samling* stepped up its propaganda towards the Jews, and this was followed by separate actions by its party army, the *Hird*. In February, March, and July, several actions were carried out against Jewish shops and offices and against cultural events where Jewish artists took part. Shop windows were painted with anti-Jewish slogans in Oslo. These actions, motivated by growing frustration on the part of radical antisemitic elements within the party, were not successful. Rather than leading to hatred towards the Jews, it led to sympathy. After the last action on the night of 2 July 1941, the party leadership and Quisling forbade single actions by party branches.[19]

In July 1941, the Ministry of Police established a new police force, the State Police.[20] The State Police organization was closely knit to the German Security Police, but it still had its own agenda. In many ways, it served as the heavy fisted police of *Nasjonal Samling*. In the beginning, it was manned by policemen taken from other parts of the police system. Membership in *Nasjonal Samling* was, for all practical purposes, obligatory. In the summer of 1941, the department counted 150 men. At its largest in 1944, it had more than 340 employees. It also had its own department of border police. Its leader was Karl Alfred Marthinsen. The State Police HQ in Oslo would play a pivotal role as coordinator and executioner when the Jews were rounded up in October and November 1942.

In June 1941, the Minister of Church Affairs, Ragnar Skancke, suggested a law prohi-biting the marriage of persons of "Norwegian blood" with Jews and the Laplanders.[21] In August 1941, the Minister of Justice Sverre Riisnæs sent a circular to county judges asking them to send lists of Jewish properties to the ministry. The circular included a primitive definition of the term "Jew."[22] None of these measures was effective. A law prohibiting marriage between Jews and non-Jews was never enacted due to protests from the bishop of Oslo, Eivind Berggrav.[23] The circular from the Ministry of Justice had little practical importance and did not help to step up measures against the Jews. But these initiatives did show readiness for more radical measures.

The Norwegian contribution to the SS was to have an even more radicalizing effect. In the first group sent by the Reich Security Main Office to Norway in April 1940 was Erich Ehrlinger,[24] who was specifically instructed to start the build-up of a Norwegian branch of the SS. By January 1941, a group of 200–300 Norwegian volunteers gave their word of honor to Adolf Hitler; they were all enrolled in the SS Division *Wiking* and took part in Operation Barbarossa in June 1941. Jonas Lie, the Minister of Police, and Sverre Riisnæs, the Minister of Justice, became the leaders of the "Norwegian SS" (*Norges SS*).[25] Both took part as volunteers during the German invasion of Yugoslavia in April 1941. Jonas Lie later travelled to the Eastern Front, and more specifically to *Einsatzgruppe D* under Otto Ohlendorf, "to learn more about the situation on the ground."[26] After his visit, he participated in the NSDAP *Parteifeier* in Munich on 8 November 1941, at the invitation of Himmler. In the fall of 1942, when Jews were rounded up in Norway, Lie was a volunteer in a Norwegian SS-unit on the Eastern Front. Riisnæs, his brother in arms in the Norwegian SS, wrote to him, "We are now finishing off the Jews once and for all."[27]

That the Norwegian SS-volunteers knew of Jonas Lie's exploits in "hunting down" Jews is evident from a letter from a friend of Lie, who served in an SS unit on the Baltic front in 1944:

> You know the life at the Eastern Front from your own experience. I have learned that you managed to exterminate the lice when you were here, you have a great reputation here, and I have not seen a single louse here so far—not in my entire life for that matter! But they are present on the other side of no mans land, where they belong.[28]

Norwegian SS-volunteers were radicalized after their experiences on the Eastern Front, which undoubtedly included shootings. In the fall of 1942, when Jews were rounded up in Norway, volunteers who had already returned to Norway from the front would do their bit in taking part in arrests in Oslo. Others would contribute as prison guards in the Norwegian concentration camp Berg. Also, the volunteers would be especially bene-fited by the Quisling regime, as the belongings of Jews were divided. More importantly, it permeated a "bond of blood" between Germany and its Norwegian collaborators.

Unlike the Netherlands, the German civilian authority in Norway, Terboven's *Reichs-kommissariat*, showed no willingness to take the lead in anti-Jewish measures. In fact, a memo from an internal conference between the different branches of the *Reichs-kommissariat* in Norway shows that as late as January 1942, they had planned no mea-sures against the Jews on their part. Instead, they wanted the Quisling regime to reintroduce the part of § 2 of the Constitution of 1814 that denied Jews entry into the country.[29] A law reintroducing the ban on Jews in Norway was signed by Quisling in March 1942. It was by no means unimportant, but was still a symbolic measure: no Jews could enter Norway at that time, anyway, and it did not specify that Jews already in the country were to be expelled. As late as 28 November 1942, the Finance Department of the *Reichskommissariat* made it clear in an internal memo that a directive to implement the 11th amendment to the Reich Citizen Law (concerning the confiscation of Jewish property from deportation victims) was not to be implemented in Norway. Rather, this issue would be regulated through an internal agreement with Norwegian authorities.[30] The German occupation regime in Norway even tried to implement a sexual prohibition between Jewish refugees and Norwegian women through an order to the rabbi of Oslo, the German-born Julius Samuel. In February 1941, Samuel wrote to the Jewish Aid Society, instructing them that "by order of German authorities" they should make known among "Jewish emigrants" that relations with Aryan women were illegal "even in Norway."[31] German authorities in Norway would go to lengths to avoid issuing public anti-Jewish decrees. The only anti-Jewish decree eventually made public by the *Reichskommissar* in Norway was a ban on letters in Hebrew, published along with a ban on carrier pigeons.[32]

Definition by decree

Even the German Security Police had no plans for measures on their own. Instead, they ordered the Norwegian Ministry of Police to introduce an identification decree. In

October 1941, the leader of the German Security Police, *Standartenführer* Heinrich Fehlis, sent a letter to the Norwegian Ministry of Police asking them to prepare such a measure and accordingly to make clear who was to be considered a "Jew." Rather than immediately telling his Norwegian collaborators how to do this, it became a process that lasted 2 months. Originally, the Ministry of Police was of the opinion that it had to be a German decree rather than a Norwegian one. Secondly, the Ministry questioned the necessity of such a decree at all. It would be enough, they believed, if the Jewish communities were ordered to carry out the registration themselves.[33] To the German Security Police, this was far from enough. They wanted to introduce a systematic measure. It was not to be a German decree and not a Norwegian law, but rather a small announcement to be printed in Norwegian papers all over the country. It took until January until the announcement was ready. The Norwegian police was responsible for carrying out the measure, and everything worked smoothly. Even if the anti-Jewish propaganda at this point had been accelerated, the announcement was hardly commented on in the press and there was little opposition to it. In an anonymous letter of protest to the Minister of Police Jonas Lie, the writer claimed, "the announcement would be met with indignation from the Norwegian population and even outside the country."[34] But no such opposition took shape; the marking of identification papers went smoothly. Some Jews, in particular refugees from Germany or German-incorporated territories, did note that this was the beginning of the end. After all, they had been through the whole process before.[35] But most Jews chose to be registered. All in all, the police registered 1,536 Jews.

Norway was a latecomer in defining and registering Jews. In the Netherlands, the term "Jew" was defined by a decree by *Reichskommissar* Seyss-Inquart on 22 October 1940. The same month, Jews were defined by decree by the Military commander in Belgium. In the occupied zone of France, Jews were defined by decree on 27 September 1940. In the Netherlands, Belgium, and France, it was soon followed by other decrees restricting the freedom of movement of Jews.

Maybe the leader of the German Security Police had wanted more measures to be taken. If so, he was discouraged from doing this by his own expert on Jewish affairs, the leader of office IV B in the Gestapo Headquarters in Oslo, *Hauptsturmführer* Wilhelm Wagner. After the war, he explained his approach to anti-Jewish measures in a police interrogation:

> He had been called to Fehlis who told him that they were to proceed towards the Jews in the same way as was done in Germany, with marking of businesses, the Jewish star, prohibition to use public parks etc. The accused [Wagner] was of the opinion that there was no Jewish problem in Norway. Quite the opposite, the accused was of the opinion that a Jewish problem would arise if the same measures were taken in Norway as had been taken in Germany. What was done for the time being was to stamp the passport of Jews with a J.[36]

It remains a fact that the marking decree was the only really systematic measure to be taken until the destruction policy accelerated in October and November 1942. The Jewish star was never introduced. This is an anomaly compared with all other western European countries, and shows how the anti-Jewish policy in Norway took its own course, but without relinquishing the very necessary systematic registration of the Jews.

Rarely would German offices step out from the shadows as measures against the Jews were stepped up in Norway. They preferred Norwegian offices to do the job, and they would continue to remain in the background even as Jews were rounded up and deported.

Deportation and destruction

How can one explain the speed with which one destructive step after another was introduced in quick succession in October and November 1942? It would be fair to say that the period from January to October 1942 was a "waiting game," in which the perpetrators were waiting for the right occasion to make their move. Raul Hilberg notes how the process of destruction was undertaken:

> The implementation of Hitler's prophecy was a vast administrative undertaking. To start with, the preliminary process of defining the victims, attaching their property, and restricting their movement had to be extended to all areas from which deportations were to be conducted. Before the completion of these steps in a particular territory, that area was not 'ready.' Even a segregated community could still be tied in countless social and economic relationships to its neighbors.[37]

The process of destruction in Norway did not follow the outline of Hilberg, even though it is important to note that, even in Norway, the destruction was indeed "a vast administrative undertaking." The Jews in Norway, both Norwegian Jews and Jewish refugees alike, had been duly registered by early 1942, but there was no further attempt to restrict their movement or otherwise systematically take their property away. The German Security Police had arrested a handful of Jews by the fall of 1942, and deportations had indeed taken place.[38] Four Jews had been executed after a mock German trial in Trondheim in March 1942.[39] But otherwise, most Jews were little affected. Among the Jews, however, most knew someone or heard of other Jews that had been arrested or even deported. Marcus Levin was a Jewish social worker, and noted in a report written in 1943:

> Most Jews prior to October 1942 thought they would be liquidated one by one after being accused of breaking some law or regulation from the German occupation regime. Most Jews were therefore very careful not to break any regulations and thought they could avoid arrest by not sticking their head out.[40]

The arrest of all male Jews above the age of 15 in Trondheim in early October was a sign that impatience was growing. The order for that particular operation came from the German Security Police in collaboration with *Reichskommissar* Terboven personally. The operation was executed during a state of emergency declared to squash the resistance movement in the area. Norwegian order police carried out the arrests.[41] Even earlier, in September 1942, the German Security Police confiscated a few villas and houses belonging to Jews in Oslo. At that point, a major in the German Army reported to his Norwegian anti-Nazi contacts that the Jews should be brought to Sweden as soon as possible.[42]

But the events in Trondheim were only a prelude to what was to come. As the end of October approached, a "border pilot," a person guiding refugees to Sweden, shot a border policeman. The group he was guiding were Jews who wanted to leave Norway before events accelerated. This incident happened on 22 October and was used as propaganda to attack the Jews in unusually ferocious language.[43] It was the pretext the German occupation regime and the Quisling regime wanted, and this time the bureaucracy moved with enormous energy. The Germans were to remain in the background, however, watching and in some areas guiding what was to happen.

Only 2 days after the border policeman was shot, a temporary amendment to a year-old law was enacted by the Quisling regime, granting the police the right to arrest anyone suspected of "certain violations."[44] The day before, on 23 October, *Hauptsturmführer* Wilhelm Wagner of the Gestapo met with the Chief of the Norwegian State Police Karl Alfred Marthinsen and the top echelon of the State Police to plan the arrest of all male Jews.[45] No written report was ever made from the meeting. Formalities usually so important to bureaucratic procedures were no longer rendered necessary, and certainly not useful.[46]

The activity was now at its peak and preparations were made in double time. Lists were written out based on the registration carried out earlier that year.[47] On 25 October, a telegram was sent by Marthinsen and the State Police to police authorities all over the country. All male Jews over the age of 15 (with a "J" stamped in their identification papers) were to be arrested the next day.[48] In Oslo alone, 124 policemen and auxiliaries participated. The auxiliaries were mostly from the *Nasjonal Samling* party army (the *Hird*) and from *Norges SS* (veterans from the *Waffen-SS*).[49] As was the case in most other western European countries, most—but certainly not all—participants were politically loyal to the regime. In Oslo, where more than half of the Norwegian Jews lived, the arrests were carried out by mixed patrols of State Police officers, officers from the Crime Squad of the Oslo Police, along with selected members of the *Hird* and the Norwegian SS. This was not the case around the country, however. In local municipalities and small towns across Norway, local police or county sheriffs carried out the arrests. All in all, 336 Jewish men were arrested and eventually concentrated in a not yet fully prepared concentration camp outside the town of Tønsberg.[50]

In this, the first phase of the destruction process, the Quisling regime was busy legalizing the measures it wanted to take. During the weekend of 23–25 October, the Quisling regime prepared a law to confiscate all Jewish property. This was a separate move not coordinated with the Germans. The Quisling regime wanted to take control of Jewish properties before the Germans could. The law was published in newspapers on 26 October, mostly through editorial articles. The law included no definition of the term "Jew."[51] *Reichskommissar* Terboven, however, did not want to be left out. In mid-November 1942, he made sure that all gold and silver belonging to Jews, as well as all wristwatches, were to be handed over to the German Security Police as "a voluntary contribution to the war effort."[52]

Later, on 17 November, the Quisling regime introduced another anti-Jewish law, a law obligating all Jews to report their "Jewish status." Unlike the marking decree introduced in January 1942, this law registered all persons "of Jewish blood," including so-called half-Jews and quarter-Jews. Consciously, Quisling later used this law to attack what the regime considered persons with "mixed blood."[53] The propaganda was intended to drive these unwanted people out of Norway. And indeed, most of them made the choice to escape to Sweden.[54] This law was more in compliance with German lawmaking, though the definition of the different classes of Jew was more severe even than in Germany.[55]

The law introduced in order to confiscate all Jewish property was in fact a point of no return. It was not an "Aryanization" decree; its purpose was total—to eliminate the Jewish minority economically. The practical instrument in the liquidation of Jewish property was "The Board of Liquidations of Jewish property." They proceeded to liquidate Jewish property according to the principles of the probate courts. Estate managers were appointed and an administration set up in a Jewish flat in Oslo. The actual process of liquidation varied according to each estate manager. In some cases, they would prepare public auctions. In other cases, property was sold off at a relatively cheap price to organizations in the *Nasjonal Samling* party system or other interested parties. In Oslo, furniture, clothes, and other effects were collected and showed to SS-volunteers at specially prepared "collection centres." SS-volunteers were able to purchase from these collection centres at half price.[56] The work of the Board of Liquidations was not completed at the end of the war.[57]

The period from 26 October to 25 November was another waiting game. This time the pressure was high, for organizations and employers sent letters to the State Police and even to Quisling personally to ask for the release of individual Jews.[58] Norwegian Church Leaders also formulated a moral objection to the Norwegian people, asking the regime "to end the persecution of the Jews and racial hatred."[59] After the German Security Police had secured a ship transport, Wilhelm Wagner ordered the arrest of all remaining Jews in Norway on 24 November.[60] This time, a blitz operation was prepared. Rather than concentrating the women and children in a transit camp before departure, the victims were to be brought directly to the ship in Oslo harbor. This meant that the operation was to be conducted in two stages. The first stage was on 25 November, and included the arrest of Jews who had to be transported a relatively long way to Oslo. The next stage was the arrest of Jews in Oslo and its immediate vicinity, which was to take place on 26 November. The ship was to leave Oslo on that day. Yet again, the preparations were frenzied and had to be made with 1–2 days' warning. This time, the telegram from the State Police HQ ordered the arrest of all remaining persons with a "J"-stamped identification paper.[61]

The leader of the Oslo department of the State Police, police inspector Knut Rød, organized the operation in Oslo. This time, 300 men were organized in 100 patrols. A hundred taxicabs were hired. Buses and trucks were also organized. A special roster was prepared: the 100 patrols were all given lists of addresses to visit. To secure the victims, two members of each patrol were driven to the first two addresses on the list. The third policeman would then drive to the third address and bring the victims directly to the harbor. He would then drive to the first address to pick up the next family, and so on.[62] At Oslo harbor, a reception center was organized. Present were Wilhelm Wagner and Knut Rød. A guard party from the German 17 Order Police Regiment was ordered to follow the transport, and to provide guard duty at the harbor.[63] The operation started at 4 o'clock in the morning and ended only when the ship, the DS *Donau*, left Oslo harbor at a quarter to 3 in the afternoon. On board were 532 Jews. More were on the way to Oslo. The blitz-like action was in many ways a success for the perpetrators, but a second transport still had to be organized. This did not leave Oslo until 25 February 1943 with 158 Jews on board.

Simultaneously with the preparations in Oslo, the HQ of the German Security Police in Oslo notified the office of Eichmann in Berlin on 25 November 1942.[64] Eichmann's office was asked to organize the transport of the Jews when they reached the harbor in

Germany. It is interesting to note that the Reich Security Main Office seemed to be totally unaware that an action was taking place in Norway. The most important indication of this fact is a telegram from office IV B 4 in the Reich Security Main Office to the German Security Police in Oslo, received only at 6 o'clock in the evening of 25 November. In this telegram, Eichmann's assistant, *Sturmbannführer* Günther, gave the security police in Oslo numerous new regulations that neither the Germans nor the Norwegian police had taken into consideration. Günther made clear that Jews in so-called mixed marriages were not to be deported. Jews from neutral countries should not be deported, and even Jews from Britain or the USA were exempt.[65] These regulations were not known by the German Security Police in Norway, and the Norwegian State Police had made no preparations for such specialized orders. Far from it: the leader of the State Police complained in his report about the operation that these new rules, made known to him so late in the process, further complicated the execution of the arrests.[66] Indeed, "selections" had to be made in concentration camp Berg and around the country as the police had arrested Jews in mixed marriages—in many instances so-called half-Jews, and in some cases even their children.[67]

Conclusions

Most Norwegian historians have originally accepted the testimony by Wilhelm Wagner and many others who claimed that the deportation of the Norwegian Jews was ordered from Berlin and was accepted by the Quisling regime.[68] But it would be wrong to assume that Eichmann or his office supervised the operation in Norway. Far from it, the operation in all its stages was prepared and led from Norwegian soil and carried out as a result of initiatives, both German and Norwegian, in collaboration and sometimes in opposition to each other's intentions. In the short period from October 1942 to February 1943, initiatives were taken on several levels simultaneously and without any hesitation.

The actual conduct of the arrests and concentration of Jews in Norway was a matter of discussion between the German Security Police and the Norwegian State Police. The Security Police led the operation only insofar as establishing the goals to be achieved. Otherwise, the actual planning and execution was left to the Norwegian police. At higher levels, both the Quisling regime and *Reichskommissar* Terboven had obviously given their go-ahead to carry out the operation and the Quisling regime had, mainly on its own initiative, provided a "legal" framework.[69] No-one doubted where they were heading. At the outset, the operation had obvious goals, in many ways unlike the situation in most other parts of western Europe. Even if the perpetrators in Norway chose a different path, the result was just as lethal.

No direct orders to execute the destruction of the Jews were given from Berlin. Except for the execution of the arrests and deportations, there was no clear and discernible leadership. Different parts of the bureaucracy took the initiative at will, organizing the different types of measures to be taken. These measures were not entirely logical. For example, after the first deportation, when all registered Jews were either deported or concentrated in preparation for a second transport, the Ministry of the Interior moved to step up its anti-Jewish legislation by preparing a "Law on Certain Provisions Concerning Jews." In its early draft, the Jews were forbidden to marry non-Jews, not allowed to visit parks, not allowed to employ "Aryan" domestic servants under the age of 45, etc.[70] In short, the ministry prepared a law that would bring Norway onto a par with

Germany in anti-Jewish legislation. The only problem was that there were no more Jews. The deportation of Norway's Jews had simply been implemented at such a speed that a follow-up was completely unnecessary.

In all, 772 Jews were deported from Norway. Only 34 survived. In addition, 28 persons were executed or died of other reasons directly or indirectly connected to anti-Jewish actions in Norway. In all, this brings the number of victims to 766, more than 49 percent of the 1,536 Jews registered by the Norwegian Police in early 1942. In western Europe, only the Netherlands and Germany had a higher percentage murdered victims.

At the Wannsee conference, Luther from the Ministry of Foreign Affairs had recommended caution and restraint in the Nordic countries. In the final analysis, no such restraint was shown in Norway. The result was that half the Jews registered were deported. The rest of the Jews, most of them with good help from "export groups" and the Norwegian resistance, managed to escape to Sweden. Even before all Jews had been deported from Norway, the German intelligence community in Norway noted that the Norwegian people soon would forget "the radical solution of the Jewish question."[71] In other words, the German occupiers were content. Their conclusion was that the action against the Jews did not disturb the economic life of Norway.

Abbreviations

BArch: Bundesarchiv Berlin (German Federal Archives, Berlin)
DMT: Archives of Det Mosaiske Trossamfund, Oslo (Oslo Jewish Community)
OJM: Oslo Jewish Museum
RA: Riksarkivet (Norwegian National Archives)

Notes

1 The Report from the Wannsee Conference is printed in various books, including Towiah Friedmann, *Dokumentensammlung über "Die Deportierung der Juden aus Norwegen nach Auschwitz"* (Haifa, Israel: Stadtverwaltung Ramat Gan, 1963). The original report is also available in high resolution at www.ghwk.de/deut/proto.htm (accessed 15 November 2009).
2 The latest figures according to the *Database of Shoah victims in Norway*, developed by the author, and maintained by Oslo Jewish Museum.
3 This includes some 40 children taken in by Norwegian aid societies in what later has been called "Kindertransporten."
4 Parts of the Norwegian Army, Navy and Air force leadership left Norway along with the Government. The Norwegian officers who negotiated the surrender of Norwegian forces in Trondheim specified that the surrender did not include forces that had left Norwegian soil. The surrender was signed on 10 June 1940.
5 Hans Fredrik Dahl, Guri Hjeltnes, Berit Nøkleby, Nils Johan Ringdal and Øystein Sørensen, eds, *Norsk krigsleksikon 1940–45* (Oslo: Cappelen, 1995), 354–55.
6 Hitler had been enticed by Alfred Rosenberg not to accept a solution along the Danish lines in order to allow Quisling a hand on the steering wheel in Norway. Robert Bohn, *Reichskommissariat Norwegen. "Nationalsozialistische Neuordnung" und Kriegswirtschaft* (Munich: R. Oldenburg Verlag, 2000), 11, 12.
7 Dahl *et al.*, eds, *Norsk krigsleksikon*, 219–20.
8 Quisling was invited as party leader to attend the opening of the Institut zur Erforschung der Judenfrage in Frankfurt a. M. from 26 to 29 March 1941. In a memorandum from the Institut zur Erforschung der Judenfrage to the Foreign Ministry in Berlin, Quisling is noted first among the foreign guests of Reichsleiter Rosenberg. Archives of Das Auswärtiges Amt, Berlin, Eröffnung des Instituts zur Erforschung der Judenfrage in Frankfurt a/M, Aufzeichnung

(Memorandum) from the Institute to Staatsserkretär Luther of Das Auswartiges Amt, 18 February 1941. Quisling also spoke at the conference, and excerpts of the speech were printed in Norwegian papers shortly thereafter. The Nasjonal Samling party later printed a brochure with the whole speech, to be used in party work and as propaganda. Vidkun Quisling, *Kampen mellom arier og jødemakt (The Battle between Aryan and Jewish Power)* (Oslo: Nasjonal Samlings Rikstrykkeri, 1941).

9 Dahl *et al.*, eds, *Norsk krigsleksikon*, 335–37.

10 Dahl *et al.*, eds, *Norsk krigsleksikon*, 304–5.

11 Ulrich Herbert, ed., *Nationalsozialistische Vernichtungspolitik 1939–45. Neue Forschungen und Kontroversen* (Frankfurt: Fischer, 2001), 172.

12 Ian Kershaw, *The Nazi Dictatorship: Problems and Perspectives of Interpretation* (London: Arnold, 2000), esp. chapter 4, "Hitler: 'Master in the Third Reich' or 'Weak Dictator'"?

13 Michael Wildt, *Generation der Unbedingten: Führungskorps des Reichssicherheitshauptamtes* (Hamburg: Hamburger Edition, 2003), 508–11. Stahlecker was later the leader of Einsatzgruppe A during the invasion of Soviet Russia in June 1941. He was killed in battle with partisans in March 1942. The later Befehlshaber der Sicherheitspolizei und des SD in Norway, Heinrich Fehlis, was also part of the Einsatzgruppe Norwegen as the leader of Einsatzkommando Oslo.

14 In fact, *Kriminalkommissar* Wilhelm Esser, the actual executor on the side of the German Security Police, in his letter specifically ordered that he wanted the measure *not* to be mentioned in the press.

15 Samuel Abrahamsen, *Norway's Response to the Holocaust: A Historical Perspective* (New York: Holocaust Library, 1991), 79.

16 Abrahamsen, *Norway's Response to the Holocaust*, 80. Kristian Welhaven (1883–1975) was replaced as chief of police in Oslo in September 1940. Welhaven had opposed the attempted coup d'état by Vidkun Quisling in April 1940. He was later interned in Landsberg, Germany. He returned to Oslo in May 1945 and served again as chief of police until 1954. Dahl *et al.*, eds, *Norsk krigsleksikon*, 447.

17 Letter from Hans S. Jacobsen Moss to General von Kemski, Commander of the *Wehrmacht* in Oslo, dated 29 May 1940. RA, Statspolitiet, Mappe 25 Sachakten C II B 2. Judische Geschäfte. Hans J. Jacobsen (1901–80) was a well-known Norwegian publicist, editor of *Ragnarok*, an extreme-right monthly. He was briefly a member of *Nasjonal Samling* from 1933 to 1934, but later supported the pan-German *Norges Nasjonalsosialistiske Arbeiderparti*, virtually a minuscule variant of NSDAP in Norway. In the fall of 1940, he once again became member of *Nasjonal Samling* and later became county governor in Østfold.

18 Flesch explained in his affidavit after the war that he had experience from similar confiscations in Berlin before the war. RA, L-sak 41 730–31 D Trondheim, affidavit titled "Komplex Landgraff." Flesch was undoubtedly one of the most radical of the local German Security Police commanders. He was executed in Trondheim in 1948.

19 Tagesrapport No. 2 from Befehlshaber der Sicherheitspolizei und des SD in Oslo, dated 3 July 1941, IV C 3–B. Nr. 455/41g. RA, Reichskommissar 1940–45, Der Höhere SS-und Polizeiführer Nord. Sipo/SD. Tagesrapporte June–October 1942, box 2.

20 The Norwegian name "Statspolitiet" was also used by a special branch of the Norwegian police from 1932 to 1937. At that time it was organized as a special riot police with some intelligence functions as well.

21 The suggested law included a definition of the term "Jew" that was more severe than in the German Erste Verordnung zum Reichsbürgergesetz from 14 November 1935. Letter from Minister Ragnar Skancke to the Bishop of Oslo, dated 13 June 1941. RA, Kirke-og undervisningsdepartementet, copy book June 1941.

22 Circular from the Minister of Justice Sverre Riisnæs to county judges 2 October 1942. RA, L-sak Riisnæs, folder: "Justisministerens kontor. Eiendommer tilhørende jøder."

23 Letter from the Bishop of Oslo, Eivind Berggrav, dated 9 September 1941, printed in *Kirkelig hvitbok*, ed. Sigmund Feyling (Oslo: Kirke-og Kulturdepartementet, 1942).

24 Wildt, 511. Ehrlinger later became leader of Einsatzkommando 1b during the attack on the Soviet Union. See Michael Wildt, "Erich Ehrlinger: Ein Vertreter 'kämpfender Verwaltung,'" in *Karrieren der Gewalt. Nationalsozialistische Täterbiographien*, eds Klaus-Michael Mallmann and Gerhard Paul (Darmstadt: Wissenschaftliche Buchgesellschaft, 2004).

25 Later renamed "Germanske SS-Norge."

26 Andrej Angrick, *Besatzungspolitik und Massenmord: Die Einsatzgruppe D in der Südlichen Sowjetunion 1941–43* (Hamburg: Hamburger Edition, 2003), 305–6.

27 Nils Johan Ringdal, *Gal mann til rett tid* (Oslo: Aschehoug, 2004), 106–7.

28 Letter from SS-volunteer to Jonas Lie, dated 9 May 1944. RA, L-sak D4135.

29 RA, Reichskommissariat 1940–45, Hauptabteilung Volkswirtschaft Allgemeine Abteilung (Zentralabteilung), correspondence and memos, box 7. Memo (Vermerk über die Besprechung der Hauptabteilung Verwaltung mit den Dienststellen-leitern) 9 January 1942.

30 RA, Reichskommissariat 1940–45, Hauptabteilung Verwaltung, Abteilung Finanzen 2 500, box 44. Letter from Regierungsrat Korff, Abteilung Finanzen to Ministerialrat Dr Breyhan, Reichministerium der Finanzen, Berlin, 28 November 1942.

31 DMT, Archives of Jødisk Hjelpeforening (Jewish Aid Society). Letter from rabbi Julius Samuel to the board of the aid society, 25 February 1941.

32 Verordnungsblatt No. 5, Verordnung über den Nachrichtenverkehr für Norwegen 30 July 1942, §7.

33 The letters from Der Befehlshaber der Sicherheitspolizei, Heinrich Fehlis, to the Norwegian Ministry of Police 10 October, 22 November and 15 December. Letters from the Ministry of Police to the Befehlshaber der Sicherheitspolizei 3 and 29 November. RA, Pol.dep., folder "Registrering av jøder."

34 OJM, archive of a private donor. Anonymous letter to Minister of Police Jonas Lie, dated 9 April 1942, marked "The Minister J.nr. 578/J."

35 Max Tau, *En flyktning finner sitt land* (Oslo: Den norske bokklubben, 1967),100. Max Tau (1897–1976) was born in Bytom (Beuthen), Silesia. He was a well-known publisher of Norwegian authors in Germany, and escaped Germany in 1939 to settle in Norway. Norwegian author Knut Hamsun wrote a letter on his behalf to German authorities in 1938. In 1942, Tau escaped to Sweden. He acquired Norwegian citizenship in 1944 in Stockholm.

36 RA, L-dom 2479/47. Interrogation of Wilhelm Wagner, dated 12 April 1946.

37 Raul Hilberg, *The Destruction of the European Jews* (New York: Holmes and Meier, 1985), 407.

38 At least 16 Jews were deported individually before the start of systematic arrests and deportations on 26 October 1942. Source: *Database of Shoah victims.* A majority were politically active Jews.

39 The four Jews were arrested in Trondheim 8 February 1942, accused of listening to British radio broadcasts. They were executed on 7 March 1942 in Trondheim.

40 DMT, the archives of Marcus Levin, box 4, Lists and letters from 1943. Report from Marcus Levin, the Norwegian representative of American Jewish Joint Distribution Committee (JOINT).

41 The Norwegian Police was put under direct German command during the state of emergency in Trondheim.

42 National Library of Norway, Private archives of Didrik Arup Seip. Report from Wolfgang Geldmacher concerning his activities in helping Jews escape to Sweden, dated 22 December 1945. Geldmacher was a German engineer who settled in Norway in 1932. He had contacts inside the German *Wehrmacht* and with the German Army major Theodor Steltzer. Steltzer was peripherally connected to the so-called "Kreislauer Kreis" and Helmuth James von Moltke. Moltke had visited Norway and warned Steltzer that sooner or later the Norwegian Jews would be deported.

43 The propaganda included quotes from Martin Luther. See, for example, Aftenposten, 24 November 1942: "Martin Luthers mening om jødene."

44 The law itself did not mention Jews specifically. *Norsk Lovtidend 1*, No. 55. The law had the curious title: "Law on the amendment to the temporary decree of 6 October 1941 concerning securing persons suspected of certain violations." Dated 24 October 1941.

45 RA, L Dom 3323–25. Interrogation of former police inspector Sverre Dürbeck, 28 August 1945: "…present was in addition to M[arthinsen] also Hauptsturmführer Wagner of the SS. In addition there was present another German whose name he cannot remember [probably Wagner's assistant Untersturmführer Erhard (Harry) Böhm], and his colleague police inspector Knut Rød."

46 Much in the same way as described by Hilberg, *The Destruction of the European Jews*, 55. The original study of this aspect of the anti-Jewish policy was made by Uwe Dietrich Adam in

Judenpolitik im Dritten Reich (Düssseldorf: Droste Verlag, 1972). An even more substantial study of Hitler's unwritten order was made by Peter Longerich in *The Unwritten Order: Hitler's Role in the Final Solution* (New York: The History Press, 2004).

47 RA, Statspolitiet (State Police), Jødeaksjonene STAPO. OV 5000/42. Report from police officer Houmb, assistant to police inspector Knut Rød, 5 November 1942. According to the report, eight men worked round the clock that weekend to prepare the lists and divide them up according to national police districts and precincts in Oslo.

48 RA, Statspolitiet (State Police), STAPO C II B 2, folder "Jødiske forbund." Telegram from the leader off the State Police to all police districts 25 October 1942 at 10:30.

49 RA, Statspolitiet (State Police), Jødeaksjonene STAPO, OV 5000/42. Report from police officer Houmb, assistant to police inspector Knut Rød, 5 November 1942.

50 According to the prison protocol from the Berg concentration camp. Statsarkivet Kongsberg (State Archives of Kongsberg). The actual transport from different parts of Norway could take several days.

51 *Norsk Lovtidend 1* No. 55, Lov om inndraging av formue som tilhører jøder (Law on the confiscation of property belonging to Jews). In § 2 was specified: "Property of any kind belonging to a Jew who is a Norwegian citizen, or stateless Jew who lives in this country, is confiscated on behalf of the Norwegian State treasury. This regulation includes property belonging to a Jew's wife and children."

52 Letter from Vidkun Quisling to the leader of the State Police Karl Alfred Marthinsen, 12 November 1942. RA, Tilbakeføringskontoret, box marked: "Del E III Jødeboer, sønnenfj. alfabetisk J-K." Folder marked: "Jødeloven av 26. Oktober 1942. Beslutninger om jøder. Frigivelse av inndratte formuer av billighetshensyn."

53 Quisling held a speech on a party gathering in Trondheim on 6 December 1942 that was widely published in the press. In his speech, Quisling defended the action taken against the Jews. Additionally, he made an attack on persons of "mixed blood:" "These days many tragic events happen in Norway. Many Norwegians have married Jews, and their children are half-Jews, which means they are really Jews, because their Jewish side is so dominant. These are tragedies of the most agonizing kind." *Aftenposten*, 7 December 1942.

54 There were approximately 120–30 so-called "mixed marriages" in Norway. Some 70 men in mixed marriages remained in the Norwegian concentration camp Berg until 2 May 1945, when they were sent to Sweden according to a deal struck between the representative of the Swedish government and the Red Cross and the Gestapo in Oslo. Five women in "mixed marriages," interned in the German camp Grini outside Oslo, were also freed at that time.

55 Norsk Lovtidend 1 No. 59, Lov om meldeplikt for jøder (Law on the registration of Jews).

56 RA, Tilbakeføringskontoret, Del A III Div. saksomslag fra Finansdepartementet I, letter from the Ministry of Finance to the Board of Liquidations, 5 April 1943.

57 The work of the Board of Liquidations was extended and included a large staff. There is no room within the framework of this article to discuss the liquidation of Jewish property. For a more complete description, see Berit Reisel and Bjarte Bruland, *The Reisel/Bruland Report on the confiscation of Jewish Property in Norway during World War II. Part of Official Norwegian Report 1997 No. 22* (Oslo 1997).

58 Examples of such letters are widespread and can be found in RA, Archives of Statspolitiet.

59 Oskar Mendelsohn, *Jødenes historie i Norge gjennom 300 år* (Oslo: Universitetsforlaget, 1986), 2:102–3.

60 RA, L Dom 2479/47 Trial against Wilhelm Arthur Konstantin Wagner, folder "Dok. 12–50." Report from the leader of the State Police Karl Alfred Marthinsen to Vidkun Quisling entitled "Evacuation of Jews" on 27 November 1942. According to the report, Marthinsen received the order on 24 November at 8 o'clock in the evening.

61 RA, L sak 627, Telegram from the leader of the State Police to Police Districts, 25 November 1942. In the telegram was specified that the Jews were to bring food for four days, blankets and necessary personal items as well as rationing cards. Their flats were to be locked and sealed.

62 RA, L Dom 2479/47 Trial against Wilhelm Arthur Konstantin Wagner, folder "Dok. 12–50." Report from the Leader of the State Police Karl Alfred Marthinsen to Vidkun Quisling, titled "Evacuation of Jews" on 27 November 1942.

63 Letter from II./Pol.Rgt. 17 Feldposteneinheit 40562C to Der Befehlshaber der Ordnungspolizei, Abt. I a, dated 26 November 1942. RA, Der Reichskommissar für die Besetzten Norwegischen

Gebiete 1940–45 – Befehlhaber der Ordnungspolizei, box 98. Fifty men were picked from the regiment, under the command of *Oberleutnant* Manig.

64 BArch, ZB 7687 A2 Judendeportationen aus Norwegen. Telegram from the leader of the Gestapo, Sturmbannführer Helmuth Reinhard to Stapoleitstelle Stettin 25 November 1942 at 00.55 hours. In the telegram, Reinhard specifies that the transport will include 700–900 Jews of all ages. The telegram begins thus: "AUS BESONDEREN GRUENDEN KANN ICH ERST HEUTE MITTEILEN DAS AM 26.11.42 EIN SCHIFFTRANSPORT VON UNGEFAEHR 7–900 MANNLICHEN UND WEIBLICHEN JUDEN IN ALLEN ALTERSTUFEN VON OSLO NACH STETTIN DURCHGEFUEHRT WERDEN WIRD."

65 BArch, ZB 7687 A2 Judendeportationen aus Norwegen. Telegram from RSHA, office IV B 4 to the HQ of the German Security Police in Oslo and Stettin 25 November 1942, 6 o'clock.

66 RA, L Dom 2479/47 Trial against Wilhelm Arthur Konstantin Wagner, folder "Dok. 12–50." Report from the Leader of the State Police Karl Alfred Marthinsen to Vidkun Quisling, titled "Evacuation of Jews" on 27 November 1942.

67 This happened, among other places, in Bergen, where the State Police arrested "full Jews" and "half Jews," including children in mixed marriages. Late in the evening of 25 November 1945, these Jews were "sorted out." Twenty-five Jews were arrested that day and ten were eventually transported to Oslo on a train late in the evening. The transport did not arrive in Oslo until after the *Donau* had left the harbor. RA, L-dom 585. Report from the State Police in Bergen to the leader of the State Police, 30 November 1942.

68 RA, L Dom 2479/47. Interrogation of Wilhelm Wagner, 12 April 1946.

69 These laws (and other laws prepared by the Quisling government) were considered illegal by the Norwegian government in exile in London.

70 OJM, archive of private donor. Letter from the Ministry of Interior to the Ministry of Finance, 13 January 1943, marked 247/1943. The letter includes a draft of the law (*Lov om visse bestemmelser for jøder*).

71 RA, mikrofilm Helge Paulsen. "Niederschrift über die Ic-Besprechung beim AOK Norwegen in der Zeit vom 8.-11.12.1942," Anlage 120 zum Tätigkeitsbericht Dezember 1942. Quote: "Die Gesamtkirche Norwegens hat für die Juden interpelliert, als bekannt wurde, dass die Juden zum Osten transportiert wurden. Die radikale Lösung der Judenfrage wird jedoch der egoistische Norweger vergessen."

22

THE SPECIAL CHARACTERISTICS OF THE HOLOCAUST IN HUNGARY, 1938–45

Kinga Frojimovics

As an introduction, let us examine how two very different institutions belonging to different time periods, which nonetheless both devoted themselves to confronting the historical trauma of the Holocaust, have defined the main characteristics of the Holocaust in Hungary. A Hungarian Jewish relief organization that was established to assist Holocaust survivors in the immediate aftermath of the Holocaust, the Budapest-based National Relief Committee for Deportees in Hungary (*Deportáltakat Gondozó Országos Bizottság*, DEGOB), took testimonies from about 5,000 survivors between June 1945 and April 1946. DEGOB thus created one of the largest early post-Holocaust testimony collections.[1] Its staff collected testimonial protocols from survivors according to a previously prepared questionnaire that consisted of more than 300 questions.[2] The questionnaire focused on the following 12 question-clusters.[3]

1 Personal data (recorded on the headings of the protocols)—10 questions.
2 The situation and status of the Jews in the deportee's place of residence—18 questions.
3 Ghettoization and its antecedents—27 questions.
4 Deportation—21 questions.
5 Arrival in the concentration camp—16 questions.
6 Life in the concentration camp—60 questions.
7 The organization of, and life in, the work camps (*Arbeitslager*)—55 questions.
8 Evacuation—34 questions.
9 Characteristics of camps passed through during evacuation—19 questions.
10 Circumstances of liberation—12 questions.
11 Life in the camps after liberation—24 questions.
12 The journey towards home—14 questions.

For DEGOB, in the summer of 1945, a few months after the liberation of Hungary in early April, the historical concept that later became called the Holocaust almost exclusively consisted of the ghettoization and deportation of the Jews and their subsequent fate in various concentration camps (death and work camps). Two-thirds of the 12 question-clusters (numbers 3–10) and almost 80 percent of the questions themselves (244 questions) were concerned with these topics. According to DEGOB's implicit definition, therefore, the most characteristic or most important phase of the Holocaust in

Hungary was the so-called German phase, which started on 19 March 1944, when the German army occupied Hungary, and did not end with the liberation of Hungary by the Red Army. According to DEGOB then, the Holocaust of the Jews of Hungary ended only when all the concentration camps—death and labor camps—as well as all the Jews on the roads who were marched in forced marches or taken by train or trucks from camp to camp, had been liberated, which almost coincides with the end of the entire World War II in early May 1945.

In contrast to this early view of a Jewish organization of what the Holocaust is, the definition of the Holocaust Memorial Center, which was established as a state organization in 2004 in Budapest, is very different. The main objective of the Memorial Center is "to present the history of both persecution based on race, religion, and political beliefs and its consequences, and the Jewish and Gypsy Holocaust as part of the national tragedy and as a shameful chapter in the European culture and history."[4] The Memorial Center's permanent exhibition, entitled "From Deprivation of Rights to Genocide," defines the Holocaust as follows:

> The dominant motif of the exhibition is the relationship between state and its citizens. 1938 marks the beginning of the process where *the Hungarian state deprived a specific group of its citizens from all that makes a man a man*—from their rights, property, freedom, human dignity, and in the end, their very existence. This process accelerated fatally in 1944, after the German occupation. Accordingly, the exhibition does not present the events in chronological order; it is based on units that present the different phases of the persecution—the deprivation of civil rights, property, freedom, human dignity, and existence.[5] [My italics, K.F.]

From the distance of six decades, the official memorial place of the Hungarian Republic defined the Hungarian Holocaust in a much broader sense than did the DEGOB. According to the definition underlying and informing the permanent exhibition, the most characteristic phases and events of the Hungarian Holocaust are: the anti-Jewish legislation of the Hungarian state (from 1938 onward), ghettoization and deportation after the *Wehrmacht* occupied Hungary (spring and summer of 1944), and the Arrow Cross reign of terror (from October 1944 onward). The conception of the exhibition emphasizes that it was the Hungarian state that deprived its Jewish citizens first of their rights, then of their possessions and of their freedom and human dignity, and finally, of their lives. In the implementation of this process, the occupying German forces seemed to be relegated to the level of mere partners.

Now let us summarize the events of the Hungarian Holocaust by paying attention to the viewpoints described above.

The stages of the Holocaust in Hungary until the German occupation of the country, 1938–44

Anti-Jewish legislation

If we focus on the phases of the process by which the Hungarian state increasingly deprived its Jewish citizens of their basic human rights, we can observe that the

Hungarian regime, years before the German occupation of the country, reached the stage of murdering Jews. The state started with the complete exclusion of the Jews from Hungarian society by means of enacting anti-Jewish legislation.

In March 1938, Prime Minister Kálmán Darányi openly announced an armaments program and stated that in order to solve the Jewish question, political as well as legal means were needed.[6] With this statement, the solving of the Jewish question, which until then had been kept on the political agenda only by extreme right-wing organizations, for the first time since 1920 rose once again to the level of government policy. This component of Darányi's program was implemented after Hungary became an immediate neighbor of Nazi Germany as a consequence of the annexation of Austria (12–13 March 1938). Then the Hungarian Parlement enacted Act 1938: XV, the First (anti-)Jewish Law.[7]

The First (anti-)Jewish Law, which came into force on 28 May 1938, stipulated a reduction within 5 years of the percentage of Jews within the liberal professions, as well as within financial, commercial, and industrial enterprises that employed more than 10 people, to no more than 20 percent.[8] Yet this law did not satisfy the extreme Right, which demanded more radical laws in order to eliminate the Jews from social and economic spheres. In order to appease the extreme Right, the Second (anti-)Jewish Law (Act 1939:IV), entitled "On Limiting the Expansion of Jews within the Public and Economic Spheres," was enacted, and came into force on 5 May 1939.[9] This law emerged in the context of the euphoria following the reclaiming of territories lost by Hungary in the aftermath of World War I. According to the First Vienna Award (2 November 1938), Hungary regained from Czechoslovakia the majority of the so-called Upper Region (Felvidék). Between 15 and 18 March 1939, the Hungarian army occupied the Sub-Carpathian Region (Kárpátalja).

According to the Second (anti-)Jewish Law, Jews were those who belonged to the Jewish religion and those who had one parent or two grandparents who belonged to the Jewish religion at the time of the enactment of the Second (anti-)Jewish Law. Individuals in this latter category were dubbed "half Jews" in the detailed explanation. Those who had converted to the Christian faith before 1 August 1919 were not to be regarded as Jews if their ancestors had been born in Hungary before 1 January 1849, or if they had converted to Christianity before they reached their seventh birthday.

The Second (anti-)Jewish Law limited Jewish participation in the various branches of industry, commerce, religious life, and liberal professions to 6–12 percent. After the Second (anti-)Jewish Law came into force, Jews could not become Hungarian citizens by means of either marriage, naturalization, or legitimization. Moreover, the Ministry of the Interior had to review the documents of those who had been naturalized after 1 July 1914. These measures created masses of Jews with unsettled citizenship status, who were deported in 1941. Their deportation culminated in the mass murder at Kamenetsk-Podolsk in Galicia on 27–28 August 1941.[10]

It was obvious for the Jews of Hungary that the Second (anti-)Jewish Law did not merely signify some kind of a limitation of civil rights, but rather the complete exclusion of the Jews from the entire political, social, and economic life of the country. Therefore, unlike on previous occasions, the Jewish elite adamantly, albeit entirely in vain, protested against the measures by drawing upon the support of foreign Jewish organizations.[11] In effect, the first two anti-Jewish laws deprived about 90,000 Jews of their livelihoods, which led to the impoverishment of about 200,000–220,000 Jews.

The enactment of the Third (anti-)Jewish Law and two large-scale massacres at Kamenetsk-Podolsk and Újvidék happened within less than a year, while László

Bárdossy was prime minister (3 April 1941–9 March 1942). The Third (anti-) Jewish Law (Act 1941:XV), entitled "On the Amendment and Alteration of Act 1894:XXXI on Marriage Law as well as the Racist Regulations Necessary to Accomplishing This," came into effect on 2 August 1941.[12] This law, which was based on the 1935 Nuremberg Laws, forbade marriages as well as sexual relations outside marriage between Jews and non-Jews. It defined as Jewish everyone who had at least two Jewish grandparents or were of the Jewish faith. From among those who had converted to Christianity, people were not considered Jewish if they were born as Christians and, at the time of their birth, their parents had already been converted to Christianity. However, if they had two grandparents of the Jewish faith, then they were still Jewish according to the new law. With the enactment of this law, then, the process of wholly separating out and excluding the Jews from Hungarian society, a process that began in 1938 with the First (anti-) Jewish Law, was completed.[13]

The first mass murders, 1941–42

A few months after the completion of the process of legal elimination of the Jews from Hungarian society, the first steps towards their physical elimination were also carried out. The events, policies, and decisions leading up to the mass murder at Kamenets-Podolsk in Galicia occurred in the 1930s, when the National Central Alien Control Office (Külföldieket Ellenőrző Országos Központi Hatóság, KEOKH), which was established in 1930, overrode its original commission—the control of foreign citizens staying in Hungary—and aimed at drawing under its authority as many Jews as possible, Hungarian Jews included, as all Jews had been deemed "undesirables" by the policy-makers of the KEOKH.[14] In June 1941, Hungary entered World War II, and the clerks of the KEOKH suggested expelling from Hungary all the Jews whom it considered undesirable. Jews were to be expelled to those territories of Galicia that had recently come under the Hungarian military administration. This deportation was designed primarily to expel Polish and Russian Jews from Hungary, but, in reality, KEOKH rounded up many Jews, most of the time together with their families, who had been born in Hungary but could not prove it. Furthermore, in the Sub-Carpathian region, entire communities were deported. In July and August 1941, the Hungarian authorities deported tens of thousands of Jews to Galicia.[15]

On 25 August 1941, the German authorities in Galicia held a conference in Vinnitza and called upon participant *SS-Obergruppenführer* Friedrich Jeckeln, the commander of the local SS and police force, to liquidate the Jews who had been expelled from Hungary, and were wandering in the area, by 1 September.[16] On 27–28 August 1941, 23,600 Jews were murdered at Kamenets-Podolsk.[17] While local Jews were also executed, the majority of the victims had been expelled from Hungary. Those Jews from Hungary who were not killed at Kamenets-Podolsk, were taken to various ghettos in Galicia, such as Gaysin, Delatin, Horodenka, Kolomea (Kołomyja), Nadwórna, and Tarnopol. There, they shared the fate of the local Jews.

At the end of the summer of 1941, then, the first large-scale mass murder of Jews from Hungary occurred. Here, the exclusive responsibility of the Hungarian authorities in the murder of tens of thousands of Jews cannot be established with complete unanimity. However, in the case of the second mass murder, carried out in Novi Sad (Újvidék), the Hungarian authorities were solely responsible. On 11 April 1941, the Hungarian army occupied part of the so-called Southern Territories (Délvidék). Serb partisans made frequent raids. The Hungarian authorities decided to eliminate the threat posed by the partisans when they had killed four gendarmes in Zsablya in early January 1942.[18] What they meant by eliminating the threat, however, was a large-scale massacre. The Hungarians murdered 3,309 people, about 2,500 Serbs and 700 Jews. Historian Enikő Sajti explains the massacre, for which the punishment of the partisans was merely a pretext, by reasons having to do with Hungary's foreign policy.[19] Both mass murders demonstrate that the Hungarian political leadership, by closely collaborating with the army, made efforts on its own to dispose of a large part of its Jewish population well before the German army occupied Hungary.

A special feature of the Holocaust in Hungary: the history of the Jewish forced labor service[20]

The new Home Defense Act, Act 1939:II, came into force in 1939. This act was not created specifically against Jews, but many of its articles were later used to discriminate against Jews. According to the act, in times of war or those of war-menace, all men between the ages of 14 and 70 could be called up for labor in order to protect the nation. Paragraph 230 stated that Hungarian citizens above the age of 21 who were found unfit for military service could be compelled to do "forced labor service for public utility" in special work camps for not more than 3 months. Even though the law did not state it, Hungary's aim was to exclude the "untrustworthy elements" from the army. These were, at the time, communists, members of ethnic minorities, and Jews.

Forced labor service as an institution began in July 1939, and the first ones to be called up were those born in 1916. In 1940, Jewish forced laborers worked in Hungary in many localities; they were engaged mainly in forest-clearing, building canals, draining swamps, constructing railroads, airfields and roads, unloading and loading freight cars, road maintenance, etc. At this point they were still working under relatively "normal" circumstances.

Forced labor service on the Eastern Front

After Hungary attacked the Soviet Union, forced laborers were typically working on constructing roads and bridges in the Carpathian Mountains. Then, in the spring of 1942, the Minister of Defense ordered that the majority of the Jewish forced laborer companies had to be commanded to the theater of military operations. Tens of thousands of Jewish men were called up, not according to age, which left room for arbitrary practices and corruption. Leftists and Zionists, Jewish leaders, members of the Jewish intelligentsia, and successful businessmen were drafted together with anyone who could be deemed a troublemaker or a potential economic competitor to non-Jews.

The Second Hungarian Division under the command of Gusztáv Jány left for the front on 11 April 1942. More than 50,000 Jews served in the forced laborer companies between the spring of 1942 and 1944. The forced laborers were compelled to perform all sorts of terrible tasks in inhuman conditions, such as clearing minefields with their bare hands. Clearly, the aim of the majority of their guards was for them not to survive. On 12 January 1943, the Red Army near Voronezh breached the German–Hungarian front line. According to estimates of the Minister of Defense, Vilmos Nagybaczoni Nagy, only about 60,000–70,000 Hungarian soldiers and 6,000–7,000 Jews returned to Hungary.

Forced labor service in Bor

In 1943, as a consequence of the advance of the Red Army, Nazi Germany lost crucial sources of raw material. Therefore, the Germans wanted to increase the productivity in their remaining mines. Fifty percent of the copper needed by the German war industry was provided by the copper mines of Bor in former Yugoslavia. On 2 July 1943, a German–Hungarian agreement was signed according to which Hungary lent 3,000 Jewish workers to Germany. The forced laborer companies that had been lent remained under Hungarian military command in Bor. In reality, 6,200 forced laborers were sent; the overwhelming majority of them were Jews, but Sabbatarians and Jehovah's Witnesses were also among the conscripts. These forced laborers worked in the mines in terrible conditions.

In August 1944, the Germans decided to evacuate the mines. The first group of forced laborers from Hungary (3,200–3,600 men) was marched on foot through Hungary to work on the construction of defense lines around Vienna. Many of the workers were killed during the forced march by both the Hungarian soldiers and the Germans. In Cservenka, in one night, SS soldiers massacred 700–1,000 Jews. Those who survived the march were eventually taken to concentration camps in Germany. The second group, about 2,600, was liberated by Serb partisans.

Forced labor service in the spring and summer of 1944 and in the Szálasi era

In March 1944, before the German Army occupied Hungary, about 63,000 Jewish forced laborers had been working within the framework of the Hungarian army. After the German occupation of Hungary, the Ministry of Defense called up forced laborers—more than 21,000 men—to form additional forced laborer companies from Jews and members of other ethnic groups in Hungary.

When the Jews of Hungary were ghettoized and, except from the capital, were deported, forced labor paradoxically became a possible—even though very difficult and far from sure—way to survive. In June 1944, Minister of Defense Lajos Csatay called up every Jewish male between 18 and 48 years of age for forced labor service. In some localities, draft notifications were delivered to the ghettos and internment camps. The main reason for this was that Hungary was increasingly suffering from a labor shortage. Soon, therefore, authorities began to call up women as well. First, women between 18 and 30 years old were called up. In the summer and fall of 1944, many forced laborers—women among them—who had been drafted from Budapest were working in war factories, on clearing away rubble, digging trenches, constructing and mending railroads and airfields, etc.

As is well-known, Hungary's fascist movement, the Arrow Cross, led by Ferenc Szálasi, came to power through a coup on 15 October 1944. A week later, its Minister of Defense, Károly Beregfy, ordered the calling up of every Jewish male between 16 and 60 years of age and every Jewish female between 16 and 40 years of age. After the deportations of the Jews from the Hungarian provinces, Jews who could have been called up remained only in Budapest. Those forced laborers who returned from Bor and the Eastern Front also remained in service. On 26 October, Beregfy gave the Germans dozens of forced laborer contingents to construct defense lines for Vienna and fortification lines in western Hungary. These forced laborers—men and women—were sent towards the western border of Hungary. Some of them were taken by train, but the majority were marched on foot. Many were murdered during these forced marches, which were called death-marches. The people reached the border in such a terrible state that, on numerous occasions, the Germans did not even want to take them. All-in-all, about 50,000 Jews were given to the Germans during what would be the last winter of the war. These Jews were working in awful conditions on constructing the German fortification line. The overwhelming majority of both Hungarian and German guards were exceptionally cruel. Jews who survived were marched to concentration camps such as Mauthausen and Günskirchen. In the work camps and concentration camps, and during the death-marches, about two-thirds of the forced laborers given to Nazi Germany perished. All told, at least 70,000 Jewish forced laborers from Hungary lost their lives during World War II.

The stages of the Holocaust in Hungary after the German Army occupied the country, March 1944 to April 1945

Anti-Jewish legislation effectively excluded the Jews from Hungarian society in what might be called the first phase of the Holocaust—the so-called Hungarian phase—between 1938 and 1942. The killing of the majority of the Jews characterized the second phase of the Holocaust in Hungary, the so-called German phase, which began with the German invasion of its ally on 19 March 1944, prompted by concerns that Hungary was trying to extricate itself from the war. Even though, in this phase, the fate of the Jews was decided by the Germans, we have to realize that without the active and effective participation of Hungarian authorities, the stripping of the Jews of all their belongings, their ghettoization, and their deportation could not have been carried out. Rather than occasionally lending a hand to the Germans, the Hungarian administrative apparatus regarded the preparation of the Jews for deportation entirely as its own business.

After the German Army occupied Hungary, the new Hungarian prime minister, Döme Sztójay, and his government employed the legislative system in order to facilitate the anti-Jewish policy of Nazi Germany. The Hungarian government, together with local authorities, made stripping the Jews of all their belongings and their ghettoization possible by issuing a series of decrees. The entire Hungarian administrative apparatus actively participated in carrying out these decrees—members of the government, ministerial and local clerks and functionaries, gendarmes, policemen, etc. According to László Karsai, about 200,000 state officials carried out the anti-Jewish policy of the government.[21]

The creation of a legal framework by employing an avalanche of decrees instead of enacting laws is unique in the legal history of Hungary. Randolph L. Braham, in the appendix of his monograph, compiled the most important decrees concerning Jews after the *Wermacht* had occupied Hungary. He lists 107 decrees.[22] The first decree, which appeared on 29 March 1944, concerned Jewish telephone subscribers.[23] On 31 March, five new decrees appeared: Jews could no longer employ non-Jews in their households; Jews could not work as lawyers or hold public service positions; Jews were expelled from the Chamber of Journalists as well as that of the theatre and motion picture industry; Jews had to register their automobiles; and through perhaps the most invasive executive order, Decree No. 1240/1944, Jews were forced to wear a discriminatory sign.[24] This decree, the first measure taken in order to identify and separate the Jews from the rest of society, was issued by Prime Minister Döme Sztójay. According to the decree, from 5 April onwards, when not at home, every Jew over the age of six had to wear a textile, canary-yellow, six-pointed star, 10 by 10 centimeters in diameter, sewn onto the left side of the upper part of his or her overgarment.[25] Besides children under the age of six, there were other Jews who were exempt from wearing the yellow star, mainly those who received medals in World War I. Two decrees appeared on 7 April as well: one prohibited Jews from traveling; the other forced Jews to register their radios.[26]

The fact that, on the same day, Jews were denied the right to enter certain professions and at the same time forced to wear the yellow star of David demonstrates that Hungarian authorities proactively aimed at eliminating Jews from Hungary's economic and social life. That decrees concerning property and sources of information[27] were published together with decrees preparing ghettoization and deportation also points to a similar conclusion.

The last stage: ghettoization and deportation, spring and summer of 1944

When, on 19 March 1944, the *Wehrmacht* occupied Hungary, about 800,000 Jews lived in the country.[28] A secret decree (6136/1944. BM VII. res. [confidential]) that appeared on 4 April 1944 concerned all of them. By this decree, the Minister of the Interior ordered that within 4 days (by 8 April), in all localities (villages, towns, etc.), authorities had to draw up lists containing the names of Jewish residents. In theory, these lists would facilitate the ghettoization of the Jews. However, in the majority of instances, officials appear not to have prepared such lists as there are so few of them in the archives.

Another secret decree (6163/1944. BM VII. res. [confidential]) contained the results of a conference held in the Ministry of the Interior on 7 April, in which the two Under-Secretaries of State of the Ministry of the Interior, László Baky and László Endre, who were charged with the task of "settling the Jewish question," and two members of the *Sonderkommando* headed by Eichmann, participated along with other functionaries. This conference was held in order to begin the ghettoization of the Jews, and its rulings were issued to local authorities on the same day. The secret decree signed by Baky (6163/1944. BM VII. res. [confidential]) contained the following:

> Subject: Designation of the place of residence for Jews.
>
> The Hung. Roy. Government will soon cleanse the country of Jews. I order the cleansing to be done according to territorial sections. Jews, without distinction as to their gender and age, had to be transported to designated camps. In towns and larger villages, a portion of the Jews will be placed in Jewish buildings or ghettos designated by the authorities...This decree is strictly confidential, and the authorities as well as the commanders of the headquarters are responsible so that no one should learn about all this before the commencement of the cleansing action.[29]

The decree divided Hungary into six zones. In the first zone, which consisted of Sub-Carpathia and North-East Hungary, ghettoization started on 16 April 1944, on a Sunday following the last day of Passover. In other words, the first phase of the physical elimination of the Jews started in Hungary well before the cabinet's ghetto-decree ordering the "moving together" of the Jews, which was published on 28 April.[30]

On 22 April 1944, Decree No. 1520/1944. ME., concerning Jewish leadership, was published.[31] The decree ordered the establishment of a new central Jewish council called

"The Alliance of the Jews of Hungary [*Magyarországi Zsidók Szövetsége*]," a name Hungarian authorities preferred to "The Central Council of the Hungarian Jews [*Magyar Zsidók Központi Tanácsa*]," which had already been established in compliance with German orders. Simultaneously, Minister of the Interior Andor Jaross dissolved all Jewish organizations. Local Jewish councils were established on the basis of this decree whenever Hungarian authorities ordered the Jews to form them as branches of the Alliance of the Jews of Hungary. Typically, local Jewish councils organized the transfer of Jews into ghettos, as well as certain aspects of life in the ghettos. They also were responsible for maintaining contacts with Hungarian and German authorities.

On 28 April 1944, after the beginning of ghettoization, the ghetto-decree (Decree 1610/1944. ME.) officially appeared.[32] With the exception of Budapest, ghettos were established in 185 localities.[33] Through the 28 April decree, leaders of towns and villages that did not have a population larger than 10,000 could compel the Jews to move to another designated town or village. The administrative head of towns or villages with a population over 10,000 could designate parts, streets, or buildings of the town or village as places for the Jews to live. The decree made clear that it did not need to be enforced in cases of Jews who were exempt from wearing the yellow star of David. Therefore children under the age of six should not have been ghettoized, but there was not one locality in Hungary where authorities did not confine children to the ghetto together with adults.

Administrative leaders of those settlements in which ghettos would be established issued decrees concerning the exact territories of the ghettos and the processes of moving in. In some places, these decrees also considered moving the non-Jewish population out of the designated territory of the ghetto. These decrees were advertised on posters and placards. Ghettos were established in various places. There were localities in which the ghettos were established in the inner city, where many Jews lived; and there were settlements where the ghettos were established in slums without sewage systems, at the outskirts of the settlements. There were ghettos that were established in deserted factories and industrial units unfit for human occupancy. Mostly women, children, and older men had to move into the ghettos, since the majority of the men were drafted for forced labor.

The process of moving into the ghettos lasted many days, and the Jewish councils were responsible for its implementation. In the small settlements with fewer than 10,000 inhabitants, policemen or gendarmes imprisoned the Jews for a few days, usually in Jewish communal buildings. The Jews were cruelly interrogated in order to give up their hidden valuables. After this, they were sent to ghettos established in larger settlements with more than 10,000 inhabitants. At the same time, moving local Jews into the ghettos commenced in the larger settlements. Money confiscated from Jewish sources financed the entire operation.

A mayor, head of the police department, or, in ghettos guarded by gendarmes, a gendarme-commander, controlled life in the ghettos. In the majority of cases, the Jewish councils also formed Jewish police forces in order to maintain order. Food should have been provided by municipal authorities by using money and provisions confiscated from Jewish sources. In reality, however, in most of the ghettos, Jews received hardly any food after the supplies they brought with them ran out. In the overwhelming majority of the ghettos, Jews were cruelly interrogated by detectives and gendarmes. Torture was used, and women were submitted to invasive body-searches.

In general, Jews spent a period from one month to six weeks in the ghettos in the provinces of Hungary. After this period, they were transferred to transit camps of the counties, the so-called entrainment centers. These ad hoc sites were usually set up in deserted factories, in which thousands of people could be "accommodated," and they were either close to railway stations or beside railway lines. In these entrainment centers, Jews lived sometimes for a whole week without sufficient food or water.

The majority of the deportations were carried out between 15 May and 8 July 1944. However, the first deporting train left for Auschwitz from the Kistarcsa Internment Camp on 28 April 1944, and the last left from Sárvár for Auschwitz on 25 July, well after Regent Miklós Horthy had already prohibited further deportations on 6 July 1944.

From Hungary, almost all Jewish deportees were sent to Auschwitz. In the spring and summer of 1944, altogether 145 trains arrived in Auschwitz-Birkenau from Hungary, carrying more than 430,000 deported Jews.[34] Only six trains had a different destination. The famous Kasztner-train with 1,684 Jews reached Bergen-Belsen (and then ultimately Switzerland), and five trains carrying about 1,500 Jews arrived in Strasshof (in Austria), from where they were sent to labor-camps in the vicinity of Vienna.

The fate of the Jews of Budapest in the summer and early fall of 1944 as well as after the Arrow Cross coup

According to the plans of Hungarian and German authorities, the ghettoization and deportation of the Jews of Budapest would have been carried out after the Hungarian provinces were declared "free of Jews." As the first step of the concentration of the Jews of the capital, the mayor of Budapest issued several decrees in June 1944 in order to designate so-called "yellow-star houses." These houses were established in all 14 districts of the capital, and from 24 June 1944, the more than 200,000 Jews of Budapest were compelled to live in some 2,000 buildings, designated by virtue of the fact that 50 percent or more of their occupants were Jewish. Officials believed that, by concentrating Jews in these dwellings, spread out all over Budapest, they would deter the Allies from bombing the city. Moving in to the yellow-star houses had to be accomplished within a week— by 24 June—and it was to be organized by the eight-member Jewish Council led by Samu Stern.

Of course, Allied bombing did not spare the yellow-star houses, and by the fall, dozens of them were in ruins. In the beginning, Jews were allowed to leave the dwellings only between 2 and 5 pm; later, between 11 am and 5 pm. During these timeslots they had to manage to buy provisions as well as to complete any other routine daily obligations.

In response to threats and pleas by neutral countries and the Allies, Regent Miklós Horthy stopped the deportation of the Jews on 6 July 1944, before the deportation of the Jews of Budapest could begin. Thus, while Jews remained in the yellow-star houses, the danger of deportation was averted for a while.

The situation of the Jews of Budapest suddenly changed for the worse when, on 15 October 1944, Horthy agreed to Hungary's surrender to Soviet forces. The Germans then deposed and arrested Horthy and helped Szálasi's Arrow Cross stage a coup and begin a reign of terror in the city. Almost immediately following the fascist takeover, men aged 16–60 and women aged 16–40 were assembled from the yellow-star houses in order to be taken to forced labor. By 26 October, about 25,000 Jews were assembled. As described above, at first the majority of Jews were taken to work on fortifications around the capital and in various military factories, and on 6 November the infamous death-marches from Budapest to German territory commenced.

The first ghetto in Budapest, the so-called little or international ghetto, was set up in the city in November 1944 for about 15,600 Jews who held protective documents or passports issued by embassies of neutral countries. These "protected" Jews had to move into apartments in which, until then, only 3,969 people lived. The diplomats of the embassies of neutral countries thought that it was easier to defend the Jews under their protection from the Arrow Cross if they lived in one area. The little ghetto was established in Pest, near the Danube in the vicinity of Szent István Park. Jews holding protective documents issued by Switzerland, Sweden, Portugal, Spain, and the Vatican had to move into the so-called "protected houses" of the little ghetto by 20 November. The population of the little ghetto constantly increased, as many Jews with fake protective documents also moved into these seemingly safer houses.[35]

On 29 November 1944, Gábor Vajna, the Minister of the Interior, issued the decree (No. 8935/1944. BM.) ordering the establishment of the ghetto of Pest, the so-called "large ghetto," designated for the Jews of the capital in the 7th District, which was densely populated by Jews living in the vicinity of the city's three grand synagogues (the Dohány Street synagogue, Rumbach Street synagogue, and Kazinczy Street synagogue). The Jews had to move into the large ghetto from the yellow-star houses by 2 December. The large ghetto, which was surrounded by a plank fence, was sealed off on 10 December. The four gates of the ghetto were guarded by Arrow Cross men and policemen. Gentiles were forbidden to live or work in the ghetto.

In the beginning of January 1945, about 10,000 Jews from the protected houses moved into the large ghetto, as Arrow Cross men frequently raided the protected houses under the pretext of checking the validity of the protective documents of the inhabitants; they shot people they rounded up into the Danube. In January 1945, about 70,000 Jews lived in the large ghetto. Some of them moved into the ghetto of their own accord during December and January, as they could no longer stand the dangers of hiding in the city. From 12 December 1944, about 6,000 Jewish children from children's homes outside the ghetto, under the aegis of the International Red Cross, were taken to the large ghetto. The majority of the Jews living in the ghetto were children and older people; others had either been drafted into the Hungarian forced labor service or handed over to the Germans for work.

The Jewish Council presided over many aspects of the life of the large ghetto. Officially, the Jewish Council had 800 employees, but in reality, many more people worked for it. The Jewish police under the command of Miksa Domonkos was responsible for maintaining daily order. Several soup kitchens operated in the ghetto, but the lack of food supplies in the ghetto was terrible. Ghetto inhabitants did not all perish of hunger because the International Red Cross and diplomats of neutral countries were able to get food into the ghetto from time to time. In addition, the Jewish Council was able to buy food for starving inhabitants. When the Red Army surrounded Budapest completely at the end of December 1944, supplying food for the ghetto became even more difficult. Until the liberation of the ghetto and during the weeks following liberation, many Jews died of starvation.

The sanitary and medical situation constituted the other most crucial problems for ghetto inhabitants. There was neither enough water nor detergent for washing. There was neither enough space in the hospitals nor enough medicine or medical equipments. And there was no space in the inner city, jam-packed with many-storied houses, to dispose of garbage and to bury the dead. Until 24 December 1944, corpses were buried outside the ghetto, in the Rákoskeresztúr cemetery. Later, however, it became inaccessible as a consequence of the siege of Budapest. For a while, the dead could be buried in the old cemetery on Kerepesi Street, but from the beginning of January 1945, Jews could not leave the ghetto. From then on, dead bodies were placed on a square in the ghetto and in the building of the Orthodox ritual bath. Later, they were placed in the court of the headquarters of the Jewish Council as well as in the courts of the hospitals. At the time of the liberation of the large ghetto, about 3,000 unburied bodies were lying all over in the territory of the ghetto. The majority of them were buried during the weeks after liberation in mass graves in the courtyard of the Neolog Synagogue in Dohány Street.

Those who remained in the little ghetto were liberated on 16 January 1945, while all of Pest was liberated by the Red Army 2 days later. In the large ghetto, about 70,000, and in the little ghetto about 30,000–35,000, Jews were liberated. In addition to the Jews in the ghettos, several thousand Jews survived in hiding (with false papers, with the help of various individuals, and many Jews were hidden in convents) or in protected houses outside the little ghetto, such as the famous Glass House, located at No. 29 Vadász Street. (The official name of the Glass House after 24 July 1944 was the Swiss Embassy's Office for the protection of Foreign Interests, Emigration Division: *Svájci Követség Idegen Érdekek Képviselete Kivándorlási Osztály*.) The entire city was liberated on 13 February 1945, and the whole of Hungary was liberated on 4 April 1945. In the end, the death toll was catastrophic. About 550,000 Jews from Hungary had been murdered over the course of the war.

Special characteristics of the Holocaust of the Jews of Hungary as they emerge from survivor testimony

Testimonies of survivors bear witness to the unique characteristics of the Holocaust in Hungary—its belatedness, quickness, and efficiency. I want to include here just one representative example from a witness account at the Eichmann Trial in 1961, as this was the first large war crimes trial in which the voices of survivors were assigned central importance. One of the witnesses of the prosecution was Moshe Rosenberg, who, as one of the Zionist leaders in Hungary, had aimed at rescuing Jews from the ghettos in the Hungarian provinces in the spring and summer of 1944. The Zionists wanted to provide the Jews escaping from the ghettos with false papers to enable them to go into hiding in Budapest, or to smuggle them through the border into Slovakia or Romania. At one point, the presiding judge asked for the reason why so few people could have been persuaded to escape. Rosenberg then related the story of his own Orthodox brother, whom he could not convince to go into hiding with the false identity documents that he had sent him and his family. Rosenberg explains this very painful failure as follows:

> Such a Jew had to take a decision overnight, had to take this action, and, from being a devout, religious Jew, to turn into a complete non-Jew, so that he could traverse the distance of four hundred kilometers between his village and Budapest. If I thought that he was capable of doing this or that some other Jew was capable of doing such a thing overnight, then I was naive. We did not have time...He did not leave, because what we required—and this murderer succeeded in robbing us of this—was time, so that we could prepare ourselves for something like this.[36]

In the eyes of the survivors, then, what characterized the Holocaust in Hungary more than the actual events was the efficiency and quickness of the destruction. The Jews of the Hungarian provinces were deported to Auschwitz at a time when the Red Army had already been so close that in some of the ghettos people could hear the fighting. In addition, when the Arrow Cross implemented its murderous policies, the Red Army, the Hungarian army, and the Wermacht were fighting on Hungarian soil.

Rita Horváth, in her analyses of survivor testimonies and literary works by Jews from Hungary, sheds light on the trauma inflicted by the speed and efficiency of the destruction of the Jews of Hungary by the Hungarians and Nazi Germany. Exacerbating this trauma is the question of what the Jews of Hungary actually knew, believed, and were willing or capable of believing about the unfolding genocide. For the survivors of the Holocaust in Hungary, this question remains especially urgent because they feel that they could have done more to prevent what happened to them and to their loved ones.[37]

> Since the Jews of Hungary were systematically destroyed at a very late stage of the Second World War—it was the last sizable community annihilated in Europe—the story of the Jews of Hungary is fraught with cognitive and ethical questions connected to the value and possibility of witnessing and listening to witnesses. The overwhelming majority of Hungarian survivors express the feeling that had they listened better to witnesses telling unbelievable tales about the destruction of the Jews all over Europe under Nazi rule, they would have behaved differently during the destruction of their communities. The survivors are constantly tortured by this feeling at a time—in the aftermath of the Holocaust—when they are faced with the task of becoming witnesses to the events and the trauma of the Holocaust.[38]

This shock concerning the last stages of the Holocaust in Hungary accounts largely for the implicit Holocaust definition of the DEGOB questionnaire that was put together in order to obtain witness accounts. Whereas the definition of the Holocaust by the Hungarian Holocaust Memorial Center reflects the tensions and opportunities afforded by confronting the role of the Hungarian state in the fate of its Jewish citizens during World War II.

Conclusion

The general political history and the history of the events of the Holocaust in Hungary, particularly the role of the Hungarian state and that of the German occupying forces, have been comprehensively addressed during the past decades. However, the so-called Jewish viewpoint (indeed plurality of viewpoints) is still glaringly missing from the overwhelming majority of the works concerning the Holocaust in Hungary. By the inclusion of the Jewish viewpoint, I mean to call attention to the necessity of conducting research from the point of view of the victims, focusing on questions such as: how did they understand and experience the events? Within the narrow and constantly narrowing scope for action, what kind of choices did they make during the various phases of the Holocaust? How did they react as individuals and as Jews? How did ordinary Jews, Jewish leaders, and Jewish organizations react to the events occurring between 1938 and 1945? All these questions need to be addressed more extensively in future research.

Notes

1 For the history of the DEGOB, see Rita Horváth, *A Deportáltakat Gondozó Országos Bizottság története, 1944–1952* [*The History of the National Relief Committee for Deportees*], in *MAKOR Magyar Zsidó Levéltári Füzetek vol. 1*, ed. Kinga Frojimovics and Zsuzsanna Toronyi (Budapest: Magyar Zsidó Levéltár [The Hungarian Jewish Archives], 1997); Rita Horváth, "Jews in Hungary after the Holocaust: The National Relief Committee for Deportees, 1945–50," *Journal of Israeli History,* vol. 2 (1998): 69–91. Concerning DEGOB in the context of the other large-scale Jewish testimony-collecting projects in the early postwar era, see Rita Horváth, "'A Jewish Historical Commission in Budapest': The Place of the National Relief Committee for Deportees in Hungary [DEGOB] among the Other Large-Scale Historical-Memorial Projects of *She'erit Hapletah* After the Holocaust (1945–48)," in *Holocaust Historiography in Context: Emergence, Challenges, Polemics and Achievements*, eds David Bankier and Dan Michman (Jerusalem: Yad Vashem, 2008), 475–96.

2 A complete collection of all the DEGOB testimonial protocols cannot be found in any single archive. The most complete collections of original protocols and their duplicates can be found in two archives: The Hungarian Jewish Archives (Budapest, Hungary): DEGOB Protocols (XX-G-1), and Yad Vashem Archives (Jerusalem, Israel): Collection of the DEGOB Testimonies (H.15.E).

3 Gábor Murányi reconstructed a large part of the questionnaire, or rather a set of guidelines, as he discovered them written on the back of some protocols. Gábor Murányi, "'Hallottam, amikor azt válaszolta: Alles ins Gas!': A Deportáltakat Gondozó Bizottság jegyzőkönyvei 1945-ből," *Phralipe*, vol. 11–12 (1990): 32–41. Kinga Frojimovics and Rita Horváth added a few questions to Murányi's reconstruction on the basis of a document kept in the Memorial Museum of Hungarian Speaking Jewry in Safed: *Jewish Agency Dokumentációs Ügyosztály, Kérdés-komplexum*, H.476.1570. At present, Frojimovics and Horváth are working on a monograph comparing the testimony-collecting projects of various Jewish organizations in the early postwar years.

4 www.hdke.hu/index.php?menu=010302& mgroup = 1& app = info& page = main& artid = 6df71354fa2207a2238379689d14925e (accessed 4 January 2010).

5 www.hdke.hu/index.php?menu=030101& mgroup = 1& app = info& page = main& artid = 4ddb04e6d8e013776a928b5476583685 (accessed 4 January 2010).

6 *Darányi Kálmán miniszterelnök beszéde a Nemzeti Egység Pártja nagygyűlésén Győrött 1938. március 5-én. [Prime Minister Kálmán Darányi's Speech at the Rally of the Party of National Unity in Győr in 1938]* (Budapest: Budapesti Hírlap Nyomdája, 1938), 6–7.

7 For the text of the so-called First Jewish Law, that was entitled "Act 1938:XV. *On more effectively ensuring the balance of social and economic life*" ["1938. évi XV. tc. a társadalmi és a gazdasági élet egyensúlyának hatályosabb biztosításáról"], see Miklós Degré and Alajos Várady-Brenner, eds, *Magyar törvénytár. 1938. évi törvénycikkek* (Budapest: Franklin, 1939), 132–44.

8 The Law did not apply to those who participated in World War I or had lost a husband or a father in it; therefore it did not apply to war-disabled people, ex-front soldiers, war widows and war orphans. It did not affect those people who were regarded as fully assimilated, that is, those who had converted to the Christian faith before 1 August 1919 and belonged continuously to any of the Christian denominations since then, and their offspring, if they did not return to Judaism.

9 For the text of the so-called Second Jewish Law, that was entitled "Act 1939:IV. *On Limiting the Expansion of Jews within the Public and Economic Spheres*" ["1939. évi IV. tc. a zsidók közéleti és gazdasági térfoglalásának korlátozásáról"], see Miklós Degré and Alajos Várady-Brenner, eds, *Magyar törvénytár. 1939. évi törvénycikkek* (Budapest: Franklin, 1940), 129–48. For in-depth analyses of the economic and social consequences of the first two (anti-)Jewish laws, see Yehuda Don's articles: "The Economic Effect of Antisemitic Discrimination: Hungarian Anti-Jewish Legislation, 1938–44," *Jewish Social Studies,* vol. 1 (1986): 63–82, and "The Economic Dimensions of Antisemitism: Anti-Jewish Legislation in Hungary, 1938–44," *East European Quarterly*, vol. 4 (1987): 447–65.

10 For an in-depth assessment of the policy of the Hungarian authorities towards Jews termed as stateless, or having unsettled citizenship status, see Kinga Frojimovics, *I Have Been a Stranger in a Strange Land: The Hungarian State and Jewish Refugees in Hungary, 1933–1945* (Jerusalem: The International Institute for Holocaust Research at Yad Vashem, 2007).

11 See documents of the discussions between the Board of Deputies of British Jews and the representatives of the Jews of Hungary: Nathaniel Katzburg, *Hungary and the Jews, 1920–1943* (Ramat Gan: Bar-Ilan University Press, 1981), 277–84.

12 For the text of the law entitled "1941:XV: *A házassági jogról szóló 1894:XXXI. tc. kiegészítéséről és módosításáról, valamint az ezzel kapcsolatban szükséges fajvédelmi rendelkezésekről,*" see Miklós Degré and Alajos Várady-Brenner, eds, *Magyar törvénytár. 1941. évi törvénycikkek* (Budapest: Franklin, 1942), 56–66.

13 The laws that came to force after the completion of the process, such as Act 1942:VIII, which annulled the reception of Judaism, or Act 1942:XV, which concerned the agricultural and wooded properties of Jews, were merely the last touches in the process described above. (The Hungarian state seized hundreds of thousands of acres of land from Jews as a consequence of the 1942 land law.)

14 For the most comprehensive treatment of the massacre, see Artur Geyer, "Az első magyarországi deportálás", *Új Élet Naptár, 1960–1961* (Budapest: MIOK, 1960), 75–82; Tamás Majsai, "A kőrösmezei zsidódeportálás 1941-ben", *Ráday Gyűjtemény Évkönyve, IV–V. 1984–1985* (Budapest: Egyetemi Nyomda, 1986), 59–86, 195–235; Frojimovics, *I Have Been a Stranger in a Strange Land*, chapter VI. In addition, one of the survivors of the massacre, Zoltán Szirtes, published a selection of documents concerning the massacre: *Temetetlen halottaink 1941. Kőrösmező, Kamenyec-Podolszk* (Budapest: published by the author, 1996).

15 On the 1941 deportations, see Frojimovics, *I Have Been a Stranger in a Strange Land*, 104–45.

16 See the document in *Nazi Conspiracy and Aggression* (Washington, DC: Government Printing Office for the Office of United States Chief of Counsel for the Prosecution of Axis Criminality, 1946), 3: 210–13.

17 Daniel Jonah Goldhagen, *Hitler's Willing Executioners: Ordinary Germans and the Holocaust* (New York: Alfred A. Knopf, 1996), 273.

18 Artur Geyer, "Az 1942 évi újvidéki 'razzia,'" *Új Élet Naptár, 1959* (Budapest: MIOK, 1959), 42.

19 Enikő Sajti, "Megtorlás vagy konszolidáció? Délvidék 1941–44," in *The Holocaust in Hungary: Fifty Years Later*, eds Randolph L. Braham and Attila Pók (New York: Columbia University Press, 1997), 379–88.

20 For a detailed treatment of the subject, see two books by Randolph L. Braham: *The Politics of Genocide: The Holocaust in Hungary, Vol. 1* (New York: Columbia University Press, 1994), chapter 10: "The Labor Service System", 294–380, and *The Hungarian Labor Service System, 1939–1945* (New York: Columbia University Press, 1977). See also Elek Karsai, *Fegyvertelen álltak az aknamezőkön...Dokumentumok a munkaszolgálat történetéhez Magyarországon, Vol. 1* (Budapest: MIOK, 1962); Tamás Stark, *Hungarian Jews During the Holocaust and After the Second World War, 1939–1949: A Statistical Review* (Boulder, Colorado: East European Monographs/New York: Columbia University Press, 2000). For the individual phases of forced labor, see Szabolcs Szita's works, *Halálerőd. A munkaszolgálat és a hadimunka történetéhez, 1944–1945* (Budapest: Kossuth Könyvkiadó, 1989), and *Utak a pokolból. A magyar deportáltak az annektált Ausztriában* (Budapest: Metalon Manager Iroda, 1991).

21 Karsai László, *Holokauszt* (Budapest: Pannonica, 2001), 240.

22 See Braham, *The Politics of Genocide*, Appendix 3, 1371–84. See the analysis of the decrees in Judit Molnár, "Út a holokauszthoz," in Judit Molnár, ed., *Csendőrök, hivatalnokok, zsidók. Válogatott tanulmányok a magyar holokauszt történetéből* (Szeged: Szegedi Zsidó Hitközség, 2000), 11–28.

23 Decree No. 1140/1944. M.E., *Budapesti Közlöny No. 71*, 1–2.

24 Decree No. 1200/1944. M.E., *Budapesti Közlöny No. 73*, 1; Decree No. 1210/1944. M.E., *Budapesti Közlöny No. 73*, 2; Decree No. 1220/1944. M.E., *Budapesti Közlöny No. 73*, 2; Decree No. 1230/1944. M.E., *Budapesti Közlöny No. 73*, 2–3; Decree No. 1240/1944. M.E., *Budapesti Közlöny No. 73*, 3.

25 *Budapesti Közlöny, No. 73*, 31 March 1944. See the decree in its entirety in Ilona Benoschfsky and Elek Karsai, eds, *Vádirat a nácizmus ellen, I* (Budapest: MIOK, 1958), 53–54.

26 Decree No. 1270/1944. M.E., *Budapesti Közlöny No. 79*, 4; Decree No. 1300/1944. M.E., *Budapesti Közlöny No. 79*, 4.

27 The registering of Jewish owners of radio sets was soon followed by a decree ordering the requisition of radio sets (21 April 1944). Decree No. 33000/Eln. 18–1944, *Budapesti Közlöny No. 89*, 2.

28 According to the last census that was taken before the German occupation of Hungary, in January 1941, 725,007 Jews of the Jewish faith and 61,548 Jews who had converted to Christianity lived in Hungary. See József Kepecs, *A zsidó népesség száma településenként, 1840–1941* (Budapest: Központi Statisztikai Hivatal, 1993), 32–33.

29 See the text of the decree in Braham, *The Politics of Genocide,* 573–75.

30 Decree No. 1610/1944. M.E., *Budapesti Közlöny No. 95,* 2–3.

31 *Budapesti Közlöny,* No. 90, 22 April 1944. See the entire decree in *Vádirat a nácizmus ellen, I* (Benoschfsky and Karsai, eds), 191–94.

32 *Budapesti Közlöny,* No. 95, 28, April 1944. See the entire text of the decree in *Vádirat a nácizmus ellen, I* (Benoschfsky and Karsai, eds), 244–50.

33 Concerning all the individual ghettos in Hungary, see the entries written by Kinga Frojimovics in *The Yad Vashem Encyclopedia of the Ghettos During the Holocaust, Vols* I–II, eds Guy Miron and Shlomit Shulhani (Jerusalem: Yad Vashem, 2009).

34 See Braham, *The Politics of Genocide,* 674.

35 All-in-all, in Budapest there were 14 diplomats in the Arrow Cross era who received the distinction of Righteous Among the Nations from Yad Vashem for rescuing Jews (for example Carl Lutz, Angelo Rotta, Raoul Wallenberg, Friedrich Born, the Langlet couple, and Giorgio Perlasca). See the relevant entries at Yad Vashem's *Righteous Among the Nations Encyclopedia* series, Israel Gutman, ed., *The Encyclopedia of the Righteous Among the Nations: Rescuers of Jews during the Holocaust* (Jerusalem: Yad Vashem, 2003–07).

36 The Trial of Adolf Eichmann, Session 60 (Part 4 of 6). See www.nizkor.org/hweb/people/e/eichmann-adolf/transcripts/Sessions/Session-060-04.html (accessed 5 January 2010).

37 Rita Horváth, "Wiesel and Kertész: Night in the Context of Hungarian Holocaust Literature," in *Approaches to Teaching Wiesel's Night,* ed. Alan Rosen (New York: Modern Language Association of America, 2007), 69–75.

38 Horváth, "Wiesel and Kertész," 69–75.

23

THE FINAL SOLUTION IN SOUTHEASTERN EUROPE

Between Nazi catalysts and local motivations

James Frusetta

Most studies of the Holocaust focus tightly on Nazi perpetrators and their Jewish and other victims.[1] In terms of the origins, intent, and scale of the catastrophe, this approach is logical and appropriate. However, it neglects the local context of eastern Europe and the ways that its inhabitants assisted, resisted, or were bystanders to genocide.[2] This is particularly problematic with reference to southeastern Europe. German-allied and puppet regimes in the region took an active part not just in assisting overall Nazi designs, but in developing indigenous antisemitic laws, deportation policies, and even murderous campaigns of their own.

This is not to deny Nazi Germany's role as the central catalyst in the attempted destruction of European Jews, nor its primary agency in realizing the Final Solution. But it does raise the question of why elements of the state apparatus in both German-occupied and autonomous, German-allied Balkan countries took part. Critical historical accounts frequently accord these regimes a sense of banality, of collaboration in return for financial or territorial gain.[3] Apologetic accounts stress these states' wartime weakness compared with Nazi Germany.[4] Each approach understates the region's contemporary perceived crisis of national integration. This crisis both created precedents for antisemitic actions, and suggested the opportunistic use of wartime disruption to pursue indigenous programs of cleansing of other ethnic groups.

The wars of 1912–13 and 1914–18 shifted territorial boundaries in southeastern Europe, creating in each state a sense that unifying national identities must be strengthened.[5] Bulgaria's territorial losses and concerns that co-nationals across the borders were being forcibly de-Bulgarianized fostered revisionism, émigré terrorism and fears that its own minorities might serve as a "fifth column."[6] In Greece, the relatively small minority population after the Greco-Turkish population exchange of 1923 was stigmatized in national politics and feared as potentially disloyal.[7] For Romania, the doubling of territory and population in 1918 meant questions over whether ethnic Romanians in the newly annexed regions ascribed to a "correct" Romanian identity and whether acquired minorities were over-represented in the country's economic life.[8] Finally, the Kingdom of Serbs, Croats and Slovenes (hereafter, Yugoslavia) faced multiple questions of how the "triune" identity of the three dominant south Slavic groups would be forged into a national identity, and whether minorities (including the "unrecognized" Albanians and Macedonians) would be loyal to the state.[9]

Such concerns prompted discourses in each country over how to realize the national idea, influencing the authoritarian regimes that came to power across the region in the late 1920s and early 1930s. Wartime antisemitic state policies in the Balkans emerged amidst existing questions over the loyalty of minorities. Concepts of legal separation or suppression of ethnic groups had already been instituted in each state in the interwar era. This provided precedents for the stigmatization of Jews; new anti-Jewish measures radicalized existing exclusionary (but not eliminationist) policies with regard to other ethnic groups.

The role played by southeastern European states offers insight into the Holocaust as a European event. Even if Germany's role in the Holocaust cannot and should not be unduly historicized, can the actions of its satellites profitably be related to existing local trends of inter-ethnic relations, particularly since few Balkan states shared the singular Nazi vision of the total physical elimination of the Jews?[10] Similarly, even if indigenous Balkan antisemitic acts were catalyzed by Nazi Germany, debates in the historiography of the region have emerged only in the 1990s concerning whether these acts were shaped by *local* intent to destroy Jews and others, or if this represented an attempt by elements of the state apparatus to work towards German demands. What emerges below, in a consideration of recent historical debate on the region, as well as of Bulgaria as a specific case study, is the need to weave these threads into the larger, European picture.[11]

Historical background

On 6 April 1941, the German army invaded Yugoslavia after a coup removed the country's regent, who was on the verge of joining the Axis. With the help of Italian, Bulgarian, and Hungarian forces, the *Wehrmacht* overwhelmed the Yugoslav Army and proceeded to dismember the country. German forces occupied Serbia (because of Belgrade and because of Serbia's pro-Russian, Orthodox character); Italy took the Dalmatian coastline (until it left the Axis in 1943); and a puppet state under German and Italian watch was created in Croatia. (Hungarians took regions in the north, and Bulgarians annexed Macedonia.) Although technically a military zone of occupation, Serbia also had a native, collaborationist government under Milan Nedić, who came to office in August 1941.

Serbia's 12,000 Jews were persecuted almost immediately following the German victory. They lost jobs, had their property confiscated, and were forced into labor brigades, but this fell short of murder until the outbreak of partisan activity in the summer of 1941. Mass shootings of Serbian Jewish men by German army units began in the fall. The survivors of these massacres, mostly women and children, were placed in a concentration camp built on the Belgrade exhibition grounds across the Sava River. The Germans called the site Semlin, while Yugoslavs called it Sajmiste. Nearly 7,500 Jews, again mostly women and children, were murdered there via gassing in gas vans.[12]

Unlike in Serbia, Croatia had an indigenous fascist movement steeped in antisemitism that implemented a policy of persecution on its own, impacting over 30,000 Croatian Jews. The puppet state created after the German defeat of Yugoslavia consisted of Croat territories as well as Bosnia and Herzegovina. Croatian fascists, the Ustaša, assumed nominal control of the new state, and its leader was Ante Pavelić. During the spring and summer of 1941, the Ustaša enacted discriminatory legislation against Jews and Roma, and murdered Serbs by the thousands. The Ustaša also established a network of concentration camps to intern Jews, Roma, Muslims, Serbs, and Croatian political opponents. The most infamous of the Croatian camps were the five facilities of the Jasenovac complex, located 60 miles south of Zagreb, operational from August 1941 to April 1945. Ninety thousand people were murdered there—mostly Serbs, but some 20,000 Jews as well.[13] Several hundred thousand Serbs were murdered by Croatian forces over the course of the war.

With respect to Greece, for Hitler the country was a peripheral theatre, but he sent troops to bail out Mussolini's flagging campaign and invaded Greece on the same day he began his military offensive in Yugoslavia, delaying the invasion of the Soviet Union. Greece surrendered at the end of April 1941, and the country was divided into three occupation zones. German forces took western Macedonia (and the important port city of Thessaloniki or Salonika), eastern Thrace, close to the border with Turkey, western Crete, and the islands of the north Aegean. Bulgaria occupied western Thrace, and, until September 1943, Italy occupied the bulk of the Greek mainland (including Athens, which they jointly occupied with the Germans), eastern Crete, and the Greek islands in the south Aegean. Not surprisingly, policy towards the country's 80,000 Jews varied in the three zones. Half of Greece's Jewish population was located in the city of Thessaloniki, under German control. The Nazis began systematically deporting the Jews of Salonika from the city's ghetto to Auschwitz in March 1943. Most of the nearly 50,000 Jews on these transports were gassed upon arrival. The situation for the smaller Jewish community in Athens was different; there, Archbishop Damaskinos exhorted priests to help Jews, and many were saved as a result. Yet Greece had one of the highest percentages of Jews murdered in German-occupied Europe, with over 80 percent of the country's Jews losing their lives.[14]

Romania's history is complicated by its shifting territorial gains and losses between 1918 and 1940. Aligned with the Entente (Allied) Powers in World War I, Romania gained territory from Hungary, Austria, and even Russia (Bessarabia). This enlarged the number of Jews under Romanian dominion to 750,000 people. Not initially aligned with Nazi Germany, Romania lost territory in 1940 to Hungary, Bulgaria, and the Soviet Union. And yet Romania was certainly a more natural ally of Germany than the latter, with strong conservative forces and a fascist movement—the Iron Guard. Although serious struggles within the Right took place over the course of the 1930s, leading to the establishment of a royal dictatorship under King Carol II, aimed at thwarting a fascist takeover, in September 1940, in the wake of the territorial losses, the Romanian military and General Ion Antonescu toppled the king and sealed an alliance with the Iron Guard. Romania joined the Axis powers two months later. In January 1941, the Iron Guard attempted and failed to seize power from Antonescu. Jews suffered violent attacks in Bucharest during the putsch, and yet this was merely the beginning. When Germany invaded the Soviet Union in June 1941, Romania recaptured the territories of Bessarabia and Bukovina and facilitated the slaughter of thousands of Jews in the area known as Transnistria between the Dniester and Bug Rivers. The number of Romania's Jews murdered during the war is estimated at between 300,000 and 400,000.

Opportunism and agency: Balkan historiography and the Holocaust

Historiography throughout the Soviet bloc in the Cold War era faced a shared problem in contemplating the Holocaust. Acknowledgement of a particular Nazi targeting of the Jews for extermination threatened the preferred characterization of fascism as an anti-proletarian force whose chief victims were the working classes.[15]

In Romania, Marshal Antonescu's postwar trial set a precedent for distorting events and subsuming Jewish victims into communist ones.[16] Although Lucreţiu Pătrăşcanu argued in 1944 that antisemitism was a "Romanian phenomenon" indigenously responsible for the Holocaust, official historiography subsequently presented wartime atrocities as directed against communists.[17] By the 1980s, rehabilitation of Antonescu saw arguments that the destruction of the Jews "happened outside the knowledge of the regime" and that Romania *rescued* Jews from Hungarian-occupied Transylvania.[18] A similar argument was advanced in Bulgaria, where the Bulgarian Communist Party was cast as both the historical partner of the country's minorities, and also the principal actor in resisting German demands for Jewish deportation.[19] The need for national unity after civil war meant that Greek and Yugoslav accounts stressed the shared suffering under German occupation. For Greek historians, engaging Nazi atrocities against the Jews were problematic less in raising questions of indigenous collaboration than in raising questions about intra-Greek struggles over collaboration and resistance, themselves linked to the Civil War. In Yugoslavia, the state's focus on *bratstvo–jedinstvo*—brotherhood and unity—was a response to the memory of inter-ethnic strife in both the interwar and wartime era, and scholarly attention to the unique attributes of the Holocaust was politically problematic. This did not mean that atrocities against the Jews were ignored by historians in the socialist era, but it did mean that they were embedded in the concept of sacrifice against ethnic lines.[20]

The transition to a more open scholarly climate after 1989 (in Greece, 1974) invited reappraisals of the past. But historical accounts of the Holocaust in the Balkans face an additional challenge in that genocide against the Jews took place simultaneously with *other* ethnic conflicts in the region. In wartime Yugoslavia, the Ustaša Croatian puppet government began an indigenous campaign against Jews in June 1941, while the puppet Serbian government of Milan Nedić assisted the *Wehrmacht*'s shooting operations.[21] Scholars have studied both groups, as well as the Četnik and Partisan resistance movements, more for their role in fratricidal violence. Ustaša attempts to cleanse Serbs, for example, overwhelm attention to the Jewish Holocaust in much of the scholarship.[22] Macedonian or Kosovar historiography has similarly regarded the Holocaust as one element of a larger pattern of national suffering.[23] This was reflected in the growing use of the past during the mid-1980s as nationalists sought to redeem co-national figures from the 1930s and 1940s, castigate the leaders of other ethnic groups, and correlate wartime violence with the crisis of Yugoslav dissolution. The "numbers game" with respect to the total victims of the Ustaša death camp at Jasenovac reflects this.[24] This has not prevented the study of atrocities against the Jews,[25] but it has meant that such studies are part of a larger local historical context, even as the nationalist historiography that marked the Yugoslav Wars of Secession increasingly gives way to more nuanced scholarship.

As in Yugoslavia, Greek historiography in the 1990s saw a similar rise of nationalistic historiography concerning the emergence of an independent Republic of Macedonia accused of misappropriating the symbols and history of ancient Macedonia.[26] Public furor over the dispute helped prompt historians to examine inter-ethnic relations in northern Greece. But the question of the Slavic minority in the region remains paramount, particularly given its role in the Bulgarian occupation zone during the war and the pro-communist allegiance of the (Macedonian) National Liberation Front during the Greek Civil War.[27] Here, too, the study of the Holocaust is overshadowed by the larger context of inter-ethnic conflict.

Unlike the Yugoslav or Greek cases, or the Bulgarian case explored below, Romanian scholarship has sustained attention to wartime policy towards the Jews. In part, scholarly engagement may be due to relative scale: 280,000–375,000 Jews were killed on Romanian territory, most by autonomous Romanian actions, with a further 132,000 killed after deportation to Germany from Hungarian-controlled Transylvania.[28] It also comes in response to nationalist scholars' practice of trivializing the Holocaust in comparison with claims that Romanians themselves were systematically victimized during World War II[29] and in the postwar period by a Judeo-Bolshevik "Red Holocaust."[30] Socialist historiography flirted with the rehabilitation of Marshal Ion Antonescu for his nationalist credentials; this, combined with his anti-communism, made him attractive to some for rehabilitation after 1989.

Romania's initial post-socialist historiographical debate on the Holocaust built a scholarly consensus on the country's complicity.[31] It also recognized that Antonescu's regime targeted Jews in particular fashion, although select scholarly studies linked anti-semitism in Romania with broader interwar concerns over minorities.[32] Such studies have led to the questions of why the Holocaust happened in Romania and how it can be understood within Romanian history. In the Romanian case, scholars have actively raised the need both to engage and utilize the historiography on Nazi Germany to understand indigenous Romanian actions,[33] as well as to place the Holocaust within the context of Romanian nationalism.[34] It further invites comparisons with the Romanian Gulag, not to minimize Jewish suffering, but to seek the continuities and similarities between the two in terms of both material sites (such as Sighet prison), the Romanian state and legal system, and the experiences of the victims.[35]

Agency and opportunism in the Bulgarian case

Unlike the historiography on Greece, Romania, and Yugoslavia, since 1989 there has been a sharp increase in monographs on the Holocaust in Bulgaria. Nearly all of these, however, have focused on the debate over "who saved" Bulgarian Jews from deportation and death at Nazi hands.[36] An independent but German-allied Bulgarian government enacted strict antisemitic laws in 1941, and subsequently collaborated in the deportation of over 11,000 Jews from Macedonia and Thrace into German hands and, ultimately, extermination. The same regime, under significant domestic pressure from the Orthodox Church, professional societies, and parliamentary members, would first postpone, then refuse to deport Jews who had possessed Bulgarian citizenship in 1940. Unlike the Romanian case noted above, the history of the Holocaust in Bulgaria remains sufficiently ambiguous as not to spark prolonged or serious scholarly debate over the motives for Bulgarian collaboration. This is unfortunate: the Bulgarian case raises its own insights into the ways in which local inter-ethnic conflicts interacted with the Holocaust.

Historians usually ascribe opportunistic motives to the wartime Bulgarian government, inspired by the hopes that the German government would award it claimed Greek, Romanian, and Yugoslav territory.[37] The relative lack of populist antisemitism is the basis of arguments that the Holocaust was a profoundly alien event in Bulgaria, either instigated by, or adopted to curry favor with, Nazi Germany.[38] Except for a small fringe of antisemitic activity among White Russian émigrés and the small Bulgarian fascist movements, there was an absence of intent before World War II to destroy Bulgaria's Jewish minority. Although this may be true with regard to eliminationist antisemitism, concepts of social segregation of *other* minorities were already prevalent. Boris III's regime lacked the genocidal intent of Nazi Germany, but this did not mean that anti-semitic actions within Bulgaria as part of the larger, European Holocaust did not fit an *indigenous* intent towards national purification. The need to "purify" or "revive" the Bulgarian nation had been widely debated before World War II. Antisemitic policies drew on this, even as antisemitic laws were used to model additional restrictions on other minority groups within Bulgaria during World War II.

The creation of a Bulgarian state in 1878 raised the concurrent question of what role ethnic and confessional minorities would play in a country defined as the national homeland of Orthodox Christian Bulgarians. Turks, Roma, Greeks, Jews, Romanians, and Muslim ethnic Bulgarians (Pomaks) made up nearly 30 percent of the population. Guarantees of legal equality were provided in the constitution of 1879, but the Ministry of Foreign Affairs and Confession (*Ministerstvoto na vunshnite raboti i izpoviadaniiata*, MVRI) formally oversaw the religious hierarchies of both Muslims and Jews, subsequently intervening in Muslim religious institutions and limiting Roma voting rights, contributing to the emigration of some 350,000 Muslims before 1912.[39]

The Balkan Wars and World War I radicalized Bulgarian minority policy, prompted by military conflicts over disputed borderlands in Macedonia, Thrace, and Dobrudzha. Ethnic cleansing in these borderlands by the warring states was intended to bolster their territorial claims by favorably homogenizing the local ethnic landscape.[40] Bulgaria rarely used violence against domestic minorities, with the exception of the attempted conversion to Christianity of Muslim ethnic Bulgarians in the Rhodopi mountains in 1912.[41] Bulgarian regimes did, however, encourage the continued emigration of minority groups after World War I, including a mandatory exchange with Greece after 1919 and a voluntary exchange with Turkey after 1925. Combined with the immigration of almost a quarter of a million ethnic Bulgarian refugees, by the mid-1920s, minority groups had slipped in proportion to roughly a fifth of the state's inhabitants.[42]

State policies took a new direction after elements of the army and the *Voenniia Suioz* (Military League) staged the 19 May 1934 coup that put the *Zveno* (Link) group in power.[43] Proclaimed as above party politics, *Zveno* was a reaction to two decades of political crises. Roughly one in five adult males in the country had died in the wars (and defeats) of 1912–13 and 1915–18.[44] Domestic political turmoil stemming from the wars led to a postwar revolutionary agrarian government under Aleksandur Stamboliiski, then a conservative coup in June 1923. A failed communist counter-coup in September 1923 triggered a sustained white terror and communist bombings. It also assisted the spread of terrorism by various émigré political groups—most notably by the Internal Macedonian Revolutionary Organization, which raided into Greece and Yugoslavia and conducted a campaign at home against unsympathetic elements in government and dissident factions. Finally, the Great Depression devastated the agricultural economy and saw real incomes in the country fall as much as 50 percent.[45]

As in other European countries, the interwar years in Bulgaria saw broad discussion in public media over the perceived problems in Bulgarian society, politics, and the economy, and possible solutions. Within this broad debate, journals on the Right, such as *Otets Paisii* and *Arhiv za stopanska i sotsialna politika*, considered the nature of the Bulgarian nation itself. The "Bulgarian spirit" was seen as in need of revitalization after foreign rule, the strains of the wars, and foreign influence.[46] Defining the nation in terms of religious confession, language, and (rarely) biology, the conservative Right and multiple small fascist movements increasingly advocated a strengthening of national spirit, but without addressing the fate of minorities.[47] Only the *Rodina* (Homeland) movement specifically and publicly advocated a forceful minority policy—in this case, hoping to "re-Bulgarianize" ethnic Bulgarian Muslims and diminish Turkish influence over them.[48]

Zveno favored an étatist vision in which problems would be overcome by state management of the economy, politics, and society. Issuing emergency decrees under Article 47 of the Bulgarian constitution, *Zveno* dissolved all political parties, restructured parliament, and redrew provincial boundaries in an effort at rationalization. The new government went further in stating that it would "direct the spiritual and intellectual life of the country towards union and renovation for the benefit of the nation and of the state" and "organiz[e] the citizens into an ideologically homogenous national group" by instilling a healthy national spirit in all aspects of life.[49] The resulting Directorate for Social Renewal (*Direktoriia na obshestvenata obnova*) oversaw public entertainment, publishing, and education. These policies would continue even after the *Zveno* group lost power in 1935 to authoritarian governments backed by Tsar Boris III.

What role would minority groups play in building "a healthy national spirit"? Already in the 1920s, the Ministry of the Interior and National Health (*Ministerstvo na vutreshnite raboti i narodnoto zdrave*, MVRNZ) regarded Turkish Kemalist and Jewish Zionist reform movements with concern, fearing that either group might work against Bulgarian interests. The MVRI actively intervened on behalf of traditionally minded leaders of both groups.[50] Police informers and agents warned that the country's Muslim population was vulnerable to influence from the Republic of Turkey.[51] Border police reported of Muslim families crossing the border illegally to emigrate.[52] The MVRNZ was accordingly tasked to report on "Zionist" and "Kemalist" fraternal, cultural, and educational organizations within the country—expanding to surveillance of other minority cultural organizations, schools, charities, and publications.[53] By the 1930s, preventing subversion led to closing suspect Turkish schools and most Turkish-language newspapers.[54] In the late 1930s, the government ordered local police to discreetly encourage emigration by ethnic Turks, partially in the hope of obtaining agricultural land for redistribution to ethnic Bulgarians.[55] Exclusionary policies were enacted by the Bulgarian state before its alliance with Germany in 1941, but generally with attention to concerns over Muslim minorities.

It is in this context of concern over "alien" groups that the Bulgarian state collaborated with Nazi Germany in the Holocaust. Even prior to its formal alliance with Germany, the Bulgarian government adapted its minority policies. Foreign Jews were prohibited from entering the country; in November 1939, police were instructed to treat Jewish Bulgarian citizens with visas to Palestine as emigrants (who could then be refused re-entry to Bulgaria).[56] Existing restrictions and secret police surveillance of pro-fascist organizations were relaxed: members of such groups were allowed into the civil service, and antisemitic publications were increasingly tolerated by the state.[57] Such pro-German policies were credited with the reclaiming of Southern Dobrudzha from Romania in the Second Vienna Award in August 1940.

In late 1940, the Law for the Defense of the Nation (*Zakon za zashtitata na natsiiata*, ZZN) was proposed as an expansion of the country's pro-German orientation. Drawing on the Nuremberg Laws, the ZZN restricted Jewish employment, property ownership, and access to education. Socially, it excluded Jews from Bulgarian life by forbidding marriage with ethnic Bulgarians and the use of Bulgarian names. The second part of the law specified a fundamentally religious approach in defining Jews, excluding converts to Christianity and those married to ethnic Bulgarians.[58] Although triggering considerable opposition within parliament, the measure was passed into law in January 1941. Additional antisemitic laws were added that year, including a tax on Jewish property[59] and a requirement for mandatory service in labor battalions (replacing obligatory military service, now barred to Jews). Antisemitic legislation was matched by legislation targeting other alien groups, notably Muslims, drawing on the structure and logic of antisemitic legislation. The 1941 Law for the Purity of the Nation (*Zakon za chistotata na natsiata*, ZChN), for example, forbade marriage between ethnic Bulgarians and Turks.[60] Further restrictions targeted traditional Muslim clothing.[61] Both acts not only restricted Turks from Bulgarian society, but were vehicles for increasingly forcible assimilation of ethnic Bulgarian Muslims.

Measures against both Jews and Muslims intensified throughout 1942. The Decree-Law of 26 August 1942 expanded antisemitic legal measures, including the creation of the Commissariat for the Jewish Question (*Komisarstvo po evreiskite vuprosi*, KEV).[62] New acts (albeit sporadically enforced) included the mandatory display of the star of David, further confiscations of property, narrower racial definitions of Jews, deportations of Jews out of Sofia and the major cities, and restrictions on the ability of Jews to marry Muslims or convert to Islam.[63] In the Decree-Law of 26 August, the KEV's mandate was expanded to include the Roma community, who were now also subject to service in labor brigades, forbidden to marry Bulgarians, and restricted in employment and rationing.

Over the winter of 1942–43, the Reich Security Head Office approached the KEV to develop a plan for the eventual transfer of Bulgaria's resident Jewish community to German control. Eleven thousand Jews living in the "New Territories" of Thrace and Macedonia were deported in March 1943, first to transit camps within Bulgarian territory, then on to Poland. The KEV anticipated further deportations from Bulgaria proper to Germany in the summer of 1943; these measures, ultimately, did not come to fruition. A combination of popular protests, concern over Allied victories, and (later, in August) political turmoil following the death of Tsar Boris III led to the government refusing to carry through with further deportations to Germany.[64] This did not, however, prevent the expulsion of Jews (and, in August 1943, Roma) from Sofia and other cities; nor did it mean an easing of attempts to further regulate Muslim life, which continued throughout the year and into 1944. Restrictive minority policies in both cases were repealed only after the 9 September 1944 coup that allowed the Fatherland Front to come to power.

The similarities in how the Bulgarian government shaped policy with regard to both Jews and Muslims are suggestive. In this regard, I argue that the contextualization of the Holocaust in Bulgaria provides insight into how Germany's allies used its disruptions for their own ends. As a radicalizing event, Bulgarian antisemitic policies saw an unprecedented and extended campaign not merely to segregate, but to withdraw rights and citizenship. In this regard, I find it highly suggestive that only five years after World War II, the socialist regime undertook a state-organized deportation of its Turkish minority that saw over 150,000 flee over the course of a single year.

Conclusion

The history of state antisemitism in Bulgaria was, on the scale of the Holocaust in Europe, a relatively marginal event. Even the much more significant Romanian case pales next to the actions of Nazi Germany. Scholarly consideration of the role of Balkan regimes during World War II reminds us that not all countries that participated in the European persecution and destruction of the Jews shared all Nazi goals. This is not to exculpate collaborationist regimes; but it does challenge scholars to consider the gamut of motivations that drove them, and how each Axis state hoped to alter local ethnic geographies differently.[65] In this latter regard, the contextualization of antisemitic policy within inter-ethnic relations and the role of the state is valuable. It provides a better understanding of how the Holocaust related to local traditions of antisemitism and to broader indigenous fears of minorities. It further challenges local historiography that may seek to minimize past actions. Recognition of the role of many Bulgarians in stopping the deportations to Germany should go along with consideration of the moral responsibility of the same regime and its supporters in creating indigenous policies that stigmatized minorities and were involved in the deaths of tens of thousands of non-citizens in the occupation zones. In this light, scholars can also move wartime inter-ethnic violence in southeastern Europe from the restrictions of national historiographies into the wider theoretical and methodological discussions of Holocaust scholarship. This may well engender a better understanding of the causality behind the extreme violence undertaken against groups which had cohabited in the region for centuries.

Notes

1 In using the term Holocaust, I stress the broad process by which Jews were isolated from and expelled from society as well as physically eliminated. This follows Raul Hilberg's holistic conception of the "destruction" of Jewish life and Jewish society, in Raul Hilberg, *The Destruction of the European Jews: Volume II* (New Haven: Yale University Press, 2003).
2 Omer Bartov, "Eastern Europe as the Site of Genocide," *Journal of Modern History*, vol. 80, no. 3 (September 2008): 557–93. One exception is Jan Gross, *Neighbors* (Princeton: Princeton University Press, 2001).
3 Raul Hilberg, *Perpetrators, Victims, Bystanders: The Jewish Catastrophe, 1933–1945* (New York: HarperCollins, 1992), 83.
4 Michael Bar-Zohar, *Beyond Hitler's Grasp: The Heroic Rescue of Bulgaria's Jews* (Holbrook: Adams Media, 1998).
5 For an overview of this regional process, see John Lampe, *Balkans into Southeastern Europe* (New York: Palgrave, 2006), 63–140.
6 Richard Crampton, *Bulgaria* (New York: Oxford, 2009), 421–36.
7 John Koliopoulos, *Modern Greece: A History since 1821* (New York: Wiley-Blackwell, 2009), 98–100; Bruce Clark, *Twice a Stranger: How Mass Expulsion Forged Modern Greece and Turkey* (London: Granta Books, 2007), 229.
8 Irinia Livezeanu, *Cultural Politics in Greater Romania* (Ithaca, New York: Cornell University Press, 1995), *passim*.
9 Ivo Banac, *The National Question in Yugoslavia* (Ithaca: Cornell University Press, 1984); Andrew Wachtel, *Making a Nation, Breaking a Nation* (Stanford, California: Stanford University Press, 1998), 67–127.
10 Saul Friedländer, "The 'Final Solution:' The Unease in Historic Interpretation," in *The Holocaust: Theoretical Readings,* eds Neil Levi and Michael Rothberg (New Brunswick, New Jersey: Rutgers University Press, 2003), 71. Yehuda Bauer questions comparisons of the Nazi goal of total destruction of the Jews versus the partial destruction of other groups, such as Roma. The Balkan states exempted *some* Jews from destruction, usually on the basis of past patriotism or economic need; in this, they were distinct from Germany. See Yehuda Bauer, *Rethinking the Holocaust* (New Haven, Connecticut: Yale University Press, 2001), 49.
11 Paraphrasing Sybil Milton, "The Context of the Holocaust," *German Studies Review*, vol. 13, no. 2 (May 1990): 269–83, 270.

12 Christopher Browning, "The Final Solution in Serbia: The Semlin Judenlager—a Case Study," *Yad Vashem Studies*, vol. 15 (1983): 55–90.

13 See Barry Lituchy, ed., *Jasenovac and the Holocaust in Yugoslavia* (Zagreb: Jasenovac Research Institute, 2006).

14 For recent English language sources, see Steven Bowman, *The Agony of Greek Jews, 1940–1945* (Stanford, California: Stanford University Press, 2009); Erika Kounio-Amarillo, *From Thessaloniki to Auschwitz and Back: Memories of a Survivor from Thessaloniki* (London: Vallentine Mitchell, 2000); Mark Mazower, *Salonica, City of Ghosts* (New York: Vintage, 2006); Rebecca Fromer, *The House by the Sea: A Portrait of the Holocaust in Greece* (New York: Mercury House, 1997).

15 Zvi Gitelman, "Politics and the Historiography of the Holocaust in the Soviet Union," in *Bitter Legacy: Confronting the Holocaust in the USSR*, ed. Zvi Gitelman (Bloomington, Indiana: Indiana University Press, 1997), 14–42; Lucy Dawidowicz, *The Holocaust and the Historians* (Cambridge, Massachusetts: Harvard University Press, 1983), 68–84; Jeffrey Herf, *Divided Memory* (Cambridge, Massachusetts: Harvard University Press, 1999).

16 Jean Ancel, *Documents Concerning the Fate of Romanian Jewry during the Holocaust* (Jerusalem: Beate Klarsfeld Foundation, 1986), 11: 13–19. For an example of the disappearance of Jewish victims, see Marcel-Dumitru Ciuca, ed., *Procesul Maresalului Antonescu: Documente* (Bucharest: Saeculum I.O., 1996), 1: 109–18.

17 Lucreţiu Pătrăşcanu, *Probleme de baza ale Romaniei* (Bucharest: Socec, 1944), 171; Mihail Roller, ed., *Istoria Republicii Populare Romane* (Bucharest: Editura de Stat Didactica si Pedagogica, 1952), 373.

18 Ioan Scurtu, *Viaţa Politică din România 1918–1944* (Bucharest: Editura Albatros, 1982), 233, 266–67; also Miron Constantinescu, *Istoria Romaniei. Compendiu* (Bucharest: Editura Didactica si Pedagogica, 1969), 482, 529. On post-socialist rehabilitation, see Mihai Chioveanu, "A Deadlock of Memory: The Myth and Cult of Ion Antonescu in Post-Communist Romania," *Studia Hebraica*, vol. 3 (2003); for examples, see Ion Ardeleanu and Vasile Arimia, eds, *Ion Antonescu: Citiţi, Judecaţi, Cutremuraţi-vă!* (Bucharest: Editura Tinerama, 1991), 90–91; Iosif C. Dragan and Ion Antonescu, *Antonescu: Marshal and Ruler of Romania, 1940–1944* (Bucharest: Editura Europa Nova, 1995), 375–400.

19 David Koen et al., eds, *Borbata na bulgarskiia narod za zashtita i spasiavane na evreite v Bulgariia prez Vtorata svetovna voina: dokumenti i materiali* (Sofia: Bulgarska akademiia na istoriia, 1978); Ivan Memishev, *Uchastieto na Bulgarskite Turtsi v Borbata Protiv Kapitalizma i Fashizma, 1919–1944* (Sofia: Partizdat, 1977).

20 Zdenko Levental, ed., *Zločini fašističkih okupatora i njihovih pomagača protiv jevreja u Jugoslaviji* (Belgrade: Savez jevrejskih opština Jugoslavije, 1952).

21 See Jozo Tomasevich, *War and Revolution in Yugoslavia, 1941–1945: Occupation and Collaboration* (Stanford, California: Stanford University Press, 2001), 583–95, 186–90; Stevan Pavlowitch, *Hitler's New Disorder: The Second World War in Yugoslavia* (New York: Columbia University Press, 2008), 37–43, 69. On Serbian collaboration, see Stanislav Krakov, *General Milan Nedić* (Belgrade: Nova Iskra, 1995), *passim*.

22 Jovan Byford, "When I Say 'The Holocaust,' I mean 'Jasenovac,'" *East European Jewish Affairs*, vol. 37, no. 1 (April 2007): 51, 62.

23 Novica Veljanovski et al., eds, *Istorija na Makedonskiot narod: Makedonija vo Vtorata svetska vojna* (Skopje: Institut za nacionalna istorija, 2003), 135–37.

24 For extreme positions, see Franjo Tudjman, *Bespuća povijesne zbiljnosti* (Zagreb: Hrvatska sveučilišna naklada, 1994); Milan Bulajić, *Ustaški zločini, genocida i sudjenje Andriji Artukoviću*, four volumes (Belgrade: Rad, 1988–89).

25 Ženi Lebl, *Until the Final Solution: The Jews in Belgrade, 1521–1942* (Bergenfield: Avotaynu, 2007); Milan Ristović, *U Potrazi za utočištem* (Belgrade: Službeni list, 1998).

26 For an introduction to the dispute, see Kyril Drezov, "Macedonian identity: an overview of the major claims," in *The New Macedonian Question*, ed. James Pettifer (New York: Palgrave Macmillan, 2001), 47–59. A pro-Greek account is George Papvizas, *Claiming Macedonia: The Struggle for the Heritage, Territory and Name of the Historic Hellenic Land, 1862–2004* (New York: McFarland, 2006); a pro-Macedonian account is John Shea, *Macedonia and Greece: The Struggle to Define a New Balkan Nation* (New York: McFarland, 1997).

27 See the essays in Peter Mackridge and Eleni Yannakakis, eds, *Ourselves and Others: The Development of a Greek Macedonian Cultural Identity since 1912* (New York: Berg, 1997). See also John Koliopolous, *Plundered Loyalties: World War II and Civil War in Greek West Macedonia* (New York: New York University Press, 1997).

28 Elie Wiesel et *al.*, *Final Report of the International Commission on the Holocaust in Romania* (Iaşi: Polirom, 2005).

29 On the historiography of Romania's victimization in World War II, see Mihai Chioveanu, "'Victimizing Romania' – A Fictional History of German Expansion Toward East Revisited," *Studia Hebraica*, 7 (2007).

30 Florin Mătrescu, *Holocaustul roşu sau crimele în cifre ale comunismului internaţional* (Bucharest: Fât-Frumos, 1998); Gheorghe Buzatu, *Românii în arhivele Kremlinului* (Bucharest: Univers Enciclopedic, 1996), 57.

31 Key works include Dinu C. Giurescu, "Evreii din România (1940–44)," in *România în al Doilea Război Mondial (1939–1945)* (Bucharest: All, 1999), 152–72; Lya Benjamin, *Prigoană şi Rezistenţă în Istoria Evreilor din România, 1940–1944: Studii* (Bucharest: Editura Hasefer, 2001); Andrei Pippidi, *Despre Statui şi Morminte. Pentru o Teorie a Istoriei Simbolice* (Iaşi: Polirom, 2000); Radu Ioanid, *The Holocaust in Romania: The Destruction of Jews and Gypsies Under the Antonescu Regime, 1940–1944* (Chicago: Ivan R. Dee, 2000); Jean Ancel, "The German–Romanian Relationship and the Final Solution," in *Holocaust and Genocide Studies*, vol. 19, no. 2 (Fall 2005).

32 See Livezeanu, *Cultural Politics in Greater Romania.*

33 Viorel Achim and Constantin Iordachi, eds, *România şi Transnistria: Problema Holocaustului. Perspective Istorice şi Comparative* (Bucharest: Curtea Veche, 2004), 23–77.

34 Irina Livezianu, "The Romanian Holocaust: Family Quarrels," *East European Politics and Societies*, vol. 16, no. 3 (2003); Achim and Iordachi, eds, *România şi Transnistria*, 86.

35 On Sighet, see Andrei Oişteanu, "Sighet—The Capital of the Holocaust and of the Gulag in Romania," *Caietele Echinox* [Echinox Notebooks] 13 (2007). For legislative and legal continuity, see Julie Trappe, "Justişie în Tranzişie: Gulag şi Holocaust în Memoria Judecătorească," *Caietele Echinox* [Echinox Notebooks] 13 (2007); Corneliu Pintilescu, "Gulag şi Holocaust: Legislaşie Discriminatorie şi Represivă," *Caietele Echinox* 13 (2007).

36 Tsar Boris III, the Bulgarian Orthodox Church, the Bulgarian Communist Party and parliamentarian Dimitur Peshev have been advanced as the key agents in opposing deportations from Bulgaria. Michael Bar-Zohar, *Beyond Hitler's Grasp* (Holbrook, Massachusetts: Adams Media, 1998); Stephane Groueff, *Crown of Thorns: the Reign of King Boris III of Bulgaria* (Lanham, Maryland: Madison Books, 1987); Tzvetvan Todorov, *The Fragility of Goodness* (Princeton, New Jersey: Princeton University Press, 2001); Nir Baruh, *Otkuput: Tsar Boris i sudbata na bulgarskite evrei* (Sofia: Univ. Iz-vo Sv. Kliment Ohridski, 1991); Gabriel Nissim, *Chovekut koito spria Hitler* (Sofia: NS, 1999); Hristo Boiadzhiev, *Spasiavaneto na bulgarskite evrei prez Vtorata svetovna voina* (Sofia: Univ. Iz-vo Sv. Kliment Ohridski, 1991).

37 See Christopher Browning, *The Origins of the Final Solution* (Lincoln, Nebraska: University of Nebraska Press, 2004), 211–12; Michael Mann, *The Dark Side of Democracy* (Cambridge, Massachusetts: Cambridge University Press, 2004), 307–8.

38 William Brustein and Ryan King, "Balkan Anti-Semitism: The Cases of Bulgaria and Romania before the Holocaust," *East European Politics*, vol. 18, no. 3 (2004), 430–54. Anti-Jewish violence in Bulgaria receives little scholarly attention, but see Tsvi Keren, "Subdbata na evreiskite obshtnosti v Kazanluk i Stara Zagora po vreme na Rusko-turskata voina ot 1877–78," *Istorichesko Budeshte*, vol. 11, nos 1–2 (2007): 202–19.

39 See Georgeta Nazarska, *Bulgarskata durzhava i neinite malinstva, 1879–1885* (Sofia: LIK, 1999), 9; Illona Tomova, "Roma," in *Communities and Identities in Bulgaria,* ed. Anna Kraseva (Ravenna: Longo Editore, 1998), 258.

40 Carnegie Endowment, *The Other Balkan Wars* (Washington, DC: Carnegie Endowment for International Peace, 1993), 73–75, 99.

41 Velichko Georgiev and Staiko Trifanov, eds, *Pokrustvaneto na bulgarite mohamedani, 1912–1913: Dokumenti* (Sofia: Izdatelstvo "Prof. Marin Drinov," 1995).

42 Glavna direktsiya na statistika, *Statisticheski godishnik na Bulgarskoto Tsarstvo* (Sofia: Glavna direktsiya na statistika, 1937).

43 Vladimir Migev, *Utvurzhdavane na monarho-fashistkata diktatura v Bulgariia, 1934–1936* (Sofia: BAN, 1977); Vladimir Migev, "Politicheskata sistema v Bulgariia ot 9 iuni 1923 do 9 septemvri 1944," *Istoricheski pregled,* vol. 46, no. 1 (1990); Crampton, *Bulgaria,* 240–48.

44 Richard C. Hall, *The Balkan Wars, 1912–1913: Prelude to the First World War* (Oxford: Routledge, 2000), 135; Joseph Rothschild, *East Central Europe between the Two World Wars* (Seattle, Washington: University of Washington Press, 1983), 325.

45 John R. Lampe and Marvin Jackson, *Balkan Economic History, 1550–1950: From Imperial Borderlands to Developing Nations* (Bloomington, Indiana: Indiana University Press, 1982), 450.

46 "Kum Chettsite," *Otets Paisii,* vol. 1, no. 1 (1928): 1; Bogdan Popov, "Natsionalno Samo-chuvstie," *Zveno,* vol.1, no. 23 (3 June 1928): 10.

47 For typical views, see "Duh na Natsiia," *Otets Paisii,* vol. 2, no. 1 (1929): 6–10; L. Vladikin, "Narodnostniiat Printsip i durzhavata," vol. 8, no. 12 (1935) *Otets Paisii,* 287–91; Legion "Ivan Asen II" – Varna, *Nashata Borba* (Varna: Otdel za ideologiia i propaganda, 1938), 8–16. For an overview of illiberal thought in Bulgaria in the interwar period, see Rumen Daskalov, *Bulgarskoto obshtestvo Tom I* (Sofia: Gutenberg, 2005), 214–26; Nikolai Poppetrov, *Fashizmut v Bulgariia: razvitie i proiavi* (Sofia: Kama, 2008).

48 *Sbornik Rodina, tom I (1937–1938)* (Plovdiv: Izdanie na bulgaro-mohamedanskata kulturno-posvetna i blagotvoritelna druzhba "Rodina," 1939).

49 Cited from the translated attachment of Zveno's proclamations on taking power in Shoemaker, Sofia to Washington DC, dispatch #23, 11 June 1934. *Records Relating to the Internal Affairs of Bulgaria,* 10/44.

50 On Muslims, see Mary Neuberger, *The Orient Within* (Ithaca, New York: Cornell University Press, 2004), 44–54; on Jews, see Frederick Chary, *The Bulgarian Jews and the Final Solution, 1940–1944* (Pittsburgh, Pennsylvania: University of Pittsburgh Press, 1972), 30–32.

51 See, for example, this sentiment expressed in Tsentralen Durzhaven Arhiv (TsDA) [Central State Archive], Fond 264K (Records of the Ministry of the Interior and National Health), opis 1, a.e. 440, list 1; District Police Manager to MVRNZ, undated.

52 Local police records record numerous instances of illegal border crossings by Muslims; see, for example, TsDA, Fond 370K (Police Records of the Ministry of Internal Affairs and National Health), opis 6., a.e. 421, l. 39, Agent M1315 to Chief of the "B" Directorate, MVRNZ Police Directorate, 30 September 1934.

53 Police surveillance was similarly applied to the former political parties, suspect communists, pro-fascist movements and émigré organizations, particularly those affiliated with the Internal Macedonian Revolutionary Organization, which *Zveno* moved to disband in 1934. See TsDA, Fond 370K, opis 6, a.e. 1708 for examples of MVRNZ local police reports on these groups.

54 Bilal Simsir, *The Turks of Bulgaria* (London: K. Rustem, 1988), 101–34.

55 TsDA, Fond 370K, opis 6, a.e. 424, l 54, MVRNZ Central Bureau Order #4074 to district police governors and inspectors, dated March 9, 1937. On the question of land, see Neuberger, *The Orient Within,* 180–82.

56 MVRNZ, Fond 370K, opis 6, a.e. 424, list 3–4, MVRNZ Directorate of Police to District Administrative police, Order #IV-24, 314 of 16 November 1939. This order addresses several of the state's minorities, including Greeks, Turks, Vlachs, Roma, and Albanians. Section III provides specific instructions regarding Jewish citizens requesting passports for the British Mandate of Palestine: a "flamboyant 'emigrant'" stamp is to be marked on their passports.

57 For example, see N/A, "Zoshto Legionar e posveshtenen anti-Semit," *Prelom* (8/1940).

58 For the final version of the law in published form, see *Durzhaven Vestnik,* vol. 63, no.16 (23 January 1941): 1–5.

59 *Durzhaven Vestnik,* vol. 63, no. 151 (14 July 1941): 1–2.

60 Neuberger, *The Orient Within,* 50–51. Bulgarian anti-Islamic laws, unlike the antisemitic laws, were often enacted secretly due to concerns that they might spark a backlash among the Muslim population in the country. See, for example, TsDA, Fond 264K opis 1, a.e. 440, l 31, letter from Petur Gabrovski, Minister of the MVRNZ to district and sub-district chiefs. Gabrovski states that "these measures of clarification and enforcement need tact and consideration, possibly as soon possible and *without formalities and written orders*" (author's emphasis).

61 TsDA, Fond 264K, opis 1, a.e. 308, l 11, Letter from parliamentarian Sirko Stanchev to the MVRNZ, 26 April 1941. Stanchev specifically proposed restrictions on clothing worn by Muslim ethnic Bulgarians.

62 "Naredba...na evreiskiia vupros," *Durzhaven Vestnik,* vol. 64, no. 192 (26 August 1942): 1–3.

63 On antisemitic laws, see Chary, *The Bulgarian Jews and the Final Solution,* 60–68; on Muslim–Jewish interactions, see TsDA, Fond 471K (Records of the Grand Mufti), opis 1, a.e. 1059, MVRI to the Grand Mufti, "Directive on Confession #18147–38-V," 29 May 1942; TsDA, Fond 471K, opis 1, a.e. 1059, l 1–3, MVRI to the Grand Mufti, "Directive on Confession #1847–38-V."

64 On the blocking of deportations from Bulgaria, see Todorov, *The Fragility of Goodness,* 14–40; Chary, *The Bulgarian Jews and the Final Solution,* 129–71.

65 Note the synthetic, if still German-centric, approach in Mark Mazower, *Hitler's Empire: How the Nazis Ruled Europe* (New York: Penguin Press, 2008), esp. 319–470.

24

TRANSNISTRIA
The Holocaust in Romania

Ronit Fischer

Since the end of World War II, Transnistria has not been among the prominent topics of the Holocaust period, and many historians of modern European history have only a vague idea of the region. Dubbed the "Romanian Auschwitz," Transnistria became the graveyard of thousands of Ukrainian and Romanian Jews at the hands of German, Romanian, and Ukrainian forces. Situated between the Bug and Dniester rivers in southwestern Ukraine, this 24,840-square-mile area of hundreds of small towns and villages existed as a political zone only during World War II.[1] Thus, in order to achieve a comprehensive understanding of the historical events of the Holocaust in Transnistria, it will be necessary to examine the policies of both German and Romanian authorities in the region.

The political creation of Transnistria

Romania has one of the more complex histories in the period from 1914 to 1940, and the same is true when studying its place in the narrative of the "Final Solution." With respect to territory, Romania benefited after World War I because it was on the side of the victorious Allied Powers. For its efforts, it received Transylvania from Hungary, as well as parts of Bessarabia (which had been a part of Russia), Bukovina (a part of Austria), and the Banat (also Hungarian). There were over 750,000 Jews in the Kingdom of Greater Romania (4 percent of the general population). With this number, Romania had the third largest Jewish community in Europe, after the Soviet Union and Poland.

In the interwar period, Romania was officially non-aligned, but it relied on the postwar arrangements of the Allied Powers and was probably closest to France diplomatically. With France's defeat in June 1940, Romania was alone; Nazi Germany supported demands for Romanian territory by the Soviet Union, Hungary, and Bulgaria. During the summer and autumn of 1940, Romania lost about 30 percent of its territory and population. The Soviet Union received Bessarabia and northern Bukovina on 28 June 1940. On 30 August 1940, Romania ceded northern Transylvania to Hungary, and in September, Romania lost southern Dobruja to Bulgaria.

The first of many ironies in all of this was that by the summer of 1940, Romania had as right-wing a government as any in Europe. Yet there was an internal struggle between the conservative and fascist forces in Romania that was very different from other places where the Right took hold. The fascist movement in Romania was known as the Iron

Guard; this was initially the paramilitary wing of a broader fascist movement known as the Legion of the Archangel Michael, founded by Corneliu Codreanu in 1927. (By the 1930s, the Iron Guard was essentially the Legion.) This movement differed from others in Europe in that it was overtly religious—and in this case, it was an aggressive, anti-semitic defense of Romanian Christian Orthodoxy. The main symbol of the Iron Guard was a triple cross—the Archangel Michael Cross.

In 1933, Romania's liberal Prime Minister, Ion Duca, banned the Iron Guard, but it retaliated by assassinating him on the platform of the Sinaia railway station. King Carol II, in particular, did not support the radical policies of the Iron Guard and, fearing violence countrywide, he established a royal dictatorship in 1938 to prevent a fascist take-over. Codreanu was put in prison and murdered, as were other members of the Iron Guard. In 1939, the dictatorship ended, and political instability returned with continued assassinations and street carnage. With the defeat of France and the looming loss of territory, the Romanian fascists did not seem unpalatable; in fact, they seemed like the answer to Romania's problems. In July 1940, Carol made his peace with the Iron Guard and its new leader Horia Sima, appointing a pro-Nazi Prime Minister in Ion Gigurtu. On 6 September 1940, the Iron Guard outmaneuvered the king and sealed an alliance with the Romanian military and General (later Marshal) Ion Antonescu. Carol was blamed for the loss of territory and for creating as a result a national malaise, and he was forced to turn over the throne to his 18-year-old son Michael. The coalition government of military officers and fascists, known as the National Legionary State, joined the Axis in November 1940.

With respect to Jews, after the loss of the three territories, there were maybe 400,000–450,000 Jews in Romania. This was a country that had a tradition of mostly religious antisemitism, and there were some antisemitic restrictions before 1940, but these were not enforced consistently prior to the National Legion State. In the months of that regime (September 1940–January 1941), there was a fresh wave of antisemitism. Jews were expelled from professions, they were arrested, Jewish stores were boycotted, and synagogues were plundered. The violence spiraled almost out of control, and then on 21 January 1941, the Iron Guard staged a coup against the military and Antonescu. During this 3-day uprising, there was an unprecedented orgy of antisemitic violence in Bucharest. Dozens of Jewish civilians were rounded up and executed in the city's slaughterhouse, where their bodies were hanged from meat hooks and displayed with labels that read: "kosher meat."

Antonescu may have opposed the Iron Guard for reasons of power, but he was just as vicious as they were towards the Jews—more so because the butchery reached new levels under his rule. After suppressing the Iron Guard's rebellion, Antonescu threw himself wholeheartedly into the Axis effort, assisting in the invasion of the Soviet Union, and moving against Jewish civilians in that theater. On 27 June 1941, Romanian forces launched an assault against Jews of the city of Iasi, near the Soviet border, accusing them of supporting the Red Army. Romanian police went into Jewish homes and killed people on the spot. On Sunday, 29 June, over 2,000 Jews who were brought to the Iasi train station were crammed into two trains, some 100 people per car, in searing heat, without water or food, and dispatched to Calarasi and Podu Iloaiei—neither was that far away, but the trains traveled slowly and it took 17 hours to reach the destinations. Over half were dead by the time they arrived. Romanian authorities identified 13,266 victims of the pogrom. As Jean Ancel has described, the murder of Romanian Jewry during World War II took place in stages—a first stage beginning at the end of June 1941 and lasting until August of that year, during which Romanian and German soldiers murdered some 100,000 Jews. During the second phase, from September to November 1941, 180,000 Romanian Jews were deported to Transnistria, "of whom 140,000 died of cold, starvation or disease, or were killed."[2]

Following the German invasion of the Soviet Union in June 1941, Romania re-annexed Bessarabia and northern Bukovina, which had been seized by the Soviets a year earlier. After the conquest of the Ukraine by German and Romanian troops in July and August 1941, Hitler granted the territory between the Dniester and Bug Rivers to Antonescu as a reward for Romania's participation in the war against the Soviet Union. A Romanian administration was established in Transnistria at the end of August 1941 (Tighina Agreement).[3] Until December 1941, the headquarters of the Romanian High Command was in Tiraspol; afterwards, it was moved to Odessa. The Romanian regime declared Gheorghe Alexianu as Governor of Transnistria, which was divided into 13 județe (counties) for administrative purposes: Ananiev, Balta, Berezovca, Dubăsari, Golta, Jugastru (Yampil), Movilău (Mohyliv-Podilskyi), Oceacov (Ochakiv), Odessa, Ovidiopol, Rîbnița, Tiraspol, and Tulcin (Tulchyn).[4] Although cities in these districts were led by mayors, in effect, Romanian police units were in charge of all law enforcement and security matters in Transnistria. The headquarters of the Gendarmerie was in Odessa under the command of General E. Brosteanu[5] and later General N. Iliescu. According to a Soviet census, the population of Transnistria in 1939 was around three million people. The majority were Ukrainians and Russians, and next to them were three large ethnic groups: Jews (311,000), Romanians (Moldovans, 300,000), and Germans (125,000). Alongside these were also a number of smaller groups: Tartars, Lithuanians, Bulgarians, Gypsies, Greeks, and Armenians.[6]

A new law codex included two decrees (from 9 August 1940), which redefined the status of Jews throughout all of the Romanian territories: Decree-law No.2650, "The Law Defining the Legal Status of Romanian Jews," and Decree-law No.2651, "The Law for Ceasing Intermarriage between Romanians by Blood and Jews."[7] The two new laws were published after Romania's Prime Minister, Gigurtu, met with Hitler in July 1940. At that meeting, Gigurtu gave his word to immediately remove all Jews from the economic sphere of Romania. The language, contents, and even the division of the new laws can be attributed to the strong influence of "The Reich Citizenship Law" of 15 September 1935, known as the "Nuremberg Laws."[8] The Romanian laws, shaped by native antisemitism and buttressed by the rapidly growing Romanian fascist movement, became the basis for Romania's implementation of the "Final Solution to the Jewish Question" as executed in Transnistria. Beginning in the summer of 1941 and lasting until the spring of 1944, Romanian army and police units, supported by German SS and *Einsatzkommandos*, massacred several hundred thousand Ukrainian and Romanian Jews (especially from Bessarabia and Bukovina) in Transnistria.

The fate of the local Jewish population of Transnistria

According to reports of the Nazi *Einsatzkommandos*, who entered the area in July 1941 in the wake of the occupying troops, two-thirds of the local Jewish population had fled the area. Many of the local Jews had been mobilized into the Soviet army. It was clear to the Romanian troops, who marched to liberate Bessarabia and Bukovina, that this was the time for "a complete ethnic liberation," as Mihai Antonescu (vice -president of the Council of Ministers) had described it: "The time has come for a complete ethnic liberation and purification of our lineage from elements that are foreign to our nation's soul, who have grown like a plague to darken our future. Let us be ruthless so as not to miss this opportunity. No one should allow himself to be seduced by humanitarian philosophy, which makes the interests of a most aggressive race...behind which we find a rapacious religion. The act of ethnic cleansing will involve removal or isolation of all Jews in labor camps, from which they will no longer exert their nefarious influence...."[9]

By Romanian order, given on 1 August, all the remaining local (Ukrainian) Jews had to move to Jewish concentrated "colonies."[10] That was the first official decree of the Romanian Interior Ministry for the deportation of Jews beyond the Dniester.[11] Most of the remaining native Jews of Transnistria (many men unfit for the army, as well as women, children, and the elderly) were murdered by German troops and Romanian gendarmes before the Jewish deportees from Romania arrived. The dominant German unit active in Transnistria was *Einsatzgruppe D* under the command of Otto Ohlendorf. The fate of the Jewish community of Dubossary, one of the towns on the east bank of the Dniester, illustrates the magnitude of the murder actions perpetrated by *Einsatzgruppe D*; two massgraves contained the bodies of 3,500 Jews from Dubossary itself and 7,000 from the vicinity, who were killed in the town after being rounded up by General Ohlendorf's unit. Another extreme example of the murderous actions taken against the local Jewish population during the occupation occurred in Odessa during 23–25 October 1941. When Romanian and German troops captured the town, after a 2-month siege, 25,000 Jews were killed on the personal orders of Antonescu after a Russian-made time bomb exploded in a building housing high-ranking Romanian officers. The rest of Odessa's Jews were expelled from the city and were marched in long convoys in the direction of Dalnik, a nearby village. There, they were placed into groups of between 40 and 50, thrown into an anti-tank ditch, and shot. When this method proved too slow, Jews were crammed into four warehouses, which had holes in the walls. Through these holes, Romanian troops and Ukrainian militiamen were able to mow down their victims with machine gun fire.[12]

The status of the Jews in Transnistria was determined by Order No. 23 (signed by governor Alexianu and submitted to Antonescu on 11 November 1941[13]). This order served as a follow up to the Tighina Agreement, which expressly referred to the imprisonment of Jews in ghettos. By the end of 1941, Romanian troops had killed more than 25,000 of the local Jews of Odessa and Dalnik, and had relocated thousands of Jewish deportees from Bukovina and Bessarabia in ghettos and camps in the northern part of Transnistria.[14] Other Jews from Bukovina and Bessarabia were deported to several large ghettos in the Golta district, in the southern part of Transnistria. At Bogdanovka camp, by the estimation of General Isopescu, there were by mid-December more than 52,000 Jews.[15] Other Jews from Bessarabia were put in the Domanovka camp (about 12,000) and 18,000 in the Acmechetka camp. Of these Jews deported to Bogdanovka camp, 48,000 were murdered in the massacre, which began on 21 December on the initiative of Fleischer, the German adviser to the district commander, and the Romanian General Isopescu. The massacre was committed by Ukrainian police, Romanian troops, and local German members of the SS and Sonderkommando D.[16] The inhuman conditions in those camps caused the deaths of 30–40 Jews each day, and, together with massacres which caused the death of thousands of Jews in Acmechetka and Domanovka, by March 1942 there were only 810 Jews who remained at Bogdanovka and 1,900 in Domanovka.[17]

The deportations of Jewish communities from Romania to Transnistria: the first wave

Immediately after the German–Romanian occupation, Transnistria became the destination for deported Romanian Jews, without any outlined program. It is estimated that during the combined Romanian and German military actions in Bukovina and Bessarabia, more than 10,000 Jews were murdered in July 1941 alone.[18] As soon as the end of July 1941, 25,000 Jewish survivors from towns in northern Bessarabia were expelled to Transnistria by the Romanians, but they were sent back to Bessarabia by the Germans[19] after 4,000 refugees were murdered on the way. Other groups sent to Transnistria wandered about the area of Mogilev, Skazinets, and Yampol for about two weeks before the Romanians agreed to their return. Finally, on 17–18 August, another 20,500 were re-admitted to Bessarabia; many were shot or thrown into the river, by both German and Romanian troops.

More programmatic and systematic deportations to Transnistria began on 15 September 1941. During the time of the Jewish holidays (September and October 1941), all the surviving Jews of Bessarabia and Bukovina (except for some 20,000 Jews of Czernowitz) and a part of the Jewish population of the Dorohoi district in the Regat (Romania in its pre-World War I borders) were sent away from their homes, across the Dniester river to Transnistria. Tens of thousands of Jews from Bessarabia and Bukovina were killed during July and August 1941. On 1 September 1941, officials counted more than 126,630 Jews still alive in these districts. The estimated number of deported Jews from Romania, who were driven out to Transnistria in this first wave, reached 118,840 deportees by mid-November 1941.[20]

The second and third waves

The second wave of deportations began at the beginning of the summer of 1942, affecting 4,200 Jews from Czernowitz and some 450 Jews from Dorohoi. The third series of deportations, in July 1942, consisted of Jews from the Regat, Jews who had evaded the forced labor decrees, as well as their families, and Bessarabian Jews who had been in the Regat and in Transylvania during the Soviet occupation of Bessarabia in June 1940, and had asked to be repatriated to their homes. Of the latter group, 350 Jews were shot to death by SS troops on their arrival at Berezovka (in Transnistria). In this wave, there was also a large group of communist sympathizers (among them many socialists) and their families, who were sent to a special concentration camp in Vapnyarka Transnistria. Some individual deportation orders were directed against Jewish merchants and industrialists accused of economic sabotage, bribery, and similar "economic crimes."

During the summer of 1942, the Romanian general staff submitted an additional list of 12,000 Jews from the Regat who had violated forced labor laws. In the meantime, however, official Romanian policy had changed and the deportation of this group was not implemented; the Romanian government also refused to give its consent to Germany's insistence on the deportation of all Romania's Jews.

Arriving at Transnistria

The thousands of Romanian Jews, expelled from their homes in Bessarabia and Bukovina, were herded by Romanian soldiers in long convoys along muddy dirt roads to the northern part of Transnistria. These were the early forms of death-march. Those convoys of men, women, children, the elderly, sick and disabled people were driven aimlessly from place to place as some towns refused to accept them. Many deportees died on these convoys, of exhaustion, cold, hunger, and illnesses, before they reached the camps. People who could not keep up with these aimless marches were shot or beaten to death. Many bodies were thrown into the rivers, ditches or mass graves, or simply left on the side-roads. Some groups from southern Bukovina had money and bribed local authorities for the right to stay (for example, in Mogilev). In some cases, entire communities were expelled as a group together with the community leaders, such as the communities of Radauti and Suceava; the latter also saved the community's funds, with which they managed to obtain better living conditions. In places where the local Jews still survived, the deportees received shelter in homes or in synagogues that had not been destroyed. Due to lice infestations, lack of food and pure water, and a lack of medical assistance, the local Jews were exposed to all the diseases and epidemics that befell the deportees. Most of the local Jews attempted to help the unfortunate deportees by whatever means they could. Many Jewish refugees from the Ukraine (who had crossed the Bug River) and from Romania were hidden by local Jews. In some cases, they were able to procure forged identification papers.

In the ghettos and camps of Transnistria

The region of Transnistria was also known as a concentration camp zone, created to solve the "Jewish problem" of Romania. But it was not the same type of concentration camp as those built by the Nazis in Germany or Poland. In addition, there were a number of ghettos that dotted the Transnistrian landscape. The largest ghettos in Transnistria were in Odessa, Shargorod, Bershad, Golta, Verhovka, Luchinetz, Sadova, Tibulovca, and the largest, Mogilev.[21] There were hundreds of hamlets and settlements that were too small to be noted on maps, which became concentration, transit, labor or annihilation camps. In many of these ghettos or "Jewish Colonies" were no more than a thousand people.[22] Many of the deportees found shelter in animal barns, where they lived in the most crowded and dirty conditions. The first winter (1941–42) was extremely harsh, with temperatures dropping to many degrees below zero. Deportees died of frostbite and other diseases, or they starved to death. The bodies of the dead accumulated in the cemeteries or in the camps until the spring, when graves could be dug for them. Various epidemics, such as typhus and dysentery, also claimed tens of thousands of victims. The doctors among the deportees in the various camps had tried, despite a lack of adequate medical equipment, to combat the further spread of contagious diseases, and many of them were among the victims.

In Dzhurin, Shargorod, and Mogilev, local committees succeeded in organizing the internal life of the refugee communities. These committees were led by Jewish community leaders from Romania and representatives of the local Jewish population. In other places, Romanian officials appointed committee members and forced them to collaborate with the regime.[23] In some ghettos, the committees established public kitchens, hospitals, orphanages, bakeries, and soap factories, and organized sales cooperatives. All this helped make life more bearable. Jewish police detachments were formed but, as Theodor Lavi points out, these not infrequently became a tool in the hands of the occupation powers, who used them for drafting men and women for forced labor.[24] Improved internal organization controlled epidemics. In the second winter (1942–43), only four out of 25 patients died in an epidemic in the town of Shargorod, as compared with 1,400 the year before. The doctors among the deportees vigorously combated the epidemics, and many died in the execution of their task. In camps where little internal organization was created, the mortality rate was extremely high (almost 100 percent). In some camps there were local initiatives by groups of people or by individuals who made efforts to repair and rebuild local factories. There were few major examples, as the case of the deportees group in the Mogilev Ghetto, who had managed to undertake repairs of the local electric power station and a local foundry, and some of them had also established a repair workshop for automobiles.[25]

Slave labor in Transnistria

Transnistria was an autonomous region run by Romanian authorities. Nevertheless, the Germans had various units there, working together with the Romanians and especially promoting and preserving Nazi interests in that area. They had two main strategic missions: the first mission was to build the *Durchgangstrasse IV* [Highway IV] between Poland and southern Ukraine (for military and economic purposes). Thus the situation was especially grave for the Jews in the area adjoining the Bug River, as from time to time the Germans crossed the west bank to use Jews for forced labor on the other side of the river. At Pechora, a sign at the camp entrance identified it as a "death camp." Following this German decision, many of the Jewish deportees who arrived at Transnistria were set to this task as a slave labor force. The technical supervision of this project was provided by the *Organisation Todt*, and the SS and Ukrainian and Lithuanian auxiliaries handled recruitment.

Labor camps held the slave labor pool in conditions that mirrored other German concentration camps. Before work groups were organized, children under 15, adults over 50, and the sick were "selected" and "eliminated." Those who remained were housed in terrible barracks where they were crammed into tiers of wooden bunks. A Jewish capo (foreman) was selected for each group. All "laborers" were forced to wear the yellow star of David on their chest and on the back of their rags. There was a roll-call twice a day, and with it the threat of "selection" of those unfit to work.[26] As in other concentration camps, there were beatings and executions during work if prisoners showed any signs of fatigue, but, unlike in the German camps, in Transnistria the bodies were left in the ditches at the side of the road: "The piles of bodies outside our house kept growing. The snow storm and the tremendous cold made it impossible to bury them."[27] There were also other cases, such as those in Berezovka district, when, during March–April 1942, German policemen executed 4,067 Jewish labor workers, burned the corpses, and then donated their clothes to the local German population.[28]

Initially, most of the forced laborers were Jews from the Ukraine and Soviet POWs, but because of the harsh conditions in the camps, by the summer of 1942 most had perished, which led the SS to seek fresh "recruits" from the Romanian side of Transnistria. In August 1942, about 3,000 Jewish deportees (mostly from Czernowitz) were taken across the Bug River into slavery.[29] The second project of *Organisation Todt* in Transnistria was the building of a bridge from Trihati to Nicolaev, across the Bug River. This project, which began in the spring 1943 and lasted for the bulk of the year, also resulted in the deaths of thousands of Jewish deportees.[30]

In order to accomplish these missions, the Germans launched several raids from across the Bug, and in the fall of 1942, 1,000 Jews were dragged across the river. In the camp at Bar, which was over the Bug River and in Germa-occupied territory,12,000 Jews were put to death on 20 October 1942. The people who had been taken to eastern Ukraine for forced labor were put to death as soon as their job was done, while those who were unable to work were murdered on the spot. During the spring of 1942, Romanian authorities transferred to the Germans about 31,000 Jews from Berezovka district, none of whom survived (as far as is known).[31]

In the Tulchin area, the head of the district was particularly efficient in handing Jews over to the Germans, especially to *Organisation Todt*. Tens of thousands were murdered in the second deportation to the German-administered territories beyond the Bug, in such places as Gaisin, Krasnopolye, and Trihati. These Romanian initiatives of massive deportation in spring 1942 did not fit in with Eichmann's overall plans for the "Final Solution," and he protested to the German Foreign Office; as a result thousands of Jews were returned to Transnistria, while some of them were murdered during the dabbled forced journey. (Jewish Virtual Library).[32] On 14 March 1944, the Soviets reconquered Nicolaev. The Germans began to liquidate the remaining workforce, but the arrival of a Romanian patrol staved off the massacre of 370 Jews at the last minute.[33]

The "Final Solution" of the Jewish problem in Transnistria

The order to execute the Jews and to cremate their bodies was issued by the Governor of Golta, M. Isopescu.[34] A number of camps were created to complete this task. The Bogdanovka camp consisted of 40 cowsheds on a former state farm. Interned in the camp were 48,000 Jews, most of them from Odessa, and about 7,000 from southern Bessarabia. Another 18,000 Jews who had been brought from three different districts in southern Transnistria, together with a small group from southern Bessarabia, were incarcerated in the Domanovka camp. About 4,000 sick, elderly, and women, described by the gendarmes as unfit for any forced labor, were incarcerated in the Acmechetka camp located on the outskirts of the village, half-way between the other two camps. The Nizkor Project site describes the executions that followed:

> The order to begin executions was transmitted verbally to the Prefect of Golta, who in turn passed it down to his deputy, A. Padure. The murders were carried out jointly by Romanian gendarmes, Ukrainian auxiliaries, and a number of local volunteers. The operation was under the command of a Ukrainian-born Romanian called Kazachievichi. The killings began on the morning of 21 December 1941, the last day of Hanukkah. Some 4,000 Jews were packed into two cow sheds and then burned alive. The method was the same as in Odessa: straw was thrown inside, all openings were barricaded, the building was doused with gasoline and set on fire. The remaining Jews were lined up in rows (three to four hundred at a time), marched to the woods, ordered to undress at the edge of a ravine by the River Bug, and shot in the head. Now and then, grenades were lobbed into the ravine to finish off those who might still be alive. The executions went on until the evening hours of December 24 and stopped on Christmas Eve only to enable the troops to celebrate Christmas. The massacre resumed on 28 December and was completed, with considerable effort,

on 31 December, just in time for the New Year's parties. After the liquidation of the camp at Bogdanovca, the same team liquidated the camp at Domanovca. At Acmechetca, there was no need to shoot anyone. The camp was fenced off with barbed wire, and the Jewish prisoners were left to die of hunger. Prefect Isopescu was fond of visiting every few days to see and report what was happening; he even took photographs of the dying Jews.[35]

The problem of arriving at an accurate figure for the number of Jews murdered in Transnistria by the Romanian and German armies is a significant and well-known difficulty.[36] It is estimated that, during the Antonescu regime, more than 410,000 Jews were murdered by the Romanian army and gendarmerie, together with Nazi Storm Unit *Einsatzgruppe D*. Of those, there were approximately 180,000 Jews of Ukrainian origin and a quarter of a million Jews who had been Romanian citizens. About 100,000 of the Romanian Jews were murdered during the waves of deportations, and more than 140,000 Jews were murdered in the various camps of Transnistria: 18,000 in Domanovka, 48,000 in Bogdanovka, 5,000 in Acmechetka, 23,000 in Vertujeni, 25,000 in Odessa, 16,000 in Dalnik, and some thousands more were shot along the River Bug.

The Romanian government halted the deportations of Jews from Romania to Transnistria at the end of 1942, but by then two-thirds of the Jewish deportees were already dead. On 1 November 1943, Romanian army headquarters reported that more than 70,700 Jews were still alive in Transnistria. In December of that year, the Romanian Ministry of the Interior informed its government that 50,741 of them were deportees from Romania (especially from Bukovina and Bessarabia) who were still alive at that time in Transnistria.[37]

Rescue and aid operations

The idea of an "organized emigration of Jews from Romania" had gained popularity by the state's leaders before the war, culminating in a proposal by Armand Calinescu in mid-1939. On 1 December 1942, the idea of Jewish emigration from Romania surfaced for the third time (after the second try, half a year earlier), but this time it concentrated on having those Romanian Jews who were deported to Transnistria forcibly transferred to Palestine (or to other places). On 3 December, Radu Lecca summoned W. Fildermann and most of the Jewish leaders of the Regat to a meeting. There, he informed them that the Romanian government was willing to permit the emigration of 70,000 Jews "for humanitarian reasons."[38] In fact, there were attempts to help Jews deported to Transnistria since the beginning of the deportations in September 1941. These attempts were made not only by W. Fildermann and many of the prominent Jewish leaders of the Regat, but also by all the heads of the Jewish institutions in Bucharest, as well as important non-Jewish figures. A secret committee was formed in Bucharest, with Fildermann and Zionist leaders participating. Their main purpose was to stop the deportations. The second, but no less important, purpose was to provide all possible assistance to the deportees.

Their first breakthrough came in autumn 1941, when Antonescu chose not to deport 20,000 Jews from Czernowitz, considered essential for the smooth functioning of the city. A month later, in December 1941, the Council received permission from Antonescu himself to extend aid to the deportees in Transnistria. To achieve this goal, Fildermann's committee collected money and contributions in kind, and dispatched financial aid, clothing, and medicine to the deportees. Another success came in the fall of 1942, when pressure from Jewish leaders and other forces persuaded the Romanian "Conductor" to cancel the deportation of the Jews of Southern Transylvania. This deportation was intended to be the first stage in the deportation of all the Jews of Romania to the death camps in Poland.[39] The protests against this deportation came not only from the central Jewish committee, but also from non-Jews, notably members of the Royal Family (in particular, Queen Mother Helena); foreign diplomats (American officials and ambassadors of neutral countries); and religious leaders in the Christian world, such as the papal nuncio. There were also protests from representatives of the International Red Cross, leaders of the Romanian Church, and some of the leaders of Romanian political parties. The turning of the tide against German forces in Stalingrad was also a factor. It is not entirely coincidental that, in the month when the Russians launched their counter-offensive (November 1942), Romanian authorities were negotiating with Jewish leaders in Bucharest about the return of the Transnistrian deportees and the emigration of the 75,000 survivors to Palestine.

Rescue and assistance

Mihai Antonescu expressed the turn in the Romanians' policy regarding the Jews in these words, in November 1942: "I prefer to strike at the economic activity of the rich, rather than carry out massacres and engage in hostile acts against the poor...The Hungarians are watching, photographing and producing propaganda abroad against us about our so-called barbarism against the Jews. The abuses are not the work of the government, and I have already intervened three times to ensure that the Jews are treated in an orderly fashion. Some peripheral agencies have made mistakes and carried out abuses that must come to an end...."[40] The change in attitudes towards the "Jewish issue" is especially illuminating if one compares this statement with his words in the summer of 1941.

It was only with the change in Romanian policy regarding the "Jewish problem" that the central aid committee was finally granted permission, at the beginning of 1943, to send a delegation to visit the camps in Transnistria. Jewish leaders in Bucharest obtained financial aid from Jewish organizations abroad for the deportees. The most significant sources of aid were the American Jewish Joint Distribution Committee, the Rescue Committee of the Zionist Organization, the World Jewish Congress, and OSE (Œuvre de secours aux enfants). During 1943–44 about 500,000,000 lei were sent in aid to the Jews in Transnistria. Non-Jews who were horrified by the situation in Transnistria also raised money to help.[41]

The change in Romania's Jewish policy caused an immediate German reaction. Officials from the German Foreign Ministry, the German ambassador in Bucharest (Manfred von Killinger), and Eichmann's representative in the SS, Gustav Richer, lodged a protest with the Romanian government in December 1942. This document expressed anger at the new position of the Romanian leadership on the Jewish question, and rejected any decision to repatriate Romanian Jews from Transnistria. In March 1943, a special commission was sent to Transnistria by the Romanian government, and in April, Antonescu agreed to Fildermann's appeal to permit the return of all the deportees. In the first stage, Antonescu approved the repatriation of 5,000 orphaned children from Transnistria.[42]

In reaction, Eichmann informed Himmler of the planned emigration of Jewish orphans from Transnistria to Palestine, and once again asked the German Foreign Ministry to prevent it.

It was only six months later, on 7 September 1943, that the Central Jewish Office in Bucharest gave Radu Lecca its request for the repatriation of the following categories of Jews (orphans, widows, invalids, medal recipients of the 1916–18 war, etc.), and only in mid-December 1943 did the selective repatriation of the Jewish deportees from Transnistria begin. Then it ended almost as quickly, at the end of January 1944. As Soviet forces crossed the Bug River on 15 March 1944 and advanced northward to the Dniester, additional repatriations followed.

The extermination of the Romanian Gypsies in Transnistria

During the war, the Romanian administration and military forces were also preoccupied with the "dispersal" and impoverishment of thousands of Gypsies in Transnistria.[43] The deportation and extermination of the Romanian Gypsies started in May 1942, based on Law Order No. 70S/1942 and Law Order No. 33911, which facilitated the deportation of about 25,000 Gypsies (both nomadic and sedentary) from Romania to Transnistria.[44] Of these, 11,500 Gypsies were executed by SS forces in the train station of Trihăti.[45] An additional 6,000–8,000 Gypsies were murdered in Golta by the Romanian army. Only 1,500 of the Romanian Gypsies who had been transported to Transnistria survived.[46]

The historical significance of Transnistria within the historical narrative of the Holocaust in Romania

On 23 August 1944, King Michael (with the backing of Allied and communist elements) staged a coup against Antonescu and placed him under house arrest. Antonescu was remanded in Soviet custody, but he was eventually sent back to Romania to face trial after the war. He was found guilty of numerous crimes and executed. King Michael joined the Allied cause, but the Soviets marched into Romania nevertheless, and forced an armistice in September 1944.

Over the course of World War II, Romania's Jewish population was halved—falling from 756,000 in 1930 to 375,000 in 1945.[47] Most of Romania's Jews who died during the war went to their deaths in Transnistria. As the graveyard of Romanian Jewry during the Holocaust, Transnistria was a distinctly Romanian solution to the "Jewish problem." Romanians proceeded from a stridently independent position, at first exceeding German expectations by conducting massacres of Jews with vigor, and then opposing deportations of Jews to the death camps in Poland. The reasons for this change in policy are complicated, but it was heavily influenced by a different perception of the ethnicity of the Jews. The great majority of the 420,000 Romanian Jews who perished in the Holocaust came from recently acquired territories, not from the Regat, or Romania proper. This latter group, while it suffered vicious local pogroms in Bucharest and Iasi at the hands of nationalist militias, was not expelled to Transnistria or annihilated. This difference in *modus operandi* indicates ethnic in addition to religious differentiation, and the need to bring ethnic terminology into the frame of reference of historical research of the Holocaust in Romania. The different ethnic affiliations in two of the "new" heterogenous regions, Bessarabia and Bukovina (where once "people spoke and sung in four languages, and understood one another"[48]), is crucial for understanding of the acts and responsibilities of the army, the civil authorities and the public in past days and now.[49]

The commemoration of Transnistria

More than 60 years after the Holocaust, there is still a difference in the tendencies of the Romanian and Ukrainian governments to assume responsibility for the murder of hundreds of thousands of Jews and Roma in Transnistria. The area is strewn with mass graves, along country roads and ditches, forests, fields, and anti-tank trenches. Today, these fields and trenches are the final resting place of thousands of Romanian and Ukrainian Jews. They conceal the heinous crimes of a great number of killers—Germans, Romanians, Ukrainians, and Lithuanians alike. In the vast Ukrainian grainfields, there is no monument, or any kind of marker alerting visitors to the gruesome carnage committed under the lush orchards and beautifully landscaped parks.

It was only after *The Report of the International Commission on the Holocaust in Romania*, submitted to President Ion Iliescu in Bucharest on 12 November 2004,[50] nearly 60 years after the end of the war, that the Romanian government changed its traditional position of denying its role in the tragedy of Transnistria. This committee and its report were the outcome of the sharp remarks of Romanian President Iliescu and other leaders, in the summer of 2003, that "there was no Holocaust in Romania, among the Jewish population."[51] The International Committee, composed of politicians and Holocaust historians, was established in the wake of the anger aroused by his remarks. The response of the President and of the Romanian government was surprising. It finally assumed responsibility for the murder of hundreds of thousands of Jews and tens of thousands of Gypsies in Romanian territory during World War II.

Notes

1 J.S. Fisher, *Transnistria: The Forgotten Cemetery* (New Brunswick, New Jersey: T. Yoseloff, 1969).

2 Jean Ancel, "The Opposition to the Antonescu Regime: Its Attitude Towards the Jews during the Holocaust," in *Nazi Europe and the Final Solution,* eds David Bankier and Israel Gutman (Jerusalem: Yad Vashem, 2009), 346.

3 J. Ancel, ed., *Documents Concerning the Fate of Romanian Jewry during the Holocaust* (Jerusalem: Beate Klarsfeld Foundation, 1986), 5: 62, 59–63.

4 J. Ancel, *Transnistria, 1941–1942: The Romanian Mass Murder Campaigns* (Tel Aviv: Goldstein–Goren Diaspora Research Center, Tel Aviv University, 2003), 1: 21–22; see also http://ftp.nizkor.org/hweb/people/c/carmelly-felicia/transnistria-forgotten-cemetary.html

5 One of the most important documents of the deportations was written by the Transnistrian gendarmerie commander Colonel Emil Broșteanu on 17 January 1942. His report, sent to the gendarmerie headquarters in Bucharest, sheds light on technical aspects of the deportations:

> I have the honor to inform you that on 2 January 1942, the evacuation of the Jews from Odessa began. In accordance with the order issued by the Transnistrian administration, the Jews about to be evacuated have been assembled in the Ghettos after each (Jew) has appeared before the committee for the Assessment of Property (Jewelry) and surrendered his money in return for RKKS. Convoys of 1,500–502,000 individuals are put together inside the Ghetto and loaded onto German trains. They are transported to the Mostovoye–Veselyevo region, in the Berezovka district. From the Berezovka station, they are escorted to the relocation area. To date, 6,000 have

been evacuated, and the transports are continuing daily. It is very difficult to find shelter for them in the relocation villages, since the Ukrainian population does not accept them. Consequently, many end-up in stables of the collective farms. Because of the freezing temperatures (−20°C) and the lack of food, and their age and miserable condition, many die along the way and freeze where they fall...Bodies are strewn along the route and buried in antitank trenches...

Report No.76, 17 January 1942, in Ancel, *Documents Concerning the Fate of Romanian Jewry during the Holocaust*, 5: 222. See also http://ftp.nizkor.org/hweb/people/c/carmelly-felicia/transnistria-forgotten-cemetary.html

6 Institutul central de statistica, *Annual Statistic al Romaniei*, Bucuresti (1937): 58–61, cited in Irina Livezeanu, *Cultural Politics in Greater Romania* (Ithaca, New York: Cornell University Press, 1995), 10.

7 *Monitorul Oficial (Partea I)*, Nr.183, 9 August 1940.

8 Yitzhak Arad, Israel Gutman and Abraham Margoliot, eds, *Holocaust Documents: A Selection of Documents on the Annihilation of German, Austrian, Polish, and USSR Jews* (Jerusalem: Yad Vashem, 1978), 72–74. The translation was taken from *Reichsgesetzblatt*, I, 1935, 1146.

9 M. Antonescu, *Pentru Bessarabia si Bucovina, indrumari date administratiei desrobitoare* (Bucuresti, 1941), 60–61.

10 Ancel, *Transnistria*, 1: document 15, 546, 2: document 16, 27.

11 Archives of the Prime Minister's office, Military Cabinet Collection, file 86q1941. Copy in United States Holocaust Memorial Museum Archives, USHMM/RG 25002m, reel 18, 48.

12 A. Dallin, *Odessa 1941–1944: A Case Study of Soviet Territory under Foreign Rule* (Santa Monica, California: Rand Corporation, 1957), 45–110. See also http://ftp.nizkor.org/hweb/people/c/carmelly-felicia/transnistria-forgotten-cemetary.html

13 Order 23, 11 November 1941, in Ancel, *Documents Concerning the Fate of Romanian Jewry during the Holocaust*, 5: 176–77.

14 Radu Ioanid, *The Holocaust in Romania* (Chicago: Ivan R. Dee, 2000), 182.

15 J. Ancel, *Transnistria*, 1: 114–18.

16 Ioanid, *The Holocaust in Romania*, 183, 184.

17 Ioanid, *The Holocaust in Romania*, 185, 186.

18 Raul Hilberg, *The Destruction of the European Jews* (New York: Holmes and Meier, 1985), 2: 771.

19 We can learn about the German dissatisfaction from a report of Einsatzgruppe D from 21 July 1941: "The Romanians take action against the Jews without any preconceived plan. There would be nothing to criticize about the many executions of Jews had their technical preparation and their manner of execution not been inadequate. The Romanians leave the bodies of those who are executed where they fall, without burying them." From Henry Monneray, *La Persecution des Juifs dans les Pays de l'Est* (Paris, 1949), 291, cited in Ioanid, *The Holocaust in Romania*, 108.

20 Matatias Carp, *Cartea Neagra* (Bucharest: 1948), 3: 39.

21 Yad Vashem Archives, Sharaga Files O-11/42,JM/3356, JM/2824, JM/2808, and in USHMM/RG 54001 M, Reel I.

22 Dennis Deletant, "Ghetto Experience in Golta, Transnistria, 1942–44," *Holocaust and Genocide Studies*, vol. 18, no. 1 (Spring 2004): 5–6.

23 www.jewishvirtuallibrary.org/jsource/judaica/ejud_0002_0020_0_19998.html

24 www.jewishvirtuallibrary.org/jsource/judaica/ejud_0002_0020_0_19998.html

25 Ancel, *Transnistria*, 65–74.

26 See the above description of the Transnistrian gendarmerie commander Colonel Emil Broşteanu in his report on 17 January 1942 (note 5).

27 Avigdor Shachan, *Burning Ice: The Ghettos of Transnistria, East European Monographs* (New York: Columbia University Press, 1996), 200.

28 Ioanid, *The Holocaust in Romania*, 187.

29 Ancel, *Transnistria*, 1: 786–87; http://ftp.nizkor.org/hweb/people/c/carmelly-felicia/transnistria-forgotten-cemetary.html

30 Ancel, *Transnistria*, 1: 808.

31 Hilberg, *The Destruction of the European Jews,* 2: 771.

32 Otto Ohlendorf admitted at his trial that Einsatzgruppe D under his command murdered approximately 90,000 Jews between June 1941 and June 1942. *Trials of War Criminals before the Nuremberg Military Tribunal under Control Council Law No. 10, October 1946–April 1949, Case No. 9, U.S. vs. Ohlendorf (Einsatzgruppen Case)* (Washington, DC: US Government Printing Office, 1948–53), 168, as cited in Ancel, *Transnistria,* 1: 50–51.

33 Ioanid, *The Holocaust in Romania,* 256.

34 Statistics and data of the different camps as cited in Ancel, *Transnistria,* 1: 509–32; http://ftp. nizkor.org/hweb/people/c/carmelly-felicia/transnistria-forgotten-cemetary.html

35 http://ftp.nizkor.org/hweb/people/c/carmelly-felicia/transnistria-forgotten-cemetary.html

36 See the relevant chapters in Ioanid, *The Holocaust in Romania,* 170–75; Ancel, *Transnistria,* 530–32.

37 Radu Lecca to Antonescu, 20 November 1943, cited in Ancel, *Documents Concerning the Fate of Romanian Jewry during the Holocaust,* vol. 7, no. 393, 547.

38 Shachan, *Burning Ice,* 310.

39 Ioanid, *The Holocaust in Romania,* 238–42.

40 Ancel, *Documents Concerning the Fate of Romanian Jewry during the Holocaust,* 10: 241–42.

41 The papal nuncio, Monsignor Andrea Cassulo, made a lengthy visit to various camps in Transnistria from 27 April to 5 May 1943, and as a result, the pope donated 1,300,000 lei to alleviate the conditions of the Jews of Transnistria. In December of that year, an International Red Cross mission also arrived there. See Ioanid, *The Holocaust in Romania,* 243–45.

42 Shachan, *Burning Ice,* 321–32.

43 October–December 1942, Nikolayev Archives, 2178-1-457, 432, as cited in Ancel, *Documents Concerning the Fate of Romanian Jewry during the Holocaust,* 1: 812–29.

44 Yad Vashem Archives, 00A, roll 14, fond 9721.

45 Ancel, *Documents Concerning the Fate of Romanian Jewry during the Holocaust,* 5: 541.

46 *Procesul marii trădări,* 305, cited in Ioanid, *The Holocaust in Romania,* 235.

47 About 150,000 of the 756,000 ended up under Hungarian rule in northern Transylvania as a result of the wartime changes in borders.

48 "Vier Sprachen / Vier Sprachenlieder / Menschen/ Die sich verstehen," from a poem by Rosa Auslander of Bukovina, quoted in Zvi Yavetz: "Ein Jahr in Czernowitz zwischen den beiden Weltkriegen," *Kaindl Archiv,* 42 (2000): 60–71.

49 Ronit Fischer, "Between Ethnic Cleansing and Final Solution: The Fate of Bukovinian and Bessarabian Jewry and the Neighborly relations during the Holocaust with regard to the Minority Policy of the Romanian Nation State in the 20th Century," PhD dissertation, Haifa, 2005.

50 This can be found at the Yad Vashem website: www.yadvashem.org/about_yad/what_new/data_whats_new/report1.html

51 The Israeli daily *Haaretz* (Tel Aviv), on 18 June and 25 July 2003, reported that on 13 June, the Romanian government declared: "Within Rumanian borders there was no Holocaust between 1940 and 1945." While on June 18 President Ion Iliescu criticized this pronouncement by his government, he added: "While some Rumanians participated in the Holocaust, the persecution of the Jews in Rumania did not resemble their persecution in Germany." Such statements aroused official responses from Israel and from Jewish organizations elsewhere, including the Anti-Defamation League and the Wiesenthal Institute. On 15 June, the Israeli government protested formally to the Romanian ambassador Aleria Mariana Stoiko, stating: "Israel takes a most serious view of the Romanian declaration, which does not accord with historical truth."

25

NATION-BUILDING AND MASS VIOLENCE
The Independent State of Croatia, 1941–45

Alexander Korb

This chapter deals with the Independent State of Croatia (ISC), a German satellite which was created after the Axis attack on Yugoslavia and the destruction of the state in April 1941. The ISC was governed by the fascist Ustaša movement under its leader, Ante Pavelić. The translation of Ustaša is "insurgent"; beginning in the 1930s, extreme Croatian nationalists sought to subvert the Yugoslav state, by which they felt oppressed.[1] After the Ustaša came to power in April 1941, they tried to take control of a multi-ethnic and multi-confessional society comprising 3.3 million Catholic Croats, almost two million Orthodox Serbs, 800,000 Muslim Bosnians, 175,000 Germans, 40,000 Jews, 20,000–30,000 Roma, and 170,000 others.[2] The Ustaša took over the existing bureaucracy and formed armed militias and a Croatian army. The regime established the first Ustaša concentration camps and introduced discriminatory laws against Serbs, Jews, and Roma. The Ustaša ideological program put the blame for the alleged subjugation of the Croatian people onto the Serbs and the Jews, setting out to purge them from Croatia proper. A German–Croatian agreement enabled Ustaša militias and Croatian state agents to unleash a campaign of ethnic cleansing directed against the Serbs who lived on the soil the Ustaša claimed was part of Greater Croatia.

During the summer of 1941 alone, up to 200,000 Serbs were expelled to Serbia, and more than 100,000 were killed in the countryside by Ustaša units. Simultaneously, mass murders of Jews, Serbs, and other prisoners occurred in the Ustaša's concentration camp system. In the context of military campaigns against partisans, thousands of civilians were killed in the war zones. Ustaša forces shot hundreds of prisoners in the cities. As early as July 1941, the Serbs resisted against the murderous campaigns and reacted with a large-scale uprising. The ISC was soon ravaged by a bloody civil war that lasted for the next 4 years. Historians estimate that up to 600,000 people perished while the Ustaša was in power; however, not all were killed by the Ustaša.[3]

The Ustaša is traditionally viewed as a small, collaborationist movement who ruled over a German puppet regime.[4] It is true that the Ustaša was not backed by mass support, and that the "Independent State of Croatia" was a misnomer. In reality, it was divided into an Italian sphere of interest and a German occupation zone. Yet an analysis of its policies of persecution reveals that the Ustaša acted quite independently. The chapter distinguishes between phases of greater and lesser Ustaša autonomy by looking both for the ways in which Nazi Germany influenced the shape of Croatian policies, and for conflicts between the two partners. Forced resettlements, deportations, and various kinds of camps were the means by which the Ustaša regime pursued its population policies. Therefore this chapter is also a survey of the magnitude and the functions of Croatian concentration camps.

Scholars have failed thus far to establish a link between the violent acts perpetrated against different minority groups. Mainstream research has perpetuated a generic narrative of the "Ustaša genocide of Serbs, Jews, and Gypsies," which blurs the differences between the persecution of various victim groups, and at the same time confuses who the respective perpetrators were.[5] The aim of this chapter is to understand better the ways in which the persecution of Serbs, Jews, and Roma in the ISC were intertwined. In the first section of this chapter, I examine the radicalization of Ustaša policies, starting with forced resettlements and the deportations of Serbs by the Croatian state. These experiences created a process and an infrastructure for the different camps that the Croatian government instituted, which will be described in the second part. Resettlement of Serbs increasingly involved plans to resettle Jews and Roma from and within Croatia, which I discuss in the third section. The fourth part addresses the failure of such plans, which led to deportations of both groups into the concentration camp system and to an increasing level of mass violence. Although deportations to Ustaša camps threatened almost all of Croatia's Jews, German officials were dissatisfied by the Ustaša's rather unsystematic persecution of Jews. This led to increasing German efforts to deport Croatia's Jews to German extermination camps, to be discussed in the fifth part.

The forced resettlements of Serbs, July 1941

On 4 June 1941, Ambassador Siegfried Kasche hosted a reception for 18 high-ranking representatives of the German occupation apparatus and the Croatian government on the premises of the German Embassy in Zagreb. The occasion for the meeting was the Germans' search for a possibility to deport almost 200,000 Slovenians to another country from the Slovenian areas which had been annexed in April 1941. The Croatian government declared its willingness to accept the persons expelled from Greater Germany. Tying their offer to the condition that they could deport the same number of Serbs from Croatia to Serbia enabled the Croatian leaders to pursue their project of transforming Croatia into a nation-state by force. The charter for the deportation of 200,000 Croatian Serbs to Serbia signified the beginning of an unprecedented series of expulsions, forced resettlements, and deportations that would affect hundreds of thousands of people over the coming years.[6]

Following the dismantling of Yugoslavia, the German Empire and Croatia were not the only states to take advantage of the situation in order to execute expulsion and deportation policies. Italian, Hungarian, Bulgarian, Albanian, and Serbian authorities, armies or militias all viewed expulsion as the proper method to homogenize the nation-state or to cement claims to newly acquired territories. These ethnic cleansings followed an international frame of reference, following a so-called "racial reallocation of land," a concept that Adolf Hitler had already employed in order to create a new racial ordering of eastern central Europe in 1939, which would in turn bring about political and social stability. According to Hitler's comments to Pavelić during their first meeting, only clear spatial boundaries between ethnic groups would enable peaceful conditions. Relocations were painful, but better than constant suffering, and they had already proven to bring great advantages to the children of the resettled.[7] The guiding principle of the Ustaša was similar. In order to legitimate the expulsions, the Croatian government compared the expulsion of Serbs with the reciprocal Greek and Turkish mass expulsions in 1922 and 1923. The Croatian Minister of Economic Affairs, Lovro Šušić, announced in July 1941 that there would be no bloody cleansings; instead, only evacuations would take place, which would bring about order, based on the example of the Greek–Turkish population exchanges.[8] Although the number of resettled Greeks was much larger than the number of Serbs that were to be resettled, the resettlement had been successful.[9] The reference to Asia Minor served as evidence for the feasibility of the population exchange.

The German–Croatian agreement on expulsion policies on the scale covering southeast Europe required the creation of new institutions that were interlocked with one another, and that would be assigned to executing the resettlement policies. On 1 July 1941, in the ISC, the State Authority for Economic Renewal (henceforth *Ponova*) was commissioned to execute the expulsion of the Serbs.[10] In the beginning of July, in each of the 141 districts of the ISC, a resettlement office base of the Ponova was established to execute the deportations. This signified the creation of a network that was used by the Croatian government not only for population policy functions. In the offices and bases, local officials worked together with the ISC, and their participation in the deportation of the Serbs tied them more closely to the Ustaša state and expanded its local power base. Without the cooperation of the local elites, the expropriations and deportations of a portion of the Serbian population would hardly have been possible.

The Croatian government counted on being able to deport approximately 10 percent of the Serbian population.[11] But despite such national guidelines, decisions regarding specific deportees were made chiefly at the local level.[12] Meanwhile, the districts thoroughly prepared the campaign of arrests, and struck with surprising force on the night of 10/11 July 1941. In Zagreb alone, approximately 800 persons were arrested by the police; in Sarajevo the number of arrested was 1,143.[13] The average number of arrested per district was approximately 100. Mostly, whole families were arrested and interned in gymnasiums or in empty factories in the district capitals and thereafter deported by train to one of the three newly established collection camps in Caprag, Požega, and Sisak.[14] Between July and September 1941, about 5,000 Serbian prisoners were held in the camps and almost 18,000 Serbs were deported in 27 transport actions to Serbia, some after waiting for weeks for further transport.[15] Once in Serbia, Serbian officials under the supervision of the Germans organized their distribution throughout the country.[16] The deportations were often poorly organized and ended in chaos. In Ruma, close to Belgrade, the Croatian gendarme reported that 57 train cars filled with Serbs had to wait to be dispatched for 9 days.[17]

In the meantime, the resettlement staff of the German security service began with the arranged forced resettlement of Slovenians. From 5 July 1941 onwards, almost daily a train carrying 500 deportees left Maribor to one of the resettlement camps of the Ponova in Croatia, from which they were distributed among the individual districts. In this case, there were also delays, and many had to hold out in camps for weeks.[18] As only 26,000 persons arrived, it is not possible to speak of a nationwide settlement of Slovenians in Croatia.[19]

The deportations spurred a dynamic of violence that experienced a significant radicalization through Ustaša practices. Since June 1941, violence perpetrated by the Ustaša militias escalated and took on the character of a coordinated annihilation campaign in certain districts. Many of those deported were murdered shortly after their arrival in the camps. As the German authorities were highly dissatisfied with the deportation violence of the Ustaša, the German military commanders in Serbia decided to hinder further deportations to Serbia, and closed the border to Croatia in July 1941.[20] Although German pressure gradually had an impact, the Croatian government was nonetheless often not able to limit the mass expulsions, as the local actors operated independently. German–Croatian tensions over the expulsions therefore continued.

The foundation of a concentration camp system, April–June 1941

The first mass arrests of Jewish lawyers, Serbian politicians, and leftist activists occurred in April 1941. On the estate of Karestinec, near Zagreb, the first camp for so-called opponents of the new state was established.[21] The arrests did not follow according to unified categories, but rather according to the perception of the enemy as judged by the local Ustaše. Throughout Croatia, arrests were made and provisional camps were set up. The central camp intended as the first permanent fixture was established on the grounds of the fertilizer factory Danica, close to Koprivnica. Already in June there were over 2,000 prisoners in the camp. Most were Serbs, followed by Croatian communists, Jews, and Roma.[22]

The first months of the Ustaša regime in the camps were marked by arbitrary violence, symbolically demeaning forced labor, personal retribution, activism, and improvisation. The Ustaša's policing apparatus, however, soon made an effort to centralize the camp system in Croatia. Close contact with the small staff of the SS (*Schutzstaffel*, Protection Squadron) and the SD (*Sicherheitsdienst*, Security Service) under *SS-Sturmbannführer* Dr Wilhelm Beisner helped in this endeavor. In June 1941, Beisner brought the Croatian State Secretary of Security, Eugen Kvaternik, as well as some Ustaša men, with him to Berlin. They visited the SS main office in Oranienburg and toured the concentration camp Sachsenhausen. From the Croatian perspective, the visit to Oranienburg was a success. The Croatian envoy Benzon thanked the SS and from then on tried to intensify contacts with the SS.[23]

"Territorial solutions" for Jews and Roma?

Research on "territorial solutions to the Jewish Question," such as the Nisko and Madagascar plans, demonstrates that they were located on the threshold between concrete projects and fantasy. They signified ciphers for the physical disappearance of the victims.[24] They provided the perpetrators a way of rationalizing the murderous deportations, for example into ghettos in eastern Europe, which were understood as the first step of a "settlement" of Jews. The failure of such unrealistic resettlement plans led to further radicalization, as those responsible were demanding not provisional, but rather final solutions. The displacement of victims to inhospitable locations led to epidemic disease, famines, and black markets in the ghettos. From the perspective of the perpetrators, these represented a danger to the non-Jewish population. Lacking a realistic possibility of deporting the Jews to even more remote areas, the slaughter of the ghetto inhabitants soon became a concrete option for the responsible German organs. The inhumane projects always contained a readiness to accept the deaths of a large portion of the victims. Still, the physical annihilation of the deportees was not an inevitable component of the original plans.[25]

To a certain extent, a similar process can be observed in Croatia. There, resettlement plans could equally be directed against Serbs, Jews, and Roma. A certain kind of euphoria broke out amongst the Ustaša with the possibility of deporting hundreds of thousands of Serbs from Croatia in the wake of the German–Croatian agreement. Never had they been closer to the projected Greater Croatian nation-state than in the summer of 1941. In view of concrete possibilities to take action, this radicalized the Ustaša's horizon of expectations and likewise stimulated their lust for action. The conclusion can be drawn that the possibility of decimating the number of Serbs in Croatia and the attendant bureaucratic activism radicalized persecution policies towards the Roma and the Jews, and revealed ideas among the Ustaša that amounted to the physical removal of these minority groups. Only one day after the order to execute the deportation of the Serbs was dispatched, the Ministry of the Interior ordered the regional administrations to register the Roma with the ISC.[26] Jews were perceived as agents of the Serbs and occasionally as the actual founders or backers of Yugoslavia.[27] Roma were also identified with either the Balkans or with Serbia, and under no circumstances with the Croatian nation-state that was to be created. Because the Jews and the Roma could not be deported to Serbia, policies of internment and physical isolation in particular areas were first implemented.[28] It is possible that it is because of these policies that both minorities were increasingly deported to the camps. This affected Jews since June 1941 and the majority of Roma in the spring of 1942.

From their public deliberations on how "the Jewish question could be solved," the top brass of the Ustaša were guided by thoughts that the Jews were to be deported to do forced labor in remote provinces or to camps.[29] In the end of September 1941, representatives of the Ustaša submitted a proposal to establish a 250-square-kilometer "Jewish Reservation," in which all Croatian Jews would be settled. The area was to be located in close proximity to the concentration camp Jasenovac, and 11 former Serbian villages had supposedly been made available to populate.[30] Furthermore, it was claimed that "Jews from Zagreb [would be brought to] an island in the Adriatic Sea, where they would perform labor."[31] These territorial resettlement fantasies were always linked to large-scale forced labor projects. In terms of the Dalmatian Islands, the talk was of "land improvement and [work] in the salt fields."[32] Images were created that envisioned the future of the Jews as some kind of helot-people who would excavate salt or drain swamps for the Croatians. Their physical distance from society was a demand that followed this logic. Even if it was clear that the Ustaša government did not have a colony in mind in which the Jews could have lived in peace, the Jewish communities appeared to have taken the offer seriously, as they spent the effort to work out plans accordingly. The plans regarding Jewish reservations and forced labor schemes were, however, never merely propaganda tricks.[33]

As all these plans failed, the Croatian government attempted unsuccessfully to transfer Croatian Jews to the German Empire, as a quasi-territorial solution in a foreign country, in October 1941.[34] Although the Croatian request to the German empire has most often been interpreted as a particularly radical push of the Croatian ally on the path to mass murder, the early point in time appears rather to offer evidence of the opposite. The Ustaša in fact had a resettlement project in mind and not the systematic annihilation of the Croatian Jews in the eastern areas, as annihilation could not yet be predicted in the fall of 1941, particularly not from the perspective of a German vassal state. Indeed, the agreement with the Germans on the resettlement of the Serbs demonstrated to the Croatian government that the German government was ready to accept the resettling, in the sense of an ethnic reallocation of land, of populations in third-country states. It was increasingly obvious, however, that the territories on which the Jews had supposedly been resettled were exclusively camps.[35] However, within a few months, following the logic that it was necessary to evacuate the Croatian Jews led to Croatians actively participating in deporting the Jews to annihilation camps.

Quite possibly, attempts to limit the mobility of "nomadic gypsies" and force them into conditions of settlement and labor can also be seen as a type of "territorial solution."[36] In fact, the Roma, who were mobile and lived in caravans, were always the first to be deported.[37] Roma with permanent homes as well as those who had been forced to settle down were, however, to be territorially bounded and finally assimilated. The disappearance of the ethnic group of the Roma was a goal of the Ustaša, and, in terms of territorial solutions, resettlement (in camps) and forced assimilation were means for achieving this goal.

Alongside the expulsions of Croatian Serbs to Serbia, occasionally other concrete resettlement plans were discussed. In terms of the self-contained evacuation of Serbs from certain areas, the Adriatic Islands again were brought up as a possible resettlement area.[38] Nevertheless, it remained the Ustaša's highest priority that, if at all possible, Serbs should be deported to Serbia. This marked a significant contrast between the treatment of Serbs on the one hand, and Jews and Roma on the other. In terms of the latter, camps, first supposedly perceived more as a station on the way to a "territorial solution," were established as the final place for admitting the deported. In the case of the deportation of non-Jewish and non-Roma Serbian prisoners, Serbia, as a concrete place, existed, and in some instances the prisoners were released from existing concentration camps in order to be deported to Serbia.[39]

These resettlement plans were all publicly communicated. While some press statements mentioned the deportation of the Jews in connection with the evacuation of the Serbs from Croatia, other media spoke of the liquidation or the disappearance of the Jews in ISC.[40] Such grim advance notifications, also expressed by Pavelić himself, perhaps marked the step when the threshold from unrealizable resettlement fantasies to concrete intentions to annihilate was crossed along the way to realizing the intention of physically removing the Jews from Croatia.

Centralization and mass deportations

June 1941 marked the beginning of a new phase of Ustaša violence that saw the expansion and intensification of persecution. The reasons for this can be found, alongside the radicalizing effect of the mass resettlements, in the German attack on the Soviet Union on 22 June 1941, an event that significantly intensified internal tensions within the ISC. Four days after the attack, Pavelić issued a decree in which he announced the mass arrests of Jews and their deportation to camps. These arrests took place all over Croatia, and for the first time were directed at women and children. Initiatives at the local level corresponded with the assault on the national level. The radicalization from below of policies towards the Jews becomes clear in evidence that the communal authorities made demands on the central authority that the Jews had to be deported.[41] Up to 2,500 Jews were deported during this phase of the Croatian concentration camp system.[42]

Following his study trip to Berlin and Oranienburg, Eugen Kvaternik began with the centralization and expansion of the Croatian camp system.[43] In the area around Gospić in the Lika region of Croatia, a camp complex was erected that, according to the plans of the Ustaša-Inspectorate (UNS), was to become the central camp for Serbs and Jews. Up to 30,000 prisoners were deported there. Two isolated concentration camp satellites, one on the island of Pag and one in the Velebit mountain range, were part of the camp complex. The island of Pag could only be reached via boat from Karlobag. One fisherman remembered that he transported approximately 3,000 prisoners to the island in July 1941. Both were located in an inhospitable environment, and in both, the conditions for the prisoners were murderous.[44] The code of practice in those two camps followed a particular dynamic. Outside of all public view, without the possibility of being profitably exploited in forced labor projects, and dependent on food from outside the camp, the prisoners found themselves in a space of violence, in which the camp personnel of the Ustaša could exercise violence without restraint. Already in the first weeks, the Ustaša guards began to kill some of the prisoners. Presumably, in the internal logic of the Ustaša, these killings served to prevent the overpopulation of the camp.[45]

In the end of August 1941, shortly before the invasion of Italian troops in Croatia, the camps were hastily closed. On the command of the Zagreb central office, the camps of Gospić, including its prisoners, were to be relocated; however, the camp personnel was only able to deport approximately 3,500 of the prisoners to the eastern part of Croatia, while a majority of the prisoners were killed right before the camp was dismantled.[46] The Ustaša was not willing to let the prisoners fall into the hands of the Italians, which de facto would have meant liberation for the prisoners. Many Jewish prisoners were among the murdered. Historians have interpreted the murder of the prisoners as the beginning of the genocide of the Croatian Jews. In the late summer of 1941, it is more appropriate to speak about the Ustaša in terms of a situational annihilation drive, as the Ustaša government had not yet committed itself to killing the totality of the Jews in the ISC, even if they were interested in the widespread disappearance of Croatian Jews from the cities. Fleeing from the country was in general still tolerated by the Croatian authorities, as, for example, the Jewish exodus to the Italian-occupied areas, or the emigration of small groups to Palestine.[47] At no point in time was a ban on emigration of Jews issued.

With the Italian occupation of west Croatia, the concentration camp system of the Ustaša fell into a crisis. Up to 4,500 Jewish and Serbian men, women, and children were temporarily held in two makeshift internment camps. One was located between Zagreb and Karlovac on an estate near Jastrebarsko, the other in Kruščica, in Central Bosnia, in an internment camp that had already existed during the Yugoslavian period.[48] This led to a new paradigm shift and to the speedy expansion of the third generation of Croatian concentration camps. Again, the visit of high-ranking Ustaša officers to Nazi concentration camps intensified this paradigm shift. The head of the Office III of the UNS, Maks Luburić, who was responsible for the camp system of the ISC, spent 10 days in Oranienburg in September 1941, in order to observe the workings of the concentration camp Sachsenhausen.[49] Two new concentration camps, Đakovo and Loborgrad, detained female prisoners and children and did not possess any production facilities. Loborgrad did not even have a railway connection. On 23 August 1941, Jasenovac, a new type of concentration camp called a "transit camp," opened.[50] The camp contained five main sites and a number of smaller commands. It developed into one of the largest military bases of the Ustaša, with up to 1,500 militiamen. In contrast to the earlier camps, Jasenovac was located outside the reach of the Italian army, was planned for a far higher prisoner capacity, and was to contain industrial production plants. The camp was located only 70 miles from Zagreb, was connected to the railway system, and was located at a river junction. The large estate of a Serbian family that had fled became the actual grounds for the camp, where there were already a few production facilities. Jasenovac was surrounded by Serbian villages, to which the Ustaša did not need to pay any particular consideration.

After the completion of the Jasenovac camp, the months of September and October 1941 constituted the highpoint of inner-Croatian deportations. The commencement of the deportations nevertheless lacked uniformity throughout the country, and was dependent on the initiatives of individual districts. Some were not active themselves; others sought the assistance of the security forces to arrest the Jews in their areas. In many areas, there were long phases in which no deportations were carried out: for example, between September 1941 and January 1942, no deportation transports left the city of Zagreb. In other cities, the entire Jewish population was deported. For example, in the end of October 1941, the Ustaša Inspectorate sent the head of their Jewish division, Vilko Kühnel, to Sarajevo to carry out the "measures to solve the Jewish question."[51] A few weeks later, two deportation trains with almost 700 people left the city.[52] At the end of November 1941, the great majority of Sarajevo's Jews were finally deported. The poor organization of the deportations ended in a humanitarian catastrophe. The city administration also recognized that the path that they had embarked on would lead to the annihilation of Sarajevo Jews, and tried unsuccessfully to reduce the extent and consequences of the deportations.[53] The Ustaša police apparently accepted the physical destruction of the deportees. The particularly ruthless praxis in Sarajevo was probably linked to the view, in the eyes of the responsible parties in the Ustaša, that the Sephardic community there represented the Balkans or the Orient, which ran contrary to the Ustaša's claim that Sarajevo was a Croatian city.[54]

In this phase, it is possible to identify significant differences in the Ustaša's respective policies towards the Serbs, Jews, and Roma. German and Italian pressure, and above all the strength of the Serbian insurgents, led to a successive de-radicalization of the Croatian persecution of the Serbs. As early as September 1941, the Ustaša launched a policy of forced assimilation of Serbs, rather than continuing with mass killings.[55] Yet this was not a choice, but rather the consequence of pressure under which the Ustaša felt itself. However, the same factors contributed to a radicalization of the persecution of the Jews. One might argue that the regime sought to draw internal cohesion from the persecution of Jews. Jews were perceived as an unreliable group that became even more dangerous in times of the life-and-death struggle with the Serbs. The perception of the Jews as pro-Serbian was an important factor that contributed to the radicalization of anti-Jewish policy in 1941. The concentration camps, which had first been erected to target primarily the Serbs, were now ready to be used for the internment, and subsequently mass murder, of Jews and Roma, and were committed by Ustaša militias and camp guards that had been brutalized in the course of the previous months.

The constant arrival of new groups of prisoners led to extreme violence on the side of the camp guards, irrespective whether it was directed against Serbs or Jews. In May and June 1942, at least 10,000 Roma were deported to Jasenovac. By the end of 1942, the majority had been murdered by the Ustaša. After the dismantling of the concentration camp Đakovo in the end of June 1942, 3,000 Jewish women and children were sent to

Jasenovac. The prisoners were in terrible condition when they arrived, and directly after their arrival they were ferried to the other side of the Sava and killed.[56] In July 1942, in connection with a German–Croatian offensive, up to 68,000 captured village inhabitants were deported to the camp. This explosion in the number of prisoners changed the camp and its functions. Jasenovac became a supra-regional distribution center for refugees, forced laborers, and Jews who were to be deported to Auschwitz.[57]

The Holocaust

On 24 February 1942, the Croatian Minister of the Interior, Andrija Artuković, announced that the Jewish question had been solved.[58] From the perspective of the Germans, however, this was not at all the case. The Croatian leadership, together with the Germans, had indeed already progressed far along the path to the annihilation of the Jewish minority in the country. The efforts of the Croatian government to expand the deportations to the rest of the still-free Jews, however, had slowed down. The reasons for this were the differences between the German and Croatian motivations for their anti-Jewish policies. The Ustaša's project of ethnically cleansing the Croatian state was, in the first instance, driven by national–political concerns and less so racial–biological ideas. Despite the appropriate rhetoric, reasoning and theoretical derivations, the persecution practices of the Ustaša were contradictory and malleable. Evacuations of Jews and their deportation into concentration camps, but also forced assimilations of Jews, were to lead to the disappearance of Jews as a minority in Croatia. Mass murder was one part, but not the exclusive goal, of this policy. Therefore the percentage of Jews who were excluded from persecution, or who were at first able to survive within the concentration camp system, was markedly higher than in the Nazi-controlled empire. For the Germans, there was no question that Croatia would be included in the program for the "final solution of the Jewish question in Europe" through deporting all Jews to annihilation camps. The German side did not want to rely on the Ustaša eliminating all the Croatian Jews in their camp system. Above all, the fact that numerous Jews had found refuge in the Italian-occupied zone convinced the German authorities that the Jews had to be deported from the ISC.[59]

In May 1942, the German embassy thus requested the Croatian government to deport the remaining Jews to the territory of the German empire. The Croatian government did not object; instead, they assumed the usage of the German term of "evacuation to the East," and intensified propaganda against the Jews in the lead-up to the deportations.[60] In total, in five deportation trains, almost 5,000 Jews were deported from Croatia to Auschwitz in August 1942. The Croatian State Railway provided the trains, German police the escort.[61] Of those deported, it appears that none survived the year of 1943. In the beginning of 1942, the Croatian and German police arrived at an agreement to deport the remaining Croatian Jews.[62] In the spring of 1943, a further 2,000 men and women were transported to Auschwitz and, with the exception of 95, all were gassed directly after their arrival.[63]

The deportations render visible the diminishing German trust in their Croatian partners as the German police closely monitored the individual steps in the process.[64] In April 1944, the German police attaché in Zagreb, *SS-Obersturmbannführer* Hans Helm, reported that "overall, the Jewish question should be seen as having been solved" in Croatia.[65] Croatian–German cooperation, however, did not run smoothly on the path to this goal. From the German perspective, the Croatian parties appeared unreliable and unorganized.[66] Moreover, the German police attaché and the head of his Jewish division expressed their frustrations with the fact that they were not allowed entry into the Croatian camp system, and they demanded access to the 2,000 Jewish prisoners who they suspected were still in the camps. They furthermore blamed Croatian politicians for denying them access to numerous Jews through their interventions.[67]

Conclusion

The chapter generated a narrative of radicalization of Ustaša mass violence. The hopes of the Ustaša to create an ethnically homogeneous nation state led, step by step, to the physical annihilation of a significant part of the Jewish and Roma minorities, even though the death of the deportees was neither intended nor planned from the beginning. Ustaša policies of persecution became increasingly murderous. Yet their main goal always remained to ethnically cleanse the Croatian state. This goal was partly achieved by mass murder, but mass murder was not the goal as such.

The mass killings drove the ISC into an existential crisis, as tens of thousands of peasants joined the partisans, and Germans and Italians started making the Ustaša responsible. By the fall of 1941, the Ustaša had to re-evaluate their policies directed against the Serbs. However, such a change did occur regarding the policies directed against Jews and Roma. This was partly due to German influence, which finally resulted in the deportation of Jews from Croatia to Auschwitz. But it was also due to internal developments. Tens of thousands of Jewish and Roma prisoners were interned in Ustaša concentration camps after all plans to resettle them had failed. The readiness of the Ustaša to kill civilians increased once they were incarcerated in the Ustaša camp system. Thus radicalization and de-radicalization of Ustaša mass violence must be understood as an expression of local developments. German and Italian influences, though, can be identified at every stage of the process.

Notes

1 The members of the Ustaša are called "Ustaše" (insurgents). For the classification of the Ustaša as fascist, see Stanley Payne, "The NDH State in Comparative Perspective," *Totalitarian Movements and Political Religions*, vol. 7, no. 4 (December 2006): 409–15.

2 Holm Sundhaussen, *Wirtschaftsgeschichte Kroatiens im nationalsozialistischen Großraum 1941–1945. Das Scheitern einer Ausbeutungsstrategie* (Stuttgart: Deutsche Verlags Anstalt, 1983), 99ff.

3 Tomislav Dulić, "Mass Killing in the Independent State of Croatia, 1941–45: A Case for Comparative Research," *Journal of Genocide Research*, vol. 8, no. 3 (September 2006): 255–81, 270ff; Marko Hoare, *Genocide and Resistance in Hitler's Bosnia: The Partisans and the Chetniks, 1941–1943* (Oxford, New York: Oxford University Press, 2006), 23.

4 N. Bartulin, "The Ideology of Nation and Race: The Croatian Ustasha Regime and Its Policies toward Minorities in the Independent State of Croatia, 1941–45" (PhD dissertation, University of New South Wales, 2006), 247ff; Damir Mirković, "Victims and Perpetrators in the Yugoslav Genocide 1941–45: Some Preliminary Observations," *Holocaust and Genocide Studies*, vol. 7, no. 3 (Winter 1993): 323.

5 See Herbert Hirsch, "Genocide in Yugoslavia," in *Encyclopedia of Genocide*, ed. Israel Charny (Jerusalem: ABC-Clio, 1999), 2: 634; Damir Mirković, "Victims and Perpetrators," 317–32, 323.

6 Jozo Tomasevich, *War and Revolution in Yugoslavia, 1941–1945. Occupation and Collaboration* (Stanford, California: Stanford University Press, 2001), 393f.

7 Notes of Ambassador Schmidt, 6 June 1941, *Documents on German Foreign Policy, 1918–1945*, vol. 12 (Washington, DC: Department of State, 1962), doc. nos 603, 979.

8 Speech delivered at an Ustaša assembly in Slunj, printed in *Hrvatski Narod*, 9 July 1941.

9 German Information Office III to German Foreign Office, State Secretary Weizsäcker, 8 July 1941, Political Archive of the Foreign Office, Berlin (PA AA), Büro StS, Kroatien vol.1, 283f.

10 Fikreta Jelić-Butić, *Ustaše i Nezavisna Drzava Hrvatska 1941–1945* (Zagreb: Liber, 1977), 168.

11 Decree issued by Marshal Kvaternik, 7 June 1941, United States Holocaust Memorial Museum Archives, 1999.A.0173/2, fr. 288f.

12 Districts Ilok and Šid to Ponova, 19 June 1941, Croatian State Archives (HDA), 1076.1/441, no. 58/41.

13 German General in Agram to Higher *Wehrmacht* Command, 12 July 1941, Federal Archives–Military Archives, RH 31 III/1, no. 68; Slobodan Milošević, *Izbeglice i preseljenici na teritoriji okupirane Jugoslavije 1941–1945. godine* (Beograd: Nar. Knjiga, 1982), 161.

14 Serbian Ministry of Transportation to Prime Minister Nedić, 17 September 1941, Hoover Institution Archives, Tomasevich Collection/11, no page number; Miodrag Bijelić, *Sabirni ustaški logor u Slavonskoj Požegi 1941. godine* (Beograd: Muzej žrtava genocida, 2008).

15 Milošević, "Izbeglice i preseljenici na teritoriji okupirane Jugoslavije," 161ff.

16 Tomasevich, *War and Revolution in Yugoslavia*, 395.

17 Croatian Army Registration Office to Ministry of Interior Affairs, 16 June 1941, HDA 223/26, Pr. 24958/41.

18 Ponova to the Counties, June 1941, Historical Museum of Bosnia and Hercegovina (HM BIH), NDH/1941, no. 1255.

19 German Embassy, final report on the resettlements, 20 November 1941, printed in *Quellen zur Nationalsozialistischen Entnationalisierungspolitik in Slowenien 1941–1945*, ed. Tone Ferenc (Maribor: Založba Obzorja, 1980), doc. no. 179.

20 Klaus Olshausen, *Zwischenspiel auf dem Balkan. Die deutsche Politik gegenüber Jugoslawien und Griechenland von März bis Juli 1941* (Stuttgart: Deutsche Verlags-Anstalt, 1973), 226.

21 Mirko Peršen, *Ustaški logori* (Zagreb: Globus, 1990), 53.

22 Zdravko Dizdar, "Logori na području sjeverozapadne Hrvatske u toku drugog svjetskog rata 1941–45. g.," *Časopis za suvremenu povijest*, vol. 22, no. 1–2 (1990), 88; Zdravko Dizdar, "Ljudski gubici logora 'Danica' kraj Koprivnice 1941–1942," *Časopis za suvremenu povijest*, vol. 34, no. 2 (2002); Peršen, *Ustaški logori*, 67–75.

23 Berger to RFSS, 12 April 1941, German Federal Archives, NS 19/2223, 1ff; see also Chief Security Police/ SD to Berger, 27 November 1941, NS 19/3461, 2.

24 Peter Longerich, *Politik der Vernichtung. Eine Gesamtdarstellung der nationalsozialistischen Judenverfolgung* (München: Piper, 1998).

25 Longerich, *Politik der Vernichtung*, 273ff.

26 Ministry of Interior Affairs to the Croatian Counties, 3 July 1941, HM BIH, NDH/1941, no. 1312.

27 Ante Pavelić, *Die kroatische Frage* (Berlin: Institut für Grenz-und Auslandstudien, 1941).

28 Jews and Roma were targeted by deportation through the Ponova individually, see *Quellen zur Nationalsozialistischen Entnationalisierungspolitik in Slowenien* (Ferenc, ed.), doc. 131; Mark Biondich, "Persecution of Roma-Sinti in Croatia, 1941–45," in *Roma and Sinti: Under-studied Victims of Nazism. Symposium Proceedings*, eds Paul Shapiro and Robert Ehrenreich (Washington, DC: Center for Advanced Holocaust Studies, 2002), 33–48; for Jews emigrating from the ISC, see Chief Ravsigur to Command of the 4th Gendarmerie Regiment, 23 June 1941, Military Archives Belgrade, NDH/143a, 1/35–1.

29 *Neue Zürcher Zeitung* no. 1094, 13 August 1941.

30 Ivo Goldstein and Slavko Goldstein, *Holokaust u Zagrebu* (Zagreb: Novi Liber, 2001), 310.

31 *Neue Zürcher Zeitung* no. 1058, 8 July 1941.

32 *Neue Ordnung* no. 3, 13 July 1941, 6.

33 Goldstein and Goldstein, *Holokaust u Zagrebu*, 310 argues in that direction.

34 Christopher Browning, *The Final Solution and the German Foreign Office* (New York: Holmes and Meier, 1978), 93f, 115.

35 Eugen Kvaternik, "Staatssekretär Kwaternik über die Entjudung Kroatiens," *Die Judenfrage*, vol. 6, no. 10 (1942).

36 For such attempts see *Novi List* no. 55, 23 June 1941; Theodor Uzinorac, "Das Problem der Balkannomaden," in *Kroatien baut auf. Jahreslese in Wort und Bild aus der Wochenschrift "Neue Ordnung"* (Zagreb: Europa, 1943), 2: 15–20.

37 Narcisa Lengel-Krizman, *Genocid nad Romima. Jasenovac 1942* (Zagreb: Jesenski i Turk, 2003).

38 Slobodan Milošević, "Izbeglice i preseljenici na jugoslovenskom prostoru 1941–45," *Vojnoistorijski glasnik*, vol. 44, nos 1–2 (1994): 105–44, 116.

39 Peršen, *Ustaški logori*, 71ff.

40 *Neue Ordnung*, 24 August 1941.

41 Croatian Ministry of Interior Affairs, 7 June 1941, Yad Vashem Archives (YVA), M.70/9, 3.

42 *Narodne novine* 61, 27 June 1941; Antun Miletić, ed., *Koncentracioni logor Jasenovac 1941–1945: Dokumenta* (Beograd: Narodna Knjiga, 1986), 1: 47–49; Dizdar, "Logori na području sjeverozapadne Hrvatske," 99.

43 Goldstein and Goldstein, *Holokaust u Zagrebu*, 20.

44 Peršen, *Ustaški logori*, 90ff; Goldstein and Goldstein, Holokaust *u Zagrebu*, 282ff.

45 Peršen, *Ustaški logori*, 84.

46 Goldstein and Goldstein, *Holokaust u Zagrebu*, 291f.

47 Klaus Voigt, *Zuflucht auf Widerruf,* vol. 2 (Stuttgart: Klett-Cotta, 1993).

48 Peršen, *Ustaški logori*, 100.

49 Goldstein and Goldstein, *Holokaust u Zagrebu*, 312.

50 For Đakovo and Loborgrad, see Goldstein and Goldstein, *Holokaust u Zagrebu*, 304; Peršen, *Ustaški logori*, 155; Miletić, *Koncentracioni logor* Jasenovac, vol. 1, 269f.

51 Goldstein and Goldstein, *Holokaust u Zagrebu*, 156ff.

52 Police Sarajevo to Ustaša Police, Jewish Section, 27 October 1941, HDA, 252/9, nos 28750ff.

53 E. Balić, "A City Apart: Sarajevo in the Second World War" (PhD dissertation, Stanford University, 2008), 98.

54 Balić, "A City Apart," 160ff.

55 Mark Biondich, "Religion and Nation in Wartime Croatia: Reflections on the Ustaša Policy of Forced Religious Conversions, 1941–42," *The Slavonic and East European Review,* vol. 83, no. 1 (January 2005): 71–116.

56 Albert Maestro's testimony, in *Sećanja Jevreja na Logor Jasenovac*, ed. Dušan Sindik (Belgrade: Savez jevrejskih opština Jugoslavije, 1972), 128.

57 John Lampe, *Yugoslavia: Twice There Was a Country* (Cambridge: Cambridge University Press, 1996), 223.

58 Tomasevich, *War and Revolution in Yugoslavia*, 595.

59 Browning, *The Final Solution and the German Foreign Office*, 93.

60 Croatian Ministry of Foreign Affairs to Pavelić, 7 May 1942, HDA, 227/1, no 4; Goldstein and Goldstein, Holokaust *u Zagrebu*, 424ff.

61 Ustaša Police (Jewish Section) to Croatian State Railways, 29 August 1942, HDA, 252/15, no. 29861.

62 Goldstein and Goldstein, *Holokaust u Zagrebu*, 465.

63 Goldstein and Goldstein, *Holokaust u Zagrebu*, 434, 473f.

64 Bogdan Krizman, *NDH između Hitlera i Mussolinija* (Zagreb: Globus, 1980), 560.

65 German Police Attaché, Zagreb, "Overview of the Jewish Question in Croatia", 18 April 1944, YVA, O.10/60, 4f.

66 German Embassy Zagreb to German Foreign Office, 13 April 1942, PA AA, R 100.874, fr. H299714.

67 Tomasevich, *War and Revolution in Yugoslavia*, 595; Goldstein and Goldstein, Holokaust *u Zagrebu*, 326f.

Part IV

THE RESPONSES FROM VICTIMS, BYSTANDERS, AND RESCUERS

26

SWEDEN'S COMPLICATED NEUTRALITY AND THE RESCUE OF DANISH JEWRY

Paul A. Levine

On 1 October 1943, German forces in Denmark began their operation to arrest and deport that country's small Jewish population. However, because information about the *Aktion* was leaked by leading German officials to Danish authorities, that Yom Kippur evening most of Denmark's Jews went into hiding. Though some 435 people were eventually arrested, the implementation of the "final solution" in Denmark (primarily Copenhagen) also signalled the start of one of the largest rescue operations of the Holocaust. The justifiably famed rescue of Danish Jewry (including several hundred German and "stateless Jews") was, however, only made possible because Sweden declared its borders open, announcing that any Jew who could escape would be welcomed. This was made abundantly clear when, on the following day, Swedish state radio broadcast the following:

> Several days ago information became available in Sweden that measures were being prepared against Jews in Denmark similar to earlier unlawful actions in Norway and other occupied countries. In accordance with [his] instructions, on 1 October, Sweden's minister in Berlin told German officials of the serious consequences such measures will cause in Sweden.
>
> Furthermore, the minister has put forward an invitation from the Swedish Government that it is prepared to accept all Danish Jews in Sweden.[1]

For the first time since Hitler obtained power in 1933, a sovereign European state openly declared its willingness to offer sanctuary to any Jew who could escape the Nazis. In this case, the offer was directed to Danish Jewry, but in fact it meant more than that. With this broadcast, the world learned of Sweden's now open doors. In the days and weeks to follow, it would learn even more of the salvation of some 7,700 Jews, the vast majority of Denmark's Jews, including even some non-Jewish family members. This remarkable episode of the Holocaust deeply influenced both contemporary and postwar under-standing of Denmark's and Sweden's responses to the Holocaust. Though elements of this episode remain enveloped in myth and misunderstanding, it has rightly taken its place within Holocaust history as one of the few bright spots on the tragic canvas of an unprecedented tragedy. Less familiar today, but not entirely unknown at the time, was the extent and importance of Sweden's then ongoing trade with Nazi Germany. The paradox of the Kingdom of Sweden saving more Jews than any other country, while stubbornly refusing to cease its militarily vital trade with Hitler's genocidal regime, continues to vex Sweden's memory of the Holocaust. This trade finally ended only in late 1944, months after the Allied invasion of Nazi-occupied Europe, and only as a result of intense Allied pressure.[2]

In order to understand both the response of the Danish people and that of Sweden's government in 1943, it is necessary to review briefly both nations' earlier responses to the persecution and then murder of European Jewry. When doing so, we see some fascinating similarities and yet some important differences. Furthermore, if these Scandinavian responses to the horrors of Nazism are to be understood as part of Holocaust memory today, it is necessary to review each country's "master narrative" which evolved from the war. These narratives were first articulated by political and academic elites, and played a highly significant role in shaping memory in each country. Only in the past decade or so have they been challenged and adapted by younger historians.

From the beginning of Hitler's rule, proximity gave leaders and citizens of Denmark and Sweden considerable knowledge of Germany's anti-Jewish policies. As the 1930s progressed and Germany's (and later Austria's) Jews endured increasingly severe persecution, newspaper readers in both countries learned of the Jews' ever-worsening plight. Importantly, such information was supplemented by a constant flow of visitors to Germany. During the 1930s, both Scandinavian democracies responded in virtually the same way: Jews were not welcome because they were Jews. So-called political refugees (not least Social Democrats) were often given immediate refuge, but Jews were not (even though very limited numbers were let in by both countries). Bureaucrats and politicians in both countries worked assiduously to strengthen their nations' administrative "paper walls" in order to keep Jews out. In Denmark, there were instances when Jews were not only turned back at the border, but handed over to the Gestapo.[3] In Sweden, politicians, bureaucrats, prominent members of the intelligentsia, and even university students' organizations made it clear that Jews were not welcome. Swedish officials not only made it extremely difficult for Jews to obtain either entry or transit visas, in October 1938 they (along with their Swiss counterparts) also negotiated with Germany's Foreign Office—immediately prior to *Reichskristallnacht*—for the infamous, large red "J" to be stamped into Jewish passports.[4] These and other egregious, even immoral responses to the plight of desperate refugees characterized both countries' response in the 1930s. Yet, as Danish historian Hans Kirchoff has pointed out, "[They] were no better and no worse than other Nordic countries, or for that matter other democratic states, where a restrictive attitude was justified by economic costs or considerations of security policy and a greater or lesser degree of antisemitism and xenophobia."[5]

Of course, everything changed for Scandinavia on 9 April 1940, when Nazi Germany attacked Denmark and Norway. Though Hitler decided not to attack Sweden (knowing that he could get what he wanted without the necessity of occupying the country), that country's history was also fatefully changed. It was now virtually cut off from the outside world, severely jeopardizing fuel and some food supplies. Yet both countries, under very different circumstances, continued their extensive economic trade and collaboration with Germany. Hitler and his leadership quickly decided that a rather benign occupation policy would be implemented in Denmark, knowing that by doing so, Germany's economy would be able to exploit Denmark's industry, agriculture, and labor force to the maximum. Quite differently from its policies in most other occupied countries, Germany allowed a ministerial Danish government to retain most aspects of government,

Danish political leaders understanding that as long as they collaborated, Nazi occupation would remain non-violent. Further to the north, Swedish political leaders, believing they had no alternative, embarked on a series of political and economic concessions to Nazi Germany that scarcely squared with genuine neutrality. Here it is important to note that international law gives a neutral nation full right to trade with belligerent powers, but now, cut off from the west, Sweden became almost entirely dependent on trade with Germany. Extensive shipments of coal and coke, vital for both industry and the heating of homes, offices, and factories, increased Sweden's dependence on Germany.

For both Denmark and Sweden, a status quo developed which lasted through the summer of 1943. Things changed dramatically, however, in August of that year when, following some limited sabotage by the small Danish underground movement, German authorities ended the policy of benign collaboration and declared martial law. At the same time, planning for the strike against the country's Jewish population began. As will be seen, Swedish officials in Copenhagen caught wind of these plans, and began making their own preparations to help those Jews they could. Yet it is important to emphasize that in late August, no-one could have known that things would eventually turn out as happily (for most Danish Jews) as they did. But before proceeding with the most important elements of the events of late summer and autumn 1943, some comments are necessary about the tone and content of the historiography that prevailed for decades in both countries.

As is well known by now, each country in Europe (and elsewhere, for that matter) compelled to respond to the Nazi genocide formulated its own particular response during the 1930s and 1940s. Equally true is the fact that this response formed the basis for a diverse, but still similar, decades-long process of evolving Holocaust memory in each individual nation. Even though their wartime experiences were radically different, Denmark and Sweden fit this basic pattern.

In Denmark, the wartime "master narrative" was shaped decisively by the role played by the Danish people in helping its Jewish population largely escape to Sweden. This narrative is, to some extent, also formed by the underground resistance's history. Regarding the rescue, Danish historian Michael Mogensen has written:

> In contrast to virtually all other nationalities, the Danes did not let down their Jewish fellow citizens in [sic] the crucial moment. The account of how the Danes assisted them safely across the water to Sweden has been widely praised, and even as it occurred the rescue operation gained an almost mythical status. The rescue is seen as a unique example of courage and altruism during the Holocaust. Especially in the US and Israel, the rescue established Denmark as a model of respect for human rights.[6]

The response of the Danes has, of course, a particular background. Because the Danish armed forces gave up virtually without a fight, the Germans instituted the above-mentioned benign occupation. Norway was also invaded at the same time, but its armed forces, aided by British forces in the north of the country, resisted the Germans for a couple of months, delaying the complete occupation of the country. This and other factors, not least the role played by Vidkun Quisling, made the occupation of Norway a much more brutal affair. Crucially, though, in Denmark (and again differently from Norway), politicians and citizens alike made it explicitly clear to the Germans that if effective collaboration was to be maintained, the country's Jewish population was to be left alone. As a result, even in a German-occupied country, its Jews were for most part able to continue their normal lives, and the typical Nazi anti-Jewish measures were never implemented. This highly unusual circumstance was largely the result of attitudes maintained by Danish leaders and the population.

Indeed, as reported in November 1941 by Sweden's diplomatic representative in Copenhagen, this attitude also existed at the highest level of Danish society. Swedish Minister Gustaf von Dardel (who would play a crucial role in formulating Sweden's diplomatic response in October 1943) reported to Sweden's Foreign Office (*Utrikesdepartementet, UD*) that he had been told that Germany's highest diplomatic representative in Copenhagen told Danish King Christian X that Nazi Germany was planning to move against Denmark's Jews. "The King answered," wrote von Dardel, "... that he saw no reason for this." He then informed his German interlocutor that, "We Danes don't need to do anything in this matter because we don't feel inferior to Jews."[7] In this connection, a still widely believed myth may be put to rest. It is said that King Christian X daily rode his horse around the capital, wearing a "yellow star" in a sign of solidarity with his Jewish subjects. Not only did he never do this, the "yellow star" was never imposed on the country's Jews.[8] Indeed, it is virtually unthinkable that a royal member of a Scandinavian Protestant nation would have responded in such a fashion. Though the King clearly disdained Nazi antisemitism, it was the attitude of Danish leaders and most citizens that convinced the Germans that the mutually favourable collaboration would cease if the country's Jews were attacked. And this is, in fact, what occurred.[9]

Yet it took an "outsider" to commence the academic study of Denmark's response to the Holocaust, which, as will be shown, is similar to the Swedish case. This is odd because in both cases the national narrative concerning the Holocaust is overwhelmingly positive, yet in both cases historians of the countries themselves maintained for decades a "hands-off" approach towards the subject. In Denmark's case, this "outsider" was the Israeli academic Leni Yahil. Her landmark 1969 study *The Rescue of Danish Jewry: Test of a Democracy* (originally published in Hebrew in 1966) set for decades the discourse narrating Denmark's response to Nazi genocide. As Mogensen writes, the core of the Danes' response was, according to Yahil, "... the special national character of the Danes, that is, their particularly high moral standards and love of freedom and democracy."[10] To speak of a "national character" is obviously problematic, not least with reference to how the Danes responded during the 1930s. After decades as an iconic publication, Yahil's thesis was by the mid- to late-1990s subjected to scholarly scrutiny by a cadre of younger Danish historians, who, informed by the dynamism of Holocaust studies internationally, began investigating the myriad aspects of Denmark's response to Nazism. Most particularly, her analysis of the October raid and the actual escape to Sweden has been revised by historians able to utilize documentation unavailable to Yahil. One particularly sensitive "flaw" in the dominating narrative was that many Danish boat-owners and other officials were in fact paid by those Jews seeking safety in Sweden. Motives for helping based on a wish both to profit and to minimize costs hardly fit into Yahil's "national character" narrative.[11]

Though Yahil's thesis that the Danes' "special" moral character determined their response is scarcely accepted by modern Danish historians and commentators today, the basic premise that a remarkable, and remarkably widespread, humanitarian spirit prevailed at the time, with few exceptions, continues. As Mogensen concludes, "It is difficult to explain in detail why many Danes took such an active part in the illegal rescue work which resulted in the salvation of some 7,700 Jews."[12] The timing of the German decision to strike, the war's circumstances, along with the attitudes of thousands of Danes, all played an essential role in determining what was possible to accomplish and what actually happened.

Because it avoided occupation, Sweden's postwar "master narrative" is naturally very different from Denmark's. Yet its historiographical development followed a similar paradigm. A narrative more comforting than factually true was advanced by those working in the postwar years, and was supported by both the political and academic establishment. Here it is salient to note that politically, the postwar decades were completely dominated by Sweden's ruling Social Democrats. As a result, in a country where most academic research was funded by the state, research topics and trends favorable to the Social Democrats dominated the wartime narrative, which became almost reflexively defensive of the choices made by Sweden's wartime coalition government, dominated in most things that mattered by Social Democratic Prime Minister Per Albin Hansson. Though domestic politics was his metier and his lack of experience in foreign affairs sometimes a problem, "Per Albin," as he was universally known, was able to rely on Christian Günther, his non-partisan Foreign Minister, to ensure his wishes were essentially followed. In a nutshell, this narrative stated that even though Sweden's government had "no choice" but to make concessions that clearly violated any notion of strict neutrality, these were the right choices anyway. Importantly for our concerns, between the 1960s and mid-1990s, Sweden's historians in the main not only accepted this paradigm of explanation, they all but ignored study of the Holocaust itself, Sweden's reaction to it, and all other related questions.[13]

The epistemological problem for them was, and is, that Swedish concessions to Germany were so flagrant that they created discomforting, even embarrassing questions that have, over the decades, refused to go away. These issues include, but are not limited to, imposing occasional censorship on the country's free press at the Germans' behest— so as not to "irritate" Hitler and his henchmen; allowing and facilitating the transfer of over two million combat troops on Swedish railroads to occupied Norway; permitting German merchant ships to use Swedish territorial waters to escape marauding Soviet submarines; and allowing German combat and courier aircraft frequent access to secure Swedish airspace. One of the most egregious violations of neutrality took place in conjunction with Germany's invasion of the Soviet Union in June 1941. After insistent German demands, the Swedish government permitted a fully equipped combat division to move from Norway to Finland. This "Mid-Summer's Crisis" became a constitutional concern because of the involvement of King Gustav V, and exercised the imagination of Swedish historians for many years. In essence, it was a bagatelle when considering the gigantic numbers of German and Soviet troops engaged in combat on the Eastern Front after June 1941, but it is seen, still today, as a highly problematic concession to Germany and an "unforgivable" violation of Sweden's dearly held neutrality.

However, even more important in the long run was Sweden's insistence on maintaining a massive trade with Nazi Germany, even long after the government knew that Hitler's government was gassing Jews to death in purposely-built facilities in ever greater numbers. This knowledge became well known in Swedish governing and industrial circles by late summer 1942, yet trade continued apace. By late 1944, Sweden had shipped some 50 million tons of high-quality iron ore, great quantities of precision ball bearings made by SKF (*Svensk Kullager Fabrik*, the world's leading manufacturer of this critical machined product), timber and other products. These raw and machined materials, particularly the iron ore and ball bearings, were essential products for the Nazi war machine.[14] As part of their economic war-fighting, the Allies sought to halt this trade, with the issue becoming of particular importance in Sweden's relations with the Americans, who were far less understanding of Sweden's increasingly unconvincing explanations for continuing to trade with Nazi Germany than were the British. As German military losses mounted, American pressure on Sweden to lessen and eventually cease supplying the Nazi regime with vital supplies grew—mostly to no avail.[15]

Simultaneously with these geopolitical developments came the remarkable shift in Sweden's response to the ongoing genocide. This shift, which for long seemed highly unlikely, was the result of two major factors. The first was the quantity and quality of information coming into Sweden from a number of credible sources about the rapidly accelerating murder of Jews by bullets, gassing, and starvation. By late summer 1942, this information had a significant impact on the attitude of a Swedish diplomat named Gösta Engzell. Significantly, Engzell (an Under-Secretary at *UD*) was head of the ministry's Legal Division, which handled visa and immigration issues, and had become, somewhat by default, the leading unit of Sweden's government which handled "Jewish issues."

One fascinating German source made himself known to the Swedes in August 1942. On a night train from Warsaw to Berlin, Kurt Gerstein, an *SS* officer, approached a Swedish diplomat, Göran von Otter. Gerstein had just been to Belzec, the death camp in southeast Poland. Horrified by what he saw, he approached a man he understood to be a Swedish diplomat, and for a number of hours described what he had seen. He pleaded with the Swede to tell the world, and though von Otter didn't write a formal report (for reasons unknown), it is certain that Engzell absorbed this and other information available to him. There is no question that such information had a dramatic impact on Engzell's previously rather unfavorable attitude to Swedish assistance for Jews.[16] This shift in attitude had an almost immediate and dramatic effect. When, in autumn 1942, Germany and its Norwegian collaborators attacked that country's tiny Jewish community, Swedish border guards were instructed by *UD* to let those Jews who had escaped into the country. Another crucial reason for this shift was that no longer was it Polish, German or other Central European Jews in question, but rather a *broderfolk* (a "brotherly people")—that is, fellow Scandinavians. Their plight neither could nor would be ignored by the Swedish people or government—even if they were Jews.

Thus began the dramatic Swedish shift from "indifference to activism." From this point on, to the end of the war, any Jew who could make it to Sweden's borders, or who managed to obtain Swedish diplomatic help (almost always in the form of citizenship papers, or an entry visa), was certain to receive Swedish assistance. Yet as Sweden helped Jews, it continued selling Nazi Germany what it wanted and needed.

In Swedish historiography, similarly to that of Denmark, the first scholarly studies of the nation's response to genocide were conducted by outsiders. American-Jewish historian Steven Koblik first published his *The Stones Cry Out* in Swedish in 1987 without footnotes. Though subsequently published in English with proper scholarly citations, this unfortunate decision enabled the Swedish academic establishment, if not to dismiss entirely Koblik's pioneering collection of essays, then at least to severely diminish its genuine importance.[17] This delayed the growth of Holocaust studies in Sweden. The second scholarly monograph on Sweden and the Holocaust was the present author's doctoral dissertation, "From Indifference to Activism...," first published in 1996.[18] Both publications disturbed the dominant narrative, yet both also brought into the open some previously unknown and positive aspects about Swedish diplomacy and the Jews. This author argued that Sweden did not belong in the category "bystanders." In fact, its diplomatic activism on behalf of some Jews during the Holocaust, an activism directed by Gösta Engzell and his colleagues, shows unequivocally that Sweden's government did try to save some Jews from the Nazi killing machine.

This diplomacy peaked in Budapest. There, in 1944, diplomats Ivan Danielsson and Per Anger employed a tactic dubbed by this author as "bureaucratic resistance." This tactic enabled them to engage in ever-more expansive assistance and rescue activities on behalf of Jews in Budapest (there was little if anything they could do for the hundreds of thousands of Hungarian Jews rounded up and deported in spring 1944 from the countryside). Then, in July 1944, they were reinforced by the presence of Raoul Wallenberg, a scion of one of Sweden's most powerful banking and industrial families. Wallenberg took the methods and precedent established earlier, and pushed Swedish rescue and assistance activities to entirely new levels. Eventually, he and his colleagues were able to assist or rescue, in one way or another, some 20,000 Jews in Budapest.[19]

These and other aspects of Sweden's response to genocide came under increasing scrutiny, and beginning some 10 years ago, a trickle of doctoral dissertations and other publications about Sweden and the Holocaust were published that shattered the established paradigms. Not least, moral issues raised by Sweden's paradoxical response to war and genocide were raised. These studies have now established a more nuanced and credible view of Sweden's response to the Holocaust. This new picture is no longer hegemonic, but rather diverse, diffuse, and often contradictory. This, of course, makes it both much more interesting and more difficult to encapsulate under one title or another.[20] That said, Sweden's response to the plight of Danish Jewry was unequivocal, and overwhelmingly positive. Yet it too was also determined largely by the geopolitical situation which then prevailed.

When, in August 1943, German officials ended their collaboration with the Danes, they also began preparing their strike against Denmark's Jews. Engzell understood the implications of martial law, and on 31 August he wrote to von Dardel in Copenhagen:

> We are rather clear on what you can do under current circumstances *to rescue Danish Jews by bringing them here*. I'm thinking mainly about the Swedish-born and their nearest relatives, husbands and children. If there is anything to be gained by issuing emergency passports you may do that, still with some caution concerning the non-Swedish born.[21] [emphasis added]

On 2 September, he informed von Dardel that, "As expected we have received a stream of requests and applications concerning Jewish relatives in Denmark ... we are prepared to do what is possible to allow them to come over to Sweden."[22] In a vivid demonstration of official Swedish attitudes a full month before the Danish *Aktion* began, Engzell wrote to von Dardel that, "p.s. entry visas may be given to all Jews in question without prior clearance from [us]." During this exchange, von Dardel wrote, [the] "Jewish question is hanging in the air ...".[23] Sweden's government was prepared to respond when, as now seemed inevitable, Nazi Germany would strike Danish Jewry.[24]

Remarkably, this *Aktion* was revealed to Danish officials and the Jews, and it was leaked by one of Germany's most adept "desk-top" killers, Dr Werner Best. Appointed months earlier as head of Germany's occupation in Denmark, Best—for a variety of reasons—decided that deporting to death Denmark's Jews was not entirely in Germany's interests.[25] As Mogensen writes,

> Dr. Best was aware that an extensive deportation of Jews would make a political comeback difficult ... This is most likely the main reason why [he] leaked information of the up-coming raid to...Duckwitz. He in turn informed his Danish contacts, and soon the warning reached a large section of the Jewish population. When the raid was carried out, a large majority of the Jews were not at home. This is the main reason why the German operation caught so few members of the Jewish community in Denmark.[26]

Yet, as noted, had not Sweden chosen to open its borders, these thousands would have had nowhere to go. Early Saturday morning on 2 October 1943, von Dardel cabled Stockholm: "Last night at 21.00 1000 Gestapo and [Danish] Free Corpsmen, since Danish police refused, turned out and arrested a large but still unknown number of Jews and taken to a vessel. Telephone out in whole country. Himmler said to be in Copenhagen."[27] In the following days and weeks, the rescue of Danish Jewry was carried out, with literally hundreds of vessels of various sizes carrying Jews in numbers large and small to Sweden.

Crucially, Best had decided that Denmark would be satisfactorily "cleansed" of Jews even if they escaped to Sweden, and were not deported to a gassing chamber. Some days later, he reported to Berlin that, "As the objective goal of the *Judenaktion* in Denmark was the de-judaization of the country, and not a successful headhunt, it must be concluded that the *Judenaktion* has reached its goal. Denmark is de-judaized, as no Jew who falls under the relevant legislation can stay or work here any more."[28]

Engzell pressed his envoy in Berlin to convince the Germans to "give" Denmark's Jews to Sweden. Though these particular negotiations had mixed success, there is no question that Best and other German authorities in Denmark did not press their "hunt" for Jews too forcefully. As a result, another leading Swedish diplomat in Stockholm could write in his diary, on 7 October 1943, that,

> "Our démarche about the Jews [in Denmark] has not been answered, but in any case it has brought positive results, because Denmark's Jews know that they would be made most welcome in Sweden, if they succeeded in coming here. And happily they have, they have come in their thousands and they are streaming across the Sound in boats large and small. It seems that the Germans are 'closing their eyes' about this mass flight ... and perhaps this is a result of our representations in Berlin."[29]

Yet even as Denmark's fortunate Jews settled into a comfortable and relatively short-lived exile, Sweden's government and business leaders continued their shipments of militarily vital supplies to Nazi Germany.[30] It is estimated that some 600,000 Jews died in the last 12 months of World War II. The majority were Hungarian Jews in the spring and summer of 1944, but this dire figure also includes tens of thousands who died during the infamous "death marches" that occurred during the war's last months.

The salvation of Danish Jewry made headlines around the world, and Sweden justifiably reaped a "public relations" bonanza that it desperately needed as the Allies applied intense pressure to cease trading with Nazi Germany, pressure Sweden resisted until very late in the war. There is no question that Sweden's government acted to save, in 1944 and 1945, tens of thousands of Jews. Yet it remains justified to ask, even if no quantitative answer can be given, how many more would have survived had Sweden decided to cut off trade with Nazi Germany at the same time as it was rescuing Danish Jews. Moreover, we may also ask how many more brave soldiers of the Soviet Union and the Western Allies would have survived rather than sacrificing their lives in the common effort to destroy Hitler's genocidal regime? Before these important questions can be answered satisfactorily, more research is needed.

Notes

1 Text of statement given to public media, 2 October 1943, *StatensRiksarvkivet, Utrikesdepartementets 1920 års dossiersystem* [*RA UD*], Hp 21 AD 1056, vol. 2.
2 Beginning in late 1942, when Sweden quietly admitted approximately 1,000 Jews escaping from Norway through the Danish rescue in October 1943, the assistance and rescue operations in Budapest throughout 1944, the "White Buses Red Cross operations" headed by Count Folke Bernadotte, and the acceptance of debilitated survivors from a variety of countries in the spring and summer of 1945, Sweden assisted or rescued, at a minimum, between 40,000–50,000 European Jews.
3 L. Rünitz, "The Politics of Asylum in Denmark in the Wake of the *Kristallnacht*," in *Denmark and the Holocaust*, eds M.B. Jensen and S.L.B Jensen (Copenhagen: Institute for International Studies, Department for Holocaust and Genocide Studies, 2003), 14–32.
4 On this, see Paul A. Levine, *From Indifference to Activism: Swedish Diplomacy and the Holocaust, 1938–1944*, 2nd edn (Uppsala, Sweden: Studia historica Upsaliensa, 1998), 104–9.
5 H. Kirchoff, "'Doing All That Can Be Done'—The Swedish Foreign Ministry and the Persecution of Jews in Denmark in October 1943: A Study in Humanitarian Aid and Realpolitik," *Scandinavian Journal of History*, vol. 24, no. 1 (March 1999): 1–43.
6 M. Mogensen, "October 1943—The Rescue of the Danish Jews," in *Denmark and the Holocaust* (Jensen and Jensen, eds), 33.
7 G. Von Dardel to S. Söderblom, 17 November 1941, *RA UD* Hp 21 AD 1056, vol. 1. During this time, Sweden's highest representatives in foreign countries were called ministers rather than ambassadors.
8 See V. O. Vilhjálmsson, "The King and the Star: Myths Created during the Occupation of Denmark," in *Denmark and the Holocaust* (Jensen and Jensen, eds), 102–17.
9 Though Denmark did "enjoy" a quite lenient occupation compared with most other European countries and regions occupied by the Nazis, this refusal to accept German demands regarding the "customary" range of anti-Jewish measures does provide acute comment on possibilities that existed for many other Europeans—possibilities rarely, if ever, utilized.
10 Mogensen, "October 1943," 33–34.
11 For a concise bibliography in both Danish and English on this issue, see Mogenson, "October 1943," 60–61.
12 Mogensen, "October 1943," 43. Mogensen reports that of 474 Jews deported to the Theresienstadt ghetto, 53 died, mostly elderly and ill deportees. Thirty died trying to escape; fewer than 100 remained in hiding in Denmark. Mogensen, "October 1943," 33.
13 For more on this, see postscript to Levine, *From Indifference to Activism*, 286–301.
14 Germany's production of armaments reached its quantitative height during the summer of 1944, and though never perfectly measured, there seems little question that Swedish products were crucial to this development, and thus helped to keep the *Wehrmacht* and other arms going—surely lengthening the war to some extent.
15 For more detail on these issues, see P. A. Levine, "Swedish Neutrality during the Second World War: Tactical Success or Moral Compromise," in *European Neutrals and Non-Belligerents*

during the Second World War, ed. N. Wylie (Cambridge: Cambridge University Press, 2002), 304–30. Though Sweden did not trade in "Nazi gold" as did the Swiss, their trade with Nazi Germany was of significant benefit to the latter's war economy.

16 On this episode and other highly detailed information becoming available to Engzell and *UD*, see Levine, *From Indifference to Activism*, 123–33.

17 S. Koblik, *Om vi teg, skulle stenarna ropa; Sverige och judeproblemet 1933–1945*, trans. E. Frykman (Stockholm: Norstedts, 1987); *The Stones Cry Out: Sweden's Response to the Persecution of the Jews 1933–1945* (New York: Holocaust Library, 1988).

18 Professor Koblik was the author's mentor at the Claremont Graduate School, Claremont, California.

19 See the author's new study, "Raoul Wallenberg," in *Budapest: Myth, History & Holocaust* (London and Portland: Vallentine Mitchell, 2010) for a full account of Wallenberg's historical activities.

20 For an important example of this historiographical progress, see L. M. Andersson and M. Tydén, eds, *Sverige och Nazityskland; Skuldfrågor och moraldebatt* [*Sweden and Nazi Germany: Questions of Guilt and the Moral Debate*] (Stockholm: Dialogos Förlag, 2007).

21 G. Engzell to G. von Dardel, no. 37, 31 August 1943, *RA UD* Hp 21 AD 1056, vol. 1.

22 G. Engzell to G. von Dardel, no. 46, 2 September 1943, *RA UD* Hp 21 AD 1056, vol. 1.

23 G. von Dardel to G. Engzell, no. 103, 6 September 1943, *RA UD* Hp 21 AD 1056, vol. 1.

24 See Levine, *From Indifference to Activism*, esp. chapters 8–10.

25 Werner Best was a top *SS* official and lawyer who had both played a major role in legitimizing Hitler's regime in the 1930s, and in the deportation and murder of French Jews in 1942–43.

26 Mogensen, "October 1943," 37–38.

27 Von Dardel to *UD*, no. 21, 2 October 1943, *RA UD* Hp 21 AD 1056, vol. 2.

28 Mogensen, "October 1943," 58.

29 S. Grafström: *Anteckningar 1938–1944* (Stockholm: Kungliga Famfundet för utgivande av handskrifter rörande Skandinaviens historia, del 14), 509–10.

30 The vast majority of Danish Jews returned home after the war and found, for the most part, their apartments and possessions intact.

27

THE RESCUERS

When the ordinary is extraordinary

Michael Berenbaum

Now I know I owe my survival to the fact that there are admirable people in this world.[1]
The Wartime Diary of Edmund Kessler

Raul Hilberg, the incomparable scholar of the Holocaust, entitled his book *Perpetrators, Victims, Bystanders: The Jewish Catastrophe 1933–1945*.[2] Though Hilberg's work, most especially *The Destruction of the European Jews*, is monumental and enduring, the division that he suggested in this later work was too neat, too simple. Given his assessment that resistance was of marginal importance, its omission was to be expected, but omitting rescuers was most curious.

When the Israeli Parliament, the Knesset, passed legislation creating Yad Vashem, Israel's and the Jewish People's Memorial to the Holocaust, it defined its basic functions as including recognition of the "Righteous among the Nations." By 1962, a formal apparatus was in place, a Commission for the Designation of the Righteous, whose chair since its inception has been an Israeli Supreme Court Justice. To date, more than 22,000 people have been so honored by Yad Vashem and the State of Israel, people from each of the countries of German occupation or allied with Germany, as well as from neutral and Allied countries. The largest number honored have come from Poland, where there has been an organized campaign to find, research, verify, and nominate Poles. Poles who saved Jews during the war were subject to the death penalty and therefore put themselves and their family at great risk, therefore their deeds of rescue are even more impressive. The reason why Poland has been so concerned with documenting its rescuers is not unrelated to its desire to change the image of Poland in the western world, and most especially in the eyes of the Jewish community, where Poles are often perceived as being antisemitic, a reputation reinforced by survivors' accounts. Many survivors often manifest in their testimonies and memoirs greater anger at the Poles who were their neighbors than they do at the Germans. From the latter, little was expected; the betrayal of a person whom one had experienced as a friend and fellow countryman stings even decades later. Only one nation has refused individual recognition. The people of Denmark are honored as one, not as individual Danes.

Despite the undeniable importance of Yad Vashem's efforts over the past decades, most especially under the superb leadership of Mordecai Paldiel, who headed the Department of the Righteous for some two decades, there have been three significant

315

criticisms of its efforts, largely directed at its criteria. Yad Vashem honors non-Jews who risked their lives to save the life of a Jew without substantial reward and without the expectation of reward. It also insists on verification of these claims by the recipients' testimony or by "bona fide archival material."[3]

By honoring *non-Jews*, Yad Vashem has deliberately eliminated any consideration of Jews who rescued Jews. Research efforts to document individual Jews who rescued Jews are thus far less advanced than those considering non-Jewish rescuers. Thus the entire question of self-help during the Holocaust is under-researched, both as a phenomena of pre-armed stages of resistance and also as counterevidence to the perception of Jewish passivity in the face of their powerlessness. One should recall that Swiss historian Werner Rings lists self-help as a characteristic of resistance in all German-occupation territories, along with symbolic resistance and polemical resistance, all of which preceded armed resistance.

By honoring only those who have endangered their lives to save Jews, Yad Vashem has excluded almost all diplomats, who, because they enjoyed diplomatic immunity, were not at risk when they rescued Jews. It has also excluded some high-ranking church officials because, despite political risks and perhaps even career risks, their lives, too, were not in a life-threatening situation, unlike lesser-ranking church officials whose removal would not have caused public uproar. There are a few notable exceptions, the most famous of which is clearly Raoul Wallenberg, who exploited his diplomatic immunity to save Budapest's Jews by issuing "protective" passports. Although these documents had no standing in international law, they did impress those who inspected them and helped save many Jewish lives. Adolf Eichmann allegedly threatened Wallenberg, and in the end he died under mysterious circumstances. He was last heard of in Soviet custody on the day when Budapest was liberated. Soviet officials formally claimed that Wallenberg died of natural causes 3 years later. Rumors that Wallenberg was alive persisted into the 1980s.

A second notable exception to Yad Vashem's criteria is Mehmet Selahattin Ulkemen, the World War II-era Turkish Consul General in Rhodes, and the only Turk to be awarded the honor of Righteous among the Nations by the State of Israel for his rescue work. Although his country was neutral and Germany was reticent about challenging its diplomatic protection, Ulkemen defied a direct order of a German general and protected Jews of Turkish origin in Rhodes. His life was in danger, as were the lives of his wife and children. Eric Saul, who prepared an exhibition of various diplomats who saved Jews, has petitioned Yad Vashem for their recognition, but to no avail.

The third problem with Yad Vashem's important efforts is the title bestowed on these rescuers, "Righteous *among the* Nations." It transforms the behavior of the rescuer into a religious sphere, which often misrepresents the motivation of some, if not most, rescuers who were not motivated by religious aspirations. Furthermore, it does not allow us to account for other rescuers, including someone of the stature of Oskar Schindler, a Nazi war profiteer, who enjoyed a life of hedonism even as he worked to save Jews who worked for him. Above all, Yad Vashem's epithet also provides a misleading model of what is required in order to assist those in need, even those in dire need.

Reading through Yad Vashem's *The Encyclopedia of the Righteous Among the Nations*,[4] a massive compendium of those who rescued Jews, one is struck not by how lofty their motivations or how powerful their aspirations were, but by the *ordinariness* of the rescuers, *their* banality—though one hesitates to use this term since Hannah

Arendt's work on Eichmann has given it such a negative connotation. Her understanding of banality would have been far more applicable to what happened in the Shoah had she written of the banality of the *perpetrator*, and not the banality of evil.[5] The rescuers were ordinary people from virtually every walk of life—religious and secular, upper-class and peasants, communists and even fascists, scholars and illiterates, and everyone in between, who maintained humane values of decency, hospitality, assistance to one's neighbors, shelter for young and defenseless children, feeding those who were hungry, offering clothing and shelter, deeds that would not be heralded in ordinary times. Nevertheless, given the extraordinary circumstances in which rescuers lived—and given the life-and-death stakes of their simple offers—we view their actions differently. Some rescuers were religious, but many were not. Some aspired to piety, many more maintained a seamless value system that they applied to their circumstances, and many more behaved instinctively, trusting in intuition rather than thinking through all the consequences, sorting through all the moral judgments. It is the ordinariness of the good, its routineness, its naturalness, its simplicity, and its banality that strikes me as an appropriate understanding of what actually happened. The deeds were ordinary, and yet out these deeds came the extraordinary.

Bryan Mark Rigg, who has written a controversial and inappropriately titled book *Hitler's Jewish Soldiers*,[6] detailed the story of individuals of Jewish and partially Jewish origin who served in the *Wehrmacht*, demonstrating that some who wore a German uniform, even some SS men, engaged in rescue, particularly when they felt a human bond, the solidarity that one feels toward a fellow combat soldier, toward a comrade who has saved a life, or shown bravery and decency. On the one hand, a German soldier could implement the policy of the "Final Solution," yet when faced with a personal relationship or competing values, admiration for one as a soldier for instance, that same soldier could overlook, disregard, and even on occasion falsify the record of a fellow soldier to protect him against that very "Final Solution" that he was implementing. Not all who served in the *Wehrmacht* were antisemitic, even as their service facilitated the killing process.

We mystify the behavior of the rescuer not because they expect it, but because *we* require that mystification. Our language is exaggerated and disproportionate because it is asked to assume an impossible burden: to balance an unrelenting story of evil and despair that is the core of the Holocaust. Yet it is essential because without it, pedagogically and psychologically, the Holocaust would be a story of impotence and rage, defeat and destruction. Few would have the courage to confront it. We need these stories of good to relieve our despair, knowing in part that a true measure of the historical situation escapes us. These stories of goodness allow us to confront the darkness of the Shoah and remain as whole as one can remain in a journey into the abyss, and they are essential to our students if they are not to be left with the feeling of powerlessness.

Recall that paradoxical line at the end of Anne Frank's diary, written before she and her family were captured, before she entered the gates of Auschwitz:

> In spite of everything, I still believe that people are really good at heart. I simply can't build up my hopes on a foundation consisting of confusion, misery, and death.

Hope died at Auschwitz; so too illusions.

Many scholars of the Holocaust properly treat these lines as a self-willed denial of the experience outside the attic. We may also be denying that experience, if we do not insist that the rescuers be understood in context.

If there are 22,000 men and women who were honored by Yad Vashem for their efforts to save Jews, there are at least 22,000 stories. It is clear that there were many more than 22,000 rescuers. Some rescuers acted alone; most did not. Children assisted their parents. Spouses helped one another or, even if they objected to what was being done under their own roof, at least refused to betray their loved one. Neighbors kept quiet about what they knew, or pretended not to know. Store clerks cast a blind eye to the purchase of extra supplies, additional food. Some survivors never knew the name of those who rescued them, never had the chance or even bothered to thank them, although this work has often been taken up by the children and grandchildren of survivors.[7] Many were saved for a time, but did not survive the entire war due to circumstances not of their temporary rescuers' doing. Many survivors who were rescued have more than one person to thank for their rescue; they can tell more than one story. In Poland, there may be as many as 10,000 survivors of the Holocaust who, for the longest time, did not know—even now still do not know—that they were even survivors, for example, Jewish children born between 1939 and 1942 who were given over to non-Jews, who raised them as their own and who did not tell them that they were Jewish when such information was perilous both to the child and to the rescuing family. After the war, if the biological parents did not return, custodial rescuers became adoptive parents, who continued to raise these children as their own and did not tell them of their Jewish origin. Only in death have some, but by no means all, of these adults learned of their Jewish origin and of their parents' deeds. In the anecdotes of survivors that follow, I want to expand our understanding of rescuers and their motivations, and challenge some simplifications.

Even some antisemites were rescuers

Aaron Elster was born in Sokołów Podlaski, a Polish town of some 5,000 Jews, one in three of the general population.[8] Born in 1932, he was only seven when the Germans invaded, and 10 when, on Yom Kippur 1942, the Jews of Sokołów were gathered together awaiting deportation. Aaron's father, a non-kosher butcher who, because of his work, had many contacts with Polish non-Jews, forced his 10-year-old son to run away. He kept his younger daughter at his side for a journey to the unknown, what we now know as the death camp of Treblinka.

Aaron was left alone. He tried to remain inconspicuous, unseen, but he sought out the familiar and went to his uncle's home, where he found his aunt and cousin hiding in a pre-designated hiding spot. The next morning, he peered out of the hiding spot and saw a woman outside the ghetto, who motioned to him to come over to her. He never knew her name, merely her gesture. Crawling under the barbed wire, he cut his leg and ripped his pants. The woman had no strategy for the boy's survival. Seemingly, she knew that life in the ghetto was not possible. Aaron escaped to the Aryan side and approached a restaurant-owner who had been one of his father's customers. He was given some bread and pushed away; his presence was just too dangerous. German soldiers were eating inside, and Poles who hid Jews put their own lives at risk. Even the offer of bread was a momentary rescue.

An ordinary farmer placed 10-year-old Aaron in the cellar. He wanted to help, but he feared being discovered by the Nazis. He hid the young boy for a short while, but soon his fears overwhelmed his humane instincts. This behavior was not uncommon. Aaron then went to acquaintances of his parents, the Gorskis; at first they cast him away, but later they relented and let him stay in the attic. Mrs Gorski said: "Your mother was a shrew, a Jewish shrew, who talked me into taking your sister [Irene] and jeopardizing my safety as well as my husband's. You two are a curse to me."[9]

It was the first that Aaron knew his sister was alive. He was hidden apart from his sister. He was alone in the attic, day and night. He had straw to sleep on and a bucket for his bodily functions. He was given food each evening. From time to time, he would see his sister, who would pay a brief visit. Aaron wasn't sure whether her fleeting presence made life easier or more difficult. For a moment, his loneliness was over, but soon it only intensified. He lived like that for more than a year and a half.

Aaron recalled the days before liberation. The Russians were coming. They were bombing the town, attacking German soldiers. The Gorskis sought shelter in their basement. They forced Irene to join her brother in the attic. They did not want to die with Jews, fearing that dying with Jews would cost them their eternal reward. The paradox of the Gorskis was this: *even though they had rescued two Jews, they remained antisemites*. They could not turn a young boy and his sister away.

Even heroes have their limitations

Flora Mendelewicz was a Jewish child in Belgium, one of many who made contact with the resistance and successfully sought to hide. In her powerful memoir *Flora: I was but a Child*, she relates the following story. Flora had many rescuers during the course of the war. One rescuer was an important leader of the Belgian resistance, Georges Ranson, an industrialist who owned a local factory that manufactured technical equipment. He provided Flora and her mother with false identity cards and also with a gold cross, which his wife had lent Flora's mother to give credence to her newly established Christian identity. He gave her mother a job in his factory, while Flora and her sister remained in the apartment as her mother went to work. As conditions for Jews deteriorated, the children were separated. Flora's sister, Charlotte, went to live with Monsieur Ranson's brother, and finding no other place for Flora, he brought her home with him. His wife treated her graciously; his own children were also mindful of the situation, but clearly annoyed that they could no longer bring school friends home. Flora relates that after 2 weeks, Madame Ranson had misgivings: "Georges, you want to work with the underground ... you want to defy the law ... you want to risk your life for a few Jews, that's fine ...You have the right ... but you don't have the right to risk my life and the lives of our children."[10] Ten-year-old Flora then sprang from her bed: "I begged him: 'Please Monsieur Ranson take me to my mother. I don't want you and Madame Ranson to fight because of me.' He turned to me, pointed his hand with an outstretched forefinger at me and in a harsh voice I had never heard him use before, he almost shouted at me. 'You get back into bed immediately. This is none of your business.'"[11] The next morning, she was taken to a convent of the Sisters of St Francis, where Monsieur Ranson's cousin lived. This was but the first of many convents to which she was transferred, where she lived as a modern *marrano*.

What makes Flora Mendelewicz Singer's account so memorable is that it presents the real-life situation of the rescuer, the clash of loyalties, the balance that had to be weighed between the multiple commitments of real life—wife and family, causes, and values, loyalty to a child, love for a spouse, and the responsibilities to protect those under one's care. Even heroes had limits.

Mixed motives for rescue

Fanya Gottesfeld Heller's *Love in a World of Sorrow: A Teenage Girl's Holocaust Memoir*[12] is a controversial work not because it is untrue, but precisely because it reveals too much of the truth and thus makes its readers, survivors among them, uncomfortable. Born in 1924 in Skala, Poland [now Ukraine], a mixed town of some 5,500 inhabitants, some 3,000 Greek Orthodox, 1,000 Roman Catholics and 1,500 Jews, Fanya was nearly 15 when the war began. Her area of Poland came first under Soviet not German domination until the invasion of 1941, when at first Skala was under the control of Hungary, a German ally. It was then that she met Jan, a Ukrainian militia man several years her senior, who took an interest in the young Jewish girl of 17. It was Jan's increasing interest in Fanya, an interest encouraged by her father, which led to his providing a haven for the family. After hearing rumors of an impending raid, Jan brought Fanya to his room, much to the disapproval of his family. Over time and with much persistence, a romance ensued with the encouragement of Fanya's parents, who saw it as an essential means of survival. For Fanya, the romance was welcome, as love is for any young woman; it was intensified because it was a respite of normalcy and kindness in a world of danger and madness. As conditions deteriorated and the ghetto was liquidated, Jan provided a hiding place at the home of a friend, Sidor Sokolowski, and his wife Marynka, who resented their presence. Sidor's motivations were unclear even in the retelling, and yet it was in this situation that the Gottesfelds survived the war. Upon liberation, Fanya's father returned to Skala in advance of his family. He disappeared and was presumed dead. Suspicion fell upon Jan. Under the post-liberation circumstances, the class, cultural, and religious differences that separated Jan and Fanya re-emerged and, at least for her father, proved insurmountable. She writes: "It was never clear what happened. No one ever had factual information or concrete evidence but things must have gone very wrong and I was, and remain to this day, convinced that Jan killed my father."

Clearly, Heller's narrative is a story of rescue but not of righteousness, and one not without ulterior motives. Her rescuer was her lover, who was also a Ukrainian militia man who risked the ire of his family and of his community to save a Jewish family. He did not force himself on the young Jewish woman; in fact, the love scenes are tender and caring. He risked his life for her out of love for her, and rescued her family. Jan's reward was Fanya; his motive for rescue was, again, Fanya, and if she is to be believed, his motive for murder was Fanya. Sidor's motivations were less clear—concern for a friend, compassion, and decency. He received no favors; he was merely a witness to young love under conditions of distress. The word righteousness here seems strange at best.

There was good, pure good

Still, there were instances of righteous behavior. Philip Hallie's path-breaking study of Le Chambon, *Lest Innocent Blood Be Shed,* tells the story of the heroic behavior of the town and its Protestant Huguenots. Le Chambon's efforts were led by Pastor Andre Trocme, who preached a simple gospel. Characteristically, he ended his sermons with the following scriptural verses: "Love the Lord your God with all your heart and with all your soul and with all your strength and with all your mind" and "Love your neighbor as yourself." Then he would add, "Go practice it."

And practice it they did. Villagers in Le Chambon and in surrounding communities opened their homes and their institutions to Jewish children, and served as a haven for some 5,000 Jews, whom they rescued. When asked to describe the goodness of their deeds, a villager demurred:

> How can you call us 'good?' We were doing what had to be done. Who else could help them? And what has all this to do with goodness? Things had to be done, and we happened to be there to do them. You must understand that it was the most natural thing in the world to help these people.[13]

[handwritten margin note: no expect, of being thanked]

Students of rescue would be wise to heed not just the language, but the tone of the interview that Hallie recorded.

> What has this to do with goodness?
> Things had to be done.
> We were there to do them.
> It was most natural thing in the world.

Often when goodness was practiced, no credit was claimed, no grand decisions were involved. For some rescuers, goodness was natural; the very way in which they conducted themselves, seamlessly, unconsciously. But Le Chambon was an exception, a community founded on a religious ideology knit together by a charismatic religious leader and joined together in a common purpose. Other rescuers and other havens had mixed motives even as they rescued Jews.

Bulgaria and Denmark: few comparisons, but what a difference

Though there were many individuals who saved Jews, some important institutions and a few diplomats, there was only one nation that rescued its Jewish population—the people of Denmark. Danes were respected by Germany for their racial proximity to Aryans, and the occupation of Denmark was particularly light. Its governing institutions remained in place, as did its King, who contrary to legend, did not wear the yellow star, as Danish Jews were not required to wear the star. When Germans raised the issue of the Jewish question in Denmark, Danish leadership said: "We have no Jewish question."[14] Jews were accepted as citizens of Denmark, nothing less and nothing more.

German officials were initially reluctant to push for the "Final Solution" in Denmark. In the fall of 1943, well after its implementation in other countries throughout Europe, and despite the objection of some German diplomats in Denmark, who were less concerned about the fate of the Jews than they were about alienating the Danish population, the deportation of Jews was set.

The situation of Danish Jews was unique in two other ways. Deportation occurred after the German defeat in Stalingrad, when the tide of the war had changed. And neutral Sweden, which had offered to receive Scandinavian Jews, was but miles away across the sea. One wonders, but can never know, if Sweden would have been willing to receive less-assimilated Jews; or would it have opened its shores at an earlier time, when German defeat seemed less likely and when it was less concerned about its postwar reputation after profiting from trade as a neutral power?

Danish Jews also received the most unexpected of help: German naval attaché Georg Duckwitz warned Hans Hedtoft, the leader of the Social Democratic Party in Denmark, that a German *Aktion* was underway. "Your poor fellow citizens are going to be deported to an unknown destination."[15] The day of deportation was to be 1 October—the first day of Rosh Hashanah, the Jewish New Year. When Hedfort told C.B. Henriques, the chairman of the Jewish community, of the pending deportation, his response was as swift as it was surprising. He did not believe it. He used the words uttered by so many other victims and bystanders when they first learned of the Final Solution. As in all other cases, information about a pending deportation was not sufficient. It had to be internalized and accepted as true for it to be acted upon. But Henriques was soon persuaded of the seriousness of the warning and the accuracy of the information.

Jews believed the warning and prepared to go underground. Synagogues stood empty on Rosh Hashanah as Jews left Copenhagen for the sea coast, the lone escape route. The Danish people sprang into action. Ministers opened their churches, fisherman ferried Jews by boat, communities along the sea coast sheltered Jews awaiting their escape to freedom, ambulances served to bring Jews to the sea and from the sea to the harbor. German patrol boats were hoisted up for repair and therefore unable to chase the fleeing population. Still, funds were required to pay for transport and to reimburse fishermen for the risks they were taking. These funds were not easy to come by. Unlike many other countries, Danish church leadership condemned the treatment of Jews: Bishop Hans Fuglsang-Damgaard of the Danish Lutheran Church sent a letter of protest to the German government, which was read in every Church in Denmark on 3 October 1943.

> Race and religion can never be in themselves a reason for depriving a man of his rights, freedom, or property...We shall therefore struggle to ensure the continued guarantee to our Jewish brothers and sisters [of] the same freedom which we ourselves treasure more than life. We are obliged by our conscience to maintain the law and to protest against any violation of human rights. Therefore, we desire to declare unanimously our allegiance to the work, *we must obey God rather than man.*[16]

It must be emphasized that the Bishop's letter is a simple expression of the most profound of values: common human rights for all, freedom for all, the need to protest its violation, obedience to God.

In the end, some 7,200 of Denmark's Jews were ferried to freedom. Of the remaining Jews, 464 were arrested and deported to Theresienstadt, and the government of Denmark, unlike other governments in Europe, continued to inquire into their fate, which led to a Red Cross inspection of the "model ghetto" transit camp. Nine in ten Jews of Denmark were saved. While elsewhere, native people helped themselves to Jewish property, the property of the deportees was protected. Even churches hid the sacred possessions of the synagogues. And when Yad Vashem wanted to honor individuals, Denmark insisted that only the "people of Denmark be honored."

Bulgaria is wont to depict itself as the second Denmark. Its record is rather different and its history has been contested. Bulgaria became a reluctant ally of Germany. Having sided with Germany in World War I and lost, it was at first hesitant to repeat the mistakes of the past. The lure for Bulgaria came in the restoration of territory, which it regarded as its own. Bulgaria was given Thrace and Macedonia, which it occupied, and Dobrudja, which it incorporated into Bulgaria proper. According to Michael Bar Zohar's apologetic account, King Boris III regarded Thrace and Macedonia as German-controlled territories administered by Bulgaria, while he saw Dobrudja, which had been officially annexed in an agreement with Romania, as authentic Bulgarian territory. Its residents, Jews and non-Jews alike, received Bulgarian citizenship upon annexation. With the occupation of Thrace and Macedonia, the non-Jewish population was granted Bulgarian citizenship if they so chose, but the Jews were formally exempted and were in a no-man's-land with regards to rights, in a zone administered by Bulgaria but not considered its own by Bulgarian leadership. This was to prove lethal to the Jews in these territories.

Those who venerate Bulgaria's rescue of its own Jews offer an interesting argument. Bulgaria was not antisemitic: the evidence is quite compelling: German Ambassador to Bulgaria Heinz Beckerle, a former SA *Obergruppenführer* (Lieutenant General) and former Frankfurt Chief of Police, complained to Berlin:

> The Bulgarian society doesn't quite understand the real meaning of the Jewish question. Beside the few rich Jews in Bulgaria there are many poor people who make their living as workers and artisans. Partly raised together with Greeks, Armenians, Turks and Gypsies, the average Bulgarian doesn't understand the meaning of the struggle against the Jews...so the racial question is totally foreign to them.[17]

This complaint was reiterated time and again by Nazi officials who were disturbed by the unwillingness of Bulgarian officials to implement the "Final Solution" and by the less than zealous levels of their cooperation.

King Boris was not particularly antisemitic. Here, too, the evidence is quite compelling. Michael Bar-Zohar writes: "He had a good relationship with his Jewish subjects. He exchanged warm telegrams with the leaders of the Jewish community at every important Bulgarian holiday. His clothiers, dentists and court suppliers were Jews. He was considered by Jews as a friend."[18] His Italian queen is also credited with directly rescuing Jews and intervening on their behalf. The King unenthusiastically supported the so-called Law for the Defense of the Nation, the Bulgarian equivalent of the Nuremberg Laws, regarding it as essential to keep the Germans at bay. More ominously, he signed the deportation order for the 11,000 Jews of Thrace and Macedonia as they were not his subjects. Although the King did not have the Jews of Bulgaria proper deported, this was due more to the groundswell of objections from church officials and the efforts of Deputy Speaker of the Bulgarian National Assembly and Minister of Justice, Dimitar Peshev, one of 19 Bulgarians recognized by Yad Vashem as "righteous among the nations."

There were elements of the Bulgarian population that were deeply committed to the constitution and to respect for human dignity and the rights of citizens, including the Jews. As in Denmark, the role of the Christian clergy was indeed impressive, most especially the actions of Metropolitan Stefan, who enlisted all of Bulgaria's Metropolitans in a joint letter and who first protested the Law for the Defense of the Nation:

This bill and some of its other decisions against the Jews include some measures which cannot be considered just and useful to the defense of the nation... A harmful impression is being created that this bill's goal is a special treatment of a national minority in Bulgaria. All men and nations should defend their rights and protect themselves against dangers but in a justified effort they shouldn't admit injustice and violence against others.[19]

A letter to the Prime Minister, with a copy to the King, said the following:

The Saint Synod [the supreme body of the Bulgarian Church] decided to ask the following from your honor:

1 Not to deprive the Christians of Jewish origin and the Jews in general of their elementary rights as human beings and citizens, not to deprive them of the right to live in our country and to work here to assure a fair human living.
2 To ease the restrictions that have been imposed on the Jews and not to implement them firmly and cruelly.
3 To cancel the unjustified rule that Christians of Jewish origin should wear both a Christian cross and a Jewish star, and pay taxes to the Jewish consistory.

The Church cannot avoid reminding [you of] God's word: "With the measure you use, it will be measured back to you."[20]

The King vacillated; he did not want to confront either Hitler or his own leadership. At critical moments he was absent, and one has to question whether that absence fore-stalled consequences for the Jews of Bulgaria proper, or merely absolved the King of direct involvement in handling something he did not quite want to do, but did not have the courage or the political will to oppose. He lashed out at the Jews when politically convenient, reiterating standard antisemitic rhetoric regarding Jewish profiteers, accusing them of fomenting conflict and wars.[21] Even the King's death in 1943 from a heart attack is shrouded in mystery, with some suspecting that he was poisoned by German agents. Boris's role in the rescue of the bulk of Bulgarian Jews remains controversial to this day, and an effort to honor him in Israel has been withdrawn.

Despite recent attempts to portray Bulgaria as a second Denmark, its record can most charitably be portrayed as mixed. Jews were discriminated against, and they were sub-jected to legal constraints. Bulgaria presided over the deportation of Jews under its occupation, and work camps were set up for the Jewish population. The final deporta-tion order was signed, but not implemented. Only in the context of the Holocaust could such a record be depicted as heroic.

In conclusion: further research is desperately needed on Jewish efforts at self-help in order to complete our understanding of Jewish activity under conditions of power-lessness. We must also understand the role of Jews in initiating efforts of rescue. We must resist the term "righteous," for it is neither historically nor pedagogically useful, and we must heed the complexity of the stories of those who were rescued, as well as the rescuer, to understand the mixed motives for such acts in context. In the end, we may well find that the rescuers were ordinary men, women, and children, whose deeds, while extraordinary in their results, were quite often unremarkable in nature.

Dedication

In respectful memory of Stephen Feinstein

Notes

1 Edmund Kessler, *The Wartime Diary of Edmund Kessler: Lwów, Poland, 1942–1944* (Brighton, Massachusetts: Academic Studies Press, 2010), 99.

Raul Hilberg, *Perpetrators, Victims, Bystanders: The Jewish Catastrophe 1933–1945* (New York: ...n Asher, 1992).

Paldiel, *The Righteous Among the Nations: Rescuers of Jews During the Holocaust* ...Vashem and Jerusalem Publishing House, 2007).

...d., *The Encyclopedia of the Righteous Among the Nations: Rescuers of Jews* ...*ust* (Jerusalem: Yad Vashem, 2004).

...ng's use of the term "ordinary men" has not raised much concern. In fact, ...agen's exception, Browning's phrase has been quite essential to our happened during the Holocaust.

...'s *Jewish Soldiers: The Untold Story of Nazi Racial Laws and Men of* ...*rman Military* (Lawrence, Kansas: University Press of Kansas, 2002).

...ous film *Hiding and Seeking* details his search for the rescuers of his ...h he taught his sons to appreciate the non-Jewish world by forcing ...some Poles, who rescued their grandparents. In a remarkable bit ...enly states that, were the situation the reverse, he would not ...scuers. Conventional *halakhic* rulings would not insist that one ...n-Jew, perhaps not even to save a Jew.

...Miller, *I Still See Her Haunting Eyes: The Holocaust and a Hidden Child Named Aaron* (New York: BF Press, 2007).

9 Interview with Aaron Elster, USC Shoah Foundation Institute.

10 Flora M. Singer, *Flora: I was But a Child* (New York and Jerusalem: Yad Vashem: The Holocaust Survivors Memoir Project, 2007), 61.

11 Singer, *I Was But a Child*, 62.

12 Fanya Gottesfeld Heller, *Love in a World of Sorrow: A Teenage Girl's Holocaust Memoir* (Jerusalem and New York: Devorah, 2005).

13 Philip Hallie, *Lest Innocent Blood Be Shed* (New York: Harper & Row, 1979), 20.

14 Leni Yahil, *The Rescue of Danish Jewry* (Philadelphia: Jewish Publication Society, 1969).

15 Yahil, *The Rescue of Danish Jewry*, 148.

16 Daniel Jonah Goldhagen, *A Moral Reckoning: The Role of the Catholic Church in the Holocaust and its Unfulfilled Duty of Repair* (New York: Alfred A. Knopf, 2002), 51.

17 Michael Bar-Zohar, *Beyond Hitler's Grasp: The Heroic Rescue of Bulgaria's Jews* (Holbrook, Massachusetts: Adam's Media Corp., 1998), 60.

18 Bar-Zohar, *Beyond Hitler's Grasp*, 24.

19 Bar-Zohar, *Beyond Hitler's Grasp*, 34.

20 Bar-Zohar, *Beyond Hitler's Grasp*, 172–73.

21 Bar Zohar, *Beyond Hitler's Grasp*, 174–75.

28

JEWISH RESISTANCE AGAINST NAZISM

John M. Cox

In March 1937, two young Berlin Jews, Kurt Berkheim and Ernst Prager, were arrested for possessing illegal material. Unlike many others arrested by the Gestapo on such charges, they were carrying not a communist newspaper, but rather a satirical poem lampooning Robert Ley, the head of the German Labor Front. Ley was a notorious alcoholic; even his Nazi colleagues dubbed him *Reichstrunkenbold*, the "drunkard of the Reich." The incriminating poem referred to Ley as a lecher and morphine addict as well as a drunk (*Saufsack*), concluding that it was "high time" for the "working class to be rid of these riff-raff (*Gesindel*)."[1] Berkheim, who had never been a member of any political organization, copied the poem out of a communist periodical given to him by someone he knew via a Jewish youth organization. Berkheim was sentenced to one year's imprisonment and Prager received 18 months; their culpability for possessing the scandalous material was compounded by their "declaring themselves ready to continue" engaging in such "high-treasonous" activity, according to the judgment rendered against them.

Three-and-a-half years later, approximately 50 people—most of them Jewish—met in northern Berlin at the large Jewish cemetery, the *Weissensee*. This risky gathering was organized by a left-wing, predominantly Jewish resistance group led by Herbert Baum to protest the murder of a Jewish communist, Rudi Arndt, who had led the underground resistance at Buchenwald. Arndt "encouraged his fellow prisoners to write poems and songs," according to one source, "and made the greatest efforts to combat the degradation of humanity" that characterized camp existence. He was permitted to assemble a string quartet that performed works by Mozart, Haydn, and Beethoven. Arndt was also acknowledged by the Buchenwald authorities as a spokesperson for the prisoners, and derisively termed the "king of the Jews."[2]

One year later, in August 1942, German troops murdered 1,800 Jews outside the Byelorussian town of Lenin. Among the two dozen survivors was the 22-year-old Faye Schulman, who later fled to the woods outside the town and joined a Soviet partisan band. Initially confined to "women's work," as well as photography—she had trained to be a photographer, and kept her equipment when she fled—she was eventually allowed to use a rifle, which became "a friend. It meant survival, vengeance and self defence."[3]

While Schulman was making contact with the partisans, another Jewish woman of the same age helped sabotage some important rail lines in Warsaw. Yuri Suhl told the story of "Wanda," the *nom de guerre* of a slender young woman from Warsaw's leftist student movement. She reportedly shot and killed several German officers, sometimes in scenarios that would make for memorable cinema. She and her People's Guard (communist) comrades also bombed the offices of a collaborationist newspaper, as well as a club frequented by Gestapo and *Wehrmacht* officers.[4] Although the details of "Wanda's" exploits are fragmentary and difficult to prove, there is a natural tendency for later generations of scholars and others with an interest in the Holocaust to *want* them to be true. But it would be misguided to look for "uplifting" tales within the history of the Holocaust. On the whole, Jews responded as any other people would, through a wide range of behaviors and survival mechanisms. It is best to approach this topic without any inclination toward hagiography or in a search for redemptive or uplifting tales, but rather with humility, based on the knowledge that we cannot predict how we would ourselves act under such extreme circumstances and pressures.

None of the anecdotes that opened this chapter convey typical Jewish responses. While Berkheim and Prager possessed anti-government propaganda, their parents almost certainly knew nothing of their "subversive" activities and would not have approved, and most of the members of their own generation engaged in less dramatic strategies to persevere and attempt to "wait out" their oppressors. And, like many of the Nazis' victims, Schulman's parents and siblings had no time to weigh their options: they were captured with little warning and marched to their deaths.

Defining "resistance"

For many years after World War II, public and scholarly understanding of the anti-Nazi resistance—Jewish as well as non-Jewish—was distorted by Cold War-inspired political considerations. Many of the early studies of German opposition to Nazism advanced a very narrow definition of "resistance." Only a force that could have potentially overthrown Hitler was worthy of the term "resistance" and merited serious study. Accordingly, most West German and US studies of resistance focused nearly exclusively upon Claus von Stauffenberg and his fellow conspirators, who attempted to assassinate Hitler on 20 July 1944. "A rehabilitated and democratized [West] Germany needed heroes," pointed out historian Theodore Hamerow—preferably conservative ones.[5] Numerous books were published that examined only von Stauffenberg and his allies, but that were adorned with titles or subtitles referring to "*the* Resistance," suggesting (not so subtly) that this was the extent of conscious or organized opposition to Nazism.

By limiting the "resistance" in this manner, Western politicians and academics could also ignore or denigrate all opposition that originated in Germany's leftist parties—further reinforcing Cold War prejudices. Meanwhile, many East German historians reversed this approach, countering that the only true "*Widerstand*" (resistance) consciously struggled against the system responsible for fascism—that is, capitalism. Such tendentious definitions turned "resistance" into a posthumous honorific to be bestowed by historians on both sides of the Berlin Wall.

Eventually, an evolution in research—as well as in the social and political climate—engendered subtler understandings of resistance, particularly in the West. In 1979, Konrad Kwiet asserted that "any action aimed at countering the ideology and policies of National Socialism" should be deemed resistance, including those that, "even without the intention, were nonetheless directed against" Nazism.[6] Other historians have supplemented Kwiet's argument, if not establishing quite as broad a definition. In an essay published in 1991, Detlev Peukert outlined a continuum of more tangible and conscious oppositional behavior, from "occasional, private nonconformity, proceeding to wider acts of refusal, and then to outright protest, in which some intentional effect on public opinion is involved."[7] The Nazi state's totalitarian ambitions and its fear of any sort of independent thinking converted relatively innocuous acts into "resistance." Therefore the distinction between *conscious* and *unconscious* resistance should further discourage us from establishing rigid, static definitions.

Meanwhile, historical research into specifically Jewish resistance had first to confront Raul Hilberg's controversial assessment—in his pioneering 1961 *The Destruction of European Jewry*—that the Jewish victims had in fact exhibited little, if any, outward defiance. "The reaction pattern of the Jews" was characterized "by almost complete lack of resistance," Hilberg asserted, consistent with a "2,000-year-old experience" of "placating and appeasing" rather than resisting their enemies.[8] By the end of the 1960s, though, several scholars were chipping away at this assertion of Jewish submission and exposing the thinness of Hilberg's argument, which rested on a very narrow definition of "resistance." In a perceptive historiographical essay published in 2004, Robert Rozett noted that by the 1970s "consensus was forming" for an "inclusive definition," and that by the end of the 1990s "researchers began considering Jewish resistance less and less as a special category of behavior, and started to discuss it in the context of a broader exploration of the life of Jews" under Nazism.[9]

Key to the reframing of the topic was the concept of *amidah*, a Hebrew term that translates directly as "stand," but that has a deeper meaning in this context. At an important conference on resistance, held at Yad Vashem in 1968, Mark Dworzecki described *amidah* as "all expressions of Jewish 'non-conformism' and for all the forms of resistance and all acts by Jews aimed at thwarting the evil design of the Nazis," a design that included not only physical destruction, but also to "deprive them of their humanity, and to reduce them to dregs before snuffing out their lives."[10] For Yehuda Bauer, a pioneering historian of the Holocaust and of resistance, *amidah* includes "smuggling food into ghettos; mutual self-sacrifice within the family to avoid starvation or worse; cultural, educational, religious, and political activities taken to strengthen morale; the work of doctors, nurses, and educators to consciously maintain health and moral fiber to enable individual and group survival; and, of course, armed rebellion or the use of force" against the "Germans and their collaborators"—in short, "refus[ing] to budge in the face of brutal force."[11] These discussions of *amidah* are part of the larger process of redefining "resistance" and recognizing that most individual and group responses cannot be easily categorized; that is, the lines separating "resistance" from defiance or non-conformity—or even "compliance"—were often very thin, and that one could shade into the other almost imperceptibly.

Like many historical issues and controversies left over from the war, Jewish resistance was also exploited for political purposes. This exploitation derived not only (or primarily) from the exigencies of the Cold War, but also from the slow, uneven progress toward an engagement with the Holocaust through the 1960s, '70s, and '80s in Europe, Israel, and the United States. Israeli debates over national identity and Jewish history have also shaped—and occasionally distorted—the historiography of Jewish resistance. In particular, Israeli ideologies often advanced the myth of the "weak" Diaspora Jew versus the strong, new Israeli Jew; as Raul Hilberg phrased it in his memoir, resistance was sometimes intertwined with a mythology that "depicted the Exile as weak, feminine, and passive, and the Yishuv as strong, masculine, and active."[12] The task for historians and others is to sift through these competing agendas to gain an understanding that is as accurate as possible. "We historians are in the truth business," as Raul Hilberg once reminded us.[13] We do not honor Nazism's victims by exaggerating resistance, which can imply a condemnation of those who did *not* resist. Nonetheless, the notion that the Jews "went like sheep to the slaughter" has been convincingly disproved.

Obstacles to resistance

All opponents of the Nazis faced a multitude of obstacles, but for Jews who wished to fight back, the impediments were even greater. These included the lack of support from surrounding populations, a prerequisite for successful partisan warfare. Centuries of anti-Jewish prejudice had conditioned the populace of German-occupied eastern Europe to be indifferent, if not hostile, to Jewish refugees and partisans. A justified fear of the Nazi occupiers further discouraged local citizens from helping the Jews. And it was not only the local populace that Jewish partisans in the East had to fear: even the Russian-led partisan units would sometimes kill their own Jewish members.[14]

A lack of armaments and military training also impeded armed resistance by Jews. For example, the Warsaw ghetto fighters received few arms, but plenty of high-minded plaudits from the Polish nationalists and the Allies, who refused to believe that Jewish resisters could constitute an effective fighting force. The German policy of harsh reprisals provided another powerful deterrent. In March 1942, 1,540 inhabitants—half the Jewish population—of the town of Dolhynov in Belarus were murdered as punishment for the escape of two resistance fighters who were hiding in the town's ghetto.[15] Six months later, a prisoner at Treblinka killed an SS officer; 160 inmates were killed in retribution.[16] Similar examples abound, from the ghettos, to the camps, to the countryside. The effectiveness of reprisals was enhanced by a sense of Jewish responsibility for the welfare of the community and the traditional cohesion of the Jewish family.

Another psychological obstacle to resistance was the absence of any hope of military victory. Fighters in Yugoslavia, the Soviet Union, France, and elsewhere could realistically believe that, with the eventual help of the Allies, their efforts could eventually succeed in liberation, or at least deal a severe blow to the enemy. Jewish fighters, on the other hand, could not recruit to their cause through false promises of eventual victory. Mordechai Anielewicz bluntly informed a friend that his planned uprising in the Warsaw ghetto would lead to the ghetto's destruction. "He was sure that they would die like stray dogs and no one would even know their final resting place," recorded Emanuel Ringelblum.[17]

An additional psychological factor was the lack of comprehension of the totality of Nazi plans. As we now know, the Nazi leadership itself did not decide until the middle of 1941 that its mission was to physically annihilate all Jews; for the future victims, "the ultimate horrors were inconceivable," as a surviving German Jew later said.[18] In December 1941, Abba Kovner told a *Hashomer Hatzair* gathering in Vilna that the Jews faced a systematic effort at annihilation, from which there was no escape. His comrades were not yet prepared to accept this.[19]

Related to this incomprehension, the hope for survival—by making oneself useful as a laborer in the ghetto, for example—mitigated against actions that would presumably invite destruction. Most people believed in the *Judenrat* policy of survival through compliance. Ironically, and sometimes tragically, the Jews of a ghetto such as Vilna's would sometimes adopt a hostile attitude toward the resistance, which they saw as a threat to the survival of the community, "not as a source of protection or hope."[20]

But it was the debilitating conditions within the ghettos and camps that presented the greatest obstacle. The daily struggle to keep body and soul together usually precluded individual or collective action against the oppressors. In his 2004 meditation upon the moral complexities of Jewish resistance, James M. Glass painted a vivid picture of the horrors of daily life: "Individuals and families disintegrating emotionally; catatonic children wasting away, fouling themselves against ghetto walls; shrieking women roaming the streets; suicides increasing daily."[21] And Glass was describing a typical scene in a ghetto, not the death camps.

Resistance inside Nazi Germany

To the degree that German Jews organized to combat the Nazi state, they did so primarily by joining groups that originated in the pre-1933 working-class, leftist, and Zionist movements. Even for conservative Jews who sought allies, there was very little room within the bourgeois resistance, whose leaders had no intention of restoring the civil rights denied Jews.[22] The Herbert Baum groups offer a striking example of German-Jewish resistance. Herbert Baum had begun building his network of dissident groups and circles in the last years of the Weimar Republic, and during the Third Reich the groups loosely under his command encompassed more than 100 members. The Baum groups engaged in covert forms of resistance, surreptitiously dropping leaflets around Berlin, scrawling anti-Hitler graffiti on walls, and seeking allies among the forced laborers in the factories where they worked. But the main activities of the Baum groups were semi-informal evenings—usually called by the members *Heimabende*, literally "home evenings" or study groups—that revolved around discussions of novels, political texts, and music. These evening meetings imparted cohesiveness, helped the participants maintain morale, and attracted new members to Baum's resistance network.

On 8 May 1942, the "Soviet Paradise," an exhibition staged by Goebbels depicting the degradation of Russia under its supposed "Jewish-Bolshevik" regime, opened with great fanfare in Berlin. Baum and several comrades resolved to sabotage the exhibit, and one close colleague, Werner Steinbrinck, was able to steal a kilogram of explosive black powder, as well as a flammable solution, from his workplace.[23] On the evening of 18 May, despite some logistical difficulties, Baum and several associates, including his wife, Marianne, managed to place one firebomb that burned a small part of the "Soviet Paradise." This rare act of direct, public resistance, however, led quickly to the demise of the Baum groups. Over the next two months, the police arrested four dozen people, some of whom were only tangentially linked to the Baum groups. All told, 32 members and supporters of Baum's groups were executed or otherwise murdered by the German authorities over the next year-and-a-half. Sixteen of those executed were no more than 23 years old.

The Baum groups, most of whose members were non-doctrinaire leftists, do not fit easily into such categories as "Jewish resistance"—where their Marxist loyalties are difficult to reconcile—or, for that matter, "communist" or socialist resistance, although postwar East Germany exploited their memory in a dishonest, self-serving fashion, burying their Jewish identity. Baum's groups demonstrate the difficulty in acknowledging the intersections of Jewish and leftist resistance, as evidenced by the missing "First they came for the Communists" in the truncated version of Martin Niemöller's famous poem that adorns a wall of the US Holocaust Memorial Museum.

The Baum groups were not the only formations of young German Jews who engaged in varied, often creative forms of dissidence and resistance. In 1971, a survivor of a small "Berlin anti-fascist Jewish girls' group" wrote a letter to Arnold Paucker; if not for this letter, we would know nothing of the existence of this extraordinary group. The young women knew each other from their time in the *Bund Deutsch-Jüdischer Jugend*, a non-Zionist Jewish youth group with a large membership in Berlin. "Already before the war, the group's leader, Eva Mamlok, had been caught distributing anti-fascist propaganda," wrote Paucker. During the first two years of the war, "the group's members, working as forced labour in Berlin, concentrated their efforts on anti-war propaganda. In September 1941, the girls were denounced, accused of subverting the defensive will of the German people," and eventually all but one of them perished in the camps.[24]

Resistance in the ghettos

The evolving emphasis over the past 30 years on the multiple forms of anti-Nazi action should not detract attention from the fact that Jews *were* involved in substantial—in fact, disproportionately large—numbers in armed resistance. Jewish prisoners staged armed revolts in five concentration camps and 18 forced-labor camps, according to Nechama Tec.[25] And the inhabitants of the ghettos of at least seven "major" and 45 "minor" ghettos formed underground organizations that conducted myriad acts of defiance.

The Warsaw Ghetto Uprising is understandably the best known case of Jewish armed revolt. The Jewish Combat Organization (*Żydowska Organizacja Bojowa*, ŻOB), composed of members of Zionist and non-Zionist groups as well as Bundists and communists, emerged in the middle of 1942 during the massive deportations that reduced the ghetto population from about 350,000 to roughly 65,000. Revisionist (right-wing) Zionists and their youth movement, *Betar*, established the Jewish Military Union (*Żydowski Związek Wojskowy*, ŻZW) in the fall of 1942.

The ŻOB ambushed the German forces during the 18 January 1943 deportation *Aktion*, firing on the Germans and claiming a few casualties. Within the ghetto, this bold act greatly enhanced the prestige of the underground, which became more assertive, executing a handful of "traitors," including the second-in-command of the Jewish police, over the next 3 months.[26] By the inception of the final *Aktion*—19 April 1943, the eve of Passover and the day before Hitler's birthday—the two forces had about 750 fighters, two-thirds of them under the command of the ŻOB, and had acquired revolvers and a few rounds of ammunition for each fighter, as well as about 10 rifles and two machine guns. "Only God knows how they obtained them," wrote Goebbels in his diary. We know how they did *not* obtain them: from the Allies, who provided little assistance and rebuffed emissaries from the ghetto resistance even after the uprising had begun.[27] To arm themselves, the ghetto fighters resorted to such inventive tactics as smuggling arms in carts transporting corpses to the cemeteries.[28] They also produced 2,000 of the inexpensive, easily assembled device favored by urban guerrillas since the Spanish Civil War a few years earlier: the Molotov cocktail.[29]

The Germans' April 19 *Aktion* was met with a stronger, better prepared military response by both the ŻOB and the ŻZW, which had made some progress toward coordinating their forces. The Jewish combatants fought with great courage and creativity. Tovia Bozhikowski, a young fighter who survived the war, later recounted the first hours of the uprising:

Our bombs and grenades exploded over their heads as they returned our fire. They were excellent targets in the open square, while we were concealed in the buildings. They left many dead and wounded. The alert, confident attitude of our men was impressive...Liaison officers scurried between positions with messages. The battle went on for two hours. Rivka, an observer, watched the enemy retreat...Zachariash returned beaming from his survey of the battlefield; 40 dead and wounded Germans were left behind, but we suffered no losses. But even in our satisfaction we realized we would eventually be crushed. It was, though, a triumph to gladden the hearts of men who were about to die.[30]

Open warfare persisted until 28 April, and only on 16 May could the German commanding general proclaim success. It is not possible to gain an accurate estimate of German casualties; probably two or three dozen, at a minimum, were killed. Most ŻOB and ŻZW fighters died, and the overwhelming majority of the ghetto's remaining population was either killed or deported to Treblinka or other camps. ŻOB leader Yitzhak Zuckerman remained in Warsaw, hiding in the "Aryan" section, and helped mobilize several hundred Jews to fight with the communist partisans (the *Armia Ludowa*) in the ill-fated nationalist uprising of August–October 1944.

In the ghetto of Vilna, Lithuania, the Jewish Fighting Organization (JFO; sometimes called the United Partisan Organization: *Fareynikte Partizaner Organizatsye*, FPO) formed in early 1942. The JFO succeeded in some acts of sabotage, for example, destroying a German military train carrying armaments to the front.[31] Vilna's *Judenrat* and the JFO were blackmailed into surrendering Yitzhak Wittenberg, the group's founding commander, in a heart-rending drama in July 1943: the Nazis threatened to rain bombs upon the entire ghetto if Wittenberg, who had escaped a German trap and was hiding in the ghetto, was not turned over. Ghetto residents frantically searched for him while the underground and Council leaders agonized over a decision. In the end, the resistance reluctantly voted to hand their leader over.[32]

Largely because of this fateful decision, the JFO was prevented from launching the rebellion it had hoped would at least impede the destruction of the ghetto and its 20,000 inhabitants. Instead, in carefully coordinated actions during September 1943, Abba Kovner, who now commanded the FPO, and most of the fighters slipped out of the ghetto to fight in the forests, where they fought until Lithuania's liberation in July 1944. According to some reports, Kovner led his group—now dubbed "the Avengers"—back into the city on the heels of the Red Army to "engage the Germans in battle and exterminate them by the score."[33] Kovner's group lived up to their name in the early postwar months, hunting down Nazi criminals and, in at least one case, killing SS prisoners being held by the Allies.[34]

The Warsaw and Vilna underground movements give insight into the motivations of Jewish resisters, especially in the later stages of the Holocaust. Jewish resisters were driven by a thirst for revenge; the prospect of striking back at their tormentors; the possibility of escape; and, in many places by 1942, a desperation born of a growing awareness that other options would not spare them. Some Jewish fighters were consciously motivated by the desire to make a statement for posterity, to show the world that the Nazis had to pay a price. For Mordechai Aneliewicz, the fight was an end unto itself: "Jewish self-defense in the Warsaw ghetto has become a fact. Jewish armed resistance and retaliation have become a reality," he wrote from his bunker shortly before his death. "I have witnessed the magnificent heroic struggle of Jewish fighters."[35]

Jewish Councils often conducted activities that fit clearly into *amidah*, such as organizing lectures, theatrical productions, and other cultural events, and establishing soup kitchens.[36] It is also in the ghettos' underground groups that we have more sources to investigate gender dynamics in relation to resistance, a topic that has yet to be fully explored. Women "made up the bulk of couriers in clandestine operations in general and in Jewish resistance groups in particular," observed Nechama Tec.[37] Women could take advantage of Nazi ideology, which held women incapable of aggressive or military action. One courier said, "the Germans had a tendency to pass a smiling young girl....It was simply difficult [for them] to imagine that I was doing what I was doing with the way I looked."[38]

Against all hope: defiance and resistance in the concentration and death camps

In the concentration and death camps, "the Jews were enervated by exhaustion, starvation, and disease and crushed by the most complete totalitarian structure to have been devised by man."[39] Under these extreme circumstances, many Jews and other prisoners lost the physical and psychological ability to persevere, sinking to the level of the so-called *Musselmänner*, the most downtrodden and hopeless prisoners, who were only one "selection" away from death. Others succumbed to the Nazis' divide-and-rule tactics, and rose a few steps above the mass; others survived through luck, organizational skill, connections, solidarity, or other means. "The paths to salvation are many, difficult and improbable," concluded Primo Levi.[40]

Despite these conditions, there were several notable examples of organized resistance. In Sobibor and Treblinka, Jewish prisoners staged armed rebellions in 1943; the following year, the underground organization in Auschwitz blew up a crematorium. Smaller-scale Jewish-led armed revolts erupted in 18 labor camps.[41] In most camps, prisoners undertook other, less visible forms of resistance, holding secret political or religious meetings, swapping information, assisting one another (in defiance of the Nazi goal of fomenting a pitiless struggle of "all against all," as Levi termed it), and organizing escapes.

The Treblinka and Sobibor camps had similarly small numbers of prisoners as well as guards by 1943. Treblinka held only about 850 prisoners at the time of the revolt, while Sobibor housed roughly 500; both camps were policed by about 20–30 SS guards, supported by 80–120 Ukrainians.[42] For this reason, as well as the nearly identical camp layouts, the uprisings in Sobibor and Treblinka followed a similar pattern: Resisters would lure SS officers to locations where they could be quickly and quietly killed; the prisoners would then procure weapons and initiate a mass break-out. The Treblinka uprising occurred on 2 August 1943; after the resistance had killed a few guards and set several buildings ablaze, several hundred prisoners escaped. Perhaps 30 or 40 survived, while the large majority were hunted down and executed.

In Sobibor, Leon Feldhendler, the son of a rabbi in a nearby town, helped start a resistance group in July 1943. Two months later, the Germans made the mistake of shipping several Red Army officers, among other Soviet Jews, to the camp. Among the officers was Alexander Pechersky, who quickly made contact with the underground and lent his military expertise to its planning. On 14 October 1943, they staged the revolt, killing 11 Nazi guards, including the commandant; 200–300 prisoners escaped, and while most of them were killed within a few hours or days, several dozen survived the war.[43]

Some of them, like Pechersky, joined partisan groups after fleeing the camp. For his troubles, Lieutenant Pechersky was imprisoned for 5 years by his own government after the war, a victim of the paranoid and antisemitic atmosphere of Stalin's final years.[44]

In Auschwitz-Birkenau, a resistance group composed of Jews and non-Jews planned an uprising that never took place, but it was the *Sonderkommando* that organized a desperate, ill-fated revolt in October 1944. They succeeded in blowing up a crematorium, and instigated a break-out of several hundred prisoners, but virtually everyone was captured or killed while fleeing.

Jews in the partisan war

Jews served in disproportionately high numbers in the partisan armies that hounded German forces in all corners of the Nazi empire. An estimated 20,000–30,000 Jews fought in Soviet partisan groups, and four-fifths of them perished.[45] Many thousands of other Jews served in armed groups based elsewhere in the forests of eastern Europe; roughly 1,600 members of the Slovakian partisans were Jewish, for example, and Tito's Yugoslav army included about 7,000 Jews.[46] There were about 30 Jewish partisan detachments and some 21 additional non-Jewish partisan groups in which Jews fought.[47] And to the west, perhaps one-sixth of the fighters of the French *Maquis* were Jewish, although Jews constituted less than 1 percent of the country's population.[48]

The Bielski Brothers partisan army, led by Asael, Tuvia, and Zus Bielski, "harried Nazis and saved Jews," as the headline for Zus's 1995 obituary in *The New York Times* stated.[49] Led principally by the charismatic Tuvia, these Belorussian Jewish peasants organized a partisan army that was integrated into a large compound resembling a shtetl in the Naliboki Forest. The Bielskis sent emissaries and scouts to find Jews and bring them to their compound, and they ultimately saved more than 1,000 people, while conducting such effective actions against the occupying forces—killing several hundred German troops and sabotaging transports—that the Nazis placed a bounty of 100,000 Reichmarks on Tuvia's head.[50]

A survey of Jewish anti-Nazi resistance would be incomplete without mention of the 6,000 Jews who fought in the Spanish Civil War, many of them German Jews looking for a new front, after the defeat of the German workers' movement in 1933, on which to fight Nazism and fascism.[51] The outbreak of the Spanish civil war "acted as the clarion call" for many Jews, recalled Arnold Paucker many years later. "This was the beginning of the military response by Jews."[52]

Conclusion

It is only possible here to provide a brief overview of anti-Nazi activities in the ghettos, camps, and forests of German-occupied Europe; a fuller overview would also chronicle resistance in Belgium, France, and elsewhere in western Europe. But this summary should make clear that, whether by organizing hundreds of clandestine religious schools (*yeshivot*) in Poland; arranging secret libraries and archives throughout the ghetto system; raising money to support prisoners' families; producing and distributing prohibited literature; or fighting with guns in hand, European Jewry defied and resisted the Nazis in numerous ways.

And ultimately, history is best served by avoiding a simplistic dichotomy between resistance and submission. It is better, and more accurate, to think in terms of a spectrum of responses and survival strategies, not always distinct from one another: non-conformity, defiance, self-assertion, and *amidah*, as well as resilience and the refusal to submit—that is, simply attempting to continue civilized life under uncivilized conditions.

Notes

1 Indictment of Berkheim and Prager, 23 March 1937, Bundesarchiv Zwischenarchiv Dahlwitz-Hoppegarten (BA Zw), Z-C 4862.
2 Stephan Hermlin, *Die erste Reihe* (Dortmund: Weltkreis-Verlag, 1975), 37–43.
3 Faye Schulman, *A Partisan's Memoir: A Woman of the Holocaust* (Toronto: Second Story Press, 1995), 100.
4 Yuri Suhl, "Little Wanda With the Braids," in *They Fought Back: The Story of the Jewish Resistance in Nazi Europe*, ed. Yuri Suhl (New York: Crown Publishers, 1967), 51–54.
5 Theodore Hamerow, *On the Road to the Wolf's Lair: German Resistance to Hitler* (Cambridge: Belknap Press of Harvard University Press, 1997), 6.
6 Konrad Kwiet, "Problems of Jewish Resistance Historiography," *Leo Baeck Institute Yearbook*, vol. 24 (1979): 41.
7 Detlev Peukert, "Working-Class Resistance: Problems and Options," in *Contending With Hitler: Varieties of German Resistance in the Third Reich*, ed. David Clay Large (Washington, DC: German Historical Institute, 1991), 36–37.
8 Quoted by Michael Marrus, *The Holocaust in History* (New York: Penguin, 1987), 109.
9 Robert Rozett, "Jewish Resistance," in *The Historiography of the Holocaust*, ed. Dan Stone (New York: Palgrave Macmillan, 2004), 341.
10 Rozett, "Jewish Resistance," 346.
11 Yehuda Bauer, *Rethinking the Holocaust* (New Haven, Connecticut: Yale University Press, 2001), 120.
12 Raul Hilberg, *The Politics of Memory: The Journey of a Holocaust Historian* (Chicago: Ivan R. Dee, 2002), 134–35.
13 Quoted by Bauer, *Rethinking the Holocaust*, 166.
14 Nechama Tec, *Resilience and Courage: Women, Men, and the Holocaust* (New Haven: Yale University Press, 2003), 293.
15 Yehuda Bauer, *A History of the Holocaust* (New York: Franklin Watts, 1982), 248.
16 Yitzhak Arad, "Jewish Prisoner Uprisings in the Treblinka and Sobibor Extermination Camps," *The Nazi Holocaust: Jewish Resistance to the Holocaust*, ed. Michael Marrus (Westport, Connecticut: Meckler, 1989), 7: 247–48.
17 Saul Friedländer, *The Years of Extermination: Nazi Germany and the Jews, 1939–1945* (New York: HarperCollins, 2007), 524.
18 Arnold Paucker, Lecture at the US Holocaust Memorial Museum, 11 October 2005.
19 Bauer, *A History of the Holocaust*, 250–51.
20 Eric Sterling, "The Ultimate Sacrifice: The Death of Resistance Hero Yitzhak Wittenberg and the Decline of the United Partisan Organization," in *Resisting the Holocaust*, ed. Ruby Rohrlich (New York: Berg, 1998), 64.
21 James M. Glass, *Jewish Resistance During the Holocaust: Moral Uses of Violence and Will* (New York: Palgrave Macmillan, 2004), 73.
22 See Theodore Hamerow, *On the Road to the Wolf's Lair*, esp. 126–30, 157–62, 294–311, 381–85.
23 BA Zw, Z-C 12460. 22 May 1942, Werner Steinbrinck interrogation record.
24 Arnold Paucker, *German Jews in the Resistance 1933–1945: The Facts and the Problems* (Berlin: Gedenkstätte deutscher Widerstand, 2005), 37.
25 Nechama Tec, *Jewish Resistance: Facts, Omissions, and Distortions* (Washington, DC: Miles Lerman Center for the Study of Jewish Resistance of the US Holocaust Memorial Museum, 2001), 1.
26 Friedländer, *The Years of Extermination*, 522–23.

27 Israel Gutman, *Resistance: The Warsaw Ghetto Uprising* (Boston: Houghton Mifflin, 1994), 241–42.

28 Bauer, *A History of the Holocaust*, 254.

29 Gutman, *Resistance*, 204.

30 Jacob Glatstein, Israel Knox and Samuel Margoshes, eds, *Anthology of Holocaust Literature* (Philadelphia: Jewish Publication Society of America, 1969), 309–10.

31 Sterling, "The Ultimate Sacrifice," 73.

32 Sterling, "The Ultimate Sacrifice," 67.

33 Isaac Kowalski, ed., *Anthology of Armed Jewish Resistance*, Vol. 2, *1939–1945* (Brooklyn: Jewish Commemorative Publishers House, 1985), 62, quoted by Sterling, "The Ultimate Sacrifice," 74.

34 Rich Cohen, *The Avengers* (New York: Knopf, 2000).

35 Gutman, *Resistance*, xx.

36 Tec, *Jewish Resistance*, 7.

37 Tec, *Resilience and Courage*, 264–65.

38 Tec, *Resilience and Courage*, 265.

39 Michael Marrus, *The Holocaust in History* (New York: Penguin, 1989), 147.

40 Primo Levi, *Survival in Auschwitz* (New York: Collier, 1993), 90.

41 Tec, *Jewish Resistance*, 1.

42 Arad, "Jewish Prisoner Uprisings," 241–42.

43 Miles Lerman Center for the Study of Jewish Resistance, *Resistance During the Holocaust* (Washington, DC: US Holocaust Memorial Museum, n.d.), 27.

44 Thomas Blatt, "Excerpts from an interview with Alexander Aronowicz Pechersky," www.sobibor.info/hero.html (accessed 1 January 2010).

45 Rueben Ainsztein, *Jewish Resistance in Nazi-Occupied Eastern Europe* (New York: Barnes & Noble, 1974), 394–95.

46 Amos Goldberg and Yehuda Bauer, "Patterns of Jewish Response and Resistance: Excerpts from Interview with Yehuda Bauer," www1.yadvashem.org/odot_pdf/Microsoft%20Word%20-%203881.pdf (accessed 15 December 2009), 5.

47 Miles Lerman Center, *Resistance During the Holocaust*, 31.

48 Tec, *Jewish Resistance*, 2.

49 Robert Thomas, "Alexander Z. Bielski, a Guerrilla Fighter Who Harried Nazis and Saved Jews, Is Dead," *The New York Times*, 23 August 1995.

50 Nechama Tec, *Defiance: The Bielski Partisans* (New York: Oxford University Press, 1993).

51 See Arno Lustiger, *Shalom Libertad!: Juden im spanischen Bürgerkrieg* (Frankfurt am Main: Athenæum, 1989).

52 Paucker, Lecture at the US Holocaust Memorial Museum, 11 October 2005.

29

"BUT I FORSOOK NOT THY PRECEPTS"
(PS.119:87)

Spiritual resistance to the Holocaust

Stephen Howard Garrin

The Holocaust, or *Shoah*, was an unprecedented tragedy in the long, often cataclysmic history of the Jewish people. In the aftermath of the *Shoah*, the structure of European Jewry, which had comprised the largest concentration of Jews in the world, was profoundly and irrevocably altered. Indeed, the entire face of world Jewry was forever transformed. Religious institutions, languages, and cultures, and long-established communities, were either decimated or relocated. This is not to suggest that pre-World War II European Jewry represented a monolithic religious demographic. There were certainly Jews who had adopted a secular life style and departed, to a greater or lesser degree, from orthodox practices. However, the epicenter of traditional Judaism was located in eastern Europe, with its renowned rabbinic seminaries (*yeshivot*), venerated rabbinic figures, and charismatic Hasidic leaders. After the Holocaust, that world was no more.

The abandonment of faith in many instances was a distinct casualty of the Nazi genocide. Aside from those who had rejected traditional Judaism even before the war, the religious commitment of many victims, who were previously observant, could not withstand the theological challenges engendered by the Holocaust. But the large number of Jews who clung to their religious beliefs, and even intensified their faith, while confined to a universe of depravity and imminent death, or previously unaffiliated Jews who committed themselves during the Holocaust to become observant, and the emergence of an invigorated religious life in the decades following the Holocaust, all merit the attention of historians, theologians, and sociologists.[1]

Esther Farbstein notes that scholarly interest in spiritual resistance to the Holocaust first began in the 1960s. Previously, resistance to the Nazis was examined solely within the framework of armed or physical response.[2] Yet resistance is not only, and perhaps not even primarily, manifest in displays of physical defiance. The human soul is endowed with a spiritual arsenal from which to draw strength and courage in the face of persecution and oppression. In this chapter, I endeavor to show that the struggle to preserve one's faith and core religious beliefs in catastrophic times was an enduring and meaningful victory for survivors. For the purpose of this contribution, spiritual resistance will include representative religious activities in the early phase of the Nazi rise to power, in the ghettos, concentration camps, and the post-war period, by individuals, communities, and organizations. The theological implications of spiritual resistance are also addressed.

The examples of "spiritual resistance" evinced during the Nazi reign are far too numerous to recount in the limited space available. Therefore I have limited myself to a few exemplary cases to support my contention that the retention of spirituality constituted a legitimate and significant form of resistance against the Nazis.[3]

Before the Deluge: *"I am a friend to all who fear You and to those who keep Your precepts"* (Ps. 119:63)

As the Nazi threat became ever more ominous, the Union of Orthodox Rabbis of the United States and Canada formed a relief and rescue committee in November 1939, known as the *Vaad Hatzala*. The purpose of the *Vaad* was initially to aid rabbis and *yeshiva* students who had escaped Poland and settled in Lithuania following the Soviet invasion. Realizing the importance of saving the standard-bearers of normative Judaism and the vital role they played, and would play, in the continuity of the Jewish people, the *Vaad* spared no effort in securing safe havens and educational opportunities for Torah scholars caught in the net of Nazi terror. In 1942, the *Vaad* announced its decision to extend rescue efforts to all Jews regardless of affiliation or status. After the liberation of the Nazi concentration camps, the *Vaad* assumed a major role helping to provide for the spiritual needs of the *she'erit ha peleta*, the saving remnant[4] quartered in displaced persons' camps, and obtaining visas for rabbis and rabbinical students who wished to occupy pulpits and teach in the United States.

While the *Vaad Hatzala* was among the first organizations committed to saving the spiritual leaders of European Jewry, it was not the only one.[5] Other organized groups, as well as outstanding rabbinic and communal leaders, contributed their voices and labors to the rescue effort. However, the myriad anonymous individuals who risked their lives under conditions of extreme privation to remain believing and practicing Jews were, in many ways, the true foot soldiers and heroes on the "spiritual resistance" front.

In the ghetto: *"Had not Your Torah been my preoccupation, I would have perished in my affliction"* (Ps. 119: 92)

In September 1939, after the German army occupied Poland, ghettos were established in order to isolate and concentrate one of the largest Jewish populations in Europe. Ghettos were conceived as self-sustaining entities wherein the occupants would eventually succumb to disease and starvation. The most famous was constructed in Warsaw. In October 1940, the German occupiers set the boundaries for the Warsaw ghetto, which was closed off 1 month later. On the eve of the German invasion, more than 368,000 Jews lived in Warsaw. After the construction of the ghetto, the number increased with the influx of Jews from neighboring areas, who sought the "security" in numbers that a solely Jewish community could offer in perilous times.

The first school year in Warsaw under German occupation began in October 1939. Occupation authorities allowed only elementary and vocational schools to open.[6] Two months later, all Jewish educational facilities were shuttered, despite appeals by the *Judenrat* authorities to rescind the order. Lacking a legitimate educational system, the Jewish community began to operate an underground network of schools. As one chronicler observed: "Jewish children learn in secret. In back rooms, on long benches near a table little schoolchildren sit and learn what it is like to be *Marranos*."[7] Despite the draconian conditions and the official banning of religious instruction, Jewish education flourished,[8] along with organized, albeit clandestine, congregational prayer.[9] At one point, there were 46 elementary religious schools with 132 teachers, and four *Beis Yaakov* academies with a staff of 20 instructors, ostensibly functioning as soup kitchens in order to circumvent the aforementioned restrictions. However, along with the meager food rations the children did receive, 3,000 youngsters were provided spiritual nourishment in the form of Torah studies.[10] There were also a number of *yeshivot* established for teenage boys. In the Warsaw ghetto, a group of young men set up an "underground *yeshiva*" at Nalewki 35, where they studied in makeshift classrooms under the guidance of prominent Talmudic scholars.[11]

A major factor in the successful operation of the underground religious education network was the work of the *Beis Yaakov* graduates in Poland. Prior to World War I, Jewish girls and young women were, for the most part, deprived of the religious educational opportunities their male counterparts enjoyed. Sarah Schenirer, a seamstress living in Cracow, decided to remedy this inequity. In 1917, she founded a school for women and trained them to teach their peers. Schenirer set up similar institutions in cities throughout Europe, which came to be known as the *Beis Yaakov* movement. In the Polish ghettos, these *Beis Yaakov* alumnae employed the pedagogical and inspirational skills they had mastered before the war. As noted above, in 1941 Warsaw, there were at least six *Beis Yaakov* schools. Three of them were under the aegis of Rabbi Yehuda Leib Orlean, the other three were run by Rabbi Eliezer Gershon Friedenson and Rivka Alter-Rappaport. Rabbi Orlean, the driving force in this effort, had assumed the leadership of *Beis Yaakov* in 1930.

Among the prominent rabbinic personalities in the Warsaw ghetto was Rabbi Kalonymus Kalmish Shapira, known as the Piaseczner Rebbe.[12] In the ghetto, the Rebbe compiled a volume of weekly sermons delivered to his students, treating issues of faith in light of the deteriorating conditions. It was published posthumously as *Aish kodesh (The Holy Fire)*.[13] Faith, *emunah*, was the refrain that echoed throughout his ghetto homilies. Speaking on *Shavuot* (Pentecost) in June 1940, the Piaseczner Rebbe expounded upon a verse in the 121st Psalm: "A song of ascents. I lift up my eyes unto the mountains from whence shall my help come? My help cometh from the Lord who made heaven and earth." For the Rebbe and his followers, Divine intervention was axiomatic. The Creator of heaven and earth; the God who brought forth a universe, *ex nihilo*, would without question save His chosen people.[14] Nothing was beyond His power, emphasized the Rebbe. His children had only to preserve their belief. The Rebbe's personal example of unquestioning conviction, evident in his passionate sermons, provided a welcome infusion of hope and faith that lightened the burden of intense suffering for countless victims.

Jewish uprisings in Treblinka and Sobibor in the summer and fall of 1943 led the Germans to fear further insurrections. In response, Waffen-SS units surrounded the Trawnicki labor camp to which the Piaseczner Rebbe and others had been transferred after the destruction of the Warsaw ghetto. All the workers there, including the Rebbe, were shot to death on 3 November 1943.

Warsaw was only one of the numerous cities where the Nazis erected a ghetto, and in which Jews defied the odds to preserve religious life. After the Germans overran Lithuania, two ghettos were built in Vilnius (Vilna) on 24 June 1941. Vilna had a prewar Jewish population of 200,000 and a long and vibrant history of Jewish scholarship, earning it the epithet the "Jerusalem of Lithuania" by Napoleon, who stopped at the entrance of its Great Synagogue in 1815 while retreating from Russia. Among the inmates of the Vilna ghetto was Zelig Hirsch Kalmanowich (1885–1944), a secular Jewish philologist, translator, and historian, a renowned scholar of Yiddish and early director of YIVO.[15] During the Nazi occupation of Vilna, he was forced to work in the YIVO offices under Nazi supervision, sorting through the pillaged YIVO library and selecting volumes to be sent to Germany. Although Kalmanowich had been an assimilated Jew, his experience in the ghetto transformed and inspired him. In a secret diary, Kalmanowich describes a *Simhat Torah* (Festival of the Rejoicing of the Law) celebration he attended on 11 October 1942:

> On *Simhat Torah* eve at the invitation of the rabbi, I went for services in a house that had formerly been a synagogue and was now a music school... I said a few words: 'Our song and dance are a form of worship. Our rejoicing is due to Him who decrees life and death. Here in the midst of this small congregation, in the poor and ruined synagogue, we are united with the whole house of Israel, not only with those who are here today...And you in your rejoicing, atone for the sins of a generation that is perishing. I know that the Jewish people will live...And every day the Holy One, blessed be He, in His mercy gives us a gift which we accept with joy and give thanks to His holy name.'[16]

Sometime thereafter, Kalmanowich was sent to a death camp in Estonia, where he was murdered in 1944. Prior to his martyrdom, Kalmanowich professed his belief in the eternity of the Jewish people:

> For a Jew is part of the sacred triad: Israel, the Torah, and the Holy One, blessed be He. This means the Jewish people, the moral law, and the Creator of the universe. This sacred triad courses through history. It is a reality that has been tested many times...To be sure, history rages now, a war is waged against the Jews, but the war is not against one member of the triad, but against the entire one: Torah and God, against the moral law and the Creator. Can anyone doubt which side is stronger?[17]

Ghetto life revolved around two fundamental Jewish concepts—*Kiddush Ha-Shem*, the sanctification of God's name through martyrdom; and *Kiddush Ha-Chaim*, the sanctification of life.[18] Ever cognizant of their precarious existence and prepared for martyrdom at the hands of the Nazis, the Jews trapped within the ghetto walls nevertheless strove with exceptional zeal to infuse meaning into their lives by defying their victimizers. They practiced the religion of their ancestors, they educated their children in order to guarantee Jewish continuity, and they maintained their moral dignity in a barbaric world as befits the children of Abraham, Isaac, and Jacob. The ghettos, however, were but a station on the road to the crematoria. Notwithstanding the deplorable conditions endured by the ghetto inmates, an unimaginable man-made hell was awaiting them. Even Dante could not have envisioned an inferno to rival the Nazi death camps. Nor could Abraham have faced a more demanding test of faith.

In the camps: *"Though I walk through the valley of death...Thou art with me..."* (Ps. 23:4)

In the third week of January 1942, a meeting was held in an elegant villa on the shore of the Wannsee in a Berlin suburb. The infamous Wannsee Conference was the setting for finalizing the process of genocide that had already begun with the advance of the *Einsatzgruppen* in the east. The plan called for the systematic removal of all Jews in Nazi-occupied Europe, including those already confined in ghettos. While concentration camps had been operating since the mid-1930s, the transformation of the camps into highly technologized death factories began in earnest in 1942. The ultimate phase of the Nazi agenda for the eradication of Jewish life was now set to be implemented.

Leon Szalet, a Polish Jew living in Berlin, had already been taken prisoner by the Gestapo in September 1939 and sent to the Sachsenhausen concentration camp, where he remained until May 1940. The Jewish high holidays arrived shortly after Szalet was interned. In his memoirs, he recalled *Yom Kippur* (the Day of Atonement) in Sachsenhausen:

> The moon shone through the window. Its light was dazzling that night and gave the pale, wasted faces of the prisoners a ghostly appearance. It was as if all the life had ebbed out of them. I shuddered with dread, for it suddenly occurred to me that I was the only living man among corpses. All at once the oppressive silence was broken by a mournful tune. It was the plaintive tones of the ancient *Kol Nidre* prayer. I raised myself up to see whence it came. There, close to the wall, the moonlight caught the uplifted face of an old man, who, in self-forgetful, pious absorption, was singing softly to himself...His prayer brought the ghostly group of seemingly insensible human beings back to life. Little by little, they all roused themselves and all eyes were fixed on the moonlight-flooded face. We sat up very quietly, so as not to disturb the old man, and he did not notice that we were listening. [...] When at last he was silent, there was exaltation among us, an exaltation which men can experience only when they have fallen as low as we had fallen and then, through the mystic power of a deathless prayer, have awakened once more to the world of the spirit.[19]

Szalet, like Kalmanowich, was an acculturated Jew. Born in Poland in 1892, he came to Berlin in 1921, where he became active in the real estate business. While he did not come to embrace orthodox Judaism as Kalmanowich did, his response to the inmate supplicant quietly chanting *Kol Nidre* produced a spiritual awakening in him that made clear the vigor and strength of man's soul, which can transcend even the specter of omnipresent death.

The eleventh-century Spanish-Jewish poet Judah ha-Levi taught that prayer is to the soul what food is to the body. Food for the body was a rare commodity in the concentration camps, but food for the soul could be obtained without recourse to the victimizers, albeit at great risk. In the twentieth century, Viktor Frankl, a Viennese Jewish psychiatrist and Auschwitz survivor, observed that the power of supplication could create a spark of comprehension in an otherwise incomprehensible world. Frankl, a secular Jew, noted that those of his fellow inmates who continued to pray were able to perceive a purpose in their suffering and a teleological plan for this world.[20]

Even in Auschwitz, the spiritual *élan vital* could not be extinguished. Testifying before the trial of Adolf Eichmann in 1961, Rivka Liebeskind recalled her first Friday night in Birkenau. She was crowded, with hundreds of other women, into one of the huts or "blocks" in the camp. Somehow, several girls were able to acquire candles and kindle the Sabbath lights. She reminisced how, "We lit the candles and quietly began singing the songs for the Sabbath. We did not know what was happening around us, but after a few minutes we heard stifled crying from all the shelves around us. First we were frightened, then moved. Then we saw that they could jump from one shelf to another. There were Jewish women who had already been there for years. They gathered around us and listened to our prayer and singing; soon there were those who came off their own shelves and asked to be allowed to bless the candles."[21]

The enduring faith of many camp captives is poignantly illustrated in an episode that took place in the Starachowice camp during the Passover holiday in 1943.[22] Inmates of the camp wished to bake the *matzot* required by biblical law. The commandant of the camp, Bruno Pape, was a sympathetic German who not only allowed the Jews to bake the unleavened bread, but also assisted the inmates to garner enough flour. When Pape entered the Jewish mess hall several days later and saw the Jews eating the *matzot*, he inveighed against them: "*Ihr fromme Dummköpfe!*" [You religious fools!] "*Der liebe Gott hat euch verlassen und ihr seid Ihm immernoch treu!*" [Dear God has abandoned you and you remain true to Him!]. The assembly was understandably shaken by the unexpected rebuke. After a hushed pause a Hasidic Jew, Akiva Goldstoff, who later perished in the Holocaust, rose from his seat and replied: "*Herr Chef, vielleicht haben Sie Recht. Aber das ist nicht Total und nicht auf Ewig!*"[23] [Sir, perhaps you are right. But not totally and not forever!] Goldstoff's rebuttal anticipates the Jewish philosopher Arthur Cohen, who distinguishes between "finality" and "ultimacy" in his theological interpretation of the Holocaust. Had the "Final Solution" succeeded in its aim of total annihilation of Jewry, Cohen maintains, history would, in effect, have reached its conclusion as well (finality). However, "ultimacy," which acknowledges the enormity of the Holocaust, but leaves room for the exercise of human freedom of choice, preserves transcendental control, a "not total and not forever," as it were.[24]

Postwar rebuilding: *"I will walk before the Lord in the land of the living"* (Ps. 116:9)

The prophet Ezekiel speaks of three men, Noah, Daniel, and Job, renowned for their piety, who were saved by their righteousness.[25] Each of the three experienced the destruction of their world: Noah by the Flood, Daniel through the destruction of the Temple and the state, and Job through the loss of his family. While each of them saw their world disappear, they lived to witness its revival. Death followed by rebirth, destruction succeeded by rebuilding, the darkest night giving way to the breaking dawn, might serve as a mantra for Jewish history in general, and the Holocaust in particular.

When the war ended in 1945, a blood-soaked, alien, and defiled European landscape greeted the survivors. Jews who could not, or would not, return to their former homes were often placed in Displaced Persons' (DP) camps established by the Allies in the occupied zones of Germany, Austria, and Italy. The first DP camp set up solely for Jewish survivors was Feldafing, after an American Chaplain, Abraham Klausner, prevailed upon the commandant of Feldafing to relocate the non-Jewish DPs. Subsequently, educational and religious life flourished there. A *Talmud Torah* (religious elementary school) as well as a *yeshiva* and a number of seminaries were established in the camp.

Föhrenwald was one of the largest DP camps in post-World War II Europe, located some 15 miles from Munich. In June 1945, the camp was appropriated by the US Army for homeless international refugees. Under the spiritual leadership of Rabbi Yehuda Yekutiel Halberstam, known as the Klausenberger Rebbe, Föhrenwald became a center for renewed Jewish and Hasidic life in the American zone of occupation. The Rebbe established a *yeshiva* there and provided for the various religious needs of his followers, as well as for Jewish DPs throughout the occupied zone. The Rebbe himself had survived the indignities of the ghetto and the horrors of the *Lager*. He lost his wife and all 11 children, but he never lost his abiding faith or his love and concern for his fellow Jews. The Rebbe visited other camps by jeep, sometimes traveling all night, in order to teach, encourage, and provide for the Jewish residents. Any place where there were Jewish survivors, the Rebbe was prepared to travel and aid in the long road to physical, psychological, and spiritual healing.

As in Föhrenwald and Feldafing, *yeshivot*, *mikvaot* (ritual baths), kosher provisions, and religious books were provided for in other DP camps thanks to the tireless efforts of rabbinic leaders and American military chaplains. These individuals were crucial in the reconstruction of a semblance of prewar Jewish life in many DP camps, including Zeilsheim, Krumbach-Leipheim, Wetzlar, and Landsberg, where in 1924 Hitler wrote his hate-filled manifesto *Mein Kampf*.

A report released by the American Joint Distribution Committee[26] in 1947 recounts the eagerness with which survivors sought to rebuild the spiritual structure of their shattered lives.[27] In that dispatch, the myriad religious needs of the DPs in the US Zone of occupation were enumerated—prayer books, prayer shawls, facilities in which to conduct religious services, and ritual baths. Religious movements such as *Agudath Israel* and *Mizrachi* were reorganized by the few surviving European rabbis, and communication with the related organizations in America and Europe was re-established. When the Central Committee was formally constituted in January 1946, a rabbi was appointed chief of the religious council, and an attempt was made to organize religious activities throughout the zone. The director of religious activities within the AJDC assisted in the promotion of these activities, conferred with United Nations Relief and Rehabilitation Administration and military officials concerning special religious needs, and in July 1946, established a special bureau in order to consolidate the program of the Rabbinical Assembly of the Central Committee and enhance religious life in the zone.

In a report prepared by Rabbi Alexander Rosenberg, the Religious Director of the AJDC for the US Zone, for the period July/August 1946, he remarked how the influx of displaced persons in newly established camps and "the change of hearts of many former residents" had greatly increased the demand for kosher provisions and necessitated the creation of new kosher slaughter-houses.[28] As the DPs recovered physically, requests for religious articles increased apace. Providing prayer books, phylacteries, and facilities for communal prayer became a major activity of the army chaplains. US Army chaplains were also actively involved in rescuing religious books that the Germans had put in large warehouses, distributing the books to survivors, and to Jewish centers around the world.

The German Jewish poet Heinrich Heine wrote: "There where they burn books, in the end they will also burn people." On 10 May 1933, Nazi officials burned books they deemed "un-German" or "degenerate." Among them were Jewish religious tomes and volumes authored by Jewish writers and anti-fascist figures. In the course of the Third Reich, it has been estimated that hundreds of thousands of holy books were destroyed, some by fire, others ripped to shreds, and many shipped off or warehoused for some future museum chronicling a soon-to-be extinct race. Among the volumes were priceless rarities and entire libraries. And foremost amongst the desecrated holy books was the Talmud.

Throughout modern European history, the Talmud had been maligned and burned in public. Monarchs, popes, and ordinary people from the thirteenth century onwards have chosen the Talmud, the compendium of Jewish law, philosophy, and morals, to vilify the Jews and their religious beliefs. The fiercely antisemitic Nazi journal *Der Stürmer* repeatedly attacked the rabbis and Talmudic scholars, referring to them as *Talmud Juden*, a derogatory epithet originating in Christian Europe. For the Nazis, the Talmud and its students epitomized the moral and ethical values they abhorred.

When the Joint, in cooperation with the US Army of Occupation, took over the evacuation of the DP camps in 1945, they found there were children among the inmates who had never seen a book, and adults who desperately wished to once again hold a book in their hands. The AJDC realized the necessity of filling this void by publishing basic religious texts for use in the camps. Also, the newly established *yeshivot* in the DP camps required sets of the Talmud. It was a pressing need that the Joint set out to satisfy. In 1946, Rabbi Samuel A. Snieg, a Dachau survivor serving in the US Zone in Germany, proposed printing the Talmud in Germany, and in 1947 plans for the project were drawn up by the AJDC. Working in close cooperation with the Civil Affairs Division of the US Military Government, the Joint provided two sets of the Talmud to serve as a template for printing the basic text. Then they set out to procure paper, ink, and other printing supplies necessary for its production. A German plant in Heidelberg, requisitioned by the Military Government, handled the printing.[29] On 13 May 1949, in the Berlin headquarters of the US Army, Rabbi Samuel Rose presented General Lucius Clay, Commander of the US forces in occupied Germany, with the first copy of the Talmud published in Germany. Rabbi Rose, in a moving ceremony, expressed his gratitude to General Clay and the US Military, saying: "I bless your hand in presenting to you this volume embodying the highest spiritual wisdom of our people."

The sense of profound gratitude to the US Army and the exceptional message embedded in the "Army Talmud" or "Survivors' Talmud" are clear from the words of dedication:

> This edition of the Talmud is dedicated to the United States Army. This Army played a major role in the rescue of the Jewish people from total annihilation, and after the defeat of Hitler bore the major burden of sustaining the DPs of the Jewish faith. This special edition of the Talmud published in the very land where, but a short time ago, everything Jewish and of Jewish inspiration was an anathema, will remain a symbol of the indestructibility of the Torah. The Jewish DPs will never forget the generous impulse and the unprecedented humanitarianism of the American forces, to whom they owe so much.

"The scoffers have held me greatly in derision, but I have not departed ... from your Torah" (Ps. 119:51)

The philosopher Hans Jonas, in an essay titled "The Concept of God after Auschwitz," maintains that there are two possible theological responses to the Holocaust. He writes:

After Auschwitz, that is to say, after the Holocaust for whose widely dispersed reality that single name serves as a blindingly concentrating lens, the Jew can no longer simply hold on to the time honored theology of his faith that has been shattered by it. Nor, if he wills Judaism to continue, can he simply discard his theological heritage and be left with nothing. "Auschwitz" marks a divide between a "before" and an "after," where the latter will be forever different from the former.[30]

For Jonas, the *Shoah* produced a dichotomy: a before and after, an either/or, a violent and irreparable rupture with the past. This response to the Holocaust is echoed in the theological discourse of a number of post-Holocaust theologians and philosophers, Jewish and Christian alike.[31]

To be sure, the *Shoah* presented a challenge to all believers unparalleled in the annals of universal or Jewish history. However, to reconfigure a 2,000 year heritage of faith and survival into a vision of two lone sentries standing guard on opposite sides of a spiritual abyss denigrates Judaism and its followers, and belies reality. If one considers the innumerable examples of spiritual endurance during the Holocaust, of which a minuscule sample has been given here, and the postwar blossoming of traditional Jewish life, one perceives a continuum—a catenate transmission of an ancient religion and sanctified writings—not a theological breach or a spiritual disconnect.

At the outset, I summarized the efforts of the *Vaad Hatzala* to save the rabbis and *yeshiva* students who were threatened by the Nazi juggernaut. While at the time there was criticism in some quarters for its alleged narrow focus, the importance of the *Vaad*'s attempts to save rabbinic figures and Talmudic scholars is fully justified in view of a stunning and revealing directive from I.A. Eckhardt, High Commander of the German Occupation Forces in Poland. The dispatch, dated 23 November 1940, instructs the authorities in the General Government to bar the emigration of eastern European Jews. The objective was to preclude the possibility of a permanent and revitalized religious world Jewry. The document reads, in pertinent part:

> The continued emigration of Jews from eastern Europe spells a continued spiritual regeneration of world Jewry, as it is mainly the eastern Jews who supply a large portion of the rabbis and Talmud teachers, etc. owing to their orthodox-religious beliefs. And they are urgently needed by Jewish organizations active in the United States. Further, every orthodox Jew spells a valuable addition for these Jewish organizations in the United States, in their constant efforts for the spiritual renewal of United States Jewry and its unification.[32]

The Nazi ideologues understood fully that an attempt at physical extermination of the Jewish people would not suffice to annihilate the Jewish faith. Only by forever silencing Judaism's spiritual trustees—the rabbis, scholars, and men of faith—could they guarantee a "Final Solution." Conversely, the spiritual resistance manifest during the Holocaust and the subsequent years of personal and communal rebuilding scored a direct and fatal blow at the very heart of the Nazi agenda. Indeed, as the German novelist Thomas Mann wrote, "Deep is the well of the past. Should one not say, bottomless?"[33] From the cavernous cisterns of Jewish faith, Holocaust victims were able to quench their spiritual thirst during the *Shoah* and irrigate the fertile fields of faith-based regeneration in the years that followed.

Notes

1 Hillel Zeitlin, journalist, writer, and philosopher, in response to a questionnaire from Lucy S. Dawidowicz, opined that "Characteristic is the rebellion against God, against Heaven, which is noticeable among many religious Jews who no longer wish to declare God's Judgment right." A communal leader in the ghetto, however, suggested another reaction: "The truly pious have become even more pious, for they understand and see God's Hand in everything." See Lucy S. Dawidowicz, *The War Against the Jews, 1933–1945* (New York: Holt, Rinehart and Winston, 1975), 249.

2 Esther Farbstein, *Hidden in Thunder: Perspectives on Faith, Halachah and Leadership During the Holocaust* (Jerusalem: Mossad Harav Kook, 2007). Farbstein's monograph provides an exhaustive catalogue of spiritual resistance. See also Simcha Bunem Unsdorfer, *The Yellow Star* (New York: Thomas Yoseloff, 1961).

3 That is not to suggest that physical or armed resistance was rejected by Orthodox Jews or rabbinic authorities. Rabbi Leiner, the Radziner Rebbe, for one, attempted to organize his followers to join the partisans in their fight against the Germans.

4 *She'erit ha peleta* refers to the survivors of the Holocaust. The term is taken from Jeremiah, 44:14: "There will be no fugitive or survivor from the remnant of Judah."

5 In 1938, Rabbi Dr Solomon Schonfeld, Director of the Chief Rabbi's Religious Emergency Council (UK), undertook the rescue of thousands of Jews from Nazi forces. His efforts included saving rabbinic figures as well as other Jews, and providing religious education and other religious needs of these refugees.

6 See Susan M. Kardos, "'Not Bread Alone': Clandestine Schooling in the Warsaw Ghetto during the Holocaust," *Harvard Educational Review*, vol. 72 (Spring 2002): 33–66. (Kardos examines secular and cultural schools.)

7 Chaim Kaplan, *Scroll of Agony: The Warsaw Diary of Chaim A. Kaplan*, trans. and ed. Abraham I. Katsh (Bloomington: Indiana University Press, 1999), 129.

8 Various religious tomes were published in the ghetto, and religious books were even bought and sold on the street. See Joseph Friedenson, "Of Spiritual Heroes and Compassionate Leaders," in *The Jewish Observer*, vol. XLII, No. 2 (March, 2009): 42–47.

9 Emanuel Ringeblum estimates that there were 600 illegal *minyanim*, groups of Jews praying together throughout this period, in Warsaw alone.

10 The "Patronate," a committee under the direction of Meshulam Kaminer, assisted ghetto inmates who dedicated themselves to Torah study. See also Friedenson, "Of Spiritual Heroes."

11 Joseph Rudavsky, *To Live With Hope, To Die With Dignity: Spiritual Resistance in the Ghettos and Camps* (Northvale, New Jersey: Jason Aronson, 1997), 71.

12 Other Hasidic leaders in the Warsaw ghetto included the Alexander Rebbe, the Sochatchover Rebbe, the Radomsker Rebbe, the Krimilover Rebbe, and the Strickover Rebbe.

13 Kalonymus Kalman Shapiro, *Aish Kodesh: With a Biographical Sketch by Aharon Suraski* (Jerusalem, 1960).

14 Shapiro, *Aish Kodesh*, 52

15 YIVO was founded in 1925 in Vilnius, Lithuania as the Yiddish Scientific Institute (*Yidisher Visnshaftlekher Institut*). It is dedicated to the history and culture of Ashkenazi Jewry.

16 Zelig Hirsch Kalmanowich, "A togbuch fun Vilner Ghetto" ["A Diary of the Vilna Ghetto,"] in *A Holocaust Reader*, ed. Lucy S. Dawidowicz (New York: Behrman House, 1976), 225.

17 Kalmanowich, "A togbuch fun Vilner Ghetto," 232.

18 Rudavsky, *To Live With Hope*, 15.

19 Leon Szalet, *Experiment "E,"* trans. Catherine Bland Williams (New York: Didier, 1945), 70–71.

20 Viktor Frankel, *Man's Search for Meaning* (New York: Simon & Schuster, 1984), 54.

21 Testimony of Rivka Cooper Liebeskind, Eichmann Trial, 3 May 1961, Session 26, as cited in Martin Gilbert, *The Holocaust* (New York: Holt, Rinehart and Winston, 1985), 521.

22 Joseph Friedenson, "Nokh di zibetzik yohr un vos ikh gedenk mit a dopelt zikorn," in *Dos yidishe vort*, Summer 2009, 27. Pape: "You religious fools! Dear God has abandoned you and you remain true to Him." Goldstoff: "Not totally. And not forever."

23 Friedenson, "Nokh di zibetzik."

24 Arthur Cohen, *Tremendum: A Theological Interpretation of the Holocaust* (New York: Crossroads, 1981).

25 Ezekiel,14:14.

26 The American Joint Distribution Committee (the "Joint" or AJDC) was established in 1914 to aid the Jewish communities in eastern Europe and the middle east. Subsequently the Joint has been involved in preserving and fostering Jewish communal life wherever it is threatened.

27 Report N. 391, Joint Distribution Committee (JDC) 1/13/47.

28 Report N. 391, Joint Distribution Committee (JDC) 1/13/47.

29 See Alex Grobman, "The U.S. Army and the Talmud," in *Battling for Souls* (Jersey City: Ktav, n.d.), 187–205; Gerd Korman, "Survivors' Talmud and the U.S. Army," in *American Jewish History*, vol. 30 (1984): 262.

30 Hans Jonas, "The Concept of God after Auschwitz: A Jewish Voice," in *Echoes from the Holocaust: Philosophical Reflections on a Dark Time*, eds Alan Rosenberg and Gerald E. Myers (Philadelphia: Temple University Press, 1988), 292–305.

31 See Richard L. Rubinstein, *After Auschwitz: Radical Theology and Contemporary Judaism* (Princeton, New Jersey: Princeton University Press, 1996). Rubinstein contends that after the Holocaust, a belief in the covenanted God is impossible.

32 Yitzhak Arad, Yisrael Gutman and Abraham Margoliot, *Documents on the Holocaust: Selected Sources on the Destruction of the Jews of German and Austria, Poland, and the Soviet Union* (Jerusalem: Yad Vashem, 1981), 219.

33 "Tief ist der Brunnen der Vergangenheit: Sollte man ihn nicht unergründlich nennen," in Thomas Mann, *Joseph und seine Brueder* (Stockholm: S. Fischer Verlag, 1952), 9.

30

THE CHURCH, THEOLOGY, AND THE HOLOCAUST

Franklin Hamlin Littell and Marcia Sachs Littell

The cornerstone of antisemitism is the superseding or displacement myth. This is the myth that the mission of the Jewish people was finished with the coming of Jesus, that "the old Israel" was written off in favor of the "new Israel." The superseding myth has two foci: 1.) God is finished with the Jews; 2.) the "new Israel" (the Christian church) takes the place of the Jewish people as a carrier of history. The third step culminates when the Gentile tribes go over into apostasy to expunge the Jewish component altogether. To teach that a people's mission in God's providence is finished, that they have been relegated to the limbo of history, has murderous implications which murderers in time did spell out. The murder of six million Jews by baptized Christians, from whom church membership in good standing was not (and has not yet been) withdrawn, raises the most insistent question about the credibility of Christianity.[1]

Since the emergence of the Gentile church, and especially in the millennium and a half between Constantine the Great and the Enlightenment, antisemitism in Christendom has been expressed in three levels of thought, speech, and action. The three levels of antisemitism to which we refer are 1.) the theological, 2.) the cultural, and 3.) the political. At the time of the Gentile church fathers, theological antisemitism was already an ideology. In its political form we see antisemitism used as an ideological weapon—first to conquer men's (and women's) minds, and finally to shape their souls (i.e. to determine the patterns of the millennium to come).

Advocates of religious liberty have long held that when Christians ceased to be a non-resistant and persecuted remnant and became prosperous persecutors, the nature of Christianity was fundamentally altered. Often a "Fall of the church" has been dated by the union of church and state under Emperor Constantine, or perhaps by the enforcement of approved doctrine under the same Augustus. The teaching and style of life of early Christianity and the way of Christendom was accompanied by drastic decrees passed in the synods and councils against the Jews. The Nazi war against the Jews exposed and built on this endemic antisemitism which had been a malaise of Christendom for centuries.

In theological terms, Nazism was the true, if illegitimate, offspring of a false relationship between the Christian church and the ethnic bloc or nation (*Volk*). When ethnic history is infused with "spirituality," and a political program is mounted on disciplined cadres to return a people to a mythical monism of the past, a frontal challenge emerges to the "True Church," on pilgrimage and supranational grounds. It was to the great credit of the Confessing Church in Germany (the *Bekennende Kirche*) that its members confronted this challenge. Still, the Christian church as a whole has much for which to account. Karl Barth put it directly:

> National Socialism, according to its own revelation of what it is—a self-revelation to which it has devoted all the time and chance till now allowed—is as well without any doubt something quite different from a political experiment. It is, namely, a *religious institution of salvation*.[2]

The men of the Barmen Synod who presented the Memorandum of May 1936 to the *Führer* rightly identified the offense to the "True Church":

> When blood, race, nationality, and honour are regarded as eternal values, the first commandment obliges the Christian to refuse this evaluation. When the Aryan is glorified, the Word of God teaches that all men are sinful. If the Christian is faced by the Anti-Semitism of the Nazi *Weltanschauung* to hate the Jews, he is, on the contrary, bidden by the Christian Commandment to love his neighbor.[3]

Dietrich Bonhoeffer, martyred as the war was ending, drew one concrete conclusion, but a conclusion on which there is still little guidance in Christian theological literature:

> If we claim to be Christians there is no room for expediency. Hitler is the Anti-Christ. Therefore we must go on with our work and eliminate him whether he is successful or not.[4]

The problem of discerning and defining the Christian obligation and style to resist illegitimate authority, not to mention illegitimate action by legitimate authority, remains one of the most excruciating agonies of Christians today. The word "Anti-Christ" is the clue; for the Anti-Christ is not the honest and open adversary, but the one who was once numbered within and has now gone over to the opposition. The misery of those involved in the "Church Struggle," or *Kirchenkampf*, is not in the first place battle with an open opposition; it is the apostasy of the baptized, the convulsion of Christendom.

Before the Church Struggle with Nazism, the Christian corpus gave very little guidance on the matter of resistance. Representative government, in which each citizen shares the responsibility (and on occasion the guilt) for policies implemented by heads of state, is too new a thing in human history for any large body of interpretation to have emerged. But the experiences of the Third Reich remind us that not just absolute monarchs who rule by divine right must be warned and confronted on occasion, but perhaps especially those governments which claim to have substantial, if sometimes "silent," majorities acquiescing in their actions. In a police-state, without free access or egress, the moral burden of national wrong-doing is certainly no greater than in a society which still has some room for organizing public opinion and pressure.

For those who believe in repudiation of "religion-in-general" and "spirituality" without content or integrity, but are not prepared to accept the Christian theological formulation, let me state it this way: we are so situated in our various national and racial contexts, that we cannot in fact love humanity without loving concrete, earthy, historic persons and groups. Under pressure we shall love that Israel whose prophets and seers point us toward a day of universal justice and righteousness, mercy and peace. Hatred of the Jews is often the first seismographic reading of the covert emergence of a false particularism, and we must learn to recognize it as such.

Precisely for this reason, we bring together the Church Struggle and the Holocaust. For Christians, and not just for the Jewish people, the Holocaust is the most important event in recent church history. For working theologians, it has called into question the whole fabric of Christendom, indeed the very language of traditional religion, just as among youth and students it has rendered the churches uncredible. For scholars of other disciplines and vernaculars, political antisemitism is a code to identify the totalitarian ideologies and systems which are the curse of our time.

Reference was made to the false "spirituality" which was so strong in the Third Reich, and against which the men of Barmen and the Confessing Church made their particular stand. In practical terms, the interchangeability of this base core of devotion was recognized by Hitler himself. He told Rauschning on one occasion:

> There is more that binds us to Bolshevism than separates us from it...I have always made allowance for this circumstance and have given orders that former Communists be admitted to the Party at once.[5]

In theological terms, it is this interchangeability which gives special pathos to the irresponsibility of the German intellectuals. For while the common folk were left to the credulity and quick switch of the "true believer," the liberal academics had been very largely rendered incapable of *any* unqualified loyalties, especially to institutional religion. Yet in the end they proved as unable to stand against the claims of the *Volksgemeinschaft* as the most unlettered farmer or laborer. Looking on from the balcony, the men of the universities and professions were quite able to perceive the naive and faulty character of unquestioned obedience to any party or group. But again, when the day of reckoning came they were without moorings to withstand the overpowering demands of the ideological one-party state. As Albert Einstein noted in a famous statement, resistance came not from the universities, but primarily from simple Christian laymen and their pastors. The people of the congregations who remained faithful, and the pastors who held true to the covenant, were living at a level of trust which men who lived from the Fall, from *Techne*, could neither understand nor identify with.

A "spirituality" which has no relation to a known tradition, a "religious moment" which involves no loyalties to a known alternative, is what contemporary political gnosticism offers us. But the gnosticism, the closed system of secret knowledge, of the twentieth century carries political force not noted in the Gnostic heresies which tormented the Early Church.[6] "Faith" which is divorced from Judaism or Christianity, the "faith in faith" of which Will Herberg wrote in his classic review of the American Religion—*Protestant/Catholic/Jew* (1955), in our day sooner or later finds a political channel.

Let our view of the future then, and it is precisely the hope of things to come which gives history its meaning and shape, be governed by a clear vision. As Moltmann has written in his *Theology of Hope*, in criticism of the vague perspectives which mar the contemporary neoliberalism, the transposed eschatology of the Greek *moment*, the *Nun* of existentialism, is far different from the *promise* given Israel:

It is one thing to ask: where and when does an epiphany of the divine, eternal, immutable and primordial take place in the realm of the human, temporal and transient? And it is another thing to ask: when and where does the God of the promise reveal his faithfulness and in it himself and his presence?[7]

We are thrust back upon the essential Jewishness of our *Heilsgeschichte*, in spite of all awareness of the dangers of a linear view of history, pointed out by contextual ethicists and illuminated by linguistic analysis. The irony of our recent decades as men of education is severe: those who have found the particularity of "Jewish folklore and fable" too confining, too earthy, too finite, have ended in the pitiful vulgarisms of Teutonic or Anglo-Saxon or other Gentile ethnicity.

Gandhi was once asked to state his greatest grief, and he answered, "the hardness of heart of the educated." It may be that Søren Kierkegaard's iconoclastic word can fix the point: "...the greater a man's equipment of knowledge and culture, the more difficult it is for him to become a Christian";[8] anyway, for the purposes of this discussion, the harder it is for him to accept involvement or commitment. Romain Rolland telegraphed an international congress of philosophers just before the opening of World War I: "Think as men of action. Act as men of thought." This has not been the record: in the face of one totalitarian threat after another the men of the universities have copped out. Kierkegaard's presentation of "the Professor" certainly remains the most perceptive exposure of that permanent tentativeness, that spectator's stance, wherein the confusion of the scientific objectivity of accurate reporting and the moral objectivity of the irresponsible has reduced technical progress to frivolity and self-destruction. The professor, if he could have seen the crucifixion, would have asked if possible to have it repeated, that he could be sure to have an accurate report of all the details.

Bonhoeffer, of course, knew the academic world well. And he knew the terrible prejudice against involvement (*Engagement*) in conflict, especially "political" conflict. Many of the opponents of the *Gleichschaltung* of the universities, and of the *Dozentenführer* installed by the Party, took the conservative ground: the university, as a reservation for objective scholarship and research, must be kept free of turmoil and conflict. The conservatives of the German universities scorned the vulgarization of the Nazi effect, which dishonored the classical standards that had made the German universities and scholarship the center of the literate world. What a difficult decision it was for Dietrich Bonhoeffer, who knew and loved the academy, and could have survived the war in a theological faculty in America, to decide to go back home. Morally, it meant to reaffirm involvement in that most ambiguous of civil acts: tyrannicide. Professionally, it meant to abandon forever any chance of enjoying the academic preserve of "objectivity," of non-complicity. The decision to oppose Nazism was long since made: the decision to cut off the world of liberal scholarship, and those who defend its aloofness with such feline passion, was the last and hardest step.

In discussing the lessons of the Church Struggle and the Holocaust for the man of the university, we are not only speaking, of course, of university-trained mechanics/technicians with university degrees who were as empty of humane education as the bookkeeper at Dachau or the plumber at Bergen-Belsen, and just as ready to follow orders. We are referring to university men of humanistic training. The truth is, and this is the tragedy of the intellectuals in many places during the century of the Holocaust, that the academics have proven ineffectual in the face of totalitarian thrusts for power and shatteringly confused in the face of the most inhumane of all modern irrationalities: hatred of the Jews. In her study of the university professors in Weimar Germany, 1925–33, Alice Gallin likens the university professors in Weimar Germany to midwives. They paved the way for Nazism, assisting in its birth at the crucial moment with no responsibility for how it turned out.[9]

Looking back on the Church Struggle, in which he played such an important fraternal part, Josef L. Hromadka once wrote:

> The Liberal theology in Germany and in her orbit utterly failed. It was willing to compromise on the essential points of divine law and of "the law of nature"; to dispose of the Old Testament and to accept the law of the Nordic race instead; and to replace the "Jewish" law of the Old Testament by the autonomous law of each race and nation respectively. It had made all the necessary preparation for the "Germanization of Christianity" and for a racial Church.[10]

Nor is the problem yet resolved in German Protestantism, in spite of the testimony of the Confessing Church. As Samuel Sandmel pointed out in a critical essay on Rudolf Bultmann's treatment of Judaism, the danger point remains exposed. In contrast to the Early Church, where, except for Marcion, Jesus and His message were understood to be a continuation of Judaism, Professor Bultmann presses Judaism into the cramped mold of a distorted view of the Law: he describes "a Judaism that never existed so that he can set a special view of Jesus over against it."[11] The parallel to Arnold Toynbee's rejection of the Jews as a "semitic fossil" is striking.[12] Both reveal the covert antisemitism of liberal culture–religion. And the references explain why they and their colleagues and followers instinctively respond in opposition to the current manifestations of religious and cultural renaissance in world Jewry.

The lessons to be learned from the Church Struggle and the Holocaust have hardly penetrated the Protestant seminaries, the liberal Protestant press, the church literature, or the thinking and writing of even the majority of our ablest older theologians. Rather than embracing these lessons, "objectivity" has led to a rejection of overt involvement in this earthly conflict and the debate which attends it; "humanity" has become the enemy of any avowed concrete attachments.

A general religious and ethical framework has led to rejection of any special holy history, especially any that has to do with the Jews. In consequence, when push comes to shove, the covert cultural antisemitism (*Kulturantisemitismus*) erupts into implied charges that behind the theological study of a group of troubled theologians must lie a sinister Zionist influence.

The German Christians (*Deutsche Christen*)

American liberal Protestantism can be summarized by saying that it stands solidly on the ground but lately vacated by the *Deutsche Christen*. The inevitable result of such academic aloofness and doctrinal uncertainty in the German universities and churches was the fatal weakening of the two centers which might have been the chief barriers to the Nazi system. More than that, they predictably produced a generation which came to power amiably inclined toward "spirituality" and "religion-in-general" but ill-informed as to the particular claims of the Christian faith.

Although there were in fact great differences of opinion among the Nazi leaders concerning the church, the result of the Party's emphasis was that an increasing number of members left the churches and registered themselves as "believers" without affiliation (*gottgläubig*). The leaders who were not hostile appear to have been poorly informed as to Christian doctrine. Many displayed that emancipation toward historic community and confession of faith which Article 24 of the National Socialist Workers' Party (*Nationalsozialistische Deutsche Arbeiterpartei*) Platform encouraged: "The party as such represents the point of view of a positive Christianity without binding itself to any particular confession. It fights the spirit of Jewish materialism...." Goering's statement during the trial at Nürnberg seems to have been typical:

> I myself am not what you might call a churchgoer, but I have gone now and then, and have always considered I belonged to the Church and have always had those functions over which the Church presides – marriage, christening, burial, *et cetera* – carried out in my house by the Church.[13]

This is about as clear a statement based on culture–religion as one is likely to find: it implies the privatization of religion, and leaves no doubt as to basic loyalty should conflict arise between state and church.

The most complete formulation of a Christianity which accommodated doctrinally was made by the *Deutsche Christen*, and the best written statement of that position would seem to be Cajus Fabricius's *Positive Christianity in the Third Reich* (1937). Basing his rejection of any objective "Semitic" basis or unassimilatable dogmatic formulae upon the nineteenth-century liberal tradition of experiential and non-dogmatic religion, Fabricius set out to define the new religion of Germany "in accordance with the basic principles of National Socialism." He is sure that Christianity and National Socialism have the same basic principles because they both have "grown and become as one with the spirit of the German nation throughout the history of centuries." "The living religion of the *Volk* cannot be confined within a narrow scheme..."[14] Such a "narrow scheme" would be a historical or doctrinal definition which challenged the mystical base of the *Volksgemeinschaft*—an entity which Hitler said would be the Nazis' greatest contribution.

The men of the Christian resistance did not view holy history or doctrine so light-heartedly, although they did not always speak as bluntly as Hermann Sasse:

> The Evangelical Church has to start every discussion with the avowal that its doctrine is a permanent affront to the morality and ethical feeling of the German race.[15]

Nevertheless, they spoke plainly enough to be accused constantly of "meddling in politics," to be charged with "fundamentalism" for asserting doctrines not negotiable, and to be answered by a swarm of pamphlets like the neo-Lutheran "Ansbach Counsel" (of 11 June 1934) which affirmed a general revelation made manifest in the nation and its divinely appointed *Führer*.

One is inevitably reminded of the ecstatic affirmation of "non-sectarian religion" to be found in Robert Welch's *The Blue Book*:

I believe there is a broader and more encompassing faith to which we can all subscribe....And I believe it is an ennobling conception, equally acceptable to the most Fundamentalist Christian or the most rationalist idealist, because its whole purpose is to strengthen and synthesize the ennobling characteristics of each man and the ennobling impulses of his own personal religion. It is hard for man to realize that the Infinite still remains infinite, untouched in its remoteness and unreduced in its infinity by man's most ambitious approaches or that all of man's increasing knowledge leaves the Unknowable just as completely unknowable as before. But I think that, being allowed now to grasp this truth, we should cease to quarrel and disagree over how close we are to God. For we are using a term which, in a literal context, or objectively, has no meaning.[16]

This is, from a Biblical point of view, the language of atheism. From the point of view of fascists, it avoids the reproach of outright atheism by appearing tolerant and *gottgläubig*.

The *Deutsche Christen* were at least logical enough to press the religion of the ethnic base, infused with "spirituality," through to its logical conclusion: Antisemitism. In their 1932 platform, they appealed to all Christians "of German type" and affirmed "heroic piety." Repudiating all confessional parties, they cited the experience of German foreign missions which "have for a long time called to the German nation: 'Keep yourself racially pure.'" They then went on to condemn association with Jews, especially inter-marriage, and even missions to the Jews—"the entryway for foreign blood into our national body."[17]

We are returned to the original issue: the relationship of the *Kirchenkampf* and the Holocaust. When an effort is made to cut Christianity from its essentially Semitic base, when an artificial effort is made to re-establish the myth of Christendom, when the culture–religion of a Gentile race or nation becomes infused with spirituality and historic destiny, we are face to face with the Adversary. Those who attempt to domesticate the church, to make it in corrupted form a mere creature of the state, were of necessity compelled to do two things of grave theological import. For one thing, they were driven to oppose international contacts, to close off all communication with the Ecumene. The importance of the Church Struggle and the universal Christian fellowship to each other is an extensive theme, treated on another occasion.[18] Martin Bormann's model program for the "final solution to the church problem," subsequently published and ably analyzed in the German *Kommission*'s volume on the Warthegau,[19] gives further evidence on how important Bormann, the ablest and most implacable of Christianity's enemies in the Nazi inner circle, thought cutting off contacts with the world Christian fellowship to be. On the second matter, the "final solution to the Jewish problem," the church, even the hard core of the Confessing Church, did less well; and the elimination of European Jewry is the one plank of Hitler's platform which he could count a major success.

In the final paroxyms of "Christendom," as anxious powers strive to resist the process of secularization and the pattern of pluralism which modernity has thrust upon it, Jews and Christians of the pilgrim church have alike been sacrificed to bad politics and low-grade Gentile religion. The crisis in credibility faced by the churches, which has alienated the youth and students and driven the younger theologians to seek a new form of words, has created a wasteland where only a few flowers of renewal give color and bring hope. One is reminded of a child's poem which survived from the extermination center at Theresienstadt, where 15,000 Jewish children were murdered.

Then,
A week after the end,
Everything will be empty here.
A hungry dove will peck for bread.
In the middle of the street will stand
An empty dirty
Hearse.[20]

Even in America, behind the facade of statistical and institutional success are heard the rumblings of the preliminary stages of a Church Struggle which affects even the budgets of the boards and agencies. Pathological study of the German *Kirchenkampf* can teach us a great deal about political and theological realities. One of these realities is the fact that retrogression to sacral society, to a mythical and therefore false harmony, is accompanied by outbursts against the historical people the Jews, even before "the struggle of the church against the church for the church,"[21] sets in. The Jew, who cannot disappear into pre-history, is a surrogate for the Christian, who can.

The Holocaust is an event in history—the continuum of past, present, and future; in Jewish history; in the history of Christendom; in the history of Western civilization; and in the history of human kind. These are concentric circles with their own terms of reference and settings. In the history of the Jewish people, the Holocaust is the story of a destroyed civilization and culture (note the Valley of the Destroyed Communities at Yad Vashem in Jerusalem), the story of the cost of powerlessness in societies latently or actively hostile, and also the story of the recovery and flowering of post-Auschwitz Jewish energy in Israel and in the diaspora.

In the history of Christendom, the Holocaust is the record of the murderous consequences of the preaching and teaching of contempt, of the price to be paid for spiritual and political assimilation, of low standards of training and discipline for the clergy and in the membership as a whole, of the loss of authority and even of credibility amidst the welter of alternative faiths and systems of being.

In the history of western civilization, the Holocaust documents what happens when all the systems and structures fail—when the schools and universities become training grounds for technically competent barbarians rather than wise citizens, when the legal profession uses its technical skills in order to subvert rather than serve justice, when the medics use their skills in order to torture and murder rather than to heal, when the religious teachers subvert higher truths for the sake of transient and self-serving aims, and when the stewards of violence (the police and the military) become the tormentors and killers, the tools of wickedness rather than protectors of the good and barriers against evil. Other lessons must include the continuing vulnerability of open societies to populist demagogues and terrorist movements that, unless thwarted and crushed in time, may become criminal governments with the power to implement and commit genocide.

The problem is basically theological: it concerns the nature of man, his ultimate loyalty, his final identity, his end-time. The nature of the historical process is itself at stake as well as its consummation. Such affirmations cannot be proved inductively, they are not objects of "the historical method." We can, however, establish in negative terms and critical analyses the indissoluble relationship of the *Kirchenkampf* and the Holocaust. As for the question whether Jews and Christians share a common future, which may move a theologian to read and think about the evidence, each of us must use his own vernacular and begin to understand each other's languages in the university and to do something for interdisciplinary cooperation. As we do that, we shall again begin to speak for man, and not continue to contribute to his fragmentation, alienation and dehumanization at the hands of political and academic machines. We shall also perceive that the most awful figure of the Holocaust century is the technically competent barbarian, especially when he claims the sanction of religion for his politics of pride.

In human history, the story of the Holocaust is a warning of the continuing power of evil at large and of wickedness in the unchastened human heart; a warning that progress is not inevitable; a warning that technological advance by no means guarantees the elevation of the human spirit; a warning that man, called to be a partner in creation, instead may be the author of his own destruction.

Notes

Portions of this article were presented as the Opening Address at the first Annual Scholars' Conference on the Holocaust and the Church struggle, 1970, held at Wayne State University in Detroit, Michigan. The conference name was changed to the Annual Scholars' Conference on the Holocaust and the Churches in 1993.

1 Franklin H. Littell, *The Crucifixion of the Jews: The Failure of Christians to Understand the Jewish Experience* (Macon, Georgia: Mercer University Press, 1996), 2.
2 Karl Barth, *The Church and the Political Problem of Our Day* (New York: Charles Scribner's Sons, 1939), 41, 43.
3 Hugh Martin et al., *Christian Counter-Attack* (New York: Charles Scribner's Sons, 1944), 135.
4 Dietrich Bonhoeffer, *Gesammelte Schriften*, ed. Eberhard Bethge (Munich: Chrs. Kaiser Verlag, 1958), 1: 297–98.
5 Quoted by Horace Kallen, *Secularism is the Will of God* (New York: Twayne, 1954), 162n.
6 Eric Voegelin, *The New Science of Politics* (Chicago: University of Chicago Press, 1952).
7 Jürgen Moltmann, *Theology of Hope*, transl. James W. Leitch (New York: Harper & Row, 1967), 43.
8 Quoted by Gabriel Vahanian, *The Death of God* (New York: George Braziller, 1961), 225.
9 Alice Gallin, *Midwives To Nazism: University Professors in Weimar Germany, 1925–1933* (Macon, Georgia: Mercer University Press, 1986).
10 Josef L. Hromadka, *Doom and Resurrection* (Richmond, Virginia: Madrus House, 1945), 102; for more extensive discussion of this point, with citations, see my article, "The Protestant Churches and Totalitarianism (Germany, 1933–45)," in *Totalitarianism*, ed. Carl J. Friedrich (Cambridge: Harvard University Press, 1954), 108–19.
11 Samuel Sandmel, "Bultmann on Judaism," in *The Theology of Rudolf Bultmann*, ed. Charles W. Kegley (New York: Harper & Row, 1966), 218.
12 Arnold Toynbee, *A Study of History* (New York: Oxford University Press, 1957), 8, 22, etc.; see the brilliant critique by Eric Voegelin in *Order and History, I: Israel and Revelation* (Baton Rouge, Louisiana: Louisiana State University Press, 1956), 120.
13 *Trial of the Major War Criminals before the International Military Tribunal, Nuremberg, 14 November 1945–1 October 1946* (Nuremberg: Allied Control Council, 1947–49), IX: 268.
14 Cajus Fabricius, *Positive Christianity in the Third Reich* (Dresden: Püschel, 1937), 23–4.
15 Cited in *Kirchliches Jahrbuch, 1933–1944* (Gütersloh: C. Bertelsmann Verlag, 1948), 2.
16 Robert Welch, *The Blue Book* (Boston: privately printed, 1959), 68–9, 147.
17 Translated in full in *The German Phoenix* (New York: Doubleday, 1960).
18 "Die Bedeutung des Kirchenkampfes für die Ökumene," XX *Evangelische Theologie*, vol. 1 (1960): 1–21.

19 Paul Gürtler, *Nationalsozialismus und Evangelische Kirchen im Warthegau* (Göttingen: Vandenhoeck & Ruprecht, 1953), Appendix Doc. 8, pt. 4.

20 Hana Volavkova, ed.,...*I Never Saw Another Butterfly: Children's Drawings and Poems from Terezin Concentration Camp, 1942–1944* (New York: McGraw-Hill, 1962), 13.

21 Arthur C. Cochrane, *The Church's Confession Under Hitler* (Philadelphia: Westminster Press, 1962), 19.

31

MODEL DENOMINATION OR TOTALITARIAN SECT?

Jehovah's Witnesses in Nazi Germany

James Irvin Lichti

> During the military court proceedings, the captain asked him: "What wo·
> people were like you?" He responded: "This would be the end of the ·

This was the response of a man on trial for a capital crime. T
named Gustav Stange—had refused to perform military servic
Jehovah's Witness, he would have refused this service for an·
tians share Stange's conviction against military service, and presumably no one did in
the courtroom. But Stange's logic must have caught the cross-examining captain off
guard: If all people were like Stange, then all war *would* end.[1]

Stange's behavior epitomizes the manner in which the response of Jehovah's
Witnesses—as Christians—stood apart. True, there were other Christian opponents of
Nazism in Germany, and there were other Christian communities in Nazi Germany with
principles against military service. But only the Jehovah's Witnesses were in the Nazi
concentration camp system in sufficient numbers to merit a distinctive badge—the
Lilawinkel, or Purple Triangle.[2] No other Christian community in Nazi Germany stood by
their convictions more steadfastly or faced and endured a more systematic persecution.

This assessment is not new. The Lutheran Bishop of Hanover offered it as early as 1948,[3]
and during the ensuing decades, various church and mainstream scholars have echoed it. For
example, Detlev Garbe, author of the most comprehensive study of Jehovah's Witnesses in
Nazi Germany, asserts that the "courageous attitude [of the Jehovah's Witnesses] in the
Third Reich merits respect and recognition." Yet in almost the same breath, Garbe also
acknowledges that the Jehovah's Witnesses' attitude cannot serve

> as a model for a democratically oriented society. [...] This position should be
> reserved for Herbert Baum, Dietrich Bonhoeffer, Mildred and Arvid Harnack,
> Helmuth Hübener, Julius Leber, Max Josef Metzger, Carl von Ossietzky, Sophie
> and Hans Scholl, Claus Schenk Graf von Stauffenberg, Hilda Monte, and others.[4]

Garbe's list is compelling, but it is a list of individuals, not of a community. Do we have
to abandon communities in search of models? Were there no "democratically-oriented"

communities in Nazi Germany that could serve as such? More to the point, why can the Jehovah's Witnesses not serve as a model?

In the first monograph on the Jehovah's Witnesses in Nazi Germany by a mainstream historian, which appeared in 1969,[5] Michael H. Kater advanced the notion that the confrontation between Jehovah's Witnesses and the Nazi regime was that of two totalitarian systems. In 1982, Christine Elizabeth King summarized this dynamic as a face-off between "two non-democratic, anti-liberal and uncompromising bodies."[6] This characterization of Jehovah's Witnesses as totalitarian has persisted and surfaces also in sociological analyses of Jehovah's Witnesses.[7] And indeed, Jehovah's Witnesses openly adhere to a theocracy; they possess no democratic or liberal pretensions, and are uncompromising in their convictions. Although none of the above scholars would suggest that, despite their use of the term "totalitarian," the Jehovah's Witnesses are as objectionable as the Nazis, this characterization raises fundamental questions as to how to assess their response to Nazi Germany. Are they a model denomination or a totalitarian sect?

The characterization of the Jehovah's Witnesses as totalitarian is in some respects understandable but analytically problematic, as Garbe pointed out in his study.[8] The landmark totalitarian regimes of the twentieth century were utopian, human-created, and murderously coercive societies; the Jehovah's Witnesses are a voluntary and millennialist sect utterly lacking in worldly political ambitions. Labeling the Jehovah's Witnesses as totalitarian trivializes the term totalitarian and defames the Jehovah's Witnesses.

Nonetheless, if our aim is, as Garbe suggests, to hold up models for a "democratically oriented society," we cannot turn to Jehovah's Witnesses. How, then, did "democratically oriented" Christian communities fare under Nazi Germany, and can they serve as models *on a par* with the Jehovah's Witnesses? For example, the Confessing Church, as a body, did not match the bravery of the Jehovah's Witnesses. But there were several democratically-oriented denominations in Nazi Germany that, like the Jehovah's Witnesses, possessed teachings or traditions against bearing arms on behalf of the state.

To consider their witness in comparison with that of Jehovah's Witnesses, a review of the history of the Jehovah's Witnesses during the Third Reich is in order. This will provide a basis for a contrast between the response of Jehovah's Witnesses and that of other Christian communities with traditions against military service. This will be followed by closer consideration of the "democratically-oriented" denomination that most closely approaches the Jehovah's Witnesses' response—the very small community of German Quakers.

Jehovah's Witnesses and Nazi Germany

Jehovah's Witnesses are one of a number of millennialist movements that arose in the United States during the nineteenth century. Their founder, Charles Taze Russell (1852–1916), developed his doctrines in the 1870s after his encounter with an Adventist community, and the teachings of the Jehovah's Witnesses still bear an Adventist imprint. The followers of American Adventism believed that they were living in the "Advent" of the apocalypse; for them, the end of history was near and the authority of the coming Kingdom overshadowed everything else. As a consequence, they placed their primary allegiance in the imminent Kingdom and viewed all worldly allegiances as secondary. As one New England Adventist put it in 1861: "We are a nationality of ourselves."[9] The totality of this commitment has endured among Jehovah's Witnesses. There was, for them, no confusion of loyalties as experienced by many Christians in Nazi Germany.

But Russell never called himself an Adventist, and pursued his own analysis of scripture. He established a network of congregations and founded Zion's Watch Tower Bible and Tract Society in 1884; this same incorporated body persists as the organizational focus of Jehovah's Witnesses today. From the start, Russell was intent on avoiding all churchly trappings. His followers described themselves simply as "Bible students"—*Bibelforscher*. Until 1933, German followers of the movement described themselves as associated with the International Bible Students Association.

After Russell's death in 1916, his successor Joseph Franklin Rutherford (1869–1942) transformed Russell's comparatively decentralized network of congregations into a tightly managed theocracy. He did this gradually, but the process was largely complete by about 1930. In 1931, he chose the designation "Jehovah's Witnesses" for his followers.

As a consequence of Rutherford's centralization, his views on government predominated. Henceforth, the Jehovah's Witnesses condemned "financial, political and ecclesiastical power groups" as the "visible organization of the devil." This gave their refusal to perform military service an ironclad logic, but Bible Student opposition to bearing arms had begun during World War I on the basis of specific biblical passages.[10]

By the 1930s, Germany had the largest community of Jehovah's Witnesses—about 25,000—outside of the United States. Rutherford was understandably concerned when Hitler became chancellor in 1933. But during the first two years of Nazi rule, government policy on the Jehovah's Witnesses was inconsistent. To be sure, Nazi literature had long condemned the International Bible Students as part of a wider Jewish–Bolshevist conspiracy. And a month after Hitler became chancellor, the regime already had the means for targeting the Jehovah's Witnesses with the Decree of the Reich President for the Protection of People and State, often referred to as the Reichstag fire decree.[11] But the decree's immediate target was Communists, not Jehovah's Witnesses.

But just a few weeks later, Jehovah's Witnesses stood out during the 5 March 1933 parliamentary elections. During the Weimar Republic, voting had been voluntary; now, Nazi canvassers roamed from house to house, calling all Germans to the polls and taking note of those who stayed home. Based on their convictions, Jehovah's Witnesses refused to vote. This started a pattern of Nazi harassment during ensuing elections. Jehovah's Witnesses set themselves apart further by refusing to use the Hitler greeting or salute the Nazi flag. Such expressions of non-conformity led not only to harassment but also to loss of employment and even arrest.[12]

On a more systematic level, four German states used the Reichstag fire decree to outlaw the Jehovah's Witnesses as early as April 1933. Also in that month, the police occupied the Magdeburg Bible House, the publishing and organizational center for Jehovah's Witnesses in Germany. When the US State Department intervened, the regime backed off. Nonetheless, it proceeded to enact a federal ban on 24 June based on the Jehovah's Witnesses' "cultural–Bolshevik activities."[13]

Oddly, a convention of the Jehovah's Witnesses in Berlin was scheduled for the very next day. It proceeded to take place, and 7,000 members heard an address that suggested a certain compatibility between Nazi and the Watch Tower viewpoints. Some statements even appeared to agree with Nazism's antisemitic rhetoric. This apparent attempt to "curry favor" with the regime, as M. James Penton puts it, ranks among the most controversial incidents raised by the Jehovah's Witnesses in Nazi Germany.[14]

The address did not resonate with the regime, but the regime's position on the Jehovah's Witnesses was far from clear. Over the summer of 1933, government officials occupied the Magdeburg office again on 28 June, but assured the US consul that they would not appropriate any American property; then, at the end of August, truckloads of Watch Tower literature were burned outside Magdeburg.[15] But a complaint by Secretary of State Cordell Hull in September led to the return of Watch Tower property, and a decree by the Prussian minister later that month even permitted limited resumption of Watch Tower activities. While an order from Reinhard Heydrich—at this point leader of the Bavarian Political Police—called for increased surveillance in December 1933, "the authorities seemed to be more accommodating" by the middle of 1934. By fall, Jehovah's Witnesses were permitted to print and distribute Bibles "and other unobjectionable publications," although "all other activities of the Earnest Bible Students" were prohibited.[16]

At the outset, both the American and German Watch Tower leaders advised patience and moderation. By contrast, the German rank and file was divided. Their independence is striking: some agreed to make the best of things, while others were anxious to "confront the 'powers of Satan.'" As a result, not all adhered to the restrictions set down by their leaders.

Initially, Rutherford's statements to the regime were conciliatory. He maintained that the Watch Tower Society had "never accepted Communists or Marxists," did not "include any Jews," and appreciated "the National Socialist government because of the fact that Hitler and his State profess to be Christians."[17] At face value, Rutherford's position approached that of German nationalists in the mainstream churches who were pressuring their own church leaders to exclude Jews if not from the pews, at least from the pulpit.[18] But Rutherford's position soon fell in line with the dissenting and more radical sector of German Jehovah's Witnesses.[19]

Eventually, the Nazi regime also lost patience. Over the course of 1935, they shifted to systematic and state-wide persecution of the Jehovah's Witnesses, and Hitler's reintroduction of conscription on 16 March provided yet another point of conflict. But the most frequent basis for arrest was the Jehovah's Witnesses' door-to-door mission. Increasingly, they employed greater discretion, restricting the first visit to more general biblical topics and introducing their specific teachings only on later visits with responsive households. As surveillance and repression increased, they devised methods to surreptitiously import, reproduce, and distribute their literature. Their tactical ingenuity rivaled that of any underground movement; their code for the Watch Tower Society in Brooklyn, for example, was "mother."[20]

This persistence led to increasingly severe persecution. This included public harassment, loss of employment, loss of and/or limitations on pensions and public assistance, removal of their children to Nazi foster homes,[21] mass arrests, detention in concentration camps, and execution. By wartime, the enactment of Special Penal Regulations during War and a State of Emergency (Kriegssonderstrafrechtsverordnung, KSSVO) provided yet another framework for persecution. Article Five of the KSSVO made "any efforts of demoralizing 'the armed forces'" punishable by death. On this basis, Helene Delacher was sentenced to death for acting as a courier between Austria and Italy, Emmi Zehden for hiding Jehovah's Witnesses evading military service, and Martha Hopp for indicating "to a fellow worker and acquaintance that Germany would lose the war and that the loss in lives would surpass our imagination."[22]

The severity of Nazi repression had incremental success. Three waves of mass arrests—during August/September of 1936, March/April of 1937, and August/September of 1937—seriously curtailed the functioning of Jehovah's Witnesses throughout Germany. Dissatisfied with the length of sentences meted out by the Nazi court system, the Gestapo began selectively holding Jehovah's Witnesses through "protective detention" in the Nazi concentration camp system.[23] By 1938–39, the regime had destroyed organized resistance activity, although extant groups—consisting mostly of women—gradually re-established contact and created a cell network. In the summer of 1943, there were still printing operations in Berlin, but the Gestapo put a stop to this network during January and February of 1944.[24] By the final year of the war, no effective organization was possible outside of the camps. Astonishingly, however, effective organization arose and persisted within the camps. This was due to two key factors: first, the extraordinarily tight-knit network maintained by Jehovah's Witness inmates; second, a decline in the severity of the persecution of Jehovah's Witnesses in the camps just as this increased outside of the camps.

At first, Jehovah's Witnesses ranked among the most brutally treated inmates. Until 1939–40, they were often singled out for lower rations, beatings, standing at attention holding signs of self-ridicule, and executions. Not all killing was formal, however; in Sachsenhausen, 25 Jehovah's Witnesses were stuffed into a broom closet with the intent of suffocating them; after 12 hours, 15 had died.[25] Such "special treatment" had two aims: first, to coerce Jehovah's Witnesses into signing statements recanting their faith; second, to punish them for refusing to follow all orders imposed on them. Their intransigence was always principle-based. In particular, they refused to perform labor that would assist the Nazi war effort (since, increasingly, the camps were engaged in the manufacture of war-related materials).

But the SS eventually began treating Jehovah's Witness inmates with less severity. Since they never made attempts at escape, they could be entrusted with tasks without supervision. Increasingly, they were sent to locations—for example, as laborers on agricultural estates, or as servants for the families of SS officials—where the living conditions facilitated their survival. But they remained of enormous value in the camps; as the number of non-German inmates in the camp system swelled, the SS increasingly needed to manage the camps through German-speaking inmates whom they could trust. In isolated situations, some Jehovah's Witnesses even became camp functionaries.[26]

It was as if the Jehovah's Witnesses demonstrated that they were worthy of the Nazis' trust. To be sure, top Nazi officials came to admire their "fanaticism"; Heinrich Himmler even entertained the fanciful notion of using Jehovah's Witnesses to convert the non-German Christian ethnicities of the future Nazi empire. This strategy would provide—in Himmler's mind—the master race with pliant and pacific subject populations.[27]

While pacific, the Jehovah's Witnesses were never pliant. Seizing the opportunity provided by the trust vested in them, they resumed *within the camps* the resistance activities that had been abandoned *outside of the camps*. Publications were smuggled in, reproduced, and sent out for distribution. Secret baptisms were performed, and preaching activity was organized. Toward the end of spring 1944, the Gestapo attempted a system-wide search to stop these "prohibited activities." Ultimately, however, their interest in making use of these otherwise model inmates prevailed, and "concentration camp life went back to its normal routine."[28]

Comparison with denominations with traditions against military service

One of the convictions that put Jehovah's Witnesses decisively at odds with the Nazi regime was their refusal to bear arms. Few Christians in Germany shared these religious qualms. But in the early church, avoidance of military service was the Christian norm.[29] And for the first thousand years of Christianity, church leaders still traditionally regarded the soldier's profession as "utterly sinful and secular." It was only in the eleventh century that military service was "'Christianized,' that is, integrated into a Christian ethical structure and given a morally positive purpose."[30] Opposition to military service continued to resurface on Christendom's periphery during the next thousand years. Even in Nazi Germany, isolated Catholics and Protestants within the provincial churches refused to bear arms,[31] and a handful of clergy raised their voices against warfare.[32]

Alongside Jehovah's Witnesses, there were a number of small Christian communities with traditions against military service. A glance at their various responses to Nazi Germany reveals a clear line of demarcation. Those that would typically—and dismissively—be labeled as sects demonstrated a far greater consistency in their responses to Nazi Germany, while those closer to the modern denominations failed to show any pattern of response.

The term "sect," however, bears a pejorative burden that the terms "church" and "denomination" lack. For their part, Jehovah's Witnesses reject designation as a church.[33] As author of the most comprehensive study of Jehovah's Witnesses in Nazi Germany, Detlev Garbe chooses to refer to Jehovah's Witnesses as a denomination.

But is the designation fitting? The term "denomination" emerged during the seventeenth century in the English and English–Colonial setting to imply "that the group referred to was but one member, denominated by a particular name, of a larger group to which other Protestant denominations belonged." As Samuel Willard, minister of Old South Church in Boston, put it in 1688: "Through our knowing *but in part* [an allusion to First Corinthians 13:9], it is come to pass that professors of Christianity have been of diverse opinions in many things and their difference hath occasioned several *denominations*, but while they agree in the *foundation* they may be saved." In line with this sentiment, Jeremiah Burroughs—a contemporary English Puritan—declared: "God hath a hand in these divisions to bring forth further light."[34]

The term denomination thus arose to denote a post-churchly, modern, and pluralistic framework for Christianity.[35] It designated a new and protoliberal institution that differed radically from the premodern "church" but also from the sect, which—like the church—laid claim to a monopoly on both Christian "truth" and the means of salvation. But if the denominationalist believes that God's truth is so vast and complex that it cannot be contained by one human institution, then s/he must also make some room for variations in personal beliefs. Returning again to the seventeenth-century origins of the term, Praisegood Barebones asserted that "though the truth and true measure be one, yet the persons measuring are very various and much differing."[36] For the denominationalist, then, the seat of charismatic authority—if located anywhere other than in scripture—lies in the heart of the individual. As a consequence, true denominations rely on institutional forms that permit a greater respect for variations of conscience. They tend toward a liberal and "democratically-oriented" polity.

By contrast, the sect—in the typologies of Max Weber and Ernst Troeltsch—strives for something quite different. It aims at the realization of the "visible church" that the churches themselves could never achieve. That is, members of sects should be readily recognizable because they maintain a *distinctive* and relatively *uniform* level of piety. This collective conformity to a visible virtuosity secures for them their status as the "faithful remnant." In other words, a sect is an elite based on religious merit, and it is their collective merit that secures their salvation.[37] It would be impossible for the sect to maintain its rigorous standards of virtuosity with the more tolerant and permissive standards of the denomination.

Self-professing elites do not always arouse admiration and sympathy, but they are an integral component of modern society. Indeed, liberal modernity is based on both meritocracy and democracy; as typologies of Christian community, the sect emphasizes the former and the denomination the latter. The typological categories as advanced by Weber and Troeltsch are thus neither pejorative nor anti-modern.

It is, in part, the sectarian characteristics that have led to the characterization of Jehovah's Witnesses as "totalitarian." Meritocracies draw clear boundaries as to who is inside and who is outside. Also, Nazism and the Jehovah's Witnesses share authoritarian frameworks and "millennialist visions." But as Garbe aptly pointed out, while the Nazis sought to create their thousand-year Reich through war, terror, and genocide, Jehovah's Witnesses are a voluntary body that rely on God for the realization of His Kingdom.[38] The spirit of twentieth-century totalitarianism was utopian, and Jehovah's Witnesses are no utopians.

But the Weber–Troetlsch typology of the sect possesses analytical utility in comparing the response of Christian communities with teachings against bearing arms to Nazi Germany. To be sure, even among the "sects," the Jehovah's Witnesses still emerge as "the most stridently outspoken conscientious objectors" in Nazi Germany.[39] Still, Nazi executions extended to the ranks of Reform Adventists—who had broken away from Seventh-day Adventism during World War I—and the isolated Christadelphian congregation in Esslingen.[40]

But some Jehovah's Witnesses chose the more moderate course of evading military service. Along these lines, the small Hutterite community known as the *Rhönbruderhof* shuttled its draft-age men out of the country before it was dissolved by the Nazis—on the basis of the Reichstag fire decree mentioned above—in April 1937. A more moderate but still consistent course, which Jehovah's Witnesses advised for followers who were not yet baptized, was non-combatancy within the military. Evangelical Baptists (*Gemeinschaft evangelisch Taufgesinnte*) held to this consistently, arranging for draft-age male members to be trained as medics, and with this strategy preventing them from having to bear arms.[41]

All of the above communities stood closer to the typology of sect. But there were also three denominations in Nazi Germany with histories of opposition to military service: Mennonites, Seventh-day Adventists, and Quakers.[42] All three displayed a greater toleration of internal heterogeneity and usually presented themselves as democratic.[43] But unlike the sects described above, they did not present a unified front against Nazi militarism.

The response of German Mennonites stood at one extreme. As an active teaching, their "pacifism" had largely expired by the time of Nazi Germany. Arising from the sixteenth-century Anabaptist movement, many Mennonites had emigrated from central Europe—especially to Russia and North America—in search of countries that would tolerate their distinctive teachings, including their opposition to military service. Those who remained tended to be more open to assimilation; and the more they assimilated, the more they shifted away from sectarianism and toward denominationalism.

This shift took the form of congregations weakening their "virtuosity." While congregations did not abandon their opposition to military service all at once, they moved—one by one—toward transforming a community-binding norm into a matter of individual conscience. Most still pledged to support individuals who refused to bear arms. This process took place during the nineteenth century under the influence of German liberal thought. But by World War I, there were only scattered congregations—concentrated in southwestern Germany—in which a significant proportion of members chose to serve as non-combatants.[44]

Nonetheless, it was only with Hitler's reintroduction of conscription that the largest association of German Mennonite congregations officially cut themselves off from this historical teaching. The association even declared that its draft-age youth were "enthusiastically ready" to serve in combat alongside their fellow Germans. While some *individual* German Mennonites kept the principle alive, and isolated Mennonite congregations may have supported such individuals, opposition to military service was not a component of the collective Mennonite response to Nazism. (More disturbing was the extent to which German Mennonite periodicals expressed sympathy for Nazi racial ideals.)[45]

The second denomination, Seventh-day Adventists (SDAs), did not abandon their long-standing opposition to military service. However, their teaching on this matter—which endorsed non-combatant military service—was not binding: SDAs had always left the decision of how to respond to conscription to the individual conscience. As a consequence, a noteworthy minority of conscripted SDAs sought and obtained non-combatant positions, but most served as combatants.[46]

Interestingly, SDAs—like Mennonites—proved vulnerable to Nazi ideology. Ironically, it was one of their more distinctive teachings that provided the ideological bridge. SDAs view physical and spiritual health as fundamentally indivisible; this has long linked the denomination to the field of medicine and led to their abstinence from meat, tobacco, and alcohol. With the rise of Nazism, they finally had a national leader who shared their health-conscious habits, as Hitler was a vegetarian and neither smoked nor drank. Further, Nazism used medicine to legitimize its murderous policies of racial hygiene. Given their own bond to this academic field, SDA periodicals absorbed elements of Nazi racial hygiene.[47]

While Mennonites in Germany numbered more than 20,000 and SDAs approached 40,000, there were only 250 Quakers in the German Yearly Meeting. Of the three denominations, the Quaker response stood closest to the sectarian: its conscripted members all secured non-combatant positions within the military.[48] This raises the question of whether they should be considered a sect. But Quakerism arose in England exactly during the emergence of the notion of the denomination, and its doctrines intrinsically express denominational liberalism. The sanctity of conscience is enshrined, so to speak, in the Quaker teaching of the "inner light," which resides in every human being. This led to an embrace of democracy as a principle; commentaries to this effect surfaced regularly in the German Quaker journal *Der Quäker*.

Did, then, the Quakers in Germany present the "democratically oriented" model that Garbe called for? This question merits a closer comparison between Quakers and Jehovah's

Witnesses in their respective responses to Hitler's Germany. If a "non-democratically oriented" community can fare better than a democratically oriented community, then the original question may merit re-examination.

In one regard, both communities were remarkably successful: maintaining a clear ideological distance from Nazi ideology. True, the Jehovah's Witness leadership has been criticized for the early attempts to suggest some compatibility with Nazi ideology, as described above. Soon enough, however, it turned 180 degrees. Indeed, their periodicals waged a public campaign against Nazism. This campaign has been rightly criticized for its inaccurate portrayal of Nazi Germany as no more than a pawn of the Vatican.[49] This linking of the papacy to the forces of the Antichrist, however, also typified many Protestant millennialists. Moreover, the mainstream German churches clearly supported not only the regime's position against the Jehovah's Witnesses, but other key Nazi tenets—especially its anti-Bolshevism. While the Jehovah's Witnesses portrayed the link between the Vatican and Hitler inaccurately, the perception of an ideological link between the churches and the regime—especially from their perspective—was hardly inaccurate.

While Quakers also maintained a steady ideological distance from Nazi ideology, they did not proclaim this as adamantly. Indeed, *Der Quäker* remained legal and circulated in Germany until 1941 when the regime closed virtually all confessional periodicals. One may ask whether their commentary was so muted that it provided no real statement against the regime. In an arguably democratic fashion, content in *Der Quäker* served as a dialogue between the moderate and activist sectors of the German Yearly Meeting. Advocating moderation, Hans Albrecht—the clerk of the German Yearly Meeting—in 1940 recalled Quakerism's most famous founder, George Fox (1624–91), who always refused to doff his hat in court, but offered no resistance when the hat was removed for him.[50] (Regardless of this, however, Fox repeatedly found himself in prison for his convictions.) Advocating action, Emil Fuchs—a former Lutheran pastor—declared in the November 1934 issue that those who simply look on and do nothing "as the state thinks, acts, conducts war, etc., in an unchristian manner" contribute to "the ruin of this state and nation."[51] Both sides were, then, able to voice their opinions, at least early in the regime.

But commentary hostile to Nazi ideology, and especially Nazi practice, grew increasingly circumspect. It was, nonetheless present, and surfaced regularly in muted forms; for example, an article in January 1935 cited the *Jüdischer Rundschau*, in which the Jewish philosopher Carl Joël corrected a currently popular citation from Goethe's *Faust*: "Blood is a very special kind of sap." The racial potential of this quote is obvious, but Joël noted that these words were spoken not by Faust, but by "the tempter Mephisto."[52] Occasionally, bolder statements appeared: in 1937, *Der Quäker* published "Emil Fuchs' protest against the prohibition of interracial marriage in the 1935 Nuremberg Racial Laws."[53]

In maintaining this ideological distance, the German Yearly Meeting—founded in 1925—followed an anti-nationalist and pacifist course set by non-German Quakers. During World War I, American and British Quakers had challenged anti-German propaganda, and British Quakers had assisted German internees. After the war, they protested the continued British naval blockade that prolonged hunger within Germany, and administered the postwar *Quäkerspeisung* that provided over five million German children with free meals.[54] American and British Friends had also consistently denounced the Treaty of Versailles as punitive. During the 1923 French occupation of the Ruhr, British Friends intervened on behalf of imprisoned Germans. Once the Nazis were in power, British and American Quakers continued to speak on behalf of the rights of Germans as minority populations in non-German countries and participated in feeding programs for destitute Sudeten Germans. British Quakers even aided the families of Nazi internees in Austria and negotiated the release of Nazi activists from Lithuanian prisons in their quest to stand by and protect *all* political prisoners.[55] They refused to take sides; as Carl Heath—one of the foremost Quaker spokespersons of the period—put it, "there is neither You nor I as victor, only the path of persuasion and 'boundedness' between us."[56]

While some will admire this list of actions, others may ask whether the Quakers were out of touch with the realities of history. Did the Friends really understand the nature of Nazi and Stalinist totalitarianism? And Quaker historians have indeed acknowledged that liberal Quakers of the 1920s and 1930s succumbed to an excessive confidence regarding their capacity for historical impact, thereby leaving themselves open to manipulation.[57] A failure to assess the historical situation accurately was thus not an error unique to the Jehovah's Witnesses.

Nonetheless, those Germans attracted to Quakerism during the 1920s joined specifically because of the manner in which American and British Quakers had dealt with their German "enemies." This inspiration buttressed their Yearly Meeting against the intrusion of nationalist or racial sentiment. It also paralleled the firmly cemented "boundedness" of the Jehovah's Witnesses to a wider religious community beyond Germany's borders.

But Quakers and Jehovah's Witnesses differed dramatically in the expectations placed by leaders on each member. This was a function of their diverging democratic, as opposed to meritocratic, orientations. While the executive committee of the German Yearly Meeting openly called on members to render assistance to those suffering in Nazi Germany, it advised members not "do more than is within your resources."[58] It is not surprising, then, that meetings housed both quietist and activist sectors.[59] By contrast, the top leadership of the Jehovah's Witnesses—which, unlike the leadership of German Quakers, was located outside of Nazi Germany—called for far bolder actions on the part of each member.

Their boldness is universally admired by commentators. Nonetheless, M. James Penton asks whether it was "often an example of fanatical foolhardiness driven by J. F. Rutherford's teachings." He agrees that on many points their stance was consistent with Jehovah's Witnesses' principles, but argues that Rutherford unnecessarily inflated the persecution of his followers—subjecting them to hunger, deprivation, and torture aimed at obtaining the names of other Jehovah's Witnesses—through poorly thought-through campaigns that could have little positive impact.[60]

Penton is here putting Rutherford and the theocratic structure of Jehovah's Witnesses on trial. This is entirely legitimate and certainly points to the potential dangers of theocracy. The question of when suffering is necessary is also important.

At the same time, his challenge also raises questions. First, are foolhardy actions sometimes called for? While Penton himself acknowledges the integrity of suffering when Jehovah's Witnesses were adhering to their principles—such as refusing to use the Hitler greeting or perform military service—others may consider that same adherence foolhardy. Some of the actions by individual German Friends could be judged foolhardy, such as Gerhard Halle—in full view of passers-by—tearing to shreds a sign forbidding

Jews to enter a Berlin store, soon after the *Kristallnacht* pogrom.[61] And when the Protestant pacifist Friedrich Siegmund-Schultze called on his church publicly to denounce Nazi abuses of "Jewish shopkeepers and minor civil servants," which he witnessed from his vantage point as a settlement worker in the slums of east Berlin, his proposal was dismissed as "reckless."[62] Had the church listened to Siegmund-Schulze, could Hitler ever have got as far as he did? The line at which to designate an action as foolhardy has many determinants, and cannot always easily be drawn.

Second, separate from the judgment of the theocratic leader, did the theocratic framework contribute to the degree of consistency in the response of Jehovah's Witnesses to Nazi Germany? This consistency should not be overstated. There were many who must have left the community, and there were doubtless those who compromised and conformed in various ways. But while a visible proportion of German Friends became anti-Nazi activists, the steadfastness of the Jehovah's Witnesses is more compelling: approximately 250 were put to death by military courts, and this equals the number of the entire German Yearly Meeting at that time. An estimated one-third of Jehovah's Witnesses were arrested in Nazi Germany; for Quakers, the proportion probably lies somewhere between 5 and 10 percent.[63]

On the other hand, it is also possible to overstate the role of theocracy in maintaining the resolve of the rank-and-file Jehovah's Witnesses. To be sure, given their isolation, any contact with the Watch Tower Society must have been immeasurably sustaining. But this was also a "believers' community."[64] Members had joined—and remained—of their own volition. Further, accounts of Jehovah's Witnesses in the camps or on trial do not suggest a robotic or subservient conviction; they were repeatedly confronted with a range of situations that demanded dynamic responses. In the camps, Jehovah's Witnesses held their own in arguments with Communist inmates, creatively circumvented camp regulations, and thoughtfully drew lines as to when to conform and when to defy. Such boundaries were not always clear-cut, and led to confrontations and arguments among Jehovah's Witness inmates.[65] Much of what they were forced to deal with had to be undertaken at their own initiative. Very little was under close supervision of the Watch Tower Society. In all of this, they demonstrated profound resourcefulness and resolve.

Does this suggest that the theocratic framework was absent among Jehovah's Witnesses in Nazi Germany? It is worth remembering that, during the early years of the Third Reich, many Jehovah's Witnesses failed to conform to their theocratic authority, adopting a more radical response to Nazi Germany to which the theocratic leadership later conformed.

I am still convinced that the theocracy structure helped reinforce the sectarian—that is, meritocratic—character of the community. But in the setting of Nazi Germany, the practical functioning of the community did not easily fit the "totalitarian" mold, since so much relied so often on the initiative of decentralized cells or groups that had to function and innovate on their own.

By contrast, the German Yearly Meeting harbored a far more heterogeneous collection of convictions. Arguably, the "quietist" sector of the German Quakers acted as a drag on the community as a whole and inhibited a more appropriately bold response. But it did not keep a good number of German Friends from becoming engaged in a range of anti-Nazi endeavors. As an expression of a corporate body of Christians, the extent of the Quaker outreach to Jews in Nazi Germany is without parallel. Such outreach was also in evidence among Jehovah's Witnesses,[66] but it was pursued more systematically among Quakers.

While the mainstream churches and denominations focused on assisting their own members who had converted from Judaism, Quakers reached out to the wider Jewish population. On an open and corporate basis, German meetings sought to counter the social and economic isolation of Jews, participate in the creation of alternatives to the Nazi public school system, and assist with emigration. During wartime, a number of German Quakers—acting as individuals—did not shirk illegality in their attempts to help Jews.[67]

This comparison between the response of Quakers and Jehovah's Witnesses to Nazi Germany, then, does not lend itself to a tidy assessment. If we are to restrict ourselves to "democratically-oriented" models, the German Yearly Meeting provides significant inspiration, particularly in its efforts on behalf of Jews and other targets of the regime.[68] Their conception of democracy could not be twisted or contorted to fit the Nazi ideological context since it was based in their most fundamental principles. One of the co-editors of *Der Quäker*, Lilli Pollatz, described the central Quaker teaching of the inner light as "the democratic sense of the equal worth of all humans before God,"[69] and a November 1933 article called for a "more deeply" conceived democracy that would achieve "the triumph of the divine in humanity."[70] The democratic principles of both Mennonites and SDAs lacked this same resolve and doctrinal coherence.

But there are respects in which, as a model, the response of the Jehovah's Witnesses to Nazi Germany remains without parallel. It affirms the value of sectarian meritocracy. In particular, the works recording their experiences and steadfastness should be reviewed closely by those of us who are Christian. Their model should lead us to scrutinize very closely just who and what we aim to be.

Notes

1 Stange was executed on 20 February 1942. A military prison's chaplain, Rudolf Daur, conveyed Stange's witness in a letter to Stange's widow. Daur had "truly wanted...to save the life of this exceptional man. But [Stange] was completely convinced that he did the right thing." Detlef Garbe, *Between Resistance and Martyrdom: Jehovah's Witnesses in the Third Reich* (Madison, Wisconsin: University of Wisconsin Press, 2006), 378.

2 It was only in 1938 that the SS established a system-wide regulation for marking prisoners. Before that, Jehovah's Witnesses were already being "marked" in different camps due to their numbers. During 1936–37, Jehovah's Witnesses made up about 5–10 percent of the population in the entire system. In May 1938, they were 12 percent of the prisoners in Buchenwald; also in 1938, every fifth or sixth prisoner in Neuengamme was a Jehovah's Witness; in May 1939, 40 percent of those at Schloss Lichtenburg. As the number of prisoners increased, their proportion declined. The unified system of placing colored triangular patches on the left side of the chest emerged in 1938. Garbe, *Between Resistance and Martyrdom*, 394, 460, 480–81.

3 "'...no Christian community can stand even the slightest comparison with the number of their martyrs...they also served with us and undeniably, carried an element of humanity into the dark house...They can claim to be the only large-scale rejecters of military service in the Third Reich, who did this openly and for the sake of their conscience.'" Hanns Lilje, *Im finstern Tal*, 2nd edn (Nuremberg, 1948), 58, 59, cited by Christoph Daxelmüller, "Solidarity and the Will to Survive: Religious and Social Behavior of Jehovah's Witnesses in Concentration Camps," in *Persecution and Resistance of Jehovah's Witnesses During the Nazi-Regime*, ed. Hans Hesse (Chicago: Edition Temmen, 2001), 29–30.

4 Garbe, *Between Resistance and Martyrdom*, 541.

5 Michael H. Kater, "Die Ernsten Bibelforscher im Dritten Reich," *Vierteljahrshefte für Geschichte*, vol. 17, no. 2 (April 1969).

6 Christine Elizabeth King, *The Nazi State and the New Religions: Five Case Studies in Non-Conformity* (New York: Edwin Mellon Press, 1982), 176.

7 For a fairly recent example, see Andrew Holden, *Jehovah's Witnesses: Portrait of a Contemporary Religious Movement* (London and New York: Routledge, 2002).

8 Garbe, *Between Resistance and Martyrdom*, 517–20.

9 Peter Brock, *Pacifism in the United States: From the Colonial Era to the First World War* (Princeton, New Jersey: Princeton University Press, 1968), 847.

10 For much of this background, I have relied on James M. Penton, *Apocalypse Delayed: The Story of the Jehovah's Witnesses* (Toronto: University of Toronto Press, 1985).

11 On 28 February 1933, a Dutch Communist burned down the Reichstag (German parliament) building. For the Nazis, this act of arson justified the issuing of the decree mentioned above. It eliminated a number of fundamental democratic rights, including freedom of assembly and of expression. It is worth noting, however, that the decree was issued in the name of the Reich President, Paul von Hindenburg, who was not a Nazi. Hitler did not assume the office of President until after Hindenburg's death in August 1934.

12 The fact that, with the 5 March election, the Nazis still fell short of that mark may have fueled hostility toward a Christian community that refused to vote. An example of Nazi harassment during voting occurred already during the 12 November 1933 plebiscite: the SA forced Jehovah's Witnesses to march around with placards asserting their betrayal of the fatherland. Garbe, *Between Resistance and Martyrdom*, 139–55.

13 Garbe, *Between Resistance and Martyrdom*, 73–75.

14 Garbe, *Between Resistance and Martyrdom*, 87–90; Penton, *Apocalypse Delayed*, 148–9. Some details of this episode remain contested; for example, M. James Penton continues to favor the assertions that the Berlin convention opened with the *Deutschlandlied* and that swastikas decorated the hall. M. James Penton, *Jehovah's Witnesses and the Third Reich: Sectarian Politics under Persecution* (Toronto, Buffalo, London: University of Toronto Press, 2004), 68–71. Garbe, while initially in agreement, has come to distance himself from such assertions.

15 Also, by the end of July 1933, the regime decided to hold Watch Tower property hostage to ensure no propaganda "be made by this society abroad against the German government." Garbe, *Between Resistance and Martyrdom*, 97–95.

16 Garbe, *Between Resistance and Martyrdom*, 95, 100, 108, 109.

17 Garbe, *Between Resistance and Martyrdom*, 104–5.

18 On 9 April 1933, Nazi Germany enacted the Law for the Restoration of the Civil Service, which aimed at the removal of Jews from the civil service. Protestant pastors had been civil servants until the end of World War I. Many German nationalists within the Protestant provincial churches sought to extend this new Nazi policy to the churches, calling for the implementation of an "Aryan Paragraph" to remove all pastors or church officials with Jewish ancestry from office: Richard Guttridge, *Open Thy Mouth for the Dumb! The German Evangelical Church and the Jews, 1879–1950* (Oxford: Basil Blackwell, 1976), 91–131. Garbe is sharp in his criticism of such statements by Rutherford, yet argues that, due to their anti-racist stance, the German Jehovah's Witnesses should not be characterized as anti-Semitic. Penton cites such evidence, but argues for the pervasiveness of anti-Semitism among German Jehovah's Witnesses, presenting his own evidence: *Jehovah's Witnesses and the Third Reich*, 76–88. In an earlier work, Penton had asserted that the ranks of the Witnesses—while free of neither racism nor anti-Semitism—have been "amazingly tolerant ethnically and racially," and Witnesses probably identified more strongly with Jews than with any other single group. See Penton, *Apocalypse Delayed*, 126, 129, 130, 284–86.

19 Penton argues this shift had taken place as early as fall 1933, citing Rutherford's article in the 1 November 1933 issue of *The Watchtower*. Rutherford did not coordinate his move toward a more anti-Nazi position with German Watch Tower leaders such as Balzereit and Dollinger, who continued to seek accommodation with the regime, but faced arrest in May 1935. In April 1935, the regime dissolved the German branch office in Magdeburg, justifying the move in part with the activities of those Jehovah's Witnesses who had failed to observe the state's imposed restrictions. By 30 January 1936, Jehovah's Witnesses could not even distribute "unobjectionable materials." Penton, *Jehovah's Witnesses and the Third Reich*, 66, 116–17.

20 Penton, *Jehovah's Witnesses and the Third Reich*, 326.

21 The Nazi courts determined that parents "have to be deprived of custody if they alienate their children from the National Socialist ideology by teaching them religious fanaticism." There were 860 known cases of the children of Jehovah's Witnesses being taken away from their parents on this basis. As a believers' community, Jehovah's Witnesses only baptize adults. Yet many children refused to perform the Hitler salute, sing Nazi songs, or observe Nazi holidays in school. As a consequence, they faced state-sanctioned and sometimes violent harassment from both their fellow students and their teachers. Penton, *Jehovah's Witnesses and the Third Reich,* 169–91.

22 Penton, *Jehovah's Witnesses and the Third Reich,* 341–48.

23 Since this was an affront to the judicial system, a regulation by Heinrich Himmler on 5 August 1937 provided some "relief." As a means of less visibly demonstrating its disregard for the courts, the Gestapo began taking released Jehovah's Witnesses into custody only *after* they had left the courtroom. Penton, *Jehovah's Witnesses and the Third Reich,* 243, 250, 274, 284–85.

24 In some cases, Jehovah's Witnesses released from the camps during wartime assisted with developing networks during wartime, although this could lead to their return to the camps. Penton, *Jehovah's Witnesses and the Third Reich,* 319, 337–40.

25 Penton, *Jehovah's Witnesses and the Third Reich,* 404–13.

26 Penton, *Jehovah's Witnesses and the Third Reich,* 418, 428, 439–47, 465.

27 Penton, *Jehovah's Witnesses and the Third Reich,* 453.

28 Penton, *Jehovah's Witnesses and the Third Reich,* 434–39.

29 Adolf von Harnack, *Militia Christi: die christliche Religion und der Soldatenstand in den ersten drei Jahrhunderten* (Tubingen: Mohr, Paul Siebeck, 1905); Roland Bainton, *Christian Attitudes toward War and Peace* (New York: Abingdon Press, 1960).

30 Joseph H. Lynch, "The First Crusade: Some Theological and Historical Contexts," in *Must Christianity Be Violent? Reflections on History, Practice, and Theology,* ed. Kenneth R. Chase and Alan Jacobs (Grand Rapids, Michigan: Brazos Press, 2003), 31–32.

31 For an overview, see Albrecht and Heidi Hartmann, *Kriegsdienstverweigerung im Dritten Reich* (Frankfurt am Main: Haag und Herchen, 1986).

32 For example, the Catholic priest Stephan Rugel chastised his congregants in strong terms after the 5 March 1933 election: "If in the foreseeable future a much more horrible World War comes, then I beg you already today: don't complain because it was you who voted for it!" Georg Denzler, *Widerstand is nicht das richtige Wort: Katholische Preister, Bischöfe und Theologen im Dritten Reich* (Zurich: Pendo Verlag, 2003), 21.

33 This designation would also be a problematic in the German setting. The German term for church—*Kirche*—applies only to institutions that enjoyed a state–church status prior to 1918. James Irvin Lichti, *Houses on the Sand? Pacifist Denominations in Nazi Germany* (New York: Peter Lang, 2008), 11n.

34 Winthrop S. Hudson, "Denominationalism," in Mircea Eliade, ed., *The Encyclopedia of Religion* (New York: Macmillan, 1987), 292–94.

35 Ernst Troeltsch, for one, articulated this position for German Protestantism of the early twentieth century. In responding to Adolf von Harnack's seminal essay "The Essence of Christianity," Troeltsch rejected the notion that Christianity possessed only one true "essence," arguing that each epoch possessed its "own" Christian essence. In line with such pluralism, Troeltsch called for a positive regard for the richness and diversity in the Christian tradition. See Sarah Coakley, *Christ Without Absolutes: A Study of the Christology of Ernst Troeltsch* (Oxford: Clarendon Paperbacks, 1994; first published 1988), 112, 117. Troeltsch also believed that different modes of community constituted legitimate expressions of Christianity. For example, all three of Troeltsch's classic forms—church, sect, and mysticism—had their "germ" in early Christianity. See Ernst Troeltsch, *The Social Teachings of the Christian Churches* (Chicago and London: University of Chicago Press, 1960; first published in German in 1911), 733.

36 Further, Barebones' contemporary Jeremiah Burroughs asserted that "the things of religion are hidden mysteries. They are the secrets of God. They are hard to be understood. God reveals them in a differing way." Winthrop Hudson, "Denominationalism as a Basis for Ecumenicity: A Seventeenth Century Conception," in *Denominationalism,* ed. Russell E. Richey (Nashville, Tennessee: Abingdon, 1977), 30, 33.

37 Troeltsch associated (passively received) "grace" with the church and (actively obeyed) "law" with the sect. For his part, Weber specified that sectarian membership was restricted to the "qualified," that is, those who meet the sect's specified expectations of virtuosity. Weber also recognized the sectarian imperative to maintain an even and consistent level of religious virtuosity throughout the community. "The [sectarian] community is the instrument of selection that separates the qualified from the unqualified." This implied a charismatic authority at the level of *the sect as a whole*. It was not the individual who determined whether he or she belonged to a sect, but the sect that possessed a charismatic capacity to recognize the requisite level of religious virtuosity for membership. Max Weber, *Wirtschaft und Gesellschaft: Grundriß der verstehenden Soziologie*, ed. Johannes Winckelmann (Cologne and Berlin: Kiepenheuer und Witsch, 1954), 917 (also 880, 920–21); Ernst Troeltsch, *The Social Teachings of the Christian Churches*, 2: 993; Max Weber, *Sociology of Religion* (Boston: Beacon Press, 1964; first published in German in 1922), 65, 179.

38 Garbe, *Between Resistance and Martyrdom*, 513–20.

39 Penton, *Jehovah's Witnesses and the Third Reich*, 170.

40 Close to 20 Reform Adventists were executed for refusing to perform military service. See Hans Fleschutz, *Und Folget Ihrem Glauben Nach* (Jagsthausen and Heinbronn: Internationale Missionsgesellschaft der Siebenten-Tags-Adventisten-Reformationsbewegung). In the Christadelphian congregation, one member, Albert Merz, was executed in Brandenburg military detention prison on 3 April 1941; his brother Rudolf was also incarcerated. Both refused to bear arms. Photocopies of Albert Merz's final letter to his family are available through the Christadelphian congregation in Esslingen. The case is also discussed by L. Roy Waddoup, "Unpublished manuscript on history of Christadelphians in Germany" (Avon, 1983).

41 On the Hutterite community, see Emmy Arnold, *Torches Together: The Beginning and Early Years of the Bruderhof Communities* (Rifton, New York: Plough Publishing House, 1964). On the Evangelical Baptists, see Hermann Rüegger, *Aufzeichnungen über Entstehung und Bekenntnis der Gemeinschaft evangelisch Taufgesinnter (Nazarener)* (Zürich: Bücherverlag der Gemeinschaft Evangelisch Taufgesinnter, 1961).

42 For their part, Mennonites and SDAs actively pursued a denominational status in Germany at this time. Both actively sought to distance themselves from the label "sect," and instead sought public designation as "free churches" (*Freikirchen*).

43 Of the three, Quakers may most readily be viewed as democratic in that they adhere to consensus. However, some may question whether this is really a form of democracy. Most German Mennonite congregations had explicitly democratic structures, although a smaller number retained older hierarchal and patriarchal forms. The extent to which SDA is internally democratic is a matter of debate. SDA leaders insist that the SDA administrative structure is "representative"; however, critical commentators both inside and outside the SDA community assert that authority ultimately resides in SDA's administrative structure and institutions. Individual congregations enjoy considerable autonomy in many matters, but "it is also clear that the local church is modeled on the same hierarchical plan as Adventism in general." Malcolm Bull and Keith Lockhart, *Seeking a Sanctuary: Seventh-day Adventists and the American Dream* (New York: Harper & Row, 1989), 99–103.

44 A classic on this process was written quite early: Wilhelm Mannhardt, *Die Wehrfreiheit der altpreußischen Mennoniten: eine geschichtliche Erörterung* (Marienburg: Im Selbstverlage der altpreußischen Mennonitengemeinden, 1863). See also Dieter Götz Lichdi, *Über Zürich nach Addis Abeba: die Mennoniten in Geschichte und Gegenwart* (Maxdorf: Agape Verlag, 1983); Horst Penner, Horst Quiring and Horst Gerlach, *Weltweite Bruderschaft* (Weierhof: Verlag mennonitischer Geschichtsverein, 1984).

45 The most thorough account of Mennonites in the Third Reich is still Diether Götz Lichdi, *Mennoniten im Dritten Reich: Dokumentation und Deutung* (Weierhof: Mennonitischer Geschichtsverein, 1977). For a thorough analysis of German Mennonite periodical content, see Lichti, *Houses on the Sand?*

46 Christine Elizabeth King offers a concise overview of the SDA response in *The Nazi State and the New Religions*, 89–119.

47 On SDA susceptibility to Nazi racial hygiene, see Roland Blaich, "Health Reform and Race Hygiene: Adventists and the Biomedical Vision of the Third Reich," *Church History*, vol. 65,

no. 3 (September 1996). For a thorough review of periodical content, see Lichti, *Houses on the Sand?*

48 For a thorough review of Quakers in Nazi Germany, see Hans A. Schmitt, *Quakers and Nazis: Inner Light in Outer Darkness* (Columbia and London: University of Missouri Press, 1997).

49 Garbe, *Between Resistance and Martyrdom*, 231–34, 330.

50 Hans Albrecht, "Wo stehen wir?" *Der Quäker,* July 1940, 108.

51 Emil Fuchs, "Jesu Botschaft für unsere Zeit," address to the German Yearly Meeting, *Der Quäker*, November 1934, 265. Fuchs lost his position as a pastor soon after Hitler came to power; he had been active in the German Yearly Meeting prior to that time.

52 *Der Quäker*, January 1935, 25.

53 As Fuchs put it, neither *völkisch* nor racial theory may serve as the framework for the "choice of a life companion, the elevating experience of love." See Emil Fuchs, "Geist und Körper im Erleben der Liebe," *Der Quäker*, April–May 1937, 122.

54 E.A. Otto Peetz, *Allen Bruder Sein...Corder Catchpool (1883–1952), ein englischer Freund in deutscher Not* (London, Berlin, Bad Pyrmont: Society of Friends German and British), 31–32. Regarding an American Quaker who visited Germany during World War I to bring, with Jane Addams, a token offering of milk for German children, see "Portrait eines Quäkerbotschafters, Claire Carriere on Carolena Wood," *Der Quäker*, July 1936, 172–74. Already by 1914, Germany had become significantly dependent on importation of foreign foodstuffs. According to some estimates, as many as 750,000 Germans died of starvation during World War I. But the armistice (11 November 1918) did not bring relief: the allied blockade of Germany continued until 12 July 1919. Some have argued that hunger in Germany was greater during the postwar blockade than before the armistice. Individual British and American Friends managed to get some supplies through the blockade. James A. Huston, "The Allied Blockade of Germany 1918–19," *Journal of Central European Affairs*, vol. 10 (1950): 161–62; Suda Lorena Bane and Ralph Haswell Lutz, eds, *The Blockade of Germany after the Armistice 1918–1919: Selected Documents of the Supreme Economic Council, Superior Blockade Council, American Relief Administration and Other Wartime Organizations* (Stanford, 1924), 558–60, 670–71, 796–98, as cited by Peter Lowenberg, *Decoding the Past: The Psychohistorical Approach* (New York: Alfred A. Knopf, 1983), 254–59. In November 1919, the American Relief Administration entrusted the American Friends Service Committee with the administration of a massive program for feeding German children. The American Relief Administration was sponsored by the United States government, and was headed by the future US president Herbert Hoover, who was himself of Quaker stock. British Friends also became involved. The program became known as the *Quäkerspeisung*, the "Quaker feeding." The *Quäkerspeisung* continued from the immediate postwar period through the years of the Weimar Republic's spiraling inflation. John Ormerod Greenwood, *Quaker Encounters. Volume One: Friends and Relief* (York: William Sessions, 1975), 221–24; "Das Hilfswerk nach dem Kriege," *Monatshefte der deutschen Freunde*, January–March 1929, 14–15; Heinrich Otto, *Werden und Wesen des Quäkertums und seine Entwicklung in Deutschland* (Vienna: Sensen-Verlag, 1972), 215–16.

55 Peetz, *Allen Bruder Sein*, 24–25, 31–32, 65–71; Greenwood, *Quaker Encounters*, 232–34.

56 Carl Heath, "Schöpferische Ideen im internationalen Leben," *Der Quäker*, February 1935, 43. Early in 1938, leading German Quakers felt compelled to explain this ideological posture in regard to American and British Quaker efforts to ease suffering in the Spanish Civil War. Hans Albrecht clarified that, "as far as I have been informed, this work is supported from official [Quaker] position on the Franco side as well as on the other side": Hamburg Gestapo Report, 4 February 1938. Captured German Records Group T-175, Roll 645 (frames are unnumbered on this roll), Item No. EAP 173-b-16–14/51, Provenance: Geheimes Staatspolizeiamt/II A 2.

57 "In different ways and to different degrees [influential Quaker writers in the early years of the twentieth century] were influenced by the idealistic Neo-Hegelian philosophy which colored theological thinking in the later decades of the nineteenth century. This resulted in an optimistic view of human life and a high opinion of man as akin to God. Since then two world wars and their results in the form of totalitarian states have afforded a grim revelation of the evil that men can perpetrate." Howard H. Brinton, *Friends for 300 Years: The History and Beliefs of the Society of Friends since George Fox Started the Quaker Movement* (Wallingford, Pennsylvania: Pendle Hill Publications, 1994), ix.

58 E. Brenda Bailey, *A Quaker Couple in Nazi Germany: Leonhard Friedrich Survives Buchenwald* (York: William Sessions, 1994), 40.

59 Michael Seadle, "Quakerism in Germany: The Pacifist Response to Hitler" (unpublished dissertation, University of Chicago, June 1977). I have heard this critical tone also among some German Quakers, while others have strongly defended the accomplishments of their community during the Nazi period.

60 One example of such an activity was the distribution of anti-Hitler broadsides. See Penton, *Jehovah's Witnesses and the Third Reich*, 175–80.

61 Margarethe Lachmund provides another example, when she demanded that the Nazi Party's deputy chief for Mecklenberg end the harassment of a Jewish doctor. Seadle, "Quakerism in Germany," 143; Schmitt, *Quakers and Nazis*, 125.

62 John S. Conway, "Between Pacifism and Patriotism—a Protestant Dilemma: The Case of Friedrich Siegmund-Schultze," in *Germans Against Nazism: Nonconformity, Opposition and Resistance in the Third Reich: Essays in Honour of Peter Hoffmann*, ed. Francis R. Nicosia and Lawrence D. Stokes (Oxford and Providence, Rhode Island: Berg, 1990), 90–91. Siegmund-Schultze relatively soon abandoned the pursuit of open opposition in pursuit of a seemingly more pragmatic approach of ecumenical cooperation in assisting Jewish emigration, which—interestingly—aligned with the German Quaker approach. Yet his efforts came to naught, and he faced exile already in June of 1933. Had the provincial churches spoken out persistently with the "recklessness" that the situation called for, could Hitler ever have proceeded as far as he did?

63 The German Yearly Meeting numbered between 200 and 250 members during these years; according to one source, at least 16 German Quakers served varying terms of incarceration, some in prisons and others in concentration camps. Peetz, *Allen Bruder Sein*, 55.

64 Believers' communities do not baptize infants. They operate on the principle that membership entails an informed and conscious decision. On the significance of believers' Christianity, see Donald F. Durnbaugh, *The Believers' Church: The History and Character of Radical Protestantism* (New York: Macmillan and London: Collier-Macmillan, 1968).

65 Garbe, *Between Resistance and Martyrdom*, 385–91, 481, 483.

66 Jolene Chu provides some striking examples of assistance to Jews by Jehovah's Witnesses in "Purple Triangles: A Story of Spiritual Resistance," *Judaism Today*, Spring 1999, 15–19.

67 The corporate efforts on behalf of Jews were coordinated in part by International Centres in Germany; these were funded and managed by British and American Quakers, but the involvement of German Quakers was open and direct. For a concise overview of German Quaker assistance to Jews, see Lichti, *Houses on the Sand?* 185–96.

68 The German Yearly Meeting also did outreach to political prisoners who had been released from prison or concentration camps. See Lichti, *Houses on the Sand?* 135.

69 Lilli Pollatz, "Aus den großen Jahresversammlungen," *Der Quäker*, July 1931, 187. To be sure, access to that light is not automatic and must be nurtured. But its universal presence leads Quakerism toward the denominational mold, and Quaker decision-making—which is consensus based—is often considered a form of democratic process. See Brinton, *Friends for 300 Years*.

70 Roger C. Wilson, "Quäkertum und Demokratie," *Der Quäker*, November 1933, 285.

32

THE NEGLECTED MEMORY OF THE ROMANIES IN THE HOLOCAUST/ *PORRAJMOS*

Ian Hancock

why Hitler sought to eradicate the Romanies, a people who presented no
ally, politically, militarily or economically, one must interpret the under-
the Holocaust as being his attempt to create a superior Germanic popu-
ice," by eliminating what he viewed as genetic pollutants in the Nordic
he believed that Romanies constituted such contamination. In Nazi
ideology, two "racial" populations defined by biology were targeted for removal from
German "living space"—the Jews and the Romanies.[1] Raphael Lemkin, who coined the
term "genocide," made specific references to the slaughter of the "Gypsies" even before
World War II was over, thus linking Gypsies to the narrative of persecution and extermination experienced by Jews.[2] For most Romanies[3] today, however, the Holocaust or
Porrajmos lacks the special place it holds for Jews, and many Romanies view it as just one
more hate-motivated crisis—albeit an overwhelmingly terrible one—in their overall
European experience. Others refuse to speak about it because of its association with death
and misfortune, or to testify or accept reparation for the same reason.

The first German anti-Romani law was issued in 1416, when Romanies were accused
of being foreign spies, carriers of the plague, and traitors to Christendom; in 1500
Maximilian I ordered all to be out of Germany by Easter. Ferdinand I enforced expulsion and extermination orders in 1566; in 1659 the mass murder of Romanies took place
in Neudorf. In 1710, Prince Adolph Frederick of Mecklenberg-Strelitz condemned all
males to forced labor, had the women whipped and branded, and their children permanently removed. In 1721, Emperor Karl VI ordered the extermination of all Romanies,
220 years before the same directive was issued by Hitler. In 1725, Friedrich Wilhelm I of
Prussia condemned all Romanies 18 years and older to be hanged.

By the end of the eighteenth century, anti-Romani racism had received establishment
sanction from the Church and the Academy after Heinrich Grellmann published his
treatise demonstrating their Asian origin. He wrote that, in studying Romanies, he felt a
"clear repugnancy, like a biologist dissecting some nauseating, crawling thing in the
interests of science,"[4] echoed in the words of the Lutheran minister Martinus Zippel:
"Gypsies in a well-ordered state in the present day are like vermin on an animal's
body."[5] Acknowledgement of the physical and social differences of the Romanies was
being increasingly incorporated into German scholarly and ecclesiastical attitudes.

In 1808, Johann Fichte wrote that the German "race" had been selected by God himself for pre-eminence among the world's peoples;[6] two years later, the German nationalist Friedrich Ludwig Jahn wrote that "a state without *Volk* is a soulless artifice, while a *Volk* without a state is nothing, a bodiless, airless phantom, like the Gypsies and the Jews";[7] the fact of non-territoriality marked both Romanies and Jews as asocials, populations who did not fit in. In 1830, using the same techniques employed in the previous century, the Nordhausen city council attempted to bring about the eventual eradication of the Romani population by taking children away from their parents for permanent placement with German families. In 1835, Theodor Tetzner called Romanies "the excrement of humanity."[8] Robert Knox described them as the "refuse of the human race."[9]

In his influential treatise, Arthur de Gobineau argued that human beings could be ranked into higher and lower races, with the white "Aryans," and particularly the Nordic people within them, placed at the very top: "Aryans were the cream of mankind," he believed, "and the Germans, the cream of the cream—a race of princes."[10] This had particular impact upon the development of German philosophical and political thinking. In 1863, Richard Liebich wrote about the "criminal practices" of the Romanies,[11] and described them as *"lives unworthy of life,"* the first use of a phrase that was repeated in 1869 in an essay on Romanies by Kulemann, and which was later to have ominous significance.[12] The opinions of these scholars were having repercussions at the highest administrative levels, for just one year later, on 18 November 1870, Imperial Chancellor Otto von Bismarck circulated a brief demanding the "complete prohibition of foreign Gypsies crossing the German border," and which stated further that, when arrested, they were to be "transported by the closest route to their country of origin." When Alsace and Lorraine were annexed by the German Empire in 1871, each was made responsible for the control of Romanies at the borders into other areas of the new Reich.[13] That same year, Charles Darwin referred briefly to Roma and Jews in *The Descent of Man* in the context of the question as to the impact of climate on skin color. The exact line was: "An argument on the same side may likewise be drawn [discounting climate's effect] from the uniform appearance in various parts of the world of gypsies and Jews, although the uniformity of the latter has been somewhat exaggerated."[14] Many intellectuals twisted Darwin's science into the notion that only the "fittest survive"; in fact it was another British intellectual, Herbert Spencer, who actually coined this phrase (although Darwin incorporated the new concept in later editions of *On the Origin of Species*). Social Darwinism came to influence the discourse of a number of leading thinkers in the late nineteenth century, including Cesare Lombroso, whose influential 1876 work *L'Uomo Deliquente* contained a lengthy chapter on the genetically criminal character of the Romanies, whom he described as "a living example of a whole *race* of criminals." This was later translated into German and had a profound effect upon German legal attitudes. In 1890 or 1891, the Swabian parliament organized a conference on the "Gypsy Scum" and suggested means by which the presence of Romanies could be signaled by ringing church bells. The military was also empowered to apprehend and move Romanies out.

Under the directorship of Alfred Dillmann, the Bavarian police established The Central Office for Fighting the Gypsy Nuisance, in Munich in March 1899. Relevant documents began to be collected, particularly those pertaining to legislation and "criminality," and compiled into Dillmann's *Zigeunerbuch*, in which Romanies were described as "a pest against which society must unflaggingly defend itself,"[15] and special instructions were issued to the police by the Prussian government to "combat the Gypsy nuisance." The crimes listed in Dillmann's book consisted overwhelmingly of trespassing and stealing food.

Using Liebich's phrase in the title of their book,[16] the German jurist Karl Binding and psychiatrist Alfred Hoche argued in 1920 for euthanizing individuals who were *Ballastexistenzen*, dead weight on humanity. Three populations were considered: those with gross physical disfigurements, those carrying hereditary diseases, and those in comas considered unlikely to recover. Romanies would fall into the second category, their genetically transmitted disease being criminality; this rationalized the "preventative detention" of Romanies in Weimar Germany and was clearly racial: even if one had not committed a crime, one was likely to do so eventually because criminality was a genetic—that is, racial—characteristic.

By 1922, all Romanies in Baden were to be photographed and fingerprinted. The Bavarian parliament issued a new law "to combat Gypsies, nomads and idlers," and the Provincial Criminal Commission endorsed another decree, dated 16 July 1926, aimed at controlling the "Gypsy Plague." By 1927, legislation requiring the photographing and fingerprinting of Romanies had been introduced in Prussia, where 8,000 were processed in this way. Bavaria instituted laws forbidding Romanies to travel in family groups or to possess firearms. Romanies aged over 16 were liable for incarceration in work camps, while those without proof of Bavarian birth began to be expelled from Germany. In further direct violation of the Weimar Constitution, which guaranteed equal rights for all citizens, after 12 April 1928, Romanies in Germany were placed under permanent police surveillance. In the same year, Professor Hans F. Günther wrote that "it was the Gypsies who introduced foreign blood into Europe."[17] On 16–17 April 1929, the Munich Bureau's National Center jointly established a Division of Romani Affairs with the International Criminology Bureau (Interpol) in Vienna. Working closely together, they enforced restrictions on travel for all Romanies without documents, and imposed sentences of up to two years' detention in "rehabilitation camps" on Romanies 16 years of age or older.

On 20 January 1933, officials in Burgenland called for the rescinding of all civil rights from Romanies; in May, a law was introduced to legalize eugenic sterilization. In Germany, on 14 July, Hitler's cabinet passed the Law for the Prevention of Hereditarily Diseased Offspring, through which many "Gypsies" were eventually sterilized as "asocials." In November, the Nazis passed the Law against Dangerous Habitual Criminals, which resulted in the incarceration of Romanies in concentration camps. With the passage of the Nuremberg Laws in the fall of 1935 (and specifically the legal commentaries that followed it), Romanies were denied the right to marry or have sexual relations with other Germans. A telling policy statement issued by the Nazi Party read "In Europe generally, only Jews and Gypsies come under consideration as members of an alien people."[18]

The earliest Nazi document referring to "the introduction of *the total solution of the Gypsy problem* on either a national or an international level" was drafted under the direction of State Secretary Hans Pfundtner of the Ministry of the Interior in March 1936. In June and July, several hundred Romanies were transported to Dachau by order of the Minister of the Interior as "dependants of the Munich Bureau (of Gypsy Affairs)." In advance of the summer Olympics in Berlin, Romanies were cleared off the streets and forcibly relocated to the suburb of Marzhan, near a sewage dump. Also in 1936,

Dr Hans Globke, Head of Service at the Ministry of the Interior for the Third Reich, who served on the panel on racial laws, declared that "In Europe, only Jews and Gypsies are of foreign blood," and race-hygienist Dr Robert Körber wrote in his book *Volk und Staat* that "The Jews and the Gypsies are today remote from us because of their Asiatic ancestry, just as ours is Nordic."[19] This sentiment was reiterated by Dr E. Brandis, who wrote that besides the Jews "only the Gypsies are to be considered as an alien people in Europe."[20] German romaphobia became transnational when Interpol established the International Center for Combating the Gypsy Menace, formerly the Bureau of Gypsy Affairs. The main Nazi institution to deal with Romanies, the Racial Hygiene and Population Biology and Research Unit of the Ministry of Health, was established under the directorship of Dr Robert Ritter at Berlin-Dahlem, the expressed purpose of which was to determine whether the Romani people were Aryans or subhumans ("*Untermenschen*").

In a speech delivered before the German Association for Racial Research in September 1937, Adolf Würth of the Racial Hygiene Research Unit said "The Gypsy question is a racial question for us today. In the same way as the National Socialist state has solved the Jewish question, it will also have to settle the Gypsy question once and for all. The race biological research on Gypsies is an unconditional prerequisite for the Final Solution of the Gypsy Question."[21] An order released on 14 December stated that persons could be incarcerated on the grounds of their being inherently, as well as habitually, criminal, that is, whether they were actually engaged in criminal activity or not, but depending upon "genetic make-up" and their potential threat to Aryan security. By the end of 1937, large-scale round-ups of Romanies began. At Buchenwald, a special camp for "pure" Romanies was set up, and during the war, Romanies were incarcerated in camps in Nazi-controlled territories throughout Europe. Four hundred were sent to Taucha, others to Mauthausen, Gusen, Natzweiler, Flossenbürg, Ravensbrück, Westerbork, Malines, and elsewhere.

From 1937 onwards, the *Wehrmacht* High Command began issuing decrees ordering the exclusion of all Romanies from military service for reasons of "racial policy." In March 1938, Romanies were prohibited from voting, and in that same month, a letter to the "Imperial Leader of the SS" from Dr Werner Best, Head of the Nazi Security Police, addressed the "initiat[ion of the] Final Solution to the Gypsy problem from a racial point of view."[22] The first official, publicly posted Party statement to refer to the Final Solution of the Gypsy question (*endgültige Lösung der Zigeunerfrage*) was also issued at that time, signed by Himmler, who also ordered the Bureau of Romani Affairs to be moved from Munich to Berlin.

Between 12 and 18 June 1938, "Gypsy clean-up week" (*Zigeuneraufräumingswoche*) was in effect, and hundreds throughout Germany and Austria were rounded up and incarcerated;[23] in Mannworth, 300 Romani farmers and vineyard-owners were arrested in a single night. In a parallel development to the 1938 Jewish expulsions, Romanies were expelled from the left bank of the Rhine in August. In that month's issue of the *Bulletin of the German Association of National Socialist Physicians*, Dr Karl Hannemann wrote that "Rats, bedbugs and fleas are also natural occurrences in the same way as Jews and Gypsies. All existence is a struggle; we must therefore gradually biologically eradicate all these vermin."[24] After 4 September, Romani children were forbidden to attend public school.

An ironic footnote to the story of the persecution of Romani was the strand of thought, advanced by individuals such as Himmler, that the original Romani people hailed from regions of India where the "Aryan race" allegedly originated. Following this logic, the more Romani ancestry an individual had, the less threatening he was seen to be. And yet the standard by which Romani ancestry was determined was quite broad and damning; if two of one's eight great-grandparents were even part-Romani, that individual had too much "Gypsy blood" to be allowed, later, to live. These criteria were twice as strict as those applying to Jews; if the criteria for determining Jewishness had been applied to Romanies, some 18,000 would have escaped death (18,000 was also the total number of Romanies in Germany at the time).[25]

On 8 December 1938, Himmler signed a new order based upon the findings of the Office of Racial Hygiene, which had determined that Romani blood was "very dangerous" to Aryan purity. Dr Tobias Portschy, Area Commander in Styria, wrote in a memorandum to Hitler's Chancellery that "Gypsies place the purity of the blood of German peasantry in peril."[26] He recommended mass sterilization as a solution.

On 1 March 1939, the Order for the Implementation of the Reich Criminal Police Department was issued, stipulating that "The decree of the *Reichsführer SS* of 12 August 1938 orders the registration of persons living in the Reich territory who count as Gypsies. Once it has been established how many there are in the Reich territory, further measures can be taken."[27] Instructions for carrying out these orders were also issued in March, stating that "the aim of the measures taken by the state must be the racial separation once and for all of the Gypsy race from the German nation, then the prevention of racial mixing." Every police headquarters was to set up a unit to monitor Romani matters, and one or more persons were to be permanently responsible for Romanies. According to the minutes of a meeting organized by Reinhard Heydrich on 27 September, nearly a month after the start of World War II, Hitler instructed that German Romanies and Jews were to be moved by rail into Poland. That order came on 16 October: "With regard to the transportation of the Gypsies, we advise that the first transport of Jews is leaving Vienna on Friday, 20 October 1939; four wagons of Gypsies are to be added to that transport."[28] This may not have taken place, but in December, Hitler issued a new decree regarding these transportations, forbidding all "Gypsies and part-Gypsies" not already in camps from moving out of their areas, and trains were subsequently reported moving east "packed with Gypsies." Dr Johannes Behrendt of the Office of Racial Hygiene issued the statement that "All Gypsies should be treated as hereditarily sick; the only solution is elimination. The aim should therefore be the elimination without hesitation of this defective element in the population."[29] Justice Minister Otto Thierack would later write to Martin Bormann that he "intended to make the *Reichsführer SS* responsible for the prosecution of Poles, Russians, Jews and Gypsies; Poles and Russians can only be prosecuted by the police if they lived in the area of the former Polish state prior to September 1st. Prosecution proceedings against Jews and Gypsies, however, should be taken without observing these reservations."[30]

The first mass genocidal action against Gypsies took place in January or February 1940, when 250 Romani children in the concentration camp at Buchenwald were used as guinea pigs for testing the gas Zyklon B, later used for mass killings at Auschwitz-Birkenau.[31] Nazis in Alsace complied with an order to round up "criminals, asocials, the sick, French nationalists and of course the Jews and the Gypsies." In this year, Nazi statisticians Wetzel and Hecht estimated that "one hundred thousand Gypsies and others" were scheduled for deportation to Poland. They were shipped off between 15 and 18 May. A memorandum from Leonardo Conti, Secretary of State for Health in the

Ministry of Interior, to the Main Office of the Security Police, Kripo headquarters, and the Reich Health Department, Berlin, sent on 24 January 1940, read:

> It is known that the lives of Romanies and part Romanies are to be regulated by a Gypsy law (*Zigeunergesetz*)...I firmly believe, now as before, that the final solution of the Gypsy problem (*endgültige Lösung des Ziegeunerproblems*) can only be achieved through the sterilization of full and part Romanies...I think that the time for a legal resolution of these problems is over, and that we must immediately try to sterilize the Romanies and part Romanies as a special measure, using analogous precedents...Once sterilization is completed and these people are rendered biologically harmless, it is of no great consequence whether they are expelled or used as labor on the home front.[32]

In a speech delivered on 29 February to top-level Nazi party officials, Himmler said "The Gypsies are a question in themselves. I want to be rid of them this year if it is at all possible. There are only thirty thousand of them in the entire Reich, but they do great racial damage."[33] On 27 April, a joint order from NS Headquarters and the Chief of Police stated that "The first transport of Gypsies to the General Government will leave in the middle of May with 2,500 people." The following day, Heydrich sent out more precise instructions to chiefs of police and district governors in Germany in the so-called *Umsiedlungserlaß* for the "resettlement, arrest, and deportation of Romanies above the age of 17 from western and northwestern border zones."

On 18 May, Romanies were deported from seven assembly centers in the Old Reich to Lublin, located in the General Government. The first transport included 2,500 German Romanies, selected as full families wherever possible. The transport included 1,000 from Hamburg and Bremen, 1,000 from Cologne, Düsseldorf, and Hanover, and 500 from Stuttgart and Frankfurt. The deportation to Lublin proceeded as planned, although subsequent police reports revealed that a further 300 had been "evacuated," bringing the total number of deportees to 2,800.

On 10 October 1941, Heydrich proposed that German Romanies be sent to Riga with the Jews instead of being sent to Auschwitz and Chelmno in Poland. At the same meeting, the motion that Łódź be chosen as the final destination for non-German-born Romanies was approved, and between 9 and 11 November, five trainloads, each transporting a thousand Romanies, left from Austrian transit camps at Hartburg, Fürstenfeld, Mattersburg, Roten Thurm, Lackenbach, and Oberwart for Łódź, where they were joined by a transport of 20,000 Jews. Of the 5,000 Romanies deported, nearly two-thirds were children. In December and in January, Romanies were taken from Łódź to Kulmhof (Chelmno), where they were among the first to be killed in mobile gas vans. Clearly, the fall 1941 policy towards Gypises was to be one of systematic annihilation. On 24 November, the Commander of the *Wehrmacht* in Byelorussia stated "The Jews must disappear from the countryside and likewise the Gypsies must be eradicated."[34]

In early 1942, Romanies were selected for experimentation at Dachau and Buchenwald by Dr Adolf Pokorny, to see how long they could survive on sea water, claiming that they "must not only be conquered, but exterminated also."[35] That same spring, 1,000 Romanies were shot and buried alive in a single action on a collective farm near Smolensk. Nazi death squads entered Greece in June, murdering hundreds of Romanies. In Serbia, Military Governor Harald Turner announced—prematurely—that "Serbia is the only country in which the Jewish Question and the Gypsy Question have been resolved," warning that "one must not forget that the Jews and the Gypsies generally constitute a threat to security and, as such, pose a threat to peace and public order; it is the Jewish nature which is responsible for this war and, as for the Gypsy, by his nature he can never be a useful member of international society."[36] In Greece, 50 Romanies were murdered for each German casualty. In Croatia, an estimated 100,000 Romanies ultimately perished at the hands of the Ustaša, mostly at the Jasenovac camp.[37]

On 31 July, the Ministry of the Eastern Occupied Territories reaffirmed to the SS and police leaders in Riga the order that "the treatment of both Jews and Romanies was to be placed on equal footing (*gleichgestellt*)."[38] Romanies were being exterminated at Majdanek, Bełżec, Sanok, Sobibor, Chelmno, and Treblinka. In Bucharest, a policy statement that "for Romania, the Gypsy question is as important as the Jewish" was published. In the minutes of a 14 September meeting, Justice Minister Otto Thierack proposed that "Jews and Gypsies should be unconditionally exterminated."[39] A memo signed by Himmler requested data on Romani populations in Britain in anticipation of the eventual takeover of that country.[40]

On 26 January 1943, the president of the German Criminal Police Association issued the following statement: "Political preventative custody can be ordered to stop any further children of mixed blood issuing from the willful continuation of sexual union between Gypsies and Gypsies of mixed race, and those of German blood."[41] In February, the remaining Romanies were transported to Birkenau. The largest-ever transport of Polish Romanies was brought to the same camp in March. They were exterminated within the first month. Dutch Romanies began being transported to Auschwitz as well.[42] In his memoirs, SS Officer Percy Broad, who worked in the political division at Auschwitz, wrote that "it is the will of the all-powerful *Reichsführer* to have the Gypsies disappear from the face of the earth."[43] Eva Justin's book dealing with Romani children appeared in 1944. In it, she expressed the hope that it would serve as a basis for future race-hygiene laws regulating such "unworthy primitive elements." In May, when she had finished studying the children, they were all sent to Auschwitz and were killed there. In the early morning hours of 2/3 August 1944, 2,900 Romanies at Auschwitz-Birkenau were killed and cremated in one mass action, referred to as *Zigeunernacht*. On 26 September, a further 200 Romanies, mostly children, were shipped to Auschwitz from Buchenwald, and gassed two weeks later.

Not one Romani was called to testify on behalf of his own people at the Nuremberg Trials that began in October 1945. Some estimate that between 150,000 and 250,000 Romani perished during the war.[44] Others indicate that between one and one-and-a-half million Romanies died during the period 1933–45. If this estimate is correct, between 50 and 75 percent of the entire Romani population in Nazi-controlled Europe had perished at the hands of the Nazis, victims of racially motivated genocidal policy. At the Nuremberg Military Tribunals in September 1947, former SS General Otto Ohlendorf told presiding Judge Michael A. Musmanno that, in the killing campaigns, "There was no difference between Gypsies and Jews." As late as this date, Romani survivors from the camps were afraid to show themselves publicly because pre-Nazi laws were still in effect which would have put them back into detention centers if they were unable to show documentation proving German birth.

Despite the overwhelming documentary evidence to the contrary, in 1951, the Württemburg Ministry of the Interior issued a statement that judges hearing restitution claims should bear in mind that "Gypsies were persecuted under the National Socialist regime not for any racial reason, but because of an asocial and criminal record." Members of the shattered postwar remnants of the surviving Romani population lacked the where-withal legally to challenge this statement, and no outside agency came forward to take up the Romani case.

A report issued by the German Ministry of Finance in 1986 concluded that "all those victimized by Nazism have been adequately compensated...the circle of those deserving compensation need not be extended any further." Two years later, in February, the East German government announced its resolution to pay $100 million in war-crimes reparations to Jewish survivors, but refused to pay anything to Romani survivors. Finally, on 12 April 1990, the East German Government released a statement apologizing for the "immeasurable sorrow" the National Socialist regime had inflicted upon its victims, including Romanies, but "while the world celebrates the changes in Eastern Europe, the traditional Gypsy role of scapegoat is already being resurrected in countries like Romania and Hungary...Collective rights for minorities such as...Gypsies remains as elusive as ever."

Romani language terminology

Holocaust: O Baro Porrajmos
Nazis: Nacoci (Nacjonalne Socjalisturja)
Jews: Židovurja; Bibolde
Germans: Njamcurja
Final Solution of the Gypsy Question: O Paluno Impačimas le Rromane Pučhimaske
Final Solution of the Jewish Question: O Paluno Impačimas le Židovickone Pučhimaske
Survivors: E inkalde
Victims: Dukhadile
Gas chambers: Sobi gasoske
Ovens: Bova
Gypsy Night, Zigeunernacht: E Rjat le Rromane Phabimatangi
Kristallnacht: E Rjat la Phagerdja Vojagake
Gypsy Clean-Up Week: O Kurko e Šulavimaske le Rromenge

Notes

1 Recognition of this has been a long time coming. See Sybil Milton, "Nazi Policies toward Roma and Sinti," *Journal of the Gypsy Lore Society*, vol. 5, no. 1 (1992): 1–18; her essay "Gypsies and the Holocaust," *History Teacher*, 24 (1991): 375–87; and David Luebke, "The Nazi Persecution of Sinti and Ròma," unpublished paper, United States Holocaust Memorial Museum, 18 April 1990, 3. Richard Breitman argues that "[w]hatever its weaknesses, 'Final Solution' at least applies to a single, specific group defined by descent. The Nazis are not known to have spoken of the Final Solution of the Polish problem or of the gypsy [*sic*] problem." Richard Breitman, *The Architect of Genocide: Himmler and the Final Solution* (Hanover, New Hampshire: University Press of New England, 1991), 20. The fact that the concept of "race" has no scientific basis is irrelevant here, since Nazi ideology fabricated its own "racial" identities for Jews and Romanies and acted upon them. If we add the third group selected for elimination, the mentally and physically handicapped, then the "gene-pool pollutant" factor becomes all the more clear. One might consider, too, that male homosexuality was also documented by the Nazis as a "racially destructive phenomenon," a further weakening genetic element in the proposed "Master Race."

2 Raphael Lemkin, *Axis Rule in Occupied Europe: Laws of Occupation, Analysis of Government, Proposals for Redress* (Washington, DC: Carnegie Endowment for International Peace, 1944).

3 Called *O Baro Porrajmos* ("paw-rye-mawss"), or "The Great Devouring," in the Romani language. The Romani people are commonly, but inaccurately, referred to as "Gypsies," a label based on the false assumption that they had come into Europe from Egypt. The Romani population, numbering some 12 million throughout the world, consists of very many sub-groups, including the Sinti, the Roma, the Kalé, the Bashalde, the Romanichals, and so on. Originally from India, they left that region a millennium ago as a result of Islamic expansion, and entered Europe for the same reason some 250–300 years later.

4 Heinrich Grellmann, *Die Zigeuner* (Dessau and Leipzig: Kessinger, 1783).

5 In Johann Erich Biester, "Über die Zigeuner," *Berlinische Monatsschrift*, 21 (1793): 108–165.

6 Johann Fichte, *Versammlungen zum Deutschen Volk* (Leipzig, 1807–1808).

7 Friedrich Ludwig Jahn, *Deutsches Volksthum* (Lübeck: Niemann und Co., 1810).

8 Rainer Hehemann, *Die 'Bekämpfung des Zigeunerunwesens' im Wilhelminischen Deutschland und in der Weimarer Republik, 1871–1933* (Frankfurt am Main: Haag und Herschen Verlag, 1987), 99, 116, 127; Wolfgang Wippermann, *Das Leben in Frankfurt zur NS-Zeit: Die nationalsozialistische Zigeunerverfolgung* (Frankfurt am Main: W. Kramer & Co., 1986), 57–58.

9 Robert Knox, *The Races of Men* (London: Lea and Blanchard, 1850).

10 Joseph Arthur Gobineau, *Essai sur l'inégalité des races humaines* (Paris: Librairie de Firmin Didot Frères 1855).

11 Richard Liebich, *Die Zigeuner in ihrem Wesen und ihre Sprache* (Leipzig: Brockhaus, 1863).

12 Kulemann, in Joseph Tenenbaum, *Race and Reich* (New York: Twayne, 1956), 9.

13 Karola Fings and Frank Sparing, *Nur wenige Kamen zurück: Sinti und Roma im Nationalsozialismus* (Cologne: Stadt-Revue Verlag, 1990), 250.

14 Darwin, *The Descent of Man*, 2nd edn (New York: American Home Library, 1902), 256; John P. Fox, "The Nazi Extermination of the Gypsies: Genocide, Holocaust, or a 'minor irritant'?" Paper presented at the conference of the Association of Genocide Scholars, Williamsburg, Virginia, 14–16 June 1995, 7.

15 Alfred Dillmann, *Zigeuner-Buch* (Munich: Wildsche, 1905).

16 Karl Binding and Alfred Hoche, *Die Freigabe der Vernichtung lebensunwerten Lebens* (Leipzig: Felix Meiner, 1920).

17 As cited by Dov Freiburg, "Testimony," in Yad Vashem Archives A-361.

18 Hans Joachim Döring, *Die Zigeuner im Nationalsozialistischen Staat* (Hamburg: Kriminalistik Verlag, 1964), 37.

19 Robert Körber, *Rassesieg in Wien, der Grenzseste des Reiches* (Vienna: Wilhelm Braumuller, 1939).

20 Emil Brandis, *Ehegesetze von 1935 erläutet* (Berlin, 1946), 37.

21 *Reichsfuhrer-SS-Dokument S-Kr. 1*, No. 557 (1938).

22 Romani Rose, *'Der Rauch hatten wir täglich vor Augen': Der nationalsozialistische Völkermord an den Sinti und Roma* (Heidelberg: Wunderhorn, 1999), 347.

23 Miriam Novitch, *Le Génocide des Tziganes sous le Régime Nazi*, AMIF Publication No.164 (Paris: La Comité pour l'Erection du Monument des Tziganes Assassinés à Auschwitz, 1968).

24 Karl Hannemann, "Artfremde Gegenwart," *Bulletin of the German Association of National Socialist Physicians* (August 1938): 38.

25 Donald Kenrick, *Historical Dictionary of the Gypsies (Romanies)* (Lanham: The Scarecrow Press, 1998), 74–75.

26 Donald Kenrick and Grattan Puxon, *The Destiny of Europe's Gypsies* (London: Heinemann, 1972), 76.

27 Kenrick and Puxon, *The Destiny of Europe's Gypsies*, 74.

28 Novitch, *Le Génocide*, 9.

29 Johannes Behrendt, "Die Wahrheit über die Zigeuner," *NS-Partei Korrespondenz*, vol. 10, no. 3 (1939).

30 *Nuremberg Trial Documents* Nos. NG 558 and PS-654.

31 Emil Proester, *Vraždńí čs. Cikánů v Buchenwaldu*, Document No. ÚV ČSPB-K-135 of the Archives of the Fighters Against Fascism, Prague (1940).

32 Bundesarchiv, Document R18 Nr. 5644.

33 Romani Rose, *Der Rauch hatten*, 150.

34 Romani Rose, ed., *The National Socialist Genocide of the Sinti and Roma* (Heidelberg: Dokumentations-und Kulturzentrum Deutscher Sinti und Roma, 2003), 172.

35 Raul Hilberg, *The Destruction of the European Jews* (Chicago: Quadrangle Books, 1961), 608.

36 Raul Hilberg, *The Destruction of the European Jews*, 602, 1275.

37 Dragoljub Acković, "Suffering of the Roma in Jasenovac," in *Jasenovac and the Holocaust in Yugoslavia: Analyses and Survivors' Testimonies*, ed. Barry Lituchy (New York: Jasenovac Research Institute, 2006), 53–62.

38 *Zentrale Stelle des Landesjustizverwaltungen*, 19 August 1961.

39 *Nuremberg Trial Document* No. PS-682.

40 Document No. 66558/42, Central Office for Reich Security Dept. VI-D-7B, dated 14 August 1942.

41 Staatliche Kriminalpolizei, Memo No. K.130/43 (Z), 28 January 1943, Duisberg.

42 Jerzy Ficowski, *Cyganie na Polskich Drogach* (Cracow: Wydawnicwo Literackie, 1965), 110.

43 Percy Broad, "KZ Auschwitz: Erinnerungen eines SS Mannes," *Hefte von Auschwitz*, 9:7–48 (1966): 41. He reiterated this elsewhere, saying "the Central Office knew it was Hitler's aim to wipe out all the Gypsies without exception." See *Die Auschwitz-Hefte: Texte der polnischen Zeitschrift "Przeglad lekarski" über historische, psychische und medizinische Aspekte des Lebens und Sterbens in Auschwitz* (Auschwitz: Panstwowe Muzeum, 1959), 54.

44 Yehuda Bauer estimates that 150,000 Roma and Sinti were murdered; Donald Kenrick puts the number around 200,000, while the United States Holocaust Memorial Museum advances a figure closer to 220,000. See Yehuda Bauer, *Rethinking the Holocaust* (New Haven, Connecticut: Yale University Press, 2002), 66; Kenrick and Puxon, *The Destiny of Europe's Gypsies*, 83, 84; United States Holocaust Memorial Museum, www.ushmm.org/wlc/article.php?ModuleId=10005219

33

THE PERSECUTION OF GAY MEN AND LESBIANS DURING THE THIRD REICH

Geoffrey J. Giles

Before the Third Reich

As Germany had proven in the nineteenth century to be one of the most welcoming ... for Jews fleeing from discrimination or persecution elsewhere in Europe, so ... homosexuals flocked there in the 1920s. Major cities such as Berlin and ... came magnets for gay and lesbian culture during the Weimar Republic. As ... ...itism, there was an undercurrent of homophobia as a reaction against this ... Yet bars, clubs, and magazines flourished, and a feeling of ever-greater ... acceptance was the predominant one. Political initiatives toward the decriminalization of homosexuality seemed close to fruition. Both the powerful Social Democratic Party (*Sozialdemokratische Partei Deutschlands*, SPD) and the communists were more than once on the verge of persuading parliamentary subcommittees to endorse a vote on the issue by the whole Reichstag, only to see the motion tabled by the frequent collapse of coalitions and the formation of new governments that had more urgent items on their agenda. In 1931, the SPD dropped its crucial support, leaving the communists to carry the banner with little hope of attracting partners. What had happened? The SPD had come into possession of some private correspondence of the homosexual chief of staff of the Nazi Stormtroopers (*Sturmabteilung*, SA), Ernst Röhm. Immediately dropping its liberal stance on the gay question, the party seized the opportunity to launch a homophobic press campaign, not even hesitating to employ the Nazis' own accusations against ordinary homosexuals, by implying that Röhm was a pedophile who could not be trusted in charge of a youth organization.[1]

A minor issue for the Nazis?

For its part, the Nazi Party (*Nationalsozialistische Deutsche Arbeiterpartei*, NSDAP) had firmly rejected the relaxation of the law dealing with homosexual offenses, paragraph 175 of the German criminal code, whenever asked to declare its position. It was not, however, a topic that concerned Adolf Hitler very much, certainly not to the same degree as the Jewish question. He tolerated Röhm's proclivities and defended him against the objections of other Nazi leaders when necessary. Yet Hitler was fully aware of the considerable backlash of conservative, right-wing society against the libertarian atmosphere in Germany after World War I. Here was a useful card to play when the occasion demanded it. For the moment, Germany's homosexuals saw little threat to themselves from the Nazi movement, and some gay men actually joined the SA, attracted by the uniforms, the male camaraderie and, it must be admitted, the racist ideology. For homosexual men, like Jews, came from all sides of the political spectrum: some were as fiercely conservative as others were vigorously liberal. Indeed, when, immediately after the seizure of power in 1933, the Nazi authorities began closing down gay bars and arresting their clients in a move designed to placate Hitler's conservative coalition partners, some gay men promptly enrolled in the SA, believing that Ernst Röhm would protect them from homophobic attacks.

The Röhm Purge

That comforting illusion came to a sudden end in June 1934 with the murder of Röhm and other known homosexual SA leaders as part of the Night of the Long Knives. While Röhm's homosexuality was not the reason Hitler ordered him killed (but rather, the complaints of the army's generals that the millions-strong SA was eclipsing the German army), Propaganda Minister Joseph Goebbels left the public with the impression that the disgust he and Hitler had felt featured prominently in the decision.[2] Within days, the Bavarian *Gauleiter*, Adolf Wagner, had ordered an immediate round-up of homosexuals "to free society of this plague," and "for their own protection" in light of the repulsion felt by honest citizens. Some were sent immediately to Dachau without a trial. That concentration camp alone saw at least 600 homosexual inmates over the next decade.[3] The number is not large, but these "pink triangle" prisoners were subjected to particular brutality by the SS (*Schutzstaffel*, Protection Squadron) guards. The pink badge worn by concentration camp inmates accused of homosexual offenses is widely recognized today, having been adopted in the 1970s as a symbol of the gay emancipation movement in the United States and many other countries. Yet it was not the norm in all camps. Elsewhere, these inmates sometimes wore a badge with a large letter "A" emblazoned on it, for *Arschficker* ("ass-fucker").[4] Not a single pink triangle badge has survived to the present day. This is less a sign of its rarity than of the continuing stigma attached to homosexuals after the end of the war. Gay survivors did not want to reveal the reason for their incarceration by the Nazis. In addition, many "pink triangle" prisoners owed their survival to the fact that they had succeeded in exchanging their badge for the red triangle of a political prisoner, which significantly increased their chances of staying alive. This is the case with the badge worn by Josef Kohut, now on display at the United States Holocaust Memorial Museum in Washington, DC.[5]

Enforcing the law

The Night of the Long Knives, or Röhm Purge, is rightly seen as the major turning point away from official tolerance for homosexuals. Already in the first weeks of the Nazi regime, however, the Reichstag fire ushered in emergency legislation, giving the Nazis exceptional police powers to incarcerate alleged enemies of the state, and paved the way for the Enabling Act that cemented the dictatorial grasp of Adolf Hitler. In the policies toward homosexuals, the noose began to tighten even before the arson attack on the parliament building on 27 February 1933. Just the previous week, the Prussian Interior Ministry, headed by Hermann Göring, had ordered the closing down of known gay bars and homoerotic magazines. This initiative was explicitly welcomed by the Vatican, and may be seen as a move to increase support for the minority government of the Nazi Party among moralistic, conservative voters.[6] At this stage, few Germans believed that the Nazis would remain in power for very long, and so gay men and women simply needed to keep their heads down for a while. The open repression seemed to be but a harsher manifestation of the attitudes and legislation existing in most European countries in the early twentieth century. By the time of the Röhm Purge in the summer of 1934, the life-or-death urgency of a closeted existence was realized by many, but not all homosexuals. Gay men continued to frequent certain bars, which was risky behavior. The police had made note of such meeting places since the beginning of the century. Even before the Nazi revision of paragraph 175 made quite innocuous interaction between men punishable, the police were raiding gay bars. One evening in March 1935, Berlin Gestapo agents set out with a platoon of 20 SS men from the *Leibstandarte* Adolf Hitler, in order to round up homosexuals. They raided eight bars and netted at least four truckloads of suspects, who were first taken to Gestapo headquarters, then on the following day to the Columbiahaus concentration camp in the center of Berlin, where the torture of prisoners was routine, with the goal of making them sign false confessions.[7]

Tightening the law

The Supreme Court had established a curious twist in its interpretation of the section of the German criminal code dealing with homosexual offenses, paragraph 175, in a series of rulings since the late nineteenth century. It had become the rule that prosecutions were pressed successfully only if it could be proven in court that penetrative, or para-coital (*beischlafsähnlich*), sex had occurred—usually anal but sometimes oral. Other sexual practices, most notably mutual masturbation, generally resulted in acquittals. By the 1930s, this was well known not only in gay circles, but also, as testimony in countless criminal investigations reveals, among Germany's youth in general. Interrogated by Himmler's police officials, young men cheerfully admitted to having engaged in masturbation, secure in the belief that nothing could then prevent their immediate release. Unfortunately, the scope for prosecution had grown markedly greater in the summer of 1935. The legal profession itself, with frustrated state prosecutors in the vanguard, began to press for a tightening of the law. Already in the fall of 1933, the Ministry of Justice called together a commission to reform the entire criminal code. The existing paragraph 175 from 1871 had been taken over word-for-word from the penal code of Bismarck's North German Confederation, and read: "Unnatural indecency that is carried out between persons of the male sex, or by people with animals, is to be punished with imprisonment up to two years; the loss of civil rights may also be allowed." The Prussian penal code of 1851 had been similar in every respect, except for permitting a prison term of up to 4 years. As late as 1934, the commission still had a draft on the table that used the language of Weimar reformers in narrowing the offense to a "para-coital act."[8] Yet that was swept aside on the advice of Count Wenzeslaus Gleispach, the Berlin law professor charged with making recommendations on morals offenses.

The new version of the paragraph, promulgated on 28 June 1935, read as follows:

§175 Indecency Between Men

A man who commits indecency with another man, or allows himself to be misused indecently, will be punished with prison.

In especially minor cases the court can refrain from punishment of a participant, who was not yet twenty-one years old at the time of the criminal act.

This new paragraph 175, then, crucially deleted the word "unnatural" in order to make the reach of the law more extensive, rather than restricted to specific sexual acts. In addition, where the courts in the past had tended to see one partner as the active party and the other as passive (reflecting "Victorian" views about heterosexual relationships), now the judges could find equal guilt among both parties, if the partner of the initiator had not resisted the former's advances. The second part of the new provision seemed to reflect a common-sense acknowledgment that teenage boys not uncommonly engage in sexual experimentation with one another. Indeed, the commentary published about the new reforms reinforced that view:

> The language of the new provisions *per se* also encompasses misdemeanors that occur from time to time, as experience shows, among schoolboys, especially in boarding schools. Even if they do represent a regrettable vice to be suppressed with all the rigor of school discipline, they do not as a rule cause any lasting damage to those concerned. Such cases do not require judgment from a criminal court judge.[9]

Regrettably, common sense was not always a prominent characteristic of the police during the Third Reich, and hundreds of ordinary schoolboys were indeed dragged into the courtroom in the coming years to answer the charge of being a homosexual. The law had changed, but the problem was that the public did not become aware of the finer points of this tightening of the provisions against alleged homosexual behavior. Even at the height of the anti-homosexual crackdown in the Frankfurt area just before the war, there remained a press blackout regarding the campaign, for fear of the suggestive power among German youths of reports of homosexual acts. The state prosecutor lamented: "Publication is not possible, for this would mean an endangerment of young people."[10]

The new version of paragraph 175 removed the necessity for the state prosecutor to prove that penetrative intercourse had taken place. In fact, a man did not even have to touch the other person to be convicted of a homosexual offense. Though this rarely happened in practice, it was considered a perfectly legitimate interpretation of the law. As a commentary on the penal code put it in 1942: "Indecency with another man is committed by someone using the body of another man as a means to arouse or satisfy his sexual lust. It is not necessary for physical contact to have taken place or even to have been intended."[11] This covered situations, which indeed came before the courts, where one man had masturbated in front of another, or two men had masturbated together but without touching each other. They could still be sent to prison. There were even cases of entrapment on the Russian front. A gay soldier walking in the square of an occupied Soviet town thought he was being cruised by a civilian there. Having approached him, he did no more than lightly brush against him in passing, when the other revealed himself to be an SS sergeant and promptly had the soldier arrested for a homosexual offense. The latter was stripped of his rank and sent to jail for one whole year.[12]

Deliberate entrapment was another problem for homosexuals during the Third Reich. In one case, a pair of twins amused themselves by pretending to encourage sexual advances in the rest rooms at the Alexanderplatz in Berlin, before handing over their victims to the police.[13] The police themselves often raided public toilets (as they had done since the beginning of the century), but Burkhard Jellonnek has shown that such a proactive policy was principally confined to big cities, which boasted a larger police force, and in smaller communities they relied more on denunciations, which were certainly plentiful.[14]

The Nazis' homosexual problem

Opposition to homosexuality within the Nazi movement was rooted in separate but overlapping prejudices. Among the earliest myths was that homosexuals were generally pedophiles. That poisonous dart was launched well before the Nazis came to power. In October 1928, socialist students at a Berlin high school held a meeting with several outside speakers, including the well-known sexologist Dr Magnus Hirschfeld. In fact, the evening's discussion focused largely on student self-government, and Hirschfeld himself talked not about sex education, but about the regrettable wave of student suicides that were occurring. The Nazi Party newspaper, the *Völkischer Beobachter*, devoted fewer than five lines to his address in a three-column article, but the lengthy headline was all about Hirschfeld: "Homosexuals as Lecturers in Boys' Schools. Magnus Hirschfeld, the 'pioneer' for the repeal of §175, is permitted to speak in German high schools. The destruction of German youth! German mothers, working women! Do you want to put your children into the hands of homosexuals?"[15] The same ploy was used in the vicious campaign against the Catholic church in the mid-1930s, resulting in countless show trials against monks and priests on charges of sex abuse of boys in their care. Even if some of the charges may have had merit, the sheer scale of the campaign—there were some 250 trials in 1936–37 alone—raised doubts in the minds of the public about their validity. Propaganda Minister Joseph Goebbels knew that many of them were bogus, remarking: "When Himmler wants to get rid of someone, he just throws §175 at him." Nevertheless, the press campaign went into high gear on this subject until the Propaganda Ministry acknowledged that it was backfiring.[16]

Unpatriotic childlessness

Germany had suffered great losses to its population in World War I, with some two-and-a-half million deaths. Austria–Hungary forfeited another one-and-a-half million citizens to the war. Yet Adolf Hitler was clear in his mind from early in his political career that he would fight another war, and seize living space for Germany in the east. That would require large armies and a steady supply of recruits. During the Third Reich, women were offered inducements to produce large families, from monetary allowances to the Mother's Cross in bronze, silver, and gold for those who bore four, six, or eight children, respectively. Homosexual men were considered to be abrogating their responsibility to the nation in not marrying and siring healthy sons for the German *Wehrmacht*. Heinrich Himmler saw in this situation a serious sexual imbalance that would lead to a permanent decline in the population if allowed to continue. In a 1937 speech to SS generals, he speculated that there were some 20 million sexually capable men in the German population of 67–68 million. However, "if I assume there are one to two million homo-sexuals, the result is that seven, eight, or ten per cent of the men in Germany are homosexual. That means, if things stay that way, that our race will collapse under this epidemic."[17] Himmler's concerns about an inexorable shrinking of the population dated from his 1927 reading of a book from the lunatic fringe. Herwig Hartner's *Eroticism and Race* claimed that an unchecked expansion of homosexuality would lead quite literally to the "destruction of mankind." It was in fact a devious Jewish plot to shrink the world status of Germany to insignificance.[18] Himmler was impressed by this "valuable" and "necessary collection of evidence," and the fear never left him.[19]

The conspiratorial nature of homosexuals

SA chief Ernst Röhm indeed included homosexuals like Karl Ernst in his inner circle, but that did not mean that the Nazi Stormtroopers were run by a homosexual clique. The very conventional Himmler himself enjoyed high rank in the SA, as head of the initially insignificant SS. Yet Himmler, borrowing an idea from Hitler, believed that homosexuals would not follow meritocratic ideals (which Nazi leaders liked to think were guiding them) in choosing leaders and associates, but rather would give preferment to other men based solely on the "erotic principle." In other words, if you once gave a position of authority to a homosexual, very soon an entire party unit, or department or government ministry, would be full of them. Homosexuals were more loyal to each other than to their country or the Nazi Party. That argument was hinted at in Goebbels' and Hitler's public justification for the murder of Ernst Röhm and his associates in June 1934. And it was enunciated again and again in the Nazi press, as for example in the 1937 article in the SS newspaper, *Das Schwarze Korps*, titled "These are Enemies of the State!" The diatribe culminated in the call: "These are not 'poor, sick people' to be 'treated,' but rather enemies of the state are to be eradicated!"[20]

Homosexuality as a disease

In the Nazi stereotype, homosexuals preyed principally on teenage boys, seduced them, and infected them with a predilection for homosexual behavior. Homosexuality was catching! The literature of the period is full of disease metaphors, describing homosexuality as a plague or an epidemic. The fear was that young men would be "turned" permanently away from the path of heterosexual normality, and never become fathers. The police, who, having confiscated the address book of a single alleged homosexual, then investigated all his acquaintance on similar suspicions, often believed that they had broken into whole networks of sexual perversion, as the net widened with the address books and contacts of others. The multiple partners revealed in a landmark Weimar case in 1935 seemed to justify this alarm.[21] The fact was that many young men, who, like most Germans, remained ignorant about the tightening of the law, spoke openly and without regret about mutual masturbation, believing this quite rightly to be harmless in terms of its effect of their essential sexual orientation. The Nazi authorities, however, viewed it as the highly danger-ous first step down an extremely slippery slope to full-blown homosexuality. It was essential therefore to nip such activity in the bud. In the late 1930s and beyond, the efforts to halt the spread of this "disease" resulted in the arrest of thousands of ordinary teenagers, who had not been particularly worried about their "fooling around" in the way that teenagers always have done.[22]

Modifying the definition

Nazi racial thinking built on the turn-of-the-century debates about criminality and eugenics, which stressed the relative ease of identifying undesirables, in some measure through their physical characteristics. It also worried about the hereditary nature of these faults. Having decided that homosexual tendencies were a sign of a degenerate and distinctly un-Aryan personality, Himmler became increasingly perturbed by the repeated incidence of homo-sexual activity within the elite SS. Here were men who had passed the most stringent tests of racial superiority. These men were the super-Aryans. Surely, then, they could not be homosexuals. Indecent acts between SS men were continually being reported to him, even featuring officers in his own headquarters. Gradually, Himmler and other German officials came to believe that not all men who had engaged in homosexual activity were necessarily irremediable homosexuals. A man who had, quite out of character, succumbed to tempta-tion, especially under the influence of alcohol, might somehow be "cured" if steps were taken quickly. The cure might range from a short stay in a concentration camp to a lengthy psychotherapeutic treatment. The problem of identifying a "real" homosexual was never solved for the duration of the Third Reich. One of the most thorough discussions of the question came in the form of guidelines issued in June 1944 by the chief air force medical officer, General Oskar Schröder. He placed the men under discussion in three categories: quasi-homosexuals, experiential homosexuals, and born homosexuals. The first group did not experience homosexual desires under normal circumstances, but might be led astray under the influence of alcohol or drugs. Or they might be trying to secure favorable treat-ment from a homosexual superior by prostituting themselves. Schröder felt that the overall estimates of the number of homosexuals were unjustly skewed by this particularly large category. The experiential homosexuals were men who had not been born with a deviant disposition, but had undergone an irregular childhood and puberty. This was "extra-ordinarily often" the fault of a "cold, strict, mirthless, unfeminine" mother, and the onset of erotic feelings thus sought attachment to another male. They, too, could be saved with the help of psychotherapy. Then there were the "real" homosexuals, who had been born that way. They were "more dangerous by far" than the others, though Schröder confessed that medical science was "still completely in the dark [about] the nature of a homosexual disposition."[23] Because of the difficulty of categorizing suspects accurately, the military never solved the problem of how many suspects to dismiss permanently from the service without overly damaging the numerical strength of the troops. In the first 4 years of the war, the army alone had dealt with over 5,800 cases of homosexuality.[24]

Heightened policing

While Hitler himself rarely addressed the issue of homosexuality, Himmler became more and more obsessed with the idea of cleansing the nation of this anomaly. When he became head of all German police forces in 1936, he had unrestricted authority to direct a concentrated campaign in this direction. Already in 1934 he had set up at Gestapo headquarters a special desk to deal with the homosexual question. It solicited lists from police stations with the names of all men known to have engaged in homosexual behavior. A chart from the beginning of June 1935 showed that, just in the previous month, the Prussian Gestapo alone had incarcerated 513 suspected homosexuals for "preventive detention" in a concentration camp, where of course they had no access to legal due process. The Lichtenburg concentration camp held 325 of these individuals.[25] In October 1936, Himmler, now in charge of the police forces of all the federal states, went a step further and set up a Reich Central Office for Combating Homosexuality and Abortion. This sounded like a continuation of the rational objection to those who were confounding the call to add 1.5 million babies to the German population each year, and provided the public with reasonable grounds to support the crackdown. The police were now given detailed instructions about how to spot a homosexual, and not just those who were flamboyant. Even those men who were discreet could often give themselves away, if they were known to avoid female company, and were usually seen with other men, often walking arm-in-arm with them. Hotel receptionists, railway station porters, taxi drivers, rest room attendants, hairdressers, and bath house supervisors should be quizzed about likely suspects. Men who took a double room in a hotel were especially suspicious.[26] The problem was that there were thousands of homosexual men who did not follow the popular stereotypes, and conversely other men who were effeminate but not at all homosexual. Nevertheless, the police now proceeded to detain men on charges of violating paragraph 175 with a vengeance. Just in the 3 years 1937–39, almost 95,000 arrests were made. Nationwide, that amounted to over 600 per week. This represented a major investment of time and manpower, and underlines the Nazi obsession with the homosexual question.

The Reich Central Office was headed by Josef Meisinger, who gave a lecture to his associates in April 1937 about the extent and nature of the problem they were tackling. He emphasized the epidemic spread of homosexuality, especially among teenage youths. If an adult seducer conquered one of these youths, the latter's friends would "usually" be introduced to him and fall prey to his assaults as well. Meisinger stated that the average confessions wrested from such men included an admission to such "swinish behavior" with 50 or more boys. In the case of one recent prosecution, he claimed that the court had proven the convicted man to have seduced 800 boys under the age of 16! Citing another case running into hundreds of victims of one man, and yet another who also murdered 20 people, he was suggesting that this was not at all unusual behavior for homosexuals.[27]

The policy toward lesbians

The thrust of police prosecution was directed toward homosexual men. Lesbian relations had never been covered under paragraph 175 after 1871, and that continued to be the case even after the tightening of the law in 1935. Certainly, there was a desire to stop all non-procreative sexual activity, but even the best legal minds of the Third Reich could not fathom how to identify lesbians, given the public shows of affection displayed by all women. Kissing, embracing, or walking arm-in-arm was not the tell-tale sign of sexual deviance that it was thought to represent for men. More importantly, lesbian women were by no means incapable of producing children. Meisinger summed up the standard view to his colleagues in 1937: "Experience shows that homosexual men are inoperable for normal sexual intercourse." On the other hand, he found that "the great majority of girls engaging in lesbian behavior are anything but abnormal. If these girls receive the opportunity to fulfill the task allotted them by nature, then they will certainly not fail."[28] Whether they wanted to have sex with men or not, women could still be impregnated (raped) and produce children for the *Führer*. During the war, attempts to expand paragraph 175 still further to include lesbian activity were postponed for the duration, but some lesbians were indeed incarcerated in concentration camps as "asocials." In a particularly cruel move, they were sometimes assigned to the camp brothel.[29]

The experience in the camps

One needs to distinguish between the regular prisons in Nazi Germany, which were bad enough, and the concentration camps, which lay completely outside the justice system, in the hands of the SS and Gestapo. Homosexuals serving a prison sentence still had some recourse to lawyers and appeals, and the length of their prison term had been fixed by the court. Those who vanished behind the barbed wire of a concentration camp were held arbitrarily for an indefinite period. Within the camps, homosexuals were treated so badly that, in one bizarre instance, inmates deliberately committed homosexual acts in order to be charged by the police, brought outside before a regular court, and sent to a standard prison. Unfortunately, they were not privy to the latest developments in Himmler's policy after the beginning of World War II. From 1939, any convicted homosexual who had "seduced" more than one person, which was deemed to be the case for a second offense, was sent to prison or penitentiary in the usual way, but no longer released at the end of the appointed jail term. Instead of being freed, they were transferred immediately to a concentration camp for an indefinite period, as now happened to these re-offenders at Sachsenhausen.[30] In the camps, they were subjected to the murderous whims of the SS guards, who frequently picked out pink triangle prisoners and deliberately murdered them, despite the fact that it was more or less the policy at camps such as Mauthausen and Flossenbürg literally to work these men to death in any case. Thus, in Sachsenhausen in the summer of 1942, several reports from inmates confirm that homosexuals were deliberately taken aside in one of the workplaces and murdered. Estimates of such deaths range between 100 and 200 in the period between July and mid-September 1942. Recent meticulous research has established that at least 79 pink triangle prisoners were killed in the brick works (just one of the murder sites) during the month of July alone. Seven hundred homosexual inmates died in Sachsenhausen between 1936 (when the camp was opened) and 1945.[31]

Death sentences for homosexuals

Heinrich Himmler had always talked tough about the treatment of homosexuals. Already, in his 1937 speech to SS generals, he announced his decision that any SS man convicted of a homosexual offense would first serve out the prison sentence handed down by the judge, but would then be transferred to a concentration camp and would be shot dead there "while trying to escape."[32] In actuality, that policy was never implemented. Sometimes, despite fairly persuasive evidence, men were acquitted altogether. In a late-night conversation with Goebbels and others on 18 August 1941, Hitler held forth about the homosexual question. He stressed that his officers should act "with ruthless severity" to keep, in particular, all Nazi Party organizations and the armed services "clean." But then, reflecting the concern that teenagers were especially vulnerable to being "turned" irremediably into homosexuals, Hitler continued: "In *one* organization every case of homosexuality must be punished with death, namely in the Hitler

Youth."[33] Himmler was not present at this soirée, but when he was alerted to the comments, he quickly realized that, if the Hitler Youth was going to take such a firm stand, the Nazi racial elite of the SS could not lag behind. In fact, the Hitler Youth did not start killing the thousands of teenagers who engaged in sexual horseplay in its camps and youth hostels. But Himmler, eager to set an example, was not to be stopped, and went ahead with the preparation of an official decree mandating the death sentence to any SS or police member found guilty of a homosexual transgression. Above all, this would serve as a deterrent, but its effectiveness in that direction was severely hampered by the *Führer* himself. Upon signing the document on 15 November 1941, Hitler insisted that there should be absolutely no publicity about the new policy, because its draconian nature would give the impression to Germany's enemies that the nation had an especially high incidence of homosexuality, something that oppositional propagandists there and abroad had been claiming since the days of Ernst Röhm. The measure was never published, even in the SS newspaper, and the blackout forced Himmler to resort to a complicated process, whereby all the thousands of SS men were supposed to be called in one-by-one by their superior officers, shown the decree, and then asked to sign a form acknowledging that they had seen and understood it. There is considerable evidence that this, too, did not happen everywhere, and many arrested SS or policemen credibly insisted that they had never heard of the decree.[34]

Some death sentences were carried out against Himmler's men, but just as often the SS chief would relent and commute the sentence, if he could persuade himself that the guilty man was not a *real* homosexual, but had suffered a momentary lapse, especially under the influence of alcohol. His policy then was often to send the unfortunate man to prove himself in battle at the most dangerous parts of the front line as part of the Dirlewanger Brigade, in which the chances of survival were dim.

No gay Holocaust

Even in the SS and police, then, we cannot speak of a consistent policy to wipe out all homosexuals in the same way as Nazi thinking applied to Jews. Homophobia was pervasive among the Nazi leadership, and indeed among the German population as a whole (in similar measure to other European countries at the time). Yet the persecution of the several million homosexuals in Germany and its occupied territories was hampered by difficulties over identifying them and uncertainty about the nature of homosexuality. If only some 100,000 men were ever arrested on charges under paragraph 175 during the Third Reich, and only half of them actually convicted, a final solution of the "homosexual problem" would seem to have been elusive, or even not a particularly high priority. Yet it is clear that it remained an obsession in SS and police headquarters, and among leaders of other party organizations. It was, however, a problem that could wait for the moment. Wartime comments and discussions make it clear that, after the presumed successful conclusion of the war by the Germans, the persecution of homosexuals would be ramped up considerably. Castrations would become standard policy, lesbians would be included in paragraph 175, and death sentences for multiple offenders would become the norm. The continuing characterization of homosexuals as child molesters would make it easy to gain the support of the public for a more sweeping campaign. However, all this depended on the ability of the police to locate homosexuals, who for the most part were surprisingly successful in keeping themselves hidden in this police state. And it would require a resolution of the question of who was a homosexual. At what point did someone become *a* homosexual? When did it become too late to "cure" the person? Was this indeed, as some argued, a hereditary disease, so that an offender's whole family might need to be wiped out? The internal experience gained within the elite SS did not augur well for a ready solution to all this. Identifying a man as a full-blown homosexual worthy of punishment was not as easy as picking out a Jew, or a gypsy, or a Freemason, or a Catholic, or indeed many of the putative enemies of the Reich. And frustration over the near-impossibility of a complete or final solution to the homosexual problem would doubtless have led to a more consistent radicalization, as we see in other areas of the Holocaust. As it was, homosexuals were treated worse than most other prisoners in the camps, apart from the Jews. Although it is believed that only some 5,000–15,000 homosexuals were consigned to a concentration camp, their death rate is much higher than that of other groups of prisoner—two out of three pink triangle prisoners did not survive. From 1941 onwards, the main task of the SS was to kill all the Jews of Europe. When that goal had been reached, which the Nazis confidently expected to be possible, it would have been absolutely necessary to switch to other targets of persecution in order to maintain the illusion of a permanent revolution. Numerically, homosexuals represented one of the largest domestic target groups of the Nazis. And if they could all be success-fully portrayed as potential pedophiles, even fewer people would spring to their defense than in the case of the Jews. The future for homosexuals indeed looked bleak in the case of a Nazi victory in World War II.

Notes

1 W.U. Eissler, *Arbeiterparteien und Homosexuellenfrage: Zur Sexualpolitik von SPD und KPD in der Weimarer Republik* (Berlin: Winkel, 1980). At this time, the Hitler Youth stood formally under the overall command of the SA.
2 "Die Aktion des Führers," *Völkischer Beobachter*, Sondernummer, 1 July 1934.
3 Barbara Distel, ed., *Konzentrationslager Dachau 1933 bis 1945: Text- und Bilddokumente zur Ausstellung* (München: KZ-Gedenksta?tte Dachau, 2005), 77.
4 "We Were Marked with a Big A," United States Holocaust Memorial Museum, VHS, 1994.
5 Kohut was the author of the early autobiographical work, *The Men With the Pink Triangle* (Boston: Alyson Publications, 1980), which he wrote under the pseudonym Heinz Heger.
6 Günter Grau, ed., *Homosexualität in der NS-Zeit: Dokumente einer Diskriminierung und Verfolgung*, 2nd edn (Frankfurt: Fischer, 1993), 56–60.
7 Meldung SS-Obersturmführer Carl Marks, 11 March 1935, Bundesarchiv Militärarchiv Freiburg (BAMA), LSSAH v.57. The late Dr Sybil Milton was kind enough to share this document with me.
8 Kai Sommer, *Die Strafbarkeit der Homosexualität von der Kaiserzeit bis zum Nationalsozialismus* (Frankfurt: Peter Lang, 1998), 362–71.
9 Geoffrey Giles, "Legislating Homophobia in the Third Reich: The Radicalization of the Prosecution Against Homosexuality by the Legal Profession," *German History*, vol. 23, no. 3 (2005): 339–54.
10 Lagebericht Oberstaatsanwalt Frankfurt/Main, 24 January 1939 [Klein, 1999 #170], p. 504.
11 Quoted in Joachim Müller, "'Unnatürliche Todesfälle':Vorfälle in Außenbereichen Klinker-werk, Schießplatz und Tongrube," in *Homosexuelle Männer im KZ Sachsenhausen,* eds Joachim Müller and Andreas Sternweiler (Berlin: Rosa Winkel, 2000), 255.
12 John Borneman, ed., *Gay Voices from East Germany: Interviews by Jürgen Lemke* (Bloomington, Indiana: Indiana University Press, 1991), 33.
13 Gabriele Rossbach, "'*Daß ein weiteres Streiten für mich keinen Zweck mehr hat*': Vorbestraft und vorverurteilt," in *Wegen der zu erwartenden Strafe: Homosexuellenverfolgung in Berlin 1933–1945,* eds Andreas Pretzel and Gabriele Roßbach (Berlin: Rosa Winkel, 2000), 278–86.

14 Burkhard Jellonnek, *Homosexuelle unter dem Hakenkreuz: Die Verfolgung von Homo-sexuellen im Dritten Reich* (Paderborn: F. Schöningh, 1990).

15 *Völkischer Beobachter*, Bayernausgabe, 31 October 1928.

16 Hans Günter Hockerts, *Die Sittlichkeitsprozesse gegen katholische Ordensangehörige und Priester 1936/37. Eine Studie zur nationalsozialistischen Herrschaftstechnik und zum Kirchenkampf* (Mainz: Matthias-Grünewald Verlag, 1971), 62.

17 Himmler deducted women, children and the elderly from the total population in his calcula-tion. Speech to SS-*Gruppenführer*, 18 February 1937, in *Heinrich Himmler: Geheimreden 1933 bis 1945 und andere Ansprachen*, eds Bradley F. Smith and Agnes Peterson (Frankfurt am Main: Propyläen Verlag, 1974), 93.

18 Herwig Hartner, *Erotik und Rasse: Eine Untersuchung über gesellschaftliche, sittliche und geschlechtliche Fragen* (München: Deutscher Volksverlag, 1925).

19 Library of Congress (LC) Himmler file, container 418.

20 "Das sind Staatsfeinde!" *Das Schwarze Korps*, 4 March 1937.

21 Giles, "Legislating Homophobia in the Third Reich."

22 Geoffrey Giles, "The Institutionalization of Homosexual Panic in the Third Reich," in *Social Outsiders in Nazi Germany,* eds Robert Gellately and Nathan Stolzfus (Princeton, New Jersey: Princeton University Press, 2001), 223–55.

23 Anweisung für Truppenärzte zur Beurteilung gleichgeschlechtlicher Handlungen, Schröder, 7 June 1944, BAMA H20/479. The memo was prepared without consultation with the army, which rejected several key points.

24 Handwritten note on OKH memo, Entlassung von Soldaten aus dem aktiven Wehrdienst wegen widernatürlichen Unzucht, 22 July 1943, ibid.

25 Grau, *Homosexualität in der NS-Zeit*, 89.

26 Giles, "The Institutionalization of Homosexual Panic," 243.

27 Extracts in Grau, *Homosexualität in der NS-Zeit*, 147–53.

28 Grau, *Homosexualität in der NS-Zeit*, 147–53.

29 Borneman, *Gay Voices from East Germany*, 23.

30 Andreas Pretzel, "'*Ich wünsche meinem schlimmsten Feind nicht, daß er das durchmacht, was ich da durchgemacht habe*': Vorfälle im Konzentrationslager Sachsenhausen vor Gericht in Berlin," in *Wegen der zu erwartenden Strafe* (Pretzel and Roßbach, eds), 119–68.

31 Müller, "Unnatürliche Todesfälle'," 234–58.

32 Smith and Peterson, eds, *Heinrich Himmler: Geheimreden 1933 bis 1945 und andere Ansprachen*, 97.

33 Geoffrey Giles, "The Denial of Homosexuality: Same-Sex Incidents in Himmler's SS and Police," in *Sexuality and German Fascism*, ed. Dagmar Herzog (New York: Berghahn, 2004), 265–70.

34 Herzog, ed., *Sexuality and German Fascism*, 265–70.

DOUBLE JEOPARDY
Being Jewish and female in the Holocaust

Myrna Goldenberg

The will to live is nourished only by hope.[1]

The philosopher Joan Ringelheim has remarked that genocide is an equal opportunity victimizer and, in fact, that "every Jew was equally a victim in the genocide of the Holocaust."[2] Indeed, Nazi policy marked every Jew for murder, but Nazi practice differentiated men and women in most phases of the Holocaust.[3] Yet, for decades, the Holocaust was known through the experiences of men. Their experiences became *the* Jewish experience.[4] Obviously, men's experiences are true for men—but not necessarily, and in some aspects not at all, true for women—for example, the issues of menstruation, rape, pregnancy, and childbirth. Undoubtedly some men were raped, but, for sure, no man was pregnant. As a partial response to critics who claim that the study of women and the Holocaust trivializes the subject, John Roth argued that it is through the particularities of the victims that we develop a reliable knowledge base about this genocide.[5] The fact is that women faced a double jeopardy: First, they were targeted for death because they were Jews; second, they suffered, and those who survived often attribute their survival in large part to behaviors they learned, as women.[6]

The Nazi treatment of women and children was largely unprecedented and unthinkable, just as the Holocaust itself was unimaginable,[7] and the murder of women and children could not be anticipated. Jewish women in Nazi Germany sought ways to emigrate, even though they could not imagine that they too would be subjected to forced labor and worse.[8] In 1935, women were not targets for work crews, and, in fact, both the history of women and war and the Law for the Protection of German Blood and Honor, of 15 September 1935, forbidding sexual contact between Aryans and Jews, deluded Jewish women and men into thinking that women were relatively safe from deportation and sexual aggression. Despite the law, though, sexual exploitation played a part in the process of emigration. One woman, Marion Kaplan writes, expressed gratitude that her mother had "sex with a bureaucrat who then provided their exit paper,"[9] thereby establishing physicality or sexuality as an actual or potential instrument for survival. Jewish women were more likely to be hidden because they were less likely than men to be identified as Jews (in the absence of indelible circumcision), but at the same time, women were more vulnerable to sexual abuse by their "rescuers."[10] Beauty provided Katarina Horowitza with an opportunity for revenge. Horowitza was a dancer who killed SS Sgt Schillinger in the vestibule of a gas chamber. In August 1943, this beautiful young woman, who was part of the transport from a Polish town (Bedzin), mesmerized Sgt Schillinger by undressing very slowly in what amounted to a strip tease. Unable to control himself, Schillinger approached her and she smacked him, catching him totally off guard, grabbed his gun and shot him several times in the abdomen. She also fired at another SS man. Both died soon after. Then she and her whole transport were quickly locked into the gas chamber and gassed, but she had the satisfaction of killing two of her killers.[11]

The situation for German Jews worsened after *Kristallnacht*, on 9/10 November 1938. The increased public violence against Jewish men led to changes in Jewish women's roles that included assuming family economic responsibilities, and rescuing husbands sent to concentration camps.[12] Although men were by far the majority of victims of the pogrom, the violence of *Kristallnacht* was not limited to them. One Viennese woman who had been raped multiple times during *Kristallnacht* pleaded in vain with the American consul to let her leave for the United States. She was raped again a few days later and returned to the consulate to beg for an exit visa. Exasperated, the Consul told her she could not leave unless she had a sponsor who would guarantee that she would not become a welfare case for an American city. Handing her the New York City telephone directory, he challenged her to find a sponsor, and she picked a name at random: Schiff. She had phenomenal luck. She called and spoke with Mrs Schiff, the wife of the Jewish investment banker, who heard her story and promised help, not only for rape victims, but for other women who needed to leave. Schiff sent money and helped about 20 women to emigrate. Then the borders were closed.[13]

In July 1942, when Parisian Jews still thought that they were relatively safe and that only men were in danger of being deported, reality proved otherwise. This large round-up could not be kept a secret, so most men went into hiding, never dreaming that women and children would be taken. In the end, 4,500 gendarmes rounded up 13,000 Jews in Paris and its suburb: 3,031 men, 5,802 women, and 4,051 children. After 3 days of misery, in an unbearably overcrowded sports arena to which they were taken, with little food and no sanitary facilities, with temperatures never below 100 degrees, they were shipped to transit camps and from there, to Auschwitz.[14]

Though not apparent before the onset of the war, the Final Solution depended on the annihilation of Jewish women not *only* because they were Jews, but for two other reasons: first, they were women and, as women, they were perpetuators of future generations of Jews who could be expected to avenge their families' deaths; second, they had to be "eliminated" because, according to Nazi propaganda, they could and would seduce Aryan men and thereby contaminate the Aryan race for generations to come. In his speech on 24 May 1944 to a gathering of German generals at Sonthofen, Heinrich Himmler defended the decision to murder Jewish women:

> I believe, gentlemen, that you know me well enough to realize that I am not a bloodthirsty man nor a man who takes pleasure or finds sport in the harsher things he must do. On the other hand, I have strong nerves and a great sense of duty—if I do say so myself—and when I recognize the necessity to do something, I will do it unflinchingly. As to the Jewish women and children, I did not believe I had a right to let these children grow up to become avengers who would kill our fathers [sic] and grandchildren. That, I thought, would be cowardly.[15]

Several sources, including women's memoirs, oral histories, websites devoted to the subject of women and the Holocaust, and recent histories of the Holocaust, shed light on the way biology and socialization led to specific ways in which Jewish women were targeted, as well as to the ways they responded to Nazi atrocities.[16] Anecdotes from these sources do not constitute incontrovertible evidence, but they merit investigation, if only to determine authenticity and rule out coincidence. This repetition is true for sources by and about women and the Holocaust. Women's narratives, whether spoken or written, reveal themes that are unique to their biology, such as amenorrhea and its psychological effects, pregnancy, childbirth, and physicality, which included sexual humiliation, rape, and torture. For example, Gerda Klein could not believe that her barrack-mates were relieved when they stopped menstruating. She feared that she would never again menstruate and thus, even if she did survive, that Hitler could claim a victory. Desperately wanting to have a baby, the possibility of forced sterilization and the reality of amenorrhea terrified her.[17] Isabella Leitner opens her memoir with a chilling understatement that she had not "menstruated for a long time," casting the Final Solution as planned sterility.[18] Elli Bitton Jackson worried that if she were caught bleeding, she would be accused of sabotage and killed, since Jewish women were not allowed to be fertile. She asked, "Does menstruating constitute sabotage?"[19]

In the concentration camps, the Nazis perfected a process that, at the least, disoriented girls and women. Those who survived the initial selection process underwent a gamut of humiliations, including exposure, crude body searches for hidden jewelry, painful body shaves, and sexual ridicule. Even in the moments before death, SS men tried to demoralize Jewish women. As a Sonderkommando, Leib Langfuss wrote his observations and hid his manuscript for posterity: one SS officer, he wrote, "had the custom of standing at the doorway...and feeling the private parts of the young women entering the gas bunker. There were also instances of SS men of all ranks pushing their fingers into the sexual organs of pretty young women."[20] Many women describe their horror at being required to undress in front of leering SS men and at being shaved by male prisoners. Rose Meth, one of the women who smuggled gunpowder to the Sonderkommandos in Auschwitz, said, "They made us undress completely naked in front of the Nazi soldiers. We wanted to die. They shaved our heads. They shaved all our hair, everywhere."[21] Sarah Nomberg-Przytyk, an Auschwitz prisoner, explained that they were treated like cattle and hit and kicked as they were "processed": "In silence with tears streaming down our cheeks, [we] were made to spread [our] legs and the body hair was shorn too."[22] "Imagine," says one religiously observant survivor, "women and girls from very sheltered areas and from Orthodox homes—what it meant to get undressed in front of these German officers and soldiers. They were standing there with their big rubber whips. We did as we were told...."[23]

The ordeal of deliberate humiliation began in the ghetto for Cecilie Klein, just before being loaded onto cattle cars:

> ...we were marched off in groups to a brick factory near the station for a degrading body search. First we were ordered to strip naked, men and women together. Then the women and the girls were lined up on one side and were ordered to lie on our sides on a wooden table. While an SS officer gawked and jeered, a woman with a stick poked around our private parts. My burning cheeks betrayed my sense of shame and humiliation. I sobbed for my mother, subjected to this bestial invasion.[24]

Klein was to endure more degradation upon her arrival at Auschwitz, where she and other naked women were required to stand on stools: "Five male prisoners appear alongside the stools, scissors in hand....In seconds, the men cut off the [the women's] hair, shaved their heads, then their intimate parts. The cut hair around the stools was collected by three male prisoners."[25] In one account, a survivor reported the chilling story she heard from a "mother who told [her] that she was forced to undress her daughter and to look on while the girl was violated by dogs that the Nazis had specially trained for this sport." That particular brutality was not an isolated event, but rather a "favorite form of amusement" of the SS guards in Auschwitz.[26]

Under what category of sexual abuse does one classify the experience of one Jewish woman imprisoned in Stutthof, who recalled "a hand going into [her] vagina and pulling" in an attempt to find hidden gold? In Stutthof, women also experienced sexual torture; in one testimony, a woman described the punishment meted out for an attempted escape. In retaliation, the women in the camp were forced to stand naked in the cold for 12 hours. Then four or five women were pulled from the ranks and repeatedly raped by all the male kapos, blockleaders, and other men who were nearby and, when the men were exhausted, they violated the women using sticks. The women died.[27]

Felicia Berland Hyatt, raised in strict Orthodoxy in Chelm, was cautioned by her mother to "do anything anybody asks you to do, just so you save your life." Hyatt and her mother parted, convinced that separation increased their chances to survive. She was grateful for her mother's parting words, which had stunned her at the time: "The instructions she gave me when we parted were truly a revelation and they became even more meaningful when months later I was faced with a situation in which I had to make a snap decision about bestowing a sexual favor in exchange for a temporary rescue from the German authorities."[28]

Ironically, as Hyatt's testimony and Kaplan's analyses reveal, the same sexual vulnerability that victimized women sometimes provided them with a small but significant measure of control. At times, they were able to use their sex and sexuality to save themselves. Some scholars label bartered sex or sex for survival as prostitution or selling one's body for food, thereby judging the women's morality by standards appropriate for a civil society rather than for a concentration camp.[29] Pawelczynska argues that adaptation was necessary for survival, specifically, adapting to the reduction of needs and standards. Without such an adjustment, prisoners were doomed unless they received help and care from others. Humanism, the supposed norm, prevailed in the camps among those prisoners who willfully and successfully lived on two planes and found a way to "lessen the dissonance between [one's] convictions and [one's] conduct."[30] For women, bartered sex was such an accommodation, consciously or otherwise. For those male prisoners who sold food or clothing to women in return for sex, I can only suggest that they exploited the women and victimized them further. Condemning the women for exchanging their bodies for food in order to live is a form of blaming the victim: "Yet it was rarely pity that made the men share their not-too-abundant food. For food was the coin that paid for sexual privileges. It would be heartless to condemn women who had to sink so low for a crust of bread. The responsibility for the degradation of the internees rested with the camp administration."[31] Yet, to continue to blame the women and never consider the role of the men who had food to give is to ignore predatory behavior and complicity—however passive—in an inhumane environment.

Nazi policy made pregnancy for Jewish women a death sentence. Abortions were not uncommon in the ghettos, but less likely in the camps, where childbirth was a particularly horrible experience. Visibly pregnant women were taken off the trains and sent to the gas chambers immediately, but some pregnancies went unnoticed or ignored. Several memoirs by survivors and incarcerated female physician survivors document the horrors of delivering babies in such circumstances. Gisela Perl saw "SS men and women" amuse themselves by beating pregnant women "with clubs and whips, [being] torn by dogs, dragged around by the hair and kicked in the stomach with heavy German boots. Then, when [the pregnant Jewish women] collapsed, they were thrown into the crematory—alive."[32] Sometimes, pregnant women were spared until they delivered, after which the Nazis killed both baby and mother. Mengele thought it was inhumane to send a new born baby, infant, or child to the gas chamber without its mother.[33] To save the lives of these women, Perl and other Jewish women doctors "pinched and closed" the newborn's "nostrils and when it opened its mouth to breathe...gave it a dose of a lethal product"[34] or drowned it in a pail of whatever liquid was available, rather than watch it starve to death for one of Mengele's so-called scientific experiments.[35]

As noted above, women were vulnerable to rape, even though intimate conduct with Jewish women was prohibited. Emmanuel Ringelblum recorded numerous instances of rape of Jewish and Polish women by German soldiers early in the occupation. Although such cases of rape were illegal and heavily punishable, the Gestapo did not consistently report them.[36] For example, men in the *Wehrmacht* who raped Tunisian Jewish women were also unreported despite the threat of reprisals[37] for "race defilement." Owing to the advanced age of the survivors, it is unlikely that we will learn much more about rape: many of the women are still ashamed and want to keep it from their husbands and children. A woman I interviewed whispered to me that she had been raped by a soldier in the *Wehrmacht* who was returning from the eastern front and stopped at Auschwitz. He kept watching her as she sorted clothes in one of the "Kanada" storehouses. When she finished her shift, he made his way to her bunk and raped her. To whom could she report him? He would have denied it and she would have been shot. She was still embarrassed about it, and years later had never told her husband.[38]

We do not know what motivated survivor–scholar Susan Chernyak-Spatz to speak out, but she did. In her recent memoir, she described being raped in Birkenau—although there is no "rape" entry in the index. She never mentioned this violation in hundreds of lectures in the 55 years since her liberation. Assigned to work in the construction department as a typist and cleaning woman, she was invited by a German *kapo* named Jupp to follow him to the store room, where he would give her food. Because she was starved, she went: "What followed was a plain quick rape on the floor of the store room and a bit of sausage thrown at me for payment." Jupp, an Aryan who was imprisoned as a habitual criminal, was unafraid that Chernyak-Spatz would report him, for to do so would incriminate herself, and she would assuredly suffer more consequences than he, possibly by gassing or by another form of murder.[39]

Sexual violence took other forms besides rape.[40] We have substantial documentation showing that, prior to being murdered in 1941 by the *Einsatzgruppen*, single girls and young women were often tortured before they were raped, then murdered.[41] In fact, perhaps the most chilling examples of sexual violence come from the *Einsatzgruppen* reports. It is patently clear that rape and other forms of sexual torture were, besides wholesale killings, the specialty of the murder squads.[42] Their reports and photos show women stripped naked and abused in front of their husbands, fathers, and sons before they were shot into pits. Thus terror was accompanied by the humiliation of public nakedness, and made all the more painful by the presence of their male relatives and friends, who were forced to stand by helplessly. In these actions, both men and women suffered the leers and laughter of the killers. But for the sadistic, murder itself was not enough.

As was true of other Nazi strategies or potentially incriminating actions, the record of sadism by the *Einsatzgruppen* is not to be found in official reports. Those reports, found by American soldiers in the Gestapo offices of Berlin, detail the trumped-up charges of crimes that the Jews perpetrated on the Germans, the Ukrainians, the Bylorussians, and so forth—possibly to justify the murders for posterity.[43] Of course, the official reports also boast about the statistics—the lists of the number and place of dead Jews—and say nothing of the crimes committed by the Germans. For that, we look at *The Black Book of Soviet Jewry,* a contemporaneous compendium of eyewitness reports, letters, and diaries of the victims and survivors of the *Einsatzgruppen,* compiled when the memories of horror were fresh. They tell harrowing tales of mass executions, rape, and other sexual abuses that are not and would not have been covered in official reports to Berlin Headquarters. For example, in early July 1941, in Riga, the Nazis celebrated their successful mass murders by herding "several dozen Jewish girls to their orgy, forced them to strip naked, dance, and sing songs. Many of these unfortunate girls were raped right there, and then taken out in the yard to be shot. Captain Bach surpassed everyone with his invention. He broke off the seat cushions of two chairs and replaced them with sheets of tin. Two girls, students of Riga University, were tied to the chairs and seated opposite each other. Two lighted Primus stoves were brought and placed under the seats. The officers really liked this sport. They joined hands and danced in a ring around the two martyrs. The girls writhed in the torment, but their hands and feet were tightly bound to the chairs; and when they tried to shout, their mouths were gagged with filthy rags. The room filled with the nauseating smell of burning flesh. The German officers just laughed, merrily doing their circle dance."[44]

The *Einsatzgruppen* seemed to have no end to their perversion. In the Minsk ghetto, *Hauptscharführer* Ribbe selected 13 beautiful Jewish women and led them down a street that led to the cemetery. "The animals stripped the women naked and mocked them. Then Ribbe and Michelson personally shot them. Ribbe took Lina Noy's [one of the women's] bra and put it in his pocket: 'To remember a beautiful Jewess,' he said."[45] In Brest, Osher Zisman testified that he "saw the Germans [through a ventilation opening in a hiding place] herd the young girls into a shed next to the graves and rape them before the execution. I heard one girl call for help; she hit the German in the snout, and for that the Germans buried her alive."[46] As part of a chain gang in Bialystok that was ordered to dig up and cremate the bodies, Nukhim Polinovsky reported digging up a "pit with 700 women...The bodies were absolutely naked. The breasts of many of the victims had been cut off."[47] Mutilation is thus added to the breadth of Nazi crimes against Jewish women.

Father Patrick Desbois, author of *Murder by Bullets,* knew little to nothing about the Holocaust until he found himself in Rawa-Ruska to learn more about the slave labor camp to which his grandfather was deported. After inquiries about his grandfather, some townsperson suggested that "others" were murdered. These "others" were Jews. Desbois asked some penetrating questions about the Jews and their cemeteries, which were unmarked and often unknown. In June 2002, he began study of Jewish cemeteries in Ukraine. He interviewed eyewitnesses of murder at the killing pits and the "infinite sadism" and obscenities performed on women and children. He quoted the peasants who witnessed mass murders. In the town of Busk, near Lvov, a peasant described what happened before the ghetto was destroyed:

> The young girls—there was one who went to school with me, Silva, who was very beautiful—weren't killed straight away. Silva had to live with the German commander. The other girls waited on the other soldiers. When the girls got pregnant, they were killed, because they couldn't have children with these people. They asked the police to take these girls, who were really beautiful, to a place ten kilometers from Busk to kill them because they didn't want to do it themselves.[48]

However, while the liabilities were certainly greater than the assets, women were more likely to pass as non-Jews than men, again because of circumcision. Their bodies could not betray them. Thus women could more easily pass as couriers, gun-runners (when they were able to get arms), and informal spies. We can all define armed resistance, but recognizing unarmed resistance is more challenging. Consider the proposition put forth by an eminent Polish resistance fighter that couriers were remarkably brave: "The average life of a woman courier did not exceed a few months."[49] Vladka Meed, born Feigele Peltel in 1922 in Warsaw, became a member of the underground in 1939. She looked more Polish than Jewish, spoke fluent Polish, and had extraordinary resourcefulness and bravery. She was a courier, smuggling messages and guns across the ghetto wall to the Jewish Fighting Organization, the Żydowska Organizacja Bojowa, ŻOB. She found Polish homes in which to hide Jews she smuggled from the ghetto. She faced danger and death every time she sought and found a non-Jewish home for a Jewish ghetto child whom she also smuggled out. She made connections and contacts with partisans fighting in the woods, and was betrayed and arrested and released. She had many narrow escapes, including the time when she was caught with a map of the Treblinka extermination camp hidden in her shoes. The Nazi lieutenant ordered her to undress and examined her clothes closely, holding them up to the light and fingering the hems and the seams. He ordered her to give him her shoes. She dawdled, taking a long time to unlace them. Finally, he whipped her. Just as he was about to grab her shoes, a guard rushed in and shouted that a Jew had escaped. The Nazi rushed out. Vladka put her clothes back on, walked out calmly, and joined a group of detainees headed for the Aryan side. At one point, she posed as a Polish smuggler, using the identity card of a dead Aryan woman born in 1922, her own birth year. She now was a "full fledged Aryan with two generations of Gentile forebears."[50] But she was suspected by neighbors and had to find yet another room and get yet another card. She did this often, usually using forged cards. After the ghetto was burned, she continued her false identity and worked to get arms to the Jewish partisans fighting in the forests.

Almost never allowed to engage in active combat in partisan groups, occasionally women were given intelligence or scout assignments. Except for the Bielski Otriad, they were few in number, five percent at most.[51] Most Jewish women who were allowed to join non-Jewish partisan groups did so under the "protection" of a man, often one high up in rank.[52] These "transit wives," as they were called, had no chance of survival other than as a mistress. The braver and more fearless the protector, the greater status of his woman. Although there were no official weddings, couples were treated as if they were married, and, more often than not, the match was asymmetrical. In the main, refined women were matched to uneducated, lower-class men who provided them with status and security. While there were undoubtedly couples who lived together because of love, most women accepted men who could raise their own status. The irony is that many of these "marriages" lasted 40 or 50 years—until death separated them.[53]

In addition to biological differences between men and women which, to a large extent, defined the nature of their experiences, gender-based socialization accounts for a variety of subtle behaviors that may have positioned women to recognize what was happening to the Jews. Because of the way they were raised, women were more apt to adapt than men were. Kassow quotes the Oneg Shabbas' valorization of women because of their resiliency and courage; when they had to assume economic responsibility, they did so. Out-numbering the men by a significant ratio, women were needed as fighters and responded admirably; according to Ringelblum, "Their courage, ingenuity, and combat skills left the men far behind."[54] When men were deported or assigned to forced labor groups, they had been left without a means of restoring their former identities. They were stripped suddenly of their economic status, their social and civic status, their family status.[55] Women had been socialized to use their domestic skills to improve their living conditions, and, writes one woman, even in the concentration camp, "men had to learn behaviors that women already knew."[56] Most women describe situations in which they confronted their new reality and devised strategies that actively engaged them in fighting for their survival. Essentially, as women cleaned their surroundings, sewed pockets into their ragged clothes, fantasized menus to mitigate their hunger, nursed and nurtured one another, they created the illusion of taking some measure of both control and responsibility for their wellbeing. In these efforts, they worked collaboratively and, in doing so, imparted a sense of being needed by others. I want to emphasize that survival was more a matter of luck than any-thing else. Still, most women in twentieth-century Europe were socialized to perform in the private sphere—the home, to be a nurturer and caregiver and to be proficient in daily chores, and these learned characteristics may have enhanced their chances for survival.[57]

Informal surrogate families played an incredible role in sustenance; prisoners often knew one another and expressed concern for their fellow inmates, thereby encouraging them to ward off depression and maintain personal hygiene. Their concern for one another eliminated "systematic thieving" among a relatively large group of women, dis-tributed victims' goods that were housed in storerooms among the group, contacted similar groups of women, and enabled them to persevere in the face of random brutality. These surrogate families, bound by shared origins or ideology, "showed the most stabi-lity and perseverance in their activities and from these groups developed the camp underground…in that hell called Auschwitz."[58] Obviously, the bonding among women was an important factor in their day-to-day and ultimate survival.

Women's coping strategies, and thus their chances for survival, consciously or unconsciously, reflected their pre-camp experiences, their early training—their socializa-tion. I became aware of the emphasis in women's memoirs on relationships, nurturing, and bonding in Isabella Leitner's memoir. She captured the significance of bonding in her statement, "If you are sisterless, you do not have the pressure, the absolute responsibility to end the day alive."[59] Frances Penny tells about the women who saved a barrack-mate from the gas chamber when she was very feverish. They dragged the sick woman to the courtyard for roll call and placed her in the middle of the line of five and supported her on either side: "Since she was unable to stand on her feet, we supported her and propped her up, so that her weakness would not be noticed by the German commandant."[60]

Clearly, women were expected to nurture and take responsibility for caring for others. Just as clearly, however, no amount of nurturing could counteract a bullet, a beating, a capricious attack, a vicious *kapo*, an Irma Grese or a Dr Mengele, or the thousands of others like them. Again, I have to emphasize that luck was the most important factor in survival. But, according to many memoirs, nurturing was also a significant element in survival. It led to both feeling and being needed in concrete ways, such as sharing a morsel of bread, seeking members of the family for mutual sustenance, and building surrogate families to restore the sense of oneself as an integral member of a group. These connections helped negate the anonymity of the concentration and labor camp systems. One survivor told me that the friends she made in Stutthof remained her closest friends; she even considers their children part of her extended family.[61] Surrogate families were motivated not by trivialities, but rather by a genuine sense of solidarity among people who shared each other's grisly fate and felt responsible for one another. These friendships and surrogate families also helped to balance the humiliation designed to break the spirit and the will.[62]

A daughter of a survivor told me that her mother, Lily Kasticher Hirt, a Hungarian survivor, devised a plan of spiritual resistance to help raise the morale of the women in her barracks. She ran a contest for the best poem, artwork, or song. She was the judge who would give out the three prizes. First prize was a piece of bread, second prize, a sewing needle, and third prize, a palm reading (she had taught herself to read palms). Hard as it is to imagine—in a barrack in Birkenau in 1944, she was offering bread that she had saved from her own portion as a prize for poems or artwork. Lily was able to provide paper and colored pencils for artwork because her *kapo* had asked her to decorate the love letters she was writing to her boyfriend in the *Wehrmacht*, who was fighting on the Russian front. According to Lily's daughter, the romance wasn't going as well as this *kapo* had expected, and she hoped that cheerfully decorated sentimental love letters would do the trick. She gave Lily the necessary paper and pencils, which Lily made available to her barrack-mates. Yad Vashem has the originals of the poetry and artwork. The women knew the value of a sewing needle, which was probably made from a piece of wire or a sliver of wood.[63]

Gender difference is also conspicuous in the inmates' response to, and memory of, hunger. Even before they were sent to the camps, both male and female Jews were subjected to starvation in the ghettos. Łódź ghetto scholar Michal Unger writes about women's inventiveness with ersatz coffee, which they would transform into ersatz cake, and potato peels, which became ersatz soup dumplings.[64] In labor and concentration camps, sharing their memories of the wonderful meals eaten in better times was a diversion for both women and men. Prisoners "dined" out, explains Elie A. Cohen, and exchanged recipes; in the words of two survivors, such discussions were called "culinary dry screwing" and "gastric masturbation."[65] Hunger also very often brought out ruthlessness in the struggle to survive. On the other hand, Cohen, himself an Auschwitz survivor, suggests that compassion and altruism were not altogether absent. Citing the German edition of Adelsberger's memoir, Cohen confirms the assertion that there were those who sold their bread rations to "buy potatoes for a dying comrade, and thus give him [sic] a last happiness."[66]

In a close examination of both men's and women's memoirs, I found a striking difference in the way they spoke about food and hunger. In men's memoirs, hunger was usually rooted in the stomach and in memory; they evoked the meals—usually their mother's cooking—that they had enjoyed in a state of freedom. Men spoke and wrote about their hunger and distress, and confessed their willingness to do just about anything to alleviate that hunger. Thus, for them, starvation was a manifestation of Nazi power, and their hunger, devastating proof of their own vulnerability and dependency.

In women's memoirs, hunger is just as devastating a presence as it is in men's, but often it evokes a different type of response, one rooted in the imagination, situated in the kitchen, and remembered through conversations with sister prisoners. Traditionally, cooking or sharing recipes was a "practice [that united] women across social barriers.... food [became] a common language for all through need and hunger."[67] For many women in the camps, it did just that. As they recalled their domestic roles of pre-Nazi days, women *created* communities that grew out of sharing recipes and food-preparation experiences. In describing the food they once cooked to another prisoner, they shared an experience familiar to both of them, an experience that connected them to another person and briefly broke the isolation and despair brought on by prolonged hunger. Thus, for many women, hunger led to a social relationship, just as food preparation and food consumption had created, reinforced, or defined social relationships for women before the Nazi era. In a sense, these women prisoners created oral cookbooks and, in the process, organized themselves into a temporary, loose but purposeful community shaped from and by their kitchen experiences. These communities gave women someone to cling to, another person who knew their name, a way to break the loneliness of imprisonment. Their shared memories about food gave them not physical sustenance, but emotional sustenance.

Food, and its connected rituals of cooking, determining menus, and setting a table, reminded these imprisoned women of their former status when they were not trapped and starving victims. They reminded themselves of their earlier connections. They reminded themselves that they had been part of a family, a family with a rich heritage, with love, and with a future as well as a past. These positive reminders of their past status contributed to their emotional strength.

Since most Jewish cooking is sooner or later connected to a Jewish holiday, the women engaged in such talk and teaching were, in essence, transmitting and perpetuating Jewish custom and observance. For Jews, there is a special way to prepare the food, as well as special dishes on which to eat specific sorts of food; special blessings to be said over the food and over the cooking. In the life of a woman who prepares food in this way and maintains the kosher kitchen, with all its ritual complexity, God can become almost as tangible as the stove.[68] Hence we see that the act of sharing recipes not only took on cultural significance, but ironically reinforced religious identity.

"Food talk" was a distraction from the horrific conditions and from the fear of starving to death. Acknowledging that it was a "terrible thing to be hungry all the time," one survivor wrote: "We used to get together for sessions to try to make each other stronger. Also, when we were very hungry we used to cook in our imaginations. You wouldn't believe the recipes that were flying around. We used to say that when we were free we would make potatoes in every possible way—baked with sour cream, boiled with butter, fried with onions and so on."[69] And one woman teaching another how to cook makes *her* feel needed. She is giving information that assumes a future. The act of teaching, in fact, is based on some expressed or unexpressed acknowledgment of one's importance or utility. Teaching establishes a relationship and renders each participant in the process a role, a job to fulfill, that presupposes a future. And a future means hope.

Furthermore, teaching someone how to cook very often involves recollection of a dead person. We teach Aunt Esther's recipe for noodle pudding, Grandma's recipe for sponge cake, and mama's recipe for *hamantashen*. Indeed, Jewish women learn to create menus and prepare dishes that are related to the Jewish calendar. Chicken soup is a Sabbath dish; sponge cake is traditionally a Passover dessert; *hamantaschen* is a Purim cookie. Recipes carry both our culture and our past. A recipe, asserts cookbook writer Joan Nathan, is "about a heritage, a family. [Recipe collections] are oral history."[70] So it was in the unlikely setting of the concentration camp, when women spoke rather than wrote recipes and cookbooks. Attributing a recipe to a grandmother or aunt or mother, who was absent from the conversation because she had been starved, beaten, or gassed to death, figuratively restored her to the circle of women and embedded her in the memory, not only of the woman describing the recipe, but also in the memories of the audience of women listening to the recipe-giver. Through her recipes, a dead woman would be remembered in her life-affirming identity, that is, through a validation of her life in the domestic sphere.[71]

Batsheva Dagan, survivor of six German prisons and a 20-month veteran of Auschwitz-Birkenau, wrote about an illegal newspaper, written by women prisoners on strips of paper, and read aloud to other prisoners who gathered between the barracks. One issue of the newspaper, the *Kanada Observer* (read aloud on Sundays, the day the Kanada Kommando did not work), was all about food. The first article, "Practical Suggestions for successful 'Kanada' Women," was a list of four bullets, two of which say, "One who cannot steal/Is too dumb to have a meal." And "Cut the bread in seven slices/To avoid tomorrow's crisis." Next followed four "Original Recipes for Camp Soup." These included "Cutlet à la Peter," which called for the cook to add "edible 'herbs'" the Latin name of which may be "Herba Suepina Auschwitziana." The recipe for meat begins, "Firstly take a microscope. Position the lens and search carefully. With luck you may find something! 'Acquire' some mustard or horseradish—to avoid putting on too much weight." Finally, the excerpt of the newspaper concludes with a "Did you know that?" list, all of which is biting tongue in cheek: "On Thursday at 4:10 exactly a transport of female inmates will be moved to a sausage and chocolate factory."[72] Thus we have women collaborating to write a newspaper, as well as to read it to their sister prisoners. Both actions are obviously dangerous and, if discovered, likely to result in serious beatings or worse.

Survivors recalling "food talk" often laugh and nod in recognition of Susan Chernyak-Spatz's comment that she was never as good a cook in the kitchen as she was with her mouth. This "food talk" among women went on for hours and encouraged them to bond with one another, to anticipate the next day, to recall their dead relatives and friends, and, to an extent, to sabotage the Nazi plan to annihilate them and their culture. For some women, sharing recipes was an act of defiance, heroic resistance, and a refusal to become dehumanized.[73] In the end, however, although it distracted them, food talk did not overcome starvation. "Food talk" was clear proof that the Nazis couldn't really control every inch of the prisoners' minds. Through this sharing and teaching, women resisted the dehumanization that was part of Nazi systematic debilitation. Unconsciously and temporarily, these women defied their status by reiterating their previous importance as food-givers. Thus, not only was recipe sharing a social and educational activity, it was also a spiritual one that assumed there would be a next holiday meal, a next family gathering around a table, a future.

The daily acts of nurturing are quiet and undramatic, but they are the stuff of sustenance, survival, and resistance. While the Holocaust was once unthinkable, it is no longer so. Regrettably and obscenely, the rest of the twentieth century witnessed genocide, mass murder, and ethnic cleansing, and in all cases, women were and have been singled out for extreme violence. To be sure, there are few lessons to be learned from the Holocaust, but among those is the example of traditional socialization of European Jewish women in the early to mid-twentieth century: in large measure, women's experiences in the Holocaust place a "new emphasis on values that had traditionally been the purview of women."[74]

Notes

1 "Double jeopardy" has been used quite commonly to describe the status of Jewish women in the Holocaust. For example, see Judith Tydol Baumel, *Double Jeopardy: Gender and the Holocaust* (London: Vallentine Mitchell, 1998). See also Vera Hajkova, "Such was Life," *The World Without Human Dimension: Four Women's Memories* (Prague: State Jewish Museum, 1991), 114.

2 Joan Ringelheim, "The Split between Gender and the Holocaust," in *Women and the Holocaust*, eds Dalia Ofer and Lenore Weitzman (New Haven, Connecticut: Yale University Press, 1998), 344.

3 Myrna Goldenberg, "Different Horrors, Same Hell: Women Remembering the Holocaust," Joan Ringelheim, "Thoughts about Women and the Holocaust," in *Thinking the Unthinkable: Meanings of the Holocaust*, ed. Roger S. Gottlieb (New York: Paulist Press, 1990), 143: "There is no time, there is no place that is the same for everyone, not even Auschwitz." Myrna Goldenberg, "Lessons Learned from Gentle Heroism: Women's Holocaust Narratives," *Annals of the American Academy of Political and Social Science*, vol. 548 (November 1996): 78–93. See also Claudia Koonz, *Mothers in the Fatherland: Women, the Family and Nazi Politics* (New York: St Martin's Press, 1987), 363. Concerning the mid-1930s, before the Nuremberg Laws: "Frequently, family discussions about the future divided men from women because each sex encountered antsemitism in different ways."

4 Joan Ringelheim, "The Unethical and the Unspeakable," *Simon Weisenthal Annual*, vol. 1, no.1 (1984): 69–87. See also Joan Ringelheim, "Memory, Oral History, and Gender," paper for United States Holocaust Memorial Museum, 11 June 1995, especially for her discussion of Claude Lanzmann's *Shoah*, 21–23.

5 John K. Roth, "Equality, Neutrality, Particularity: Perspectives on Women and the Holocaust," in *Experience and Expression: Women, the Nazis, and the Holocaust*, eds Elizabeth R. Baer and Myrna Goldenberg (Detroit: Wayne State University, 2003), 5–22. See also Baer and Goldenberg, "Introduction," in *Experience and Expression*, xiii–xxxiii.

6 Sybil Milton, "Women and the Holocaust: The Case of German and German-Jewish Women," *When Biology Became Destiny*, eds Renate Bridenthal, Atina Grossman and Marion Kaplan (New York: Monthly Review Press, 1984); Jonathan Friedman, *Speaking the Unspeakable: Essays on Gender, Sexuality, and Holocaust Survivor Memory* (Lanham, Maryland: Rowman & Littlefield/University Press of America, 2002); Marion Kaplan, *Between Dignity and Despair: Jewish Life in Nazi Germany* (New York: Oxford University Press, 1998), esp. chapters 2 and 4.

7 Charlotte Delbo, *Auschwitz and After*, trans. Rosette C. Lamont (New Haven: Yale University Press, 1995), 4: "They expected the worst, not the unthinkable."

8 Kaplan, *Between Dignity and Despair*, chapters 2 and 5. Kaplan provides a thorough, invaluable study of Jewish family life as it affected men, women, and children in Germany. See also Koonz, *Mothers in the Fatherland*, 375, concerning the role of women in arranging for emigration: "...the number one best seller...the Manhattan telephone book. We spent hours, days looking for Jewish sounding last names and writing letters...And many, many answered back. But not enough." See Jacob Apenszlak, ed., *The Black Book of Polish Jewry: An Account of the Martyrdom of Polish Jewry Under the Nazi Occupation* (The American Federation for Polish Jews in cooperation with The Association of Jewish Refugees and Immigrants from Poland, 1943; Reprint, Waterbury, Connecticut: Brohan Press, 1999), 28–29.

9 Kaplan, *Between Dignity and Despair*, 72.

10 Such abuse is seldom talked about unless the survivor is prodded; the women apparently feel shame and are reluctant to appear ungrateful.

11 Sarah Nomberg-Przytyk, "Revenge of a Dancer," *True Tales from a Grotesque Land* (Chapel Hill, North Carolina: University of North Carolina Press, 1985), 106–9; Tadeusz Borowski, *This Way for the Gas, Ladies and Gentlemen* (1958; reprinted New York: Penguin, 1976), 143–46; Filip Müller, *Eyewitness Auschwitz: Three Years in the Gas Chambers* (New York: Stein and Day, 1979), 87–89.

12 Kaplan, *Between Dignity and Despair*, 128. For a striking picture of the change in women's roles as a result of Nazi deportation and incarceration of men in Warsaw, see Samuel D. Kassow, *Who Will Write Our History? Rediscovering a Hidden Archive from the Warsaw Ghetto* (New York: Vintage Books/Random House, 2009), 239–51.

13 Gregory Weeks, International Association of Genocide Scholars, Sarajevo, 13 June 2007.

14 Saul Friedländer, *The Years of Extermination: Nazi Germany and the Jews 1939–1945* (New York: HarperCollins, 2007), 414–15; Tatiana De Rosnay, *Sarah's Key* (New York: St Martin's Press/Griffin, 2007), 42–43, 50–51, 59–62; Susan Zuccotti, *The Holocaust, the French, and the Jews* (New York: Basic Books/HarperCollins, 1993), 103–17.

15 www.scrapbookpages.com/dachauscrapbook/HimmlerSpeeches.html

16 In addition to published memoirs, oral interviews, and the website *Women and the Holocaust* (www.theverylongview.com/WATH), all of which are among my primary sources, other sources recently used to study women/gender in the Holocaust are the Shoah Foundation Oral Testimonies Archive (see Helene Sinnreich's "'And it was something we didn't talk about': Rape of Jewish Women during the Holocaust," *Holocaust Studies: A Journal of Culture and History*, vol. 14, no. 2 (Autumn 2008): 1–22; The Jewish Historical Institute in Poland, the Historical Commission in Munich, and the Boder Collection (see Na'ama Shik, "Infinite Loneliness: Some Aspects of the Lives of Jewish Women in the Auschwitz Camps According to Testimonies and Autobiographies Written Between 1945 and 1948," *Lessons and Legacies*, vol. 8 (2008): 124–56. The Shoah Foundation is the largest collection of survivor interviews, which, despite problems in the interviewing process, are being used extensively.

17 Gerda Klein, *All But My Life* (NewYork: Hill and Wang, 1957), 155–56.

18 Isabella Leitner with Irving Leitner, *Fragments of Isabella: A Memoir of Auschwitz* (New York: Bantam Doubleday/Dell Publishing, 1978), 44.

19 Livia E. Bitton Jackson, *Elli: Coming of Age in the Holocaust* (New York: Times Books, 1980).

20 Leib Langfuss, "The Horrors of Murder," *The Scrolls of Auschwitz*, ed. Ber Mark (Tel Aviv: Am Oved, 1985), 209.

21 Oral History, Interviewer, Bonnie Gurewitsch, *Women of Valor*, vol. 6, no. 4 (28 October 1985): 38–41.

22 Nomberg-Przytyk, "Revenge of a Dancer," 14.

23 Lydia Brown, *Voices from the Holocaust,* ed. Sylvia Rothchild (New York: New American Library, 1981), 280.

24 Cecilie Klein, *Sentenced to Live* (New York: Holocaust Library, 1988), 73, 77.

25 Klein, *Sentenced to Live*, 73, 77.

26 Olga Lengyel, *Five Chimneys* (reprinted New York: Granada, 1972), 193.

27 Judith Meisel and Dora Goldstein Roth, Oral Testimonies, Wexner Learning Center, United States Holocaust Memorial Museum.

28 Felicia Berland Hyatt, *Close Calls: The Autobiography of a Survivor* (New York: Holocaust Library, 1991), 76–77.

29 Kassow, *Who Will Write Our History?* 240, 242; Goldenberg, "Sexual Violence and the Holocaust: An Interim Analysis," paper presented at the International Association of Genocide Scholars, June 2007.

30 Anna Pawelczynska, *Values and Violence in Auschwitz: A Sociological Analysis* (Berkeley, California: University of California Press, 1980), 135–44, esp. 139: "Prisoners at Auschwitz had to be capable of creativity in the sphere of moral standards…The highly developed system of values which was created…clashed with a set of conditions for which that system was incongruous."

31 Lengyel, *Five Chimneys*, 190.

32 Gisela Perl, *I Was a Doctor at Auschwitz* (1948, reprinted Salem, New Hampshire: Ayer, 1984), 80.

33 Nomberg-Przytyk, "Esther's First Born," 67–71.

34 Lengyel, *Five Chimneys*, 11.

35 Perl, *I Was a Doctor at Auschwitz*, 80–86.

36 Szobar, 136–44.

37 Richard J. Evans, *The Third Reich at War* (New York: Penguin Press, 2009), 52–53.

38 Interview with M, survivor of Auschwitz, Philadelphia, Pennsylvania, November 1996.

39 Susan Chernyak-Spatz, *Protective Custody: Prisoner 34042* (Cortland, New York: N & S Publishers, 2005), 178–79.

40 *The Black Book: The Nazi Crime Against the Jewish People* (New York: The Jewish Black Book Committee/Duell, Sloan and Pearce, 1946), 245, 249, 325, 342–43, passim. See also Apenszlak, ed., *The Black Book of Polish Jewry*, 25–28.

41 Ilya Ehyrenberg and Vasily Grossman, eds, *The Black Book of Soviet Jewry: The Ruthless Murder of Jews by German-Fascist Orders throughout the Temporarily Occupied Regions of the Soviet Union and the Death Camps of Poland during the War of 1944–1945*, trans. John Glad and James S. Levine (New York: Holocaust Library, 1981). See also Apenszlak, ed., *The Black Book of Polish Jewry*, 9, 28–29.

42 Yitzhak Arad, Shmuel Krakowski and Shmuel Spector, *The Einsatzgruppen Reports: Selections from the Dispatches of the Nazi Death Squads' Campaign Against the Jews, July 1941–January 1943* (New York: Holocaust Library, 1989), 9. See also Evans, *The Third Reich at War*, 159, who cites acts of sadism by the Croatian Utaša, who "gouged out the eyes of Serbian men and cut off the women's breasts with penknives."

43 Arad *et al.*, eds, *The Einsatzgruppen Reports*, 9.

44 Ehyrenberg and Grossman, eds, *The Black Book of Soviet Jewry*, 302 (report by USSR Capt. Yefim Gekhtman, war correspondent for the newspaper *Krasnaya Zvezda* during the war).

45 Ehyrenberg and Grossman, eds, *The Black Book of Soviet Jewry*, 173 (based on information provided by A. Machiz, Grechanik, L. Gleyzer and P.M. Shapiro; prepared for publication by Vasily Grossman).

46 Ehyrenberg and Grossman, eds, *The Black Book of Soviet Jewry*, 221.

47 Ehyrenberg and Grossman, eds, *The Black Book of Soviet Jewry*, 244.

48 Patrick Desbois, *Murder by Bullets: A Priest's Journey to Uncover the Truth behind the Murder of 1.5 Million Jews* (New York: Palgrave Macmillan, 2008), 136.

49 Nechama Tec, *Resilience and Courage: Women, Men, and the Holocaust* (New Haven: Yale University Press, 2003), 264.

50 Vladka Meed, *On Both Sides of the Wall* (New York: Holocaust Library, 1979), 213.

51 Nechama Tec, *Defiance: The Bielski Partisans* (New York: Oxford University Press, 1993), 156.

52 Anna Hyndrakova-Kovanicova, "Letter to my Children," *World Without Human Dimension*, 177–79, who describes being told that she needed a protector during an evacuation march from one camp to another or would be "passed from one to the other and [she] wouldn't be able to fend them off." Hysterical, she fought three men for three nights but concluded "Actually I don't even know if I lost my virginity or not."

53 Tec, *Defiance*, 154–69.

54 Kassow, *Who Will Write Our History?* 239–51. For the ratios of women to men in 1939 and later, see 241: at the end of October, 1939, women accounted for 54 percent of the Jews in Warsaw; the disparity gets much more dramatic by age cohort. In January 1942, men comprised 43 percent of the total Jewish population, women 57 percent.

55 Koonz, *Mothers in the Fatherland*, 382–83.

56 Koonz, *Mothers in the Fatherland*, 381.

57 It is interesting to note that, to some scholars, differences in socialization account for little or nothing, and that women's coping with hunger through recipe sharing was atypical, as was the formation of women's surrogate families. More distressing is the charge that such differences were universal and therefore untrue. One cannot ignore the fact that these "strategies" were learned in the course of living in early to mid-twentieth-century Europe, and that so many women's narratives/memoirs in fact mention both cooking and surrogate family formation as contributing to their survival, while many, many fewer men (perhaps the most conspicuous exception is Primo Levi) did the same. The critics of feminist scholarship of the Holocaust

rarely identify men's memoirs that support their opposition. To my knowledge, no scholar who writes/wrote about women and the Holocaust ever claimed that learned socialization strategies were the sole, or even the most important, factor in survival, although a substantial number of survivors assert that it was true. Nor do feminist scholars ignore the horrors—filth, disease, hunger, savage beatings, medical experimentation, sexual abuse—of the ghettos and camps. It is indisputable that luck was the most important factor in survival, but how one lived contributed to the chances of survival. And how one lived during imprisonment was influenced considerably by how one lived before the Nazi takeover.

58 Ber Mark, *The Scrolls of Auschwitz* (Tel Aviv: Am Oved Publishing, 1984), 79; see also 94–96 for more descriptions of male and female groups organized to rebel against Nazi control.
59 Leitner and Leitner, *Fragments of Isabella*, 44.
60 Frances Penney, *I Was There,* trans. Zofia Griffen (New York: Shengold, 1988), 103.
61 Interviews with B.M.B., fall and spring, 1998–99, Derwood, Maryland.
62 Lucie Adelsberger, *Auschwitz: A Doctor's Story,* trans. Susan Ray (Boston: Northeastern University Press, 1995), 99.
63 Interviews with Daniela Sela and Lili Ben Ami, daughter and granddaughter, respectively, of Lily, Jerusalem, August 2005. Yad Vashem holds her collection.
64 Michal Unger, "The Status and Plight of Women in the Łódź Ghetto," in *Women and the Holocaust*, eds Dalia Ofer and Lenore Weitzman (New Haven: Yale University Press, 1998), 134–35.
65 Elie A. Cohen, *Human Behavior in the Concentration Camp*, trans. M.H. Braaksma (New York: The Universal Library, 1953), 132.
66 Cohen, *Human Behavior in the Concentration Camp*, 138, 139.
67 Cecilia Lawless, "Cooking, Community, Culture: A Reading of *Like Water for Chocolate*," in *Recipes for Reading*, ed. Anne L. Bower (Amherst, Massachusetts; University of Massachusetts Press, 1997), 219. Lawless quotes from Susan Leonardi's groundbreaking article, "Recipes for Reading: Summer Pasta, Lobster à la Riseholme, and Key Lime Pie," *PMLA,* vol. 104 (May 1989).
68 Rachel Naomi Remen, *Kitchen Table Wisdom: Stories that Heal* (New York: Riverhead Books, 1996), 268–69.
69 Brown, in Rothchild, 283.
70 "Recipes as Oral History," *The Washingtonian Magazine*, December 2001, 92.
71 Marion Bishop, "Speaking Sisters: Relief Society Cookbooks and Mormon Culture," in *Recipes for Reading* (Bower, ed.), 95.
72 Batsheva Dagan, *Imagination: Blessed Be, Cursed Be*, trans. Anna Sotto (Newark, UK: Memoir Publications in conjunction with the Holocaust Centre, Beth Shalom, 2001).
73 Cara De Silva, ed., *In Memory's Kitchen: A Legacy from the Women of Terezin* (Northvale, New Jersey: Jason Aronson, 1996), ix–xvi, xxv–xliii.
74 Kassow, *Who Will Write Our History?* 241.

35

THE JEWISH DP EXPERIENCE

Boaz Cohen

About 250,000 Jews, survivors of the Holocaust and refugees, were stranded in occupied Germany, Austria, and Italy in the immediate aftermath of World War II. It was only with the establishment of the state of Israel in 1948 and the opening of other immigration possibilities that these people found a home outside of Europe. While on German soil (mostly) these Jewish Displaced Persons rebuilt their lives, forged new communities, and made their voice heard on the political scene. This chapter deals with the major issues and points of contention in the research of their experiences during these years.

Scope, periods, and numbers

When the Allies occupied Germany and Austria, they were faced with an immense humanitarian challenge—taking care of about eight million foreign workers, slave-laborers, camp inmates, and prisoners of war, and repatriating them to their homes. The Allies were not unprepared. Already in 1943, they had established the United Nations Relief and Rehabilitation Administration (UNRRA), whose role was to administer aid and relief to liberated populations and to repatriate them to their home countries. The people who were to be returned home were termed Displaced Persons (DPs).

In a feat of organization and logistics by UNRRA and the occupation authorities, the Allies repatriated about six million DPs between May and September 1945. All over Europe, slave laborers, camp inmates, and prisoners were going home. But to the authorities' surprise, more than a million from eastern Europe (Poland, Baltic countries, etc.) refused to be repatriated. Of these, between 10 and 20 percent were Jews.[1] The first estimates of surviving Jews, made in June 1945, counted 100,000, chiefly in Germany and Austria.[2] Many tried to return to their home towns only to find out that none of their family members had survived and that their property had been taken over by their neighbors. Disillusioned, they returned to the DP camps in Germany.

The original camp survivors were soon joined by a massive influx of Jewish refugees fleeing eastern Europe ("infiltrees" in the official jargon). Driven by antisemitism and anti-Jewish violence, the 80,000 Jews who survived the Holocaust in Poland and the 150,000–200,000 repatriated Jews who joined them from the USSR poured over the borders into Austria and the American zone of occupation in Germany. By the beginning of 1946, there were more than 90,000 Jewish DPs in Germany, Austria, and Italy, of these 70,000 in Germany alone. By the end of the year, there were 230,000 Jewish DPs, 180,000 of them in Germany. The numbers peaked in the spring of 1947 with almost 190,000 DPs in Germany and 250,000 in all.[3] Ironically, it was occupied Germany, the land of the perpetrators, where the survivors of the Holocaust in Europe found a haven where they had security and cultural autonomy for a few years after the Holocaust. This paper deals with the Jewish DPs and their experience in the early postwar years.

Self-leadership and political struggle: the emergence of the DPs as a political force

Jewish survivors in the camps began organizing in the months leading to liberation. They were emaciated, physically and mentally exhausted, and scarred by their experience in the Nazi camps. Liberating soldiers, viewers of film reels, and readers of magazines saw them as living skeletons bereft of humanity and agency. It was therefore more surprising for contemporaries to find out that this faceless mass of survivors was capable of organizing itself and of formulating and fighting for a national agenda. On 1 July 1945, in the Feldafing camp, DP representatives established the Central Committee of the Liberated Jews in Bavaria. On 25 July, 94 DP representatives from all over occupied Germany met in the St-Ottilien hospital and confirmed the Committee's leadership.

By 12 January 1945, the Central Committee of the Liberated Jews held its first major conference in the Munich Town Hall. It was attended by 120 DP delegates and by a bevy of dignitaries from the allied occupation authorities, German municipal and state institutions, and even David Ben Gurion as the representative of the Jewish community in Palestine. The organizers, aiming as they were to raise public awareness of the plight of the DPs and their demands, enhanced the public relations aspect of the event. Journalists covering the Nuremberg Trials were invited and attended, and a film, *These are the People*, utilized footage from the conference and scenes from DP life.

The Jewish DPs called themselves the "surviving remnant," *She'erith Hapletah* in Hebrew, and they were making a point: "We are Here" (*Mir Zaynen Do*). What were the issues at hand? First and foremost, Jewish survivors demanded recognition of Jewish DPs as a distinct national group. At first, Allied authorities and the UNRRA refused to do so, and treated Jews according to their country of origin. As a result, Jewish survivors were refused camps for themselves and were placed with non-Jewish and at times antisemitic groups of DPs that victimized them.

Another burning issue was the treatment of the Jewish survivors by the US military. Jewish survivors were still under guard in camps and were subject to harsh military regulations. The overall atmosphere was one whereby it seemed that American GIs were sympathizing with the German population much more than with the Jewish victims. Letters home and reports from Jewish soldiers in the US army about the mistreatment of survivors brought about the appointment, by President Truman, of Earl G. Harrison to a fact-finding mission to occupied Germany. Harrison's report was scathing; he claimed that "As matters now stand, we (the American Occupying forces) are treating the Jews as the Nazis treated them except that we do not exterminate them." He claimed that Jews were victimized as Jews and that the granting of special recognition was not favoritism but an act of justice. The highly publicized report with its passionate tone brought about a major change in American policy *vis-à-vis* the Jewish survivors. President Truman reacted sharply to the report and directed General Eisenhower to take action. The latter appointed a special adviser on Jewish Affairs and met Jewish demands for separate camps with improved rations and a measure of internal autonomy. The importance of Harrison's report cannot be underestimated, but did he judge the US military and its actions fairly? Atina Grossmann emphasizes the difficulties facing the Americans and claims that on the whole they tried to make the best of an impossible situation.[4]

But the report had another important recommendation; it accepted the DPs' demands for immigration to Palestine and called for the immediate granting of 100,000 entry permits to Palestine for surviving Jews. Current research shows the importance of the impression that the DP leaders themselves made on Harrison. In interviews and visits, they ably presented their case to the American envoy. But they were not alone. Researchers show the impact of relief workers, American officials, and US army chaplains on Harrison and his report. They differ as to the relevant importance of these persons.[5] Harrison's recommendations were in fact an acceptance of the Jews as a national community. It was an acknowledgment of DP claims that the only solution to their problems was emigration to *Eretz-Israel*. This issue became the focal point of DP politics and identity, and a contested point for contemporaries and historians.

The Zionist choice

A major factor in the evolution of the Jewish DP phenomenon was their refusal to be repatriated "home" to their prewar homelands. There were no Jewish communities to return to; their houses and property were taken over by their neighbors who, in places, also aided or colluded with the extermination of the Jews. Those who did come back found a very cold welcome and anti-Jewish violence as well. It was obvious to them that they had no future in Europe. It was not surprising therefore that the DP population and its leaders adopted a Zionist stand, demanding that DPs be allowed to emigrate from Europe and to immigrate to Palestine and establish there a Jewish homeland.[6]

Prior to the Holocaust, Zionism was but one ideology on the Jewish political scene; it had hard competition from the socialist Bund, which called for Jewish cultural Yiddishist autonomy in the framework of a socialist politics, and from ultra-religious movements such as *Agudath Israel*, which opposed the secular underpinnings of Zionist ideology and practice. But the Holocaust and the post-Holocaust anti-Jewish violence in eastern Europe brought about a radical change in Jewish politics. Koppel Pinson, working in relief work for the Joint Distribution Committee (JDC), was an on-the-spot observer of DP life. He wrote of DP Zionism:

> …the events of 1939–45 seemed to discredit completely those philosophies of Jewish life prevailing before the war which were not centred around Palestine. The Zionists were the only ones that had a program that seemed to make sense after the catastrophe…Without Palestine there seemed to be no future for them. Anti-Zionism or even a neutral attitude toward Zionism came to mean for them a threat to the most fundamental stakes in their future.[7]

For many prewar Zionists, the postwar Zionist sentiment was a continuum of the prewar one. But for the mainstay of the DP community, Zionism was a practical stand born out of the experience of the Holocaust and its aftermath. The Jewish people had no future in Europe, whose soil was soaked by the blood of their compatriots. A Jewish state would provide security for the Jews, and a supportive community for those who lost so much.

"The Jewish people is sick...the best specialists have presented us with a diagnosis: statelessness," wrote Meir Gavronsky, the editor of Feldafing DP camp's Yiddish paper *Dos Fraye Vort* (The Free Word). "The cure is our own soil, our own home, our own state."[8] The adamant demand by DPs to be allowed to immigrate to *Eretz-Israel* became the lynchpin of Jewish DP identity. Paradoxically, the loss of their real homes, citizenship, and past enabled the construction of a new identity based on their ties to a homeland most of them never saw, and which did not yet exist.

DPs as a political force and a political problem

The DPs' demand for *Aliyah* ("ascent" in Hebrew, referring to immigration to *Eretz-Israel*) led to a head-on collision with the British, who refused to grant DPs immigration visas to Palestine. In spite of election promises to the contrary, the postwar British government opted to continue the harsh immigration restrictions on Jews who wanted to go there. Thus, in the eyes of the DPs, languishing as they were in the camps, the British underwent a change from liberators to heartless enemies perpetuating the work of the Nazis. The British government's repressive measures against illegal immigrants to Palestine and against the Jewish community there added to the animosity. The US government, while not enabling the DPs to immigrate to the USA, supported the DPs' demand to immigrate to Palestine.

DPs also partook in underground attempts to immigrate illegally in small boats, which the British seized for the most part, and had their occupants expelled to detention camps in Cyprus or, more radically, back to Germany. All this was done under the eyes of the international press and created an enormous concern for the British.[9] While privately many DPs were willing to immigrate elsewhere, publicly they argued for Jewish immigration to *Eretz-Israel*. When the Anglo-American Commission of Inquiry on Palestine toured the DP camps in April 1946, they found that more than 80 percent of the DPs, 118,570 in all, demanded to go to *Eretz-Israel*. The existence of the DPs and their unified voice for Palestine exerted pressure on the British government to open the gates of Palestine.

Until their dream to leave Europe for *Eretz-Israel* could materialize, the quest for Zion introduced an inherent tension into DP life. Everything was aimed at immigration from Europe, preferably to *Eretz-Israel*. But immigration there was blocked and no other destination was available. So, unwillingly, the DPs had a unique opportunity, which they used to the fullest, to rebuild Jewish society and Jewish cultural, ideological, and religious life in a society oriented on the dream of a Jewish homeland.

Contested history—evaluating DP politics: agency or manipulation?

Lately, some researchers have claimed that the Zionists manipulated the DPs and used them to their own ends in order to advance the Zionist goal of a Jewish state in Palestine. It was not the best interests of the DPs, but rather a political agenda which the Zionists had at heart. In this narrative, DPs had no agency and were either forced or misdirected into Zionism through the actions of active Zionists or emissaries from Palestine.[10] Modern research on the DP community, its development, and its concerns refutes this claim.[11] Survivors chose the Zionist option as a pragmatic and ideological solution to their plight in the post-Holocaust world. It was they who fashioned themselves into a political and cultural force, and their decision to partake in political struggles was a conscious decision by people who had the agency and ability to do so. A chronological exploration of the DP entry into politics and the emergence of the DPs as a political force can be antedated to the early postwar days, and was done by the DPs themselves—before Zionist leaders made contact with them. Researchers working on the immense corpus of historical, cultural, and social materials left by the DPs are those who show the DPs' concerns, discussions, choices and, above all, their agency. The connection between the disempowerment of DPs and the attempt to show them as pawns in the hands of the Zionists in the post-Zionist and anti-Zionist discourse has still to be explored.

Commemoration

The issue of commemoration of the fate of European Jewry was paramount for the DP community. It was seen as a commitment to the dead and also as a way to reiterate the lessons of the past and counter attempts to obliterate Nazi crimes. Commemoration and documentation by DPs challenged the commonplace view on silence and silencing of survivors in the post-Holocaust world.

Memorial days

Commemoration was to become one of the building stones of the emerging DP identity. It was felt that a day should be set apart as a "Unified day of Remembrance and Liberation." The question was: should the day of liberation be commemorated as a day of mourning or a day of thanksgiving?[12] The Central Committee decided to set up the fourteenth day of the month of Iyar (which fell on 15 May 1946). It was to be a day emphasizing "both our sadness and bitterness in the face of the great tragedy that consumed European Jewry and as a commemoration symbolizing national rebirth, underlining that 'Am Yisrael Chai'—the Jewish people lives."[13] DPs evolved ceremonies for such commemoration days, incorporating traditional Jewish religious rituals and secular and Zionist readings and songs. Commemoration events were an opportunity to invite allied and UNRRA officials for an official affirmation of DP ideology.

Mourning academies

In addition to organizing full-scale commemoration days, DPs developed other ways to commemorate their murdered communities. Among the more unique communal commemorations were the "mourning academies" (troyer akademyen—literally, academy of tears). Such mourning meetings were organized by survivors from a prewar community or from a camp, and were an opportunity to reminisce about the prewar years and the war experiences. At such academies, survivors would start with a visit to grave sites of Holocaust victims, then come together in one of the DP camps and tell stories about prewar life and Holocaust experiences. DP newspapers and poster boards were used to inform the public about impending academies whose dates were according to major Nazi killing actions and ghetto liquidations. Sometimes academies were held in honor of Jewish armed resistance to the Nazis. The academies were a grass roots commemoration tool enabling survivors to share their losses with others who shared a common fate.

They also facilitated the establishment of a common memory for survivors who had different wartime experiences. By providing lectures and expositions on the different aspects of the Holocaust, they enabled survivors to integrate their own experiences within the general story.[14]

History writing and documentation

In December 1945, the Central Committee of the Liberated Jews in Germany established the "Central Historical Commission." Two survivors, Israel Kaplan, a teacher from Kovno, and Moshe Feigenboim, an accountant, were appointed to head the Commission. "To work!" Kaplan urged his fellow survivors: "The work must not be postponed, because it is actually a matter of saving [the past] from oblivion." Now is a crucial moment in history, insisted Kaplan, because the survivors who were about to disperse "across the seven seas" still had vivid memories of the horrors of the past:

> History is on the tip of every one of our Jews' tongues; each fold of our memory is actively sparring with historical events. Living springs of history trickle inside us, around us, from every individual—truly an abundance! Let us amass it, draw it up, gather it—rescue it![15]

Under Kaplan's and Feigenboim's leadership, the Commission's team collected 2,500 testimonies, 8,000 questionnaires in Yiddish (largely), Hebrew, Polish, Hungarian, and German. The Commission sought to collect all Holocaust-related material available and acquired the card-index register of the Dachau camp. It also conducted a survey of unknown concentration camps through German mayors and regional officials. The effort was not only on collecting information, but also on disseminating it through books and pamphlets.[16]

But the central publishing project of the Commission was its Yiddish-language journal, entitled *Fun lezten Hurban (From the Last Extermination, Journal for the History of the Jewish People during the Nazi Regime)*. Established in 1946, the journal was a major tool in the Commission's effort to collect testimonies. They distributed a total of 10,000–12,000 copies of the journal. By publishing eyewitness accounts and testimonies, the Commission aimed to "inspire every Jew from among the [Holocaust] survivors to give their testimony of their experiences under the Nazi regime." And indeed, claimed Kaplan: "Since we started with the Journal we get a wider response from survivors."[17]

The journal was seen by Kaplan as a "people's project" (*folks arbeit*). "It is still too early for serious scientific research," he said, "Therefore, our purpose is simply a peo-ple's (folk) journal with the participation of the masses...It is the role of the people themselves to recount their experiences and fill in 'the great blank in our historiography.' These testimonies will 'furnish the historical material for future scientific research and evaluations.'"

Contested history—a silence that never was

The work of the Historical Commission and the discourse on commemoration and memorial days debunks the claim that survivors and DPs were silent, did not want to speak, and were not listened to in the early post-Holocaust years. Actually, it was indeed "a silence that never was." The work of the Historical Commission, its journal, and the widespread attendance at memorial ceremonies and mourning academies show that the Holocaust was talked and written about, researched, and ritualized at an early stage. It is but another example of a widespread Jewish post-Holocaust consciousness that is now coming to light.[18] While some of the DP "memory activists" continued their work in the ensuing years, especially in the new state of Israel, on the whole, this "society" of memory dissolved with the DPs' integration into their absorbing countries.[19] Much research is done now on the issue of Holocaust awareness in the early postwar years. The issue of the disappearance of the DPs' voice has still to be researched.

Family and babies—the re-emergence of the Jewish family

Research on the DP community has moved lately into uncharted ground. Works by Atina Grossmann and Margarete Myers Feinstein have opened new insights into sexuality, gender, childbirth, and motherhood in the DP society. The DP baby boom, which has been discussed by contemporaries in a celebratory fashion, is now the subject of academic research.

The DP "baby boom"

The Jewish DP population in Germany, composed as it was of survivors and refugees, needed physical rehabilitation from the ravages of wartime. One of the early steps was the establishment of health centers and hospitals by UNRRA and by survivors themselves. Once physical health was restored (outwardly at least), survivors started to establish families. The DP camps were the scene of numerous weddings and an accompanying baby boom.

The urge to establish a family was for survivors an answer to the loss of nuclear and extended families and the ensuing sense of loneliness and abandonment. It provided intimacy and security which were so lacking. Culturally, most DPs insisted on Jewish traditional weddings, thus affirming a commitment to Jewish culture and identity and establishing a link between the pre-Holocaust world and their current lives.[20] But it was also the scene of a baby boom. The birth rate of the DP population in Germany was amongst the highest in the postwar world. The birth rate of the Jewish DP population in Bavaria in 1945 was 14.1 births per 1,000 persons. The birth rate of the German population at the time was five births per 1,000 persons.[21] At the time, contemporaries noted that "nearly one third of Jewish women between the age of 18 to 45 in the American zone were either expectant mothers or had new-born babies."[22] Estimates for 1947 were up to 50.2 births per 1,000 persons.[23] While many other countries experienced a postwar baby boom, the DPs' birth rate outstripped most of them.

Why were so many survivors, exhausted and spent as they were, insistent on having children so soon after their terrible ordeal? First and foremost, it was a personal decision. It was a reclamation of personal agency by survivors over their body and their future. It provided survivors with material evidence of their survival and a continuity of their family. This continuity was affirmed in the custom of naming children after murdered family members. For the DPs who had no permanent home or viable destination, having a baby guaranteed a future and a promise of a "normal" home and family.[24]

For the DP community, the baby boom had a cultural and national dimension: "Children have become a kind of religion here…a symbol of the continuity of a people," wrote one of the relief workers.[25] Childbirth was encouraged by the community as a whole and by religious and medical authorities: "One entire generation of Jewish children has been exterminated," wrote a contemporary. "Of all the irreparable losses we have suffered this is the gravest."

> Thus, every Jewish child survivor, every Jewish child to be born, represents for us the most precious and inestimable treasure. We may not freely renounce any single one of them...So we must help these mothers in their task of giving life to the children, we must aid them to bring up the little ones to become good and useful members of the community.[26]

The number of births and babies brought about an interesting chapter in Jewish–German relations. There were not enough DP doctors, nurses, and midwives to cater to the burgeoning baby population and their mothers. As a result, DP women were treated by German gynecologists, gave birth in German hospitals and clinics, and had their children treated by German pediatricians. Young DP mothers, exhausted by their war experience and with no extended family members surviving to help and to instruct in child care, turned to German nannies and domestic helpers. These either were allotted by the authorities or were found independently. While the need to rely on German professional and non-professional help did create tensions, these were assuaged by the urge to keep the babies alive and well.

Contested memory: Jews and Germans, the dynamics of coexistence

Researchers differ as to the depth and meaning of these relations in the early years of the postwar era. Atina Grossman emphasizes the way in which both Jews and Germans muted the immediate dark past in favor of an advantageous present. She shows extensively how survivors forged working relations and modes of interaction with the German population. Margarete Feinstein, on the other hand, focuses on the negative memories of DPs from their lives with the Germans. She analyzes traumatic memories of some of the DP women who experienced antisemitism or indifferent German doctors and medical personnel. According to Feinstein, there were German doctors working with DPs who were "still practicing Nazi Medicine."[27]

The future generation and its education

Research on surviving children and their education has only just begun, and much of what has been published in Hebrew has yet to be translated. Even so, there is already a substantial body of work in English on the children in the camps, their education, and their place in the community's concerns.[28]

The children

Very few children survived the Nazi annihilation of European Jewry. Only 11 percent of Jewish children alive in 1939 were still alive by the end of the war.[29] A census from July 1945 showed that of the 250,000 Jewish survivors in Germany and Austria, only 3.6 percent were under the age of 16. Close to 90 percent were between 18 and 45 years old, and 7.3 percent over 45. This changed rapidly with the influx of survivors and refugees from eastern Europe. In 1946, the number of children aged under 18 in the American zone rose from 7,600 at the beginning of the year to 20,000 children by the end of it. This was also due to the high birth rate in the Jewish DP population.

Educating these children received top priority in the DP society, and schools were established right after liberation. In Bergen Belsen, a Jewish elementary school with 200 students was established by July 1945, and shortly afterwards a makeshift high school opened. Schools were staffed by survivor teachers from the DP population. Later on, they were joined by teachers from the Jewish Brigade of the British Army and by teachers sent over from the Jewish Community in Palestine.[30] This phenomenon repeated itself in other camps as well.

The educational system had to cope with children and teenagers scarred by the experience of the Holocaust. They had no schooling for the years preceding liberation and were speaking a multitude of languages. Many of them had no remaining family members and were caught in the postwar competition between Jewish political, religious, and ideological movements seeking at once to provide for children and to indoctrinate them with their values. The fate of the children became a national issue debated and fought over by the DP leadership. Thus, for example, when 1,000 temporary visas were offered by the British to child survivors, the offer was refused by DP leaders. They insisted that the only possible haven for Jewish children was Palestine. They also spoke of the importance of *Eretz-Israel* as a redemptive force for the children and the adults as well:

> Having gone through such an agonizing life experience, people could so easily fall into a life of killing and stealing and become the dregs of humanity. Only the inspiring idea of building the Land of Israel as a homeland gives both young and old the courage and belief to prepare themselves for a new life based on social justice.[31]

Through the work of survivor leaders and teachers, and workers of UNRRA and other relief organizations, the DP society was the scene of varied educational endeavors. Five children's camps were established for the organized groups of unaccompanied children arriving from eastern Europe. *Yeshivot* (traditional Talmud academies) and other ultra-Orthodox-style schools were established, as were general secular schools. In a way, this was a continuation of the prewar divisions in Jewish education, with stronger orientation towards Hebrew and Zionism. Strongly apparent were the *Kibbutzim* and their training centers. In 40 such farms, about 3,000 teenagers and young people were able to form their own communities while training in farmwork towards immigration to Palestine.

Contested memory: the Zionists and the children

The ideological decision gave rise to criticism, both by contemporaries and in later historical writing, that the children's welfare was sacrificed on political grounds.[32] But Margarete Feinstein has shown that there was a strong case for those who refused the idea of dispersing surviving children in Britain instead of letting them be educated with their peers who shared similar experiences. The fact that the British offer was for a limited period was seen as detrimental to the children. A permanent (hoped-for) home in Palestine was also seen as a much better option for the children. Moreover, one has to remember that adult and children DPs shared a common experience, and that child survivors could find, so it was claimed, much more understanding in DP society than elsewhere in Europe or the USA.[33]

Conclusion

The story of the Jewish DPs in the postwar period is fascinating for the striking abnormality it presents. Here were the remnants of a European community who survived several years of Nazi terror and who attempted to rebuild their community and culture (occasionally in the space of that terror, as in the case of Bergen-Belsen) while finding a territory they could ultimately call home. By and large, non-Jewish DPs rebuilt their communities in the space of their former homes and homelands. Jewish DPs forged a national and communal identity on totally temporal grounds. This identity was built on two pillars—the Holocaust that was, and the Jewish homeland that was soon to be. When almost all Jewish DPs left Europe for Israel and the United States by the end of the 1940s, the unique DP community and culture came to an end.

The scope of this chapter does not allow a discussion of several other important aspects of the DP experience, including the DP cultural scene, religious life and religious strife in the camps, and inter-Jewish political divisions in DP society. Research into these issues is an ongoing project, as works published in recent years and their bibliographies demonstrate.[34]

Notes

1 Hagit Lavsky, *New Beginnings: Holocaust Survivors in Bergen-Belsen and the British Zone in Germany 1945–1950* (Detroit, Michigan: Wayne State University Press, 2002). The time was one of transition and great fluidity, and there are other estimates of the total number of people needing repatriation and of those repatriated.

2 Lavsky, *New Beginnings*, 27–28 discusses various estimates of Jewish DPs and is cited as an authority by most later works.

3 Lavsky, *New Beginnings*, 32–33.

4 Atina Grossmann, *Jews, Germans and Allies: Close Encounters in Occupied Germany* (Princeton, New Jersey and Oxford: Princeton University Press, 2007), 137–42.

5 See Zeev W. Mankowitz, *Life Between Memory and Hope: The Survivors of the Holocaust in Occupied Germany* (Cambridge: Cambridge University Press, 2002), 52–67; and Grossmann, *Jews, Germans and Allies*, 137–42.

6 In this paper, I use interchangeably the terms Palestine and *Eretz-Israel* (The Land of Israel) as they were used by DPs.

7 Koppel Pinson, "Jewish Life in Liberated Germany," *Jewish Social Studies*, 9 (1947): 101–26; here 117, quoted by Mankowitz, *Life Between Memory and Hope*, 70.

8 Meir Gavronsky, *Dos Fraye Vort*, no. 14 (4 January 1946), quoted by Mankowitz, *Life Between Memory and Hope*, 72.

9 Arieh J. Kochavi, *Post-Holocaust Politics: Britain, the United States and Jewish Refugees, 1945–1948* (Chapel Hill, North Carolina: University of North Carolina Press, 2001).

10 See Idith Zertal, *Israel's Holocaust and the Politics of Nationhood*, transl. Chaya Galai (New York: Cambridge University Press, 2005); Yosef Grodzinsky, *In the Shadow of the Holocaust: The Struggle between Jews and Zionists in the Aftermath of World War II* (Monroe: Common Courage Press, 2004).

11 See works by Lavsky, Mankowitz, Finestein, and Brenner, cited in the footnotes.

12 Leo W. Schwartz, *Congress Weekly*, vol. 22, no. 15 (1955), quoted by Mankowitz, *Life Between Memory and Hope*, 197.

13 Schwartz, *Congress Weekly*, 197.

14 Margarete Myers Feinstein, *Holocaust Survivors in Postwar Germany 1945–1957* (New York: Cambridge University Press, 2010), 77.

15 Israel Kaplan, "Day to Day Work in the Historical Commission," lecture given at the meeting of the Historical Commissions, Munich, 12 May 1947, published by the Central Historical Commission of Liberated Jews in the American Zone (Yiddish), 24.

16 On the Historical Commissions, see Boaz Cohen, "Holocaust Survivors and the Genesis of Holocaust Research," in *Beyond Camps and Forced Labour: Current International Research on Survivors of Nazi Persecution*, eds Johannes-Steinert Dieter and Weber-Newth Inge (Osnabrück: Secolo Verlag, 2005), 290–300; Ada Schein, "'Everyone Can Hold a Pen': The Documentation Project in the DP Camps in Germany," in *Holocaust Historiography in Context: Emergence, Challenges, Polemics and Achievements*, eds David Bankier and Dan Michman (Jerusalem and New York: Yad Vashem and Berghahn, 2009). On the general phenomenon of Jewish Historical Commissions, see Laura Jokush, "Khurban Forshung: Jewish Historical Commissions in Europe 1945–49," in *Simon Dubnow Institute Yearbook*, vol. 6 (2007): 441–73.

17 Israel Kaplan, The protocol of the first meeting of the [historical] workers of the Historical Commission, Munich. 11–12/ 5/1947 (Yiddish), YIVO Archive 1258/476.

18 See Hasia Diner, *We Remember with Reverence and Love: American Jews and the Myth of Silence After the Holocaust 1945–1962* (New York: New York University Press, 2009).

19 Boaz Cohen, "Holocaust Survivors and Early Israeli Holocaust Research and Commemoration: A Reappraisal," in *How the Holocaust Looks Now: International Perspectives*, eds Martin L. Davies and Claus-Christian W. Szejnmann (New York: Palgrave Macmillan, 2006), 139–49.

20 Feinstein, *Holocaust Survivors in Postwar Germany*, 128–33.

21 Michael Brenner, *After the Holocaust: Rebuilding Jewish Lives in Postwar Germany* (Princeton: Princeton University Press, 1997), 24.

22 Grossmann, *Jews, Germans and Allies*, 188.

23 Grossmann, *Jews, Germans and Allies*, 190.

24 Grossmann, *Jews, Germans and Allies*, 184–200.

25 Dr Joseph Schwartz, JDC European director, quoted by Grossmann, *Jews, Germans and Allies*, 196.

26 O. S. E. *Report on the Situation of the Jews in Germany, October/December 1945* (Geneva: Union O.S.E., 1946), 66–67. Grossmann, *Jews, Germans and Allies*, 192.

27 Feinstein, *Holocaust Survivors in Postwar Germany*, 133–45.

28 See Feinstein, *Holocaust Survivors in Postwar Germany*, 159–97; Mankowitz, *Life Between Memory and Hope*, 131–60; Lavsky, *New Beginnings*, 167–87; Ada Schein, "The Struggle for Uniform Education in the Displaced Persons Camps in Germany 1947–49," *Moreshet: Journal for the Study of the Holocaust and Antisemitism*, vol. 6 (Spring 2009): 30–72; Boaz Cohen, "The Children's Voice: Post-War Collection of Testimonies from Child Survivors of the Holocaust," *Holocaust and Genocide Studies* (Spring 2007): 74–95.

29 Deborah Dwork, *Children With a Star: Jewish Youth in Nazi Europe* (New Haven, Connecticut: Yale University Press, 1991), xv.

30 Brenner, *After the Holocaust*, 23–24.

31 Leo Srole, 1946, quoted by Mankowitz, *Life Between Memory and Hope*, 126.

32 Grodzinsky, *In the Shadow of the Holocaust*, 71–86.

33 Feinstein, *Holocaust Survivors in Postwar Germany*, 172–78.

34 For up-to-date research, see Avinoam J. Patt and Michael Berkowitz, eds, *We are Here!: New Approaches to Jewish Displaced Persons in Postwar Germany* (Detroit, Michigan: Wayne State University Press, 2010).

Part V
THE HOLOCAUST IN LAW, CULTURE, AND MEMORY

36

PUTTING THE HOLOCAUST ON TRIAL IN THE TWO GERMANIES, 1945–89

Devin Pendas

The political crimes of the Nazi regime before and during World War II are among the most heavily prosecuted in the history of the world.[1] In part, this has to do with the simple fact that, because Germany was utterly defeated in World War II and then occupied, the Allies had unlimited access to Nazi documents, and it was reasonably safe for survivor witnesses to come forward and testify. It was also relatively easy to find and capture defendants, at least in comparison with many later cases, where the perpetrators often remained in power or were protected by sympathetic governments.[2] Yet this merely explains why it was possible to vigorously prosecute Nazi atrocities. It says nothing about why the decision was taken, by the victorious Allies, by the various formerly occupied countries of Europe, and by the Germans themselves to treat Nazi atrocities as actionable crimes, rather than as objects for rough justice or as unavoidable horrors of war best handled politically, if at all.

Broadly speaking, trials for Nazi atrocities can be divided into four categories: an international trial, occupation trials, domestic trials outside Germany, and domestic trials within Germany. First, there was the International Military Tribunal (IMT) at Nuremberg, the Nuremberg Trial proper, which put 22 leading Nazis on trial. It was intended to demonstrate to the world that the Nazi regime was thoroughly criminal and that Nazi aggression and atrocities were part of a wide-ranging and longstanding plan originating at the very top of the party and state hierarchies. Second, alongside the IMT trial, there were numerous trials for Nazi atrocities before the courts of the occupation authorities (American, British, French, and Russian) in Germany. These included the 12 so-called successor trials, likewise held at Nuremberg, but before an American, rather than international, military tribunal. They also included the American Dachau Trials held directly by the US military, as well as French military trials, and British Royal Warrant courts. Third, there were tens of thousands of trials for Nazi atrocities conducted in the domestic courts of virtually every European country touched by World War II and even in a few non-European countries, such as Canada and, later, Australia. Finally, even before the founding of the two German states in 1949, German domestic courts began to hold thousands of trials for Nazi crimes, a practice which continues to the present day, as John Demjanjuk's recent deportation to stand trial in Germany shows.

The numbers of people convicted for participating in Nazi atrocities is staggering. Altogether, more than 95,000 Germans and Austrians were convicted of Nazi crimes after the war.[3] This does not include the tens of thousands of other Europeans convicted of collaboration in Nazi crimes.[4] Most of the cases against Germans and Austrians (at least 52,721) were tried in eastern Europe.[5] In western European courts, 2,890 Germans/Austrians were convicted of Nazi crimes.[6] The four major allied powers together convicted 8,812 Germans or Austrians in occupation courts on German soil. The Germans themselves convicted just under 20,000 people of Nazi crimes. This includes 6,656 in the German courts of the Western Occupation Zones/Federal Republic and at least 12,776 in the German courts of the Soviet Occupation Zone/German Democratic Republic.[7] Only partial, and in many cases approximate, figures are available for the total numbers of investigations and indictments for Nazi crimes.[8] Nonetheless, based on the available data, one can say that there were at least 329,000 investigations or indictments of individuals for Nazi crimes after the war.[9] Presumably, the true figures are higher (likely much higher) but, since reliable data are unavailable for Hungary, Romania, or Yugoslavia, it is impossible to be more precise.

Although the British and the Americans in particular wanted to postpone any reckoning with Nazi atrocities until after the war, in large part because they feared retaliation against Allied flyers held in German PoW camps, trials nonetheless began even before the German surrender in May 1945. France, Poland, and the Soviet Union all began holding trials as early as the fall of 1944. Still, the trials held during the war were few in number and played a minor role overall. The real story during the war was the debate over what to do after the war. Beginning in 1942, when the exile governments of the smaller occupied countries of Europe issued the so-called St James Declaration demanding "the punishment, through the channel of organized justice" for perpetrators of Nazi atrocities, pressure began to mount for a systematic legal response to Nazi atrocities.[10] On the other side were those who, like both Churchill and Stalin for a time, favored a largely extra-legal response, calling for drumhead court-martials and the summary execution of a sizable number of suspected "war criminals." (Stalin once suggested a figure of 50,000.)[11] Even in the United States, proponents of drastic measures initially seemed to hold sway. The so-called Morgenthau Plan (named for its architect, Treasury Secretary Henry J. Morgenthau Jr), which Roosevelt briefly favored, called for summary executions as well.[12] In the end, though, the party favoring criminal prosecution, centered on Secretary of War, Henry L. Stimson (a former Wall Street lawyer and US Attorney), won out and the Americans were able to push their Allies in that direction as well.[13] The Nuremberg Trial was the direct result.

Brainchild of the Americans, the IMT at Nuremberg had three important features. First, Robert H. Jackson, US Supreme Court justice, chief negotiator for the Americans at the London Conference that drafted the Charter authorizing the IMT, and then chief prosecutor at Nuremberg, felt strongly that the Nazis' fundamental sin had been in launching a war of aggression. As Jackson said in his opening statement, "This inquest represents the practical effort of four of the most mighty of nations, with the support of 17 more, to utilize international law to meet the greatest menace of our times—aggressive war."[14] For Jackson (and ultimately the Nuremberg Court as well), it was this aggressive war that led to all the diverse horrors laid out in the indictment, including many of the crimes that would later come to be called the Holocaust; war, not genocide or mass atrocity, was the chief crime of the Nazis. Second, on the Americans' view, this war had been the result of a longstanding and widespread plan. "This war did not just happen," Jackson insisted, "it was planned and prepared over a long period of time and with no small skill and cunning."[15] Finally, although the Americans put tremendous emphasis on Nazi crimes against peace, virtually everyone involved in preparing the IMT trial recognized that many Nazi atrocities went beyond what could be prosecuted as traditional war crimes (which largely covered crimes against foreign nationals and PoWs). To this end, the London Charter included a newly formulated international legal category: crimes against humanity. This covered atrocities (murder, deportation, inhumane acts, etc.) committed against non-combatants, including stateless persons and German citizens, as well as "persecutions on political, racial, or religious grounds."[16]

Given the interpretation of Nazi criminality as, in the first instance, a conspiracy to launch a war of aggression, from which all other Nazi misdeeds flowed, it is hardly surprising that the distinctive quality of Nazi genocide would recede at Nuremberg. Yet because the accused were indicted for crimes against humanity as well, evidence of what would come to be called the Holocaust—the systematic attempt to exterminate European Jewry in its entirety—was ubiquitous at Nuremberg, ranging from Otto Ohlendorf's admission that his unit (*Einsatzgruppe D*) murdered at least 90,000 "Jews and Communists" to Soviet film footage of the liberation of Auschwitz in 1945.[17] The Soviets, who had responsibility for presenting the prosecution's case concerning crimes against humanity in eastern Europe, and hence for prosecuting the Holocaust, largely failed (or refused) to distinguish between the genocide of the Jews and other Nazi mass murders. Consequently, while the Holocaust was by no means completely absent from the IMT trial, neither did it emerge with any great clarity during the course of the trial.[18]

Similarly, in the other Allied trials, the extermination of the Jews only rarely emerged as the principal crime on trial. Most of the Allied trials—both those of the occupation courts and those in the domestic courts of the formerly occupied countries—were concerned with crimes committed against their own citizens. To the extent that these included crimes against Jews, as was true for the French or Dutch, it was inconvenient to accentuate this fact overly much, since it would have highlighted the full extent of the cooperation by local authorities in the deportation of local Jewish populations. Meanwhile, in eastern Europe, the emerging communist regimes had every reason to prosecute Nazi atrocities vigorously, but not to highlight the special character of anti-Jewish violence. The Marxist narrative of the war was a class narrative, in which the peaceful workers of Europe were assaulted by Nazi hordes operating at the behest of revanchist capitalists. The genocidal mass murder of Jews for racial reasons fit uneasily with this interpretation. The Poles, for instance, convicted a number of the most important mid-level perpetrators of the Holocaust, including Rudolph Höß, commandant of Auschwitz, and Amon Goeth, commandant of the Plaszow labor camp depicted in Stephen Spielberg's film *Schindler's List*. Yet in these cases, the defendant's crimes were framed not as crimes against Jews, but as crimes against Polish citizens.[19] The major exception to this rule was the trial of Otto Ohlendorf and others (the *Einsatzgruppen* Case), one of the 12 so-called successor trials held before American Military Tribunals at Nuremberg.[20] Since the *Einsatzgruppen* had initiated the mass killing of Jews in the summer of 1941, this, the "biggest murder trial in history," as the prosecution called it, was one of the few early trials to deal explicitly with the genocide of the Jews.

More generally, the Holocaust as such emerged only gradually in the context of trials for Nazi atrocities. Broadly, such trials can be divided into three main periods. First, there was a relatively brief period of rigorous and extensive prosecution in the immediate aftermath of the war. This was initiated by the major Allies, but the rest of Europe eagerly followed their lead. Even the Germans got in on the act, prosecuting the vast majority of their Nazi cases during the occupation period (over 4,000 of the western German and 8,000 of the eastern German trials took place between 1945 and 1949). The second phase, which began with the founding of the two German states in 1949, was marked by what one observer called an "amnesty fever."[21] By the end of the 1950s, hardly any Nazi criminals were still in prison anywhere in Europe (even eastern Europe). Alongside this, there was a precipitous drop in prosecution rates in those countries (such as the two Germanies) that still bothered to prosecute Nazi crimes at all. Then, beginning at the end of the 1950s and picking up steam over the course of the 1960s, a counter-reaction set in to this policy of clemency and amnesia, one critical of its "moral and legal deficits."[22] As a result, the few Nazi criminals still in prison found it much harder to secure an early release and there was a new wave of prosecutions, especially in the two Germanies.

The trials for Nazi crimes in German courts broadly followed the general European trajectory, with an initial period of intensive prosecution, followed by a period of quiescence and amnesty and then, starting in 1958, a new wave of trials. Between 1945 and 1949, 13,333 defendants were indicted for Nazi crimes in German courts in the three western occupation zones. Of these, 4,667 were convicted, 3,703 were acquitted, and 491 had the charges dismissed.[23] In the Soviet occupation zone, meanwhile, there were 33,654 investigations or indictments from 1945 to 1949. Of these, 8,059 resulted in convictions.[24] In the course of the 1950s, these figures dropped markedly in both Germanies, though more dramatically in West than in East Germany. In the Federal Republic, there were 1,438 convictions for Nazi crimes from 1950 to 1959, more than half of these occurring in 1950 alone.[25] After 1953, the number of convictions for Nazi crimes would only twice exceed 50 per annum in West Germany (67 in both 1965 and 1968). In the German Democratic Republic, there were 4,717 convictions from 1950 to 1959.[26] In both 1956 and 1957, there was only a single conviction for Nazi crimes before East German courts.[27]

During the occupation period, German courts had jurisdiction over Nazi cases only on Allied sufferance. The Allies initially explicitly excluded Nazi crimes from the jurisdiction of the newly reconstituted German courts (Allied Control Council Law No. 4, 30 October 1945).[28] Then, in December, the Control Council issued Law No. 10, which formed the basis for all subsequent prosecutions for Nazi crimes in Germany, including those before Allied courts (such as the successor trials at Nuremberg). Containing the same criminal charges as the London Charter (crimes against peace, war crimes, and crimes against humanity), as well as membership in an organization declared criminal by the IMT, CC Law No. 10 essentially extended the logic of Nuremberg to the rest of the Allied war crimes prosecution program. Importantly, Article III 1 d authorized the four occupying powers to grant German courts jurisdiction over the crimes covered, insofar as these were committed "by persons of German citizenship or nationality against other persons of German citizenship or nationality, or stateless persons."[29]

Thus it became possible for Germans to prosecute Nazi crimes in their own courts. It is important to note that the restriction of German jurisdiction to crimes against German citizens or stateless persons meant German courts could be granted jurisdiction only over crimes against humanity, not war crimes (which were committed against foreign, especially Allied, nationals) or crimes against peace. A great many German judges and prosecutors were deeply hostile to the whole project of trying Nazi crimes at all. In part this was because, despite the strident rhetoric of denazification, the legal system remained among the least denazified in postwar Germany.[30]

CC Law No. 10 only authorized the transfer of jurisdiction to German courts. It did not require it. The four occupying powers each handled the matter somewhat differently. The French and the British both issued military government ordinances that granted German courts jurisdiction over Nazi crimes against humanity in quite general terms.[31] The Americans, on the other hand, declined to grant German courts jurisdiction over crimes against humanity at all, insisting instead that German courts in their zone prosecute Nazi crimes against German citizens under existing German statutory law.[32] The Soviets granted German courts jurisdiction over Nazi crimes against humanity broadly, but on a case-by-case basis, through August 1947. After that, under the provisions of Soviet Military Government Order 201, the Soviets shifted their strategy. Henceforth, German courts were given general permission to prosecute Nazi crimes, but were to do so simultaneously as crimes against humanity and as part of a broader denazification process in accordance with Control Council Directive 38, which called for the removal from public life and punishment of anyone who had been a member of organizations deemed criminal by the IMT.[33] As a result, after August 1947, Nazi trials in the German courts of the Soviet zone became increasingly instrumentalized for political purposes, as the Stalinist Socialist Unity Party increasingly consolidated its power.

German courts during the occupation period thus had broad jurisdiction to prosecute Nazi crimes against German citizens and stateless persons. Even in the American zone, German courts were allowed to pursue such cases, albeit under German rather than occupation law (for example, as murder or assault rather than as crimes against humanity). The fact that crimes against humanity had been devised at the London Conference as a way of prosecuting Nazi atrocities that seemed to go beyond ordinary war crimes might seem to imply that these trials were largely for Holocaust-related crimes. The opposite is in fact the case. From 1945 to 1949, only 1.2 percent of all the cases tried in the three western zones concerned mass extermination crimes.[34] Rather, the dominant categories of cases tried in German courts during the occupation period were criminal denunciations (38.3 percent) and crimes against political opponents (16.3 percent). There is one important exception to this general rule that these early trials did not concern themselves extensively with the crimes of the Holocaust. 15.4 percent of all trials from 1945 to 1949 in the German courts of the three western occupation zones concerned crimes committed in connection with so-called *Reichskristallnacht*, the organized anti-Jewish pogrom of November 1938.[35] Included among these cases were numerous instances of arson (for the destruction of synagogues), assault, and, in a few cases, homicide.

In addition, there were other kinds of crimes against Jews that were prosecuted under the broad rubric of "persecution." For instance, in February 1947, the Chamber Court in Berlin convicted a former air-raid warden for crimes against humanity for refusing to allow a Jewish neighbor into an air-raid shelter during an attack, as well as for denouncing the victim to the Gestapo for not wearing the requisite yellow star on his clothing. This case, in particular, reveals one of the central problems for German courts in dealing with many crimes against Jews under the Nazis. As the court put it: "The facts of the case, which the court has determined to be crimes against humanity, did not constitute punishable offenses at the time they were committed."[36] Consequently, the court continued, this case "violated the generally acknowledged principle, now reinstituted in German law, that a crime can only be punished if the punishment was determined by law prior to the commission of the act." The court, however, concluded that the Allies, as the sovereign authorities in Germany, had the authority to punish "particularly abhorrent acts" committed under the Nazis, even retroactively. This included, according to the court, racial persecution. Both the denunciation of the victim to the Gestapo and his exclusion from the air-raid shelter constituted persecution, and hence a crime against humanity, the court ruled. Denunciations intended to disadvantage the victim were generally crimes against humanity, the court held. Similarly, "a persecution can also be some other act against a person that is intended to harm or even merely to expose and humiliate him."

A great many German judges and prosecutors were deeply troubled by this seeming violation of the prohibition on ex post facto law, and protested vociferously.[37] Hodo von Hodenberg, president of the State Court in Celle, registered one of the first and most influential objections to prosecuting Nazi crimes as crimes against humanity, initially in a letter to appellate judges on the Superior Court for the British zone, then in a long article published in the influential German law review, the *Süddeutsche Juristienzeitung*.[38] Prosecuting Nazi atrocities retroactively, von Hodenberg argued, was both morally wrong and politically unwise, as it would undermine efforts to democratize German society. "In this way, however, a fundamental principle is damaged, the violation of which during the Nazi period was justifiably subject to severe attacks." Such prosecutions would, he insisted, do irreparable harm to the "public's legal consciousness." In other words, von Hodenberg argued that the effective pursuit of justice for Nazi crimes would, in fact, undermine the democratic principles such trials were supposed to help promote.

It would be a mistake to read Hodenberg's argument as a principled liberal critique of an abuse of law. Hodenberg, though not a former Nazi, was an ardent nationalist and ultra-conservative. He was a leading member of the so-called Heidelberg Circle, a lobbying group of prominent German jurists dedicated to bringing an end to the prosecution of Nazi crimes and securing the release of all those already convicted by the Allies in such cases.[39] Thus, for Hodenberg, as for many of the German critics of the seeming retroactivity of prosecuting Nazi crimes as crimes against humanity, arguments of legal principle also served an ulterior purpose, which was to undermine the entire project of prosecuting Nazi crimes at all.

This is perfectly in keeping with the situation in Germany, where the percentage of Germans who saw the Nuremberg verdict as "fair" fell from 78 percent in 1946 to 38 percent in 1950.[40] Moreover, the Germans came increasingly to view themselves as the primary victims of World War II over the course of the early postwar years.[41] In this context, it is hardly surprising that calls for amnesty mounted, led by jurists such as those in the Heidelberg Circle and, to greater effect, by the churches, which retained considerable moral authority as supposedly untainted by any association with the Nazi regime.[42] In response, the government of the newly formed Federal Republic passed two amnesties for Nazi crimes in 1949 and 1954. Also in response to the criticisms of those such as Hodenberg, who felt that prosecuting "crimes against humanity" violated the prohibition on ex post facto law, the West German courts stopped prosecuting Nazi cases on that charge as soon as the Allies let them in 1950. Thereafter, in West Germany, Nazi crimes had to be prosecuted under ordinary statutory law, which in the 1950s meant manslaughter or murder and, after 1960, only murder.

Meanwhile, in East Germany, the pace of prosecution actually accelerated dramatically in 1950, when the Soviets decided to close their "special camps" in Germany and transfer the remaining inmates to German custody. In January, the Soviets transferred 3,400 prisoners to German jurisdiction. Special tribunals were created within the State Court at Chemnitz, formally under Soviet Order 201. Judges and jurors were directly selected by the Socialist Unity Party and the Saxon justice ministry was explicitly prohibited from exercising any influence on the proceedings. Party head Walter Ulbricht himself declared the prisoners to be "undoubted enemies of the building [of socialism]" and demanded that no sentences under 10 years be passed.[43] A special commission was created to review all cases where the sentence was less than 5 years, and the "clemency" commission created subsequently mostly increased the severity of the sentences imposed. In addition, the police regularly spied on judges and jurors to ensure their compliance with the desire of the Socialist Unity Party of Germany (*Sozialistische Einheitspartei Deutschlands*, SED) for draconian, politically correct verdicts.[44] Between April and July 1950, 3,324 defendants were convicted, almost all sentenced to the requisite 10 years or more. The only evidence in most cases was a German translation of the Soviet report on the prisoners, generally quite vague. Most telling, however, was the fact that the defendants were convicted primarily as enemies of socialism, their alleged Nazi crimes being only the pretext.[45]

Thereafter, the rate of prosecution for Nazi crimes fell dramatically in both German states. Perhaps somewhat ironically, the complex and antagonistic relations between the two Germanies actually led to an upswing in prosecutions, especially in West Germany, starting in the late 1950s. In practical terms, the decisive development was the founding of the Central Office for the Investigation of National Socialist Crimes in Ludwigsburg in 1958. For the first time, there was a coordinated national effort to investigate Nazi crimes. This led to a dramatic rise in the number of investigations and to a somewhat less dramatic revival in convictions.[46]

The Central Office was founded by agreement among the Justice Ministers of the various German states. This agreement followed shortly on the heels of the so-called Ulm *Einsatzgruppen* trial. The Ulm trial was the result of the entirely coincidental discovery of the identity of Bernhard Fischer-Schweder, who had been deeply involved in the massacre of Jews in Lithuania in the early days of Operation Barbarossa. The trial revealed the glaring inadequacy of previous efforts to investigate Nazi crimes, which had relied largely on allegations being made by survivors. Yet it would be too simple to maintain, as Adalbert Rückerl has, that the Ulm Trial provided the "decisive impulse for the intensification and concentration of the criminal prosecution of National Socialist crimes."[47] There is little indication that Germans somehow dramatically changed their mind about prosecuting Nazi crimes in the wake of the Ulm trial. Indeed, the polling data indicate that throughout the 1960s, a majority of Germans favored terminating such prosecutions altogether.[48] Rather, a handful of prominent liberal journalists pushed the issue.[49] In and of itself, this would not have been enough to generate the political willpower required to found the Central Office, however. Rather, it was the fact that the East Germans had begun to enjoy considerable success with their propaganda campaign against the all-too-real failings of Federal Republic's handling of Nazi crimes that made the West German political elite nervous.[50] The Central Office was a way to de-fang East German criticism, without, it should be added, being intended to lead to a thorough purge of former Nazis from elite positions in West Germany.[51]

The most prominent result of this enhanced investigation and prosecution of Nazi crimes was the so-called Frankfurt Auschwitz Trial of 1963–65.[52] With 20 defendants (and 17 convictions), 350 witnesses and 183 trial sessions, it was the largest and most important Nazi trial in Germany since Nuremberg. If it would be going too far to claim, as one historian has, that the trial "broke the wall of silence" surrounding the Nazi past, the trial nonetheless did help, together with the Eichmann Trial in Jerusalem a few years earlier, to highlight the Holocaust as a distinct and central element within the broader universe of Nazi atrocity.[53] It also helped establish Auschwitz as the dominant symbol of Nazi genocide. Not to be outdone, the East Germans staged an Auschwitz Trial of their own in 1966.[54]

In the end, then, the Holocaust did eventually emerge as a central focus of Nazi trials in the two Germanies, but not until well after the war. Between 1960 and 2005, fully 23 percent of all Nazi trials in the Federal Republic dealt with mass extermination actions.[55] In this respect, the prosecution of Holocaust crimes, like the broader awareness of the distinctive place of the genocide of the Jews within the broader panoply of Nazi atrocities, took time to emerge. The enduring impact of the Americans' legal strategy at Nuremberg, with its emphasis on aggressive war, as well as the desire by the governments of occupied countries to highlight their national suffering (and downplay their national collaboration), played an important role in this. So, too, did the resistance of German jurists to prosecuting Nazi crimes as crimes against humanity. Prosecuting such crimes as ordinary homicide downplayed the systematic character of Nazi criminality and made it harder to grapple with the scale and scope of the genocide of the Jews. The eventual emergence of the Holocaust as a central focal point for Nazi trials in the two Germanies owes much to the dedicated efforts of a handful of activist prosecutors, such as the Hessian attorney general Fritz Bauer, who initiated the Auschwitz Trial.[56] The global impact of the Eichmann Trial in Jerusalem in 1961 also played an important role. Above all, the weight of the evidence, once it began to be systematically evaluated with the founding of the Central Office in 1958, spoke for itself. The Holocaust lay at the heart of Nazi criminality, and gradually the courts came to recognize this as well.

Notes

1 Rwanda marks an important exception. If official statistics are to be believed (and they may be inflated), the *gacaca* courts in that country had rendered at least 1.1 million judgments as of April 2009, with 3,000 cases still pending. *Chambres Specialisées* tried an additional 9,721 individuals prior to the onset of the *gacaca* jurisdiction. See Jens Meierhenrich, *Lawfare: The Formation and Deformation of Gacaca Jurisdictions in Rwanda, 1994–2009* (Cambridge: Cambridge University Press, forthcoming). This does not even count the relatively small number of verdicts issued by the International Criminal Court for Rwanda.
2 Of course, many Nazi perpetrators managed to escape, either to sympathetic third-party countries in South America and the Middle East or, often enough, to the allied countries themselves.
3 Unless otherwise indicated, all numbers come from Norbert Frei, "Nach der Tat: Die Ahndung deutscher Kriegs-und NS-Verbrechen in Europa—eine Bilanz," in *Transnationale Vergangenheitspolitik: Der Umgang mit deutschen Kriegsverbrechern in Europa nach dem Zweiten Weltkrieg,* ed. Norbert Frei (Göttingen: Wallstein, 2006), 30–31.
4 István Deák, Jan T. Gross and Tony Judt, eds, *The Politics of Retribution: World War II and its Aftermath* (Princeton: Princeton University Press, 2000).
5 Frei, "Nach der Tat." This includes trials within the USSR, Poland, and Czechoslovakia. Statistics are not available for trials against Germans and Austrians in Hungary, Romania, and Yugoslavia, so the total numbers in eastern Europe are presumably much higher. These totals represent minimum figures. For instance, the numbers here include 25,921 Germans or

Austrians convicted in the Soviet Union. See Andreas Hilger, "'Die Gerechtigkeit nehme ihren Lauf'? Die Bestrafung deutscher Kriegs- und Gewaltverbrecher in der Sovjetunion und der SBZ/ DDR" in *Transnationale Vergangenheitspolitik* (Frei, ed.), 193. By contrast, Martin Lang gives a figure of 37,000 convictions in Soviet courts. See Martin Lang, *Stalins Strafjustiz gegen deutsche Soldaten: Die Massenprozesse gegen deutsche Kriegsgefangene in den Jahren 1949 und 1950 in historischer Sicht* (Herford: Mittler, 1981), 47–48.

6 Frei, "Nach der Tat." Includes France, but not French trials within Germany, the Netherlands, Belgium, Denmark, Norway, Greece, and Italy.

7 The West German figures come from Andreas Eichmüller, "Die Strafverfolgung von NS-Verbrechen durch westdeutsche Justizbehörden seit 1945," *Vierteljahrshefte für Zeitgeschichte* 56/4 (2008): 621–40. The East German figures are from Frei, "Nach der Tat."

8 For instance, the total number of allied investigations is unknown. Total figures for investigations are available at the moment only for West Germany but not for East Germany. In many cases, the available figures are best-guess approximations. Given the state of many eastern European archives and the limits on access still in place for former Soviet archives, more precise figures may never become available in some cases.

9 Frei, "Nach der Tat," 30–31. These numbers include figures for the two Germanies only down to 1959. One must also treat these figures with caution, since many of the investigations were merely pro forma, with entire rosters of *Wehrmacht* or SS units being registered as suspects, without each of them being actually investigated at an individual level.

10 St James Declaration, 13 January 1942, cited by Arieh J. Kochavi, *Prelude to Nuremberg: Allied War Crimes Policy and the Question of Punishment* (Chapel Hill, North Carolina: University of North Carolina Press, 1998), 20.

11 Annette Weinke, *Die Nürnberger Prozesse* (Munich: C.H. Beck, 2006), 12.

12 In general, see Warren F. Kimball, *Swords or Ploughshares? The Morgenthau Plan for Defeated Germany, 1943–1946* (Philadelphia: Lippincott, 1976).

13 This story is best told by Kochavi, *Prelude to Nuremberg*.

14 International Military Tribunal, *The Trial of the Major War Criminals before the International Military Tribunal, 14 November 1945–1 October 1946* (Nuremberg: Secretariat of the Tribunal, 1947), 2: 99.

15 International Military Tribunal, 104.

16 "Charter of the International Military Tribunal," in *International Military Tribunal*, vol. 1. The court would restrict its jurisdiction over persecutions to the war years, for reasons having to do with the somewhat opaque wording of the charter. For subsequent trials in both allied and German courts under Allied Control Council Law No. 10, this self-imposed restriction was lifted by rewording the definition of crimes against humanity.

17 *International Military Tribunal*, 4: 315, 318. On the use of Soviet film footage, see Lawrence Douglas, *The Memory of Judgment: Making Law and History in the Trials of the Holocaust* (New Haven, Connecticut: Yale University Press, 2001), 11–37.

18 For a quite critical assessment of the treatment of the Holocaust at Nuremberg (and in early postwar trials more generally), see Donald Bloxham, *Genocide on Trial: War Crimes Trials and the Formation of Holocaust History and Memory* (Oxford: Oxford University Press, 2001). For somewhat more positive views, see Michael R. Marrus, "The Holocaust at Nuremberg" in *Yad Vashem Studies,* ed. David Silberklang (Jerusalem: Yad Vashem, 1998); Douglas, *The Memory of Judgment*, 38–64.

19 Włodzimierz Borodziej, "'Hitleristische Verbrechen': Die Ahndung deutscher Kriegs-und Besatzungsverbrechen in Polen," in *Transnationale Vergangenheitspolitik* (Frei, ed.), 424–27.

20 Hilary Earl, *The Nuremberg SS–Einsatzgruppen Trial, 1945–1958: Atrocity, Law, and History* (Cambridge: Cambridge University Press, 2009).

21 Robert Kempner at a colloquium on Nazi trials in 1966, "Kolloquium über die Bedeutung der Nürnberg Prozesse für die NS-Verbrecherprozesse," in *Rechtliche und politische Aspekte der NS-Verbrecherprozesse: Gemeinschaftsvorlesung des stadium generale Wintersemester 1966/67,* eds Peter Schneider and Hermann J. Meyer (Mainz: Gutenberg-Universität Mainz, 1968), 14.

22 Frei, "Nach der Tat," 22.

23 Eichmüller, "Die Strafverfolgung von NS-Verbrechen," 626. The discrepancy between indictments and verdicts is due to the number of cases still pending.

24 Frei, "Nach der Tat," 31. Figures are not available for acquittals or dismissals.

25 Eichmüller, "Die Strafverfolgung von NS-Verbrechen," 626.

26 Frei, "Nach der Tat," 31.

27 Annette Weinke, "'Alliierter Angriff auf die nationale Souveränität': Die Strafverfolgung von Kriegs- und NS-Verbrechen in der Bundesrepublik, der DDR und Österreich," in *Transnationale Vergangenheitspolitik* (Frei, ed.), 58.

28 *Amtsblatt des allierten Kontrollrats*, 30 November 1945, 20.

29 *Amtsblatt des allierten Kontrollrats*, 20 December 1945, 50.

30 Ingo Müller, *Furchtbare Juristen: Die unbewältigte Vergangenheit unserer Justiz* (Munich: Knauer, 1987).

31 In the French zone, the military government of Baden granted jurisdiction to German courts for Nazi crimes against humanity in May 1946. See *Amtsblatt der Landesverwaltung Baden* (1946): 49. The French extended this jurisdiction to the German courts throughout their entire zone in September 1948. See "Verordnung 173," *Amtsblatt des französischen Oberkommandos in Deutschland* (1948): 1684. The British granted German jurisdiction through Military Government Ordinance 47 of August 1946. See *Amtsblatt der Militärregierrung, Britisches Kontrollgebiet* 13 (1946): 306.

32 The various *Länder* in the American zone all issued identical laws to this effect in May 1946. See Christian Meyer-Seitz, *Die Verfolung von NS-Straftaten in der Sowjetischen Besatzungzone* (Berlin: Berlin Verlag, 1998), 85.

33 Meyer-Seitz, *Die Verfolgung von NS-Straftaten*, 155–70.

34 Eichmüller, "Die Strafverfolgung von NS-Verbrechen," 628. At present, it is unclear how many of the early East German trials would have concerned Holocaust-related crimes. For reasons outlined below, it is unlikely to have been significantly higher than in the western zones.

35 Eichmüller, "Die Strafverfolgung von NS-Verbrechen," 628. See also Alan E. Steinweis, *Kristallnacht 1938* (Cambridge: Belknap Press of Harvard University Press, 2009).

36 Verdict of the Kammergericht, Berlin, 2 February 1947 (1 Ss 136.46), printed in *Deutsche Rechts-Zeitschrift*, 10 (1947): 345.

37 Devin O. Pendas, "Transitional Justice and Just Transitions: The German Case, 1945–50," *European Studies Forum*, vol. 38 (Spring 2008): 57–64.

38 Von Hodenberg to Oberlandesgerichtspräsident der britischen Zone, 3 October 1946, Bundesarchiv Koblenz, Z 21, Bd. 784, Bl. 23–24. For his published critique, see Hodo von Hodenberg, "Humanitätsverbrechen und ihre Bestrafung," *Süddeutsche Juristienzeitung*, Sondernummer (March 1947): 113–24

39 Norbert Frei, *Vergangenheitspolitik: Die Anfänge der Bundesrepublik und die NS-Vergangenheit* (Munich: C.H. Beck, 1996), 166.

40 Anna J. and Richard L. Merritt, eds, *Public Opinion in Occupied Germany: The HICOG Surveys, 1949–1955* (Urbana: University of Illinois Press, 1980), 11, 101.

41 Robert G. Moeller, *War Stories: The Search for a Usable Past in the Federal Republic of Germany* (Berkeley: University of California Press, 2003).

42 See Frei, *Vergangenheitspolitik: Die Anfänge der Bundesrepublik und die NS-Vergangenheit*, 137–38.

43 Falko Wentkertin, "Strafjustiz im politischen System der DDR: Fundstücke zur Steuerungs-und Eingriffpraxis des zentralParteiaparates der SED" in Huberg Rottleuthner ed., *Steuerung der Justiz in der DDR* (Cologne: Bundesanzeiger, 1994), 99.

44 See, for example, "Abschluß-Bericht über die Durchführung der Kriegs-und Nazi-Verbrechen in Waldheim," Bundesarchiv Berlin-Lichterfelde, SAPMO DY 30/IV2/13/432, Bl. 360–88.

45 Meyer-Seitz, *Die Verfolgung von NS-Straftaten*, 234.

46 There were more than 1,000 investigations opened in both 1959 and 1960, for instance. See Weinke, "'Alliierter Angriff auf die nationale Souveränität'," 74.

47 Adalbert Rückerl, *NS-Verbrechen vor Gericht: Versuch einer Vergangenheitsbewältigung* (Heidelberg: C.F. Müller, 1984), 140.

48 See Devin O. Pendas, *The Frankfurt Auschwitz Trial, 1963–1965: Genocide, History, and the Limits of the Law* (Cambridge: Cambridge University Press, 2006), 346.

49 Claudia Fröhlich, "Die Gründung der 'Zentralen Stelle' in Ludwigsburg: Alibi oder Beginn einer systematischen justitiellen Aufarbeitung der NS-Vergangenheit?" in *Justiz und*

Nationalsozialismus—Kontinuität und Diskontinuität: Fachtagung der Justizakademie des Landes NRW, Recklinghausen, am 19. und 20. November 2001, eds Gerhard Pauli and Thomas Vormbaum (Berlin: Berliner Wissenschafts-Verlag, 2003), 213–50.

50 Annette Weinke, *Die Verfolgung von NS-Tätern im geteilten Deutschland: Vergangenheitsbewältigung, 1949–1969, oder, eine deutsch-deutsche Bezieungsgeschichte im Kalgen Krieg* (Paderborn: F. Schöningh, 2002).

51 Marc von Miquel, *Ahnden oder amnestieren? Westdeutsche Justiz und Vergangenheitspolitik in den sechziger Jahren* (Göttingen: Wallstein, 2004).

52 In addition to Pendas, *The Frankfurt Auschwitz Trial*, see Rebecca Wittmann, *Beyond Justice: The Frankfurt Auschwitz Trial* (Cambridge: Harvard University Press, 2005).

53 Irmtrud Wojak, "'Die Mauer des Schweigens durchbrochen:' Die Erste Frankfurter Auschwitz-Prozeß 1963–65" in *"Gerichtstag Halten über uns selbst..." Geschichte und Wirkung des ersten Frankfurter Auschwitz-Prozesses*, ed. Irmtrud Wojak (Frankfurt: Campus Verlag, 2001), 21–42.

54 Christian Dirks, *Die Verbrechen der anderen: Auschwitz und der Auschwitz-Prozess der DDR. Das Verfahren gegen den KZ-Arzt Dr. Horst Fischer* (Paderborn: F. Schöningh, 2005).

55 Eichmüller, "Die Strafverfolgung von NS-Verbrechen," 628.

56 Irmtrud Wojak, *Fritz Bauerr, 1903–1968: Eine Biographie* (Munich: Beck, 2009).

37

MUSIC IN THE NAZI GHETTOS AND CAMPS

Shirli Gilbert

From Hitler's rise to power in 1933 until the liberation in 1945, music played an integral role in daily life under Nazism. In diverse contexts—political rallies and ghetto youth clubs, opera houses and military bands, concert halls and concentration camps—music was a medium through which the Nazi Party imposed its racist and nationalist ideals, and through which its victims expressed their opposition to the regime and confronted what was happening to them.

This chapter focuses on musical life amongst Nazism's victims, Jews and others, in the ghettos and camps. Prisoners were most likely to encounter forced music of various kinds, particularly in the camps, where music often functioned as a means of torture. Forced singing of German marches was a regular feature of the daily roll-call, and official inmate orchestras played regularly at hangings and executions. At the same time, many inmates engaged in, and derived great benefit from, voluntary music-making, despite the restrictions and risks involved. Most of the larger Jewish ghettos established choirs, orchestras, theatres, and chamber groups that existed for periods of months and even years. In the camps, prisoners held clandestine sing-songs and concerts and established musical groups. The music they performed ranged from popular prewar songs to opera and operetta, folk music, jazz, classical repertoire, choral music, film hits, religious music, and dance melodies. In addition, hundreds of new songs and pieces were created, in Yiddish, Polish, Czech, German, Russian, and other languages.

Musical life under Nazi internment was as varied as the inmate populations themselves, which included people of diverse ages, nationalities, religions, sexualities, and political affiliations. It thus has much to tell us about the spectrum of prisoners' responses. This chapter offers an overview of key issues in the history and historiography of the subject, and concludes with some thoughts on how music enriches our understanding of the Holocaust and the experiences of its victims.

Historiography

Music during the Nazi period has become an increasingly popular area of study, covering a broad range of topics and issues. A prominent focus has been the Nazi leadership's effort to reform and "cleanse" Germany's musical world, a far-reaching though conflicted process that affected performers, composers, musicologists, concert halls, opera houses, and educational institutions throughout the Reich. The *Reichsmusikkammer*

(Reich Chamber of Music), founded just months after the Nazi accession to power, aimed to centralize and regulate musical life as well as to purge the musical scene of Jews, foreigners, and political leftists. The *Jüdischer Kulturbund* (Jewish Cultural League), by contrast, was an exclusively Jewish organization established in 1933 to employ temporarily the thousands of Jews fired under Nazi legislation.

Music was an effective means of propaganda and indoctrination, and in 1938, the infamous *Entartete Musik* (*Degenerate Music*) exhibition was mounted in order to identify to the German public what music was "degenerate" and to demonstrate its dangers. Many promising musical careers were destroyed and musicians forced into exile, concentration camps, or "inner emigration." Although the Nazi Party vilified hundreds of "undesirable" individuals and works, and appropriated older composers (notably Beethoven, Bruckner, and Wagner) as archetypal "German" musical icons, it never succeeded in defining a coherent Nazi aesthetic.[1]

The earliest work on music in the ghettos and camps began during the war itself and continued into the immediate postwar period, when numerous independent efforts were initiated to document the Nazi onslaught. Although those involved in documentation work placed their primary emphasis on testimonies, many also consistently expressed their interest in songs, stories, jokes, and other cultural remnants of the communities they sought to memorialize. Music featured prominently in three Jewish initiatives carried out in the postwar years: the collection work of the *Tsentrale historishe komisye* (Central Historical Commission) in Munich, the interview project carried out by the psychologist David Boder in central and western Europe, and the work of Shmerke Katsherginski, a renowned Vilna poet and partisan whose monumental *Lider fun di getos un lagern* (*Songs from the ghettos and camps*), published in 1948 with H. Leivick, remains the most important collection of Yiddish songs from the Holocaust period.[2]

While these collections focused primarily on the music of Jewish victims, the passionate efforts of Aleksander Kulisiewicz concentrated on Polish prisoners in the Nazi camps. A Polish law student and musician, Kulisiewicz was arrested in October 1939 for his involvement in anti-Nazi activity, and was interned in Sachsenhausen from 1940 to 1945. In addition to composing dozens of songs himself, Kulisiewicz collected music from other inmates, and during the 1950s and 1960s gathered songs, poems, and memories of musical activity from survivors. The private archive that he amassed contained hundreds of pages of transcriptions. He also performed widely to raise awareness about the experiences of Nazism's victims.[3] Songs performed and created by German, particularly political, prisoners have been published in a number of collections.[4] Substantial material relating to many other prisoner groups is held at archives in Germany, Poland, Israel, the United States, and elsewhere, and numerous inmate testimonies provide accounts of musical life under internment.[5]

Scholarly writing on the subject began in the 1950s, particularly in the former German Democratic Republic (GDR), although it was only in the 1980s and early 1990s that more substantial work began to appear in print. Since then, growing numbers of books, articles, conferences, project groups, scholarly publications, and dissertations have been devoted to the subject, with German-language research predominating.[6] More recently, scholars have begun to consider the postwar period, exploring cultural politics in postwar Germany and Displaced Persons' camps, the relationship between music and memory, and the sizeable corpus of compositions written in response to the Holocaust.[7] Interest has also extended well beyond the academic arena. Increasing numbers of films, recordings, television and radio programmes, exhibitions, and websites have been produced, and efforts are being made to reintroduce some art music from the period into the mainstream repertory.[8]

Research in this area is still developing. Given the sheer number of internment centres established across occupied Europe (ghettos, concentration camps, labour camps, transit camps, death camps, and so on), the diversity of inmate populations, particularly after the outbreak of war, and the markedly different circumstances that characterized daily life in these places, a great deal of detailed work remains to be done to produce a rich and rounded picture. In particular, focused and contextualized research is needed into music among distinct prisoner communities including Roma and Sinti, national groups, and in women's camps.

Music in the camps

Much of the early research on the subject of music and the Holocaust focused on Theresienstadt (Terezín in Czech), a garrison town located outside Prague that became a "model" or "show" camp under the Nazis. Partly in order to serve propagandistic aims, the Nazi authorities tolerated and later encouraged an unparalleled range of cultural, educational, and entertainment activities under the banner of the well-organized *Freizeitgestaltung* (Administration of Free Time Activities). Musical offerings included operas, chamber and orchestral concerts, choirs, cabarets, jazz bands, and solo recitals by numerous professional musicians, including pianist Alice Sommer Herz and bass Karel Berman.

A good deal of new music was composed in Theresienstadt by several serious composers who had already been active in the prewar years, best known among them Viktor Ullmann, Gideon Klein, Pavel Haas, and Hans Krása. Ullmann, the most prolific, produced three piano sonatas, a string quartet, and the opera *Der Kaiser von Atlantis oder Der Tod dankt ab* (*The Emperor of Atlantis or Death Abdicates*), a thinly veiled allegory of the Third Reich, during his internment. He also wrote numerous vocal and choral compositions. Krása's children's opera *Brundibár*, composed in 1938 and re-orchestrated for performance in Theresienstadt in 1943, was performed 55 times. Some of the new music produced was performed under the auspices of Ullmann's *Studio für neue Musik* (Studio for New Music), and detailed critical reviews were produced of many performances.

This thriving musical life served as effective propaganda for the Nazis to convince the outside world of the humane treatment that Jewish prisoners were enjoying. *Brundibár*, for example, was staged for an inspection by the International Red Cross in 1944, and also appears on the propaganda film *Theresienstadt: Ein Dokumentarfilm aus dem jüdischen Siedlungsgebiet* (*Theresienstadt: A Documentary Film of the Jewish Settlement Area*).[9]

Research and recordings have focused on the classical composers from Theresienstadt and their works, in part because of a bias towards art music. To a great extent, musical life in the ghetto has been considered a case apart from other internment centres, and has even come to represent the subject of music during the Holocaust. Beyond its extraordinary cultural life, however, Theresienstadt was, like other Nazi ghettos, a place of hunger, disease, and unremitting suffering, and most musicians were not spared the fate of the majority of inmates: deportation to Auschwitz.

Research has also revealed a wide range of music-making under Nazi internment, from the earliest camps in Germany through to dozens of centres established in wartime occupied Europe. While perhaps not as abundant, musical life in these places assumed many of the same forms as it did in Theresienstadt, with inmates engaged only to a limited extent with art music alongside myriad other genres and styles. Jewish inmates regularly made music, as did non-Jewish German, Polish, and Czech inmates, Soviet PoWs, Jehovah's Witnesses, Roma and Sinti, and countless others.

Music became an integral part of camp routine as early as 1933. Despite the absence of a standardized system, common traditions and practices quickly established themselves, in part through the transfer of prisoners. Nazi camp authorities routinely used music as a means of torture and humiliation. Forced singing sessions were a common element of daily life: usually these would take place on the *Appellplatz* (roll-call square), as commandos marched to and from work, or at forced labour, and unsatisfactory performances would be punished. As well as keeping marching prisoners in formation, these sessions demoralized them and assaulted them psychologically and physically. Former Sachsenhausen inmate Eric Goodman, for example, described the forced singing to which they were regularly subjected:

> Late in the evening, when we were already tired and longed for the little bit of rest that remained for us in the day, we were made out of pure abuse to remain standing in the courtyard and to sing, sing continuously, into the depths of the night. The same happened when, now and then, someone tried to escape. Then the sirens howled eerily through the night, until the victim had been seized, but in the meantime all the prisoners had to remain standing on the big square, without food, without pause to rest, and had to sing. During this singing many perished, exhausted.[10]

Scores of former prisoners commented similarly on the forced singing they endured. Authorities would demand renditions of cheerful German marches, military songs, or songs that mocked inmates' religious or political beliefs. In some camps, music was broadcast over loudspeakers during punishment sessions. Music also, at times, formed part of the "welcoming" ritual to the camp, a practice begun in the early camps and perpetuated most infamously to deceive new arrivals on the ramp at Auschwitz-Birkenau.[11]

In many camps, official inmate orchestras were established on the initiative of the SS. These were generally composed of both amateur and professional musicians who were sought out from newly arrived transports or recruited by prisoner functionaries. Orchestras were established in several early camps, and following the restructuring and centralization of the camp system in the mid-1930s most of the larger camps—including Dachau, Buchenwald, Mauthausen, and Sachsenhausen—had their own ensembles. At Auschwitz, five orchestras of varying sizes were set up in the main camp and Birkenau alone between 1940 and 1943. Orchestras apparently functioned as symbols of power and prestige for certain camp authorities, and some ensembles accordingly enjoyed particular support, most notably the women's orchestra in Birkenau led by the accomplished violinist Alma Rosé in 1943–44. Orchestral musicians often fell into the category of "privileged" prisoners, which meant that they might receive additional food rations, cigarettes, warmer clothing, or other "rewards," or be placed in less gruelling work commandos than their fellow inmates. The conditions they experienced were not uniform, however, and in some contexts they were not given preferential treatment.[12]

One of the orchestras' primary tasks was to play at the camp gates each morning and evening as the labour contingents marched to and from their places of work, and they helped to maintain discipline and order in this way. For many inmates, however, hearing music against this background was macabre and exacerbated their suffering even further. Primo Levi believed that these "monstrous" activities had been planned with "meditated reason" in order to kill the individual will of the prisoners, and to set them "marching like automatons":

> The tunes are few, a dozen, the same ones every day, morning and evening: marches and popular songs dear to every German. They lie engraved on our minds and will be the last thing in Lager that we shall forget: they are the voice of the Lager, the perceptible expression of its geometrical madness, of the resolution of others to annihilate us first as men in order to kill us more slowly afterwards.[13]

In some camps the orchestras accompanied hangings and executions. A series of notorious photographs from Mauthausen show an orchestra accompanying the execution of Hans Bonarewitz on 30 July 1942.[14] In Monowitz, the band performed at special ceremonies conducted to celebrate the retrieval of escapees. Musician Herman Sachnowitz recounted how the captured man would be forced to shout the words "*Hurra, hurra, ich bin wieder da!*" (Hurrah, hurrah, I am back again!) while marching through the ranks of prisoners and banging on a drum. He would subsequently be hanged while the orchestra played parade music.[15]

Music also featured as an element of daily life in the death camps Treblinka, Bełżec, and Sobibór, where musicians greeted newly arrived transports and played outside the gas chambers during their daily operations.[16] For their part, the musicians experienced their forced participation in these activities as painful and distressing. Most were understandably loath, however, to jeopardize their chances of survival through rebellious behaviour.

Orchestras were frequently called upon to perform formally and informally for the Nazi authorities at public concerts, dinner parties, birthdays, and other special occasions. The repertoire performed varied widely, and musicians were sometimes asked to play forbidden repertoire, particularly jazz.[17] In these contexts, music helped the Nazis to relax and find temporary distraction from their work, often in combination with heavy drinking. While it might be tempting to view their appreciation for music and their brutal actions as irreconcilably contradictory, it seems that music was in fact an integral part of the camps' perverse logic, providing a framework within which the authorities could maintain a self-image of refined German culture and civilization, not apart from, but precisely in the context of, the activities in which they were involved.

While forced music was a feature of camp life that most prisoners encountered during their internment, voluntary music-making also took place, usually during the limited leisure time available in the evenings or on Sundays. Some activities were secret and had to be carefully guarded; others were tolerated or even sanctioned by the camp authorities. Attitudes varied over the years according to the whims of different authorities, the functions of certain internment centres, the progress of the war, and the nature of the activities themselves. Since organized music-making relied to a great extent on the assistance of prisoner functionaries, cultural life was generally more easily organized in camps where political prisoners were in charge of the prisoners' self-government.[18]

Voluntary music-making included choral groups, solo and chamber recitals in individual blocks, large-scale variety events, and religious performances. The most popular voluntary activity, however, was informal singing, usually among small groups of friends or fellow block inmates. Singing was accessible to all, including those with no musical training. It did not require preparation or instruments, could be conducted in any location, and was easily hidden. Participatory music-making of this kind provided a framework for documenting and making sense of what was happening, and strengthened unity among national and religious groups. It also afforded prisoners temporary diversion from camp existence, and helped them to reconnect with their prewar lives and reassert their agency and identity in the face of the camp's dehumanizing onslaught. As Kulisiewicz put it, "In the camps we could not use our fists to express our fury against our oppressors, so we lashed out at them with curses and disdain. [...] we took heart from the poetry and song that welled up from the depths of our ever-burning hearts and always-empty stomachs."[19] For some, music was also a medium for expressing political opposition, raising morale, and encouraging or even organizing resistance.

Inmates drew on a wide repertoire of pre-existing music. They sang songs with which they were familiar from school, the military, and particularly workers' youth movements, national and patriotic songs, love songs, film music, and prewar hits. Hundreds of new songs were also created by prisoners across the camp spectrum. These songs created and communicated information about camp life: about prisoner functionaries, the state of the war, food, the gas chambers, and other elements of camp existence. While many songwriters remain unknown, a few creative individuals stand out for their prolific camp compositions, among them Ludmila Peškařová in Ravensbrück, Józef Kropiński in Auschwitz and Buchenwald, and Kulisiewicz in Sachsenhausen.[20]

One of the earliest and best known camp songs was the "*Moorsoldatenlied*" ("Moor Soldiers' Song"), composed in Börgermoor in 1933 by Johannes Esser, Wolfgang Langhoff, and Rudi Goguel, and subsequently popularized in many other camps. Like several other songs created in the prewar period, the "*Moorsoldatenlied*" included images of camp life—marching columns, forced labour, living conditions, isolation—alongside sentiments of optimism and encouragement:

Wohin auch das Auge blicket,
Moor und Heide nur ringsum.
Vogelsang uns nicht erquicket,
Eichen stehen kahl und krumm.
Wir sind die Moorsoldaten
und ziehen mit dem Spaten
ins Moor!

Hier in dieser öden Heide
ist das Lager aufgebaut,
wo wir fern von jeder Freude
hinter Stacheldraht verstaut.
Wir sind die Moorsoldaten...

[...]

Doch für uns gibt es kein Klagen,
ewig kann's nicht Winter sein.
Einmal werden froh wir sagen:
Heimat, du bist wieder mein.
Dann ziehn die Moorsoldaten
nicht mehr mit dem Spaten
ins Moor!

~

Wherever the eye looks
All around only moor and heath.
No birdsong to comfort us,
Oaks stand bare and crooked.
We are the moor soldiers,
and march with our spades
into the moor!

[...]

Here on this barren heath
the camp is built,
where, far from any joy,
we are packed behind barbed wire.
We are the moor soldiers...

[...]

But we have no complaints,
it can't be winter forever.
One day we will cheerfully say:
Homeland, you are mine again.
Then the moor soldiers
will no longer march with their spades
into the moor![21]

Many camps similarly produced their own "signature songs" or "anthems." Some of these originated on the order of camp authorities or through specially convened competitions, such as the *"Buchenwaldlied"* ("Buchenwald song") created by Fritz Löhner-Beda and Hermann Leopoldi in 1938. Others, like the *"Dachaulied"* ("Dachau song") by Herbert Zipper and Jura Soyfer (1938), were created on the initiative of the prisoners and only later became unofficial anthems. While these camp hymns frequently expressed sentiments of defiance and longing for freedom, the SS often deliberately used them as a tool for demonstrating their control over the inmates, to mock them as they marched to and from work or at forced singing sessions.[22]

Some songwriters took pains to portray camp life in explicit detail in order to document the crimes being perpetrated. In Sachsenhausen, for example, Kulisiewicz's "*Egzekucja*" ("Execution") described the treatment meted out to rebellious prisoners:

> *Na szubienicy cień człowieka.*
> *Oczy przekorne wyszły z orbity*
> *i świecą jeszcze jak dwa guziki...*
> *Szyja oślizgła, żółta, długa –*
> *Nogi bestialsko skatowane –*
> *Gdzie jesteś ludzkie zmiłowane?!!* [...]

> ~

> On the gallows a shadow of a man.
> Defiant eyes have left their sockets
> Still shine, like two buttons...
> The neck slippery, yellow, long –
> The feet terribly tortured –
> Where are you, human pity?!! [...][23]

Songs were also a way for victims to convey their experiences to a future many feared they might not live to see. The idea of bearing witness was returned to frequently and with great intensity, both in contemporary writings and in postwar testimonies. Cut off from the world both physically and emotionally, victims felt it crucial that someone or something survive to attest to what had happened. Because they could be orally transmitted, songs were an obvious medium, and in several cases, the lyrics themselves explicitly articulate this intention. The 24-year-old Warsaw poet and journalist Leonard Krasnodębski wrote the lyrics of "*Chorał z Piekła Dna*" ("Chorale from the depths of hell"), a desperate appeal to rouse the listener's compassion: "Hear our choral from the depths of hell! Attention! Attention!"[24]

Given the atmosphere of brutality and terror that reigned in the Nazi camps, the scope of voluntary music-making that took place across a wide range of establishments is remarkable. At the same time, it must be emphasized that prisoners experienced enormous disparity in freedom of access to music, and that many were unable to engage in it at all. The spectrum of musical life to a large extent reflected the stratification of camp populations, as Szymon Laks, former conductor of the Birkenau men's orchestra, explained:

> ["Prominent" prisoners] had—except for freedom—everything their souls could want, and for them music was entertainment and an additional luxury for which they paid generously...For the class of paupers, however, if music had any effect at all, it had a disheartening one and deepened still further their chronic state of physical and mental prostration.[25]

Music in the ghettos

Jewish communities in the eastern European ghettos were able to organize cultural and social activities with less interference from the Nazi authorities than was the case in the camps. Ironically, Jews generally felt more protected in the sealed ghettos than they had previously: the severe restrictions on movement and activity they had faced initially under Nazi occupation were relaxed, and they had limited contact with Nazi officials and the surrounding population—although any sense of stability and autonomy was ultimately illusory. Jewish ghetto inmates established a wide array of artistic organizations including choirs, orchestras, theatres, and other musical institutions, many of which built on the vibrant cultural life of the interwar years.

The Warsaw ghetto, which housed the largest Polish Jewish community, offered a rich and varied programme of musical activities. One of the earliest initiatives was the establishment in late 1940 of the Jewish Symphony Orchestra, which performed classical repertoire for enthusiastic audiences. Five professional theatres also operated, in both Yiddish and Polish, staging serious dramatic pieces as well as lighter revue shows consisting of choral singing, dancing, musical comedy, and other skits. Instrumental and vocal concerts were regularly held, and numerous cafés and cabarets—the survival of which often depended on the assistance of Jewish Council members—offered live musical entertainment.

Warsaw's thriving cultural life was not unique. The Łódź ghetto similarly housed a symphony orchestra, choral society, and revue theatre, and dozens of concerts and theatrical productions were performed at the "House of Culture" established by Jewish Council leader Chaim Rumkowski. The Vilna ghetto had an orchestra, chamber groups, Yiddish and Hebrew choirs, theatrical productions and revues, and a music school with more than 100 students. The ghettos were home to scores of talented Jewish musicians and composers, many of whom had already established themselves in the interwar period and continued their creative work during their internment.[26]

In addition to musical institutions, many ghettos generated a rich culture of informal music-making in youth clubs, private homes, workplaces, on the streets, and among partisans and resistance groups. As in the camps, singing was the most popular and accessible form of entertainment. Jewish communities drew extensively on familiar prewar repertoire, but numerous new songs were also created dealing with contemporary events. Many set new lyrics to existing melodies, a long-standing tradition in Yiddish folksong and a widespread practice across the camp and ghetto spectrum. Songs of hunger and oppression (an integral part of the Jewish experience prior to World War II) were particularly adaptable, but even songs from "normal" life—lullabies, love songs, and songs about children—acquired radically altered associations and provided revealing commentary about the new reality.[27]

From the hundreds of Yiddish songs created during this period, a handful have become well known, particularly songs expressing sentiments of resistance. Prominent among them is Mordekhai Gebirtig's prescient elegy *"Es Brent"* ("It burns"), which was written in response to a pogrom in the Polish town of Przytyk. Although penned before the Nazi onslaught reached Poland, the song apparently resonated with ghetto inmates, particularly in its final stanza's urgent appeal to Jews to resist and defend themselves:

> *S'brent! briderlekh, s'brent!*
> *Di hilf iz nor in aykh aleyn gevendt.*
> *Oyb dos shtetl iz aykh tayer,*
> *Nemt di keylim, lesht dos fayer,*
> *Lesht mit ayer eygn blut,*
> *Bavayzt, az ir dos kent.*

Shteyt nit, brider, ot azoy zikh
Mit farleygte hent.
Shteyt nit, brider, lesht dos fayer—
Undzer shtetl brent!

~

It burns! Brothers, it burns!
Help is contained only in yourselves!
If the village is dear to you,
Take up arms, quench the fire,
Quench it with your own blood—
Show that you can do it!
Don't stand, brothers, like that
With folded arms,
Don't stand, brothers, quench the fire,
Our village burns![28]

The song became popular in many of the ghettos, and was a hymn of the underground Jewish resistance in Gebirtig's home town of Kraków, where he was also interned. It has remained one of the most frequently performed items at Holocaust commemoration ceremonies, alongside the well-loved partisan anthem "*Zog nit keynmol az du geyst dem letstn veg*" ("Never say that you are walking the final road"), created by the young writer and partisan Hirsh Glik in Vilna in response to the 1943 Warsaw ghetto uprising. "*Zog nit keynmol*" became the official hymn of Vilna's *Fareynigte partizaner organizatsye* (United Partisans' Organization) and spread quickly across Nazi-occupied Europe:

Zog nit keynmol az du geyst dem letstn veg,
Khotsh himlen blayene farshteln bloye teg;
Kumen vet nokh undzer oysgebenkte sho,
S'vet a poyk ton undzer trot—mir zaynen do! [...]

~

Never say that you are walking the final road,
Though leaden skies obscure blue days;
The hour we have been longing for will still come,
Our steps will drum—we are here! [...][29]

In addition to its melody, a rousing Soviet march composed by Dimitri Pokrass, it was presumably Glik's defiant assertion of collective Jewish survival that accounted for the song's enduring popularity.

While both "*Es Brent*" and "*Zog nit keynmol*" clearly struck a common chord among ghetto inmates, the vast majority of Yiddish songs created during this period have remained largely unknown, despite having survived in large numbers. The corpus of newly created ghetto songs covers a wide range of styles and sentiments, from irreverent street ballads to critical satires and militant anthems of resistance, offering us myriad different perceptions of, and responses to, life under internment.

Many songs unsurprisingly describe the grief, suffering, and hopelessness of Jewish inmates. *"Nit keyn rozhinkes, nit keyn mandlen"* ("No raisins, no almonds"), for example, written in the Łódź ghetto by Yeshaya Shpigl and Dovid Beyglman, was a poignant Yiddish lament about a father who had not gone to market, but left his home and gone away to the end of the world. The title made reference to Avrom Goldfadn's classic lullaby *"Rozhinkes mit mandlen"* ("Raisins and almonds"), which formed the basis for several other ghetto songs as well.[30] Songs also covered a wide range of topical issues relating to ghetto life. Some dealt with pressing social problems like begging, smuggling, and the allocation of welfare benefits, while others directed sharp criticism at the ghetto leadership. Many songs, for example, were directed at Chaim Rumkowski in Łódź. Several also offered satirical portrayals of the inequalities between ghetto inmates.[31] In Warsaw, the popular *"Moes, moes"* ("Money, money") exposed the ghetto as a place of economic and social inequality, and criticized the ill treatment of the ghetto masses at the hands of the powerful and wealthy elite:

> *Moes, moes, moes iz di ershte zakh.*
> *Hostu nit keyn moes, iz tsu dir a klog,*
> *Gib avek die bone un zog a gutn tog.*
> *Moes, moes, moes iz di beste zakh.*
>
> *Moes, moes, moes iz di beste zakh,*
> *Di yidishe gemine nemt fun undz danine*
> *Un git dokh undz tsu esn broyt mit sakharine.—*
> *Moes, moes, moes iz di beste zakh. [...]*
>
> ~
>
> Money, money, money is the first thing.
> If you have no money, woe to you,
> Give away your ration-card and say good day.
> Money, money, money is the best thing.
>
> Money, money, money is the best thing,
> The Jewish Council takes taxes from us
> Yet it feeds us bread with saccharin.—
> Money, money, money is the best thing. [...][32]

As in the camps, songs were also used as a means of documenting events and victims' responses to them. *"Aroys iz in Vilne a nayer bafel"* ("A new command has been issued in Vilna") chronicled carefully and with understated emotion the liquidation of the *shtetls* around Vilna during the spring of 1943, and the spontaneous resistance mounted by several of the victims when they realized they were being taken to be murdered, and not simply being relocated as they had been informed.[33] A song entitled "Treblinka," created when inhabitants of the Warsaw ghetto had begun to discover the fates of those who were being deported during the summer of 1942, documented how the Jews were chased out of their homes and transported to the Treblinka death camp.[34]

As in the camps, music was for many ghetto inmates a means of asserting Jewish identity and continuity, countering the dehumanization of Nazi oppression, and resisting the attempt to obliterate Jewish culture along with entire communities.

Music and Holocaust historiography

The music produced in the Nazi ghettos and camps offers insight not only into inmates' cultural activities narrowly construed, but also more broadly into how they understood, interpreted, and responded to their experiences. As such, it constitutes one of the most valuable historical sources from the period. While much source material relating to prisoners' experiences was produced after the war, the songs are a significant body of texts originating from the time itself. In this regard, they stand alongside the diaries, ghetto chronicles, and photographs that were preserved. Songs are also distinctive in that they were oral texts disseminated—and, ultimately, preserved—within large-scale group frameworks. The songs that survived convey to us not the retrospective understanding of surviving individuals, as do postwar testimonies, but the uncertain and shifting perspectives of prisoner communities as they made sense of lived reality.

In a world where newspapers, radios, and other forms of communication had almost or entirely ceased functioning, songs became an informal place where information and experiences could be processed and shared. They acknowledged wishes, fears, and uncertainties in the public realm; as they circulated, people identified with them, modified them, added to them, or rejected them; sometimes they did not engage with them at all. The access they offer is of course not direct or uncomplicated: the process through which songs were created and circulated was informal and unregulated, and it would be impossible to extract from them a representative collective narrative. Taken alongside other sources, however, songs from the ghettos and camps deepen our understanding of the experience of internment, offering insight into the ideas and perspectives with which victims identified and the concerns that most preoccupied them.

Cultural life under Nazi internment, particularly for Jewish inmates, has often been interpreted within the framework of "spiritual resistance," a notion that entered into Holocaust historiography partly in an attempt to counter earlier accusations that victims had gone "like sheep to the slaughter." While Jewish armed resistance during the Holocaust was infrequent and largely unsuccessful, a range of social and cultural initiatives—including religious activities, education, social welfare, diary writing, and musical and artistic life—were increasingly foregrounded in order to mitigate the critique that victims had been passively subsumed by the Nazi onslaught. Spiritual resistance is by now a familiar theme in secondary literature as well as popular representations of the Holocaust, linked with redemptive notions such as the will to live and the triumph of the spirit, and it is often associated with, though by no means limited to, music.[35]

The discourse of spiritual resistance tends to emphasize the uplifting effects of music, and to focus on songs with defiant and optimistic messages such as those produced by partisans and resistance organizations. No doubt, much musical activity during this period served genuinely encouraging and morale-building functions. Participatory music-making was one of the few ways in which inmate communities could attempt to retain a sense of

SHIRLI GILBERT

order, familiarity, and continuity in the face of Nazi oppression. It also provided a framework within which victims could laugh at, express despair at, or make sense of what was happening. Particularly when conditions in ghettos and camps worsened, inmates sought solace and reassurance in their struggle to grapple with the events, and music offered at least some comfort in sustaining past identity, affirming group solidarity, or allowing inmates to escape temporarily from reality.

Beyond these positive functions, however, music encompassed a wider range of roles. Many songs engaged directly with the actualities of camp or ghetto life—hunger, hard labour, death, disease—and expressed emotions ranging from nostalgia to anger, pain, despair, loss of faith, guilt at having survived family members, frustration, uncertainty, and the desire for revenge. While songs were sometimes used for expressing opinions about the Nazi authorities, they also provided a forum for criticism directed within the prisoner communities themselves, towards Jewish Councils, welfare organizations, and camp functionaries. Some detailed specific events—massacres witnessed, information about death camps—while others dealt with new social problems that had arisen. As well as functioning as a medium for the discussion and documentation of social disparity, music as a participatory activity was also a site where disparity was played out, particularly in the context of the camps' social hierarchies.

Finally, while voluntary music-making fulfilled valuable functions for many inmates, there were countless others for whom it played little role. Even as we focus in on the isolated times and places where music existed, we should have as a constant mental backdrop the atmosphere of fear, uncertainty, violence, illness, hunger, and death that characterized the camps and ghettos, and permeated their every aspect. At a certain point in the world of atrocity, when people were exhausted, diseased, freezing, and dying of starvation, music could simply no longer flourish.

Music contributes to a complex, multi-layered understanding of what Primo Levi called the "Grey Zone" that constituted captive life. The Nazi ghettos and camps were not homogeneous entities, but diverse societies made up of millions of individuals from across Europe. Music opens a window onto the internal world of these societies when they were not yet distant past but raw present, revealing the astonishingly divergent experiences that characterized life within the same limited spaces, and the varied ways in which people confronted the events. It thus has important implications for the ways in which we understand life under Nazi internment, and can tell us much about the Holocaust and the experiences of its victims.

Notes

1 The literature on music and Nazism is substantial, and a short overview of this kind cannot do justice to the myriad subjects and issues covered. The notes below provide only a selection of important works; for more extensive bibliographies see http://holocaustmusic.ort.org/resources-references/bibliography; Guido Fackler, "Des Lagers Stimme"—Musik im KZ. Alltag und Häftlingskultur in den Konzentrationslagern 1933 bis 1936 (Bremen: Temmen, 2000). On music in the Third Reich, see Erik Levi, Music in the Third Reich (London: Macmillan, 1994); Michael H. Kater, The Twisted Muse: Musicians and their Music in the Third Reich (Oxford: Oxford University Press, 1997); Michael H Kater, Composers of the Nazi Era: Eight Portraits (Oxford: Oxford University Press, 2000); Pamela Potter, Most German of the Arts: Musicology and Society from the Weimar Republic to the end of Hitler's Reich (New Haven: Yale University Press, 1998); David B. Dennis, "'Honor Your German Masters': The Use and Abuse of 'Classical' Composers in Nazi Propaganda," Journal of Political and Military Sociology, vol. 30 (2002): 273–95; Bryan Gilliam, "The Annexation of Anton Bruckner: Nazi Revisionism and the

448

Politics of Appropriation," *The Musical Quarterly*, vol. 78 (1994): 584–604; Reinhold Brink-mann and Christoph Wolff, *Driven into Paradise: The Musical Migration from Nazi Germany to the United States* (Berkeley, California: University of California Press, 1999); *Entartete Musik: Dokumentation und Kommentar zur Düsseldorfer Ausstellung von 1938*, rev. and exp. edn (Düsseldorf: DKV, 1993); Albrecht Dümling, "The Target of Racial Purity: The Degenerate Music Exhibition in Düsseldorf, 1938," in *Art, Culture, and Media under the Third Reich*, ed. Richard A. Etlin (Chicago: University of Chicago Press, 2002); Horst J. P. Bergmeier, Dr Ejal Jakob Eisler and Dr Rainer E. Lotz, *Vorbei...Beyond Recall: Dokumentation jüdischen Musik-lebens in Berlin 1933–1938* (Hambergen: Bear Family Records, 2001); Lily E. Hirsch, *A Jewish Orchestra in Nazi Germany: Musical Politics and the Berlin Jewish Culture League* (Ann Arbor, Michigan: University of Michigan Press, 2010). For helpful surveys of recent scholarly trends, see Pamela M. Potter, "The Arts in Nazi Germany: A Silent Debate," *Contemporary European His-tory*, vol. 15 (2006): 585–99; Pamela M. Potter, "Dismantling a Dystopia: On the Historiography of Music in the Third Reich," *Central European History*, vol. 40 (2007): 623–51.

2 *Lider fun di Getos un Lagern*, eds Shmerke Katsherginski and H. Leivick (New York: Alvel-tlekher Yidisher Kultur-Kongres, 1948). For more on these collection projects, see Shirli Gil-bert, "Buried Monuments: Yiddish Songs and Holocaust Memory," *History Workshop Journal*, vol. 66 (2008): 107–28. Additional collections of Jewish songs published in the postwar period and since include Samy Feder, *Zamlung fun Katset un Geto Lider* (Bergen-Belsen: Central Jewish Committee in Bergen-Belsen, 1946); *Ghetto- und KZ-Lieder aus Lettland und Litauen*, ed. Johanna Spector (Vienna: AJDC, 1947); Ruta Pups and Bernard Mark, *Dos Lid Fun Geto: Zomlung* (Warsaw: Yidish-Bukh, 1962); *Es brennt, Brüder, es brennt: Jiddische Lieder*, eds Lin Jaldati and Eberhard Rebling (Berlin: Rütten and Loening); *Lieder aus dem Ghetto: Fünfzig Lieder jiddisch und deutsch mit Noten*, eds Elsbeth Janda and Max M. Spre-cher (Munich: Ehrenwirth); Shoshana Kalisch and Barbara Meister, *Yes, We Sang! Songs of the Ghettos and Concentration Camps* (New York: Harper and Row, 1985); *Draußen steht eine bange Nacht: Lieder und Gedichte aus deutschen Konzentrationslagern*, eds Ellinor Lau and Susanne Pampuch (Frankfurt am Main: Fischer, 1994); *We Are Here: Songs of the Holocaust*, eds Eleanor Mlotek and Malke Gottlieb (New York: Educational Department of the Work-men's Circle); *Songs Never Silenced*, ed. Velvel Pasternak (Baltimore: Tara Publications, 2003).

3 Kulisiewicz's voluminous materials are held at the United States Holocaust Memorial Museum Archive (USHMM) in Washington, DC. See also Aleksander Kulisiewicz, "Polish Camp Songs, 1939–45," *Modern Language Studies*, trans. Roslyn Hirsch, vol. 16 (1986): 3–9; Aleksander Kulisiewicz, *Musik aus der Hölle*, ed. Guido Fackler (Würzburg: Königshausen & Neumann, 2007); *KZ-Lieder: Eine Auswahl aus dem Repertoire des Polnischen Sängers Alex Kulisiewicz*, ed. Carsten Linde (Sievershütten: Wendepunkt); Aleksander Kulisiewicz, *Songs from the Depths of Hell* (Poland: Folkways Records, 1979); Aleksander Kulisiewicz, *Ballads and Broad-sides: Songs from Sachsenhausen Concentration Camp 1940–1945* (Washington, DC: United States Holocaust Memorial Museum, 2008).

4 See, among others, *Lieder aus den Faschistischen Konzentrationslagern*, eds Inge Lammel and Günter Hofmeyer (Leipzig: Friedrich Hofmeister); *Sachsenhausen-Liederbuch: Originalwie-dergabe eines illegalen Häftlingsliederbuches aus dem Konzentrationslager Sachsenhausen*, ed. Günter Morsch (Berlin: Hentrich).

5 These are far too numerous to list. Some of the best known in English are Fania Fénelon, *The Musicians of Auschwitz* (London: Sphere, 1979); Szymon Laks, *Music of Another World* (Evan-ston, Illinois: Northwestern University Press, 1989); Anita Lasker-Wallfisch, *Inherit the Truth 1939–1945* (London: Giles de la Mare, 1996); Władysław Szpilman, *The Pianist: The Extra-ordinary Story of One Man's Survival in Warsaw, 1939–45* (London: Victor Gollancz, 1999).

6 See, among others, Shirli Gilbert, *Music in the Holocaust: Confronting Life in the Nazi Ghettos and Camps* (Oxford: Oxford University Press, 2005); Fackler, *"Des Lagers Stimme"*; Gila Flam, *Singing for Survival: Songs of the Łódź Ghetto 1940–45* (Urbana and Chicago: University of Illinois Press, 1992); Moshe Hoch, *Kolot mitokh hakhoshekh* [Voices from the Darkness] (Jerusalem: Yad Vashem, 2002); Joža Karas, *Music in Terezín 1941–1945*, 2nd edn (New York: Pendragon Press, 2008); Milan Kuna, *Musik an der Grenze des Lebens: Musikerinnen und Musiker aus Böhmischen Ländern in Nationalsozialistischen Konzentrationslagern und Gefängnissen* (Frankfurt am Main: Zweitausendeins, 1993); Gabriele Knapp, *Das Frauenorchester in Auschwitz* (Hamburg: von

Bockel, 1996); Eckhard John, "Music and Concentration Camps: An Approximation," *Journal of Musicological Research*, vol. 20 (2001): 269–323.

7 David Monod, *Settling Scores: German Music, Denazification, and the Americans, 1945–1953* (Chapel Hill and London: University of North Carolina Press, 2005); Shirli Gilbert, "'Es benkt zikh nokh a haym': Songs and Survival amongst Jewish DPs," in *We Are Here: New Approaches to Jewish Displaced Persons in Postwar Germany*, ed. Avinoam J. Patt and Michael Berkowitz (Detroit, Michigan: Wayne State University Press); Sophie Fetthauer, "Musik im DP-Camp Bergen-Belsen und ihre Rolle bei der Identitätsfindung der jüdischen Displaced Persons," in *Musikwelten – Lebenswelten. Jüdische Identitätssuche in der deutschen Musikkultur*, eds Beatrix Borchard and Heidy Zimmermann (Cologne and Weimar: Böhlau, 2009), 365–79; Abigail Wood, "Commemoration and Creativity: Remembering the Holocaust in Today's Yiddish Song," *European Judaism*, vol. 35 (2002): 43–56; Wlodarski, Amy Lynn. 2007. "An idea can never perish: Memory, the musical idea, and Schoenberg's A survivor from Warsaw (1947)." *The Journal of Musicology 24(4): 581.*

8 See, among other recordings, *The Terezin Music Anthology* (nine vols) (New York: Koch International Classics, 1991); Ruth Rubin, *Yiddish Songs of the Holocaust: A Lecture/Recital* (Global Village, 1993); Zamir Chorale of Boston, *Hear Our Voices: Songs of the Ghettos and Camps* (Newton, Massachusetts: HaZamir Recordings, 1995); *O Bittre Zeit. Lagerlieder 1933 bis 1945* (Papenburg: DIZ Emslandlager, 2006); *KZ Musik: Encyclopedia of Concentrationary Music Literature. Music Composed in Concentration Camps (1933–1945)* in 24 CDs (Rome: Musikstrasse). For films, see Michel Daeron, *La chaconne d'Auschwitz* (Cinemax Reel Life, 1999); James Kent, *Holocaust: A Music Memorial from Auschwitz*, 2004; Christopher Nupen, *We Want the Light* (BBC/Opus Arte, 2005). For websites, see http://holocaustmusic.ort.org and www.ushmm.org/museum/exhibit/online/music. See also the work of *musica reanimata* (www.musica-reanimata.de/en/0080.journal.html).

9 See Hans Günther Adler, *Theresienstadt 1941–1945: Das Antlitz einer Zwangsgemeinschaft* (Tübingen: Mohr, 1960); Karas, *Music in Terezín; Und die Musik spielt dazu! Chansons und Satiren aus dem KZ Theresienstadt*, ed. Ulrike Migdal (Munich: Piper, 1986); Max Bloch, "Victor Ullmann: A Brief Biography and Appreciation," *Journal of the Arnold Schoenberg Institute*, vol. 3 (1979): 150–77; David Bloch, "'No One Can Rob Us of Our Dreams': Solo Songs from Terezin," *Israel Studies in Musicology*, vol. 5 (1990): 69–80; Lubomír Peduzzi, *Musik im Ghetto Theresienstadt: Kritische Studien* (Brno: Barrister and Principal, 2005); Ingo Schultz, "Komponiert und geprobt im KZ Theresienstadt: 'Der Kaiser von Atlantis oder Die Tod-Verweigerung' von Viktor Ullmann," in *Musiktheater im Exil der NS-Zeit*, eds Peter Petersen and Claudia Maurer Zenck (Hamburg: Von Bockel, 2007); *Komponisten in Theresienstadt*, ed. Cornelis Witthoefft, 2nd edn (Hamburg: Initiative H. Kra?sa, 2001). See also Guido Fackler, "'Musik der Schoa' – Plädoyer für eine kritische Rezeption," in *Jüdische Musik? Fremdbilder-Eigenbilder*, eds John Eckhard and Heidy Zimmermann (Köln, Weimar, Wien: Böhlau, 2004), 219–39.

10 Eric Goodman, Wiener Library Archive, P.II.d. No. 528.

11 On music as torture, see Gilbert, *Music in the Holocaust*; Fackler, *"Des Lagers Stimme"*; John, "Music and Concentration Camps," 273–80.

12 On camp orchestras, see Knapp, *Das Frauenorchester in Auschwitz*; Hans-Ludger Kreutzheck, "Kapellen der Hölle: Die offiziellen Lagerkapellen in Auschwitz und anderen Konzentrationslagern," *Verein für demokratische Musikkulturen in Geschichte und Gegenwart*, vol. 8 (1995): 33–44; Gilbert, *Music in the Holocaust*; Fackler, *"Des Lagers Stimme."*

13 Primo Levi, *If This is a Man/The Truce* (London: Abacus, 1979), 57.

14 Kurt Lettner, "Musik zwischen Leben und Tod: Musik im Konzentrationslager Mauthausen und seinen Nebenlagern 1939–45," *Oberösterreichische Heimatblätter*, vol. 54 (2000): 55–72, here 58, 62.

15 Herman Sachnowitz, *Auschwitz: Ein Norwegischer Jude Überlebte* (Frankfurt am Main: Büchergilde Gutenberg, 1981), 98.

16 Annekathrin Dahm, "Musik in den nationalsozialistischen Vernichtungszentren Belsec, Sobibor und Treblinka," *mr-Mitteilungen*, vol. 23 (1997): 1–11; Gilbert, *Music in the Holocaust*, 192–95.

17 On the Nazis and jazz, see Michael H. Kater, *Different Drummers: Jazz in the Culture of the Nazis* (New York: Oxford University Press, 1992); *Swing Heil: Jazz im Nationalsozialismus*, ed. Bernd Polster (Berlin: Transit); Michael Zwerin, *La Tristesse de Saint Louis: Jazz Under the Nazis* (New York: Quartet, 1985).

18 Camp inmates were classified (often arbitrarily) according to the nature of the "crime" that had led to their internment. Designations included political, criminal, "asocial," Jews, Jehovah's

witnesses, and homosexuals. In most camps, inmates were also divided on the basis of a prisoner hierarchy that gave certain prisoners—often politicals or criminals—control over others; responsibilities were carried out in widely diverging ways.

19 Aleksander Kulisiewicz, "Polish Camp Songs, 1939–45," *Modern Language Studies*, trans. Roslyn Hirsch, vol. 16 (1986): 3–9, here 4.

20 See USHMM RG-55.003.83 (Peškařová) and RG-55.004.03, 55.002M.05, 55.002M.04 (Kropiński), among others. See also Gabriele Knapp, *Frauenstimmen: Musikerinnen erinnern an Ravensbrueck* (Berlin: Metropol-Verlag, 2003).

21 Gilbert, *Music in the Holocaust*, 110–12, and *Das Lied der Moorsoldaten 1933 bis 2000* (Frankfurt am Main and Potsdam-Babelberg: Papenburg: DIZ Emslandlager, 2002).

22 Paul Cummins, *Dachau Song: The Twentieth Century Odyssey of Herbert Zipper* (New York: Peter Lang, 1992); Sonja Seidel, "Kultur und Kunst im antifaschistischen Widerstandskampf im Konzentrationslager Buchenwald," *Buchenwaldheft*, vol. 18 (1983); Lammel and Hofmeyer, *Lieder aus den Faschistischen Konzentrationslagern*; John, "Music and Concentration Camps"; Kreutzheck, "Kapellen der Hölle."

23 USHMM RG-55.004.18.

24 Linde, *KZ-Lieder*, 13; USHMM RG-55.004.18.

25 Laks, *Music of Another World*, 118.

26 Gilbert, *Music in the Holocaust*; Flam, *Singing for Survival*; Rebecca Rovit, "Cultural Ghettoization and Theater during the Holocaust: Performance as a Link to Community," *Holocaust and Genocide Studies*, vol. 19 (2005): 459–86; *Hidden History of the Kovno Ghetto*, ed. USHMM (Boston, New York, Toronto, London: Bulfinch Press, 1997); Moshe Fass, "Theatrical Activities in the Polish Ghettos During the Years 1939–42," *Jewish Social Studies*, vol. 38 (1976); Stefan Hanheide, "Lieder im Angesicht des Volkermords: Zu den Funktionen der Musik im Ghetto von Wilna," *Krieg und Literatur*, vol. 6 (1994): 69–85; Franz Ruttner, "Die jiddischen Lieder aus dem Wilnaer Getto," in *Ess Firt Kejn Weg Zurik: Geschichte und Lieder des Ghettos von Wilna, 1941–1943*, ed. Florian Freund (Vienna: Picus, 1992), 123–29.

27 On the practice of recycling songs and its implications in the ghettos, see Eliyana R. Adler, "No Raisins, No Almonds: Singing as Spiritual Resistance to the Holocaust," *Shofar: An Interdisciplinary Journal of Jewish Studies*, vol. 24 (2006): 50–66; also David Roskies, *Against the Apocalypse: Responses to Catastrophe in Modern Jewish Culture* (Cambridge, Massachusetts: Harvard University Press, 1984), 185–89.

28 *Mordechai Gebirtig: His Poetic and Musical Legacy*, ed. Gertrude Schneider (Westport, Connecticut: Praeger, 2000), 77; see also Mordecai Gebirtig, *Krakow Ghetto Notebook* (Port Washington, New York: Koch, 1994).

29 Katsherginski and Leivick, *Lider fun di Getos un Lagern*, 3; Gilbert, *Music in the Holocaust*, 70–73; Theodore Bikel and Freida Enoch, *Rise Up and Fight! Songs of the Jewish Partisans* (Washington, DC: United States Holocaust Memorial Museum, 1996).

30 Katsherginski and Leivick, *Lider fun di Getos un Lagern*, 93, 306.

31 *Hidden History: Songs of the Kovno Ghetto* (Washington, DC: United States Holocaust Memorial Museum, 1997); Flam, *Singing for Survival*, and Brave Old World, *Song of the Łódź Ghetto* (Winter & Winter, 2005).

32 Katsherginski and Leivick, *Lider fun di Getos un Lagern*, 177–78.

33 Katsherginski and Leivick, *Lider fun di Getos un Lagern*, 32–33.

34 Several versions exist of this song: see Katsherginski and Leivick, *Lider fun di Getos un Lagern*, 213–16; Ruth Rubin, *Voices of a People: The Story of Yiddish Folksong* (Philadelphia: Jewish Publication Society of America, 1979), 444; Mlotek and Gottlieb (eds), *We are Here*, 37–38.

35 In describing a discourse of "spiritual resistance," I refer not only to specific use of this term, but rather to a broader interpretive narrative that tends to idealize heroism and resistance, often in a decontextualized and ahistorical manner. It is manifest in secondary writing as well as a range of popular representations such as commemorations, pedagogy, websites, concerts, and songbooks. I have discussed this issue more extensively in Gilbert, *Music in the Holocaust*, 1–20 and Gilbert, "Buried Monuments." While spiritual resistance is associated primarily with Jewish narratives, Fackler offers a related observation regarding anti-fascist narratives in the former GDR (Fackler, "Musik der Schoa").

38

HOLOCAUST DOCUMENTARIES

Lynne Fallwell and Robert G. Weiner

Since the end of World War II, the cinematic market has witnessed the production of literally thousands of Holocaust documentaries. While the largest number come from those countries in which relevant events unfolded (Germany, France, Russia, and Poland, to name a few), or areas where significant groups of survivors settled, such as the United States, Canada, England, and Israel, the actual geographic range of distribution is much broader. For example, in addition to films released in eastern and western European languages, films have appeared in Japanese, Chinese, and even Tibetan. In this regard, Holocaust documentaries are a global undertaking. Yet even this does not account for the vast range of potential documentaries. As Annette Insdorf points out in her comprehensive study, *Indelible Shadows: Film and the Holocaust,* for every documentary that makes it to the screen, another half dozen completed projects never reach circulation.[1]

Of the films that do make it to the screen, style issues such as presentation, content, and even length vary greatly. Some documentaries last only a few minutes, like the 13-minute Canadian short *Zyklon Portrait* (1999), directed by Elida Schogt and telling the story of her family's experiences in the Holocaust. At the other end of the scale are epic productions such as Claude Lanzmann's nine-and-a-half-hour undertaking *Shoah* (1985), which provides viewers with a vast array of interviews from across the eyewitness spectrum. Falling in the middle in terms of length are productions such as *The Nazis: A Warning from History* (350 minutes, 1998) and *Auschwitz: Inside the Nazi State* (300 minutes, 2005), offering detailed glimpses of the mechanized and bureaucratized machine that drove the Final Solution.

While longer documentaries are afforded room for greater explanation and exploration, the shorter films are no less powerful. This is evidenced by the enduring legacy of the 32-minute French production *Nuit et Brouillard* (*Night and Fog*) by Alan Resnais. Released in December 1955, it combines liberation footage with scene recreation and contemporary images shot in the now-vacant camps. The film opens with a panoramic view of Auschwitz 10 years after liberation, slowly shifting from an innocent-looking meadow to barbed-wire enclosure. As it unfolds, the film offers a surprisingly comprehensive look at the systematization of the Nazis' extermination plan, tracing a path from deportation, arrival in the camp, selection, and eventually death. In one instance, the wry voice of the narrator describes the architectural design employed in constructing guard towers, which has similarities to Japanese style. This compact film, with its stark images and compelling narrative, manages to capture the essence of brutality and incalculable inhumanity, which helps to explain why over a half century after its release, *Night and Fog* remains a significant educational tool and staple of Holocaust education courses.[2]

Although Resnais' work marks one of the major moments on the timeline of Holocaust documentaries, it is certainly not the first. The genre actually began in the postwar period with the Allied forces filming their liberation of the camps. Since the release of this liberation footage in the late 1940s (discussed in greater detail below), new documentaries have appeared every decade. At first, selection was sparse. *Night and Fog* remains the most widely recognized contribution from the 1950s. In the 1960s, arguably in response to the reawakening of public discourse about the Third Reich prompted by coverage of the Eichmann Trial, more documentaries began to appear. At least eight different countries were represented, including the joint French/Swiss/West German contribution *Le chagrin et la pitié* (*The Sorrow and the Pity*, 1969). Directed by Marcel Ophüls, this provocative two-part film takes a critical look at France under Nazi occupation. It centers on the city of Clermon-Ferrand, whose residents include Pierre Laval, head of the collaborationist Vichy government. The film recounts the experiences of a cross-section of the population, capturing the views of fascists, bystanders, and resistors alike. At its heart, *The Sorrow and the Pity* explores issues surrounding the human choices of complicity, complacency, and conflict, as well as the moral and ethical costs of each.

Since the 1980s, the number of Holocaust documentaries has grown exponentially, with film-makers branching out to explore not only representations of direct survival, but also other perspectives on the Holocaust. For example, in *To Bear Witness* (1984), Allied soldiers recall their reactions at liberating the camps. The film also includes excerpts from the First International Liberators Conference in Washington, DC. Other films explore themes of knowledge and awareness. *Who Shall Live and Who Shall Die?* (1981), directed by Laurence Jarvik, chronicles American understanding of events, particularly issues of antisemitism and Jewish persecution, as they unfolded in Nazi-occupied Europe. A third direction incorporates early work on matters of the legacy inherited by subsequent generations and, in particular, how the descendants of survivors and perpetrators interact (*The Third Generation: A German–Israeli Youth Exchange*, 1988).

One of the most significant films of the 1980s is Claude Lanzmann's *Shoah* (1985). Although Lanzmann himself does not feel that this film was a documentary, preferring to see it as a new type of cinematic representation, many others have come to consider *Shoah* as the model representation of the form. Eschewing the use of archival footage from camp liberation, a mainstay of many documentaries made before and after *Shoah*, Lanzmann opts instead to use the camera as accompaniment rather than directing force. Rather than pushing for a scripted linear narrative, Lanzmann allows memories of the participants to unfold in a multitude of directions. However, that does not mean the director's touch is wholly absent. Often, Lanzmann places his interview subjects in deliberately provocative settings, as in the oft-cited case of the barber Abraham Bomba, who is filmed while cutting hair in a shop in Tel Aviv. Answering Lanzmann's questions in this seemingly innocuous setting, Bomba reveals how he served on a work detail in Treblinka charged with cutting the hair of women about to be gassed. Bomba recounts how another man, a friend of his from the same town and working in the same detail, saw his own wife and sister enter the chamber. As Lanzmann pushes him to finish the story, Bomba breaks down, recalling the barbers' frustration at not being able to communicate to their loved ones what was about to happen. While the interview plays out, and amid his distress, Bomba continues to cut the hair of the client seated in the Tel Aviv shop. It is this juxtapositioning of the mundane and the grotesque that is so captivating and problematic about Lanzmann's film.

Since the 1990s, the pace of new documentary film releases continues unabated: Initiatives from Steven Spielberg's Shoah Visual History Foundation, and efforts of institutions such as Yad Vashem in Israel, the Simon Wiesenthal Center in Los Angeles, and the Holocaust Memorial Museum in Washington, DC, to name only a few, work diligently to provide a forum for survivors desiring to tell their personal stories. Also fueling this proliferation is a significant degree of consumer demand, particularly as secondary and post-secondary institutions begin incorporating Holocaust education into their curricula. This demand is not misplaced. The more time that passes, and the farther the world gets from contact with eyewitnesses who lived through the Holocaust, the more urgent grows the need to record as many perspectives as possible on what actually happened.

The purpose of a documentary

While the demand for Holocaust documentaries grows, such cinematic representations are not without issue. The first set of questions can be raised about any documentary. What is the perspective being presented? How accurately are the events being depicted? What is the documentary's overarching purpose? Just because a documentary is invested in portraying "real life," that does not mean the reality being presented is without context and a specific point of view. However, unlike fiction films, which can rely on fantasy as well as reality to construct the desired narrative point of view, documentaries, particularly historical documentaries, seek to capture a specific point in time as it was, or better said, as it was remembered. As Paula Rabinowitz points out, "Documentary cinema is intimately tied to historical memory."[3] Its purpose is to convey a particular set of memories about an occurrence in the past with the aim of educating about that event. The documentary narrative relies heavily on presenting information gained through historical eyewitness. This can take many forms: a person who lived through the event; memories shared with or about participants by subsequent generations; the physical location where an event occurred; artifacts as eyewitness; finally, written accounts such as journals, diaries, or letters, either created at the time or written after the fact. While all documentary constructions face challenges in addressing the fluidity of memory, in the case of documentaries about the Holocaust, the situation is further complicated by the added issues of trauma and memory.

Holocaust documentaries face the challenge of trying to make sense of the illogical, to imagine the unimaginable, and to explain what many consider cannot be explained. In addition to elucidating about the Holocaust, there is also the issue of education. These films are not only united by the desire to inform, but are charged with an implicit mandate that the events depicted are both never forgotten and never allowed to happen again. Due to the enormity of the moral and ethical issues raised by their subject matter, Holocaust documentaries walk a fine line, particularly when it comes to using violent film images such as those shot at liberation. How shocking is too shocking? What is the proper balance between recalling memories (presenting the past through the lens of the present) and showing images of the events themselves? At what point does the mandate of education suffer? The sizeable increase in new releases over the past decades has also led some to question whether we have reached a saturation point regarding Holocaust documentaries.[4] Documentaries are perhaps less well conceived due to their haste to contribute to this popular field (one prevalent criticism charges some directors as seeing Holocaust documentaries as an easy way to gain access to cinematic nominations and honors such as the Oscars). To what degree do subsequent releases run the risk of relying on trite formulaic constructions in order to provoke an emotional response?

Documentary categories: intent of purpose

Given the vast number of Holocaust documentaries produced over the past 60 years, it is impossible to discuss every individual film and therefore some form of categorization is necessary. One approach is to categorize these films according to cinematic terms applied to documentary films more broadly defined. Examples of techniques such as voice-over narration (a disembodied voice, often described as omniscient, narrates events as they unfold on screen), *cinema vérité*/direct cinema (the camera observes without interacting, with the goal of revealing a kind of objective truth), and the seated interview are certainly evident in Holocaust documentaries. However, rather than analyzing these films according to general cinematic criteria, a more useful approach is perhaps observing intent (how relevant documentaries choose to frame the Holocaust). In taking this approach, three different types of intent emerge: films that seek to show the results of Nazi atrocities, those that desire to show who was affected, and those that set out to explain how the Holocaust unfolded. Of course, these categories are not finite and overlap does occur, but in general the three types correspond to different phases in the broader understanding about the Holocaust.

Films seeking to depict the scale of Nazi atrocities feature among some of the earliest postwar documentaries, and comprise primarily footage shot by Allied forces. Unlike later productions, these initial films do not need to present the background context explaining in detail the formation of the Third Reich or layers of National Socialist rhetoric, because their intended audience had lived through the regime itself. These first documentaries are designed to educate through shock. Such films function through the production of vicarious trauma.[5] They set out to jolt the viewer out of perceived complacency and, in doing so, to alter perceptions of how the world functions. For example, films like *Die Todesmühlen* (*Death Mills*) aim both to document the existence of the camps and to educate the viewing public (via a version of visual shock therapy) about what Nazism actually represented. Created by the United States government (US Information Control Division) and directed by Billy Wilder, this 22-minute film was screened in the American occupation zone, starting in 1946. For German citizens living in the American zone, it was required viewing. Later, this film was also shown to American troops preparing their tour in Germany. Similarly, those Germans residing in the British zones were shown a film created from footage shot by the British Army's Film and Photographic Unit as their soldiers entered the Bergen-Belsen camp (*Atrocities—The Evidence*, 1945). This footage was also introduced into the trials of the Bergen-Belsen guards.[6] In both the British and American cases, these documentaries were intended to inform about mass inhumanity perpetrated by a regime that drew millions of followers. The films were designed to silence the claim "but I never knew."

Not all liberation footage was released immediately. Another British production, begun in 1945, remained unfinished for four decades. Stored in a vault at the Imperial War Museum in London, five reels of footage (a sixth shot by the Russians appears to be missing) and a never-recorded script were eventually edited into an hour-long documentary under its intended title *Memory of the Camps* (known as F3080). Shown for the first time on the US Public Broadcasting Service (PBS) in 1985, this film represents a unique bridge between immediate postwar shock films and later, more contextualized undertakings, and reflects how audiences have shifted in the intervening years. *Memory of the Camps* is a film within a film. While the main body of the film features a voice-over narrative reminiscent of earlier works like *Death Mills* and *Night and Fog*, the PBS introduction, which includes an accompanying website, focuses on setting the broader context of the film, explaining the discovery of the unedited reels and background of the unfinished project.[7] In this sense, the film is both an educational device and a primary document. Modern audiences are as interested about the history of the film itself as they are about its content. One reason for this is director Alfred Hitchcock's apparent involvement.

One of the criticisms leveled at these first documentaires, including Resnais' *Night and Fog*, is that they do an inadequate job of explaining the genocidal intent of the Nazis. The central importance of Jews as the primary target of Nazi aggression is omitted. Scenes such as the deportation footage included in *Night and Fog* show people wearing a yellow star, the Nazis' mandated identification symbol for Jews. However, the presence of Jewish victims is overlooked in favor of a more universalizing narrative about mass atrocities. In addition, the film's desire to maximize the shock narrative means that the voice of survivors loses out to depictions of those masses who did not survive; bulldozers push undifferentiated bodies into mass graves. More recent documentaries have undertaken to correct both these omissions. Rather than the shock value of the atrocity, these films focus on the survivors as individuals. These films are interested in capturing memories of their experiences in the survivors' own words. Some films in this category use the direct interview techniques (featuring seated interviews), for example, those using footage from the Survivors of the Shoah Visual History Foundation. Others, such as Claude Lanzmann's epic project *Shoah*, often take survivors back to sites of historical significance and interview them on location.

Unlike documentaries relying on liberation footage, this second group of films revisit the past through the present by recalling memories ranging from moments of loss to those of hope, resistance, and survival. Whether at the site where an event occurred, or showing an interviewee sitting in their own living room, these films serve to draw attention to the specific genocidal agenda of the Nazis regime. Although the Holocaust is a tragedy of humanity, or better said, lack of humanity, hearing survivors' testimony makes clear that the primary intended target for annihilation were European Jews. Like those films made immediately after the war, survivor testimony documentaries are also a product of their time. As the passage of time makes recording survivor testimony an increasingly rare possibility, the number of such films has increased significantly.

The most recent category of Holocaust documentary involves films that seek to give a more thorough understanding of the context surrounding the Holocaust. Combining contemporary site visits with archival footage and eyewitness accounts, these documentaries recreate a historical narrative that traces events as they unfold over time. Primarily designed for an audience who did not experience the Holocaust directly, these latest productions must not only explain what happened during the planned extermination attempt on Europe's Jews, but also clarify the climate that made it possible. As interest in academic study of the Holocaust increases, more and more documentaries are moving to this explanatory approach.

Documentary categories: content and themes

Context is not the only way to classify documentaries. They can also be grouped according to subject matter and themes. The following list is by no means complete.

Rather, it is meant as a suggestion of additional Holocaust documentary categories and sample films for each.

Roots of hate

Films in this group expand their temporal focus to include periods that pre-date the Third Reich and Holocaust. Their aim is to trace features that explain the roots of discriminatory thinking that created a climate in which genocidal practices were able to flourish. Some films focus on theories of hierarchical thinking and belief in superiority of races. *Homo Sapiens 1900* (1998) and *In the Shadow of the Reich: Nazi Medicine* (1996) both place Nazi eugenic practices into the broader context of Social Darwinian philosophy and the sterilization laws evident in many countries in the early part of the century.

The Cross and the Star: Jews, Christians and the Holocaust (1992), by John Michalczyk, has a slightly different focus. It traces the history of antisemitic thought and actions from early Christianity through to the exterminationist policies of the Nazis. Combining an examination of religious, political, and cultural factors, the film shows how events including the Crusades, the blood libel trials, and the Inquisition factored into perpetuating a climate of intolerance, fear, and violence.

European Jewish life pre-1933

Perhaps one of the smallest categories of Holocaust-related films is those depicting prewar European Jewish life. From remaining fragments of surviving film and photographs, these documentaries aim to capture the vibrancy of communities before they were extinguished. One example is *Fading Traces: Postscripts from a Landscape of Memory* (2001), which traces the history of pre-World War II Ukraine, highlighting the large and vibrant Jewish community that once resided there, and its contributions to arts, music, theater, and culture. For a broader focus, see *Ashkenaz—The German Jewish Heritage* (1989), which explores a millennium of German Jewish life from origins to near extinction.

Ghettos

Of those films that focus specifically on the fate of Europe's Jews in the 1930s and 1940s, one frequently selected approach is to document life in the various ghettos in the eastern occupied territories. *The Story of Chaim Rumkowski and the Jews of Łódź* (1982), directed by Peter Cohn and Bo Kuritzen, provides insight into the interactions between Jews, Poles, and Germans. Centered on the controversial figure of ghetto leader Chaim Rumkowski, the film combines photographs taken in the ghetto by Jewish Council members and others, with archival footage to describe both the functioning of daily ghetto life and Rumkowski's complicated relationship with the Nazis.

The Jewish Historical Institute produced a three-part series on the fate of Jews in the Warsaw Ghetto. *912 Days of the Warsaw Ghetto*; *Children of the Ghetto*; and *The Warsaw Ghetto Uprising* trace the lives, resistance, and extermination of ghetto inhabitants between 1939 and 1945. Utilizing both German and Polish archival sources, the film's languages include English, German, Hebrew, and Polish. A similar BBC production, titled

Warsaw Ghetto, also traces the story of Jewish life in the ghetto between 1940 and 1943. Running 150 minutes, *Not Like Sheep to the Slaughter: The Story of the Bialystok Ghetto* (1991) bridges the gap between the story of ghetto life and that of Jewish resistance. Tracing the efforts of Mordechai Tenenbaum and other resistance fighters, this film centers around the story of the Bialystok Ghetto during the summer of 1943.

Resistance

Important for many film-makers is to show that Nazi aggression did not go unopposed, and in particular to demonstrate that many Jews actively fought against the regime's genocidal agenda. In addition to the French film *The Sorrow and the Pity,* already discussed, other examples of resistance films include *Flames in the Ashes* (1985), *Partisans of Vilna* (1986), the Israeli film *Forests of Valor* (1989), *Revenge* (1998), *In Our Own Hands* (1998), and *They were not Silent: The Jewish Labor Movement and the Holocaust* (2000).

Rescue

An accompaniment to the resistance films are those depicting how not all Gentiles turned their back on Jewish suffering. The story of how the residents of a small farming village, Le Chambon-sur-Lignon, sheltered some 5,000 Jews is told in the film *Weapons of the Spirit* (1989). Written and directed by Pierre Sauvage, who, along with his parents, was sheltered by the people of Le Chambon-sur-Lignon, the film focuses on the mostly Protestant villagers, descendants of Huguenots, who remembered their own persecution.

Comme si c'était hier (*As If It Were Yesterday,* 1980) describes Belgian efforts to rescue 4,000 Jewish children from deportation. In French and Flemish with English subtitles, the film offers interviews with those directly involved in the rescue efforts, including teachers, housewives, and officials. Some of the now-grown children also talk about their experiences of being separated from family members and sent into strange new surroundings. Other films include: *Courage to Care* (1985), *An Act of Faith* (1990) about Danish efforts to help Jews escape to Sweden, *They Risked Their Lives* (1992), and *The Port of Last Resort: Zuflucht in Shanghai* (1998).

Some resistance films focus on the heroic efforts of a single individual. *Sugihara* (2005) tells the story of Japanese diplomat Chiune Sugihara as he used his post as Lithuanian consul to procure transit visas for hundreds of Jewish families. Similar efforts of Swedish diplomat Raul Wallenberg are documented in films such as *Raul Wallenberg: Buried Alive* (1984) and *Raul Wallenberg: Between the Lines* (1987), to name just two.

Reunion

Many documentaries seek to overcome the story of incalculable loss by focusing on reuniting those who lived the experience. Similar work includes *Memory of a Moment* (1990), which depicts the reunion of Robert Waisman, a camp survivor, and Leon Bass, an African-American soldier at the anniversary celebrations in Buchenwald. The film *Reunion* (1986) tells the story of the liberation of Mauthausen from the perspective of Allied soldiers and camp survivors. The film also features interviews with other notables, such as Elie Wiesel and William Wilkins, an American judge at Nuremberg. Many of these reunion films are a product of encounters that took place during the fortieth and fiftieth anniversaries of liberation.

Eyewitnesses returning

As part of the effort to explain to subsequent generations about the Holocaust, some films choose to accompany survivors back to the camps, ghettos, and similar locations. In addition to cases in Lanzmann's *Shoah*, other examples include *Kitty: Return to Auschwitz* (1979). Kitty Hart-Moxon, who was 16 when interned, revisits Auschwitz. She recalls and relives her experiences at the camp many years later. In the film, Kitty recalls to her son David the horrors of living in the camp. Visiting Auschwitz again inspired her to complete a book about her experiences, also called *Return to Auschwitz* (1981). The documentary *Fighter* (2000) follows Holocaust survivors Jan Weiner and Arnošt Lustig as they recount their survival and retrace Weiner's route of escape. In the Canadian documentary *Memorandum*, a group of survivors return to Germany on the twentieth anniversary of liberation from the camps. The film offers a comparison of Germany then and now as seen through their eyes.

Tracking the perpetrator

In an effort to address the question of how the Holocaust happened, some documentaries present information on those who took a direct role in the exterminationist policies. These are often biographical in nature, covering not only the early developmental years of the perpetrators' lives, but also, where relevant, postwar efforts to track them down and bring them to justice. For example, *Hotel Terminis: The Life and Times of Klaus Barbie* (1989) spans seven decades, including the 40-year hunt to locate the man known as the "butcher of Lyon." Similar films in this category include: *The Search for Mengele* (1985); *Hunt for Adolf Eichmann* (1998) and *The Specialist* (2002), two of the many films about Eichmann; and *In the Führer's Shadow* (1998), which followed theories about the fate of Hitler's private secretary and head of the party chancellery, Martin Bormann.

Period propaganda

While some films are made about the Nazis, others were made by them. Documentary film served the Nazis' propaganda purposes by furthering the rhetoric of the Third Reich. *Der ewige Jude* (*The Eternal Jew*, 1940) was an antisemitic production written by Ebert Taubert and directed by Fritz Hippler, both members of Joseph Goebbels' Propaganda Ministry. The film's opening scene, which juxtaposes rats scurrying through a sewer with Jews on a crowded street, was one of the many filmic pairings designed to indoctrinate audiences to Nazi racial thinking and to provide justification for their claims of racial hierarchies. The film goes on to claim that Jews were dangerous because of their ability to "pass" in Christian German society by altering their appearance, and ends with the assertion that Jews were responsible for the decline of western civilization. Another example of Nazi propaganda was the 1944 film *Der Führer Schenkt den Juden Eine Stadt* (*Hitler Gives the Jews a Town*). Created to show Hitler's benevolence, this 10-minute black-and-white film supposedly depicted idealized conditions in the Theresienstadt ghetto; however, survivors recall how this reality was manipulated for the screen.[8]

Connecting generations

The aim of films in this category is to bring generations of families together. Surviving family members, accompanied by younger generations, return to places where the family lived before the war. Often they are structured to feel like private journeys where the film audience is invited to accompany the travelers. These films are often as much about generational catharsis as they are about education. *Hiding and Seeking: Faith and Tolerance After the Holocaust* (2004) traces one father's journey with his adult sons, Orthodox Jews, to Poland to search for the family that helped hide the boys' grandfather. *Hiding in the Attic* (1988) follows multiple branches, primarily cousins, of one family back to where their family members hid in the attic of a sympathetic Christian family. *The Legacy: Children of Holocaust Survivors* (1981) follows five adults as they recount their experiences growing up as the children of survivors.

Reaching Israel

Not all documentaries are about returning. Some focus on the struggles to reach a new homeland. In *The Unafraid* (1987), film-maker Meyer Levin captures the struggles faced by Jews trying to reach Palestine in 1947, and then reconnects with them three decades later to discover how their life has been. Similarly, *Children of the Exodus* (1967) seeks to find out what became of a group of children sent to Palestine in 1947. *Long Way Home* (1997), a 2-hour film written and directed by Mark Jonathan Harris, describes the situations facing Jewish refugees after 1945 and their struggles to form the Jewish state of Israel. See also *The Last Sea* (1979).

Liberators

A different perspective on the Holocaust is taken by documentaries that focus on those who liberated the camps. Featuring interviews with American and other servicemen, these films recall the memories of these young men as they encountered the unimaginable. To help underscore the magnitude of their discovery and the liberators' feelings of shock, many documentaries contain extended scenes of camp liberation. Films here include *Opening the Gates of Hell* (1992), *To Bear Witness* (1984), *Liberation* (2004), and *The Liberation of KZ Dachau: A Documentary* (1990).

Forgiving but not forgetting

Forgiving Dr. Mengele (2006) presents the story of Eva Mozes Kor and her twin sister Miriam, two of the children selected by Dr Josef Mengele for his so-called "twin experiments" in Auschwitz. Describing the lingering nightmares suffered by Kor as a result of her traumatic experiences, the film focuses on her decision to declare forgiveness to Mengele as a way to move on with her own life.

Child survivors

Just like their adult counterparts, children's stories have been documented in film. Sometimes these stories describe efforts to save Jewish children from harm. For example,

Secret Lives: Hidden Children and Their Rescuers During World War II (2003), directed by Aviva Slesein, tells the story of non-Jewish families in both western and eastern Europe who risked their own safety to shelter Jewish children. Likewise, after the attack on Jewish homes, businesses, and places of worship during the so-called "Night of Broken Glass" (*Kristallnacht*), Britain's Jewish community lobbied for special permission to bring Jewish children out of German-occupied areas. Films such as *My Knees Were Jumping: Remembering the Kindertransports* (1996), and *Into the Arms of Strangers: Stories of the Kindertransport* (2001), describe their efforts to rescue some 10,000 children between November 1938 and the eve of World War II.

Other films track the fate of children who found themselves caught in the Nazi web. One production of Spielberg's Shoah Foundation, *The Lost Children of Berlin* (1997), reunites 50 students who were part of the last class held at the Jewish school on Berlin's Grosse Hamburgerstrasse. Presenting Jewish life in prewar Berlin and the tightening restrictions, the film documents student life until the school closed in 1942. When survivors reunited in the newly reopened school in 1996, it was the first time for many to discover who had survived. *Preserving the Past to Ensure the Future* (1990), a 15-minute montage, captures the faces of Jewish children who died in the Holocaust. The film also documents a visit to the memorial for children at Yad Vashem. *Voices of the Children* (1996), *The Journey of the Butterfly* (1996), and *I Never Saw Another Butterfly* (1999), recall the stories of some of the 200 children who survived the Theresienstadt (Terezin) ghetto. The use of the butterfly imagery comes from a poem ("I Never Saw Another Butterfly") written by Pavel Friedman, one of the young children in the ghetto. Friedman, like many of his friends, died after being sent to Auschwitz. Other films in this category include *Children Remember the Holocaust* (1995), and *When I was Fourteen: A Survivor Remembers* (1995).

Another perspective

Can a documentary film portray a real-life story without showing actual artifacts, locations, or eyewitnesses? The short animated production *Silence* (1998), co-produced and co-directed by Orly Yadin and Sylvie Bringas, challenges the idea that documentary films must contain live action. As Yadin writes, "Animation can be the most honest form of documentary filmmaking."[9] The advantage of using animation, Yadin points out, is the reduced risk of voyeurism by offering an additional layer of protection to the subject: an individual can put their story on display, but not themselves. Animation also widens the possibility of representation by portraying events for which there is no visual record, or for which the visual record is restrictive. For example, this medium can help overcome issues brought by the passage of time, such as how to portray the experiences of a child more than a half century after the fact. In the case of *Silence*, which tells the story of a young girl born in Berlin in 1940 and hidden by her grandmother in Theresiendstadt until liberation in 1945, the viewer does not have to search for the remnants of a young girl in the face of a mature woman, but can instead focus on the details at hand.[10]

Student documentary projects

Some films center not on eyewitnesses and their descendants, but rather on later generations who try to understand the Holocaust and its broader moral and ethical messages. Often these films stem from initiatives undertaken by middle- and high-school students living far from where the events occurred. They start out not to be films, but rather projects designed to make the lessons of the Holocaust more accessible to students born well after the end of World War II. For instance, the film *Paperclips* records how students in Whitwell, Tennessee developed a project to help better understand what it meant to talk about the death of six million Jews, and set out to create a visual record by collecting one paper clip for every Holocaust victim. The film ends with images of the memorial they built to house the collection. Perhaps not surprisingly, many of the projects, particularly those created by middle-school students, are generated by extended interest in classroom reading, and then they take on a life of their own (*Anne Frank in Maine*, 1983). In other projects, American students journey to sites of Holocaust atrocities to collect film images, survivor testimony, and other documentation in order to create a presentation accessible to their peers (Carlsbad students in *Never Forget*, and Youngstown State and West Chester University students in *There are No More Wise Men in Chelm*). Like so many other documentary projects, these films are created with a limited budget and spread through grassroots promotion.

Other victims

In addition to documentaries focused on the fate of Jews during the Holocaust, some films offer an examination of other groups facing persecution. *Paragraph 175* (2002), its title stemming from anti-gay laws originally created when Germany formed in 1871, traces the lives of gay men during the Third Reich. *Purple Triangles* (1991) describes what happened to Jehovah's Witnesses incarcerated in the camps, and *Porraimos* (2002) offers a look into the lives of Sinti and Roma ("Gypsies") and the persecution they faced for following traditional cultural practices.

Some concluding points

This list of films is by no means exhaustive. Nor is it intended to imply exclusivity or superiority. Instead, the films mentioned here are a cross-section of the very rich field of documentary films. Those looking for more comprehensive lists of Holocaust films may find the following resources useful:

Annette Insdorf, *Indelible Shadows: Film and the Holocaust* (Cambridge: Cambridge University Press, 2002).
"Guide to the Holocaust Video Collection," http://fcit.usf.edu/HOLOCAUST/RESOURCE/videogl.htm
www.filmsite.org/docfilms.html

Notes

1 Annette Insdorf, *Indelible Shadows: Film and the Holocaust* (Cambridge: Cambridge University Press, 2002), quoted here from Barry Gewen, "Holocaust Documentaries: Too Much of a Bad Thing?" *New York Times*, 15 June 2003, 21.
2 Ilan Avisar, *Screening the Holocaust: Cinema's Images of the Unimaginable* (Bloomington and Indianapolis, Indiana: Indiana University Press, 1988).

3 Paula Rabinowitz, "Wreckage upon Wreckage: History, Documentary and the Ruins of Memory," *History and Theory*, vol. 32, no. 2 (May, 1993): 119–37.

4 Barry Gewen, "Holocaust Documentaries," 21.

5 Joshua Hirsch, *AfterImage: Film, Trauma, and the Holocaust* (Philadelphia: Temple University Press, 2004).

6 See the essays by Toby Haggith, Kay Gladstone, and Helen Lennon in Toby Haggith and Joanna Newman, eds, *Holocaust and the Moving Image: Representations in Film and Television since 1933* (London: Wallflower Press, 2005).

7 PBS website *Memory of the Camps*, www.pbs.org/wgbh/pages/frontline/camp

8 See the essays by Lutz Becker and Zdenka Fantlova-Ehrlich in *Holocaust and the Moving Image*.

9 Orly Yadin, "But is it documentary?" in *Holocaust and the Moving Image* (Haggith and Newman, eds), 169.

10 Yadin, "But is it documentary?" 169.

39

SEQUENTIAL ART NARRATIVE AND THE HOLOCAUST

Robert G. Weiner and Lynne Fallwell

Over the past three decades, Holocaust sequential narratives have risen in popularity. Sequential art can be defined as using a form of visual art sequentially to tell a story with most narratives via a combination of art and text. Ever since the publication of Art Spiegelman's Pulitzer Prize-winning graphic novel *Maus* in 1986, no fewer than 35 different graphic novels dealing with Holocaust issues have found their way to press. Some are designed for classroom use, while others are memoirs, fictional tales, or traditional superhero fare. They have been written and translated in a number of languages in addition to English, including Hebrew, Spanish, Italian, German, and even Japanese. While *Maus* has certainly been the catalyst for the most recent round of publications, the history of graphic novels depicting the Holocaust begins even before World War II ended.

Horst Rosenthal, who perished in Auschwitz, produced perhaps the earliest sequential art narrative dealing with the Holocaust, the 15-page "Mickey Mouse in the Gurs Internment Camp (1942)." In it, Rosenthal used a very naïve Mickey Mouse to show the injustice of the Nazis. Using Walt Disney's most famous character, the short graphic novel illustrates how Jews are made into "the other"—something that is subhuman. Based simply on physical stereotypes, Mickey is charged with being a Jew, even though he proclaims, "Shamefully I confessed my complete ignorance on the subject" of what a Jew is supposed to look like. Rosenthal produced two similar booklets, *A Day in the Life of a Resident, Gurs Internment Camp 1942*; and *A Small Guide through Gurs Camp 1942*.[1]

Early sequential art writers and artists, many of them Jews, created the comic book industry (1936–50). They were keenly aware of Hitler's hate-mongering and the "Final Solution." There were literally millions of comics sold during the war years with the war itself as their plot device. The premiere issue of *Captain America Comics* by Joe Simon and Jack Kirby appeared with a cover date of March 1941, before the United States officially joined the Allied cause. It became the first comic to feature a main character slugging Hitler. Once America was in the war, comics provided a morale-booster to the servicemen by providing a real-life villain to defeat. Although Captain America quickly became successful, the German American Bund and those sympathetic to Nazi ideology were not pleased to see Hitler slugging it out with a superhero dressed up in the American flag. In fact, the publisher, Timely Comics, received threatening phone calls, and phrases like "Death to the Jews" were heard outside their offices, causing police to be called to monitor the offices.[2]

In the first issue of *Daredevil* (July 1941), Daredevil is shown punching a very scared looking Führer, and in bold letters the caption says, "Daredevil Battles Hitler...promises the 'Ace of Death to the Mad Merchant of Hate.'"[3] A more telling example appears in *All Star Comics 16* (1943), which features the Justice Society of America. In this issue, Hitler is shown thinking about a propaganda scheme that will give Europe "something to hate." He opines that "Jews were a good subject," and sends agents to America to spread the slogans "Gentile against Jew" and "Protestant against Catholic."[4] In 1943, when antisemitism and Jewish quotas were rampant in universities, country clubs, and businesses, these statements acknowledged the racial suffering Hitler's Reich wrought, and were quite radical for a mainstream comic book. Also, they show that there were those who were aware of what was happening, and sequential art characters such as Superman, the Young Allies, the Shield, the Human Torch, and the Sub-Mariner all fought Hitler and the Nazis. The cover of *Captain America Comics 46* (April 1945) depicted the Nazis marking Jews scheduled for massacre with red tags around their necks. Although the actual story in the book has little to do with what was shown on the cover, this does show awareness of some of the atrocities being committed.[5] In the 1945 issue of *Real Life Comics 26*, there was the text story, "Lest we Forget: A Story of Grim Nazi Brutality" that detailed the gruesome treatment of people by the Nazis.[6]

The Third Reich took notice of sequential art, as evidenced by Joseph Goebbels' April 1940 comments about Superman and his creator, Jerry Siegel, in the SS newsmagazine, *Das Schwarze Korps*:

> The inventive Israelite named this pleasant guy with an overdeveloped body and underdeveloped mind. Superman...Well, we really ought to ignore these fantasies of Jerry Israel Siegel, but there is a catch. The daring deeds of Superman are those of a Colorado beetle. He works in the dark, in incomprehensible ways. He cries 'Strength! Courage! Justice!' to the noble yearnings of American children. Instead of using the chance to encourage really useful virtues, he sows hate, suspicion, evil, laziness, and criminality in their young hearts. Jerry Siegellack stinks. Woe to the American youth, who must live in such a poisoned atmosphere and don't even notice the poison they swallow daily.[7]

These comments show that the Reich understood how sequential art could be a powerful form of communication.

In 1955, a story appeared as one of the first direct acknowledgments of the Shoah in sequential art stories. In EC comics, *Impact 1* had a story titled "Master Race," written and drawn by Bernie Krigstein. At a time when there was very little acknowledgment of concentration camp events, much less the Holocaust as a whole, "Master Race" was revolutionary. The story deals with the Belsen concentration camp and the "awful smell of the gas chambers...the stinking odor of human flesh burning...[and] mad experiments with human guinea pigs." In the story, an Adolf Eichmann-type character named Reissman is running and evading justice, but when he meets a Holocaust survivor on a subway train, he tries to run away, and is killed by an oncoming train, implying that justice was finally served. Pictures of torture and death abound, including the *Jude* identification, the star of David on the clothes of those sent to the camps, and eventually death and burial in mass graves.[8] Another two-page short story appeared in 1958 in *Harvey Hits 6*. In this story, when a former camp commandant becomes a prisoner in the "Elsen Concentration Camp," he fashions a clock from barbed wire as he formerly saw his captives do.[9] Both of these might be considered a revenge or retribution in a sequential art narrative.

Although war comics dominated in the 1960s, with DC's *Our Army at War* featuring Sgt Rock, and Marvel Comics' Sgt Fury and his Howling Commandoes, it was not until the 1970s that writers and artists dealt again with issues related to the Shoah. For example, Charlton Comics' *Fightin' Army 119* (1975) told the tale of the liberators[10] and the hunt for a concentration camp commander. Its cover has an image of Nazis fleeing an Allied plane with the ghosts of Holocaust victims behind barbed wire in the background. One story from *Invaders 12–13* (1976) dealt "loosely" with the question, "What if the Jews had their own protector, in the form of a Golem?" In it, Rabbi Jacob Goldstein is transformed, through a freak accident, into a half-human/Golem who can, with his faculties intact, change his form at will, and he stays in the Warsaw ghetto as a protector of the Jews. Writer Roy Thomas knew that since he wrote about World War II, he had to address the questions of Jewish persecution and the Holocaust. He did it in mainstream, sequential narratives.[11] One of the most controversial stories concerning portrayals of the Holocaust in comics appeared in 1998's *Superman: Man of Steel 80–82*, by Jon Bogdanove and Louise Simonson. It attempted to answer the question, "What if Superman were around to deal with the horrors of the Shoah?" It put Superman in the Warsaw ghetto, and received a great deal of press and controversy because it never mentioned the word Jew.[12]

The most mainstream sequential art narrative connection to the Holocaust is that of the mutant superhero team the X-Men, created by Stan Lee and Jack Kirby in 1963. But it was not until the 1970s, when the Jewish/British writer Chris Claremont took over the reins, that a blatant connection between the X-Men and the Shoah was shown. Shortly after the war, Magneto (the X-Men's main nemesis) and Professor X (the X-Men's leader) worked together in a hospital, helping Holocaust survivors cope with the trauma of the camps. It revealed that Magneto (Erik Magnus Lehnsherr—real name Max Eisenhardt) survived Auschwitz, where he saw his family murdered (*X-Men 161* [1982], and the recent *X-Men* films). Writer Claremont wanted to show the parallel between hatred of mutants, Jews, and any group that is different. Because Magneto was a survivor, the plot of the stories brought to light the problems of racism and fear of others to a wider audience. One of the most telling narratives appears in *X-Men 199–200* (1985), when Shadowcat (Kitty Pryde—a young Jewish character, whose extended family members perish in the camps) goes with Magneto to speak at the Holocaust Memorial Museum in Washington, DC. The ultimate message of her talk is "Never Again" can we allow something like the Holocaust to occur.

Originally, there was some debate as to whether Magneto was actually Jewish. Was he just a survivor, a Gypsy, or of some other ethnicity? The 2009 publication of the graphic novel *X-Men Magneto: Testament* put the debate to rest. The story tells that as a youth in Germany, Magneto was ostracized and beaten up because he was a Jew. What is unique about this fictional tale is that the author, Greg Pak, has put in many historical facts about the Shoah and Nazi Germany, and includes note-by-note annotations providing the historical backdrop of events. Clearly problematic, though, is the use of a Jewish Holocaust victim as a villainous character, and the creators of Magneto's backstory might have unintentionally crossed into antisemitic territory here. Although a tragic figure, Magneto is an extension of the broader *meme* of the Jewish villain, which sequential artists, like those who contributed the front page cartoons for Julius Streicher's *Der Stürmer*, have mined for centuries.[13]

The most important and well-known graphic novel concerning the Holocaust is Art Spiegelman's two-volume *Maus*, which was originally serialized in *Raw Magazine* and later published as a book. *Maus* won the Pulitzer Prize in 1992; it was the first and only sequential art narrative to do so. It tells the story of Spiegelman's father's life in a concentration camp, Spiegelman's attempt to deal with his father's pain, and its effect on his life. In *Maus*, Jews are portrayed as Hitler referred to them, as "dirt-covered vermin"; Germans are cats; Poles are pigs; Americans are dogs; and the French are frogs. One might question the appropriateness of depicting such a serious topic as the Shoah with "funny animals," but *Maus* is a powerful testament not only to Holocaust survival, but also to one man's attempt to deal with the pain of losing his family. Its publication showed that comics, far from being throwaway children's fare, could deal with real issues in an adult manner. *Maus* became the subject of a number of scholarly studies, and it is now taught in high schools and universities worldwide.[14]

In the post-millennium period there has been an effort to put the Holocaust in sequential art format to explain the concept to elementary- and junior high-school children. An example of such a book is *Good-bye Marianne: The Graphic Novel* (2008) by Irene Watts and Kathryn Shoemaker. This book is the story of a young girl forced to leave her home due to the hounding of the Jews by the Nazis. It is based on the 1998 young adult novel of the same title. Other examples include Eric Heuvel's works *A Family Secret* (2009) and *The Search* (2009), published by the International Center for Education about Auschwitz and the Holocaust in cooperation with the Anne Frank Foundation. Both books present fictional stories designed to educate young people about the Shoah.[15] *Mendel's Daughter* (2007), by Gusta and Martin Lemelman, is a true-life narrative, and there are at least four graphic novels that tell the famous story of Anne Frank. They include one written from a Japanese perspective by Etsuo Suzuki (2006), Elizabeth Hudson-Goff and Jonathan Brown's *Anne Frank* (2006), Nicholas Saunders' *The Life of Anne Frank* (2006), and Joeming Dunn's *Anne Frank* (2008).

In sequential art, Holocaust narratives can be assigned to a number of categories:

- Survivor depictions from the standpoint of their children. Examples: *Maus* or Bernice Eisenstein's *I Was a Child of Holocaust Survivors*;
- History of the Holocaust: Examples: Haim Bresheeth's *Introducing the Holocaust* or those that mention Shoah in the larger context of history, such as Stan Mack's *The Story of the Jews: A 4,000 Year Adventure* or David Gantz's *Jews In America: A Cartoon History*;
- Superhero stories that use the Holocaust as backdrop or allegory. Examples: X-Men, Alan Moore's Miracle Man, Robin Synder's Mainmal character, or Roy Thomas's work in the *Invaders* series;
- Serious comics. Examples: Donna Barr's *Desert Peach*[16] and *Zog Nit Keyn Mol* from a 1985 issue of *Wimmen's Comics*, for which Trina Robbins took a poem by Warsaw Ghetto poet Hersh Glik, and provided a contemporary story featuring a Holocaust survivor;[17]
- The Holocaust used as a backdrop to explain racial tensions. Examples: Eric Drooker's "JewBlack" from *World War 3: Illustrated 18*;[18]
- Fictional tales that provide a Holocaust narrative based on history. Examples: Joe Kubert's *Yossel April 19, 1943: A Story of the Warsaw Ghetto Uprising* (a fictional

retelling of the Warsaw Ghetto uprising) or *Auschwitz Croci* (the tale of an elderly couple who recall their time at the camp) by Paschal. (Both *Yossel* and *Auschwitz* caused some controversy over whether the sequential art form could really portray the horrors of the Holocaust in a realistic manner.)[19]

- Revenge tales. Example: Krigstein's "Master Race";
- Books for young people. Examples: fiction designed to teach them about the Holocaust, such as Heuvel's *The Search* and biographies for young people, like those of Anne Frank.

Finally, there are works that defy categorization, such as David Sims' *Judenhass*, the story of Shoah and the history of antisemitism told through historical quotes and images. This is a powerful work that combines image and text in a distinctive and effective manner. Sequential art Holocaust narrative has a long and unique history, one that continues to be told as new stories about the past are discovered. It will continue to be written about in this unique artistic way, despite—or perhaps because of—the kind of representation which it offers.

Notes

1 The strange history of Rosenthal's unique documents can be found in Prina Rosenberg, "Mickey Mouse—Humor, Irony, and Criticism in Works of Art Produced in the Gurs Internment Camp," *Rethinking History*, vol. 6, no. 3 (2002): 273–92; this article reproduces parts of Rosenthal's work
2 Joe Simon and Jim Simon, *The Comic Book Makers* (Lebanon, New Jersey: Vanguard Publications, 2003), 44.
3 See an example cover for *Daredevil 1* (1941) (accessed 12 March 2009), www.coverbrowser.com/covers/daredevil-comics
4 *All Star Comics 16* is reprinted in Roy Thomas, Gardner Fox, Sheldon Mayer et al., *All Star Comics Archive* (New York: DC, 1997), 3: 238.
5 An example of *Captain America Comics 46* (1945) (accessed 12 March 2009), www.coverbrowser.com/covers/captain-america#i46. See also Kathrin Bower, "Holocaust Avengers: From Master Race to Magneto," *International Journal of Comic Art*, vol. 6, no. 2 (Fall 2004): 182–94.
6 Most comics of the 1940s–1950s had narrative text stories side-by-side with sequential art narratives.
7 "Jerry Siegel Attacks!," *Das Schwarze Korps* (25 April 1940), 8, trans. Randall Bytwerk; "The SS and Superman," *German Propaganda Archive*, Calvin College (1998) (accessed 12 March 2009), www.calvin.edu/academic/cas/gpa/superman.htm
8 Bernie Krigstein, "Master Race," reprinted in *B Krigstein*, ed. Greg Sadowski (Seattle: Fantagraphics, 2002), 218–25.
9 A partial example of this tale can be found at Mike DeLisa, "Comics Exploring the Holocaust" (accessed 12 February 2009), http://mikedelisa.blogspot.com/2008/09/comics-exploring-holocaust.html
10 An example of the cover can be found at www.comics.org/issue/28611/cover/4/?style=default (accessed 12 February 2009).
11 Roy Thomas's email message to authors on 14 September 2009.
12 Eric J. Greenberg, "Superman editors sorry about omission: Comic erases Jews from Holocaust," *J Weekly,* 10 July 1998, 2 December 2009, www.jweekly.com/article/full/8618/superman-editors-sorry-about-omission-comic-erases-jews-from-holocaust
13 Greg Pak, Carmine Di Giandomenico et al., *X-Men: Magneto Testament* (New York: Marvel, 2009). See also Cheryl Alexander Malcolm, "Witness, Trauma, and Remembrance: Holocaust Representation and X-Men Comics," in *The Jewish Graphic Novel: Critical Approaches*, eds Samantha Baskind and Ranen Omer Sherman (New Brunswick, New Jersey: Rutgers University Press, 2008), 144–60.

14 See Art Spiegelman, *The Complete Maus* (New York: Penguin, 2003); Deborah R. Geis, ed., *Considering Maus: Approaches to Art Spiegelman's "Survivor's tale" of the Holocaust* (Tuscaloosa, Alabama: University of Alabama Press, 2003); Erin McGlothlin, "When Time Stands Still: Traumatic Immediacy and Narrative Organization in Art Spiegelman's *Maus* and *In the Shadow of No Towers*," in *The Jewish Graphic Novel: Critical Approaches*, eds Samantha Baskind and Ranen Omer Sherman (New Brunswick, New Jersey: Rutgers University Press, 2008), 94–110; Stephen E. Tabachnick, "Of Maus and Memory: the Structure of Art Spiegelman's Graphic Novel of the Holocaust," *Word and Image*, vol. 9, no. 2 (April–June 1993): 154–56; James Reibman, "Fredric Wertham, Spiegelman's *Maus*, and representations of the Holocaust," in *The Graphic Novel*, ed. Jan Baetens (Louvain, Belgium: Leuven University Press, 2001), 23–30. This bibliographic list just scratches the surface on the amount of analysis *Maus* has received. A similar book was awarded the Pulitzer Prize: Michael Chabon's *The Amazing Adventures of Kavalier & Clay* (New York: Random House, 2000), a novel (not graphic novel) that deals with themes of World War II and the Holocaust and comics.

15 See Paweł Sawicki, "Holocaust Comics. A Story in Drawings," *Memorial and Museum: Auschwitz-Birkenau*, 5 March 2008 (accessed 6 December 2009), http://en.auschwitz.org.pl/m/index.php?option=com_content& task = view& id = 11& Itemid = 8

16 See Robert Eaglestone, "Madness or Modernity? The Holocaust in Two Anglo-American Comics," *Rethinking History*, vol.6, no. 3 (2002): 319–30.

17 This story is reprinted in Arie Kaplan, *From Krakow to Krypton: Jews and Comic Books* (Philadelphia: Jewish Publication Society, 2008), 200–201.

18 Drooker's strip is reprinted in Paul Buhle, ed., *Jews and American Comic Books: An Illustrated History of an American Art Form* (New York: New Press, 2008), 144.

19 Roger Boyes, "Comic Book Depiction of Jews Upsets Jews," *Times Online*, 21 June 2005 (accessed 4 December 2009), www.timesonline.co.uk/tol/news/world/article535579.ece

40

THE ROLE OF THE SURVIVORS IN THE REMEMBRANCE OF THE HOLOCAUST

Memorial monuments and *Yizkor* books

Rita Horváth

Holocaust survivors took their role as witnesses extremely seriously. This phenomenon becomes evident when we take into account that the large Holocaust collections of the world in archives and libraries have accumulated nearly 1,000 *Yizkor* books (memorial books) and more than 100,000 survivor testimonies. These collections continue to increase to this day, despite the dwindling numbers of survivors. This essay addresses the personal and communal role of the survivors in shaping the memory not only of the Holocaust, but also of the Jewish world that went before it.

Witnessing the Holocaust together with the lost pre-Holocaust era became intertwined with other deep-seated needs of the survivors to commemorate, honor, and memorialize loved ones, family members, members of their geographical, social, and religious communities, as well as fellow sufferers with whom they were thrown together in the concentration camp universe. Memorialization took shape as both an individual and collective process, i.e., survivors aimed at memorializing the individual victims' ties to various communities as well as the communities themselves. The primary communities in which most survivors were especially invested to commemorate were the private community of the family, and the larger community of Jews living in the same village, small town, city, or area prior to the Holocaust.

Commemorating the intimate community of the family was chiefly part and parcel of the testimonies, memoirs, and other forms of life-accounts of the survivors, whereas the memorialization of their annihilated pre-Holocaust Jewish communities took two distinct public forms, depending on where the survivors settled down after the end of the war. The choice of their major vehicle of commemoration—erection of "communal martyr memorial monuments," to use Kinga Frojimovics's term,[1] or the creation of *Yizkor* books—depended on whether the survivors returned to live in or near their former homes, or left the landscape of the Holocaust behind and opted for living in localities free from the actual memories of the Holocaust, typically in Israel, the United States, Canada, and South America.[2]

One of the very first acts of those survivors who returned to their former places of residence from concentration camps, forced labor, or hiding was to erect a martyr memorial monument, i.e. a symbolic grave for the members of their wiped-out community. In this setting, a sense of overwhelming absence was a given physical reality. The emptiness of the place made the absence inescapably present. Béla Zsolt's conclusion to his preface to an early and anomalous Yizkor book for the Jews of Nagyvárad clearly demonstrates this point. The leftist survivor writer asserted that he could never again visit his empty town with its empty cafés and the side of the River Körös devoid of children.[3] Those who started their lives anew somewhere else also created memorials. Producing Yizkor books,[4] which also became viewed as symbolic burial places, emerged as one of the most common commemorating activities in this new environment. A space, glaringly empty of their former communities, did not surround those survivors who left Europe. Therefore, they had to create that tangible void, i.e. the physical means to spatially bind the reality of the malicious absence crushing them. Appropriately for the immigrant experience, they incorporated a spatial sense of being rooted within a portable memorial monument—a book—by including photos, maps, drawings, and descriptions.

Kinga Frojimovics, in her groundbreaking article focusing on the Jewish communal martyr memorial monuments in the context of the modern-era history of Hungary's Jews, classifies Holocaust memorial monuments into two major categories. The first category includes communal memorial monuments erected in key settings of Jewish communal life (typically the synagogue or the cemetery) by local Jewish communities, to commemorate individual members as well as the community itself. The second category consists of official memorial monuments—which she calls "Holocaust monuments"— erected in places of prominence for the general public by national Jewish organizations, regional authorities, or the state to memorialize the Holocaust of the Jews of greater political and/or geopolitical unities. While official Holocaust monuments usually carry political messages addressed to and concerning the surrounding society, martyr memorial monuments reflect internal Jewish history.[5] That her analyses concerning the martyr memorial monuments are so readily applicable to Yizkor books highlights the similarities between the main functions of the two communal commemorative genres.

What emerges from Frojimovics's research as the most relevant point for this chapter is that she shows how the martyr memorial monuments are not complete in and of themselves. On the contrary, "rituals, memorial services, and [various] forms of personal and communal commemoration, [that have] crystallized around the martyr memorial monuments soon after the war" are integral parts of the monuments. After surveying the denominational publications, Frojimovics asserts that "within a few years after the Holocaust, the Jahrzeit ceremony that was held alongside the martyr memorial monuments became established and canonized."[6]

Viewed as complex works of art, constructed not only of physical objects (the monument itself and the items buried in them), but also of the list of names, and (ritual, testimonial, and historical) texts recited and/or created during the memorial services, communal memorial martyr monuments are strikingly similar to Yizkor books. The speeches and sermons delivered as part of the Jahrzeit ceremonies were often published in the denominational presses that had extensively covered such ceremonies throughout Hungary. Yizkor books are themselves works of art, in which the list of martyrs as well as photos, maps, and drawings of a locality are surrounded by the same kinds of texts as those delivered on the occasions of memorial services held beside martyr memorial monuments.

Instruments of commemoration are usually a primary means of ensuring some kind of continuity. In our case, however, both major vehicles of commemoration—communal martyr memorial monuments and Yizkor books—are emphatically discontinuous. Martyr memorial monuments consist of fragments of various natures—different materials such as stone, ashes mixed with earth, cakes of *R.I.F.* soap,[7] parchment, paper, and all sorts of visual and textual pieces of an artistic as well as documentary nature, etc.—resulting in a collage, or rather, assemblage. *Yizkor* books are also emphatically heterogeneous in their incorporation of both textual and visual material, constituting collages.

The martyr memorial monuments, by their assemblage nature, try to dispose of the strict boundary separating symbolic and real, as survivors were forced to create symbolic graves for their murdered loved ones and community, whose absence made up their reality in very concrete ways. Frojimovics depicts the typical early martyr memorial monuments (*Yad Vashems*) as combinations of a symbolic grave and a memorial wall inscribed with the names of the victims of the Holocaust. The objects buried in the monuments were typically pieces of *R.I.F.* soap or ashes from the crematoria of Ausch-witz alongside desecrated Torah scrolls.[8] The other way to lay the dead to rest in a symbolic manner was to bury scrolls or a memorial book bearing the names of the Holocaust martyrs of the community within the monument. The Jewish community of Tapolca, for example, buried a scroll,[9] whereas the Neolog Jewish community of Óbuda "raised a martyr memorial monument in the foyer of its synagogue in November, 1948, [which includes] a memorial book in the form of a codex [...]. The book, created by artist Ervin Abádi, contains the names of the approximately 1,500 victims of the Óbuda community."[10]

In addition to their heterogeneous use of materials, both forms of communal com-memoration (martyr memorial monuments and *Yizkor* books) include a plethora of individual as well as collective voices. Multilingualism further dispels any feeling of unity. As they include periodical (that is, not continuous) acts of remembering—the memorial services of a community or *Landsleit*—both the *Yizkor* books and the com-munal martyr memorial monuments display additional facets of structural discontinuity. By these structural paradoxes of continuity and discontinuity, these memorials seem to embody the major paradox governing the memory of the Holocaust together with its memorialization, which the survivor Rebe Israel Spira, the Rabbi of Bluzhov, formulated as a piece of commentary, and which Yaffa Eliach chose to be the motto of her *Hasidic Tales of the Holocaust*:

> When Pharaoh restored the chief butler to his position as foretold by Joseph in his interpretation of the butler's dream, he forgot Joseph. "Yet did not the chief butler remember Joseph, but forgot him" (Gen. 40:23). Why does the Bible use this repetitive language? It is obvious that if the butler forgot Joseph, he did not remember him. Yet, both verbs are used, remembering and forgetting. "The Bible in using this language, is teaching us a very important lesson," said the rabbi of Bluzhov, Rabbi Israel Spira, to his Hasidim. *"There are events of such overbearing magnitude that one ought not to remember them all the time, but one must not forget them either. Such an event is the Holocaust."*[11]

Both the choric and collage/assemblage nature of the communal memorials—in sharp contrast to the testimonies, memoirs, and other forms of life-writings—radically disrupt the rules of narration, one of the basic hermeneutic devices of our civilization. Narration endows the events with meaning, that is to say, it introduces a structure, which the events "do not possess as mere sequence." In writing history proper or during testifying, facts are given meaning through the construction of narratives, a process that Hayden

White calls "emplotment."[12] In order to make sense to us, facts are organized into familiar, pre-existing narrative structures. The facts themselves, however, do not dictate the narrative genre into which they can be encoded.

The *Yizkor* book genre concerning its level of narrative fullness—or narrativity, to use Hayden White's term—differs greatly from fully narrativized historical monographs or the main forms of individual survivor life accounts, such as testimonies, memoirs or autobiographies. Individual accounts attain narrative fullness. They are stories "with central subjects, proper beginnings, middles, and ends, and a coherence that permits us to see 'the end' in every beginning."[13] By contrast, *Yizkor* books, as communal memorial projects, lack narrative fullness; they do not tell one proper story, even if certain individuals, the editors for example, strive to do exactly that. The list of the names of the martyrs is the least narrativized part of communal memorials—both *Yizkor* books and martyr memorial monuments—as lists lack narrative coherence. However, lists imply many stories. An enormous amount of individual stories are implied, for example, by the fact that the names that follow one another in alphabetical order organize themselves into families.

The under-narrativized nature of the *Yizkor* book genre was noted and criticized by many. As Jonathan Boyarin and Jack Kugelmass show in their theoretical introduction to *From A Ruined Garden: The Memorial Books of Polish Jewry*, "some historians are wary of memorial books" partly because they are not written "as professional historical monographs." They quote historian Jacob Szacki (Shatzky)'s "scathing remarks concerning the Ostrog (Ostre) *Yizkor* book: 'Perhaps all of the material sent in should have been handed over to a professional who could rework them into his narrative and give credit to everyone who sent in materials. This would result in the book's being of smaller proportions, more easily read and remembered. The way they are assembled now, they are for the most part gravestones, not books.'"[14]

The most extreme manifestation of narrative disruption can be seen in bilingually published *Yizkor* books, when one of the languages is either Hebrew or Yiddish and the other is a language that uses left-to-right script. In these books, we can see that the martyr list occupies at once two structurally key places of the book, which coincide with defining places of narratives as well—the end and the center. The martyr list, which, being a list, is the furthest from being a narrative, ends both parts of the book written in two languages, and by doing so, it physically makes up the center of the volume.

In the cases of these publications, the structure of the *Yizkor* books emphatically displays, in a very clear manner, that traditional narrative forms are not adequate to communal forms of witnessing such an enormous calamity. This is all the more salient as survivor testimonies show that the major hermeneutic structures of storytelling had to continue to be observed in testimonies and memoirs. They could not be bypassed during individual instances of witnessing; yet they do not dominate communal forms.

The problematization of narrative meaning-making concerning the Holocaust as a historical event by its survivors comes to the fore as survivor writers, notably Imre Kertész and Eli Wiesel, insistently experiment with the hermeneutic nature of narration and try to invent narrative forms that do not automatically interpret the realities conveyed through them. Kertész, for instance, strives, in a number of his works, to find a novel form that would keep the narrative, a strong hermeneutic device, from providing unequivocal explanations, from creating the illusion that the events narrated can be fully explained.[15] In addition to his special way of simultaneously employing and calling into question the explanatory powers of the most conventional form of chronological narration used in *Fatelessness*, both the topic of the lost novel in his *Liquidation* and the compulsive surfeit of explanations that make up *Kaddish for an Unborn Child* undermine the illusion of conveying universal and unequivocal explanations.[16] The family novel genre, one of the most popular genres of Holocaust literature, through its transformation by the traumatic topic on which it focuses, also registers the same problem-complex.[17]

It is not by chance that Szacki, who takes issue with the non-narrative, non-monographic nature of *Yizkor* books, complains especially bitterly about a story genre—about "the inclusion of an article on the Chelm-story genre in a book for Chelm." The historian complains that such stories "reveal nothing new, and are generally inappropriate in a book about the Holocaust, because the Chelm-story was not destroyed, and the genre actually has only a slim connection to the city of Chelm."[18] Chelm-stories are humorous tales and, in my opinion, the *Yizkor* books register precisely the fact that the genre of "good stories" has indeed been destroyed, since the possibility of any kind of continuation became nearly or entirely unattainable. The transmission of funny–wise "good stories" concerning European Jewry became deeply problematic. This is the reason why Eli Wiesel, in his memoir-novel *Night*, problematizes narrativity and storytelling through the image of an unfinished story that becomes the symbol for, and the prelude to, the deportation of the Jews of his hometown, Sighet:

> The general opinion was that we were going to remain in the ghetto until the end of the war, until the arrival of the Red army. Then everything would be as before. It was neither German nor Jew who ruled the ghetto—it was illusion.
>
> On the Saturday before Pentecost, in the spring sunshine, people strolled, carefree and unheeding, through the swarming streets. They chatted happily. The children played games on the pavements. With some of my schoolmates, I sat in the Ezra Malik gardens, studying a treatise on the Talmud. Night fell. There were twenty people gathered in our back yard. My father was telling them anecdotes and expounding his own views on the situation. He was a good story teller. Suddenly the gate opened and Stern—a former tradesman who had become a policeman—came in and took my father aside. Despite the gathering dusk, I saw my father turn pale.
>
> "What's the matter?" we all asked him.
>
> "I don't know. I've been summoned to an extraordinary meeting of the council. Something must have happened."
>
> The good story he had been in the middle of telling us was to remain unfinished.[19]

According to Wiesel, then, stories and storytelling belong to the pre-deportation, pre-Holocaust era. They belong to the times ruled by illusion. The Holocaust made storytelling and well-made stories impossible. This notion is what the *Yizkor* book genre registers by throwing open the anachronistic structure of narrative unity.

I do not suggest that underlying hermeneutic narratives do not emerge in the context of creating communal memorials. They do, and I am giving four examples of the most widespread narratives. A common meaning-making narrative that substantiates the Zionist position is exemplified by the concluding words of Ödön Groszmann, the president of the emigrants from Nagyvárad (today Oradea Mare, Romania), to the *Yizkor* book of the town, which identify the fundamental message of the historical trauma of the Holocaust to be the following: "It is forbidden for us to start walking again on the roads of the Galut. That is Auschwitz's great lesson."[20] Another frequent overriding narrative endows the Holocaust with meaning through the celebration of Jewish survival and renewal. This kind of narrative informs, for instance, one of the *Yizkor* books of Suwalk.

> This *Yizkor* book is written then, both as a memorial to our dead and as a symbol of our rebirth. It is written to show the world the spirit of the Jew. As important as mere personal survival is to each and every one of us, the survival of an idea, of a faith, of a religion, of the right to be different is more important than even life itself.
>
> Each time we take this Book in hand we reconfirm our faith that we as Jews can not be obliterated from the faith of this earth. For, no matter how many of us are gassed, or how many of us are cremated, so long as one of us survives, or so long as one of our books remains or one of our ideas endures, we survive and our culture, our tradition, our heritage is transmitted, as if by a lit candle, from one generation to the next.
>
> And so, the story of Suwalk is written to acquaint the living with the tragic events of the past. It is written so that we may take pride in our heritage, courage in our actions, and reinforce our faith in our ultimate survival and rebirth.[21]

Both Arye Moskovits in his introduction to the *Yizkor* book of Derecske and Sámuel Löwinger in his introduction to the *Yizkor* book of Debrecen characteristically emphasize that, besides their memorial book function, the *Yizkor* books need to convey clear messages to posterity. Moskovits's typical Orthodox message is that: "Because remembering them [the Holocaust martyrs] is our holy heritage, it [their memory] is an everlasting beacon guiding us and our children's children. They, who bequeathed us the True Torah, may purify us and set us an example."[22] By contrast, Löwinger's message can be understood in the contemporary historical context: he wants to ensure that future generations of Israelis would also be proud of their Galut heritage.[23] By stating a clear aim, editors and contributors try to impose a comprehensible narrative framework on the memorial volume.

After the above enumeration of typical hermeneutic narratives, it becomes all the more obvious how these narratives all fail to structure the entire works, and how the traumatic, mourning-stricken nature of these commemorative projects manifests itself in unruly, fragmented multiplicity. Communal Holocaust memorials, especially *Yizkor* books, are thus not dominated by unequivocal interpretative narratives. On the contrary, by their structure and content they problematize the possibility as well as the usefulness of such narratives. In addition, they also question with utmost anxiety one of the prerequisites of such narratives—the notion of continuity. Therefore, in comparison with the overwhelming disruption of dominant unequivocal interpretive narratives, which is one of the defining generic characteristics of communal memorials, the above-mentioned eschatological storylines, even when they reflect the thoughts of the editors, remain voiced more on the individual level (that is, not as a representative of the collective), and merely as part of an emphatically little-narrativized work.

One of the major problems of registering the enormity of the historical trauma of the Holocaust by struggling with the hermeneutic nature of narratives is that telling stories is a culturally valued form of transmitting tradition. The words of Boyarin and Kugelmass demonstrate clearly how privileged a form story-telling is: "[stories] could now be passed on from generation to generation and from land to land. Narrative not only confirms human existence; it is the core of human culture."[24] Therefore the problem pertaining to Holocaust witnessing narratives (that is, the assigning of meaning) became intertwined with another traumatic anxiety of the survivors, namely with the difficulty of ensuring continuity—physical and mental—between the generations.

Survivors feared that they would not be able to engender any kind of cultural–mental continuity, even if physically they would have children. Nancy J. Chodorow, advancing Erik Erikson's research, calls attention to the fact that one of the most painful aspects of the trauma of Holocaust survivors was that they were "losing their place in historical and generational continuity,"[25] even though participation in the continuity of the generations, mentally and/or physically, is a basic human need. Chájjim Franck's words in the introduction to the *Yizkor* book of Margitta in Transylvania poignantly demonstrate this. Franck was the driving force behind the creation of the book, undertaking its writing and financing its publication. He wrote: "I want our children to read [this book] and to learn from its letters about their grandparents, who had been wrenched away from our lives by violent deaths."[26] To create some kind of generational continuity even if it seems impossible, and to hold it up as a value that can undo at least some aspects of the utter and irrevocable destruction, explains why Holocaust survivors, both individually and communally, kept struggling and experimenting with various ways to accomplish transmission of information between the generations. Survivors aim at creating a continuity that they perceive as mostly impossible, and by this struggle, they claim their place along the generational continuity. They succeeded to create in the end an especially large volume of works that problematizes continuity and the narrative as the one culturally preferred vehicle. At the same time, however, by creating a plethora of works, they made possible some kind of continuation of knowledge and experience only if the next generations rise to the challenge of developing the hermeneutic tools necessary to enable them to receive the transmitted information.

Paradoxically, *Yizkor* books have developed into a special multi-voiced, multilingual, collage/assemblage-natured, emphatically little-narrativized genre, even though they report many stories. However, as Boyarin and Kugelmass so astutely observe, the overwhelming majority of the stories are illustrative ones,[27] and their main purpose is not to provide explanations, but effectively to commit their protagonists or the setting to memory. To demonstrate how crucial the shift towards illustrative narratives is in *Yizkor* books, Boyarin and Kugelmass quote a story from one of the first modern memorial books written "in response to the Ukrainian pogroms between the end of World War I and the early 1920s," *Khurbn Proskurov* (1924). "The Story [which they quote] points out the rebbe's almost unnatural insight into his followers. The point of retelling it in the memorial book, however, is to provide a 'narrative vessel' to fix the rebbe's memory in the reader's mind [to employ] narratives as means of observing and establishing living memory."[28] Thus also by elevating a less important function of the narrative—its illustrative role as mnemotechnic; and simultaneously downplaying a major one—its automatic meaning-making/hermeneutic function, *Yizkor* books call attention to the fact that the enormity of the historical trauma of the Holocaust brings into question one of our most valued means of cultural transmission and meaning-making alongside the notion and possibility of continuity itself.

Because of their all-inclusive nature, communal memorials also contain pieces that follow different sets of rules. This phenomenon in itself effectively dispels any notion of classical unity. The Debrecen *Yizkor* book, for example, displays photos of a martyr memorial monument founded in 1958 and unveiled in 1959, together with a picture at the foundation of the monument, in which Dr Rabbi István Végházi is praying.[29] The inclusion of a martyr memorial monument together with the documentation of memorial sermons show that, even though both forms of commemoration have the same aim, as well as structural position in the life of the survivor communities, they are also used as material for one another in order to document the most important aspects of communal life.

The fundamental difference between individual and communal witnessing pertaining to the central role of meaning-making through narratives comes to the fore when individual testimonies are included in the collective projects. They are either delivered in *Jahrzeit* ceremonies or constitute parts of *Yizkor* books. Editors of *Yizkor* books usually collect survivor testimonies to include them in the memorial volume. *Emlékkönyv Nagybánya, Nagysomkút, Felsőbánya, Kápolnokmonostor és környéke zsidóságának tragédiájáról* [*The Yizkor Book of the Tragedy of the Jews of Nagybánya, Nagysomkút, Felsőbánya, Kápolnokmonostor and their Vicinity*] is a case in point. Ichak Joszéf Kohén, the editor of the book, writes in his foreword that "We were lucky, because about 80 people took the trouble to take down their personal stories, ordeals, and experiences."[30] Kohén informs us in the foreword to the testimony section, entitled "Memories from the Shoah," that the published testimonies are lightly edited; mostly there are omissions in order to avoid much repetition, which is the consequence of the testimonies being published together. However, the editors sent the original, unedited testimonies to the Yad Vashem Archives.[31] One of the longest and least-edited testimony in the volume is that of Zvi Meron (Moskovits), who himself was a member of the editorial board.[32]

The juxtaposition of the genres of individual and communal witnessing (in this case, the juxtaposition of testimonies with *Yizkor* books) brings up a question of special interest: the role of survivors in checking one another's memories and thus validating survivor testimonies in important ways. Boyarin and Kugelmass also emphasize that "editors or at least [the] intended audience [of *Yizkor* books] had their own memories of the person or event being described."[33] In the case of the above-mentioned Nagybánya *Yizkor* book, precisely the left out "repetitions," mentioned by the editor, check and validate the individual testimonies. In this respect, *Yizkor* books come close to special Holocaust testimony-collection projects devised and carried out by individuals engaged in documenting the history of the Holocaust of their own regions. One of the most famous examples of such a project is that carried out by Leib Koniuchowsky, who collected the testimonies of Jewish survivors from Lithuania.[34]

The testimonies that Koniuchowsky took down, and particularly his group testimonies, reveal that, as a collector of protocols, he was also involved in stimulating the witnesses' memories. He was especially effective in drawing upon the communal feelings of witnesses of the same region, which both stimulated their memories and opened up the possibility of checking facts and conditions. Whenever Koniuchowsky took individual or group testimonies, he made the informants sign every page. Moreover, in cases of group testimonies, he held an official group meeting during which he read aloud the end product to the witnesses to ensure the document's accuracy.[35] Koniuchowsky's methods, and their similarities to the creation of the testimony sections of *Yizkor* books and collective memorial projects in general, demonstrate the complex relationship between individual and communal ways of remembering, bearing witness, and commemorating.

David Roskies, as well as Boyarin and Kugelmass, emphasize the special future-oriented functions of communal memorial projects, resulting in community building (and/or destruction[36]). The researchers enumerate the various circles of people who could be drawn into the community of creating memorials, such as Jews who emigrated before the Holocaust. As a ghost conveying our longing for lost ways of meaning-making, the notion of creating narratives concerning the creation of community and continuity looms large in the vocabulary of the scholars. Roskies said: "The DNA of Jewish memory is not the family; it is the institution, the *landsmanschaft*. [...] The fact that we can get together and reconstitute ourselves as a community ensures that our story will live on for many generations to come."[37] Boyarin and Kugelmass go even further by employing Walter Benjamin's notion of the story-telling circle as their main metaphor for community creation through researching *Yizkor* books: "We who were not born in Eastern Europe now try to include ourselves in the story telling round. We arrive very late. It is quite dark already; the study house is almost deserted. A book lies on the table, written in a language few of us can read. We open the book [...]"[38]

Transmitting knowledge about the Holocaust and the annihilated pre-Holocaust communities—living up to their own expectation of bearing witness and taking their role in a generational continuity—was by no means perceived as a real possibility by the majority of the survivors. However, they stubbornly, sometimes single-mindedly, continued to try and create commemorative works and render witness accounts pertaining to both the Holocaust and their wiped-out communities. This resulted in the production of a vast resource for later generations. By being engaged in witnessing, struggling incessantly with conceptions of individual and communal loss, survivors made it possible for later generations to assign personal experiences to the enormity of the historical trauma of the Holocaust. This point can be clearly demonstrated by the history of Holocaust museums and exhibitions. There is a drastic change in the concept of the museums that is connected to a basic change in their primary audience.

In earlier times, purely chronological rendering of historical facts and numbers, together with a few reminder objects, were sufficient, since the survivors themselves knew the personal stories of the victims. The Holocaust was personal for them, overwhelmingly so, and they had mourned the victims as individuals. Nowadays, all of the major museums and exhibitions emphatically trace and present personal stories of individuals, families, and communities, offering a personal entry into the unimaginable realities of the Holocaust for their audiences. This conceptual change was necessary as the majority of the members of the audience who inherited, and thus have to face, the Holocaust as a family, national, and/or universal human trauma, do not have immediate personal knowledge of the individual victims.

The conceptual change in museums incidentally parallels the processes of creating communal memorials. For the returning survivors who decided to start their life anew in or near the place from which the traumatic events of the Holocaust uprooted them, the actual place was meaningful and initially held for them the memory of the murdered majority of their communities. By contrast, those who moved away lacked even this one stable spatial point of reference to ensure continuity. Therefore, what was contained in the two major forms of communal memorial—martyr memorial monuments and *Yizkor* books—depended on the primary audience's current access to a special location. Similarly, the concept of Holocaust museums and exhibitions also depends upon the primary audience's access to personal memories of individual stories of victims.

The survivors' insistent rendering of testimonies, together with their commemorative efforts, made it possible for later generations to form links with the victims on a personal/individual human level, but paradoxically, even more so for the survivor-victims of the Holocaust themselves. Therefore it is now the role of the later generations to claim our place in the continuity of generations by actively receiving the transmitted information and to bear witness for the witnesses, despite the seemingly insurmountable difficulties in doing so. As Paul Celan asserts in his "Aschenglorie" ["Ashes-Glory"], "Niemand / zeugt für / den Zeugen" ["No one / bears witness for the / witness"].[39]

Since we have a wealth of special sources created by the survivors, it is our responsibility as researchers to devise methods that would enable us to employ the works of commemoration, testimonies, and life-writings at our disposal to their fullest as historical sources.

Notes

1 Kinga Frojimovics, "'Landmark-Stones are the Highway toward Martyrdom…': Holocaust Memorial Monuments in Hungary," *Studia Judaica*, vol. 14 (2006): 115.

2 The first *Yizkor* book that is connected to the Holocaust, the *Łódźer Yiskor Book*, was published in Yiddish in New York in 1943. Abraham Wein, one of the first researchers concerned with Holocaust *Yizkor* books, wrote about the drive of creating such memorials as follows: "Survivors and emigrants from the destroyed communities in all parts of the world met together with the purpose of attempting to perpetuate the memory of the past. They continued the age-old tradition of concluding an era by recording its history; this was done for the sake of preserving the cultural and national value of the past, as well as to bring home its lesson to future generations. This role, which had been performed in earlier periods by various chroniclers and scholars, was now an enterprise in which thousands from all classes and strata of the nation participated." Abraham Wein, "'Memorial Books' as a Source for Research into the History of Jewish Communities in Europe," *Yad Vashem Studies*, vol. 9 (1973): 255. The YIVO Institute in New York also emphasizes the same qualities: "Memorial books were compiled by ad hoc committees of survivors, as a way to commemorate their families and friends who perished in the Holocaust. The books were published privately, in limited quantities, and were intended for distribution among fellow survivors from the same town or region. These books were part of an ancient Jewish tradition to remember dead relatives on the anniversary of their death (*yortsayt*) as well as to mention their names during *Yizkor* services in the synagogue, during Yom Kippur and other major holidays." www.yivo.org/library/index.php?tid=46& aid = 254 (accessed 8 December 2009).

3 The medieval *Memorbücher* and Nathan Nata Hannover's *Yeven Metzulah* (in English: *The Abyss of Despair*) that was written following the Bogdan Chmielnicki-pogroms, are customarily identified as the antecedents of the Holocaust *Yizkor* books. Hannover's work contains not only the detailed description of the pogroms in a stylized form, but also the description of annihilated Jewish life. The first modern *Yizkor* books, such as *Khurbn Proskurov*, appeared in 1924 and were published following the pogroms in the Ukraine in the aftermath of World War I. See Jack Kugelmass and Jonathan Boyarin, eds, *From A Ruined Garden: The Memorial Books of Polish Jewry* (Bloomington, Indiana: Indiana University Press, 1998), 18. Concerning the characteristics of *Yizkor* books published after 1948, after the proclamation of the State of Israel, published by Israeli *Landsmanschaften*, see Judith Tydor Baumel, "'In Everlasting Memory': Individual and Communal Holocaust Commemoration in Israel," in *The Shaping of Israeli Identity: Myth, Memory and Trauma,* eds Robert Wistrich and David Ohana (London: Frank Cass, 1995), 150–54.

4 Béla Zsolt's preface to Béla Katona's *Várad a viharban* (Nagyvárad, Teala Kórháztámogató Egyesület, 1946), 5.

5 Frojimovics, "Landmark-Stones."

6 To reveal the symbol-system of these memorial days, Frojimovics describes one such occasion, "the memorial day observed in Debrecen in 1950 by the only *Statusquo Ante* Jewish community remaining in post-war Hungary." See Frojimovics, "Landmark-Stones."

7 According to a widespread myth, the Germans used the body fat of their burned Jewish victims to make soap. This is a misinformation which is, however, easily believable in a world where the Nazis had made use of the hair of their victims, for example. The stamp R.I.F. on the soap that Germans commonly used during the war, which people misinterpreted, actually signified "Reichs-Industrie-Fett." See Henry Huttenbach, "The Myth of Nazi Human Soap," *The Genocide Forum,* vol. 1, no. 6 (1994).

8 Frojimovics describes in detail the communal martyr memorial monuments in Szeged and Szolnok: "In Szeged, for example, on the 18th of June, 1946, two coffins were placed as foundation-stones of the martyr memorial monument erected in the Jewish cemetery. One coffin contained pieces of R.I.F. soap and the other, desecrated Torah scrolls." Besides ashes and bones, fragments of Torah scrolls desecrated during the time of the deportations were also buried in the Szolnok monument, which was unveiled on 30 October 1949. See a description of the inauguration ceremony of the Szolnok martyr memorial monument in "A szolnoki mártírok jelképes emléksírkövének felavatása," *Új Élet, 1949. november 24,* 6.

9 See a description of the inauguration ceremony of the Tapolca martyr memorial monument in "A tapolcai mártírok emlékművének leleplezése," *Új Élet, 1947. augusztus 14,* 13.

10 See a description of the inauguration ceremony of the Óbuda martyr memorial monument in "Mártíremlékműavatás Óbudán," *Új Élet, 1948. november 18,* 4.

11 Motto of Yaffa Eliach's *Hasidic Tales of the Holocaust* (New York: Oxford University Press, 1982).

12 Hayden White defines "emplotment," the operation by which we turn lists of events into stories, as "the encodation of the facts contained in the chronicle as components of specific *kinds* of plot structures"; Hayden White, "The Historical Text as Literary Artifact," in *Tropics of Discourse: Essays in Cultural Criticism,* Hayden White (Baltimore, Maryland: Johns Hopkins University Press, 1985), 83. Emplotment is a central notion for White, as we can see from his chapters, "Interpretation in History," in *Tropics of Discourse,* 51–80, and "Historical Emplotment and the Problem of Truth in Historical Representation," in *Figural Realism: Studies in the Mimesis Effect,* Hayden White (Baltimore, Maryland: Johns Hopkins University Press, 1999), 27–42. In the latter essay he addresses the Holocaust.

13 Hayden White, "The Value of Narrativity in the Representation of Reality," in *The Content of the Form: Narrative Discourse and Historical Representation,* Hayden White (Baltimore, Maryland: Johns Hopkins University Press, 1987), 24.

14 Jonathan Boyarin and Jack Kugelmass quote it from Jacob Szacki (Shatzky), "Yizkor Bicher," *YIVO Bleter,* vol. 39 (1955): 340, 345, 351, and in their "Introduction" to Kugelmass and Boyarin, *From A Ruined Garden,* 24–25.

15 In his study "Narratívátlanság," Dávid Kaposi highlights the phenomenon in *Fatelessness* of "resisting narratives" well known from Holocaust witness accounts, and analyzes the novel according to this phenomenon. See Dávid Kaposi, "Narratívátlanság," in *Az értelmezés szükségessége: Tanulmányok Kertész Imréről,* eds Tamás Scheibner and Zoltán Gábor Szűcs (Budapest: L'Harmattan, 2002), 15–51.

16 Gábor Schein in his "Összekötni az összeköthetetlent" defines *Kaddish for an Unborn Child* as "an explanation rendered unfinishable, a text of an inner debate determining the entire poetics of the narrative." Gábor Schein, "Összekötni az összeköthetetlent," 112; Rita Horváth, "Family Novels and 'Anti-Family Novels' in Hungarian Holocaust Literature," in *The Holocaust in Hungary: A European Perspective,* ed. Judit Molnár (Budapest: Balassi Kiadó, 2005), 687–700.

17 See my article: "A Changing Genre: Jewish Hungarian Family Novels After the Shoah," *Yad Vashem Studies,* vol. 32 (2004): 209–26, reprinted in *The Treatment of the Holocaust in Hungary and Romania During the Post-Communist Era,* ed. Randolph L. Braham (New York: Columbia University Press, 2004), 201–15.

18 Kugelmass and Boyarin, *From A Ruined Garden,* 25.

19 Eli Wiesel, *Night,* in *The Night Trilogy* (New York: Hill and Wang, 1987), 21–22.

20 Dezső Schön *et al.,* eds, *A tegnap városa: A nagyváradi zsidóság emlékkönyve* (Tel Aviv: Nagyváradról Elszármazottak Egyesülete Izraelben, 1981), 446.

21 Aaron Seligson, "Foreword," in *Yizkor-book Suwalk and the Vicinity: Baklerowe, Wizshan, Yelinewe, Saini, Punsk, Psherosle, Filipowe, Krasnopole, Ratzk,* ed. Berl Kahan (New York, 1961), 823–24.

22 "Mert a rájuk való emlékezés szent örökségünk, örök útmutatónk nekünk és gyermekeink gyermekeinek. Megtisztulásul és például legyenek azok, akik ránk hagyták az Igaz Tórát." See Arye Moskovits, *Derecske és vidéke zsidósága* (Tel Aviv: A Derecskei Gyülekezet Maradéka, 1984), 6.

23 Moshe Elijáhu Gonda, *A debreceni zsidók száz éve. A mártirhalált halt debreceni és környék-beli zsidók emlékére* (Tel Aviv: A Debreceni Zsidók Emlékbizottsága, n. d. (after 1966), 7. Kinga Frojimovics's study analyzes in depth the conceptual views of *Yizkor* books concerning Hungary in the historical context of the different Jewish religious trends. See: "A 'doktor-rabbik' nagy nemzedéke Magyarországon: A neológ identitás kialakítása a történetíráson keresztül." ["The Great Generation of Rabbi-Historians in Hungary: Defining Identity Through Writing History."] in *Széfer Józséf,* ed. József Zsengellér (Budapest: Open Art, 2002), 221–39.

24 Kugelmass and Boyarin, *From A Ruined Garden,* 35.

25 Chodorow calls attention to what was especially the case for Holocaust survivors, namely "losing one's native language and country, as well as—especially relevant in the case of World War II—losing many family members and the very physical space of home and community." See Nancy J. Chodorow, "Born into a World at War: Listening for Affect and Personal Meaning," *American Imago,* vol. 59, no. 3 (2002): 300.

26 "Azt akarom, hogy gyermekeink olvassák és ismerjék meg a betűkből, kiket kiragadott életükből az erőszakos halál, nagyszüleiket," in *Emlékkönyv: Margitta és vidéke zsidóságának sorsa,* ed. Kleinmann, Áháron (Jerusalem: Chájjim Franck, 1979), 1–2.

27 Social linguist Deborah Schiffrin distinguished and analyzed illustrative narratives and differentiated them from explanatory and performative narratives in oral history interviews based on "function, location, and structure." See Deborah Schiffrin, "Mother/Daughter Discourse in a Holocaust Oral History: 'Because Then You Admit That You Are Guilty,'" *Narrative Inquiry,* vol. 10, no. 1 (2000): 8–9.

28 Kugelmass and Boyarin, *From A Ruined Garden,* 19.

29 Gonda, *A debreceni zsidók száz éve,* 291–93.

30 Ichak Joszéf Kohén, ed., *Emlékkönyv Nagybánya, Nagysomkút, Felsőbánya, Kápolnokmonostor és környéke zsidóságának tragédiájáról* (Tel-Aviv: Irgun Jocze Baia Mare (Nagybánya) b'Israel, 1996), 6.

31 Kohén, *Emlékkönyv Nagybánya,* 163.

32 Kohén, *Emlékkönyv Nagybánya,* 225–53.

33 Kugelmass and Boyarin, *From A Ruined Garden,* 40.

34 The Koniuchowsky Collection is in the Yad Vashem Archives: YVA O.71.

35 See, for example, Koniuchowsky's Special Meeting held on 11 July 1948 in Feldafing with survivors of the work camps at Heidekrug. YVA O.71/164/5.

36 Boyarin and Kugelmass show how emerging and re-emerging ideological, political, and social problems oftentimes led to the destruction of the creative community, such as the case of a *Yizkor* book, which "was published in 1952, and shortly afterward the [Lublin] *landsmanshaft* split along political lines." See Kugelmass and Boyarin, *From A Ruined Garden,* 24.

37 David Roskies, "Forging the Link: The Iconography of the Felshtin Yizkor Book," 2, www.felshtin.org/yizkor/forgingthelink.pdf (accessed 15 January 2010).

38 Kugelmass and Boyarin, *From A Ruined Garden,* 37.

39 Paul Celan, *Selected Poems and Prose of Paul Celan,* trans. John Felstiner (New York: W.W. Norton, 2001), 260–61.

41

"THE WAR BEGAN FOR ME AFTER THE WAR"

Jewish children in Poland, 1945–49

Joanna B. Michlic

Introduction

In the Spring 1944 issue of the *American OSE Review*, Dr G. Bychowski, a Polish-Jewish psychiatrist, contemplated the potential range of mental disorders which Jewish and non-Jewish child survivors from Nazi-occupied Europe might suffer acutely from as a result of their traumatic wartime experiences.[1] Before he had fled Poland for the United States in 1941, first-hand medical contact with Jewish children in Warsaw had taught him that "fear, loneliness, isolation, loss of parents and all the various traumatic shocks to which children had been exposed during the war and Nazi occupation"[2] could lead to traumatic neurosis, anxiety, hysteria, and acute psychoneurotic symptoms. Regarding the potential rehabilitation of such child survivors, Bychowski attached great value to re-education, which he understood as a healing process where the children would have the opportunity to forget about hunger, fear, and hatred, while simultaneously regaining a "sense of being human, of being real citizens of their liberated countries and of a liberated Europe."[3] Rehabilitation of child and adult wartime victims had begun immediately after the end of the war, but had proved to be a challenging process requiring time, skills, effort, and funds.

For Jewish child survivors in Poland and other formerly Nazi-occupied countries, the early postwar period was still very much a turbulent era full of a magnitude of messy and confusing events, which were yet to determine the future of these children and how they were to develop, both as individuals and as members of national and cultural communities. It was at this time that many children first realized and reflected upon just how badly and deeply they had been physically neglected and emotionally scarred by the war. Many were devastated by a sense of extreme loneliness, having just learned of the physical elimination of their immediate and extended families, and the consequent realization that no familiar and loved adults would be there for them. Others, who had forgotten about their biological families during the war or could not remember them because of their very young age, had to come to terms with the fact that what had appeared to them as a solid, familial life with wartime rescuers was in reality a fragile, temporary arrangement, psychologically and socially complicated.[4] That some rescuers to whom they had become emotionally attached, thinking of them as parents, were not willing or able to support them emotionally and materially after the war, while other rescuers had kept them for purely instrumental reasons or for profit.

Furthermore, some Jewish children adopted by Jewish couples immediately after the war, either relatives or strangers, felt an acute sense of estrangement in their newly reconstituted families. And, in some cases, these same children were neglected or abused, or even returned by their adoptive parents to the Jewish children's homes and Jewish organizations. Many child survivors also experienced the torment of being objects of intense battles between former wartime rescuers and the surviving parents or other relatives or members of Jewish organizations. Therefore the sense of fear, anxiety, and uncertainty, rather than disappearing after the war, persisted and played a major part in such children's lives. As a result, some of them later, as adults, were to reflect on the early postwar period as "a time when the war for them had just begun."[5] This article aims to show the centrality of the early postwar period in any assessment of the short- and long-term impact of the war and Holocaust on child survivors. I aim to delineate a synthetic picture of how the children in Poland perceived their wartime and contemporaneous existence, and what decisions and actions they took, and how they reacted towards the world of adults.

My main arguments are as follows: First, that in spite of a multitude of individual children's wartime biographies, it is possible to detect certain clear patterns and commonalities in the children's micro-universes of wartime experience and interaction with the adult world, whereby one can conjure up a history of a generation or generations of children and youth. Second, regarding the agency of the children, many cases point to children as appendages and recipients of adult expectations, values, judgments, and decisions. This is particularly transparent in children of 11 years old or less. Cases of older children of 11 years and beyond reveal that many of them acted as autonomous beings, attempting and succeeding in making conscious life decisions, and attest to their resourcefulness under the testing conditions of war and its aftermath. However, all the children's cases attest to their immense vulnerability in the adult world. This, of course, is not unique to Jewish children, but it highlights aspects of their tragedy shared by non-Jewish child victims of traumatic episodes.

Third, cases of children cut off during the war years from the Jewish world in which they had grown up, reveal that their social identities in the early postwar period were fragile, fluid, and exposed to many shifts. These children exhibited what I call "affiliation without affiliation," as a result of having experienced two massive ruptures within family and local community under the conditions of the war and genocide. The initial primary rupture, violent and traumatic, was characterized by the loss of, and separation from, their biological families and local communities as a result of Nazi policies of extermination. It subsequently resulted in the children's transfers into a Christian Polish environment with a different cultural code, characterized to a large degree by intense anti-Jewish stereotypes. The second traumatic rupture occurred in the immediate postwar years, when the children were confronted with the news of being Jewish and consequently having to shed their acquired wartime Christian Polish identity and leave behind stable and loving family lives. Such cases suggest that children possess personality prior to developing a solid sense of social identity; that social identity is first acquired through a steady process of socialization within the family unit. And that once a brutal rupture takes place within the biological family, as in the case of Polish Jews under the conditions of war and genocide, and the surviving children are exposed to, and live in, ethnically and culturally different family unities, they easily lose the social identity acquired in their original family. Thus any return to the original ethnic and cultural identity becomes a painful and gradual process, marked by confusion, flux, hesitation, and many fears. Furthermore, it is characterized by the dynamic process of negotiations and renegotiations of one's identity. This development was manifested not only among Jewish children in Poland, but also among Jewish children from other Nazi-occupied countries who were cut off from their families and communities during the war.[6]

In this chapter, I focus mainly on Polish-Jewish children who lived on the Aryan side in Nazi-occupied Poland, passing as Christian Polish children, and those who were hidden in individual Catholic homes, state orphanages, Catholic convents, and monasteries due to their obviously Jewish appearance. The children in this study were born in 1929 and beyond. The children constituted a large cohort among the 5,000 Jewish children registered by the Central Committee of Polish Jews in the summer of 1945.[7] This figure of 5,000 Jewish child survivors was not final, as it did not include all the young survivors from Nazi-occupied Poland, nor those Polish-Jewish children who, along with their families, had survived the war in the Soviet Union.[8] Nonetheless, it clearly indicated the sheer destruction of Jewish children and youth. On the eve of World War II, Polish Jewry was considered a youthful community, and most scholars evaluate that in 1939, the number of children aged 15 years or younger was several hundred thousand.[9]

The world through the eyes of children: self-perceptions and interpretations of loss of childhood

Jewish children who were delivered, or who found their way of their own accord, to various Jewish organizations and children's homes that began to mushroom in Poland in 1945[10] were instantly forced to confront the heavy burden of matters concerning their health, identity, family, and the future. Older children and adolescents were acutely aware that their childhood had been shattered and that they had consequently been transformed into premature adults bearing little resemblance to children. Some poignantly articulated a sense of irreversible disconnection with their prewar childhood and family history Therefore they mourned their childhood, so abruptly and violently lost:

> We are young old women. Now I am an orphan.[11]
> The days of childhood for little Joasia were full of joy and carefree. At present I think about this little Joasia as though she were a totally strange girl, with whom I was connected in the past, but now I have no connection at all, except for fuzzy unclear memories.[12]

Children also had a profound sense of the loss of years of education, and felt starved of knowledge, culture, and learning. Therefore they immersed themselves in intellectual activities and pursuits, trying to make up for the lost years. They not only studied intensively at school, but also spent much of their free time learning individually and in groups, so they could be transferred quickly to a class level more appropriate for their age. The youngest ones, on the other hand, experienced, often for the first time, the pleasures of ordinary childhood, such as playing with toys and playing in nature with other children.

Discovery of physical and emotional problems

Emerging from hiding in cellars, chicken coops, and dug-outs, many children instantly realized that their eyesight and ability to walk were affected by the conditions in which they had been sheltered for three or four years. Though their eyes quickly accustomed to daily light, persistent difficulty in walking often indicated that the children were suffering from the medical condition called rickets (*rachitis, rozmiękczenie kości, softening of the bones*), and therefore they were in need of operations on one or both legs to walk properly again. Rickets was a disease common among former hidden Jewish children who, during the war, were confined to small, dim places without regular exposure to daily light, physical exercise, and movement. Lice then plagued almost all the children, and the hair on their heads had to be treated or shaved. Shaving hair was a particularly shameful and humiliating experience for older girls, while for those children who had survived death and concentration camps, this was a reminder of their most dreadful nightmarish experiences in the camps. Tuberculosis and lung infections were also common.

While most children took great joy in tasting various foods and devouring unknown or forgotten treats such as chocolate, other children found it hard to conform to the eastern European model of being the good child who eats everything that he or she is served. Prolonged hunger and severe malnutrition experienced during the war caused serious digestive problems for such children. Some also had to face a struggle with baldness, developed as a result of long-term malnutrition.

Characteristically, children were not always aware of the emotional problems and mental disorders that some of them had developed as a result of drastic experiences during the war, but the adults in charge of the children and their daily care could usually detect those children suffering from emotional or mental problems.[13] Children who exhibited such signs were usually either lethargic and socially detached, or unruly, violent, and aggressive towards other children and adults for no reason. The latter verbalized their anger, on some occasions during the interviews conducted with them in the children's homes:

> A lot of things I can tell, a lot of things I should not tell, and a lot of things I am ashamed to tell...Of a scant 3,000 Jews, there remain – in any case you will not believe me...And in what way was I saved – is not your business![14]

Nonetheless, children among themselves were able to grasp that some were more physically and emotionally damaged than others. They were capable of differentiating between the more devastating and the less challenging wartime experiences, and of conceiving a "hierarchy" of wartime experiences: "standard," "normal or boring," "horrible," and "the most horrible and embarrassing," including sexual abuse and rape over an extended period. Those who had experienced sexual abuse and rape would disclose and share such information only with their closest friends.

Some orphaned children and adolescents who had survived the war mostly due to their wits and determination did not trust any adults, non-Jewish and Jewish alike. Their wartime experiences taught them not to be dependent on any adults after the war, as one such child states:

> I did not believe people and I had to help myself alone in all cases. Today I also do not believe people. People say one thing and do something else. The family also does not bring me warmth.[15]

"Who am I?" Problems with individual and social identity

What is my name? Who are my family?

Another acute problem among children was confusion about one's date and place of birth. Children who were born in the 1930s, who had lived on the Aryan side during the war, passing as Aryans, and thereby had not been allowed to possess any documents or family photos that might reveal their true identity, forgot many aspects and details of their prewar life, such as date of birth, location, and even their original and family names. It was only long after the war that some of these children were fortunate enough to correct their dates of birth by accessing remaining documents or by garnering information from adult relatives, particularly those who lived in the west or Palestine/Israel. Such relatives were frequently the only family members who could offer to share family memorabilia with them, such as letters, postcards, and photos of parents and grandparents, and special family occasions including snapshots of their own birth.

In the early postwar period, orphaned children had their birth date estimated by Jewish educators at Jewish children's homes. The birth date estimate was usually based on an interview with the child that included questions such as which Jewish holidays the child might remember as being celebrated close to his/her birthday. However, it was impossible to estimate closely the birth dates and other important background details in the cases of the youngest children born in the late 1930s and early 1940s. For example, the so-called "luggage children" (*walizkowe dzieci*), thrown out from trains by their parents while en route to the death camps, were totally ignorant of their backgrounds and had to live with the names and birth dates given to them after the war.

Next to physical and emotional degradation, children were acutely aware of family losses. As a result, they experienced overpowering loneliness, articulated in this characteristic, common, and brief utterance: "I am now completely on my own in the world."[16] In Jewish children's homes, the total orphans often felt jealous of those children who were visited by parents, other relatives or former Christian rescuers, and felt pain that there was no-one to visit them, that no-one was writing to them. Some children's letters to their beloved former rescuers confirm that their authors had longed for a word from their previous guardians, not only because of a strong emotional attachment, but also because they did not want to stand out as different from other children in the Jewish children's home:

> Dear mummy,
>   I am happy. I am in the Children's Home in Zabrze, near Katowice. How does papa feel? Did he travel to Zakopane? What is Zbyszek doing? Does granny still work? Here I have one very good friend named Fredek. He, like myself, lived with one Polish lady. Fredek misses her a lot and I miss you a lot and therefore we are happy to be together. We will soon be leaving for France and I will write to you from there. I ask you to reply to my letters. All other children receive letters. And only I do not receive letters and am very sorry about that. I kiss all of you many times. Wiktor B.[17]

For those who had remained after the war with their Christian Polish former rescuers, and who were well looked after and loved by their rescuers, the appearance of a forgotten or an unknown relative meant a traumatic and frightening disruption of what they then regarded as a solid familial life and happy childhood. And it took them a while to adjust to the idea of leaving a familiar and stable environment of two or three years— or, in some cases—even five or six years. Reluctance to leave rescuers is evidenced in many children's early postwar testimonies, and is recalled in later videotaped oral histories and written memoirs. For example, the testimony of Jurek Adin of 3 April 1948, born on 22 June 1933 in Warsaw, speaks of his preference for staying in Poland in close contact with his private tutor from the pre-1939 period, the Polish woman who had saved his life on many occasions during the war. He preferred remaining with her to being reunited with unknown members of his Jewish family, who lived in the United States:

> I stayed there until 1945, when my tutor came and took me with her to Roszalin. Again I felt so good. My family had been found in the United States. They asked my tutor many times to place me in a Jewish orphanage. I am supposed to leave for the United States, but I would rather stay in Poland.[18]

A similar personal drama is revealed in the testimony of Barbara Blecher, who was born on 13 August 1931. Before the war, her family lived in Lviv (Lwów), where her father was a merchant. During the war, she lost her parents and three older sisters, but a couple, Mr and Mrs Bocian, saved her. In the aftermath of the liquidation of the Lviv ghetto, Mrs Bocian brought her to Warsaw, where she stayed with the Bocian family. During the Warsaw Uprising of 1 August 1944, she was separated from her foster family.[19] When the war came to an end, Barbara was reunited with the Bocian family. She wished to remain with them forever. However, she finally reconciled herself to the idea that she would depart for Palestine. As this report, based on an interview conducted with Barbara in the Jewish orphanage, attests:

> She did not wish to leave Mr and Mrs Bocian and enroll in the Jewish children's home. She was convinced that they were her family and she wished to remain with them. However, the relationship between her and Mrs. and Mr. Bocian did not work out in the end. They did not have the means to provide her with an education. Therefore, as of this time, the girl has decided to leave for Palestine.[20]

Problems with Jewishness: rejecting and regaining the Jewish identity

The youngest children, those who were born on the eve of or during the war, were the most shocked by the visits of strangers who came to claim them since, as far as they were aware, they had never had any other family, nor a different ethnic, social, and cultural background from that exhibited by their Christian Polish rescuers. Like some of the older children, they did not have any memories of their biological parents or of the main facets of Jewish identity. Thus they had to adjust not only to their new Jewish guardians, but also to the adoption of a Jewish identity that was a new and totally foreign terrain, terra incognita, and moreover that stood for and symbolized the "world of the murdered," as well as "the world of evil."

Some older children made a conscious decision not to "return to Jews" because of what they had personally witnessed during the war. They were aware of, and feared, the stigmatized Nazi image of the Jew as parasite and subhuman. The Jew, in their minds, was purely the object of Nazi extermination policies. They did not want to be associated with a people for whom others had only contempt and hatred. In some cases, these emotions persisted for a long time, and played a major part in making choices of friends and loved ones:

> I was attracted to my colleagues from the Jewish dorms and at the same time repelled by them. When I heard them speaking Yiddish, I got goose pimples. I was unable to get used to it. I thought that somebody would come soon and put an end to 'it.' It seemed impossible that they could be so calm, that they should talk and laugh. I could not find a place for myself among them. I looked at them, and the people I liked the most were those who looked the least Jewish. Those who looked the most Jewish scared me. I ran as far away from them as I could.
>
> This also happened later. I would run away from Jews, then I'd come back to them. At times I thought I could be with some Jews, but then I really couldn't. I ran away and pretended I didn't have anything in common with them. Then I'd be drawn to them again, and I would come back. From the time I was a little child, I had to deny being Jewish, and this has left traces that did not allow me to think, see, or live normally.[21]

Among such children were some who continued to pass as Christian Poles after the war, and to pretend throughout their adult lives that they were someone else. Only in the 1990s and 2000s, as mature individuals, in the new political and social climate in Poland, did they feel the need to come out into the open and come to terms with their Jewishness—what they called the return to being oneself.[22] In the past two decades, a number of these children have gradually begun to speak out publicly for the first time about their Jewish identity. They became members of the Association of the Holocaust Children, established in 1992.

Yet, in the early postwar period, other children were sometimes encouraged to admit themselves to the Jewish children's homes by their Christian Polish friends or even by strangers who recognized them as Jews. This, for example, happened to Aviva Blumberg, who as an "Aryan-looking" teenager had decided to embark on what she considered a "normal life" among Christian Poles. However, her wartime girlfriend insisted that she should visit the newly re-established branch of a local Jewish Committee. That was the trajectory that led Aviva not only to accept her Jewish roots, but also to be reunited with her father.[23]

In the early postwar period, the Jewish children's homes and *kibbutzim* served as the main centers in which the children gradually became accustomed to and accepted their Jewishness. Jewish parents, themselves Holocaust survivors, who were in despair over their children's requests that the entire reunited family would adopt Christian Polish identity, turned to these homes to help their confused children become Jewish again. On the other hand, other parents encouraged their children to continue to play a "double-identity game" until the departure from Poland—to act as Christian Poles while in a Polish environment, but not to be afraid of being oneself among Jews. For example, Yehudit Kirzner, born 1935 in Wilno (Vilna, Vilnius), reports that her father, who was an administrator in the Jewish children's home in Helenówek near Łódź, instructed her to behave in such a way:

We play, sing and put on performances. I go to a Polish school, with a Polish name. My parents do not want anyone in our school [the fourth grade of the public Polish school No. 24 in Łódź] to know that I am Jewish, because I do not look Jewish. My father said that in the meantime, [it should] be that way, because when we will leave for Palestine, I will be able to be Jewish.[24]

Both younger and older children had to unlearn viewing Jewishness in a pejorative or purely negative sense. These children had acquired strong anti-Jewish feelings and attitudes as a result of consciously and unconsciously internalizing various anti-Jewish stereotypes disseminated in the Polish Christian environment in which they had grown up during the war. For example, nine-year-old Ludwik Jerzycki, in an interview conducted on 27 September 1947 in the Jewish Children's Home in Chorzów, recalled that he at first refused to enter the place:

I cried, I did not want to return to the Jews, because they were saying that the Jews kill children. I was so afraid. But I found out that things are different here. I feel so content. I am not being beaten up. I learn and go to school.[25]

'I do not want to be touched by a Jew,' 'Do not touch me with your Jewish hand,' 'I do not want to wear Jewish shoes,' and 'I do not want to return to Jews (powrót do Żydów)' were the characteristic common complaints such children voiced in front of their surviving parents, relatives, educators and other Jewish children in the children's homes.[26]

Strong anti-Jewish feelings were often intertwined with an ardent Catholic faith. In those cases, the children wore crosses, carried with them Catholic prayer books, prayed to the Virgin Mary and Jesus in the mornings and evenings, and yearned to go to church on Sunday mornings.

The Coordinated Commission for Jewish Children (Komisja koordynacyjna dla spraw dzieci żydowskich), based at Apartment 20, 17 Zawadzka Street in Łódź, reported many such cases, some of which persisted until the late 1940s.[27] These cases were viewed as difficult and requiring understanding and care, and as ones where children should not be prematurely forced to become Jews again. Such children needed both to overcome fears caused by the wartime stigmatization of Jews as people to be killed, and to free themselves from the mosaic of anti-Jewish prejudices acquired during the war. They also had to regain trust in adult strangers. In the interview with Marysia Szpigiel (real name Elżbieta Haberger), an inhabitant of the Jewish Children's Home at Narutowicza Street 18 in Łódź, the interviewer B. Mosiężnik summarizes Marysia's personal daily practices, which demonstrate how deeply mixed her identity was still in 1948:

Marysia Szpigiel still continues to say Catholic prayers. She prays in the evenings and listens to Catholic mass on Sunday, which is played on the radio. She wears a chain with a cross on her neck and does not eat meat on Friday. Under her pillow we find two books: one Hebrew [not identified] and the other a Roman Catholic prayer book. Marysia insists that her nationality is Jewish and wants to go to Israel to join the Hagana movement.[28]

In the Jewish children's homes, older children, who began to be proud of their Jewish identity, called the children like Marysia, "Convent or Aryan children," and often reacted violently against their exhibition of Catholic rituals and habits. They verbally abused them or beat them up.[29] Such violent behavior was not only a reaction against an individual "Cross" child, but also against Christian society as a whole, which had been a source of cruelty against Jews.

Adoption of Catholicism and the antisemitic code was an essential strategy of survival during the war, common not only among adults, but also among youth and children.[30] For children, both hidden and passing as Christians, Catholic religion often was the only spiritual refuge on the Aryan side during the war. After the war, some older children were able to shed off the traces of Catholic identity and antisemitic code instantly, but the younger ones, who had internalized the antisemitic code, had an understandably hard time in divesting themselves of it. In some cases, these children were even eager to become nuns and priests after the war to prove to their former rescuers that they were free of any remaining vestiges of Jewishness.[31]

The emotional attachment to Catholicism, fused with the anti-Jewish code, was perhaps the most common feature of pre-adolescent Jewish children's experience in Nazi-occupied Europe during the war, though some did not lose all sense of their background. No doubt, there must have been a thin line between the use of anti-Jewish prejudice as a strategy of survival, and full identification with the non-Jewish identity performed under pressure over a long time. In his personal memoirs, *When Memory Comes*, the eminent historian of the Holocaust Saul Friedländer speaks poignantly about this kind of transformation, which he himself underwent as a Czech Jewish boy in hiding:

> I nevertheless felt at ease within a community of those who had nothing but scorn for Jews, and I incidentally helped stir up this scorn. I had the feeling, never put into words but nonetheless obvious, of having passed over to the compact, invincible majority, of no longer belonging to the camp of the persecuted, but, potentially at least, to that of the persecutors.[32]

The Polish-American sociologist Nechama Tec, born in 1931 in Lublin, retells similar shifts in her cultural identity. Though she remained with her parents on the Aryan side during the war and was fully aware who she was, her passing as a Christian Polish teenager girl made her undergo what one might recognize as spells of identity crisis and internalization of the negative stereotypes of Jews:

> There were times when I believed myself to be truly Stefa's niece, as Polish as any of her blood relations. It was not that I really forgot who I was, only that I became able to push my true self into the background. I liked my new name. Feeling and believing myself to be Krysia Bloch made life easier, and I felt less threatened when Jews were mentioned. I could listen to antisemitic stories indifferently, and even laugh heartily with everyone else about some Jewish misfortune. I knew that they were abusing my people, but part of me was like them.[33]

While, after the end of the war, many children were still under the spell of the main facets of Catholicism and struggled with the idea of interacting with Jews and of regaining Jewishness, other children were eager to leave their former rescuers, even with an unknown relative or a total stranger—a representative of a Jewish organization.

Those were children who were physically or mentally abused by their former rescuers and guardians, and were eager to experience a better life and to regain a sense of childhood in the care of newly encountered adults.

In an interview conducted on 2 February 1947 in the Jewish orphanage in Kraków, Maria Straucher, born in Bochnia on 4 May 1938, describes how happy she was to be reunited with her mother's sister, who found her in her rescuer's home. What emerges from her testimony is that her rescuers used her more like a servant for carrying out various heavy tasks, rather than as a child to be cared for. The rescuer, Tadeusz Połowiec, was a simple, violent, and brutal man. He physically abused his own baby as well as Maria, who was also exposed to antisemitic verbal abuse at his place. Her testimony, which reveals a drastic case of abuse, lacks any expression of sorrow over leaving her rescuers:

> Mr Połowiec appeared again and placed me with one young woman who had just given birth to a child. I washed nappies, cleaned the house, and brought water from the cellar. I worked very hard. All the neighbors knew how hard I worked and could not understand how I coped with all that work and the constant beatings. My rescuer, Mr Połowiec, married this woman. They very often beat me up. When he was angry, he even used to beat the little eight-month-old baby. Once the mother had to call for the doctor to assist with the baby's wound caused by Mr Połowiec. Once in anger he kicked me so hard that I fell over and broke a bone in my face. I lost consciousness and they threw cold water over me. After a while, when I finally woke up, Mr Połowiec ordered me to clean the floor. I liked the baby very, very much. They constantly called me "Żydowica" [a negative term for a Jewish woman], but I did not know what this meant—no one explained it to me. Połowiec never called me by my first name, but only "you little beetle" (*ty bąku*). He never cuddled me. The first time I was cuddled and kissed was by my auntie whom I now call my mother. She found me at Połowiec's house and came to visit me. She kissed me and began to cry. I did not know why she cried so much. She told me that she was my real aunt. The day she visited me I worked as usual and did not stop for a moment. Only in the evening, I slept with auntie, who spent the night with us. My aunt explained to me that she was the sister of my mother and that she finally found me after a long search in Bochnia. She promised to take me away to Kraków. I was not afraid of anything and immediately agreed to go with her. My rescuer asked me if I was going to file a complaint against him. Later they took me to a judge who asked me if I wanted to go with my aunt. I went with my aunt to Kraków where she placed me in this Jewish orphanage. I have been here for the entire month since October. I call my aunt my mother and feel so happy here.[34]

Search for family, family reunions' and new families

Children hoped to be reunited with close family members, and yet a prolonged separation caused by the war sometimes had a detrimental effect on the relationship within the reconstituted families. This was particularly transparent among families in which children were reunited with one surviving parent whom they had not seen for a period of more than five years. That separation resulted in the children and parents remaining physically and emotionally estranged from each other after the reunion. For example, Leo Arnfeld, born in Warsaw on 22 August 1939, recalls the absence of a strong bond between his father and himself in the postwar years. Leo's father, a pharmacist, had been drafted into the Polish army at the outbreak of war, when Leo was less than two weeks old. In 1941, the father had escaped from Nazi-occupied Vilnius in Lithuania, and subsequently survived the war in China. Leo met him for the first time in 1948, at a soccer match in Munich. Leo's first reaction to the news that his father was visiting him was of disbelief: "I thought that they must have made up a story about him...I did not want to meet him because they were taking me out of my soccer game....'I don't have a father,' I screamed."[35]

At that time, Leo was living with his father's sister, his aunt Regina, and her second husband. Regina had lost her first husband and child during the war, and had remarried in Munich, a city that had become one of the major centers for Jewish Displaced Persons in early postwar Germany.[36] Regina had remained informed of Leo's whereabouts, and had kept an eye on him during the war while living as a Christian Polish woman on the Aryan side. After the war, she took up the role of Leo's guardian after reclaiming the boy from Irena, the Polish Christian rescuer to whom Leo was strongly attached, and whom he treated as his biological mother. During their temporary stay in Germany, Regina and her new husband together raised Leo and acted as if they were his parents; while, as Leo himself admits, his biological father, who never remarried, remained a distant figure who played no significant role in his postwar childhood.[37] That Leo remained with his married aunt rather than his widowed father after the reunion at the football match might suggest that it was more socially acceptable for a child to be brought up by a female rather than a single male member of the family; a position in accordance with both European and eastern European traditional family models, both Gentile and Jewish, that developed in the modern period, according to which neither children nor household were considered a man's business.[38]

Many children who were adopted by their uncles, aunts, and cousins felt an integral part of such reconstituted families, whereas others felt estranged due to tensions between the newly adoptive parents and child. These tensions were rooted in widely differing expectations, differing social and cultural backgrounds, or emotionally harmful evaluations of an adoptive child against a perished biological child. In such cases, the perished child sometimes seemed "better" than the adopted one.[39]

Other children and youths experienced long, frustrating delays in being reunited with their only remaining relatives abroad, and had to confront a difficult bureaucracy for young immigrants. Those repatriated to Poland from the former eastern Polish territories, called *kresy*, seemed to face particularly complicated bureaucratic challenges on the path to reunion with their relatives in the west. Like the children who survived the war in central Poland, they possessed hardly any family memorabilia or important documents such as birth and death certificates of parents. The only proof they had of their Polish citizenship was the Repatriation Card (*Karta Ewakuacyjna*) which they had used to cross the new Polish–Soviet border. However, in Poland at that time, the Repatriation Card was not necessarily considered a sufficient document to confirm Polish citizenship and obtain a Polish passport, without which no individual could leave Poland for abroad. In such cases, the children themselves and their relatives waiting for them in the west were completely baffled and seemed powerless in the face of the bureaucratic machinery operating according to strict laws and regulations.

This happened, for example, to Józef Strauber (Sztrauber), born on 15 December 1930 in the shtetl of Potok Złoty (today Zolotyy Potik in Ukraine) in the district of Tarnopol. Józef's Repatriation Card, issued on 25 November 1945, contained information that the boy had entered Poland having only one private possession, his bicycle.[40] Like many Polish repatriates from the Soviet Union, Jewish and non-Jewish, he was settled in the western Polish territories, the so-called Recovered Territories (*Ziemie Odzyskane*). There he began life anew by himself in the town of Nowa Ruda in Kłodzko.

On 10 and 17 February 1948, his only surviving sister, Maria Kuberczyk of Brooklyn, New York, made a direct petition to the American Joint Distribution Committee (AJDC) in Poland to include her brother Józef in the Canadian Orphan Emigration Program.[41] This program, as it was stated, did not guarantee Józef's automatic entry into the United States. But in many cases when relatives in the USA could not apply directly for a child's entry to the USA, as in the case of Józef's sister, the Canadian Orphan Program was the second-best option for the family—albeit with some delay— eventually to be reunited in the USA.

On 20 February 1948, in a letter to the AJDC in Poland, Ann S. Petluck, Director of the Migration Department for United Service for New Americans, described the accompanying eyewitness documents that provided proof of Józef's background and status, which were supposed to help him obtain a Polish passport and other necessary travel documents:

> Unfortunately, Józef was not able to secure an official birth certificate. The town in which he was born, Potok Złoty, now belongs to Russia. Józef wrote there and learned that there were no Jews left and [that] the Nazis destroyed all Jewish documents. The enclosure statement which we have numbered one, states that Mr. Norbert Rajnharc, residing at the address given in the statement in the town of Nowa Ruda, and Janina Goldberg, residing at the address given in the statement, certify that Josef [Józef] Strauber, the son of David and Fryda Goldberg, was born on December 15, 1931, in Potok Złoty, near Buczacz, in the district of Tarnopol. They are giving this certificate for the documents which he needs to immigrate to Canada.[42]

In this letter, the year of Józef's birth was changed from 1930 to 1931, despite the fact that in all his previous documents Józef had stated that he was born in 1930. One could guess that this was not a mistake, but a strategically and carefully planned move to buy time, given the fact that the Canadian Immigration Program under the War Orphans Project was eligible only for children and youths up to the age of 18, and that Józef had not yet obtained a Polish passport.

By May 1948, Józef had submitted to the AJDC in Warsaw most of the necessary documents for emigration, such as the History of the Child Application, the Health Examination Form, X-rays of his lungs, four photographs, and his curriculum vitae.[43] By the end of June 1948, the additional affidavit of an eyewitness, Sara Orliansky, then a resident of Brooklyn, stating the death of Józef's parents, was sent to AJDC in Warsaw.[44] Like Józef, Sara Orliansky belonged to a tiny group of survivors born in Złoty Potok. By early November 1948, Józef received an immigration visa to Canada.[45] However, this news could not yet be fully celebrated, since he still had not succeeded in obtaining a Polish passport. On 28 December 1948, Józef again wrote out his CV as part of the passport application. The laconic one-page CV is written in child-like language and style, more appropriate for a child in fifth grade, which Józef had completed before the outbreak of the war, than for a youngster of his age. The CV is a chilling account of what had happened to Józef, and reveals his state of mind:

> I was born on December 15 1930 in Złoty Potok Tarnopol district. I lived in Złoty Potok and completed fifth grade of primary school there before Hitler's occupation. In 1943, Germans killed my parents and a sister. My brother and I ran to a forest where we created a military unit with other Jewish boys. After the liberation of Złoty Potok, my older brother volunteered to go to the Front where he was most likely killed, whereas I had worked on temporary basis until I was repatriated to Lower Silesia. I arrived in Lower Silesia in 1946 and settled in Nowa Ruda where I have been living until now. I work as a tractor driver. Except for the only sister in New York, I have no other relatives.
> Strauber Józef, Nowa Ruda, 28 December 1948[46]

The search for relatives in Poland and abroad, in which orphan children placed many hopes and expectations, did not always result in the long-hoped-for happy family reunion.[47] Deeply disappointed and heartbroken when they did not find any relatives, some children tried to find comfort with other children who, like them, did not have any relatives to turn to. Those orphans supported and relied on each other and, not infrequently, made joint decisions concerning their future lives, such as departing for children's *kibbutzim* in Palestine/Israel to begin life anew there.

Some of these orphan children replaced the yearning and hunger for family love and belonging to an individual family with the new, promising passion for *Eretz-Israel* and Zionism in all its various shades. However, among orphan children there were also those who experienced painful internal torments between beginning life anew in Palestine/Israel, and yearning for their deceased parents and vanished prewar childhood. Attempts at committing suicide were the most extreme manifestations of such torment, as reported in Jewish children's homes in Poland and in the special *kibbutzim* in the west, the temporary stations for Palestine/Israel. For example, Chava Meir, born in November 1931, attempted suicide twice, first in the Jewish Children's Home in Otwock, and second in the Zionist Kibbutz in Germany, because "no-one from her relatives came for her."[48] The burden of loneliness and the knowledge of the total destruction of her immediate family were, for her and others alike, an overwhelming tragedy that could not be so easily solaced with the idea that *Eretz-Israel* would, from then on, be their new "substituted family."

But the idea of moulding out of these orphan children "new, content Jews and individuals" was not voiced and implemented only by the Zionists.[49] The early postwar publications of the Jewish Labor Committee, with headquarters in New York, are also filled with comments and photos suggesting that the young survivors from Europe were instantly transformed into happy, healthy individuals with smiles constantly on their faces.[50] Yet those who worked with the orphan children on a daily basis knew how devastated they were by the loss of their families, and how the pain and sorrow associated with that loss might never truly abate.

Notes

1 G. Bychowski, "Neuro-Psychiatric Rehabilitation of Children in Post-war Europe," *American OSE Review*, vol. 3, no. 1 (1944): 12–17.

2 Bychowski, "Neuro-Psychiatric Rehabilitation," 12.

3 Bychowski, "Neuro-Psychiatric Rehabilitation," 16.

4 On a variety of relationships between Jewish children and their rescuers in wartime Poland, see Joanna Beata Michlic, *Jewish Children in Nazi-Occupied Poland: Survival and Polish–Jewish Relations During the Holocaust as Reflected in Early Postwar Recollections, Search and Research – Lectures and Papers* (Jerusalem: Yad Vashem, 2008).

5 See, for example, the interviews with child survivors in Aviva Slesin's documentary film *Secret Lives: Hidden Children and their Rescuers During WWII* (2003).

6 For the study of hidden Jewish children in western Europe, see, for example, Suzanne Vromen, *Hidden Children of the Holocaust. Belgian Nuns and their Daring Rescue of Young Jews from the Nazis* (Oxford: Oxford University Press, 2008); Diane L. Wolf, *Beyond Anne Frank. Hidden Children and Postwar Families in Holland* (Berkeley, California: University of California Press, 2007). Comparative analytical studies of hidden Jewish children in Nazi-occupied Europe are highly desirable.

7 On the history of the re-emergence of Jewish child survivors and Jewish organizations in the early postwar period, see Lucjan Dobroszycki, "Re-emergence and Decline of a Community: The Numerical Size of the Jewish Population in Poland, 1944–47," *YIVO Annual* 21 (1993): 3–32. See also Natalia Aleksiun, *Dokąd dalej? Ruch syjonistyczny w Polsce (1944–1950)* (Warsaw: Wydawnictwo Trio, 2002); August Grabski, *Działalność komunistów wśród Żydów w Polsce (1944–1949)* (Warsaw: Wydawnictwo Trio, 2004).

8 For some basic observations about the differences between the situation of child survivors in Nazi-occupied Poland and in the Soviet Union, see Irena Kowalska, "Kartoteka TOŻ z lat 1946–47. (Żydowskie dzieci uratowane z Holocaustu)," *Biuletyn Żydowskiego Instytutu Historycznego* vol. 6, no. 7 (1995): 97–106. This topic deserves a separate historical analysis.

9 For the study of Jewish youth in pre-1939 Poland, see Moses Kligsberg, "Socio-Psychological Problems Reflected in the YIVO Autobiography Contest," *YIVO Annual of Jewish Social Science*, vol. 1 (1946): 241–49, and "Di yidishe yugnt bavegung in poyln tsvishn beyde velt milkhomes (a sotsiologishe shtudye)" ("The Jewish Youth Movement in Poland Between the Two World Wars: A Sociological Study") in *Studies on Polish Jewry, 1919–1939*, ed. Joshua A. Fishman (New York: YIVO, 1974): 137–228.

10 See Helena Datner-Śpiewak, "Instytucje opieki nad dzieckiem i szkoły powszechne Centralnego Komitetu Żydów Polskich w latach 1945–46," *Biuletyn Żydowskiego Instytutu Historycznego* 3 (1981): 37–51; Joanna B. Michlic, "The Raw Memory of War. Early Postwar Testimonies of Children in Dom Dziecka in Otwock," *Yad Vashem Studies*, no.1, vol. 37 (2009): 11–52.

11 Testimony of Hinda Dowicz (The Central Committee of Polish Jews, CKŻP), file no. 301/1328, Archives of Żydowski Instytut Historyczny ŻIH.

12 Joanna (Joasia) Hercberg, Pamiętnik without a title, but with a one-page un-numbered introduction with a dedication "To my dearest Mrs. Luba [Lena Bielicka-Blum] on her birthday," in Franciszka Oliwa, ed., *Księga Wspomnień*, p. 1. This is a separate memoir that was added to the *Księga Wspomnień*. See Franciszka Oliwa, *Księga Wspomnień*, file 037/378, vol. 2, YVA (Yad Vashem Archives).

13 See, for example, the autobiography of the educator Lena Küchler-Silberman, *My Hundred Children* (New York: Dell, 1987); and the documentary film *My 100 Children* about Lena Küchler-Silberman and some of her former charges, made by Amalia Margolin and Oshra Schwartz, 2003.

14 Testimony of F-g A, CKŻP, file no. 301/2872, ŻIH. The girl, 15 years old, was born in Deraźne, near Równe in former eastern Poland. The interviewer's note attached to F-g A's testimony states that the girl burst into tears and could not continue to relate her story: "She regretted that she had uttered her sins."

15 Testimony of Józef Himelblau, signed by Genia (Genya) Silkes, Łódź, 19 January 1948, CKŻP, file no. 301/3615, Archives of ŻIH. (Yiddish).

16 Testimony of Jankiel Cieszyński, CKŻP, file no. 301/5514, ŻIH.

17 Letter of Wiktor Baranowicz to the Barański family, 20 October 1946. A second, undated letter, also written in the Children's Home in Zabrze, contains a similar message; for both, see file no. M31/7081, Archives of Righteous Among the Nations, Yad Vashem.

18 Testimony of Jurek Adin, CKŻP, file no. 301/3695, Archives of ŻIH

19 On the Warsaw Uprising, see the classic historical study by Jan M. Ciechanowski, *The Warsaw Rising of 1944*, new edn (London and New York: Cambridge University Press, 2009; 1st edn 1974); see also Norman Davis, *Rising '44: The Battle for Warsaw* (New York: Viking, 2004), which is an impressive volume but not free of errors and unsatisfactory discussions, including the subject of Polish–Jewish relations during World War II. Ciechanowski, who is a former soldier of the Uprising, is one of its most adamant critics; see his most recent interview, "Powstanie nie powinno było wybuchnąć," *Gazeta Wyborcza*, July 30, 2009, http://wyborcza.pl/1,75515,6878163,Ciechanowski-Powstanie_nie_powinno_bylo_wybuchnac.html?utm_source=Nlt&utm_medium=Nlt&utm_ campaign=961608?utm_source=RSS&utm_medium=RSS&utm_campaign=5095994 (accessed 5 August 2009).

20 Report about Barbara Blecher, "Historia Dziecka" (The History of the Child), CKŻP, Wydział Oświaty, file no. 303/09/188, Archives of ŻIH.

21 Testimony of Irena (Agata) Boldok, née Likierman, born in 1932, "Back to Being Myself," in *The Last Eyewitnesses. Children of the Holocaust Speak*, eds Jakub Gutenbaum and Agnieszka Latala (Evanston, Illinois: Northwestern University Press, 2005), 2: 35. (Originally published in Polish in 2001 by the Association of the Children of the Holocaust.)

22 For an interesting recent account by a Jewish child survivor who was saved in the convent in Turkowice in north-eastern Poland, see the personal story of the distinguished Polish literary critic Michał Głowiński in "Zapisy Zagłady," *Tygodnik Powszechny. Kontrapunkt*, vol. 1, no. 2 (25 March 2001): 14–15. Głowiński is the author of a number of recently published personal accounts of his wartime experiences and his recent "rediscovery" of his Jewishness. See, for example, M. Głowiński, *Czarne Sezony* (Warsaw, 1999); English translation: *The Black Seasons*, trans. M. Shore (Evanston, Illinois: Northwestern University Press, 2005). See also an interview conducted by T. Torańska, "Polskie gadanie," *Gazeta Wyborcza*, 23 May 2005, http://serwisy.gazeta.pl/df/2029020,34471,272112.html

23 Interview with Aviva Blumberg, 20 January 1995, no. 587 (English), Tape 4, USC Shoah Institute, University of Southern California, Los Angeles.

24 Testimony of Yehudit Kirzner, CKŻP, file no. 301/2077, Archives of ŻIH, (Yiddish). Genia Silkes interviewed Yehudit Kirzner on 15 December 1945 in Łódż.

25 Statement of Ludwik Jerzycki to interviewer Janina Sobol-Masłowska, 27 September 1947, file no. 301/2755, 1, Archives of ŻIH.

26 On the problem of internalization of anti-Jewish prejudice and the transformation of individual identity among Polish-Jewish children, see, for example, Joanna B. Michlic, "'Who Am I?' The Identity of Jewish Children in Poland, 1945–49," *Focusing on Memorialization of the Holocaust, Polin*, vol. 20 (2007).

27 Coordinated Commission for Jewish Children to American Joint Distribution Committee (AJDC), 24 June 1948, file no. 350/2369, Archives of ŻIH.

28 Statement of B. Mosiężnik, signed on the cover page attached to the testimony of Marysia Szpigiel, CKŻP, file no. 301/3345, Archives of ZIH.

29 For accounts of such behavior, see the documentary film *My Hundred Children*.

30 On the problem of adopting an antisemitic social and cultural code among adults and children, see Małgorzata Melchior, *Zagłada a Tożsamość: Polscy Żydzi ocaleni na 'aryjskich papierach'. Analiza doświadczenia biograficznego* (Warsaw: Wydawnictwo IFiS PAN, 2004).

31 See, for example, testimony of Tamar Miran (Tamara Jarnicka), file no. 26166, Tape 2, (Hebrew), 25 December 1996, Rishon Letsion, Israel, Interviewer Uriel Reingold, USC Shoah Institute.

32 Saul Friendländer, *When Memory Comes* (New York: Farrar Straus Giroux, 1979), 121.

33 Nechama Tec, *Dry Tears: The Story of a Lost Childhood* (New York: Oxford University Press, 1984), 145.

34 Testimony of Maria Straucher, signed by the interviewer, Janina Sobol-Masłowska, CKŻP, file no. 301/3292, Archives of ŻIH.

35 Interview with Leo Arnfeld, file no. 15731, tape 3 (English), USC Shoah Institute.

36 On Jewish Displaced Persons in early postwar Germany, see Atina Grossmann, *Jews, Germans and Allies: Close Encounters in Occupied Germany* (Princeton, New Jersey and Oxford: Princeton University Press, 2007).

37 See interview with Leo Arnfeld, tapes 3 and 4.

38 For general information about the Jewish family model in eastern Europe and in the West, see Benjamin Schlesinger, *Jewish Family Issues: A Resource Guide* (New York and London: Garland, 1987). On the eastern European family pattern and the role of the father in the pre-modern period, see Gershon David Hundert, "Jewish Children and Childhood in Early Modern East Central Europe," in *The Jewish Family: Metaphor and Memory*, ed. David Kraemer (New York and Oxford: Oxford University Press, 1989), 81–94.

39 See, for example, the interview with Barbara Gesundheit (prewar family name: Tasma) conducted on 29 October 1996, file no. 21539, USC Shoah Institute.

40 Certificate confirming that Józef Strauber was a holder of Repatriation Card no. 10730. Collection postwar AJCD, 1945–49, file no. 350/384, 112, Archives of ŻIH. Strauber's file includes 45 documents altogether in this archival collection.

41 Request for inclusion in Children's Emigration Project made by Maria Kuberczyk of 558 Fairview Avenue, Brooklyn, NY, on 17 February 1948, Collection postwar AJCD, 1945–49, file no. 350/384, 157, Archives of ŻIH.

42 Letter of Ann S. Petluck, Director Migration Department, United Service for New Americans, INC to Emigration Service American Joint Distribution Committee 23 Rue Dumont D'Urville, Paris 16e, France, dated February 1948. The Warsaw branch of AJDC received it on 8 March 1948. Collection postwar AJCD, 1945–49, file no. 350/384, 153 –154, Archives of ŻIH.

43 Letter of Józef Strauber to the American Joint Distribution Committee in Warsaw dated 14 May 1948. In the letter, Józef stated that he could not obtain the requested X-ray of his entire body because there was no available technical equipment to have such a medical examination. In addition, he presented the bill for 2000 *zlotys* covering the costs pertaining to obtaining the documents. AJDC reference child case 2444/51, Collection postwar AJCD, 1945–49, file no. 350/384, 144, Archives of ŻIH.

44 Letter of Ann S. Petluck, Director of Migration Services of United Service for New Americans, INC, with an accompanied affidavit of Sara Orliansky to the AJDC in Warsaw. The letter was posted on 28 June 1948. Collection postwar AJCD, 1945–49, file no. 350/384, 141, Archives of ŻIH. At that time, a second identical affidavit was obtained from another survivor Mr Solomon Bauchman. See letter of Ann S. Petluck, Director of Migration Services of United Service for New Americans, INC, 15 June 1948. Affidavit of Mr Solomon Bauchman to the AJDC in Warsaw was enclosed with the letter. Collection postwar AJJCD, 1945–49, file no. 350/384, 140, Archives of ŻIH. See letter of 15 November 1948 of the American Joint distribution Committee, Emigration Section to Józef Strauber, Collection postwar AJCD, 1945–49, file no. 350/384, 134, Archives of ŻIH.

45 See letter of 15 November 1948 of the American Joint Distribution Committee, Emigration Section to Józef Strauber, Collection postwar AJCD, 1945–49, file no. 350/384, 134, Archives of ŻIH.

46 CV of Jozef Strauber, 28 December 1948, Collection postwar AJCD, 1945–49, file no. 350/384, 119, Archives of ŻIH.

47 For a good example of such disappointment, see the interview conducted on 22 October 1995 with Jerry Shane (Jankiel Cieszyński), file 7860, tape 4 (English), USC Shoah Institute. In the early postwar period, Jankiel wrote letters to a person who bore his family name, Cieszyński. Jankiel assumed that this Mr Cieszyński, living in Chicago, was his uncle. It turned out that the Mr Cieszyński to whom the boy addressed his letters was not related to him at all. After a long period of silence, Jankiel received a letter written by Mr Cieszyński's employer, informing him that the person to whom he wrote was neither his relative nor Jewish.

48 Interview with Chava Meir, File no. 12189, 17 March 1996, in Petach Tikva, Israel. Interview conducted in Hebrew (tape 5), USC Shoah Institute.

49 On Zionist activities among children and youths in DP camps, see Avinoam J. Patt, *Finding Home and Homeland. Jewish Youth and Zionism in the Aftermath of the Holocaust* (Detroit: Wayne State University Press, 2009).

50 See, for example, the colorful cover brochure *Our Children*, published by the Jewish Labor Committee, Child "Adoption" Program in New York at unspecified date. Ida Alter edited the brochure.

42

TOWARD A POST-HOLOCAUST THEOLOGY IN ART

The search for the absent and present God

Stephen C. Feinstein
(Transcribed and edited by Margery Grace Hunt)

Since the end of World War II, a good deal of art has been produced that has attempted to conceptualize and provide some understanding about the Holocaust. The results have been mixed. Many artists have relied on some of the symbols associated with the event to provide the impulse for artistic creativity. However, these symbols, whether stars of David, barbed wire, or camp and ghetto scenes, often have become clichés. Some provide the viewer only with nostalgia, melancholia, and at best false mourning. Others have relied on the photographic record, which has often created a pattern of repetitious images of questionable authenticity, quite different from what was achieved by earlier forms of academic art dealing with Christian, mythological, or classical subjects.

An answer to the question "What is Holocaust art?" remains elusive, suggested perhaps by the public debate centering around Nazi imagery in the New York Jewish Museum's 2002 exhibition *Mirroring Evil*. In this exhibition with postmodern edges, curator Norman Kleeblatt framed the works exhibited around the theme of the moral and ethical issues surrounding the question of exhibiting items that reflected on perpetrators of genocide whose policies often affected more than Jews. Nevertheless, the media's commentary focused on questions that the exhibit had something to do with the Holocaust, and it did.

The search for a spiritual in art, a difficult subject, is a theme in which some artists have found a subject for intellectual and theological challenges. Spiritual themes and images, of course, are found in many, although certainly not all, of the themes of Christian art. Much of Christian art seeks to be redemptive. Art about the Holocaust has more problems in seeking redemptive answers, as the subject itself is mired in negativity. The idea of creating art from such extreme negation that might affirm the vital principle of life from a creator is at best questionable, and suggests some of the difficult theological questions that have been created for Jews by the Holocaust: the presence and absence of God, the death of God, the call on mysticism as a way to understand the immensity of negativity and to affirm, perhaps, that for good to be understood, so must there be a comprehension of the nature of evil.

This chapter examines theological themes in the artistic labor of three artists: Alice Lok Cahana, Anselm Kiefer, and Samuel Bak. The unifying aspect of their work is the conflicting images of God, the use of a biblical or rabbinic text, and what may be interpreted as a *"midrashic"* approach to Holocaust art.

Alice Lok Cahana: *Shabat in Auschwitz*

Alice Lok Cahana is a native of Sarvar, Hungary, who was deported to Auschwitz during late summer 1944. Cahana has a unique history, presented in Steven Spielberg's film *The Last Days* (though the most dramatic aspect escaped the film). Cahana was in the gas chamber on 7 October 1944, waiting to be liquidated, when the Sonderkommando uprising took place. She and other women in the chamber were ordered to dress and leave. Cahana survived Auschwitz, Guben, and Bergen-Belsen. Coming from an Orthodox Jewish family, Cahana brought with her not only faith through her Holocaust experiences, but also an understanding of the power of the religious ritual. Cahana married, moved to the United States, and after a visit to her native Sarvar in 1978, where she was struck by the absence of not only the Jews, but memory of them, she began painting.

For someone deeply imbued with faith in God, the concept of the spiritual has strong links that feed back to the memory of the proximity of the Jews to God, and to the Jews as representing God's stake in the world. Therefore, even in the most adverse circumstances, one who is observant must remember the grandeur of creation, even if it is polluted by the free will of mankind, which admittedly God himself cannot control. During their stay in Auschwitz, Alice and Edith tried to maintain Jewish traditions. On one occasion, they sang and chanted the traditional prayers for Sabbath in the women's latrine at Birkenau. Other Jewish women inmates from many other countries started singing along with them. The event marked an act of spiritual resistance as well as an affirmation of God's creation and perhaps of his redemptive capabilities.

Cahana's painting, which originally followed what one might suggest is allegiance to the second commandment and utilized abstract color fields, later became more expressionist with use of collage. The figurative did enter, especially in her paintings that honor the Swedish diplomat Raoul Wallenberg, who was instrumental in saving her father by giving him a *Schutzpass*. Cahana also used photographic images in some of her works. These canvases are autobiographical in nature, using such items as a school photograph or occasionally some of the broader assemblage of recognizable photographic images from either German or Allied sources.

In 1985, Cahana painted *Shabat in Auschwitz*, a large work in acrylic that recalls not only the hellish situation in Auschwitz-Birkenau, but also the festive Sabbaths at her home in Sarvar. In this painting, however, the artist also evokes the other critical Jewish festival, Passover. In this context, Passover, the universal commemoration of the liberation of the Jews from the Egyptian bondage through the miraculous intervention of God, becomes a poignant experience. While the artist's focus was indeed the Sabbath and the memory of creation, her work also unleashes some probing and difficult questions about how one prays during and after Auschwitz.

Shabat in Auschwitz is conceived as a large tablecloth with formal edges, colored in a green-tinted white. The painting suggests a table set for the Sabbath, but the cloth has a transparent quality that reveals some uncomfortable truths as well as memory. The memory is both of better times in a family-centered Sabbath in Sarvar, and of the horrible predicament in Auschwitz, veiled by the cloth, which brings up ghostlike apparitions that fail to disappear with time. Standing figures appear as specters. On the right, a larger image looms, incomplete as a human form. The more emaciated heads on the left recall the *Muselmänner*, the "living dead" as described in the language of the camps. In the center, there are barely observable human hands. The word Shabat is inscribed in Hebrew *(shin/beth/thet)* on the bottom right in red, as if written in blood and perhaps as written with an unsteady hand. Diagonally to the left in the upper part is a mutilated red swastika, which turns into the Hebrew letter *shin*, the letter of God's name, hence affirming his presence and power for the believer in Auschwitz.

The whiteness of the canvas not only serves as a transparent curtain across these memories, but also suggests the absence of time during the Holocaust. Primo Levi has expressed this absence best in *If this is a Man: Survival in Auschwitz*. For Levi, as well as for other survivors, chronological time disappeared in the context of the camps. Certainly there was day and night, cold and heat, a sense of seasons. Levi's narrative begins in a chronological fashion, but then the notion of time fades away, reappearing, like the author's humanity, only as liberation approaches in January 1945. Just as 27 January 1945 loomed as a critical day for Primo Levi, the day of Liberation, for Cahana, a white veil covers time and memory. However, for her, the remembrance of the Sabbath, and hence God's creation of the world, remains sacrosanct.

Within the painting, Cahana has placed four distinct torn pages from Hebraic texts. These, however, are not the prayers for the Sabbath, but questions from the Passover *Haggadah*. While both the Sabbath and Passover are occasions for remembrance, Sabbath memory relates to the remembrance of creation and to the goodness of it. Passover memory is about liberation and divine intervention. The Sabbath prayer over the wine, however, also contains the memory of the intercessional God who delivered the Israelites from bondage. Thus the Sabbath and Passover are interrelated. The excerpt on the right of center in horizontal form, partially torn, is taken from the *Haggadah*. It is a midrash on Deuteronomy 26:5–8. *V'hie shamdad...*

> And it is this promise which has stood by our fathers and by us.
> For it was one man only who stood up against us to destroy us; in every generation they stand up against us to destroy us, and the Holy One, blessed be he, saved us from their hand.[1]

In this section, the "'one man only who stood...to destroy us'" can be a Pharaoh, a Hitler, or a Haman. Nearby, glued vertically to the canvas, is another section of the *Haggadah*, which asks the *ma nishtana*, the well-known beginning of the "four questions'" recited by the youngest at Passover. Here, Cahana juxtaposes the irony of Sabbath praying in what has been called the *anus mundi*, Auschwitz, with that of the story of redemption from slavery. It is not only an irony, but also the expression of disappointment. How many survivors raised in the Orthodox tradition of believing that God was everywhere found that God was nowhere, and that the redemption of the past was perhaps not to be duplicated in 1944 and 1945? But the "why is this night different from all other nights" within an Auschwitz context relates to the positive memory of being able to commemorate the Sabbath, even in horrible circumstances where the existence of God may be questioned.

The third excerpt used in the painting is from *Avudim chainu l'Paroh b'Mitzraim*. Because it is torn, the text starts with the words *B'yad hazaka*: "'With a mighty hand':

this is the blight, as it is said: 'Behold, the hand of the Lord is upon thy cattle which are in the field, upon the horses, upon the asses, upon the camels, upon the herds, and upon the flocks; there shall be a very grievous blight'" (Exodus 9:3).[2]

The textual fragment constitutes an interesting choice, as it deals with the affliction imposed upon the Egyptians. The entire section of *Haggadah* to which Cahana refers is the midrash based on Deuteronomy 26:5–8. The prelude to the midrash is focused on Mishnah Pesahim X:4, which contains two conflicting interpretations of the same section. The rabbinical debate relates to the question of whether "the appearance of the Deity in visible form is possible." This was the basis of a dispute between the Sadducees, who believed that such an incarnation was possible, and the Pharisees, who took the opposite view.[3] The most widely accepted text is also included by Cahana on the far left side of the painting: "We were Pharaoh's slaves in Egypt, and the Lord our God brought us forth from there with a mighty hand and an outstretched arm. And if the Holy One, blessed be he, had not brought our forefathers forth from Egypt, then we, our children, and our children's children would still be slaves in Egypt."[4]

The quotation underscores the necessity of telling and retelling the story of the Exodus. Cahana's excerpt includes the beginning of the story *Ma-oseth*, which reports on the rabbis from B'nai Brak who debated the meaning of the rituals of the *seder* with such intensity that they spoke through the night and suddenly discovered it was time for morning prayers. One may derive from this Passover episode the same concept of the need to tell and retell the story of the Holocaust, although God's presence in the story may be more remote.

For Cahana, quoting from the *Haggadah* and celebrating the *Shabat in Auschwitz* imply the presence of God's spirit and assert her hope of survival. Why, however, call the painting *Shabat in Auschwitz* when the collage-based artistic evidence is from the Passover *Haggadah*? The answer is given by the basic prayer for welcoming the Sabbath and blessing the wine, thus conjoining the creation story and the concept of freedom. The sense of the spiritual has never left the artist. However, *Shabat in Auschwitz* can be read as this never-ending faith in God amidst fractured families and death. But the Jews of Europe are murdered, and for many, the concept of spirituality and belief in the aftermath of such atrocity can only result in a cynical reaction to a cruel God who allows his creation to be destroyed. As a child, Cahana clung to spirituality and biblical folklore. This tradition became for her a symbol of resistance against the Holocaust. In Birkenau, she and her sister Edith inspired others through their manifestation of faith by singing "Shalom Aleichem," the song that welcomes the Sabbath on Friday nights. Cahana thus acknowledged God's presence at Auschwitz. A wider reading of her painting must also acknowledge the existence of an evil that God could not control. Hence her reliance on the two texts of *B'yad hazaka*, probably a source of theological debate among the inmates in the death camps as to whether God would take a visible form and save his people, or remain passive. There is also the question of reverse affliction: the *B'yad hazaka* is directed against Pharaoh and it is about the ten plagues. Finally, the painting also poses the question whether the Jews have sinned and are being punished at Auschwitz by the same God who has saved them in the past. This, of course, is an untenable theological or practical position, one that blames the victims. However, *Shabat in Auschwitz* offers a variety of interesting theological questions because its inspiration is the struggle to find spirituality in the worst circumstances.

Anselm Kiefer: *Breaking of the Vessels*

During the 1980s, the German second-generation artist Anselm Kiefer, already known for his examination of Nazism and the romanticized myths of German history through his immense paintings that are overlaid with shamanistic and alchemistic meaning, began studying the Kabbalah, the mystical scriptures of Judaism. They led to a series of paintings that may be linked to the tradition of alchemy, the non-representational aspects of the second commandment, and the history of the Jewish victims. Lisa Saltzman has argued that Kiefer's large paintings from the late 1970s and early 1980s, such as *Iconoclastic Controversy* (of 1977 and 1980) and *Aaron* of 1984 and 1985, addressed the problems of representing the Holocaust. Kiefer went on to produce many paintings with themes derived from the Kabbalah: *Lilith*, *The Daughters of Lilith*, *Sefiroth*, *Emanation*, *Zim Zum*, and *Merkabah*. In addition, in 1990 Kiefer produced an artist's book entitled *The Heavenly Places: Merkabah*. Each title dialogues with fragments from the Kabbalah. The result, while seen as somewhat off base by some critics, led to several important room installations reflecting his earlier ruminations about the German past.

Breaking of the Vessels is a large conceptual installation, set in a room at the St Louis Museum of Art; it is 17 feet high and measures 27 feet in length from the wall, weighs over seven tons, and is made of iron, lead, copper, wire, glass, charcoal, and aquatec. The proportions of the work are monumental, and reflect on a similar issue within the discourse about the Holocaust. The central image is of lead books on an iron bookshelf. The essential images found in this installation are a Kabbalistic "tree of life," a library of lead, hence of unreadable books, and the entire floor is littered with broken glass. The inspiration for the piece comes from the Kabbalistic conceptualization of creation and *shivrat hakelim*, the breaking of vessels. The story is essential to an understanding of theodicy and to the conceptualization of good and evil. According to the tradition, God attempted to contain all evil *(kelippot)* in glass vessels. However, the glass broke and the evil escaped into the world. Such "breaking" is the source of secularism, loss of faith, heresy, and, in the post-Holocaust era, of the search for the roots of the Shoah in human history. The result is that mankind's task since this event is to seek *tikkun olam*, the reconstruction of the world, by recapturing the escaped evil. In the Kabbalah, evil can be contained because "holy sparks" *(nizozot)* also fell into the sphere along with the evil. Kiefer's work relates directly to this theme, constituting a challenging visual manifestation of a theological conception.

A semicircular piece of glass at the top of the sculpture is inscribed with the Hebrew words "*Ain soph*" ("The Infinite, without end"). With the books of lead below arranged on three levels, lead tabs extend from the sides with Hebrew words, derived from a traditional kabbalistic "Tree of Life." In this respect, the Kabbalah, although steeped in mysticism and multiple layers of interpretation, is at the same time accessible and comprehensible to the artistic mind because the traditional Tree of Life arranged the *Ten Sefirot*, Divine Attributes, into a metaphysical configuration with a representational, hence artistic, form. In Kiefer's sculpture, the continuity of the Tree of Life is achieved with copper wires connecting the ten lead elements. These can also represent ten paths of life.

The Tree of Life in the Kabbalah represents the ten attributes of God, usually in the form of circles with Hebrew words. According to the principle of *Tsimtsum*, God contracted himself to create the first man, Adam Kadmon, God's first form. The highest of God's attributes is *Keter* (The Crown), "the source of all." Below the crown are

Hokhmah and *Binah* (Wisdom and Understanding, reading from right to left in the Hebraic tradition); *Hesed* (Mercy) and *Gevurah* (Judgment) form the upper outer pillars, and represent "the emotional principles of fear and love," which were believed to be part of Adam's heart.[5] Beneath and between *Hesed* and *Gevurah* is *Tiferet* (Beauty), "symbolizing the pivotal point at the center of the Divine realm."[6] Beneath *Tiferet* are *Nezah* and *Hod*, meaning Victory and Glory, but also "repeat or cycle" or "to shimmer and vibrate," respectively. Midway below *Nezah* and *Hod* is *Yesod* (Foundation) and below *Yesod* is *Malkhut* (Kingdom). *Yesod* may represent either sex or the ordinary mind, while *Malkhut* is the sum of the others. Kabbalists believe that the central space of the Tree of Life is the place of knowledge, the *Ruah ha-Kodesh*, the Word of God.[7]

The Tree of Life is also seen as a rendition of Jacob's Ladder, that is, a link between heaven and earth, and is hence related to the ultimate question of redemption. One tradition of the Kabbalah argues that every human is a cell in the body of the original Adam, and such cells come to earth to attempt to comprehend existence. "In this way, the three lower worlds become a three-dimensional reflection that synthesizes into a single self conscious image," which is sometimes called *tikkun*, restoration, or sometimes redemption.[8]

The dialectical qualities of the Kabbalah, especially the divisions between earth and the heavens, day and night, are mirrored in the concepts of good and evil. By dealing with mystical aspects of God, Kiefer is also dealing with the interconnectedness of God and the Jews, and with God's absence through the Holocaust.

From an artistic viewpoint, the effect of Kiefer's work on the viewer is overwhelming. The scale of the work suggests the monumental nature of the evil and the difficulty of redemption. On the simplest level, the sculpture can be read as a representation of *Kristallnacht*. However, this reading would avoid the critical questions raised. Can humanity read and learn, comprehend, and contain an evil that has spilled out to consume the Jews of Europe? Are books sealed, as Kiefer's lead representations? Will they reopen? In a more formal sense, Kiefer is suggesting that a non-figurative and hence a spiritual artistic vision is the best way to comprehend the Holocaust.

Samuel Bak: *Questioning God*

Samuel Bak was born in Vilna in 1933 and survived the Vilna Ghetto. After the war, he lived in Israel, Paris, and Rome, and became a successful modernist painter. By 1963, after he turned 30, he began to question the direction of his modernist canvasses, well embedded in the popular culture of the period. The reason for the shift, Bak now understands, was the suppression of Holocaust memory immediately after World War II and his own realization of the influence of this past on his painting: The inner traumas of his life experience, "elements of my inner self...were asking to be communicated through art."[9]

Eventually, his style has matured into what may be called a form of surrealism mixed with complex theological questions that relate to the artist's own feeling of estrangement. Bak does not describe this process as a long intellectual journey. He conceives it rather a "responding to something that was pushing out from the inside, something visceral, something that takes a long time for the mind to comprehend."[10] The result was a large body of painted work on canvas, dealing with the themes of absence, the post-Holocaust landscape of Jewish existence, technologies and people of the modern age that do not function, and metaphorical uses of specific objects, such as chess pieces or pears for a *midrash* about the post-Holocaust world.

Much of Bak's work questions God's absence during the Holocaust and what mankind is to make of this absence. Bak's most challenging work is a series based on the kabbalistic theme of *Pardes*, or the path toward God, the search for paradises, for the Garden of Eden, and for the key to knowledge. Bak has produced at least three variations of *Pardes*. Part of the kabbalistic teachings is esoteric and is based upon theosophy. They reflect a yearning for direct communication with God through annihilation of individuality. But while understanding God is perhaps beyond the intellect, "He" is most clearly perceived through man's introspection. In this tradition, theosophy reveals the hidden life of God, and the relationships between the divine on one hand and the existence of man and creation on the other. One group of kabbalists called themselves *yoredei merkabah*, or "those who descend to the chariot," perhaps alluding to Elijah's rise to God. The Merkabah terminology is found in texts of the Dead Sea Scrolls. One theme is that of angels who praise the image of "The Throne of the Chariot." The ascent of man to the Heavens, and hence to the realm of knowledge and truth, is through *Pardes*, literally an orchard, entering paradise.

Nevertheless, the path through *Pardes* is difficult and dangerous, fraught with the potential for madness and even death. That path is mentioned in the Talmud in the story of four Jewish sages who entered *Pardes*. In this story, the first rabbi, Simeon ben Azzai, entered the gate of *Pardes*, "looked and died." Rabbi Ben Zoma "looked and was smitten (mentally)." Elisha ben Avuyah, called *aher* (other), forsook rabbinic Judaism and "cut the shoots," apparently becoming a dualistic agnostic. Only Rabbi Akiva "entered in peace and left in peace," or "ascended in peace and descended in peace." This gives Akiva the central role in mysticism.[11]

Bak's visual rendition of *Pardes* from 1995 is an oil on canvas, although variations of this image appear in many of his works, sometimes labeled *Landscapes of Jewish History*. *Pardes* depicts the visual image of the tablets of the Commandments lying flat as if in a closed garden. They are sited in a bleak landscape without people. The bottom sides of the tablets become the entry wall. The word "PARDES" (four letters in Hebrew: *peh, raish, dalet, sommet*) is spelled out across the front, one letter over each of the four possible entry doors. Three doors are open or partially open, but the fourth door, on the extreme left, under the *S* in "PARDES," is nailed closed with two boards in the shape of a cross or a Roman X, signifying 10. As if the forbidden area, outside human entry, knowledge, and comprehension, this zone shows a fire burning from an oven looking like a crematorium, with the smoke rising and flowing through the air. The smoke, ironically, comes not from a chimney, but from two sources on the ground, one on the left and one on the right, suggesting other episodes of struggle to understand God, and perhaps other Jewish encounters with violence.[12]

On the opposite side of the sealed door is an open one with a small garden, a single tree, and small patches of grass. The tree sits in the rear of this section and may be the Tree of Knowledge, or perhaps a kabbalistic Tree of Life. However, it is not adorned with the *sefirot*, rather with numbers, as if to say that rebuilding the Commandments after the Holocaust necessitates entering the garden and ascending the tree as Moses ascended Sinai to bring the Commandments. Which numbered Commandment is to be taken first? We are uncertain, although the Tenth Commandment, "Thou shalt not covet thy neighbor's wife, nor his man servant, nor his maid servant, nor his ox, nor his ass, nor anything that is thy neighbor's," is closest to the ground, suggesting one aspect of contemporary "ethnic cleansing" and appropriation of property. Above is the Sixth Commandment, "Thou Shalt not Murder." These two numbers are most discernible. They stand for the artist's realization that, in cases of genocide, these are the two Commandments most often violated. After Auschwitz, there must be a desire to have the Law.[13]

The second doorway, moving from right to left, is obstructed partially by a branch that must be pushed away to enter the garden. This garden contains a path under arches that are reminiscent of the streets in the Vilna Ghetto, at the end of which are two tablets of the Law, with the Sixth Commandment, "Thou Shalt not Murder," the most obscured.

The third entry door has several trunks of trees impeding entrance, while several ladders, three with rungs missing, are also leaning against the wall as a memory of previous failed attempts to enter this garden. Pages with no text are pinned to the outside wall. Inside is a maze in the form of a partial star of David,[14] leading not to the Commandments, but into the fiery fourth garden that had been closed from the outside. The application of the parable of the four rabbis to this artistic vision poses the following possible questions. First, does the true path to knowledge go through God and his Commandments? Second, is the quest for trying to understand the Holocaust a dangerous endeavor, which can become consumptive for those who attempt it? Third, if a way to comprehend the Holocaust exists, will it lead mankind to understand the principle of free will, and hence the powerlessness of God to intervene during the Shoah? The parable from the Kabbalah does not help answer these questions. Even if one can enter the garden, the issue of establishing *tikkun* is difficult. Hope may be too much to anticipate, but *tikkun*, the artist seems to suggest, is possible.

Conclusion

This chapter has focused on a particular form of representation belonging to a group of international artists whose works can be connected to post-Holocaust narrative theology and to the search for the absent and present God of history. All of the works deal with fundamental theological questions that were asked by the victims of the Holocaust, and that have continued to be asked ever since by both Jews and Christians. God's relationship to the Jews and his presence throughout history, despite earlier suffering, met its greatest test during the Holocaust, and both scholars and artists are still wrestling with the subject. Unfortunately, it is one that provides no easy answers.

Alice Cahana and Samuel Bak are two Holocaust survivor artists who have used the instruments of Jewish knowledge, so to speak, to explain their memories of the camp, of Jewish life, and of God. Their message and analysis are found not only in a literal text, but also in the painterly surface. Thus, while content is important, the means of expression through line, quality of drawing, medium, and shift from realism to abstraction all suggest the difficulty of both depiction and interpretation. Both of these artists use references to Hebrew letters and texts. The texts that exist are of several essential varieties: in Cahana's work, the text is in Hebrew, thus pushing the viewer to further inquiry if it is not easily decipherable. The answer, however, reveals a complex *midrash* mixing the important imagery of the Sabbath and Passover. This is a critical point of convergence for identifying the presence of God and his relationship to the Jewish people.

For Bak, the text is primarily visual. His surrealist landscapes, devoid of humanity and linked to earlier Jewish themes, tie the past to the present, and suggest parables and answers regarding the path to goodness, but not its absolute resolution. One leaves Bak's works with a feeling of the loneliness of one who wishes to continue to believe in God's greatness and creation, but has difficulty doing so. Is there bitterness here? Perhaps so. But there is also hope in *tikkun*, the repair of the world. The paintings of both of these artists do not provide definitive answers. It is suggested that Judaism and Jewish texts constitute means of survival and working through trauma.

Kiefer plays the role of "the other" in this chapter. He is the German artist seeking meaning to the German past through Jewish language and text. *Breaking of the Vessels* has such monumental proportions that it manages to impress the viewers, although perhaps not to understand fully with the "why" of the Shoah. But Kiefer's approaches, using Kabbalah as a source for containing evil, suggests the potentiality for the Jewish revival. In Kiefer's imagery, German redemption comes from the Jews. Kiefer points to the post-Holocaust German-Jewish paradox: the Jews are gone physically, but not from Germany's memory.

Text, an outstanding feature of Jewish life, appears to some degree in all of the works by Jewish artists mentioned above. What appears most interesting, however, is the diversity of artistic creation about such a negative subject and its ultimate meaning. None of the artists gives up on the questions of redemption or the existence of God. But all seem to ask, one way or another, about God's absence. Whether viewed from the ground or above, art has the power to create a discourse and, in a certain way, to provide a partial answer at least to the question of how one keeps the memory of the Holocaust alive.

Notes

1 Nahum N. Glatzer, ed., *The Passover Haggadah* (New York: Schocken Books, 1953, 1989), 39.
2 Glatzer, ed., *The Passover Haggadah*, 46.
3 Glatzer, ed., *The Passover Haggadah*, 46.
4 Glatzer, ed., *The Passover Haggadah*, 27.
5 Z'ev ben Shimon Halevi, *Kabbalah: The Divine Plan* (New York: HarperCollins, 1996), 28.
6 Halevi, *Kabbalah: The Divine Plan*, 28.
7 Halevi, *Kabbalah: The Divine Plan*, 28–29.
8 Halevi, *Kabbalah: The Divine Plan*, 34.
9 Samuel Bak, "About Myself," text of talk from The Decordova Museum, Lincoln, Massachusetts, 14 December 1999.
10 Bak, "About Myself."
11 *Encyclopaedia Judaica* (Jerusalem: Keter Publishing House, 1972), 10: 499.
12 For a somewhat different interpretation, see Lawrence I. Langer, "Essay and Commentary in Samuel Bak," *Landscapes of Jewish Experience* (Waltham, Massachusetts: Brandeis University Press and University of New England Press, 1997). The other variations of *Pardes* have smoke coming only from an altar, with ladders rising along the walls of the garden.
13 In other variations of *Pardes*, Bak did not include numbers hanging from the tree in the fourth section of the garden. One version shows smoke moving from left to right through the tree, while in another version the smoke bypasses the tree. But the tree is not severed, as is found in several of Bak's other pessimistic landscapes.
14 Other versions of this section contain something closer to a maze based on a rectangular geometry.

CONCLUSION

Saul S. Friedman

This chapter was requested of me by the editor of this collection. It represents an effort to revisit one of the crucial events in Jewish history, namely the Nazi genocide of the past century. Not the process of dehumanization—*how* the Nazis and their allies adapted their schemes of mass murder to a particular situation. Rather, the *whys*—the rationalizations about cause and impact, and the devastating implications of the Holocaust for human morality and civilization. Having spent the bulk of 50 years of study exploring the Nazi system of death camps and ghettos with on-site research at Buchenwald and Dachau in 1984, and Auschwitz, Terezin, Majdanek, and Sobibor in 2002, I am still wrestling with what Karl Schleunes termed "the twisted road to Auschwitz" with no satisfactory answers to the questions posed by it.[1]

In the age of Caligula, Rabbi Simeon ben Gamaliel advised, "provide yourself with a teacher and avoid all doubt." I was fortunate to have lived in an era and in a land where, for the most part, intellectual honesty prevailed. Sons of an immigrant stone-cutter from Poland, two of my brothers became physicians. I carried mail, worked as a social worker on the East Side of Cleveland for four years, and attended classes at Harvard Law School and Dropsie College. My years of graduate study were enriched by contact with Ben Halpern and Marie Syrkin of Brandeis, Nora Levin of Gratz College, Howard Sachar of George Washington Universtity, Jacob Marcus of Hebrew Union College, Simon Wiesenthal, and Emil Fackenheim of Hebrew University.

Historian, philosopher, and theologian, Fackenheim probably influenced me as much as any contemporary Jewish writer. Born in Halle (the birthplace of Reinhard Heydrich), Fackenheim subscribed to the teachings of Rabbi Leo Baeck, the Reform rabbi who reminded Jews of their ancestral mission as outlined by Isaiah—to bear witness to the crimes of men and to advance the concept of *tikkun olam* (the obligation that people carry with them of mending the world). Expelled from Germany after *Kristallnacht*, Fackenheim emigrated to Toronto, Canada, where he was ordained a rabbi. Through the war years and beyond, he grappled with a host of issues in a world that was seriously flawed. His peers included Martin Buber, Jules Isaacs, Rabbi Richard Rubenstein, Reinhold Niebuhr, Jacques Maritain, Rosemary Ruether, and Elie Wiesel. His battle cry was forged in cities as far separated from one another in time and space as Jerusalem and Jedwabne. Fackenheim assayed the existence of evil in his world and concluded that what Jews had experienced was not a transient meanness, but "evil for evil's sake."[2]

As the remnants of a slaughtered generation again stood alone against 11 well-armed Arab states in May–June 1967, Fackenheim continued his professorial research into the life and times of Georg-Friedrich Hegel and Franz Rosenzweig. But he could not ignore renewed threats against "Zionist imperialism," particularly after 1983, when he and his wife Rose made *aliyah* to Israel. In one brief moment, our paths crossed when Fackenheim agreed to write the preface for my book on the Oberammergau Passion Play. Implicit throughout the Oberammergau text was the promise *of metanoia*, or repentance that stems from a fundamental change of heart.[3]

Fackenheim beseeched Muslims and Christians to appreciate the centrality of Israel in Jewish life and to develop more positive relations with Jews. He compared the suffering of his people with that of the German Pastor Dietrich Bonhoeffer, who was martyred during World War II, and the subsequent torment of Natan Sharansky, the Russian Jewish *refusenik* who inspired tens of thousands of Jews to leave the Soviet Union. He agreed with Lucy Dawidowicz when she labeled the Nazi genocide a war against the Jews. And he predicted that the Jewish cultural hero at the end of the twentieth century would be the man who gave no posthumous victory to Hitler or the Nazis.

Fackenheim carried with him a revolutionary proposal as he traveled to Rome to attend the scholars' conference on the Holocaust in 1967. It was, in brief, a 614th commandment, the first and only commandment issued to the Jewish people since the time of Moses. In its simplest form, it declared: *Jews are forbidden to grant posthumous victories to Hitler.* They are commanded to remember the victims of Auschwitz lest their memory perish. They are forbidden to despair of man and his world, or to escape into either cynicism or other-worldliness, lest they cooperate in delivering the world over to the forces of Auschwitz. Finally, they are forbidden to despair of the God of Israel, lest Judaism perish. It may be fair to say that rabbis have done a remarkable job in the past quarter of stressing the connection between the moral imperative inherent in Judaism and the defiance with which Jews react to threats issued against them by a perpetually diverse legion of bigots. "To do no more than remain a Jew after Auschwitz," said Fackenheim, "is to confront the demons of Auschwitz in all their guises and to bear witness against them."[4]

Fackenheim hoped to advance the cause of ecumenism with Joseph Cardinal Ratzinger (who succeeded John Paul II as Pope Benedict XVI), and did not shrink from involving colleagues in disputations challenging church dogma. Thus we read in Fackenheim's "Commanding Voice of Auschwitz" of a "uniquely/unique" genocide which permeated the Silesian death camp of "evil for evil's sake," a concept that originated in correspondence among several prominent ministers, who, noting the unfairness of comparing the suffering of Jewish and non-Jewish children starving in Auschwitz, declared such scenes not just evil in the extreme, but a "unique descent into Hell."[5]

Looking back on the state of Holocaust studies after a third scholars' conference was held in Rome in 1997, Fackenheim wrote: "It is a vast scandal that, till today historians have not explained the 'why' of the Holocaust."[6] Raul Hilberg, praised by Fackenheim as "the most thorough, exhaustive scholar of the Holocaust," concurred. The first Holocaust texts—Gerald Reitlinger's *The Final Solution* (1953), Leon Poliakov's *Harvest of Hate* (1954), and Nora Levin's *The Holocaust* (1968) —offered detailed expositions, but little in the way of theory or philosophy. There were few surprises when a second wave of Holocaust texts, expressing concern for the security of the state of Israel, appeared after 1967. Lucy Dawidowicz's *The War against the Jews* (1975), as well as books by Leni Yahil and Yehuda Bauer, had similar format and content to their predecessors. Before he died in 2007, Hilberg transformed his 1961 tome into four volumes, supplemented by texts that explored the bureaucracy which supervised the transports of

Jews and others to death camps in the East. Through mastery of documents and detail, Hilberg was the dean of Holocaust scholars. A meticulous researcher, Hilberg was the first western scholar to penetrate the Praetorian system that vested power in small cliques of ruthless men, thereby befogging responsibility for issuance of a death decree. However, just as Fackenheim's attempt at reconciling theology and history through the application of post-Holocaust *Midrashim* is arcane, Hilberg's history text can be overwhelming. Perhaps a more accessible explanation, at least of the guiding ideology of the Hitler state, can be found in the writing of Gunnar Heinsohn, head of the Raphael Lemkin Institute for Contemporary Genocide at the University of Bremen, who has argued that Hitler's *Weltanschauung* was guided by three basic principles: *Entfernung* (elimination of "unfit" peoples), *Lebensraum* (acquisition of land in the east for the "Aryan race"), and an end to the Jewish concept of the sanctity of life (which, in Heinsohn's opinion, makes the Holocaust "uniquely unique").[7]

Over 100 years would pass after Napoleon sent his armies into Russia; another four decades would be spent debating the feasibility of the Germans' winter campaign in Russia and the "whys" of Auschwitz. Most of the original participants in this second struggle are now gone. Those who remain are still arguing among themselves about which massacres in history were the worst, which attacks merit the label of genocide or acts of genocide. Rabbi H. J. Zimmels has reminded his readers of the truism that "all historical events are unique. History does not and cannot repeat itself."[8] Which should simply be cast aside as "existential peculiarities" or "literary redundancies"? The threat posed to humanity by the Holocaust was in the embracing of an ideology and program of death, pure and simple. Six years ago, I completed my own text on the Holocaust and sighed, for resting on the floor in my office were 100 pages of discarded text, most of which related to causation and ideology.

If the continuing arguments surrounding Franklin Roosevelt and his effectiveness as a champion of Jewish survival from World War II serve as a model, we probably will not resolve the uniqueness controversy for a long time.[9] Scholars who affirm use of the term employ other key words traceable to medieval German sources. In addition to "uniqueness" and the awkward tongue-twister of "uniquely unique," we have descriptions like *außerordentlich* (extraordinary), and other impenetrable phrases like "uniquely transcendent uniqueness." While victims of the Holocaust were both Jewish and Gentile, the Nazi intent to destroy European Jewry in its entirety, and the adoption by the German state of that intention as official policy, coupled with the alienation of Jews of every age, background, and condition in other hostile European societies, illuminates at the very least the singularity of the Jewish condition in the age of Hitler. Jews suffered from religious persecution and hatred dating to the age of Caligula and Antiochus Epiphanes, but no scholar has claimed that these instances, or the pogroms in Balta and Kishinev, were more extensive than the systematic brutality experienced by German Jews from 1933 to 1945 and European Jewry from 1939 to 1945. In the worst of times, when Muslims boasted of purging Jews from Arabia, when self-proclaimed Christian Crusaders slaughtered Jews in isolated settlements along the Rhine River in Germany, when barbarians led by Tigleth Pileser or Tamerlane stacked pyramids of human skulls beyond the gates of some of the greatest cities in the Near East, Jews could occasionally negotiate for their lives. This was not the case in Nazi Germany or German-occupied Europe during World War II. When 14-year-old Bill Vegh was liberated from a Nazi slave labor camp in Austria in the spring of 1945, he carried with him a UN Relief and

Rehabilitation Administration identification card. Typed on the line "Reason for detention" was a single word—"Jew."

And yet Jews were not alone as victims of the Holocaust. Roma who were gassed alongside Jews in Chelmno in the winter 1941/42 suffered the same death and were murdered for similar reasons. The targets of Nazi oppression were identified and discriminated against in employment, education, residence, culture, human relations, and citizenship. They were detained and deported, and suffered starvation and misuse of their bodies in involuntary experiments. They were targeted as slaves or murdered outright. Modern and swift transportation facilitated the removal of Jews, Russian prisoners of war, Roma, and people with disabilities to remote locations where the final act in this hideous Passion Play could be enacted. Each of the victims, Jews and non-Jews alike, were human beings who lost lives and legacies, families, friends, and wholesale communities, and whose histories would be shaped by their deaths rather than their accomplishments, however great or small, in life.

Notes

1 Karl Schleunes, *The Twisted Road to Auschwitz* (Champaign-Urbana, Illinois: University of Illinois Press, 1970).
2 Emil Fackenheim, *The Jewish Return into History* (New York: Schocken Books, 1978), 27.
3 Emil Fackenheim, "Foreword" to Saul S. Friedman, *The Oberammergau Passion Play: A Lance against Civilization* (Carbondale, Illinois: Southern Illinois University Press, 1984), xxx.
4 Fackenheim, *The Jewish Return into History*, 31.
5 Fackenheim, *The Jewish Return into History*, 27.
6 Emil Fackenheim, "Thoughts on a Conference in Rome," *Hakira: A Journal of Jewish and Ethnic Studies*, vol. 1 (2003): 5–18.
7 Gunnar Heinsohn, "What makes the Holocaust a 'Uniquely/Unique Genocide?'" *Journal of Genocide Research*, vol. 2, no. 3 (November 2000): 411–30.
8 H.J. Zimmels, *The Echo of the Nazi Holocaust In Rabbinic Literature* (New York: Ktav, 1977).
9 See also Alan Rosenbaum, ed., *Is The Holocaust Unique? Perspectives on Contemporary Genocide* (Boulder, Colorado: Westview Press, 2003).

INDEX